Operationalized Psychodynamic Diagnosis OPD-3

Operationalized Psychodynamic Diagnosis OPD-3

Manual of Diagnosis and Treatment Planning

OPD Task Force
(Editors)

hogrefe

Library of Congress Cataloging in Publication information for the print version of this book is available via the Library of Congress Marc Database under the LC Control Number 2026941426

Library and Archives Canada Cataloguing in Publication
Title: Operationalized psychodynamic diagnosis OPD-3 : manual of diagnosis and treatment planning / OPD Task Force (editors).
Other titles: OPD-3 Operationalisierte Psychodynamische Diagnostik. English.
Names: Arbeitskreis zur Operationalisierung Psychodynamischer Diagnostik, editor.
Description: Translation of: OPD-3 Operationalisierte Psychodynamische Diagnostik. | Includes bibliographical references.
Identifiers: Canadiana (print) 2026019235X | Canadiana (ebook) 20260192368 | ISBN 9780889376717 (hardcover) | ISBN 9781616766719 (PDF) | ISBN 9781613346716 (EPUB)
Subjects: LCSH: Psychodiagnostics. | LCSH: Psychodynamic psychotherapy.
Classification: LCC RC469 .O64413 2026 | DDC 616.89/075—dc23

The present volume is an adaptation of *OPD-3 - Operationalisierte Psychodynamische Diagnostik* (ISBN 978-3-456-86348-1) by Arbeitskreis OPD (Eds.), © 2024 (2nd ed.) by Hogrefe AG, published under the license from Hogrefe AG, Switzerland. Translated and adapted by the OPD Task Force.

www.hogrefe.com

PUBLISHING OFFICES

USA:	Hogrefe Publishing Corporation, 44 Merrimac St., Newburyport, MA 01950 Phone 978 255 3700, E-mail customersupport@hogrefe.com
EUROPE:	Hogrefe Publishing GmbH, Merkelstr. 3, 37085 Göttingen, Germany Phone +49 551 99950 0, Fax +49 551 99950 111; E-mail publishing@hogrefe.com

SALES & DISTRIBUTION

USA:	Hogrefe Publishing, Casemate Publishers & Book Distribution, 22835 Quicksilver Drive, Dulles, VA 20166 Phone 610 853 9131; E-mail customersupport@hogrefe.com
UK:	Hogrefe Ltd, Hogrefe House, Albion Place, Oxford, OX1 1QZ Phone +44 186 579 7920; E-Mail customersupport@hogrefe.co.uk
EUROPE:	Hogrefe Publishing, Merkelstr. 3, 37085 Göttingen, Germany Phone +49 551 99950 0, Fax +49 551 99950 111; E-mail publishing@hogrefe.com

OTHER OFFICES

CANADA:	Hogrefe Publishing, 82 Laird Drive, East York, Ontario, M4G 3V1
SWITZERLAND:	Hogrefe Publishing, Länggass-Strasse 76, 3012 Bern

Printed and bound in the Czech Republic

ISBN 978-0-88937-671-7 (print) • ISBN 978-1-61676-671-9 (PDF) • ISBN 978-1-61334-671-6 (EPUB)
https://doi.org/10.1027/00671-000

Dedication

In memory of Cord Benecke, 1965–2025.

Contents

Preface

It is with great joy and pride that we can now present the English translation of the third version of the German-language system of *Operationalized Psychodynamic Diagnosis* (OPD). OPD-3 was first published in German in 2023 and has since rapidly established itself as a standard reference in the clinical fields of psychiatry, psychosomatic medicine, and psychotherapy throughout the German-speaking world. It offers a concise and coherent synthesis of the psychoanalytic and psychodynamic diagnostic tradition across four relevant axes: The subjective experience of illness, maladaptive relational patterns, central intrapsychic conflicts, and structural capacities in terms of personality functioning.

At the same time, the OPD is more than a useful and practical synthesis of psychoanalytic traditions. It also builds bridges to other psychological and psychotherapeutic approaches and perspectives. Behavioral and systemic therapists alike find the OPD to be a valuable and horizon-broadening framework in everyday clinical practice.

Our experience with OPD 2, published in 2006, demonstrated the crucial importance of the English translation for the international dissemination of the OPD. Numerous further translations were subsequently based on the English edition. We are therefore especially pleased to take this next step with the present translation and hope that the work developed over the past decades will continue to resonate with and inspire clinicians as well as researchers in other countries.

A major driving force behind the development of the third edition of the OPD was Cord Benecke, who served as the spokesperson for the OPD Task Force from 2017 until his death in December 2025. His contributions to this process are beyond measure. We miss him deeply as a friend, colleague, and a source of inspiration, and we are committed to continuing his work in his spirit – not least as a way of preserving his legacy.

Henning Schauenburg and Stephan Doering
for the Coordinating Committee of the
OPD Task Force

Preface

With this book, the OPD Task Force presents the third version of the Operationalized Psychodynamic Diagnosis (OPD). The OPD was developed in Germany in the 1990s by a group of psychoanalytic researchers and clinicians. The first manual was published in 1996 and quickly spread both in the clinical-practical field and in psychodynamically oriented research in German speaking countries. The manual for the second version (OPD-2) was published in 2006 and is now in its third edition. OPD-2 has been translated into several languages: English, Spanish, Italian, French, Portuguese, Turkish, Czech, Hungarian, Romanian, Russian, and Chinese.

In addition to the central OPD manual and numerous research studies (including empirical validation), other supplementary writings have been published, such as OPD for substance abuse disorders, trauma-related disorders, and OPD in psychotherapy applications.

A working group of child and adolescent psychiatrists, child and adolescent psychotherapists, and developmental psychologists published a manual for Operationalized Psychodynamic Diagnosis in Childhood and Adolescence (OPD-KJ) in 2000, which is available in a second version in English (OPD-CA-2 Task Force, 2017).

Meanwhile, OPD represents a widely accepted standard in psychodynamic diagnostics for both clinical practice and research. It has also found a permanent place in psychodynamic/psychoanalytic training institutes. It is expected that OPD is to be taught in the new Psychotherapy Master's programs in Clinical Psychology, in Germany. This success story is partly due to a significant advantage that OPD has over other interview-based diagnostic systems: The OPD interview is conducted like a normal clinical conversation; it is not a structured interview where every question is pre-formulated and must be asked exactly as written to reliably assess the OPD axes. The OPD is therefore suitable for psychodynamic research and can be seamlessly integrated into any practice and clinical routine for accurate indication and treatment planning. As with the previous versions, a large group of psychodynamically oriented psychotherapists and researchers from the fields of psychoanalysis and psychodynamic psychotherapy, psychosomatic medicine, and psychiatry collaborated on OPD-3. This collaboration took place over many years, striving for innovations and the provisionally "best" result. We believe that the OPD-3 represents another significant step forward: The stronger dimensionalization has made the instrument even more suitable for research, and the stronger linkage of the axes allows a better representation of the clinically significant complexity of psychological processes. During the revision process, the OPD Working Group, and other groups, suffered a severe and unexpected loss: Manfred Cierpka passed away in December 2017. He had led the OPD Working Group for many years as a key initiator and spokesperson with wisdom, determination, and foresight. The OPD Working Group is a fairly heterogeneous group, quite contentious and conflict-prone. It is largely thanks to Manfred Cierpka that this diverse group has been so productive and has repeatedly come together over the years. We will strive to develop the work further and continue with the OPD in this spirit.

Cord Benecke†, Kassel
Speaker of OPD Task Force

OPD Task Force – Members and Their Function Within the OPD Task Force

Spokesperson

Cord Benecke (Kassel)†

Members of the Coordinating Committee

Reiner W. Dahlbender (Barmelweid)
Stephan Doering (Wien)
Johannes C. Ehrenthal (Cologne)
Miriam Henkel (Kassel)
Gereon Heuft (Münster)
Thorsten Jakobsen (Basel)
Johannes Kruse (Giessen)
Henning Schauenburg (Heidelberg)
Gudrun Schneider (Münster)
Wolfgang Schneider (Lübeck)
Gerhard Schüßler (Innsbruck)
Inge Seiffge-Krenke (Mainz)
Carsten Spitzer (Rostock)
Michael Stasch (Heidelberg)
Matthias von der Tann (London)

Spokespersons of the Axes

Axis I
Spokesperson until 12/31/2022:
Gerhard Schüßler (Innsbruck)
Spokesperson starting 01/01/2023:
Carsten Spitzer (Rostock)

Axis II
Henning Schauenburg (Heidelberg)

Axis III
Spokesperson until 12/31/2022:
Gerhard Schüßler (Innsbruck)
Spokesperson starting 01/01/2023:
Cord Benecke (Kassel)†

Axis IV
Stephan Doering (Wien)

Members of the Working Groups

Axis I
Markus Burgmer (Münster)
Reiner W. Dahlenbender (Barmelweid)
Isa Sammet (Göppingen)
Gerhard Schüßler (Innsbruck)
Carsten Spitzer (Rostock)

Axis II
Manfred Cierpka (Heidelberg)†
Ulrike Dinger-Ehrenthal (Düsseldorf)
Johannes C. Ehrenthal (Cologne)
Armin Hartmann (Freiburg)
Henrik Kessler (Fulda)
Claudia Oberbracht (Frankfurt a.M.)
Henning Schauenburg (Heidelberg)
Michael Stasch (Heidelberg)
Matthias von der Tann (London)

Axis III
Cord Benecke (Kassel)†
Markus Burgmer (Münster)
Reiner W. Dahlbender (Barmelweid)
Miriam Henkel (Kassel)
Gereon Heuft (Münster)
Gerhard Schüßler (Innsbruck)
Gudrun Schneider
Viktoriya Wörmann (Osnabrück)

Axis IV
Cord Benecke (Kassel)†
Stephan Doering (Wien)

Michael Dümpelmann (Rosdorf)
Johannes C. Ehrenthal (Cologne)
Holger Himmighoffen (Zürich)
Susanne Hörz-Sagstetter (Berlin)
Thorsten Jakobsen (Basel)
Johannes Kruse (Giessen)
Joachim Küchenhoff (Basel)
Günther Lempa (München)
Christiane Montag (Berlin)
Claudia Oberbracht (Frankfurt am Main)
Doris Pouget-Schors (Pullach)
Joram Ronel (Barmelweid)
Gudrun Schneider (Münster)
Sebastian Seifert (Dresden)
Claudia Subic-Wrana (Cologne)
Jana Volkert (Berlin)
Dorothea von Haebler (Berlin)

Authors Without Axes Affiliation

Valentina Albertini (Berlin)
Markus Bassler (Mainz)
Peer Briken (Hamburg)
Andreas Dieckmann (Berlin)
Lukas Forschner (Blankenheim)
Johanna Jedamzik (Münster)
Martin Lüdemann (Schlangenbad)
Alexander Niecke (Cologne)
Dieter Nitzgen (Müllheim/Baden)
Ole Karkov Østergård (Aalborg/Denmark)
Jan Odendiek (Möckern)
Silke Pless (Giessen)
Harald Sporn (Sprockhovel)
Darius C. Tabatabai (Berlin)
Klaus von Ploetz (Möser)

Authors Affiliated With Prior OPD Versions

Peter Buchheim
Manuela Burgmeier-Lohse
Susanne Davis-Osterkamp†
Barbara Dierse
Wolfram Ehlers
Matthias Franz
Harald J. Freyberger†
Gabriele Frevert
Tilman Grande
Karsten Hake
Sven Olaf Hoffmann
Paul L. Janssen
Peter Joraschky
Marianne Junghan
Reinholde Kriebel†
Elmar Mans
Stavros Mentzos†
Aribert Muhs
Gerd Rudolf
Ulrich Rüger
Wolfgang Schneider
Frank Schwarz
Günther H. Seidler
Michaela Strack
Bernhard Strauß
Manfred Tetzlaff
Jörn von Wietersheim

Translation

Henning Schauenburg (Coordination)
Johanna Behringer
Stephan Doering
Miriam Henkel
Florian Juen
Carsten Spitzer
Esther Stalujanis

ChatGPT 4 was used for a first English version, which was then thoroughly revised by the group.

All members of the OPD Task Force and their contact details can be found on the OPD website https://www.opd-online.net

1 Introduction and Theoretical Background

Psychodynamic diagnosis has a reputation of being unreliable, which is related to the high level of abstraction and complexity inherent to the underlying psychoanalytic concepts. Prior research has demonstrated that the diagnostic process, for instance is guided by strong stereotypes (Blaser, 1977), therapist personality play a role (Rudolf & Stille, 1984), or the inclusion of additional information can significantly impact diagnostic outcomes (e.g., Langer & Abelson, 1974).

In contemporary psychodynamic literature a differentiation of personality and the classification of mental disorders continue to be based on drive theory, with the incorporation of additional theoretical frameworks from ego psychology, object relations, and self-psychology (Shapiro, 1991). In the clinical context, these constructs are employed to elucidate psychological functions and their associated disorders. During the initial interview, for example, psychotherapists utilize these conceptual frameworks to organize the case history in order to shed light on the interrelationships between the patient's symptoms and disturbances in their emotional and cognitive development. A psychodynamic diagnosis is derived from the material reported by the patient and the observations and perceptions of the psychotherapist within their interaction. The differentiated assessment of transference/countertransference, conflict, and structural characteristics enables individualization in this process (Schüßler, 2002) and offers the advantage of describing patterns of patients and identifying information that guides action, such as that relevant for differential indication (cf. Rudolf et al., 1996). It should be noted that the determination of indication must also be considered a highly intersubjective process (Döll-Hentschker et al., 2006).

Nevertheless, this form of diagnosis is not without its own set of disadvantages: The diagnostic statements of analytical psychotherapists may be perceived by some critics as diagnoses formulated in "artistic freedom" (cf. Rudolf, 2001), which can impede the scientific discourse. For this reason, several instruments have been developed in recent years in parallel to the OPD – to operationalize psychoanalytic concepts (for overview see Section 1.1). Since 1996, the Manual for Operationalized Psychodynamic Diagnosis (OPD) by the OPD Task Force (1996; in the second version OPD-2 from 2008) has been available. The Manual presents three central psychodynamic axes "Interpersonal Relations," "Conflict," and "Structure." The OPD system allows for the formulation of clinically relevant and precise diagnoses that meet overall satisfactory quality criteria (see Section 1.3). The present OPD-3 represents a further development and refinement of both the diagnostic and therapeutic perspectives.

A further motivation for the formation of the OPD Task Force was with the recognition of shortcomings in the existing descriptive classification systems (DSM-III, -IV, and ICD-10). These systems offer limited guidance for psychotherapists with a psychodynamic orientation. They not only abandoned the concept of neurosis, but also adhered predominantly to phenomenological and biological concepts, which neglected the validity of diagnostic categories in favor of reliability (Schneider & Hoffmann, 1992). A diagnosis that is exclusively descriptive and symptom-centered provides the clinician with limited guidance for determining indications and for conducting psychotherapy. For instance, psychodynamically oriented therapists are deficient in statements regarding intrapsychic and interpersonal conflicts, the structural level, or the subjective illness concepts. With the assistance of these they establish a connection between symptomatology, the triggering conflicts, the patient's dysfunctional relationships, and their life history in the broadest sense, and therefore derive a concrete treatment strategy.

Consequently, the development of new psychiatric classification systems highlighted the necessity for a more unified instrument that would also consider other diagnostically relevant levels. In light of these considerations, an operationalized psychodynamic diagnosis should aim to capture and encompass observation-based psychodynamic constructs as an additional component to phenomenological diagnostics.

In the early 1990s, the OPD Task Force was founded by a group of psychoanalysts, psychosomatic clinicians, and psychiatrists in Germany. The objective of this task force is to expand the symptomatically descriptive classification of mental disorders to include fundamental psychodynamic dimensions.

The OPD Task Force developed a diagnostic inventory and provided a manual (OPD-1, published in 1996; a revised version, OPD-2, followed in 2008) for training and clinical application. The multiaxial psychodynamic diagnosis was based on five axes, as follows:

- Axis I: Mental Disorders, Experience of Illness, and Prerequisites for Treatment
- Axis II: Interpersonal Relations
- Axis III: Conflict
- Axis IV: Structure
- Axis V: Mental and Psychosomatic Disorders according to ICD-10

In the OPD-3, the classificatory diagnoses (formerly designated as Axis V in OPD-1 and OPD-2) have been eliminated from their own axis and are now recorded at the beginning of Axis I. Additionally, it was deemed inappropriate to categorize ICD or DSM as a sub-aspect of OPD. Nevertheless, it is evident that syndromal diagnostics remain a fundamental aspect of the diagnostic process. Accordingly, it is now situated before the entirety of the OPD. The OPD axes then serve to elucidate the etiology of the symptomatology.

Following an initial interview of between one and two hours of duration, the clinician (or an external observer) is then able to assess the patient's psychodynamics based on the OPD categories and record this assessment in the evaluation forms. The use of an interview guideline facilitates the acquisition of information pertinent to the diagnostic process within the OPD framework. In contrast to other diagnostic systems, such as the Structured Interview for Personality Organization (STIPO, German abbreviation for "Strukturiertes Interview zur Persönlichkeitsorganisation"), Scales of Psychological Competencies (SPK, German abbreviation for "Skalen Psychischer Kompetenzen"), Reflective Functioning (RF), which necessitate a highly structured and standardized interview format, the OPD interview guideline is designed to be flexible, allowing for the conduct of the interview in a manner that closely resembles a typical open psychodynamic interview. This better enables the OPD to be employed in non-research settings and renders it considerably more practice-oriented than numerous other instruments.

As a foundational premise for the development of the OPD, it was established that a clinically relevant psychodynamically oriented instrument should be created, taking into account and adapting existing approaches. This instrument should be sufficiently abstract to facilitate its use while remaining situated between pure behavioral description and pure metapsychological conceptualization.

Moreover, the objective was to develop a language with precise terminology and culture that is uniform and avoids school-specific terminology wherever possible.

The following are the purposes which operationalized diagnostics can serve:

1. The instrument provides clinical-diagnostic guidelines that, due to relatively open formulations, allow for practitioner discretion.
2. It can be a valuable tool for training in psychodynamic psychotherapy, as it permits the application of both psychodynamic and phenomenological classification.
3. It can be employed as a research instrument for scientific studies, for example, to facilitate greater sample homogenization in studies through the implementation of more rigorous diagnostic criteria. In this context, the term "basic data" can be understood to refer to the essential information required for a comprehensive phenomenological and psychodynamic baseline assessment. This includes the documentation of illness progression, the evaluation of therapeutic indications and differential indications, the identification of distinctive patterns across various domains of life, and the investigation of therapeutic efficacy beyond mere symptom alteration.
4. Furthermore, it can facilitate enhanced communication within the scientific community regarding the constructs of psychodynamic theory.
5. By identifying psychodynamically relevant foci, the OPD can be utilized for therapy planning. When significant aspects of an unconscious conflict, structural limitations, and dysfunctional relationship patterns are identified as problematic areas, the focal goals can be formulated in a planned treatment. Concurrently, process studies can investigate the extent to which addressing these defined foci during treatments is related to treatment success.

The present OPD-3 manual represents a further comprehensive revision of the OPD axes, by the OPD Task Force. In this process, the experiences gained from numerous training courses and clinical applications, as well as the findings of research projects (see Section 1.3), were considered.

1.1 Previous Approaches to the Operationalization of Psychodynamic Constructs

The lack of precision and clarity in psychodynamic terminology has been a persistent source of concern among scientists. It is therefore unsurprising that psychoanalysis has been more successful in generating new hypotheses than in validating existing ones since Freud's time. The serious admonition of the then-president of the American Psychoanalytic Association, A. Kaplan, that the validation of psychoanalytic theory is the task of our time and not the constant creation of new theories (Kaplan, 1981), was largely ignored. On the other hand, the ambiguity of psychodynamic terms is consistent with two key aspects of psychodynamic thoughts: a strong hermeneutic orientation and an emphasis on the tolerance of "not knowing" (e.g., W. Bion) in the psychotherapeutic process. The challenge is to maintain a balance between the necessary tolerance for not knowing on the one hand and the need for the operationalization of concepts for empirical research on the other.

Of course, this does not exclude the fact that psychodynamically oriented therapists with research interests have always suffered from the state of conceptual vagueness that characterizes psychoanalysis. Almost all attempts at reformulation and operationalization, therefore, come, not surprisingly, from research context.

In assessing the preceding efforts to operationalize psychoanalytic constructs, it is imperative to determine the extent to which these investigations and findings are scientifically significant. For instance, are they adequate for substantiating or refuting broader or narrower theories or concepts as unsuitable? It is of great importance to determine whether the subject areas and theoretical concepts under examination still have a substantial proximity to underlying formations or theoretical ideas, or whether, through the process of operationalization, the substantive connection between the construct and the specific research subject has been lost (Eagle, 1991). While this is a concern in any operationalization, including in experimental psychology, where a significant discrepancy can also arise between a theoretical construct and its operational observation during the "translation" of a theoretical construct into an operational and thus observable concept, this difficulty is particularly pronounced in the case of psychoanalysis. This is due to the complex nature of underlying personality and developmental concepts, as well as the intricate theory of illness and treatment

The complex psychoanalytic theories and terminology present a substantial challenge to the implementation of a research design. Frequently, subjects such as the unconscious, self- and object representations, restructurings, unconscious affects, or transferences cannot be directly quantified; instead they must be inferred from observations. This initial situation thus requires a research approach that is capable of accommodating the diversity of potential observational data, as well as the appropriate methods of systematic observation, evaluation, and interpretation.

The assessment of the value of findings depends on (often disputed) assumptions. In a multimethod and multimodal approach that considers both "hard" bio-psycho-social data and the individual and subjective side in the entirety of their biography, the issue of integrating the different levels of analysis arises. In the context of psychosocial inquiries, the integration of findings derived from disparate methodologies, namely quantitative operationalizations on the one hand (e.g., standardized questionnaire results) and those from open-ended "narrative" interviews, is inherently challenging. Interpretative "leaps" are often unavoidable, and there is frequently a notable discrepancy between these two levels of analysis. Nevertheless, an oscillating perspective can provide a more comprehensive understanding of the subject than either approach alone can. Therefore, in order to operationalize psychodynamic concepts, it is essential to identify a middle ground that allows for increased clarity and distinctness while maintaining the concepts inherent dynamism.

In the context of the development of the Hampstead Index, Sandler (1962, p. 288) notes that: "This led to a series of reformulations because the terms found in the literature were equally inadequate, imprecise, and contradictory." The challenging process of reformulation has been undertaken by numerous authors who have sought to reestablish psychoanalysis' connection to the international scientific community, which it had previously lost. In this section, we will provide a brief overview of the most significant approaches to operationalizing psychodynamic constructs. For a more comprehensive and up-to-date overview of the instruments for capturing psychodynamic conflicts, we direct the reader to Simmonds et al., 2015. For an excellent overview of instruments for capturing "structure" we refer the reader to Doering & Hoerz (2012):

In the Hampstead Index by Anna Freud (Sandler, 1962), for example, in addition to symptomatology, biography, and drive development, the development of ego functions and the superego, fixation points, and regression tendencies, as well as conflict characteristics, were to be used for diagnostic differentiation. Accordingly, the authors sought to distinguish between a developmental pathology (profound disruption of drive, ego, superego, and object relations) and a neurotic pathology, which aligns with a more advanced level of development.

The descriptive developmental diagnosis model by Blanck and Blanck (Blanck & Blanck, 1974, 1979) is grounded in ego psychology, as such, delineates the developmental trajectory of ego functions. Bellak and colleagues (Bellak & Hurvich, 1969; Bellak & Goldsmith, 1984) developed a multi-scale measurement instrument based on this operationalization of ego functions. Patients are thus classified into one of three categories of development: neurotic, borderline or psychotic. These initial systems for psychoanalytic diagnostics can also be employed in the planning and monitoring of therapeutic interventions.

Perry et al. (1989) presented an instrument for diagnosing idiographic basic conflicts with the Psychodynamic Conflict Rating Scale (PCRS). The PCRS conceptualizes conflicts as patterns in attitudes, beliefs, interpersonal behavior, and affect regulation, which predispose an individual to experience challenges in coping with specific life stressors. The PCRS assesses the focal and global cognitive, behavioral, and affective dimensions of conflicts, encompassing both pathological and adaptive aspects.

Lester Luborsky's model of the Core Conflictual Relationship Theme (Luborsky & Crits-Christoph, 1998) represents an operationalized approach to relationship diagnosis that has generated significant scientific interest but is seldom employed in the clinical diagnostic process. A semi-structured interview is conducted with the individual, who is then asked to describe characteristic relationship episodes. These are subsequently classified based on a category system. The conflictual relationship themes that emerge from the interview process can serve as foundation for differentiated therapeutic planning (Grenyer & Marceau, 2022). Disorder-specific treatment manuals have been developed based on the CCRT model, the efficacy of which has been substantiated through randomized controlled trials (RCTs; e.g., Leichsenring et al., 2008; Leichsenring & Salzer, 2014).

A variety of instruments have been developed for the operationalization of the construct of defense (e.g., Perry & Cooper, 1989; Vaillant et al., 1986; Ehlers & Peter, 1990; Ehlers et al., 1995). The effects of different forms of defense (e.g., on physiology or even on later career success) have been extensively empirically studied and well documented (for an overview see Hentschel et al., 2004; Werner & Langenmayr, 2005; Cramer, 2006). Empirical studies have also demonstrated correlations between specific defense mechanisms or levels and particular personality disorders or personality disorder clusters as defined in the DSM-IV (e.g., Lingiardi et al., 1999). Recently, there has been a growing interest in investigating the neurobiological correlates of defense processes (Schmeing et al., 2013).

The working group led by O. F. Kernberg has developed an operationalization of the structural interview which is known as the Structured Interview for Personality Organization (STIPO; Clarkin et al., 2004; German: Doering, 2004). A revised version (STIPO-R; Clarkin et al., 2016; German: Hörz-Sagstetter & Doering, 2021) comprises 55 items that are structurally queried, explored, and rated by the interviewer based on anchor examples. The items are summarized into five dimensions: identity, object relations, defense, aggression, and value orientations. Furthermore, an overall narcissism score can be calculated based on the responses to11 individual items. In conclusion, personality organization is evaluated on six levels (normal, neurotic, borderline 1, 2, and 3, as well as psychotic), and a dimensional representation of personality organization in the form of a structural profile across the five dimensions with their subdimensions is conducted.

The Karolinska Psychodynamic Profile (KAPP; Weinryb & Rössel, 1991; Weinryb et al., 1999) is a relatively comprehensive diagnostic instrument with a psychoanalytic background. The KAPP comprises 18 subscales that examine the following characteristic areas: quality of interpersonal relationships (1–3), psychological functioning level (4–7), affect differentiation (8–9), body experience as an element of self-awareness (10–12), sexuality (13–14), the image that the individual has of their social significance

(15–17) and personality organization. The interrater agreement among trained assessors is high, and the instrument has also demonstrated satisfactory validity.

The Scales of Psychological Capacities (SPC; Wallerstein, 1996; German: Huber et al., 2006) comprise 17 dimensions, each of which is subdivided into two or three subdimensions, resulting in a total of 35. The subdimensions of a given dimension are constructed in a manner that allows for the capture of varying degrees of disinhibited functioning with the other subdimension capturing degrees of inhibited functioning. The assessment of all 35 subdimensions is based on approximately one-hour of tape-recorded clinical interviews and additionally on an approximately one-and-a-half-hour semi-structured special SPC interview using an interview guide. A comprehensive manual is available for the assessment, in which each subdimension is described in detail and illustrated with several clinical vignettes. The German version demonstrates satisfactory to excellent interrater and retest reliability, validity, and change sensitivity. Additionally, norm values are available for depression, borderline personality disorders, and healthy individuals (Huber et al., 2006).

The concept of *mentalization ability* as described by the working group around Peter Fonagy (Fonagy et al., 2002) also delineates a central structural psychological dimension. *Mentalization* is defined as "the ability to imagine mental states in oneself and others" (Fonagy et al., 2002, p. 31). This is particularly pertinent to the relationship between feelings, desires and behavior. Only through this connection can actions be experienced as meaningful and intentional. The concept of mentalization is derived from research on theory of mind. An operationalization of mentalization ability is available in the form of the Reflective Function Scale (RF), which is applied to the answers provided to the "demand questions" of the Adult Attachment Interview (AAI) (Fonagy et al., 1998; Taubner et al., 2013).

The Psychodynamic Diagnostic Manual (PDM; PDM Task Force, 2006) was developed shortly after the publication of the English translation of the OPD Manual, by a group of psychodynamically oriented researchers (predominantly US Americans) with the intention of completing the categorical, symptom-oriented approaches of the ICD and DSM. The PDM-2 (Lingiardi & MacWilliams, 2017) was subsequently published as a comprehensive, empirically based, and more case formulation and treatment planning-oriented revision. Based on a clinical interview and against the background of a model of mental development towards age-appropriate adaptive health vs. age-inappropriate maladaptive disorders including psychotic states, three dimensionally designed axes are operationalized for different life stages (infancy/early childhood, childhood, adolescence, adulthood, old age), from which an individual profile is configured: The P-axis concerns personality patterns and disorders, the M-axis mental functioning, and the S-axis symptom patterns, which may be considered the subjective experience. A Likert scale is employed to quantify 12 sub dimensions of affective, cognitive-mental, and interpersonal-communicative (self-)regulatory abilities, including the development and utilization of internalized norms and ideals. The multi-axial approach is exemplified by clinical examples. Rating scales are available for rapid orientation in clinical practice, in both analog and digital formats (PDC: Psychodiagnostic Chart).

Conclusion: Much has been done to operationalize psychodynamic concepts (see review by Benecke & Schauenburg, 2020). Most of the instruments that have been developed focus on measuring structural aspects (STIPO, KAPP, RF), basic psychological functions or abilities. In some instruments, these structural aspects are combined with motivational/conflictual aspects. We believe that it is necessary to consider both motivational/conflictual aspects and structural abilities/impairments; at the same time and these aspects should be assessed separately. A systematic recording of (dysfunctional) relationship patterns is not found in the instruments mentioned above, this has been operationalized and made assessable in separate concepts, such as the Cyclic Maladaptive Pattern (CMP, Strupp & Binder, 1984) in combination with the Structural Analysis of Social Behavior (SASB, Benjamin, 1974) for psychodynamic psychotherapy (see also Tress, 1993; Benjamin, 1993). The OPD devotes a separate axis to this clinically important level: Axis II (Interpersonal Relations).

1.2 The Concept of Operationalized Psychodynamic Diagnosis (OPD)

The OPD-3 consists of four psychodynamic axes:

I. Mental Disorders, Experience of Illness, and Prerequisites for Treatment
II. Interpersonal Relations
III. Conflict
IV. Structure

The four axes are based on a psychodynamic understanding derived from psychoanalytic theories. We assume that the essential determinations in these four axes correspond to underlying concepts (personality structure, intrapsychic conflict, transference, defense, resistance), and that conclusions at the level of the unconscious are drawn only with caution and with reference to the given operationalizations.

Why these axes?

For *Axis I, the Mental Disorders, Experience of Illness, and Prerequisites for Treatment*, the obvious practical relevance of the categories (rather borrowed from cognitive psychology) spoke in favor: Patients must be "met where they are and where they expect to be" – that is, in terms of symptomatology and expectations of therapy. The focus here is less on illness behavior and more on elements of experience, motivation, and available resources and obstacles. These levels are well researched in psychology and relatively easy to operationalize.

Axis II, Interpersonal Relations is partly rooted in psychodynamic diagnostics, which is always also relationship diagnostics, and which gives crucial weight to the interplay of transference and countertransference. This axis does not prescribe ideal-typical constellations or patterns (unlike Axis III and IV) but provides a category system of observation-based behaviors with multiple possibilities of combinations. Although the axis is designed in analogy to interpersonal circle models (particularly the SASB, Benjamin, 1974; Tress, 1993), it clearly goes beyond them by explicitly capturing countertransference aspects and linking them to the patients' experiences.

Axis III, Conflict asserts to the implementation of a fundamental tenet of piece of traditional psychoanalytic diagnostics, the pivotal role of internalized conflicts. The conceptualization of conflicts is anchored in universal motivational systems. Seven conflicts are delineated, each with a passive and an active coping mode. Here, life-determining, internalized conflicts are juxtaposed with more current, externally determined conflictual situations. The resolution of such an internalized conflict can be defined as a treatment goal.

Axis IV, Structure represents qualities or deficiencies in psychic functioning. The structural functions can be understood as fundamental psychic abilities. Such functions include, for example, the capacity for internal and external differentiation, the ability to perceive and regulate one's mental states and so forth. The availability of these structural functions has a significant impact on the manifestations and ways of dealing with internal and external conflicts. The assessment of the structural axis has a decisive influence on the determination of the indication.

Upon examination of the axes, it becomes evident that they exhibit some degree of content overlap or are to be perceived as being in closely related interaction with one another.

The figure-ground relationship between the Conflict and Structure Axes is readily apparent. The psychic structure serves as the backdrop against which conflicts unfold with the effectiveness of conflict strategy being a key factor in this process. As epiphenomena, relationship patterns are more observable than psychic structure and inner conflict. Habitual dysfunctional relationship patterns can be posited as expressions and manifestations of inner conflicts and structural characteristics as well as a form of compromise coping; Consequently they reflect the problematic aspects of both areas. Chapter 6 entitled “Interplay of Axes and Individual Psychodynamics” provides a more detailed examination of this topic.

1.3 Empirical Foundation of the OPD

A unique feature of the OPD is that it bridges the gap between clinical experience and models on the one hand and research findings on the other. This resulting area of tension has been a part of psychotherapy since the beginning of scientific inquiry (Castonguay, 2011). The questions of whether, and if so, how, basic and applied research can be meaningfully linked remains part of an open debate (Gee et al., 2022). However, this also means that systems such as the OPD, as well as other clinical models, must always consider both perspectives: the practical requirements, especially the usefulness, and the findings of research, including basic research.

Since the first publication of the OPD in 1996, a large number of empirical studies have been conducted, contributing both to the empirical foundation in terms of consolidation and evidence-based support, as well as to the further development of related instruments (Zimmermann et al., 2010). The following Section provides an overview of the results of this research.

Empirical studies on the Mental Disorders, *Experience of Illness, and Prerequisites for Treatment Axis (Axis I)* provide indications of the quality criteria and significance of the corresponding Axis I of the OPD-2. In a study by Schneider, Klauer et al. (2008), 14 trained raters assessed a case regarding this axis, achieving intraclass correlation coefficients of .73–.76 for an overall rating, indicating good interrater reliability. Zuccarino et al. (2012) observed a Kappa value of .65 in a sample of young patients with eating disorders. Furthermore, in a sample of over 450 individuals the researchers found that nearly all variables of Axis I were able to differentiate between different clinical groups (outpatient psychotherapy vs. consultation service) and demonstrated correlations with self-assessed therapy motivation. In a sample of 263 patients undergoing inpatient psychosomatic psychotherapy Waage et al. (2011) identified seven factors (Somatic Orientation, Social Orientation, Psychological Orientation, Resources and Openness, Obstacles and Secondary Gain, Passive Patient Role) that could be determined. These factors demonstrated expected correlations with one another and with scales from a questionnaire on therapy motivation. The results indicate that men exhibited a stronger somatic orientation, whereas women demonstrated a psychosocial attribution of causes and a greater openness to psychological processes. Furthermore, partial effects were observed for age and disorder areas. Zuccarino et al. (2012) employed Axis I of the OPD to discern subgroups of young patients with anorexia nervosa. Kati et al. (2015) demonstrated the sensitivity to change of selected areas in the context of inpatient psychotherapy, particularly for a decrease in distress, a somatic or social concept of illness. However, it is noteworthy that therapists rated the secondary gain from illness slightly higher on average at the end of inpatient therapy than at the beginning. Higher values regarding internal obstacles to change at the conclusion of therapy was associated with diminished improvements in subscales of an instrument for measuring resource realization. Furthermore, factors to Axis I were found to be predictive of the long-term course following inpatient psychotherapy (Schneider et al., 2015).

Empirical studies on the *Interpersonal Relations Axis (Axis II)* of the OPD-1 demonstrated satisfactory interrater reliability under research conditions, with weighted Kappa coefficients ranging from .56 to .62 at the item level (Stasch et al., 2002). However, these results were less consistent with clinical setting and with student raters (Cierpka et al., 2001). Additionally, the retest reliability was deemed acceptable (Stasch et al., 2002). Zuccarino et al. (2012) reported a weighted Kappa of .63 for the interrater reliability of the Interpersonal Relations Axis (Axis II) of the OPD-2. The Inventory of Interpersonal Problems (IIP, Horowitz et al., 2000), which is also based on a circumplex model like the OPD Interpersonal Relations Axis (Axis II), was employed to assess the convergent construct validity of the latter. The resulting validity coefficients demonstrated an acceptable level of reliability for a comparison between a self-assessed and an observer-assessed procedure (Stasch et al., 2004). Additionally, it was demonstrated that the majority of OPD relationship clusters are construct-conform, exhibiting specific interpersonal content, and forming a circular pattern when plotted on a two-dimensional diagram (Stasch et al., 2004). Further validity studies on relationships with interpersonal problems, the SASB model, attachment styles, or clinical utility provide acceptable evidence of validity (see overviews in Cierpka et al., 2001; Cierpka, Grande et al., 2007; Schauenburg & Grande, 2010). Based on Axis II of the OPD-2, Zimmermann et al. (2014) developed the OPD Relationship Pattern Q-Sort, which has been well validated and can be used as a complement or alternative to OPD Relationship diagnostics. In addition to the OPD-2, the utilization of interpersonal narratives or relationship episodes in psychological diagnostics is becoming increasingly favorable (Dunlop et al., 2022). Axis II has been employed to develop personalized research paradigms, as evidenced by its use in neuroscience (e.g., Kessler et al., 2013; Wiswede et al., 2014). In a study conducted by Kessler et al. (2011) an OPD interview was administered with patients diagnosed with depression. From the OPD Interpersonal Relations Axis (Axis II) individualized sentences were derived and assessed for their relevance to the patients' depressive symptoms. Subsequently the sentences were presented to the patients while they were undergoing functional magnetic resonance imaging (fMRI) scanning. The authors demonstrated increased activation in limbic and subcortical brain regions. "The pivotal point is that the brain responses to these stimuli can be interpreted from a clinical perspective due to the individualized nature of the stimuli" (Kessler et al., 2013, p. 4).

Several findings suggest that the *Conflict Axis (Axis III)* is a reliable and valid construct (see overviews in Cierpka, Grande et al., 2007; Schneider, Klauer et al., 2008; Benecke & Brauner, 2017). Rost (2011) observed good to very good interrater reliability for four conflict areas of the OPD-2 in a sample of 72 depressive patients undergoing inpatient psychotherapy. Additionally, acceptable interrater reliability was noted for two other conflict areas. However, only for the identity conflict the observed values were deemed unacceptable. Zuccarino et al. (2012) reported slightly lower values for an overall rating of the Conflict Axis (Axis III) with a Kappa value of.56. In a study by Kaufhold et al. (2017) acceptable interrater reliability was reported in the context of relatively less structured initial interviews, with intraclass correlation coefficients ranging from.52–.65. Furthermore, Axis III may assist in the characterization of subgroups within the domain of eating disorders (Zuccarino et al., 2012). In the context of treatment-seeking individuals undergoing inpatient psychotherapy, gender-dependent differences in the distribution of conflicts have been observed (Schneider & Heuft, 2018). Specifically, a greater proportion of men have been found to have a main conflict around Submission vs. Control, whereas a greater portion of women have been found to have a Dependency vs. Individuation Conflict. The processing mode of the main conflict was passive in approximately two-thirds of cases; with no significant gender differences observed (Schneider & Heuft, 2018). In Rost (2011), approximately 50% of the subjects exhibited active processing of the main conflict, with the distribution of the In Need of Care vs. Self-Sufficiency Conflict and the Self-Worth conflict being the most frequently described main conflicts. In the LAC Depression Study, the In Need of Care vs. Self-Sufficiency Conflicts, Dependency vs. Individuation Conflicts, and Self-Worth Conflicts were frequently described, and the authors demonstrated a moderating effect of the structural level (Kaufhold et al., 2017).

Several studies have been conducted on patients from different disorder types regarding the Conflict Axis (Axis III). Results of the studies indicate that the first four conflicts, namely Dependency vs. Individuation, Submission vs. Control, In Need of Care vs. Self-Sufficiency, and Self-Worth, are diagnosed significantly more frequently (Grande et al., 1998; Böker et al., 2007; Schneider et al., 2008b; Rudolf et al., 1996).

Dependency vs. Individuation: The significance of this conflict, regardless of whether it is expressed *passively* or *actively*, is significantly and positively correlated with the expression of the implicit motive of *self-assurance* (Rost, 2011). In other words, the greater the perceived significance of Dependency vs. Individuation Conflict, the more pronounced the manifestation of the self-assurance motive. In the OPD, the active mode is conceptualized as a defense that is employed in response to or as a means of avoiding feelings of fear of closeness. Patients in active mode described themselves as exhibiting a greater tendency to reject and a diminished capacity to interact with others. In contrast, patients in passive mode described themselves as exhibiting a tendency to be less rejective (Schneider et al., 2008b). Additionally, the same patients demonstrated a notable correlation with the reported body concept. Patients who exhibited an active expression reported experiencing enhanced physical well-being and a perception of optimal bodily functioning. Additionally, they demonstrated a reduced inclination towards physical intimacy, and a greater sense of sexual fulfilment. In contrast, the passive mode of the same conflict is correlated with increased interest in physical closeness and decreased satisfaction with one's sexuality (Schneider et al., 2008a). Rost (2011) identified indications of a somewhat less favorable trajectory among individuals experiencing a conflict of Dependency vs. Individuation.

Submission vs. Control: Irrespective of the mode (active vs. passive), this conflict shows positive correlation with the implicit motives of "self-assurance" and "assertion of one's own interests" (Rost, 2011). In the OPD the active mode is operationalized in the OPD as a pronounced striving for power and control. In accordance with the aforementioned, psychosomatic patients who exhibited an active expression of the conflict were found to self-report lower levels of self-insecurity and submissiveness in relationships, as well as an enhanced capacity to assert their own interests. Patients who exhibited active coping mode of the conflict demonstrated superior physical health and efficiency, along with elevated levels of satisfaction with their own sexuality and body image. Conversely, patients who demonstrated a passive conflict coping mode exhibited significantly below-average values in all these areas (Schneider et al., 2008a). Patients in the active mode reported a significantly lower incidence of interpersonal problems associated with feelings of dominance and assertiveness (Pieh et al., 2009). In contrast adolescents who expressed the conflict passively reported experiencing themselves in relationships as "too self-insecure/submissive" and "too exploitable/yielding" (Benecke et al., 2011). In adolescents with externalizing disorders, the active mode of the Submission vs. Control Conflict is particularly prevalent (Rathgeber et al., 2014).

In Need of Care vs. Self-Sufficiency: The passive expression of this conflict is a common finding in studies of psychosomatic patients (Schneider et al., 2008a, 2008b; Pieh et al., 2009; Rost, 2011; Rathgeber et al., 2014). These patients describe themselves overall as less capable (Schneider et al., 2008b), perceive their bodies as less healthy, less efficient, and less functional, and show less interest in body care (Schneider et al., 2008a), which suggests that the primary motive of care by others postulated in the OPD may be a key factor in this phenomenon. In contrast psychosomatic patients in the active mode, as reported by Schneider et al. (2008b) perceived their own bodies as less efficient and less healthy. However, they reported more pronounced performance in non-body-related areas. The authors posit that patients with an active expression of the In Need of Care vs. Self-Sufficiency Conflict tend to overexert themselves and disregard their own limits. For patients in the active mode the resulting *physical* complaints serve as a means of expressing their need for care and neediness. Patients in the passive mode reported a significantly lower incidence of interpersonal problems, particularly those related to perceptions of being "too quarrelsome/competitive" or "too dismissive/cold" (Pieh et al., 2009).

Self-Worth Conflict (Self-Worth vs. Object Value): Psychosomatic patients in the passive mode described increased self-insecurity, reduced self-worth, and increased shame (Schneider et al., 2008b). Correspondingly, they expressed less satisfaction with physical performance, sexuality, physical appearance, and overall, less acceptance of their bodies (Schneider et al., 2008a). Patients in the active mode, on the other hand, kept their distress low for a long time by devaluing others and are therefore less likely to be in inpatient treatment. Due to the small number of cases, only tendencies can be postulated at that point, in the expected opposite direction for psychosomatic patients in the active mode with regard to the aspects described above (Schneider et al., 2008a, 2008b). Patients with an active mode of the self-worth conflict reported significantly fewer interpersonal problems in which they were perceived by others as "too introverted/socially avoidant," "too self-insecure/submissive," or "too exploitable/yielding" (Pieh et al., 2009).

Using an innovative study design, Kehyayan et al. (2013) investigated the influence of psychodynamic conflicts on the brain. Healthy subjects were presented with 24 sentences from three different categories for five seconds each: six "neutral," six "generally negative," and twelve "conflict-typical" sentences. The third category consisted of sentences typical of the *In Need of Care vs. Self-Sufficiency* Conflict (e.g., typical for active mode: "I can't say no when someone asks me for help") or the *Self-Worth Conflict* (e.g., "I often think of myself as incompetent"). Subjects were then asked to name the first three words that came to mind first after the presentation of the sentence, and then to *associate freely* with the sentences for 60 seconds. Before the next sentence was presented they were asked to indicate their current emotional mood and their personal agreement with the sentence. The audio recordings of the free associations were played to experienced psychoanalysts who were independent of the other components of the experiment.

They were asked to judge, on the basis of criteria described in the OPD for each conflict, whether the free associations indicated that the conflict in question was personally relevant or had no personal relevance. Based on this assessment, the subjects were divided into two groups: "Conflict apparent" and "Conflict absent." It was found that the presenting of the conflict-relevant sentences, the subjects in the "Conflict apparent" group reported worse mood and higher personal agreement than the subjects in the other group. Regarding the investigation of neural correlates, the authors focused on the anterior cingulate cortex (ACC), which is associated with (especially implicit) emotion regulation (Etkin et al., 2015). In a preliminary study, Schmeing et al. (2013) showed that increased ACC activity was observed during the presentation of conflict-relevant sentences compared to negative and neutral sentences. In addition, Kehyayan et al. (2013) additionally showed that this effect of increased ACC activity for conflict-relevant sentences was greater in the "Conflict apparent" group than in the "Conflict absent" group. Thus, the authors were able to demonstrate a neural effect of individually significant unconscious conflicts. Overall, despite the inherent difficulties of empirically investigating unconscious conflict, the OPD Conflict Axis (Axis III) has an acceptable database even by international standards (Simmonds et al., 2015).

Previous studies have confirmed that the OPD Structure Axis (Axis IV) has acceptable to high reliability overall (Rudolf et al., 1996; Benecke et al., 2009; Doering et al., 2014). Zuccarino et al. (2012) reported a Kappa of .62 for the overall structure assessment, Kaufhold et al. (2017) an intraclass correlation coefficient of .76. Benecke et al. (2009) found a weighted Kappa of .83 for experienced raters, and Doering et al. (2014) reported an intraclass correlation coefficient of .79 for the overall structure rating. Agreements between experienced experts and, for example, students is lower; with the latter tending to rate structural deficits lower (Zimmermann et al., 2012).

A substantial body of research provides empirical evidence in support of the validity of the OPD Structure Axis (Axis IV). In a study conducted by Nitzgen & Brünger (2000) 171 male patients with long-term substance dependence at the outset of their inpatient stay was examined. The findings indicate that patients with neurotic disorders exhibited, on average, superior structural characteristics compared to patients with personality disorders. These patients exhibited the poorest performance in the domain of self-regulation, which was also theoretically anticipated, as this structural area encompasses facets such as affect tolerance and impulse control. These findings are corroborated by a study conducted by Reymann et al. (2000), which similarly identified structural deficiencies in self-regulation (mean = 2.32) and object perception (mean = 2.44) in male alcohol-dependent individuals undergoing detoxification on an inpatient basis. In a study conducted by Uzdawinis et al. (2010), 20 subjects in the prodromal stage of schizophrenia (six classified "far from psychosis" and 14 as "near psychosis") and ten patients with paranoid schizophrenia were assessed using the OPD as a reference. The discrepancies between the two prodromal subgroups (the "near psychosis" group exhibited significantly more pronounced structural deficiencies) indicate that the implementation of the OPD meaningfully could serve as a valuable adjunct to existing early detection, prevention, and psychotherapy methodologies.

In a study conducted by Schauenburg (2000) 49 consecutive patients on a psychotherapy ward were examined. The findings indicated that secure attachment, as defined by Pilkonis and high dependency strivings were associated with a superior structural level. Conversely borderline traits, exaggerated autonomy strivings, and antisocial traits were linked to inferior structural levels. In a sample of 139 subjects, including 19 healthy control subjects, Benecke et al. (2009) also identified highly significant results ($p < .001$). Correlations were observed between the OPD structural level (both overall rating and individual structural dimensions) and various other disorder specific measures. It was found that as the structure became less integrated, the number of concurrent diagnosis (increased, including both Axis I disorders and particularly personality disorders according to SCID interviews). Additionally, higher scores on the Inventory of Personality Organization (IPO), the Borderline Personality Inventory (BPI), and the Global Severity Index of the Symptom Checklist (SCL-90R) were observed. Boeker et al. (2008) identified a correlation with self-injury, while La Parra et al. (2017) and Dinger, Löw et al. (2021) observed a correlation with self-criticism. For overviews of the correlations between the OPD structural level and the presence and number of personality disorders, personality organization, interpersonal problems, symptom severity and attachment style, see Zimmermann et al. (2012) and Rudolf (2020).

A lower structural level at the outset of psychotherapy is linked to diminished treatment outcomes (Spitzer et al., 2004; Schneider et al., 2015). In light of these findings, the decision to pursue long-term psychotherapy from the perspective of psychoanalytic and psychodynamic psychotherapists is significantly influenced by the structural level (Henkel et al., 2019).

Studies on affective mimicry (Bock et al., 2016) have yielded intriguing findings. In the study by Bock et al. (2016), the mimic-affective behavior of 80 women was coded with the FACS (Facial Action Coding System) and the MFZ system (Mimic Function Attribution, Bock et al., 2015). The 2192 negative affect expressions were assigned a reference point by including context information: interactive (the mimic affect expression is directed at the current counterpart), self (the mimic affect is directed at the self, the self-representation), and object (the mimic affect expression is directed at a third person or situation). No correlations were observed between the pure frequencies of affect expressions and the structural level. Negative affect directed at the interviewer (category *interactive*) and affects related to the overall self are positively correlated with a more deficient structural level according to the OPD. In contrast, negative affects referring only to one aspect of the self or the object or to a situational event are correlated with a higher degree of structural integration (Bock et al., 2016). Similar results were observed by Gebhardt et al. (2016). In this study individuals who exhibited a significant discrepancy between their self-assessment of structure (using IPO) and external assessment (OPD structure rating) demonstrated a notable tendency to display disgust mimicry with full eye contact with the interviewer. These findings suggest potential explanation for why patients with structural impairments frequently experience difficulties in interpersonal interactions and often elicit negative affect in their interaction partners.

Additional research has been conducted on the implementation and advancement of the OPD in other languages (Both et al., 2019; Vanegas-Osorio et al., 2020; Vicente et al., 2012) and the integration of the OPD into blended or e-learning tools (Ferber et al., 2014).

Moreover, the DSM-5 (Zimmermann et al., 2013) and the ICD-11 (Tyrer et al., 2019) consider personality disorder in the context of dimensionally graded basic psychological functions.

1.3.1 OPD Questionnaires

Given the considerable time investment required for an accepted OPD diagnosis which entails a comprehensive interview and subsequent rating, the development of self-assessment instruments for Axis III (OPD Conflict Questionnaire, OPD-KF; Benecke et al., 2018) and Axis IV (OPD Structure Questionnaire, OPD-SF; Ehrenthal et al., 2012) have become a recent trend in the field. Additionally, the OPD Structure Questionnaire is also available in a condensed format designated as OPD-SFK (Ehrenthal et al., 2015). The OPD questionnaires are in German and have been validated for German-speaking regions. English translations are available from the authors.

It should be noted that these instruments are intended to supplement, rather than replace, the OPD diagnosis via interview. For example, Ehrenthal et al. (2012) identified four key objectives for the OPD-SF: Firstly, the procedure should be more time-efficient than the interview as a potential screening method; secondly, it should facilitate the collection of large research samples and their use in routine diagnostics; thirdly, the item formulations should facilitate communication with patients regarding therapy planning and focus determination; and fourthly, it should assist in aligning the patients' subjective perspective with the experts' assessment based on individual information about the person, behavior, and life history.

The OPD Conflict Questionnaire (OPD-KF)

Benecke et al. (2018) developed the OPD Conflict Questionnaire (OPD-KF). The questionnaire comprises 66 items and is designed to capture the typical experience and behavioral patterns associated with the respective conflicts, classified according to active and passive coping modes. This enables the formulation of conclusions based on the responses to the conflict themes.

In addition to the description of the test construction, the initial study on the OPD-KF presented findings, on factorial structure, as well as reliability and validity (Benecke et al., 2018). The results indicate that the passive coping modes were more strongly correlated with current psychopathology, measures of structural impairment, and (inversely) life satisfaction than the active modes (with the exception of C3). Furthermore, the OPD-KF may prove useful in predicting symptom severity and life satisfaction. Henkel et al. (2022) demonstrated that the scales assessed with the OPD-KF exhibited distinct and meaningful correlation profiles with the eight scales of the Interpersonal Circumplex Model according to IIP.

The OPD-KF has been examined in relation to structural concepts and psychological personality models (Gisch et al., 2021), job satisfaction and burnout (Gisch et al., 2020), and in the field of sexual medicine (Koops et al., 2021). A modified version for the work context is also currently under development (Kotte et al., 2019). The next steps in the development of the OPD-KF include further development of the scales to improve reliability and a comparison with the OPD expert rating.

The OPD Structure Questionnaire (OPD-SF)

To complement the interview-based expert assessment Ehrenthal et al. (2012) developed a self-assessment instrument: the OPD Structure Questionnaire (OPD-SF). The OPD-SF exhibits excellent psychometric properties and a multitude of indications of validity (Ehrenthal et al., 2012). In addition to translations into Spanish (Lorenzini et al., 2021), Danish, French, English, and Norwegian (Østergård et al., 2019), a validated 12-item screening version exists (Ehrenthal et al., 2015).

The OPD-SF and OPD-SFK were found to correlate with levels of personality function as assessed in interviews. Dinger et al. (2014) identified a significant correlation ($r = .62$) between the OPD expert rating of the Structure Axis (Axis IV) and the combination of interview and questionnaire data which proved particularly effective in predicting external criterion (number of personality disorder diagnoses). This finding underscores the importance of integrating both perspectives into structural diagnostics. The short version (OPD-SFK) also exhibited a significant correlation with the DSM-5 Levels of Personality Functioning Scale ($r = .78$), as evaluated with the STiP-5.1 interview (Zettl et al., 2019), in addition to reflective functioning as measured with the Reflective Functioning Scale, even after statistical adjustment for symptom burden (Zettl et al., 2020).

In the fields of psychopathology and somatic medicine, studies have employed the Structure Questionnaire to assess post-traumatic stress disorders (Baie et al., 2020), eating disorders (Rohde et al., 2019), bipolar disorders (Wagner-Skacel et al., 2020), irritable bowel syndrome (Berens et al., 2021), and diabetes (Ehrenthal et al., 2019). Furthermore, the questionnaire has been used to assess other conditions, including vaginismus and dyspareunia (Koops et al., 2021), quality of life (Crempien et al., 2017), chronic pelvic pain syndrome (Albrecht et al., 2015), and the extent of change in affective experience in depressed patients with vs. without borderline personality disorders (Dinger, Fuchs et al., 2021; Köhling et al., 2016). Furthermore, it has been employed in neuroscientific studies on addiction disorders (Hiebler-Ragger et al., 2021), to elucidate the impact of adverse childhood experiences on subsequent psychopathology (Dagnino et al., 2020; Flenreiss-Frankl et al., 2021; Freier et al., 2022; Krakau et al., 2021), and the examination of conspiracy narratives (Hettich et al., 2022). Psychotherapy studies have also been conducted for the purpose of predicting therapy success (Zeeck et al., 2020), measuring changes (Lübke et al., 2021; Kraus et al., 2021), and predict treatment uptake (Nikendei et al., 2020) and treatment dropout (Immel et al., 2021). Additionally, high levels of agreement have been observed between the OPD-SF and emotional intelligence (Jauk & Ehrenthal, 2020). The OPD-SF or OPD-SFK exhibits a high degree of correlation with other internationally utilized questionnaires that encompass similar domains (Jauk & Ehrenthal, 2020; König et al., 2016; Zimmermann et al., 2015). It can also be "translated" into values of other commonly employed instruments (Zimmermann et al., 2020). Furthermore OPD-SF items can be transferred to item banks for adaptive testing based on IRT analyses (Obbarius et al., 2021).

Notwithstanding the aforementioned limitations, it is feasible to employ the OPD-SF in conjunction with other methods for individual case analysis and therapy planning (Ehrenthal, 2014; Ehrenthal & Dinger, 2019; Ehrenthal & Benecke, 2019). The German OPD-SF is available for download at no cost for non-commercial purposes at www.strukturdiagnostik.de.

1.4 What Is New in the OPD-3

This manual has been completely reorganized from the OPD-2 manual. Whereas previously each Axis was divided into at least three chapters ("Operationalization," "Manualization," and the "Checklists"), all the information for each Axis is now consolidated into a single chapter. This makes the book more organized and eliminates the need for the reader to flip back and forth.

In *Axis I, Mental Disorders, Experience of Illness, and Prerequisites for Treatment* the established descriptive-phenomenological diagnostics (ICD-10/11, DSM-IV/5) are now included in the OPD. This serves the need to accurately capture psychopathological phenomena, which must also have a place in psychodynamic diagnosis. Otherwise, the essential assessment criteria of Axis I are retained but greatly simplified. Important changes include the psychodynamic summary, the consideration of corresponding somatic-psychic-social illness concepts, and motivation. As part of the objective assessment of illness, the global severity and course of the disorder requiring treatment have been adapted to internationally accepted criteria. The Global Assessment of Functioning (GAF) has been divided into the domains of symptoms, occupational function, and social function to improve reliability and validity. The psychotherapy module of the OPD-2 is now fully integrated as a basic component of Axis I.

Axis II, Interpersonal Relations has retained its basic structure: In OPD-3, the central, repetitive, and dysfunctional relationship pattern of a patient is still described from two perspectives, namely from the patient's point of view and from the point of view of the interaction partners. Relationship episodes continue to serve as material. As in OPD-2, a list of relationship items is provided, from which the descriptions applicable to the specific case are selected. The composition of the items in the list remains unchanged. It continues to follow the circumplex logic of interpersonal behavior and makes consistent use of the structure of the Circumplex Model. Similarly, the two experiential perspectives or the interpersonal positions described by the items are summarized and integrated into a relational dynamic formulation. In this way, the relational-dynamic formulation becomes an integral part of the Axis II diagnosis.

The following *changes* have been made in Axis II of the OPD-3:

- The items are now dimensionally scaled. This means that each behavior in the circular model can exist in varying degrees of dysfunctionality. For each item, an *appropriate/ normal,* an *accentuated,* and a clearly *dysfunctional* manifestation has been formulated. These three levels are formulated for each relationship item – a table with brief descriptions of all items at all levels can be found in the appendix (Appendix A).
- Each behavior can also be marked separately as a *resource* if it is judged to be "appropriate."
- A distinction is made between research and clinical scoring. In the clinical evaluation, the significant items can be selected and dimensionally evaluated. Finally, as before, the number of items selected is reduced to three per experience perspective. In the research version, two adjacent and thus similar items are combined (intentionally related to the "clusters" of the SASB). The halved number of items must be scored individually and completely. This has several advantages: Intensities can now be mapped, profiles can be created, and the data are much easier to analyze statistically.

In *Axis III, Conflict,* although the previously described seven conflicts (each with the two coping modes) and the category "Repressed Conflict and Affective Perception" remain, some significant changes have been made:

- Clear description of the basic motivational system of the conflict.
- Description of the "normal" development: What does it look like when a person does not have this conflict, when they have psychologically integrated the corresponding motivational system?
- Distinction between "core affect" (painful, repressed) and the "leading affect" (consciously accessible feeling).
- A distinction between "lifelong" and "current" is enabled, allowing changes (e.g., in the coping mode) to be better mapped.
- The frequently contentious "current conflict" is excluded from the delineation of discrete categories. However, it can be represented by the absence of any conflicts exhibiting a "lifelong" high expression. Instead, a motivational-conflictual theme currently dominates the psychological process.
- The conflict rating is no longer limited to "better" structural levels (well integrated, moderately integrated), but conflicts should be rated at all structural levels (including poorly integrated or disintegrated).
- The manifestations of the conflicts at the structural levels well integrated, moderately integrated, and poorly integrated are formulated.
- The integration of the concept of dilemmas as proposed by Mentzos (e.g., Mentzos, 2002, 2015; Lempa et al., 2017) into the OPD-3 Conflict Axis is presented in a separate chapter (for further research see Section 4.3).

The fundamental structure of *Axis IV, Structure* remains unchanged . However, some adaptions have been made:

- *Defense* has been reintroduced as a ninth dimension and newly conceptualized. The other eight dimensions remain rather unchanged.
- Facets have undergone changes; some facets, such as, *object-related affect differentiation, pleasurable experience*, or *trust* are entirely new; some facets (e.g., *experiencing affects* and *using fantasies*) have been combined; others have been content-refined.
- The previous "intermediate levels" which were situated between the well and moderate levels, the moderate and poor levels, and the poor and disintegrated levels have now also been formulated. Consequently, the Axis IV checklist has become considerably more comprehensive, yet also more transparent and nuanced.
- The "lower" structural levels have been entirely revised, particularly to align them with the tenets of psychiatry. This revision was

undertaken with the aim to depicting both psychotic and psychopathic disintegration equally, without relying on specific psychopathologies to describe them. Noted experts in psychodynamic psychotherapy for psychoses were engaged for collaboration on the Structure Axis.

- The table that provides comprehensive descriptions of all facets at all levels and intermediate levels (Section 5.5.6) now constitutes the full text of the Structure Axis. Furthermore, a succinct overview of the primary levels is provided in Appendix C.
- Two optional variability ratings have been introduced. A temporal rating may be used to map changes in the structural level over time (e.g., following a traumatic life event) and a life domain-specific one that allows differences in the availability of structural functions in various life domains (e.g., a higher level in the work area, a lower level in the intimacy area) to be mapped. This capacity to map discrepancies in the structural level introduces a further dimension to the structural diagnosis offering a more accurate representation of a greater number of patients.

1.5 Conclusion

Experience with the OPD shows that the constructed axes are practical for clinical use and can generally be reliably assessed.

Based on empirical findings and experiences in clinical work with the OPD, as well as insights from OPD training seminars, the initiative for a further revision of the OPD has arisen. Research results and the requirements of clinical applicability demonstrate that the OPD needs to be continually modified. This need conflicts with the endeavor to provide an instrument with a certain continuity and clarity – a problem we hope to solve in a creative and user-friendly manner.

Overall, the OPD-3 is *more multidimensional* and much more *differentiated* than the previous versions. This has the advantage that the individual characteristics of patients can be represented much better, and thus psychological complexity can be better taken into account. The disadvantage is that it may take more time to learn and the complexity may seem daunting at first. Hopefully, the small amount of additional effort required to use the OPD-3 will be more than compensated for by the significant gain in clinically useful validity.

2 Axis I: Mental Disorders, Experience of Illness, and Prerequisites for Treatment

2.1 Summarized Presentation of Axis I

As an initial step for psychodynamic diagnostics, Axis I comprises the assessment of the mental disorders, the current subjective experience of illness and the prerequisites for psychotherapy.

For the indication and implementation of psychotherapeutic or psychiatric/psychosomatic treatment, the type of symptoms, the externally assessed severity of the disorder, and the patient's subjective experience of illness and treatment prerequisites are crucial.

This is an external assessment, i.e., an objective evaluation of the subjective information provided by the patient. Descriptive diagnostics according to ICD-10/1 or DSM-5, previously depicted in Axis V of the OPD, are integrated into Axis I in the present version to emphasize the necessity of accurately capturing psychopathological phenomena. Patients seek help due to complaints and symptoms, and these should be systematically recorded. The course and severity of the mental and/or somatic disorder, along with their consequences, are also assessed. Furthermore, subjective illness concepts and subjective change and treatment concepts are interrelated and influence each other mutually. These include a somatic illness concept, an external oriented illness concept with emphasis on social and/or alternative dimensions. Furthermore, an internal illness concept captures the extent to which the patient acknowledges mental and interpersonal aspects in the development of their disorder.

These subjective illness concepts lead to subjective change concepts, which essentially drive the motivation concerning the chosen treatment. The assessment and consideration of these areas of motivation must be taken into account before treatment and during subsequent therapy as they influence compliance/adherence. The change resources include the level of distress and coping resources, current psychosocial support, and openness to a psychosocial genesis of the complaints and problems.

External and internal impediments to change can oppose treatment, both in outpatient and inpatient settings. These include fears of negative social consequences. Internal impediments to change and treatment are described as conscious and unconscious resistance phenomena against change and treatment. Additionally, a distinction is made between primary and secondary gain from illness.

If there is an indication for the application of a psychotherapeutic procedure and sufficient motivation for its implementation/realization, it is helpful to understand what therapeutic activities the patient expects to achieve their goal: The primary focus is usually the desire to reduce psycho/somatic symptoms. Additionally, many patients find it important to understand how and why their symptoms developed to derive strategies for change (reflection and clarification). Often, patients seek emotional support, relief, comfort, and assistance in psychotherapy to better cope with their complaints and problems (emotional support). Lastly, patients seek varying degrees of active guidance in psychotherapy to master their complaints and problems.

Summarizing these individual and varying illness concepts and treatment prerequisites for each patient enables an initial understanding of problems/disorders and their possible treatment for all forms of psychotherapy. Initial psychodynamic descriptions (conscious and unconscious conflicts, resistance, and gain from illness) point to the psychodynamic assessment level (Axis III) and the structural framework conditions of the patient (Axis IV).

2.2 Introduction to Axis I

Axis I initially assesses the syndromal-descriptive diagnoses according to ICD-10/11 (or optionally DSM-5). These were depicted in Axis V in OPD-1 and OPD-2 and are now integrated into Axis I in the current OPD-3. Following this, the subjective experience of illness, the concepts of illness and change with existing change resources and impediments, as well as treatment motivation, are examined.

The entire Axis I is understood as an objectifying assessment of the subjective information provided by the patient. For the indication and implementation/realization of psychotherapeutic (or other) treatment, besides the type of symptoms and the externally assessed severity of the disorder, the subjective experience of illness and the subjective treatment prerequisites are of decisive importance. It is essential to understand the extent of the patient's subjective suffering, whether they can understand psychosomatic and psychodynamic relationships, and which specific illness concepts and treatment wishes they are pursuing. The indication is further influenced by a person's motivation and change resources (e.g., distress, coping with illness, psychosocial support, and openness) as well as impediments to change (external and internal impediments, secondary gain from illness). These aspects are crucial for the indication and must therefore be at the forefront of the diagnostic-therapeutic process.

In OPD-3, the essential assessment criteria are continued from OPD-2. However, several changes have been made for the purpose of systematization, simplification, updating, or better understanding. Since the descriptive-phenomenological classification of the disorder is highly relevant for diagnosis and therapy planning, it is now integrated into Axis I (formerly Axis V). Other significant changes include the simplifying integration of the experience of illness and subjective illness concepts and corresponding therapy motivation. Systematization has also been achieved by assigning subjective illness concepts to a profile that follows the attribution of external or internal causes. As part of the evaluation of the illness, the global severity and course of the disorder requiring treatment were adjusted to internationally accepted criteria. The Global Assessment of Functioning (GAF) has been subdivided into the domains of symptoms, occupational function, and social function to improve reliability and validity.

The diagnostic basis of Axis I consists of the verbal and nonverbal expressions of the patient, which are objectified by the examiner within their knowledge. Generally, the current clinical findings are assessed. The *time window* refers to the last 28 days, except for the GAF or the EQ-5D, which refer to the last 7 days according to instructions. The extent of all assessment criteria is evaluated on a scale with levels ranging from zero to four. The levels mean: 0 = not present, 1 = no characteristic present, 2 = moderately present, 3 = highly present, and 4 = very highly present. If an assessment criterion cannot be evaluated, a nine (9 = not assessable) is assigned. Anchor examples are provided for all criteria, each for levels 0, 2, and 4.

Beyond the fundamentals (Schüßler & Bertl-Schüßler, 2011), the clinical-empirical significance of these assessment criteria of Axis I (e.g., psychotherapy motivation), is underscored by the review in the *Handbook of Psychotherapy and Behavior Change* (Lambert, 2013), especially Bohart & Wade (2013).

2.3 Classification: Mental and Behavioral Disorders

As before, OPD-3 refers to the *International Classification of Diseases ICD* or the *Diagnostic and Statistical Manual of Mental Disorders DSM-5* for the descriptive-phenomenological classification of symptoms and behavioral disorders. The ICD-10 was replaced by the ICD-11 in 2022 and will only be valid for a transition period of 5 years thereafter, which should be considered.

For a detailed presentation of the categorical systems, please refer to the respective manuals. The ICD and DSM follow the general rule of coding as many (comorbid) diagnoses as necessary to describe the clinical picture. The main diagnosis is the category with the greatest current significance or the so-called "lifetime diagnosis" with the highest relevance. For the documentation of main and additional diagnoses in the field of psychosomatics/psychotherapy, no more than five additional diagnoses should be coded alongside a main diagnosis for clinical use. Only the diagnosis that has the highest relevance from clinical and psychodynamic perspectives should be considered the main diagnosis. Additional diagnoses should only be coded if they contribute to the understanding of the overall picture or if they have course- and/or therapy-determining aspects. All previous application and reliability studies have shown that proper use of the descriptive diagnostics according to ICD or DSM requires training.

It is important to note that certain ICD/DSM diagnoses do not automatically correlate with specific OPD criteria, e.g., not every patient with anorexia nervosa or suffering from personality disorder can automatically be considered to be structurally poorly integrated (OPD Axis Structure).

2.4 Objectifying Severity of the Disorder

The symptoms and severity of the disorder are recorded in the classic symptom-based diagnostic manuals ICD or DSM. In the global severity of the disorder, the somatic and/or mental components of the disorder are also assessed in terms of extent, duration, and impairment caused by the symptoms. The additional global assessment of functioning (GAF) differentiates the importance of occupational and social functioning, as well as symptomatology within the last 7 days, and allows this to be documented over the course of therapy. The modified EQ-5D, as a quality-of-life instrument, depicts the impact of the physical side of the disorder.

Since both the further course and the therapeutic prognosis are influenced by the previous course of the disorder, it is necessary to map its course to date.

2.4.1 Global Severity of the Disorder

The severity of the mental and/or somatic disorder depends on its nature, extent, and consequences. The current severity of the disorder should be assessed in terms of an objectifying evaluation. The assessment of global severity should be made for both physical and mental disorders. Problems that cannot be classified as syndromal disorders according to ICD or DSM, such as significant partnership issues or interpersonal conflicts at work, should also be evaluated.

The assessment aims to evaluate the clinical findings or impairments in the somatic, mental, and social areas, regardless of the type of underlying disease. The principle is, findings take precedence over nosology!

The current severity of the complaints and problems is determined by

- the intensity of the symptoms,
- the frequency and respective duration of the complaints,
- the medically necessary treatment measures, and
- decisively by the impairment of the patient's usual activities and life activities.

For somatic complaints, the current physical symptoms and the associated limitations of physical functioning should be assessed.

The severity of mental symptoms or issues is related to the individual intrapsychic burden on the one hand as well as to problems on the level of psychosocial adaptation on the other hand. For example, experiencing frequent and severe anxiety attacks can be extremely intrapsychic and psychologically burdensome for the affected individual; moreover, the anxiety disorder can lead to significant behavioral and relational limitations due to avoidance behavior. Therefore, the extent of psychosocial functioning and the ability to adapt socially in interpersonal relationships, work, and leisure is of decisive importance for assessing the severity of the mental disorder (Table 1).

2.4.2 Global Assessment of Psychosocial Functioning and Mental Symptoms (GAF)

The Global Assessment of Functioning (GAF) scale was introduced into psychotherapeutic practice and research to enable an objectifying assessment of psychosocial symptoms. As a global assessment of mental, social, and occupational functioning, it was part of the DSM IV (APA, 2000). To improve the differentiation between mental, social, and occupational domains of functioning and to increase the reliability of the assessment, a separate recording of these domains was proposed and reviewed (Niv et al., 2007).

Unlike the usual 28-day time frame, the assessment of the respective social, occupational (or academic) functioning level and mental symptoms here refers to the last seven days. The respective domains are assessed on a continuum from mental health to severe illness-related limitations (Table 2). The maximum value of the functioning level in the current period is to be assessed. Depending on the scope and possibilities of the diagnostic assessment, all three functional areas should be evaluated separately. However, in the context of shorter clinical assessments, at least the mental symptoms must be rated.

2.4.3 EQ-5D Modified: Physical Limitations in Essential/Crucial Areas of Life

The EQ-5D is a health questionnaire that provides a unidimensional measure of quality of life. In its original version, the EQ-5D was developed by the EuroQol Group (euroqol.org) as a self-report instrument (Rabin & De Charro, 2001; Szende et al., 2014). On a scale between level one and level three (1=not/hardly applicable, 2=moderately applicable, 3=highly applicable), the patient is to indicate which statements best describe their current health status for the last seven days prior to the assessment.

The original version of the EQ-5D has been reformulated and modified as an observer-rating instrument for the purposes of Axis I (EQ-5D modified). This concerns the physical areas, namely mobility, self-care, daily activities, and pain/physical complaints (Table 3). The assessment of anxiety/depression is omitted, as it is already included in the GAF.

Mental disorders with physical limitations are also documented here.

Table 1. Symptom level scores and anchor descriptions in the global severity of disorders

Level	Feature expressions	Anchor examples
Level 0 Not present	There are no physical or mental symptoms present (or only minor everyday complaints). In the medical-social context, there is no need for treatment.	**Example 1:** A patient, after several years of successfully treated ovarian carcinoma, currently has no physical or mental impairments. **Example 2:** A habitually cautious and reserved patient, who occasionally experiences mild anxiety, reports no current psychosocial impairments and shows no signs of anxious vegetative hyperarousal during examination.
Level 2 Moderately present	The patient exhibits clinically relevant mental and/or physical symptoms with corresponding physical and psychosocial functional impairments. Diagnosable disorders are present, which are considered treatable in the medical-social context. Thus, the patient is assigned the sick role.	**Example 1:** A patient with cardiovascular disease recently experienced cardiac symptoms (e.g., chest pain, mild shortness of breath) and increased fears of having a heart attack. **Example 2:** A young patient with a chronic rheumatic autoimmune disease complains of severe vision deterioration and bone pain due to inflammation, as well as increased dysphoric-depressive mood and heightened fears of going blind. She reports having little strength to fight her illness since her recent and very hurtful divorce and seeks treatment for this reason. **Example 3:** A patient suffers from anxiety attacks twice a week with moderate vegetative signs (tachycardia, sweating, dizziness, etc.) and shows significant avoidance behavior.
Level 4 Very highly present	The patient has significant physical and/or mental symptoms. These are generally considered to be in acute need of treatment from both a medical and social perspective.	**Example 1:** A patient with insulin-dependent diabetes mellitus has started measuring blood sugar levels hourly in recent weeks and adjusting the necessary insulin medication up and down, leading to frequent blood sugar spikes and life-threatening hypoglycemia, requiring emergency medical intervention. **Example 2:** A patient with obesity (BMI 45 kg/m^2) and a pronounced metabolic syndrome has severe depression with massive drive disorder and psychotic symptoms. She is severely restricted in her mobility and in need of care. **Example 3:** A patient with generalized anxiety and almost daily panic attacks for the past four weeks is massively restricted in his activities and shows significant withdrawal and avoidance tendencies. He can no longer leave the house alone. Others do his errands for him. During panic attacks, he has severe physical symptoms, fears of going insane, and even fears of dying. He has called the emergency medical services multiple times in the last two weeks. **Example 4:** A chronically schizophrenic patient, previously relatively well-compensated in the context of the secondary labor market, is re-admitted to the clinic after discontinuing his antipsychotic medication weeks ago and decompensating into paranoid delusions again.

Table 2. Global assessment of psychological, social, and workplace functional areas (GAF)

Level of functioning	Psychological symptoms	Social functions	Occupational/academic functions
91–100	No mental symptoms	Very good social activities	Very good occupational/ academic performance
81–90	Usual, non-clinical everyday complaints	Good social functioning	Good occupational/academic performance
71–80	Transient mild symptoms, (e.g., after stress)	Transient mild social difficulties after stress	Transient mild occupational/ academic difficulties after stress (e.g., slight performance decrease – "slump")
61–70	Moderate symptoms (e.g., ongoing mild depression or anxiety)	Moderate social difficulties (e.g., interpersonal conflicts, at most mild social withdrawal while maintaining some important interpersonal relationships)	Moderate occupational/ academic difficulties (e.g., slightly reduced performance capability)
51–60	Persistent moderate complaints (e.g., moderate anxiety or depression, affective flattening, etc.)	Persistent moderate social limitations (e.g., interpersonal conflicts with relationship crises) and/or moderate social withdrawal with important social contacts	Persistent moderate occupational/academic impairments (e.g., moderate performance limitations, absenteeism)
41–50	Serious symptoms (e.g., significant anxiety, depression, or compulsions, often intoxicated, etc.)	Serious social difficulties (e.g., frequent, very stressful social conflicts) and/or noticeable social withdrawal with still existing social contacts	Serious occupational/ academic difficulties (e.g., even with work support, significantly limited performance)
31–40	Very serious symptoms (e.g., distortions of reality, hallucinations, delusions, etc.)	Very serious social difficulties (e.g., extensive social-communicative difficulties in most social contacts, hardly any social contacts)	Very serious occupational/ academic difficulties (e.g., even with the support of others, no performance capability)
0–30	Most serious mental difficulties (e.g., most severe cognitive deficits, severe intoxications, danger of hurting self and/or others' etc.)	Most serious social difficulties (e.g., only brief communication or interactions possible)	Most serious occupational/ academic limitations (e.g., inability to work or perform, daily life cannot be organized independently)

Note. Adapted from Niv et al. (2007).

Table 3. Modified operationalization EQ-5D

Area	State of health	Level
Mobility	The patient has no problems walking around.	Level 1
	The patient has some problems walking around.	Level 2
	The patient is confined to bed.	Level 3
Self-care	The patient has no problems taking care of themselves.	Level 1
	The patient has some problems washing or dressing themselves or preparing food.	Level 2
	The patient is unable to wash or dress themselves or prepare food.	Level 3
Usual activities	The patient has no problems performing usual activities (e.g., work, study, housework, family or leisure activities).	Level 1
	The patient has some problems performing usual activities.	Level 2
	The patient is unable to perform usual activities.	Level 3
Pain/physical discomfort	The patient has no pain or physical discomfort.	Level 1
	The patient has moderate pain or physical discomfort.	Level 2
	The patient has extreme pain or physical discomfort.	Level 3
Examples		
Example 1: A patient with dementia can still move well (Level 1) but is limited in self-care (Level 2) and can no longer perform usual activities (Level 2). However, they have no pain or physical discomfort (Level 1). Example 2: An acutely delusional patient can hardly walk (Level 3), has significant problems with self-care (Level 3), has considerable difficulties with usual activities (Level 3), and suffers from pain (Level 3).		

Note. Adapted with permission from "EQ-SD: A measure of health status from the EuroQol group" by R. Rabin & F. De Charro, *Annals of Medicine, 33*(5), 337–343. © 2001 The Finnish Medical Society Duodecim.

2.5 Duration and Course of the Disorder

2.5.1 Duration of the Treatment-Requiring Mental Disorder (Main Diagnosis)

The onset, duration, and course of symptoms are significant both for assessing the severity of a disorder and for the prognosis of a psychotherapy aimed at achieving change. In the case of a prolonged chronic disorder, dysfunctional adaptation processes typically occur at the somatic, mental, and social levels (e.g., in chronic pain disorders), which develop their own dynamics and can considerably affect both personal integration and the individual's psychosocial adaptation (e.g., occupational performance).

The onset, duration, and course of the currently existing primary mental complaints or primary problems should be recorded (Table 4) in the sense of the current "primary mental diagnosis." Both disorders with predominantly mental symptoms (e.g., depression, compulsion) and those with predominantly physical symptoms, i.e., psychosomatic diseases in the narrower sense, should be considered.

The onset is defined by the age at the first manifestation of this disorder.

The duration of this disorder is recorded using the following scale:

- < 6 months
- 6–24 months
- > 2–10 years
- > 10 years

If previous illnesses with other mental and/or physical symptoms than the current main complaints have occurred in the past, these previous illnesses should be named if possible. This serves to determine the general mental burden (Table 4).

Table 4. Duration for the current primary mental disorder (main diagnosis) with examples for illustration

Duration of the current primary mental disorder (main diagnosis) with examples	
Example 1	A 24-year-old patient comes for treatment of her anxiety disorder, which has increasingly troubled her since she started her studies 2 years ago. She states that between the ages of 14 and 16 she was treated as an inpatient for a total of 2 ½ years due to severe anorexia. She was symptom-free between the ages of 18 and 22. The anxiety disorder, for which the patient is currently seeking treatment, is the current "primary mental disorder," (i.e., main diagnosis) while anorexia nervosa is considered a previous disorder. The age at the first manifestation of the current main diagnosis is therefore given as "22 years," and its duration as "6-24 months."
Example 2	A 28-year-old patient developed multiple symptoms and complaints at the age of 16, which were diagnosed as a developmental disorder in child and adolescent psychiatry. She now suffers from severe depressive moods and self-harming behavior. The current emotionally unstable personality disorder, for which the patient is now seeking treatment, is the "primary mental disorder," (i.e., main diagnosis) within which the developmental disorder is seen. The age at the first manifestation of the current main diagnosis is therefore given as "16 years," and its duration as "> 10 years."

2.5.2 Course of the Disorder

The course of the disorder (main diagnosis) influences the experience of the illness, the level of suffering, the motivation for treatment, and the prognosis. In the case of an acute first-time disorder, the patient must immediately develop an attitude towards the illness and its management. With a chronic disorder, it will largely depend on the extent to which the complaints permanently affect the patients' life or whether there are also symptom-free intervals.

Complaints lasting no longer than 6 months are considered "acute," while those persisting for more than 6 months are termed "chronic." Initially, it should be assessed whether the complaints tend to remain the same, increase, or decrease, as this can significantly influence the disease experience. It should then additionally be evaluated whether the symptoms fluctuate or whether symptom-free intervals occur in an episodic-phasic course or a relapsing progression.

Based on the course characteristics, the types of courses are distinguished in Table 5.

An illness is also considered chronic if a patient remains symptom-free for years under successful continuous medical treatment after the initial diagnosis of the disease.

Example 1, Chronic Course:
A patient diagnosed with Crohn's disease three years ago remains physically symptom-free and able to work under ongoing medication treatment ("chronically stable").

Example 2, Chronic Course:
A patient with bulimia nervosa, diagnosed six years ago, has only had about one binge-purge episode per month over the past four years with the help of psychotherapy ("chronically stable").

If a patient experiences a recurrence of the same disorder after being symptom-free for more than 10 years, it is considered a new onset and the duration is assessed accordingly (e.g., 5 months).

Example 3, New Onset:
A patient who was successfully treated for six months for a depressive episode at the age of 25 after the death of his mother and remained

Table 5. Types of disorder courses with examples for illustration

Course of the disorder (main diagnosis)	Duration
Acute course	Duration of complaints up to 6 months
Chronic course	Duration of complaints longer than 6 months
Fluctuating-decreasing	Example: A patient has been suffering from back and neck pain for 10 years with fluctuating pain intensity, sometimes better, then worse again, overall decreasing over the past year.
Fluctuating-progressive	Example: A patient has been suffering from back and neck pain for 10 years, with fluctuating pain intensities that have increased over the years.
Recurrent/episodic/phasic, thereby remitting	Example: A patient with bipolar disorder has been experiencing a moderate depressive episode each fall for the past three years, usually lasting about three months, remaining symptom-free and able to work in between episodes.
Recurrent/episodic/phasic, thereby progressive	Example: In a schizophrenic patient who chronically and repeatedly decompensates psychotically, his negative symptoms increase with each further episode of the disorder.
Stable	Example: A 40-year-old patient with anorexia nervosa has had a consistent BMI of around 16 kg/m² for 15 years, with only slight weight fluctuations of up to 2 kg.

symptom-free since then, experiences a new depressive episode (currently 4 months) at the age of 47 after losing his job and requires treatment again.

2.6 Subjective Illness Concepts

The subjective illness concept significantly influences motivation for and the desired form of treatment. It captures how the patient currently explains the bio-psycho-social aspects of their suffering (physical/mental complaints, symptoms, problems). It involves the patient's subjective explanations for the onset or course of the illness.

It is determined to what extent patients attribute their disorder internally, i.e., they understand its cause primarily as intrapsychic (internal "intrapsychic illness concept") or they attribute it to physical factors ("somatic illness concept") or to non-psychic factors outside their own person ("external illness concept"), e.g., in the social environment or other, e.g., spiritual causes. This differentiation is treatment-relevant because, unlike the former, the latter hardly assume that they can influence and change their illness themselves. Internal, external, and somatic attributions can exist simultaneously, so the different illness concepts must be assessed independently.

The examiner gains an impression of the patient's subjective understanding of their illness through spontaneously expressed ideas about their complaints and their development and through specifically asked questions about the causes of the illness. It is irrelevant whether the subjective illness theory is biomedically or psychologically appropriate or not.

In the diagnostic interview, it is essential to identify and work out what subjective meaning the patient currently attributes to a life event (e.g., neglect, deaths, separations, (sexual) experienced violence, job loss, caregiving for relatives) for the development or course of their illness.

2.6.1 Somatic Illness Concept

This feature/item/symptom captures the extent to which the patient currently has a subjective understanding of the illness that focuses on biomedical explanations/causes. Complaints and problems (e.g., relationship conflicts) are predominantly seen as caused or significantly influenced by physical mechanisms, processes, deficiencies, weaknesses, defects, damage, etc. Especially mental processes (e.g., pain, depression, or anxiety) are explained biologically (possibly even after severe external events such as accidents, experiences of violence). This refers to a predominantly mechanistic and/or somato-medical understanding of the illness, with the subjective experience that the complaints and problems are the result of medical-biological dysfunctions: "Something is wrong with my body!" (Table 6).

Table 6. Symptom level scores and anchor descriptions for the somatic illness concept

Level	Feature expressions	Anchor examples
Level 0 Not present	This level is indicated when the patient's account shows that complaints and problems are not related to medical biological causes.	**Example 1:** A patient with symptoms of fatigue, sadness, and morning sickness can only fulfill her daily duties with great effort. She does not believe that the symptoms have medical-biological causes. **Example 2:** An alcoholic patient with withdrawal syndrome denies a substance-related cause for his acute symptoms. He explains his current anxiety-driven restlessness with his recovered memories of childhood experiences of violence.
Level 2 Moderately present	This level is indicated when patients consider a somatic cause of their complaints, e.g., due to an infection, an accident, an operation, or other physical damage, but are not completely sure about it.	**Example 1:** A patient with erectile dysfunction suspects that the most likely cause is his advanced diabetes mellitus and renal insufficiency but constantly broods over whether partnership conflicts are also significant since he and his wife often have heated arguments. **Example 2:** A patient describes symptoms of fatigue, sadness, morning sickness, making it very difficult for her to fulfill her daily duties. It all started after a severe, persistent flu. The patient suspects that her body was so weakened and shattered by the flu ("immune system") that she has not been able to recover. She now hopes that thorough examinations will confirm the physical cause but also considers that the complaints could be partly due to overwork in recent times.
Level 4 Very highly present	This level is chosen when patients are convinced that almost exclusively somatic causes are responsible for the complaints. The patient names clear causal relations and demands specific investigations and first therapeutic steps.	**Example 1:** A patient is convinced that he suffers from infection-related bodily complaints. He repeatedly demands new diagnostics and new treatments from his doctors. He dismisses objections that neither typical signs of infection nor corresponding antibodies have been found and is not influenced in his subjective understanding of the illness. **Example 2:** A patient with a somatoform pain disorder insists on further predominantly organic medical examinations and specific physical therapies to finally receive the "correct" treatment, as she is clearly physically ill.

2.6.2 External Attribution

Socially Oriented Illness Concept

This feature/item/symptom covers the extent to which the patient currently has a subjective understanding of illness that focuses on external social factors. It aims to assess the degree to which the patient views external social influences as causal for their current complaints (e.g., depression, anxiety, sleep disorders, pain) and problems (e.g., emotional conflicts, interpersonal conflicts). These social conditions are perceived by the patient as largely independent of their person and mental experiences. The patient considers the complaints as caused by external factors, outside their own doing and responsibility.

The causal conditions are subjectively rooted in the external social environment, such as involuntary unemployment due to company insolvency, "mobbing" experiences following workplace restructuring, sudden financial distress due to financial fraud, partners who only argue, unavoidable caregiving for a family member, or a traumatic life event (e.g., an accident not of their own doing/an accident through no fault of their own). They are not understood as the result of life-long internalization processes or as the consequences of the emotional-interactive processing of unfavorable life experiences, but rather as external causes. In this respect, the general psychosocial/emotional-interactive or socio-economic conditions of individual upbringing are not meant here, such as warm-hearted supportive vs. cold-hearted neglectful parents or poverty vs. wealth. Rather, it is about the patient's subjective experience that, without the respective external social conditions/factors/circumstances/influences, their complaints and problems would not have occurred from their perspective: "I am not to blame. If the event hadn't happened, I would be as well as before!" (Table 7).

When intensively expressed, there is a high subjective certainty that often overshadows the possibility of other causes. If a patient identifies one or more extremely stressful external events as the cause of their complaints in the sense of a possible trauma, the additional stress- and trauma module provides further differentiation.

Table 7. Symptom level scores and anchor descriptions for the socially oriented illness concept

Level	Feature expressions	Anchor examples
Level 0 Not present	This level is indicated when the patient describes no link/relation between their complaints and external social causes. Even if these seem likely from the examiner's perspective, the patient denies them upon questioning.	**Example 1:** A patient, after a divorce, finds himself unexpectedly in financial distress due to a company insolvency and fears he will not be able to pay off his mortgage, developing a range of psychosomatic symptoms from loss of appetite to sleep disturbances. However, he does not relate these symptoms to his social changes. **Example 2:** A patient has been taking care of her dementia-stricken mother alone for several years while working part-time. Around the same time her mother became dependent on care, she began experiencing severe muscle pain. Even when the examiner suggests it is understandable for her to feel pain under such a burden, she denies it. She strongly emphasizes that taking care of her mother is not a burden and that she enjoys doing it.

Table 7. Symptom level scores and anchor descriptions for the socially oriented illness concept *(continued)*

Level	Feature expressions	Anchor examples
Level 2 Moderately present	This level is chosen when the patient can identify external factors as causes for their complaints, but these do not stand out prominently or are accompanied by uncertainty, and/or the patient fluctuates in the certainty regarding external social stressors.	**Example 1:** A patient, besides recognizing his biological vulnerability for recurrent depression, can also identify external factors as equally significant. He suspects that the current depressive episode may have been triggered by his separation from his wife and moving out of their shared home. **Example 2:** A patient is not yet sure about her illness concept. With the help of the examiner, social-external factors (e.g., job loss) can be identified and acknowledged. However, she remains uncertain about their significance.
Level 4 Very highly present	This level is chosen when the patient is confident that external social factors have caused their illness. It is without doubt for them that other people or "circumstances" are to blame for their illness.	**Example 1:** A patient reports complete chronic exhaustion that developed since the imminent bankruptcy of his company. Since employees were laid off, his supervisor has been giving him more work, which can only be managed with a 13-hour workday. This is the cause of his illness. **Example 2:** A 50-year-old patient shamefully reports physical abuse by a family member during her childhood and adolescence, which only ended after her suicide attempt at the age of 17 and blames her parents for the fact that she cannot sustain a lasting partnership.

Alternative Illness Concepts

This feature/item/symptom covers the extent to which the patient currently has a subjective understanding of their illness that focuses on alternative disease concepts. The term "alternative" refers to ideas of the patient that cannot be assigned to either a somatogenic, a sociogenetic or a psychogenetic understanding of illness. In the patient's description of their complaints, the causes of their illness, and their treatment ideas, it becomes clear that they attribute their suffering to such alternative reasons. Patients may develop a variety of alternative disease concepts, such as esoteric concepts ("moon phases") or magical-fatalistic beliefs ("fate," "bewitched"), often accompanied by pronounced self-neglect and resignation: "There's nothing I can do!" (Table 8).

2.6.3 Intrapsychic Illness Concept

This feature/item/symptom maps the extent to which the patient currently has a subjective understanding of their illness that focuses on their own mental and interpersonal aspects. The aim is to determine the extent to which the patient recognizes their complaints (e.g., depression, anxiety, sleep disturbances, pain) and problems (e.g., emotional conflicts, interpersonal conflicts) in relation to their own intrapsychic experience and interpersonal behavior. The causes of the complaints and problems are located within themselves, their own experiences and behavior, not externally. Although a patient may report that external social factors (e.g., marriage, childbirth, workplace restructuring, retirement) have served as triggers, they view the illness as rooted in their inadequate internal emotional and cognitive handling of these external social factors. Regardless of external triggers, the patient attributes their disorder to their own interpersonal vulnerability: "Others wouldn't have problems in this situation; I get sick because I can't handle ..." (Table 9).

Table 8. Symptom level scores and anchor descriptions for the alternative illness concept

Level	Feature expressions	Anchor examples
Level 0 Not present	This level is chosen when the patient has no alternative subjective notions about what has caused their illness or what could help them.	**Example 1:** A patient with lung cancer firmly believes that his long-term chain smoking made him sick, not "fate." He hopes to get help through surgery, and if necessary, chemotherapy and radiation. **Example 2:** A patient who has been suffering from an anxiety disorder for years has no idea what made her sick or what could help her. Her husband believes that amalgam in her teeth is the cause, but she thinks that is wrong. Even when asked, she cannot explain her symptoms that way.
Level 2 Moderately present	This level is indicated when the patient is not entirely sure but considers it possible that unidentified alternative factors are the cause of their illness.	**Example 1:** A patient with lung cancer suspects that his long-term chain smoking is an important factor in his illness but leans more towards the idea that his illness is ultimately "bewitched fate." **Example 2:** A patient with an anxiety disorder believes it is likely that her illness is caused by a water vein under her house and has corresponding investigations carried out, but she is not completely sure and, as a precaution, also looks for additional medically acknowledged or psychological causes.
Level 4 Very highly present	This level is chosen when the patient is certain that alternative (not recognized by conventional medicine) causes are decisive for their illness.	**Example 1:** A patient with lung cancer consistently refuses medical help because he is convinced that he has been "bewitched" and that "negative energies" made him sick. He therefore turns to a faith healer. **Example 2:** A patient believes that the causes of her anxiety disorder are predominantly or exclusively environmental toxins. She wants to trust an alternative environmental healer because she distrusts conventional medicine and only believes in the healing power of herbs.

The examiner tries to ascertain during the interview whether the patient can identify personal emotional, cognitive, or behavioral factors that they consider significant for the development and maintenance of their complaints. These can be reported spontaneously by the patient during the interview or collected by the examiner with the help of and in response to questions.

At a high level, a patient will report considering their emotions, attitudes, and/or behaviors as the decisive cause of the problem and may elaborate further, regardless of whether this is correct. At a low level, the patient reports few relations with and only vague, little-detailed ideas about triggering internal conditions.

The evaluation does not assess whether the explanatory models are coherent and correct, but only whether they refer to psychosocial-internal factors.

Table 9. Symptom level scores and anchor descriptions for the intrapsychic illness concept

Level	Feature expressions	Anchor examples
Level 0 Not present	This level is indicated when the patient does not consider any relation between their psychosocial self and their complaints, even when asked.	**Example 1:** A patient with a depressive disorder reports problems in her relationship. However, she believes these have nothing to do with her. She rejects the examiner's suggestions of an association between the symptoms and her processing of relationship problems. **Example 2:** A patient with a chronic pain disorder reports that the pain regularly worsens under stress but categorically rejects any possible link to stressors in his life situation as suggested by the examiner.
Level 2 Moderately present	This level is chosen when the patient can recognize links/relations between their complaints and internal factors but is unsure about it.	**Example 1:** A patient with chronic psychosomatic complaints can, with the help of the examiner, understand that specific changes in his life (e.g., children moving out and the resulting fear of loneliness) exacerbate his complaints. However, he repeatedly seeks for other causes. **Example 2:** A young patient, after repeated physical violence from her husband, wonders what her experiences of childhood physical abuse from her alcoholic father "have to do with it," but is still unsure.
Level 4 Very highly present	This level is chosen when the patient clearly acknowledges links between psychosocial-internal factors and their complaints and reflects on their thoughts and actions and their causal effects on the complaints.	**Example 1:** A patient with anxiety symptoms spontaneously reports that his condition is related to stress at work and laments that his colleagues do not become ill because they can better set boundaries against demands and handle stress, in contrast to him. **Example 2:** A patient is convinced that her recurring dizziness is solely due to her insecurity resulting from marital problems. She dismisses other causes (e.g., CT and MRI findings).

2.7 Change and Treatment Concepts

Subjective change concepts significantly influence the willingness and motivation for the treatment to be chosen. This item/feature/symptom captures the bio-psycho-social form of treatment through which the patient wishes and expects a change or improvement for their problems and specifically, what form of therapy they are seeking.

The focus here is not on whether the treatment forms favored by the patient are considered indicated or feasible by the clinician to alleviate the suffering. However, discrepancies between the illness and change concepts of patients and clinicians must be clarified and aligned prior to treatment to avoid jeopardizing compliance or adherence.

The psychodynamic motive constellation underlying the readiness for or resistance to therapy is depicted here. Additionally, the resources or otherwise impediments to change, are assessed, such as the resistance to an obvious and sensible opportunity for change. Regarding somato-psychic comorbidities, the treatments desired by patients should not be judged as mutually exclusive, as a patient can simultaneously consider both physical therapy and psychotherapeutic treatment, and/or social support as necessary to improve their well-being. This implies that a strong desire for one form of treatment can indeed coexist with a strong desire for another form, and thus high values for two types of treatment can be present. Therefore, under no circumstances should a strong desire for one type of treatment automatically be interpreted as the absence of a different treatment desire. For example, in psychosomatic illnesses or comorbidities of somatic and psychiatric illnesses, the desire for a somatic treatment can also be accompanied by a desire for psychotherapeutic treatment.

Patients who, even with the help of the interviewer, cannot develop any ideas about what type of treatment might help them should be classified as "Level 0." If it is not clear what concept they have, despite inquiry, they are considered "not assessable."

2.7.1 Somatic Change/Treatment Concept

This item/feature maps the extent to which the patient considers physical treatment necessary to manage their disorder or problems. Examples of patient considerations are presented in Table 10. Physical treatments refer to interventions that directly influence biological factors, such as medications (including psychotropic drugs), medical procedures, diets, or physiotherapeutic applications. Body-centered interventions within psychotherapy (e.g., relaxation therapy methods, concentrative movement therapy, body awareness, biofeedback) can be found in Section 2.7.4.

Table 10. Symptom level scores and anchor descriptions for somatic change/treatment concept

Level	Feature expressions	Anchor examples
Level 0 Not present	This level is assigned when patients neither spontaneously nor upon inquiry express a desire for interventions that act directly on the physical level or when such treatment forms are outright rejected.	**Example 1:** A patient with ulcerative colitis wants to avoid medications despite a new inflammatory flare-up, as he is not convinced of their benefit, having felt better without them during previous flare-ups. **Example 2:** A patient with a paranoid-hallucinatory psychosis refuses the prescribed neuroleptics, stating that they are "poison" for the body and that the problems are not "physical."
Level 2 Moderately present	This level is chosen when patients desire a physical form of treatment despite some doubts or agree to a proposed physical treatment or carry it out, even if they are ultimately not convinced of it.	**Example 1:** A patient with an ocular melanoma agrees to radiation therapy after lengthy discussions with doctors, although she doubts the treatment's effectiveness and is concerned about coping with the resulting vision impairment. **Example 2:** A depressive patient with bipolar disorder agrees to take lithium after several discussions about its effects, side effects, and interactions.
Level 4 Very highly present	This level is indicated when patients express a clear desire for direct physical treatment in conversation. This can apply to patients for whom predominantly physical treatment is indicated, as well as those with strong resistance to psychotherapy and poorly prepared or informed patients who see no other treatment option.	**Example 1:** A patient with chronic somatoform pain disorder following a bicycle accident hopes a new pain medication regime will improve his pelvic pain and demands the medication from the provider, accusing them of delay. **Example 2:** A patient with morbid obesity, who has failed numerous weight loss attempts, asks her general practitioner to refer her to a surgical center for a gastric bypass. **Example 3:** A patient seeking a nose correction at an ENT clinic, during a psychodiagnostic screening due to suspected non-psychotic body dysmorphic disorder, stated that only her deformed nose was responsible for her life failures and that she urgently needed surgery. She categorically excluded other treatment options.

In the diagnostic interview, attention should be paid to directly expressed desires for physical treatment, as well as scenic aspects indicating such a wish. An extensive discussion of past physical treatments in the interview can be an important indication of a strong desire for physical treatment, but it may also simply reflect the medical facts, so it must be ensured that this is currently the case.

2.7.2 External-Social Change/ Treatment Concept

This feature/item covers the extent to which patients seek changes in their external environment and social area to improve their symptoms and problems, for which they desire therapeutic help and support. These are internal concepts that aim to influence the psychosocial external world and are associated with the idea that changes in the "external" realities will positively affect the patients' illness, symptoms, or problems. These interventions can be diverse, such as social counseling and assistance, referral for rehabilitation treatment, family support from the youth welfare office, job placement, pension counseling, debt counseling, and any advice that is not considered psychotherapy in the narrow sense and therefore does not primarily focus on the patients' internal psychosocial situation but addresses external reality. For example, with the help of social counseling, a patient who has experienced real overload due to caregiving for a relative can request institutionalized help (e.g., day care, home care) to positively influence their overall condition (Table 11).

Table 11. Symptom level scores and anchor descriptions for external-social change/treatment concept

Level	Feature expressions	Anchor examples
Level 0 Not present	This level is indicated when patients do not express a desire for changes in their external and social environment during the interview and do not respond to specific inquiries.	**Example 1:** A patient who has been raising her three children alone for 2 years acknowledges that she sometimes feels a bit overwhelmed in everyday life but still sees no need for social support. **Example 2:** A patient receiving social welfare, who suffers from significant chronic sleep disorders, rejects the social worker's suggestion to give up his noisy apartment near a train station with nightly shunting operations in favor of a quieter one.
Level 2 Moderately present	This level is chosen when patients express a desire for changes in their external social environment during the interview or include corresponding possibilities in their considerations for change.	**Example 1:** A patient with a chronic pain disorder wants to change his specific work situation to avoid repeatedly finding himself in mental and physical overload situations. **Example 2:** A patient with borderline disorder, who has significant debt due to frequent job and housing changes, considers her therapist's suggestion to seek debt counseling and participate in a structured reintegration into the workforce.
Level 4 Very highly present	This level is indicated when patients express a clear desire for changes in their external social environment during the interview and prioritize this desire.	**Example 1:** A patient working in an assembly factory reports constant "bullying" at her workplace, which has made her ill. She is certain that she can only get well if she changes her working conditions. She, for example, seeks social work support to negotiate with her supervisor for a transfer to another department. **Example 2:** An older, childless patient living alone, who became depressed after losing his wife in a car accident over a year ago, is certain that only new contacts are the solution for his bad mood and has, following his outpatient therapist's suggestion, begun to become socially active again.

During the interview, attention should be paid to specific statements by patients in this regard. Most often, it is necessary to ask to what extent a patient considers changes in their external and social environment helpful for managing their symptoms and problems; they desire corresponding professional assistance and social support.

Opportunities for help and support within the social network (e.g., family, friends, etc.) outside institutional professional care are considered psychosocial support (see Table 11).

2.7.3 External-Alternative Change/ Treatment Concept

This feature/item captures the extent to which patients seek so-called "alternative" (often also called complementary, even outside professional care) strategies to improve their symptoms and problems, regardless of whether these aim to influence somatic conditions, mental conditions, or external social factors. The repertoire of alternative health-related change strategies is very broad: e.g., "special medicines," "cures," "nutritional supplements," "gut cleansing," "detoxification," "mental training," "electromagnetic therapy," elimination of "water veins," "family rituals," membership in special groups, "sects," or "secret societies" (Table 12).

Table 12. Symptom level scores and anchor descriptions for external-alternative change/treatment concept

Level	Feature expressions	Anchor examples
Level 0 Not present	This level is indicated when patients do not express a desire for alternative health-related strategies during the interview, even when prompted.	**Example 1:** A depressed patient undergoing intensive chemotherapy for an AIDS-related illness does not express a desire for complementary medical treatment and denies such a wish when asked by the examiner. **Example 2:** A patient with obsessive-compulsive disorder who is being successfully treated with psychotherapy denies any desire for complementary medical treatment when asked by the examiner.
Level 2 Moderately present	This level is chosen when patients express a desire for alternative health-related strategies during the interview or include such possibilities in their considerations for change.	**Example 1:** A patient with depression and anxiety, who is undergoing chemotherapy and radiation for breast cancer, inquires the examiner about supportive mistletoe therapy. **Example 2:** A severely obsessive-compulsive patient being successfully treated with psycho- and pharmacotherapy expresses a desire to replace the medication with "healing clay and healing water."
Level 4 Very highly present	This level is indicated when patients express a clear desire for alternative health-related strategies during the interview and prioritize this desire.	**Example 1:** A depressed patient, who has been recommended chemotherapy and radiation for breast cancer, relies exclusively on "spiritual cancer healing." She has also heard of healing by "laying on of hands." **Example 2:** A severely obsessive-compulsive patient treated with psychotherapy and a combination pharmacotherapy of an antidepressant, and a newer antipsychotic has independently stopped the medication after hearing about "shamanic healing rituals" and decided to participate in them.

2.7.4 Psychotherapeutic Change/ Treatment Concept

This feature/item maps the extent to which patients consider psychotherapy necessary for improving their symptoms and problems, desire this treatment, and are motivated to pursue it. Psychotherapy refers to types of interventions that aim to influence the psychosocial inner world, including psychotherapeutic relaxation techniques.

When assessing the desire for psychotherapy, attention should be paid to both direct expressions and indirect indications suggesting such a desire. Cultural background, education level, and patient personality must be considered as these factors can influence the desire for psychotherapy. Even if the direct desire for psychotherapy is not explicitly expressed, openness to psychotherapy may manifest in the interest in discussing personal and social life areas and engaging with the therapist's perspective. Conversely, it is important to note that not every expression of the desire to participate in psychotherapy is truly driven by the intentional motivation to understand and change oneself. The ostensibly presented desire for psychotherapy may serve another function or even a defensive function, particularly when there is strong pressure from others (e.g., "skilled" externally motivated patients). The expressed desire for psychotherapy is considered, but the extent is to be assessed by the examiner (Table 13).

Table 13. Symptom level scores and anchor descriptions for psychotherapeutic change/treatment concept

Level	Feature expressions	Anchor examples
Level 0 Not present	This level is indicated when patients show no desire for psychotherapeutic treatment in the interview or reject this desire outright.	**Example 1:** A patient with heart phobia, who has presented several times at the cardiology emergency room on weekends without medical findings, rejects the suggestion to undergo psychotherapeutic treatment: "Talking doesn't help! It's not in my head!" **Example 2:** A palliative patient who underwent surgery and chemotherapy for colon cancer develops depression during the course of the illness. He refuses the offered psychotherapeutic support without providing a reason.
Level 2 Moderately present	This level is chosen when patients express some desire for psychotherapeutic treatment in the interview, for example, to improve a specific problem, but are not fully convinced of the psychotherapeutic help, perhaps thinking "Let's try it once," or show high motivation outwardly, but the examiner can discern external motivation (e.g., substance-dependent patients, forensic patients).	**Example 1:** A painkiller-dependent patient wants to use psychotherapy to "get rid of" her dependence. However, it becomes clear that her relatives have strongly recommended this, and she is complying with their wishes (mainly externally motivated). **Example 2:** An anxiously avoidant patient, who suffers from not finding a steady partner and feels under great pressure to succeed in his job as a financial IT specialist, developed a persistent bilateral tinnitus. Following his family doctor's recommendation, he sought several initial psychotherapeutic consultations but has not yet decided to start psychotherapy. He is now seeking efficient help to quickly get rid of his tinnitus, hoping that his emotional problems will be resolved as well.
Level 4 Very highly present	This level is indicated when patients express a pronounced and persistent desire for psychotherapy in the interview or are already undergoing such treatment.	**Example 1:** An obese patient with severe medically treatable arterial hypertension and sleep apnea syndrome is fighting with his family doctor for a referral to a psychotherapist because something must be wrong with him as he gets extremely stressed over many trivial everyday situations and urgently needs help by talking. **Example 2:** A patient with severe social phobia and distressing vegetative symptoms has decided to join group therapy and is now actively seeking a therapy place.

2.8 Resources and Impediments for Change

The potential for (psycho)therapeutic work and successful change is significantly influenced by emotional, cognitive, and interpersonal resources as well as actual options for action or their limitations. Intrapsychic processing and its interpersonal effects are essential for the willingness to work on it therapeutically. The psychodynamic motivation constellation of self-experience and defense is a prerequisite for resources, but can also represent change barriers (impediments).

2.8.1 Change Resources

Change resources comprise personal suffering, coping resources, psychosocial support, and openness. The evaluation of current change resources is conducted from the phenomenological surface.

Personal suffering: Individual suffering is a prerequisite for participating in therapy and holds an important prognostic function. Whether the patient wants to change something and, if so, what they intend to change is clearly related to the extent and nature of the patient's suffering.

Coping Resources: These include structural abilities, personal behavioral, and interpersonal action strategies (see also the OPD axes Relationship, Conflict, and Structure). They significantly determine the adaptive handling of the illness and its constructive resolution. It is well established that a positive experience of self-efficacy and active engagement with the illness are fundamental for any therapy.

Psychosocial Support: This is an interpersonal variable in which the person enters into a social-interactional relationship with the environment (e.g., family, social circle, helpers) to obtain support. The quantitative possibilities of psychosocial support from others and the ability to qualitatively use this support personally are protective factors and necessary conditions for any (psycho)therapy.

Openness: It is consensus in the psychodynamically oriented psychotherapy literature that the degree of openness is predictive of therapy success. This is understood as the fundamental interest, ability and inclination to engage, possibly with professional help, in a psychosocial genesis of the complaints and problems. Openness in the sense of "mental mindedness" primarily involves the patient's desire to understand the possible meanings and causes of their internal and external experiences, especially their ability to focus on the intrapsychic and not just external factors, and to conceptualize links between their thoughts, feelings, and actions and those of others (McCallum & Piper, 1997; Lingiardi & MacWilliams, 2017).

Burden of Suffering

Here, the current subjective distress is recorded. Distress usually results from the severity of symptoms and their consequences, the treatments applied, but also the individual and societal attitudes towards the illness (stigmatization). Patients with high distress suffer greatly from aspects of their illness. The emphasis here is on the subjective: high distress can also exist when patients have only moderate symptoms but subjectively express or convey significant suffering. Distress should either be verbalized by the patients and/or inferred from their behavior. Generally, distress plays an important motivational role in shaping the respective treatment expectations (somatic – social – psychotherapeutic) and the treatment cooperation of patients. The subjectively experienced distress is to be assessed, regardless of whether it corresponds with the "objective" suffering (Table 14). High levels of personal suffering can occur in the case of severe internal and external situational stress and severe symptoms (e.g., fear of the severity of the illness and its consequences, symptom worsening, burdensome treatment procedures, loss of social support), but also in the case of only moderate or even minor stress and symptoms. It is important to assess the current subjective distress. Generally, both physical and emotional aspects are considered during the assessment. During the examination, it is of interest to see how the patient expresses their distress verbally and how the presentation of complaints is reflected in facial expressions, gestures, and/or behavior. If the feeling of distress appears to contrast with the symptom or disorder severity (e.g., trivialized, dissimulated, dramatized, aggravated), the examiner should try to clarify this impression through further observations during the interview, considering the sociocultural background. If verbal and non-verbal or scenic expressions are not congruent, the predominant impression or mode is weighted.

Table 14. Symptom level scores and anchor descriptions for the level of suffering

Level	Feature expressions	Anchor examples
Level 0 Not present	This level is to be chosen when patients do not reveal any feelings of suffering, or any emotional and/or cognitive preoccupation with stress or problems during the interview. This may be the case if the patient does not express any recognizable signs or if, due to internal demands (a brave face), signs of emotional involvement are rigorously suppressed or denied, and not just trivialized.	**Example 1:** A patient proudly explains to the consultant one week after an acute myocardial infarction that he has "no problems at all" and symptoms are "not noticeable" to him. When the consultant asks if he is trivializing his symptoms, he replies, "Not at all, I feel completely healthy." **Example 2:** A patient with severe anorexia nervosa and intensive body weight loss experiences no symptoms and restrictions subjectively and feels "healthy."
Level 2 Moderately present	This level is to be indicated when patients currently suffer noticeably from the disorder and associated impairments and stress and/or have recently suffered from it.	**Example 1:** A patient, one week after a myocardial infarction, is significantly worried about his body ("my heart"), his ability to work, and his relationship with his partner. **Example 2:** In a patient with persistent sleep disorders and job stress, the doctor notices that she visits him frequently, appears sad, and is close to tears. Without explicitly stating it, she conveys to him that she is suffering noticeably.
Level 4 Very highly present	This level is to be chosen when patients, regardless of the underlying internal and external situational stress, strive to convey their distress content-wise and with corresponding affective expression using all available means, e.g., by constantly expressing their distress gesturally-scenically (e.g., parasuicidal behavior) and/or demanding help.	**Example 1:** After being diagnosed with Multiple Sclerosis a few days ago, since then the patient feels restless, cannot be calmed down, and complains that he can no longer live like this and does not want to end up in a wheelchair. **Example 2:** The patient with severe panic attacks reports being preoccupied by thoughts and feelings of fear and being tormented by the fear of fear. She cannot sit still but paces around the examination room with an anxiety-distorted face, lamenting her distress and stating that she cannot endure this state any longer.

Coping Resources

This is an assessment of the personal resources that patients currently have at their disposal in dealing with their illness, which help them to cope with their current symptoms and problems. Positive resources help to maintain a relatively stable sense of self-efficacy and self-esteem, preserve an optimistic outlook, and actively engage with illness. Despite functional limitations, patients can often maintain an active lifestyle, achieve satisfactory quality of life, and discover new perspectives on life.

It is essential to evaluate the extent of adaptive-constructive coping abilities that could improve the management of current complaints and problems. Additionally, it must be determined to what extent these are already being applied or can be activated. Thus, it is always necessary to assess the functionality of resources concerning the health-promoting requirements of the respective illness. The mere presence of potentially "positive" resources does not automatically indicate their current usefulness or effectiveness (e.g., excessive sports behavior in anorexia nervosa).

Coping resources should be assessed over the relevant recent weeks of the current phase of illness (greater than 28 days). The evaluation focuses on current circumstances, although a longer-term perspective of previous positive coping experiences may be considered. A resource is deemed absent if the patient fundamentally has this coping ability, and it would be helpful for managing the illness, but the patient is currently unable to realize it (Table 15).

Table 15. Symptom level scores and anchor descriptions for coping resources

Level	Feature expressions	Anchor examples
Level 0 Not present	This level is indicated when patients currently have no resources to appropriately and functionally cope with their illness. They exhibit only "negative" or "passive" coping patterns, which generally do not help in dealing with illnesses. If they have "positive" resources, they are currently not using them, or they are not functional and thus not helpful in the context of the present illness.	**Example 1:** A patient with a severe accident-related pelvic ring fracture is still severely restricted in mobility after an initial phase of strict bed rest. Although she is generally a very athletic and active person, she is currently completely inactive and immobile. She cannot apply other coping strategies and contribute positively, leading to complications in the healing process, which has already been critically discussed with her by her caregivers. **Example 2:** A schizoid patient who practically never leaves his apartment states that he has no hobbies, never meets people, and cannot imagine any professional activities. He just feels bored.
Level 2 Moderately present	This level is chosen when patients have functional coping abilities in certain areas and try to maintain their life style. They begin cautiously to explore areas of life beyond current limitations. However, there are also areas where they seem overwhelmed and unable to find solutions, or they are hindered by intrapsychic influences.	**Example 1:** A patient with chronic pain syndrome has started to resume active areas of life despite complaints and functional limitations in daily life. She has already contacted a Nordic walking group in her area after several solo outings. She also seeks information about self-help groups nearby and has contacted her employer to discuss workplace changes. Nevertheless, she is limited in her self-esteem due to the illness, experiences phases of despair, and often does not dare to ask acquaintances for help.

Table 15. Symptom level scores and anchor descriptions for coping resources *(continued)*

Level	Feature expressions	Anchor examples
Level 2 Moderately present		**Example 2:** A young patient with severe circadian insomnia, who has not completed any education commensurate with his intelligence and has dropped out of or has been expelled from several apprenticeships, generally knows important sleep-promoting measures and rules (e.g., maintaining sleep windows, avoiding blue light in the evening, morning light therapy, stimulus control, activity planning) but does not always apply them consistently. Too often, he prioritizes hours of computer games with "friends" in chat, which repeatedly disrupts the already challenging establishment of a fixed activity-sleep rhythm.
Level 4 Very highly present	This level is indicated when patients have very good and diverse resources that help them to functionally cope with their current illness. This does not mean the patient is symptom-free, but they have found ways to integrate the symptoms into their life without their quality of life being too severely affected. They manage to maintain a positive outlook on life.	**Example 1:** A patient, a former endurance athlete who has been almost blind in one eye due to a vascular occlusion for years, develops a benign but not entirely operable brain tumor that threatens to gradually blind the still healthy eye. After initial despondency, she decides to "fight" the impending blindness, talks with her husband and children about the potential blindness, secures support from family and friends, and seeks information about various support options, from visual aids to self-help groups and their financing. She asks her husband to take a long-planned trip as soon as possible while she can still enjoy it visually. She works on finding a "new inner path" to life. **Example 2:** A patient with recurrent panic attacks several times a week has thoroughly informed himself about the illness on the internet and tries to adjust his life accordingly. He started endurance sports a few weeks ago, which has already had positive effects. He also participates in a relaxation group and practices regularly. He can openly discuss his illness with family and friends and confront it internally. He independently notices connections between the attacks and his tendency to overexert himself and has begun to better organize his daily life and take it easier, although it is difficult for him.

Psychosocial Support

Psychosocial support is an interpersonally accentuated personal resource that meets individual psychosocial needs (e.g., affection, recognition, comfort, encouragement) as well as practical instrumental-material needs (e.g., specific help like shopping, cooking, watering plants, caregiving, financial support) and informational needs (e.g., recommendations, advice) within the context of interpersonal relationships, particularly in stressful life situations. Psychosocial support includes both the available social support network (quantity) and the quality of partnership, family, and social support (Table 16). The key question is whether the current social network is perceived as a resource and whether interpersonal relationships can be used to manage disorders and problems.

Table 16. Symptom level scores and anchor descriptions for psychosocial support

Level	Feature expressions	Anchor examples
Level 0 Not present	This level is indicated when patients don't have or cannot mobilize any caregivers who provide instrumental and/or emotional support during the assessment period. Helpful individuals are not present, or if they are, the patient does not utilize them, either because they do not consider the help necessary or feasible or avoid it for other reasons.	**Example 1:** A patient with severe fractures of the upper and lower leg is significantly restricted in mobility and must stay in bed for recovery and rest for an extended period. Although she has family and friends available, she does not accept any help and tries to prepare food and to use the toilet entirely on her own. **Example 2:** A patient with a psychotic development lives isolated in his own apartment. He is divorced and unemployed, has withdrawn from friends, and has no contact with his family of origin.
Level 2 Moderately present	This level is chosen when patients have and can mobilize existing caregivers for instrumental and/or emotional support, which they use. Either the caregivers provide only limited support, or the patient accepts it only to a certain extent.	**Example 1:** A patient with severe fractures of the upper and lower leg is significantly restricted in mobility and must stay in bed for recovery and rest for an extended period. Her busy partner and a good friend provide practical and emotional support as much as their schedules allow, which the patient gratefully accepts. Occasionally, relatives who live far away must travel to help on weekends. However, the patient finds it difficult to accept help from them due to poor relationships. **Example 2:** After his wife's death, a patient has withdrawn significantly due to depression. The couple had a small circle of family and friends who now provide limited practical and emotional support. Since his wife used to organize everything, only the children remain to offer some support.
Level 4 Very highly present	This level is indicated when patients have several caregivers, and their instrumental and/or emotional support actively takes place to manage their illness and life problems.	**Example 1:** A patient with severe fractures of the upper and lower leg is significantly restricted in mobility and must stay in bed for recovery and rest for an extended period. He lives alone but has a large, supportive network of family and friends who take care of him diligently. The helpers coordinate all necessary support areas with him, do the shopping and laundry, visit him frequently, and provide necessary care. The patient expresses his gratitude and happiness for the help. **Example 2:** A patient with a chronic, severely limiting anxiety and obsessive-compulsive disorder, who can no longer leave the house alone or take care of herself, finally asked family and friends for support in all anxiety- and compulsion-related activities to ensure her daily care after a suicidal crisis. She is very relieved about the everyday help and encouraging support she receives.

Openness

Openness, in the sense of being "psychologically minded" describes a person's ability to mentally consider and reflect on possible psychosocial backgrounds, meanings, and causes of existing somatic, psychosomatic, and mental symptoms and problems. Openness thus denotes an inherently available resource, the interest, ability and tendency to engage with a psychosocial genesis of complaints, to reflect on them, and to report on them. The significance of one's own thoughts, feelings, unconscious or maladaptive reaction, processing, and relation-

Table 17. Symptom level scores and anchor descriptions in openness

Level	Feature expressions	Anchor examples
Level 0 Not present	This level is to be chosen when patients are retentive or when they report little emotionally significant content about themselves. They cannot establish relevant relations between internal or interpersonal processes and their problems and symptoms or do not respond to corresponding suggestions from the examiner.	**Example 1:** A patient with a chronic inflammatory bowel disease (IBD) meticulously describes his recurring abdominal cramps, pain, and bloody-watery diarrhea. This does not change even after the examiner encourages him to report a personal incident where the complaints were worse or better. The examiner gets the impression that the patient has no access to his emotional experience. **Example 2:** A patient with chronic somatoform lower abdominal pain remains solely focused on her physical complaints, especially her pain. She has no introspective access to her internal thoughts and feelings. Although the pain started during a severe marital crisis, she does not understand or even rejects corresponding questions and suggestions ("My doctor once asked if it could have something to do with home. I think he is just as clueless as I am").
Level 2 Moderately present	This level is to be chosen when patients can name emotional-internal processes, thoughts, feelings, and relationships in a differentiated way but can only laboriously relate them to their own problems and symptoms. Patients can use suggestions from the examiner to gain further symptom understanding or to open up emotionally and begin to make initial further considerations.	**Example 1:** An anxious-avoidant patient with a persistent cardiac arrhythmia after a heart valve replacement reports extensively on recurrent, extremely painful runs of extrasystoles. Only upon the examiner's inquiry does he admit that these strongly unsettle and frighten him because they make him immediately incapable of action, so he cannot even take care of his two-year-old daughter. He has also observed that the symptoms usually occur in situations of too much stress. He is willing to consider a relation to the failure of his sporting and scientific engineering ambitions but is unsure about giving these aspects importance for his illness. **Example 2:** A patient with chronic somatoform lower abdominal pain first extensively describes her entire symptomatology and then reports in several episodes on dysfunctional relationships. She repeatedly manages to incorporate parts of her internal emotional experience and relate them to her complaints (" ...it feels like my pain gets worse when everything becomes too much for me"). Such hints are not rejected by the patient but accepted questioningly, then only partially reflected upon and further elaborated.
Level 4 Very highly present	This level is to be chosen when patients can independently establish links between feelings, thoughts, interpersonal experiences, and their symptoms and behavior and report self-exploratively. The patient's insights are further deepened by the therapist's suggestions, leading to a better understanding of their illness, experiences, and behavior, and the patient is also interested in biographical links.	**Example 1:** The patient can link chronic pain symptoms and maladaptive relationship patterns with his internal emotional experience. He is open within the therapeutic contact to consider previously unconscious feelings of anger mentioned by the therapist. **Example 2:** A patient with moderate chronic depression and chronic somatoform lower abdominal pain can recognize that the first symptoms began in childhood in the context of suspected sexual abuse and resurfaced and worsened during the current marital crisis with her husband. She constructively picks up the suggestions of her general practitioner that the depression and lower abdominal pain might be related to her relationship with her husband and discusses this on her own initiative.

ship patterns for the illness is at least fundamentally acknowledged. The patient is able and willing to deal with this in therapy, i.e., to openly discuss and consider the therapist's interventions (interpersonal aspect).

The basis for openness in the sense mentioned above is the ability of a person for self-perception and self-reflection, thus insight into one's motives but also the motives of others and to link the present with the past (and vice versa). This ability is described in the framework of the OPD Axis IV (Structure) as an important structural capability.

Openness in this sense is considered essential for the course of psychodynamic psychotherapy, especially since many patients lack these abilities in a specific way (see Axis IV).

The evaluation assesses the extent to which the patient can spontaneously engage with mental processes, thoughts, feelings, and desires, establish a connection to their complaints and impairments, and reports on them (Table 17). Additionally, it is evaluated whether there is a willingness to engage with possible links between internal-emotional or interpersonal processes and one's own symptoms and problems, at least in response to suggestions from the examiner or, if necessary, with the examiner's support. In the diagnostic situation, it is important to observe if the patient can establish links between their internal experiences, feelings, thoughts, and their complaints and problems. The interest and willingness of the patients to reflect on possible psychodynamic links and report on them, as well as non-verbal reactions, are to be noted.

Openness in general also refers to open communication; the ability to frankly talk about thoughts and feelings is crucial for all (psycho) therapies. A person may perceive themselves as "open," reporting "everything," yet without addressing the significant thoughts and feelings (therefore low openness according to OPD). In objective assessment, it does not matter that people claim to be open but whether this is actually evident. It is what the examiner evaluates, not what the patient claims. In cases of deliberate withholding (especially in forensic contexts such as alcohol, drugs, crimes), it must be considered whether there is otherwise an effort to understand the psychosocial relations between problems and complaints, and these areas are only (partially) excluded ("I cannot/will not elaborate on that").

2.8.2 Impediments for Change

Indicated psychotherapeutic or psychosomatic treatment can face both external and internal barriers to change, in both outpatient and inpatient settings. External life circumstances and environmental conditions can primarily hinder or even prevent implementation. Repetitive maladaptive relationship patterns, persistent internal conflicts, and unfavorable structural conditions, as captured on the OPD Axes Relationship, Conflict, and Structure, can complicate the treatment process up to the point of discontinuation, or diminishing the success and subjective benefit of treatment, or even making it impossible.

External Impediments for Change

Whenever there is motivation for change through professional treatment, external life circumstances and environmental conditions are crucial. These include the lack of availability and/or affordability of psychotherapy, unfavorable social background conditions (e.g., shift work or prolonged absence from home due to work), and/or a rejecting attitude of significant others toward psychotherapy. Other external barriers may include the threat of job loss, lack of childcare or caregiving for dependents, fear of stigmatization, and/or negative social consequences.

It must be assessed whether the indicated psychotherapeutic measure is available, feasible, and affordable (e.g., privately or through social insurers). It is also important to clarify whether significant professional and social disadvantages are to be expected. Social obligations (e.g., caring for animals or dependents) and real or feared stigmatization must also be considered (Table 18).

Family disputes about undergoing treatment ("we don't want you to do psychotherapy") are considered external barriers to change. However, if the treatment is rejected due to the patient's own feelings and thoughts ("my mother wouldn't like it"), these are internal barriers to change.

Table 18. Symptom level scores and anchor descriptions for external change and impediments to treatment

Level	Feature expressions	Anchor examples
Level 0 Not present	This level is to be chosen when a patient has no relevant external barriers to starting and continuing a long-term psychosomatic-psychotherapeutic treatment.	**Example 1:** A young patient with a severe adolescent identity crisis, who is fundamentally motivated for change and psychotherapy, finds a suitable therapist or clinic. The cost coverage is secured, and both outpatient and inpatient treatment can be seamlessly integrated into her family and work context. If no private car is available, she can reach the therapy via public transport. **Example 2:** A civil servant patient with post-traumatic stress disorder (PTSD) after a robbery is transferred professionally. She wants to continue her previously successful long-term therapy of 90 hours with the same therapist. Therefore, she arranges further therapy sessions twice a week. The cost coverage is secured.
Level 2 Moderately present	This level is to be indicated when a patient faces external barriers to starting and continuing a long-term psychosomatic-psychotherapeutic treatment, but these are fundamentally solvable, albeit with some effort.	**Example 1:** A therapy-motivated patient with an acute anxiety disorder cannot find an outpatient treatment slot in his town of residency in the short term (waiting list over 6 months). To start outpatient psychotherapy, he would have to travel a relatively long distance (about 20 km by car) in his region. He is unsure if he can afford the fuel costs. **Example 2:** A young patient, a single mother of two toddlers, with increasing obsessive-compulsive symptoms, is fundamentally motivated for an indicated inpatient treatment. Childcare could be arranged without issues. However, she is considering postponing the treatment until she has taken her exams, so she does not have to make up for an academic year.
Level 4 Very highly present	This level is to be chosen when a patient faces significant external barriers to starting a psychosomatic-psychotherapeutic treatment, so the treatment is usually rejected or does not take place.	**Example 1:** A young patient with chronic inflammatory bowel disease (IBD) is indicated for inpatient psychotherapy. However, he is aware that another inpatient treatment will result in his temporary contract not being renewed, making him unemployed again. His social environment is also vehemently opposed to another inpatient therapy. The father even threatens not to support him financially if he loses his job again. **Example 2:** A young patient with a migration background, mother of two children aged 3 and 5, is to be treated inpatient due to a severe anxiety disorder and depression with suicidality. The patient is fundamentally motivated. The children could be cared for by a good friend she knows from kindergarten. However, her family environment is strictly against it. They see it as an intrusion into family matters and threaten to disown her, preventing any treatment from taking place.

Internal Impediments for Change

Internal barriers to change include characteristic conscious and unconscious resistance phenomena against changes and treatment. These complicate the therapy or make participation in therapy difficult or reduce its benefit. They are based on psychodynamic defense mechanisms such as repression, denial, etc., and serve to reduce the anxiety of (un)conscious conflicts and/or structural problems as well as the fear of change. The extent of the internal barriers is assessed, which results from the strength of individual resistance phenomena or the interaction of several resistance phenomena. The underlying psychodynamic conflicts and defense constellations ("Nothing must change, or everything will fall apart!") are depicted in the Conflict and Structure Axes (Table 19).

Table 19. Symptom level scores and anchor descriptions for internal change and impediments to treatment

Level	Feature expressions	Anchor examples
Level 0 Not present	This level is to be chosen when a patient has no significant internal barriers to change and treatment.	**Example 1:** A patient with persistent dizziness attacks cannot, upon the investigator's inquiry, establish any relation with her life situation. She is open to suggestions and can reflect on them.
		Example 2: A young patient with a severe obsessive-compulsive disorder is well motivated for inpatient psychotherapy and shows good prerequisites. At the beginning of therapy, he shows a marked increase in his anxiety and obsessive-compulsive symptoms (fear of change), but he faces them, so they do not pose a significant barrier.
Level 2 Moderately present	This level is to be indicated when a patient has several internal barriers or at least one significant internal barrier that reduces therapy motivation and/or treatment adherence.	**Example 1:** A patient with persistent dizziness attacks resists the investigator's attempt to initiate a psychosomatic-psychotherapeutic treatment. After the purpose of a psychosomatic examination and treatment is explained in detail, the patient becomes more receptive. However, at the end of the diagnostic interview, she states that she does not need another consultation, even though the investigator recommends it.
		Example 2: A patient with increasing psychosomatic problems and depressive moods has never sought or accepted help and support in his entire life. He expresses strong resistance to the now necessary inpatient treatment: "I don't need help!" He can only accept the proposal for inpatient treatment after these internal barriers are addressed and the assurance that he can decide and do as much as possible himself.
Level 4 Very highly present	This level is to be chosen when a patient has one or more significant internal barriers to change and treatment.	**Example 1:** A patient with persistent psychogenic dizziness attacks vehemently resists the attempt to initiate psychotherapy. She finds this an "insult" she does not have to tolerate because she "is not crazy." She breaks off the conversation.
		Example 2: A single mother of two children aged 4 and 8 suffers from progressively worsening depressive moods that have now reached a severe level. The patient is not willing to accept an inpatient treatment offer because she perceives it as a personal failure towards her family and children to not be able to care for them during the inpatient stay and to be dependent on help herself.

To capture internal barriers to change and resistance phenomena, it is important to clarify why a patient has not participated in indicated treatment so far or does not want to participate, or why they want to discontinue or have discontinued previous treatment. For example, a patient might express their beliefs and fears that they will become dependent on the therapist, that the therapist will exploit them financially, or that they will be judged and rejected by their environment for undergoing psychotherapy.

An unconscious intensification or strategically motivated aggravation of complaints and problems, which usually represents a considerable complication for treatment, is to be classified as (usually high or even very high) internal barriers to successfully completing treatment. A conscious simulation of complaints and problems is not to be evaluated as an internal barrier.

Secondary (Social) Gain as a Problem-Maintaining Condition

While the primary gain from illness through symptom formation involves the reduction of unconscious neurotic conflict tension, secondary gain refers to the external advantages and social benefits that arise from symptoms and assuming the sick role. These can include sympathy, compassion, but also release from everyday obligations and economically viable gainful employment. Such psychosocial advantages resulting from an illness and its consequences can lead to an unconscious or even conscious "gain," described in psychodynamic literature as secondary gain from illness. Over time, this can develop into an internal barrier to change, acting as a clinically relevant factor maintaining the patient's complaints and problems. Secondary gain in this sense consists of external advantages derived from existing symptoms, such as increased social attention and consideration. Objectively, it manifests, for example, in disproportionately long sick leaves and hospital stays, excessive relief from duties, and inappropriately long periods of rest and avoidance of work and normal daily life. Self-medication resulting from an illness can also become a problem-maintaining condition, e.g., in the case of ongoing sick leaves due to pain within the context of medication misuse. Disability pensions or claims from accident insurance often lead patients to cling consciously or unconsciously to their illness and its consequences, to bring to bear their unmet needs and expectations.

Assessing whether a psychosocial condition represents a secondary gain in the sense of a problem-maintaining condition for the specific patient requires a look at the patient's individual development and his or her overall psychosocial situation. Deviating from the usual time frame, it therefore refers here to the overall course of the illness to date (Table 20). The investigator must judge secondary gain, regardless of how the patient expresses or presents themselves. Naturally, not all regular consequences of illness should automatically be interpreted as gain. It should be noted that the sick role implies increased emotional and social attention from others, which should only be assessed if it significantly exceeds the culturally or group-specific norm (in time or extent). Since secondary gain is fundamentally an internal and external barrier to change, it often manifests through patients' resistance to changing their situation. It may appear that they have settled into their illness and its consequences to the extent that they at least derive social benefits from it. Due to the particular significance of social benefits, it is necessary to evaluate secondary gain as an independent criterion.

2.9 Psychotherapy: Change Strategies and Goals

When there is an indication for a psychotherapeutic procedure and corresponding motivation to undergo psychotherapy (see 2.7.4), it is helpful to understand through which professional psychotherapeutic activities the patient expects

Table 20. Symptom level scores and anchor descriptions for secondary gain from illness

Level	Feature expressions	Anchor examples
Level 0 Not present	This level is to be chosen when no secondary gain is detectable in a patient. The existing illness has only negative consequences for the patient, and the social relief that can usually be expected because of the illness is not to be understood in the sense of a subjective gain from the illness.	**Example 1:** A single patient is retired after her third severe heart attack, in addition to existing lung and back diseases. Although she receives extensive social support and a well-secured pension, she tries to remain employed. **Example 2:** A patient with recurrent severe depression is retired after a medical assessment. However, he wanted to stay in the workforce, as work is an extremely important, almost indispensable part of life for him.
Level 2 Moderately present	This level is to be chosen when clear psychosocial advantages exist for a patient, which maintain the illness or problem.	**Example 1:** A slightly anxious patient has a relapsing, chronical inflammatory bowel disease requiring recurrent inpatient treatment, which has improved enough so that he could currently be discharged from the hospital. He reports additional medically unexplainable symptoms, insists on further clarification, making it difficult to discharge him ("I need the security"). **Example 2:** A patient experiencing a threatening anxiety disorder feels hardly able to leave the house without company. She demands help from her partner, from whom she previously felt too little seen and supported. In addition to his high professional load, he now takes more responsibility for family duties than before but increasingly insists on ending the "support" over time.
Level 4 Very highly present	This level is to be chosen when significant social advantages are found in one or more areas of a patient's life due to illness (e.g., financial benefits, social security, support from relatives), leading the patient to show no desire for change.	**Example 1:** A patient, a lawyer by profession, develops chronic pain syndrome after a rear-end collision. As a result of the illness, he achieves a high material gain with an accident and occupational disability pension as well as a massive relief from all unpleasant social tasks by his relatives that exceed the usual level. **Example 2:** A patient with recurrent depression receives (only) during her depressive episodes a maximum of attention and support from her family and demands this even on the ward. She does not want to leave the ward.

to achieve their specific goals of change. Many patients expect therapeutic activities aimed at the immediate alleviation and improvement of their symptoms. Others seek reflection and clarification of psychodynamic backgrounds to change their complaints and problems. Additionally, there are desires for emotional support or specific active guidance.

This feature/item covers the desired psychotherapeutic change strategies. It is essential to note that the change strategies to be evaluated do not exclude one another but should be captured as an individual profile. For example, a patient may hope for specific treatment to reduce symptoms while also seeking emotional support. Psychotherapeutic change strategies and specific therapy goals can change during the therapeutic process. It is crucial to work on developing appropriate and beneficial treatment goals for the patient as early as possible, while at the same time to take into account unconscious dynamics. In the initial interview, the investigator usually needs to ask actively and may need to provide instructive explanations.

2.9.1 Symptom Reduction

Typically, patients with mental or psychosomatic disorders expect professional help to eliminate or alleviate their symptoms. The guiding principle is: "I want to feel better and make my symptoms disappear!"

The type of change motivation can be assessed based on the problem description and the further goals of change formulated by the patient. For existing symptoms, this describes the extent to which the patient is exclusively focused on symptom reduction (Table 21).

Table 21. Symptom level scores and anchor descriptions in relation to symptom reduction

Level	Feature expressions	Anchor examples
Level 0 Not present	This level is to be chosen when the patient's urge for change due to symptoms is not very pronounced, and symptom reduction is therefore in the background.	**Example 1:** A patient with mild chronic fluctuating lower abdominal pain shows no interest in specific medical measures to improve her symptoms. She seems focused on addressing her sexual trauma experienced in childhood and adolescence. **Example 2:** A patient who repeatedly comes into conflict with other people because of his impulse control disorder deals very little in conversation with the interpersonal consequences of his disorder, but even more with the "mistakes" of others who are "to blame" for the fact that he sometimes becomes so angry and aggressive towards others.
Level 2 Moderately present	This level is to be chosen when the patient's desire for symptom reduction is moderately pronounced.	**Example 1:** A patient suffering from a stress-dependent sleep disorder for several months after separating from her partner wants a fast-acting sleep medication. After the sleep disorder nearly disappears, she states that the treatment is essentially over for her but then accepts the therapeutic offer to tentatively discuss her current life situation regarding the sleep disorder and schedules further appointments. **Example 2:** A patient with alcohol dependence is willing to address his dependency issues in therapy. Additionally, he seeks support in resolving other family and work-related problems caused by his illness.
Level 4 Very highly present	This level is to be chosen when a patient has an exceptionally high desire for symptom reduction.	**Example 1:** A patient with a somatoform pain disorder wants only to change the physical pain symptoms and demands immediate corresponding measures in therapy. Consequently, this creates strong pressure in the countertransference that an improvement in the pain must be achieved. **Example 2:** A patient with chronic alcohol problems and alcohol-related damage seeks help only for the physical symptoms ("I can't walk anymore") and for relieving his severe craving.

2.9.2 Reflection and Clarification

For some patients, it is essential to understand the origins of their symptoms to derive strategies for change. The guiding principle is: "I want to understand why I keep having these complaints and problems so I can change them!" (Table 22).

Especially in psychodynamic therapy, it is crucial to explore the extent to which an affective and cognitive understanding of the symptom's background and the problem is sought. This includes the desire to recognize, reflect on, and change maladaptive interpersonal patterns.

Here, the focus is on assessing the extent to which problematic experiences and motivational areas are discussed and reflected upon, and how much their change is pursued with therapeutic help. The evaluation is based on the fundamental willingness, independent of the ability to do so.

Table 22. Symptom level scores and anchor descriptions in relation to reflection and clarification

Level	Feature expressions	Anchor examples
Level 0 Not present	This level is to be chosen when the patient is not striving to gain a genuine understanding of the psychosocial backgrounds of their symptoms, leaving their attitude towards their disorder unreflected. They are not interested in the relation between conflict and symptoms pointed out by the therapist.	**Example 1:** A young patient with a months-long gait disorder due to a medically unexplained leg paralysis views her illness solely as physically caused and is not open during the interview to consider whether the leg paralysis might be related to her efforts to become independent from her parents and a planned long-term stay abroad. **Example 2:** A patient with severe depression sees his problems primarily in the somatic or social realm and is hardly accessible to biographical and intrapsychic factors/dimensions. He indicates to the examiner that he does not want to work on these areas in therapy either: "The past and my relationships have nothing to do with this!"
Level 2 Moderately present	This level is to be chosen when the patient shows moderate interest in therapeutic activities aimed at illuminating the psychosocial or psychodynamic backgrounds of their complaints and problems.	**Example 1:** A patient with severe allergic asthma regards his illness solely as physically caused. Even when asked, he is only somewhat willing to consider why his asthma always exacerbates when he gets "extremely upset" about his family. **Example 2:** A patient with bulimia has started inpatient treatment to reduce symptoms. During treatment, she increasingly understands the link between her symptoms and her partnership, but she is still unsure whether this emotional insight will be helpful to her and whether she wants to use it.
Level 4 Very highly present	This level is to be chosen when the patient highly desires to gain a genuine understanding of the backgrounds of their symptoms. The desire to understand and change extends to the intra- and interpersonal aspects of their life.	**Example 1:** A pain patient uses his good emotional access to understand the problem and independently establishes links to the development and maintenance of the symptoms. His main therapeutic goal is to understand his inner conflict constellation and to change it. **Example 2:** A young patient with a dissociative disorder recognizes clear links between her seizures and currently triggering experiences of disappointment. She is therefore very eager to deepen her understanding and to work through them in therapy against the backdrop of her earlier emotional neglect.

2.9.3 Emotional Support

Patients often seek emotional support, relief, comfort, and assistance in psychotherapy to manage their complaints and problems. The guiding principle is: "I need support so that I can feel better and change my complaints and problems!" (Table 23).

Here, it is assessed how intensively emotional-supportive therapeutic support is sought and utilized and defined as an essential therapy goal. The evaluation particularly focuses on the extent to which emotional support is sought or directly demanded in the context of the interview.

Table 23. Symptom level scores and anchor descriptions in relation to emotional support

Level	Feature expressions	Anchor examples
Level 0 Not present	This level is to be chosen when the patient shows no need or interest in emotional support, comfort, assistance, or encouragement and may even reject it.	**Example 1:** A patient has lost her husband in an accident and appears devastated, but she rejects the caregivers' attempts to comfort and support her emotionally: "Thank you, but I don't need that." **Example 2:** A patient with alcohol dependence and schizoid personality disorder does not accept the supportive help of the therapist or nursing staff in an inpatient setting. He also does not wish for it.
Level 2 Moderately present	This level is to be chosen when the patient is noticeably interested in receiving emotional relief and support but also pays attention to other therapeutic activities.	**Example 1:** A patient who had to have an arm amputation due to an accident repeatedly talks about how terrible it was and is for him even after months, constantly seeking comforting support and encouragement from caregivers and family. However, he actively addresses his depressive symptoms following the accident. **Example 2:** A patient with borderline disorder initially demands only support and assistance in treatment but can increasingly set aside her emotional needs during the therapeutic process and regulate herself better.
Level 4 Very highly present	This level is to be chosen when the patient is particularly interested in therapeutic activities that provide emotional relief and support and ideally convey a feeling of being emotionally carried and supported in the relationship.	**Example 1:** A patient with malignant skin cancer is devastated after receiving the diagnosis and imperatively demands emotional support and comfort from the caregiver: "I am fighting for my life. I need you. You must help me!" **Example 2:** A patient with severe depression as part of bipolar disorder understandably wishes for his mood to improve quickly. Above all, however, he seeks comfort, support, and the reassurance that the new severe relapse will endure once again: "I can't go on. I have no strength left to fight. Without you, I can't go through this again."

2.9.4 Active Guidance

Many patients also seek active guidance in psychotherapy to manage their complaints and problems. The guiding principle is: "Tell me what to do to change my complaints and problems!" (Table 24).

This feature/item maps how intensely the patient is interested in actively instructive therapeutic activities to address their complaints and problems. The patient is oriented towards recommendations and methods for direct behavior changes. They seek a suitable therapeutic context and expects the therapist or the therapeutic system to take on an expert role. It is evaluated whether and to what extent the patient seeks and demands active help to cope.

Table 24. Symptom level scores and anchor descriptions in relation to active instructions

Level	Feature expressions	Anchor examples
Level 0 Not present	This level is chosen when the patient does not consider active instructive measures and advice as important, does not demand them, or even rejects them.	**Example 1:** A patient, a healthcare professional himself, is in a severe life crisis after the death of his partner and has started smoking again. He knows how to implement appropriate measures in his life and does not wish for active therapeutic guidance but would rather receive emotional support. **Example 2:** A patient with anxiety symptoms has developed techniques for anxiety regulation. In treatment, he even rejects therapeutic suggestions for this: "I know best what helps me!" Instead, he tries to clarify with the therapist how the symptoms came about.
Level 2 Moderately present	This level is to be chosen when the patient expects help through information dissemination and active therapeutic measures aimed at their concrete lifestyle and immediate behavior. They can participate in treatments where these active-instructive elements are not the focus, even if they view them with some skepticism.	**Example 1:** A patient with severe diabetes and comorbid recurrent depressive disorder joins a diabetes education program primarily to learn more about the disease and its treatment, to avoid dietary mistakes, and to better manage his medication. Although he views program content dealing with psychosocial aspects skeptically, he still participates. **Example 2:** A patient with chronic stress-related pain seeks targeted help through a manualized pain treatment program that provides concrete instructions for pain management. Whenever deeper interpersonal and psychosocial conflicts are addressed, she is willing to work on these as well.
Level 4 Very highly present	This level is to be chosen when the patient expects therapeutic activities with active guidance to a particularly high degree.	**Example 1:** A patient with early mild vascular dementia and depression persistently urges all members of the treatment team to give her tips and show her exercises to improve her memory. **Example 2:** A patient with burnout and an obsessive-compulsive personality structure considers himself a victim of mobbing. He urges the therapist for clear guidance on how to deal with his work situation in the future: "What do you advise me to do so they leave me alone?" All other psychosocial aspects are of no importance to him.

2.10 OPD-3 Rating Sheet Axis I

The rating scale for Axis I is shown in Figure 1 (also available in the online material for this book; numbering refers to the sections in the chapter).

Axis I: Mental and psychosomatic disorders		
Mental disorders/behavioral disorders	ICD or DSM	
Main diagnosis		
Additional diagnosis 1		
Additional diagnosis 2		
Additional diagnosis 3		
Additional diagnosis 4		
Additional diagnosis 5		
Physical illnesses	ICD	
Main diagnosis		
Additional diagnosis 2		
Additional diagnosis 3		
Additional diagnosis 4		
Additional diagnosis 5		
Age: ___ years	Gender: m/f/___	Assessment date ___/___

Axis I: Experience of illness & treatment requirements		
2.4 Current severity of symptomatology/disorder		
Global severity of the disorder	⓪ ① ② ③ ④	⑨
GAF: Highest value of the last 7 days Psychological symptoms Occupational functions Social functions	 ___ ___ ___	⑨
EQ-5D-modified Sum: ______ item scores →	1.___ 2.___ 3.___ 4.___	⑨
2.5 Duration and course of the illness/problem		
Duration of the current mental disorder	○ <6 months ○ 6–24 months ○ 2–10 years ○ >10 years	⑨
Other pre-existing conditions	Were there any prior mental conditions? Which? ___	⑨
Chronic course of the current mental symptomatology	Course of symptom severity (trend) • stable • decreasing • progressive Additional course information: • without fluctuations • fluctuating • episodic-remitting • relapsing progressive	⑨

Figure 1. OPD-3 rating sheet for Axis I. 0 = not present, 2 = moderately present, 4 = very highly present, 9 = not applicable.

Illness and change concepts						
2.6 Illness concepts						
Somatic illness concept	⓪	①	②	③	④	⑨
External-social illness concept	⓪	①	②	③	④	⑨
External-alternative illness concept	⓪	①	②	③	④	⑨
Intrapsychic illness concept	⓪	①	②	③	④	⑨
2.7 Change and treatment concepts						
Somatic treatment concept	⓪	①	②	③	④	⑨
External-social treatment concept	⓪	①	②	③	④	⑨
External-alternative treatment concept	⓪	①	②	③	④	⑨
Psychotherapeutic treatment concept	⓪	①	②	③	④	⑨

Change resources/impediments for change/psychotherapy goals						
2.8.1 Change resources						
Burden of Suffering	⓪	①	②	③	④	⑨
Coping resources	⓪	①	②	③	④	⑨
Psychosocial support	⓪	①	②	③	④	⑨
Openness	⓪	①	②	③	④	⑨
2.8.2 Impediments for change						
External impediments for change	⓪	①	②	③	④	⑨
Internal impediments for change	⓪	①	②	③	④	⑨
Secondary gain	⓪	①	②	③	④	⑨
2.9 Psychotherapy: Change strategies and goals						
Symptom reduction	⓪	①	②	③	④	⑨
Reflection and clarification	⓪	①	②	③	④	⑨
Emotional support	⓪	①	②	③	④	⑨
Active guidance	⓪	①	②	③	④	⑨

Figure 1. OPD-3 rating sheet for Axis I. *(continued)*

3 Axis II: Interpersonal Relations

3.1 Summarized Presentation of Axis II

Disturbances in interpersonal relationships occur in many mental disorders. Since these impairments often have repetitive relationship patterns, their identification is crucial for psychotherapy. This is particularly important because such relationship patterns often shape the therapeutic contact from the beginning and become the subject of therapeutic work to varying degrees.

The goal of OPD relationship diagnosis is to identify the repetitive dysfunctional relationship pattern of a patient as well as relevant aspects of transference and countertransference. Dysfunctional relationship patterns can be understood as specific interpersonal constellations in which a patient's behaviors intertwine with those of their interaction partners into a repetitive pattern. The procedure primarily focuses on the dysfunctional aspects of repetitive relationship formations. These constellations can be described from the perspective of the patient's experience and from the experience of others (their interaction partners); from each of these perspectives, both the behaviors of the patients and those of their interaction partners can be considered. These distinctions result in four analytical units called *interpersonal perspectives:*

1. How the patient experiences others: This is about the relationship behavior that the patient repeatedly experiences and possibly complains about with their interaction partners.
2. How the patient experiences themselves: The focus here is on the patient's relational behavior. It describes the interpersonal behavior that the patient repeatedly experiences and consistently portrays in their relationship descriptions.
3. How others repeatedly experience the patient: This captures how others (including the examiner) repeatedly experience the patient. This perspective usually captures more than what the patients themselves can describe, i.e. also the unconscious aspects of their (difficult) relationship offer.
4. How others repeatedly experience themselves in relation to the patient: Here we record which reactions the patient induces in the other person in the sense of a role offer (unconsciously suggested response). This element corresponds to the procedure of psychoanalytic countertransference diagnostics (for comparison, see Mertens, 2004a; Thomä & Kächele, 2006a)

These four interpersonal perspectives are "filled" based on the narratives of subjects or patients. The item lists shown below are used for this purpose. The item lists are available in two versions (see Figure 4 and Figure 5). The clinical version consists of the respective experience/behavior descriptions in a graded format (unremarkable, i.e., not clinically relevant, accentuated, dysfunctional). Each item can be rated individually; however, in clinical practice, ratings may be limited to the most prominent items. The research version is identical to the clinical version in terms of item formulations.

However, the items at a neighboring position in the circumplex model (i.e., similar in content) are combined into pairs to enable a more reliable assessment. It is also assumed in the research application that all item pairs are assessed.

The descriptions of the interpersonal perspectives can then be connected in a relational dynamic formulation to create a psychologically coherent context that explains the dysfunctionality and stability of the relationship pattern. This formulation traces how the patient, contrary to their own perspective of experience, unconsciously shapes their relationships in such a way that they always elicit responses from others that they then perceive as, for example, painful, disappointing, or threatening.

Through the Interpersonal Relations Axis (Axis II), both relational behaviors and the typical reactions of interaction partners can be described with suitable complexity. This approach also enables the depiction of reciprocal influences between these two levels, reflecting transactional reinforcement in interpersonal interactions.

3.2 The Central Importance of Relationship Experiences

Later within the chapter, the practical approach to relationship diagnostics in the OPD is described. For those interested, the following provides an in-depth explanation of the theoretical foundation of the Axis II.

The experience and shaping of interpersonal behavior is seen as a crucial factor in the development and maintenance of mental disorders, especially in psychodynamic therapy. How a person shapes and experiences their relationships with others is therefore central in this form of therapy, but presumably also in all other psychotherapies. Intrapsychic conflicts significantly shape any relational behavior, while specific relationship patterns, in turn, allow conclusions about intrapsychic conflicts. Repetitive relationship patterns can also express structural limitations of patients, i.e., impairments in interpersonal perception processes and intrapsychic self-regulation. They can reveal impairment of emotion regulation or serve to protect certain vulnerabilities.

Relationship diagnostics within the OPD framework addresses this phenomenon at the interface between the intrapsychic and interpersonal levels. It primarily relies on observable and describable relationship behavior. This includes the relational aspects that the examiner experiences and observes in the encounter with the patient. These can be formulated as the patient's relational offer and as the examiner's countertransference (i.e., the comprehensive reaction of the therapeutic counterpart to the patients' unspoken relational expectations).

We understand relationship behavior as an expression of the dynamic between more or less conscious relationship desires, the associated inner anxieties of patients, and the fears of how the counterpart might react to these desires. It is also determined by the respective structure in terms of the "psychic tools" for integrated and flexible relationship shaping. Anxieties, fears, and difficulties can be determined by conflicts or by structural conditions in varying weights. For example, a rather conflict-related relationship behavior in a predominantly actively resolved Dependency vs. Individuation Conflict can manifest as repetitive, exhausted caregiving of others while almost indignantly rejecting offers of support. A relationship behavior on a lower level of personality (i.e., "structural") functioning might be suspected behind a repeated alternation between clinging demands and devaluing contact breaks.

Habitual problematic (dysfunctional) relationship behavior can be understood as a stable psychosocial compromise formation between desires and fears in relationships, where the relationship shaping is co-determined by structural abilities. Habitual means that the behavior then appears as dominant and continuously effective in patients. The relational offers arising from the habitual relationship behavior become particularly relevant when they are ambivalent or require a high degree of understanding and self- or co-regulation from the counterpart. This is often evident in the relationship between how people experience their own reaction to the "adversity of the world" and the perception of this reaction by others. Here, something like a "central misunderstanding" can arise ("Others fundamentally reject me"). This needs to be reconstructed and diagnostically examined to determine whether it arises from an inner conflict tension with desires and their defenses, different facets of structural limitations (e.g., interpersonal misperceptions), or a mixture of both (Ehrenthal & Grande, 2014; Grande, 2007).

In an initial interview, one can obtain information about the patient's relationship behavior, among other things, from their narratives of relationship episodes with important others. Particularly stable and repetitive relationship experiences can be discerned from the depiction of these episodes. Apart from that, information can be gained during the conversation from the unfolding transference and countertransference between patient and examiner. Based on the reactions and impulses that the examiner observes in themselves, they can draw conclusions about how others might feel and behave in the encounter with the patient. Experiencing and using countertransference must be learned and practiced and can then be used as an instrument for relationship diagnostics. The diagnostics of the dysfunctional relationship pattern always encompass these two perspectives: that of the patients and that of the others, including the examiners.

3.2.1 Relationship Experiences and Their Intrapsychic Organization

From a developmental mental perspective, relationship experiences are made in various ways, mediated through different perception modalities, and stored partly in procedural memory (e.g., as attachment patterns; Ainsworth et al., 1978) and partly in episodic memory. There is much evidence suggesting that subjective experiences are highly organized by emotional experiences. What is remembered and with what specific meaning depends, among other things, on the emotional tones and intensities associated with the memory (Stern, 1985). Subjectively organized memory and meaning structures modulate how current relationship information is handled.

Psychoanalytic object relations theory assumes that relationship experiences, especially with significant caregivers during childhood and adolescence, crystallize into internalized representations (e.g., as self and object representations) at the intrapsychic level. These internalized images are embedded in the context of subject- and object-related feelings, desires, expectations, fears, and habitual interpersonal transactions. Following the traditions of Jacobsen (1964) and Mahler et al. (1975), Kernberg (1984) sees such "self-object-affect units" as primary determinants of intrapsychic structural formation. These internalized relationship schemas represent the subjective processing of interpersonal experiences and interactions, not the "objective reality." Self and object representations are always compromise formations and are partly determined by defense processes, especially when certain relationships are associated with unpleasant affects or fears. Consistent repetition of positive relational experiences, especially during childhood, is particularly important for forming these internal representations. For instance, it is a prerequisite in early development for achieving "object constancy" (i.e., the enduring and not easily disrupted inner presence of memories of significant caregivers) and later for personal "identity" (see Axis IV). The redundancy of negative experiences or the lack of reliability of positive experiences leads to structural limitations.

While Kernberg describes the early development of "ego functions" (i.e., abilities or structural features) as the differentiation of the early undifferentiated self from the early caregiver, Stern (1985) and Emde (1988) see the child from the beginning as a separate, affective, active, and controlling being. They understand its development as a sequence of increasingly complex intersubjective regulatory projects of the self in interaction with the caregiver. This tradition also includes attachment theory, which posits that children develop enduring behavior patterns in adaptation to the interaction offers of their early caregivers to ensure proximity to security-providing adults. These patterns establish themselves in the form of "internal working models of attachment," which are transactionally reinforced or modified (e.g., Bowlby, 1988).

There is now considerable evidence supporting the hypothesis that a person's psychopathology results from formative life experiences stored, as mentioned, as mental relationship representations (e.g., Pincus & Wright, 2010). Children are not only shaped by their caregivers and family relationships but also actively influence and reshape these relationships from the beginning. These constellations can be described from two perspectives: the patient's experience and the experience of their interaction partners, considering both the patient's and the interaction partners' behaviors. Thus, the child develops relationship patterns to which it has significantly contributed (Cierpka, 1992). Because remembered relationship experiences also contain contradictory self and object images, they play a crucial role in shaping intrapsychic conflicts (see Axis III).

In recent years, elements of this understanding of interpersonal impairments have also been incorporated into behavior therapy. For example, a therapy form was developed for the psychotherapy of chronically depressed patients and their relationship disorders, which very specifically addresses difficult relationship patterns and uses the interpersonal circumplex model (see Section 3.2.1), particularly in the sense of Kiesler (Cognitive Behavioral Analysis System of Psychotherapy; CBASP, McCullough, 2000). Schema therapy (Young et al., 2003) also emphasizes identifying problematic interpersonal patterns, offering a typology that includes rejection, autonomy, boundary-setting, orientation toward others, and inhibition.

3.2.2 Interpersonal Manifestation of Intrapsychic Conflicts and Structural Components

Typically, participants in an interaction aim to create a communication situation characterized by safety, personal well-being, and trust. When this is achieved, the intrapsychic balance for each participant is maintained, and relational desires can be expressed without excessive fear.

When relationship building fails, it can have various causes. Often, the perspective of past repeated experiences distorts the perception and subsequent behavior in current relationships. Freud conceptualized this perspectival shift as "transference" (Freud, 1912, 1925). Transference processes--rooted in unconscious or preconscious wishes, fears, or internalized relationship experiences--strongly influence the interpersonal roles patients assume and project onto others.

Albani et al. (2002) showed that the severity of a mental disorder closely correlates with the manifestation of negative central relationship patterns. Structural vulnerabilities likely play a crucial role in this, potentially leading to impaired emotional self-regulation; abrupt defensive reactions may become necessary, complicating interactions and heavily burdening relationships over time (Rudolf & Grande, 2002). Dahlbender (2002) formulates the relationship between these aspects as follows: Internalized relationship patterns result from intrapsychic conflicts and their defense or processing, which in turn are based on the level of structural functioning.

The more limited a person is in their structural abilities and defense mechanisms in the sense of habitual relationship behavior, the more they will attempt to restore familiar configurations in their interactions to limit the extent of new and potentially overwhelming experiences. Familiarity can then, for example, be more important than the consequences of the original trauma. It is often observed in patients that they try to establish relatively stable and consistent themes, feelings, and (unconscious) fantasies with their caregivers. The more rigid and extreme a subject's experience and behavior in relationship situations are, and the more these relationship configurations are "automatically" unconsciously established, the more likely they are to be continued and perpetuated (Cierpka et al., 1998).

For patients with inconsistent and contradictory relationship experiences, such as those with borderline personality disorders, attempts at relationship building can lead to disintegration. Adequate perception of the wishes and needs of others and the situational framework conditions is then hardly possible. Diagnostic identification of relationship patterns can be difficult and even impossible in psychotic patients with fragmented object relationships.

Interpersonal flexibility, on the other hand, is present when a patient can shape diverse and differentiated relationships. This flexibility depends significantly on the ability of the ego to mediate between the individual's inner needs, the demands of the superego, and the environment, as described by Freud (1923) in "The Ego and the Id." A well-integrated structure enables empathy with the experiences of others and perception of their desires, fears, and behavior strategies. Such an individual has more capabilities to regulate their social relationships according to situational conditions.

In relationship diagnostics, flexibility can be expressed when the patient can draw on a wide repertoire of relationship-building possibilities and describe interaction partners who do not react in a typical, dysfunctional way as experienced by the patient. Despite focusing on describing dysfunctional patterns, the examiner should look for such exceptions, as they indicate healthy parts and resources of the patient.

3.2.3 Diagnosing Transference Patterns

Psychodynamic diagnostics are centrally based on the assumption that, in the therapeutic encounter, a central relationship pattern is unconsciously induced by the patient, assigning the therapist a specific transference role (see Sandler's concept of role-responsiveness, Sandler, 1976). This role often mirrors that of a significant caregiver. Krause et al. define transference as "a specific set of behaviors with which social partners are induced to behave concordantly with specific unconscious expectations" (Hans et al., 1986). This also includes what König (1982) describes as the "interactional part of transference," involving the counterpart interactionally. For patients, this often involves compromise behavior, incorporating desires, impulses, fears, and their defenses. Subjective experiences in interpersonal relationships become internalized, creating predispositions toward specific transference patterns (also known as transference readiness).

In interpersonal relationships, the neurotic distortion moment can contribute to maladaptive vicious circles, where personal expectations are doomed to fail from the outset, resulting in a negative self-assessment (Strupp & Binder, 1993). Neurotic transference in psychotherapy is characterized by the patient selectively focusing on certain aspects of the behavior and personality of others, especially the therapist, and behaving unconsciously in a way that elicits responses aligning with their expectations (Gill & Hoffmann, 1982). The therapeutic task is to create an interpersonal space where the therapist does not react as expected (Weiss & Sampson, 1986), allowing the patient to interpret their transference readiness and make new experiences in a protected relationship (Thomä & Kächele, 2006a). It is crucial to consider that the therapist's transference readiness can also distort the therapeutic interaction. To reduce this factor, Freud (1910) already demanded the necessity of training therapy for prospective psychoanalysts, a requirement soon adopted by Carl Gustav Jung (1921/1971). This has become a cornerstone of training not only in psychoanalysis but also in many psychotherapy training programs, and it has been incorporated into the German federal law regulating psychotherapy training and education.

3.2.4 The Relationship Between Transference and Scenic (Re-)Enactment

Historically, the concept of transference evolved from the concept of displacement. Experiences are shifted from the original object to another object (or energetic cathexes are transferred from one inner object representation to another). In this concept, transference was seen as a defense mechanism, protecting the ego from remembering pathogenic early object relationships (Bettighofer, 1998). Long after Freud's technical writing (Freud, 1912), transference was understood as a one-sided process concerning only the patient. Paula Heimann (1950) was a pioneer in extending the understanding of countertransference as an affective-cognitive constellation arising from the interaction and the therapist's (sometimes neurotically distorted) inner objects. Gill (1979) in the Anglo-American context and Thomä (1981) in the German-speaking context later argued that in every therapeutic situation, both patient and therapist contribute to shaping the activated transference in the sense of an "interactional symmetry" (Ermann, 1992).

The term "enactment" refers explicitly to the interactional aspect of the actualization of generalized interaction representations in the therapeutic relationship. It corresponds most closely to behaviors in the therapist-patient relationship that arise in response to (unconscious) conflicts and fantasies activated in the therapeutic process. These behaviors are linked to both the interplay of transference and countertransference and (through memory) with thoughts, fantasies, and interpersonal experiences from the past. Jacobs (1986) explicitly emphasizes that this definition of enactment also includes aspects of re-enactment, i.e., the revival of fragments of the psychic past. Other authors (Sandler, 1983; Stolorow et al., 1987) also emphasize the relational nature of transference, which can only be understood by considering the entire intersubjective relational field (Ferro & Civitarese, 2018).

OPD relationship diagnostics are therefore oriented towards concrete experiences and behaviors in interpersonal situations, applying the concept of re-enactment. In this sense it includes not only transference phenomena but also the scenic realization of transference in the current mutual relationship structure. Reenactment as a central concept of psychodynamic psychotherapy can be empirically confirmed (e.g., Stasch et al., 2002) and has high therapeutic utility, as the manner of reenactment allows conclusions about the underlying transference tendencies of the patient and thus about intrapsychic representations of relational experiences (e.g., Dahlbender, Buchheim et al., 2004).

3.2.5 Theoretical and Empirical Roots of the Interpersonal Relations Axis (Axis II)

Without reliable identification and classification of dysfunctional relationship patterns, a corresponding theory can hardly gain practical significance in everyday clinical practice. Since the early 1970s, numerous researchers and clinicians have worked on creating formulations for the systematic description and mapping of interpersonal problems from a psychodynamic perspective (overview by Schauenburg & Grande, 2010).

To delineate the framework within which we have developed our current relationship diagnostic instrument, the following procedures originating from the psychoanalytic and interpersonal traditions will be described. Therefore, references will only be made to work from social psychology (e.g., SYMLOG; Bales & Cohen, 1979), family research (overview by Cierpka, 2003), and behavior therapy (e.g., Caspar, 2007). For Axis II of the Operationalized Psychodynamic Diagnosis, the following methods have been particularly important and influential:

1. Structural Analysis of Social Behavior (SASB; Benjamin et al. 2006; Tress, 1993);
2. Core Conflictual Relationship Theme (CCRT; Luborsky et al., 1991).
3. The Plan Formulation Method; Control-Mastery-Theory (Weiss & Sampson, 1986).
4. Role-Relationship Conflict (Horowitz, 1991).
5. Person Experience of the Therapist (PERT; Hoffmann & Gill, 1988).
6. Cyclical Maladaptive Pattern (CMP; Strupp & Binder, 1984).

All methods share the focus on interpersonal interaction. The spectrum ranges from the microscopic examination of individual speech acts (SASB) to the description of individual components of interaction (wishes, fears, reactions of objects, and their consequences for the self in CCRT or CMP) to constellations of intrapsychic and interpersonal schemas (Horowitz) and instruments aimed at capturing complex transference processes in psychodynamic therapies (e.g., "Plan Analysis," PERT).

All procedures assume the existence of one or possibly several central interpersonal patterns in patients. Likewise, the clinical judgment of the practitioner/interviewer is an essential component of all these procedures, with varying extent of required interpretative inference. In general, as complexity increases, so does the level of subjective inference ("Level of Inference" according to Luborsky & Crits-Christoph, 1998), negatively impacting the quality of inter-rater agreement. The more abstract the categories to be assessed are, the less likely it is to achieve high agreement rates.

The Structural Analysis of Social Behavior (SASB; Benjamin 1974, 1993) allows for a differentiated and simultaneously reliable representation of complex relationship events. The method can be used to identify stereotypes in the observable dyadic interaction process and represent relatively invariant interpersonal and intrapsychic behavior patterns of individuals. Fundamental to SASB assessment is the assignment of relationship acts to the two dimensions of love-hate (affiliation) and control-submission (interdependence), depicted as orthogonal axes of a circle. SASB was developed in the tradition of interpersonal circle models (Leary, 1957). Both form the basis for the item selection of the OPD Interpersonal Relations Axis (Axis II).

Luborsky's method of the Core Conflictual Relationship Theme (CCRT) examines relationship episodes reported by patients, capturing the expressed or implicit wishes, the reactions of others to these wishes, and the subject's reaction to the others. These three elements often form the basic structure of relational narratives. Difficulties with this method arise because unconscious wishes usually cannot be derived from observable behavior, while the overtly visible motives often appear trivial compared to the underlying complex intrapsychic processes from which they arise. This was one of the reasons why the Axis II incorporated the reactions in interpersonal scenes into its matrix but did not include the "wish level" (which is located on the Conflict Axis in the OPD logic).

For the SASB and CCRT methods, numerous studies demonstrate their reliability and validity (e.g., Albani et al., 2002; Schauenburg & Cierpka, 1994; Dahlbender, 2002).

The method of Cyclic Maladaptive Patterns (CMP; Strupp & Binder, 1993) has also influenced the OPD relationship diagnostics. This model conceptualizes behavior patterns as neurotic repetitions of childhood conflicts, assuming the determining influence of a core conflict. Following an interpersonal understanding of transference (Gill, 1982), therapeutic work should primarily focus on the relationship between patient and therapist. References to earlier life contexts take a back seat to the current relationship behavior, which forms the therapeutic focus. The CMP method, therefore, contains a strong action orientation and predominantly uses action-oriented formulations. It describes the expectations and thoughts someone brings into an interaction, the reactions they elicit from the other person, and how these shape or confirm their beliefs about themselves and others. A cyclic maladaptive pattern is thus defined as a repetitive sequence of interpersonal events linked in a self-confirming and transactional reinforcing loop.

This model is adopted in the OPD in the instructions for relationship dynamic formulation. Categories such as "response of the subject" and "response of the object" were borrowed from the CCRT tradition and CMP, as well as the systematic use of relationship episodes as the diagnostic material basis. As previously indicated, the interpersonal circle models, particularly the Structural Analysis of Social Behavior (SASB), were heuristic foundations for generating the items required to capture repetitive dysfunctional relationship behavior.

3.3 Relationship Diagnostics in OPD

The operationalization of psychodynamic diagnostics demands that the description of interpersonal perspectives be conducted in a standardized manner. For this purpose, an item list was generated based on the so-called circumplex model of interpersonal behavior. Circumplex models assume that people align their relationship behavior to establish a certain status and a desired level of closeness. These models share the characteristic that every interpersonal behavior is arranged on a circle (see Figure 2). The widely known Kiesler Circle (though in OPD, Lorna Benjamin's Double Circle Model is preferred; see Benjamin, 1996) is divided by two orthogonal and bipolar axes, which represent the two fundamental categories (status/degree of closeness): A vertical axis represents the control of status (dominant/controlling vs. obedient/submissive), while the horizontal axis represents the degree of desired closeness, affiliation (loving/approachable vs. hostile/distant).

The issue with this model is that the vertical axis works with the only possible opposition between dominant/controlling vs. obedient/submissive, while the opposite of control could also be granting freedom, and the opposite of submission could also be resistance. This issue was resolved by Lorna Benjamin with the development of the SASB model, which includes two interrelated circles to describe interpersonal behavior ("transitive," i.e., behavior/experience directed towards others in the upper circle and "intransitive," i.e., behavior/experience directed towards oneself in the lower circle), where the vertical axes in both circles do not represent "status" but enmeshment, better yet neutrally "interdependence." The bipolarity of dominant/controlling vs. obedient/submissive is now found by connecting the lower poles of the two circles (see Figure 2). This model allows for a much more differentiated depiction of interpersonal behavior and was therefore used as the basis for the behavior categories of the OPD Interpersonal Relations Axis (Axis II).

Various qualities of interpersonal behavior can be determined as mixtures of these basic dimensions and thus as locations on the respective circles. The circumplex models and the measurement instruments derived from them are well-researched and validated within personality psychology, social psychology, and clinical psychology (Wiggins, 1982; Wendt et al., 2019). Other works highlight their significance for capturing relevant personality variables in psychotherapy research. Moreover, they form the core framework of dimensional models developed for the interpersonal description of personality disorders (Widiger & Simonsen, 2005).

Figure 2 shows the active ("transitive") and reactive ("intransitive") levels of relationship behavior in two circles. The horizontal axis of both circles describes *affiliation*, and the vertical axis describes *interdependence*.

A closer look highlights the inner order of the circle models (see Benjamin, 1993): Behaviors that are opposite each other indicate opposite behaviors. The items located at the 45-degree angle indicate relationship qualities where the dimensions of affiliation and interdependence are partially represented. The degree of friendliness/hostility or control/submission in relationship formation is less at these positions than at the extreme poles of the two orthogonal axes. Interpersonal behaviors noted at identical positions in the upper and lower circles are in a complementary relationship to each other. This means that for each relationship offer from an interaction partner (e.g., 5 in the upper circle, "affectionately pressuring"), there is a corresponding reaction described at the same axis position in the lower circle (21, "overly engaging with affection") from the person. Complementarity also means that there is a statistically more frequent interaction of two behaviors.

Prerequisites for the assessment of relationship patterns include a clinical diagnostic interview following the guidelines of the OPD interview (see Chapter 7). The diagnostic assessment incorporates the following two sources of information:

1. The relationship experiences reported by the patient in the interview. Their narratives illustrate how they perceive others and themselves in interactions and how these typically unfold (so-called relationship episodes).
2. The interpersonal information from the direct interaction between the patient and the diagnostician. This includes the patient's observable behavior and the immediately inferred internal experienced behavior, as well as the diagnostician's experiences and reactions (countertransference) as important information.

3.3.1 The Assessment Procedure

The relationship diagnostics of OPD use a series of terms and methodological tools that are introduced and explained below: the experiential perspectives of the patients and others, the interpersonal perspectives, the item list for describing relationship aspects, the circumplex model underlying this list, and the schema for the relational dynamic formulation.

The Experiential Perspectives

According to the two different sources of information (the relationships described by the patient and the behavior and experiences observable in the assessment conversation), the central relationship pattern is captured by distinguishing between the experiential perspective of the patient and that of others (including the examiner).

Experiential perspective of the patient (perspective A): The idea that patients have about their relationships arises from their descriptions of relationship experiences. These descriptions can reveal which relationship aspects (behavior and emotional elements) the patient experiences and identifies in themselves and their interaction partners. The examiner should understand and depict this experiential perspective in their relationship diagnosis.

Experiential perspective of others, including the examiner (perspective B): This perspective concerns how others ("real" interaction partners of the patient, including the examiner) repeatedly experience the patient's relationship offers and how they react to them (i.e., what relationship behavior the patient suggests to others). Ideally, the examiner tries to put themselves in the shoes of the objects described by the patient and examine how they would likely perceive the

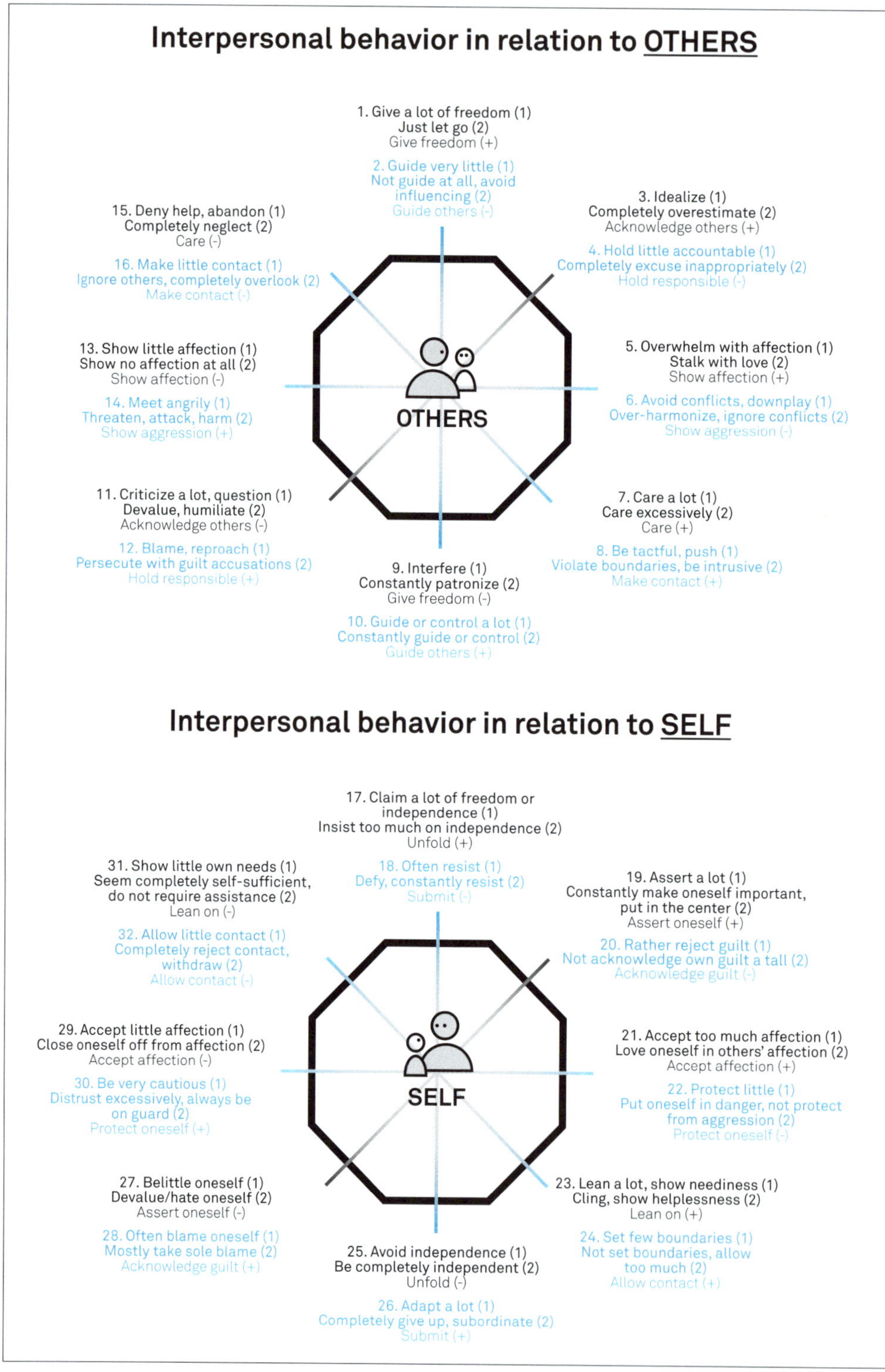

Figure 2. Circumplex model of OPD-3 Axis II. Design by Ludwig Wendt.

patient and respond interactively from their perspective. Since this can be challenging in practice, working with case vignettes on training or supervision videos might serve as a methodological "bridge" to assess the countertransference behavior of the interviewer as a basis for the suggested relationship response. Pragmatically, it often succeeds in examining one's own experience, especially one's own impulses for action, in the encounter with the patient (as a clinician or video viewer) and accounting for the impulses and feelings that the patient evokes in us. Finally, an attempt is made to align one's own experience with the ideas about the experiences of others regarding the patients. If this is done coherently, the identification of characteristic features of the dysfunctional pattern has likely succeeded. If not, further clarification is necessary: the examiner must then check whether they have possibly overlooked important aspects of the patient's relationship offer or in what specific way the patient distorts their relationships, so that the discrepancy can be explained as a result of such misperceptions.

The Interpersonal Perspectives

Dysfunctional relationship patterns are presented as specific constellations of interpersonal behaviors a) of the patient and b) of the others (their objects). This applies to both experiential perspectives, so four interpersonal perspectives can be distinguished (Figure 3).

Patient's experiential perspective:

- The patient repeatedly experiences others in such a way that they ...
  Here, the focus is on the behaviors of the objects towards the patients, as they are more or less consistently experienced and described by the patients.
- The patient repeatedly experiences themselves in such a way that they (others or towards others) ...
  Here, the focus is on the interpersonal experience and behavior of the patients themselves. Described are those behaviors that appear dominant and consistently effective in the self-experience of the patients. This

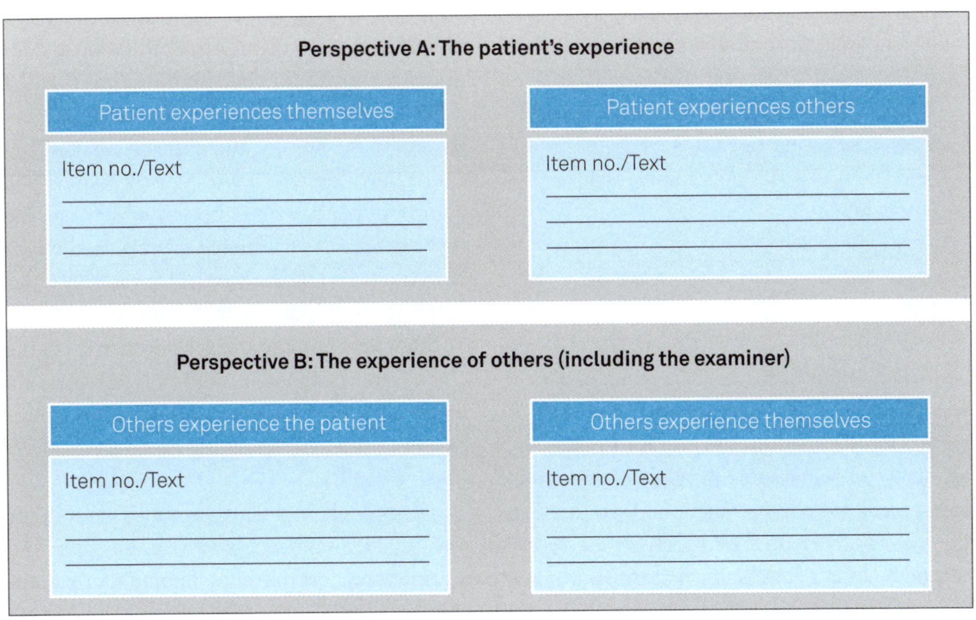

Figure 3. The four interpersonal perspectives.

includes behaviors that are conscious to the patients and typically involve defensive, reactive aspects (in conflict situations).

Examiner's experiential perspective:

- Others (including the examiners) experience that the patient (them) repeatedly ...
  Here, the focus is on the patient's relationship offers towards others, including the examiner. Described are the patient's behaviors as perceived by others. These behaviors are often unconscious to the patient And potentially difficult transference offers by the patient may play a role here.
- Others, including the examiners, repeatedly experience themselves towards the patient in such a way that they ...
  Here, the focus is on the reactions, impulses, and feelings that the patient elicits in others, including the examiner. It captures which reactions the patients induce in the counterpart in terms of a role offer (unconsciously suggested response). It is important that this is primarily not about how the examiner behaves or would behave, but about which action impulses are triggered in them. This element corresponds to the approach of psychoanalytic countertransference diagnostics (see Mertens, 2004a; Thomä & Kächele, 2006a). Benjamin (1993) assumed that these categories transcend gender differences and postulates a universality of relationships.

The Item List

The assessment of the four interpersonal perspectives is carried out using items that in OPD-3 for the first time are primarily graded by intensity (unremarkable or clinically not relevant, accentuated, dysfunctional). In this list, the four interpersonal perspectives are represented by four columns. Each of the four interpersonal perspectives is thus assessed separately by columns (Figure 4).

In the research version, the differentiation of two items in adjacent position(s) in the circle model is omitted, and only one rating is provided for both items. For example, in the clinical version (Figure 4), Items 15 ("neglect") and 16 ("ignore") should be rated separately (which can be clinically meaningful because the underlying relationship themes differ). In the research version (see Figure 5), however, only one rating is given for both Items (Figure 5), as both Items are in a neighboring position in the circle model.

Additionally, Appendix A contains the item checklist with brief explanations for all items in each manifestation, facilitating the rating of relevant items.

The Circumplex Model

The item list is based on a circumplex model (see Figure 2), whose specific logic is briefly explained here. To illustrate, consider Item 7 "care excessively," positioned at the bottom right of the upper circle and representing a mixture of positive affiliation and taking influence. In the opposite position one can find Item 15 " completely neglect" with negative affiliation and reduced positive influence (in the sense that the other is left alone). These two descriptions of relational behavior are thematically related because they describe opposing expressions of a common relationship theme, which can be termed "care." This theme is presented under both Items and marked with "(+)" and "(-)" depending on the polarity of the theme. Similarly, all other items (opposite each other on the same circle) are assigned a common relationship theme. The assignment is such that the numbering of the corresponding items differs by 8 (like 7 and 15).

The model's logic further implies that items positioned at identical places on the upper and lower circles describe complementary relationship qualities. The complementary theme to the "care" (offering support to others) is "lean on"

OPD-3 Item List Rating Sheet Axis II (Clinical Version): Relationship Topics

	OPD relationship theme	P:O	P:P	O:P	O:O	Res	Unremarkable/clinically not relevant (= 0)	Accentuated (= 1)	Dysfunctional (= 2)	
1	*Give freedom (+)*					1	Give others freedom	Give a lot of freedom	Just allow it to happen/ignore	1
2	*Guide others (–)*					2	Guide little	Guide very little	Not guide at all, avoid influencing	2
3	*Acknowledge others (+)*					3	Acknowledge friendly	Idealize	Completely overestimate	3
4	*Hold responsible (–)*					4	Hold responsible	Hold little accountable	Completely excuse inappropriately	4
5	*Show affection (+)*					5	Show affection	Overwhelm with affection	Stalk with love	5
6	*Show aggression (–)*					6	Show little aggression	Avoid conflicts, downplay	Over-harmonize, ignore conflicts	6
7	*Care (+)*					7	Care	Care a lot	Care excessively	7
8	*Make contact (+)*					8	Make contact	Be tactless, push	Violate boundaries, be intrusive	8
9	*Give freedom (–)*					9	Get involved	Interfere	Constantly patronize	9
10	*Guide others (+)*					10	Guide appropriately	Guide or control a lot	Constantly guide or control	10
11	*Acknowledge others (–)*					11	Critically acknowledge	Criticize a lot, question	Devalue, humiliate	11
12	*Hold responsible (+)*					12	Hold responsible	Blame, reproach	Persecute with guilt accusations	12
13	*Show affection (–)*					13	Keep distance	Show little affection	Show no affection at all	13
14	*Show aggression (+)*					14	Show anger	Meet angrily	Threaten, attack, harm	14
15	*Care (–)*					15	Limit help	Deny help, abandon	Completely neglect	15
16	*Make contact (–)*					16	Limit contact	Make little contact	Ignore others, completely overlook	16
17	*Unfold (+)*					17	Unfold independently	Claim a lot of freedom or independence	Insist too much on independence	17
18	*Submit (–)*					18	Assert oneself, resist	Often resist	Defy, constantly resist	18
19	*Assert oneself (+)*					19	Assert oneself	Assert a lot	Constantly make oneself important, putting oneself in the center	19
20	*Acknowledge guilt (–)*					20	Examine own responsibility	Rather reject guilt	Not acknowledge own guilt at all	20
21	*Accept affection (+)*					21	Accept affection	Accept too much affection	Lose oneself in others' affection	21
22	*Protect oneself (–)*					22	Open up	Protect little	Put oneself in danger, not protect from aggression	22
23	*Lean on (+)*					23	Show own needs	Lean a lot, show neediness	Cling, show helplessness	23
24	*Allow contact (+)*					24	Allow contact	Set few boundaries	Not set boundaries, allow too much	24
25	*Unfold (–)*					25	Unfold independently	Avoid independence	Be completely dependent	25
26	*Submit (+)*					26	Submit somewhat	Adapt a lot	Completely give up, subordinate	26
27	*Assert oneself (–)*					27	Question oneself	Belittle oneself	Devalue/hate oneself	27
28	*Acknowledge guilt (+)*					28	Acknowledge own responsibility	Often blame oneself	Mostly take sole blame	28
29	*Accept affection (–)*					29	Examine affection	Accept little affection	Close oneself off from affection	29
30	*Protect oneself (+)*					30	Protect oneself	Be very cautious	Distrust excessively, always be on guard	30
31	*Lean on (–)*					31	Show one's own needs	Show little of one's own needs	Seem completely unneedy, claim no help	31
32	*Allow contact (–)*					32	Limit contact	Allow little contact	Completely reject contact, withdraw	32

Patient ID:

Date:

Therapist:

Narrative:

Note. P:O = patients' experience others, P:P = patients' experience themselves, O:P = others' experience patients, O:O = others experience themselves.

Figure 4. OPD-3 item list rating sheet Axis II (clinical version): Relationship topics (also available in the online material).

OPD-3 Item List Rating Sheet Axis II (Research Version): Relationship Topics.

OPD relationship theme		P:O	P:P	O:P	O:O	Res	Unremarkable/clinically not relevant (= 0)	Accentuated (= 1)	Dysfunctional (= 2)	
Give freedom (+)	1					1	Give others freedom	Give a lot of freedom	Just allow it to happen/ignore	1
Guide others (–)	2					2	Guide little	Guide very little	Not guide at all, avoid influencing	2
Acknowledge others (+)	3					3	Acknowledge friendly	Idealize	Completely overestimate	3
Hold responsible (–)	4					4	Hold responsible	Hold little accountable	Completely excuse inappropriately	4
Show affection (+)	5					5	Show affection	Overwhelm with affection	Stalk with love	5
Show aggression (–)	6					6	Show little aggression	Avoid conflicts, downplay	Over-harmonize, ignore conflicts	6
Care (+)	7					7	Care	Care a lot	Care excessively	7
Make contact (+)	8					8	Make contact	Be tactless, push	Violate boundaries, be intrusive	8
Give freedom (–)	9					9	Get involved	Interfere	Constantly patronize	9
Guide others (+)	10					10	Guide appropriately	Guide or control a lot	Constantly guide or control	10
Acknowledge others (–)	11					11	Critically acknowledge	Criticize a lot, question	Devalue, humiliate	11
Hold responsible (+)	12					12	Hold responsible	Blame, reproach	Persecute with guilt accusations	12
Show affection (–)	13					13	Keep distance	Show little affection	Show no affection at all	13
Show aggression (+)	14					14	Show anger	Meet angrily	Threaten, attack, harm	14
Care (–)	15					15	Limit help	Deny help, abandon	Completely neglect	15
Make contact (–)	16					16	Limit contact	Make little contact	Ignore others, completely overlook	16
Unfold (+)	17					17	Unfold independently	Claim a lot of freedom or independence	Insist too much on independence	17
Submit (–)	18					18	Assert oneself, resist	Often resist	Defy, constantly resist	18
Assert oneself (+)	19					19	Assert oneself	Assert a lot	Constantly make oneself important, putting oneself in the center	19
Acknowledge guilt (–)	20					20	Examine own responsibility	Rather reject guilt	Not acknowledge own guilt at all	20
Accept affection (+)	21					21	Accept affection	Accept too much affection	Lose oneself in others' affection	21
Protect oneself (–)	22					22	Open up	Protect little	Put oneself in danger, not protect from aggression	22
Lean on (+)	23					23	Show own needs	Lean a lot, show neediness	Cling, show helplessness	23
Allow contact (+)	24					24	Allow contact	Set few boundaries	Not set boundaries, allow too much	24
Unfold (–)	25					25	Unfold independently	Avoid independence	Be completely dependent	25
Submit (+)	26					26	Submit somewhat	Adapt a lot	Completely give up, subordinate	26
Assert oneself (–)	27					27	Question oneself	Belittle oneself	Devalue/hate oneself	27
Acknowledge guilt (+)	28					28	Acknowledge own responsibility	Often blame oneself	Mostly take sole blame	28
Accept affection (–)	29					29	Examine affection	Accept little affection	Close oneself off from affection	29
Protect oneself (+)	30					30	Protect oneself	Be very cautious	Distrust excessively, always be on guard	30
Lean on (–)	31					31	Show one's own needs	Show little of one's own needs	Seem completely unneedy, claim no help	31
Allow contact (–)	32					32	Limit contact	Allow little contact	Completely reject contact, withdraw	32

Patient ID:
Date:
Therapist:
Narrative:

Note. P:O = patients' experience others, P:P = patients' experience themselves, O:P = others' experience patients, O:O = others experience themselves.

Figure 5. OPD-3 item list rating sheet Axis II (research version): Relationship topics (also available in the online material).

(allowing oneself to be supported), represented by Items 23 "lean a lot" and 31 "show little own needs" (difference between 23 and 31: 8) on the lower circle. Thus, each item pair of a relationship theme on the upper circle has a complementary item pair on the lower circle, in the sense that the relationship themes assigned to each item pair ("care" for items 7 and 15 above and "lean on" for items 23 and 31 below) are complementary. Therefore, 4 out of the 32 items of both circles are thematically related, with 2 of these 4 belonging to the same relationship theme (7 and 15 to "care," 23 and 31 to "lean on"). Accordingly, there are 8 complementary pairs of these themes.

This thematic grouping of items makes clinical sense as one often finds several items of a thematic complex united in dysfunctional relationship patterns. To illustrate, here are a few examples:

- A patient can process the experience of neglect (Item 15) by showing few own needs or rejecting help (31) while intensively caring for others (7) who, in turn, lean on or cling to them (23) (theme pair: care/lean on).
- A patient with self-esteem issues may display a pattern where they both belittle themselves (27) and place themselves particularly in the center of regard (19) and both devalue others (11) while idealizing and perhaps overestimating them (3) (theme pair: acknowledge others/assert oneself).

However, it must be noted that not always do these Items result in such a meaningful match. When rating, one should not seek such matches but rather map the behavior as it presents itself in all four interpersonal perspectives.

Relational Dynamic Formulation

The goal of the diagnosis is a relational dynamic formulation that links the four interpersonal perspectives. This transforms the purely descriptive recording of the relationship behavior into a deeper and more dynamic understanding (see Rudolf, Grande et al., 2004). The schema shown in Figure 6, which illustrates typical connections between the perspectives, guides this linkage process.

In the patient's perspective, the sequence of events typically proceeds from right to left (I. relational dynamic connection): Patients describe recurring relational acts of others (which are, for example, disappointing, dismissive, or hostile) to which they must respond.

From the perspective of others and the examiner, things usually appear in reverse: What a patient describes as their reaction to the other's behavior appears here as a problematic relational offer, conveyed through (problematic) interpersonal behavior (e.g., subtle devaluation, control, accusation, etc.), which challenges and involves the counterpart, for example, by putting them under pressure or scaring them. These active moments of the patient's own relational behavior are often omitted in their self-experience and create a characteristic difference between self-perception and perception by others (II. connection).

The third (III.) relational dynamic connection links the two lower fields from left to right. The patient, with their relational offer, induces certain reactions that can be experienced in the countertransference as feelings, fantasies, and impulses to act, with the focus here being on the impulses to act.

The examiner can now test: How would the patient experience the situation if I act according to the impulses suggested by their relational offer? Would they perceive my behavior exactly as they always perceive the behavior of others? This question pertains to the (IV.) connection between the fields at the bottom right and the top right.

If the latter connection can be coherently established, the interpretation of the relational dynamic event is complete and can be summarized in a compact "relationship formulation." This describes a self-reinforcing cycle and explains how the patient, through their relational

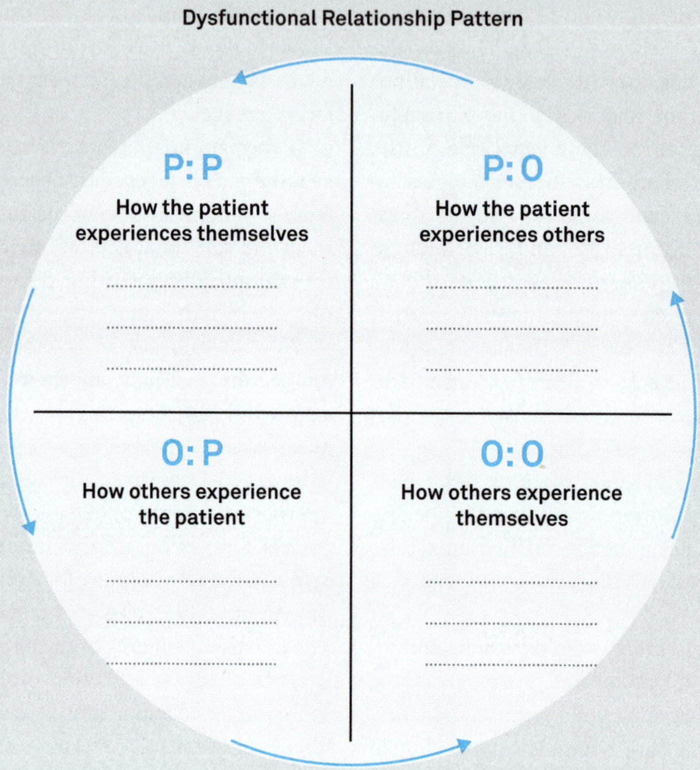

How the patient experiences others time and again:	
How the patient reacts to this typically:	
Which is the (unconscious) relational offer:	
Which are typical answers elicited through the offer:	
How is the patient experiencing the situation, if others answer as elicted:	

Figure 6. OPD-3 evaluation sheet Axis II: Dysfunctional relationship patterns; with the four interpersonal perspectives, the relation between perspectives (curved arrows), and empty fields for relationship dynamic formulation.

offers, provokes precisely those reactions they fear and wish to avoid. The coherent connection between the impulses experienced in the countertransference and the patient's object experience is an important, though not exclusive, criterion for whether the diagnosis of the dysfunctional relationship pattern was successful. It is also possible that a central dysfunctional element is found in a misinterpretation on the part of the patient, such as a patient eliciting impulses in others to take care of them but then experiencing such behavior as patronizing and devaluing.

Practical approach: Compared to Axes III and IV, Axis II is fundamentally designed to be rated closer to descriptive behavior. Thus, it focuses both on observable (relationship) behavior and on conscious affective experiences. The central question is: What does a patient (and others) do concretely in a specific relationship episode? The more precisely and specifically a patient reports on a particular episode (" ...so that I could replay the scene"), the less they make generalized considerations over multiple episodes, the easier it is to find appropriate items for an episode. However, it is also always crucial to ask whether the specific behavior in the episode might have a habitual character. Accordingly, the interviewer can condense and abstract over multiple episodes and the interview situation itself ("red thread of dysfunctional relationship dynamics").

The standard procedure for relationship diagnostics requires the examiner to take *three steps*:

1. In the first step, for each of the four interpersonal perspectives in the item selection list, all items that may describe the dysfunctional pattern are marked. These are the problematic aspects in the patient's perspective of experience (related to their own behavior and that of others) as well as the problematic aspects in the perspective of others/the examiner (again related to the patient's behavior and that of others). Helpful questions for assigning relationship behavior to one of the four perspectives might be, for example: Where do I find out how the patient experiences others (position top right, P:O)? Where is their own behavior described, which the patient is aware of (top left, P:P)? Where does the difficult relationship offer become clear, which the patient(s) themselves are mostly unaware of (bottom left, O:P)? What are the reactions of others or my own impulses to act (bottom right, O:O)? The number of items to be selected at this step is not yet limited. The assessment should ensure that only typical accentuated and dysfunctional behaviors are marked.
2. In the second step, the severity of the most important items for each of the four perspectives is determined and recorded on the evaluation sheet (Figure 6). A maximum of three salient items should be selected for each perspective. To capture the dysfunctional relationship pattern as concisely as possible, it is recommended to limit it to two or even one item per position if the case allows. There are two recommended variants for identifying the correct items, which can be mixed in practice:
(a) Orientation by themes: Simplified, there are a total of 8 themes in both circles (see above), which can be found meaningfully as the headings of Items 1-8 (Freedom, Control, Value, Guilt, Love, Aggression, Care, and Contact). There can either be too much (+) or too little (–) of these 8 behaviors, resulting in 16 items. These 16 items can be formulated either in relation to another person or centered on the self, yielding a total of 32 items. The first question for each relationship behavior is: To which of the 8 themes does it pertain? After identifying a theme/behavior, the second question is: Is there too much or too little of it? Finally, the question is whether the relationship behavior is centered on another person or the self. Example: A patient reports that in a dispute with their mother, he or she felt that she did not support them enough. An item for the P:O posi-

tion is sought, as the patient describes her or his perception of others. It is about the theme of care, there is too little of it (–), and the patient describes how others (mother) do something (too little) to them (upper circle). The recommended Item would be No. 15.
(b) Orientation by circle axes: Each of the two circles is divided into axes: the horizontal "affiliation" axis, and the vertical "interdependence" axis. For each relationship behavior in this orientation, the first question is: Is the relationship behavior centered on another person ("transitive," upper circle) or the self ("intransitive," lower circle)? This reduces the selection to the 16 items of one of the two circles. The second question is: Is the affiliative aspect of the relationship behavior positive (right half of the circle) or negative (left half)? Then, the question is: Does the behavior involve too much (lower half) or too little (upper half) interdependence? Within the now remaining "quarter" of the circle, the final decision is which of the two neighboring items/themes (e.g., 7/8) is more relevant. Example: The examiner observes in a reported episode that the patient inappropriately spoils their son, takes excessively care for him. An item for the A:P position is sought, as this may be a relationship behavior of others, but not the patients themselves. The patient does something with others (the son), so the item must be found in the upper circle. The affiliative quality of the relationship behavior is rather positive (right half), and it tends towards too much interdependence/control concerning others (lower half). Thus, the focus is on the bottom right "quarter" of the upper circle, with the choice between too much contact (8) or care (7). The latter would picture the situation more precisely.

3. In the third step, the connections between the interpersonal perspectives marked in Figure 6 are established and summarized in the "relational dynamic formulation". It is important to check whether the connection between the countertransference impulses and the patient's object experience can be coherently established as explained above. If this fails, it may be necessary to review the item selection and correct it to convincingly "close" the relationship cycle. It must also be considered that sometimes the behavior of others may be denied or repeatedly misinterpreted, which can also contribute to the dysfunctionality of a relationship pattern.

When selecting items, it is important to ensure that, in addition to the wording of an item, its positioning in the circumplex model mirrors the relational content correctly; this means that the relationship aspect must correspond to the expressions of the two dimensions of affiliation and interdependence represented by the item's position on the circle. An example: A patient reports that they "gave up." This word belongs to Item 26, assigned to the relationship theme "submit" However, the context of this statement shows that this patient "gives up" in the sense that they no longer try to contact others and go their own way. In this case, they assert themselves (positive interdependence) and simultaneously distance themselves from others (negative affiliation). This behavior is reactive and positioned in the lower circle, top left. Looking at the items noted there, Item 32 "little contact allowed" correctly describes the patient's behavior and is thus the more accurate choice.

3.3.2 Clinical Case Example

A 32-year-old patient is admitted for inpatient therapy following a depressive-suicidal breakdown. His girlfriend, from his perspective, unexpectedly and inexplicably, left him after about six years of partnership when he had to be in a clinic for a few weeks due to an illness. The problem of his relationship dynamics is evident in his relationships and behavior at his workplace: He takes on important and demanding tasks and, according to his perception, handles them well, but still repeatedly gets into conflicts with his superiors. They correct decisions he has made without consulting him and ignore agreements that he believed were binding. This apparently happens entirely arbitrarily and by virtue of their more powerful position, which infuriates the patient and leads him to stubbornly assert his position at any cost. He feels completely justified in doing so. The situation eventually escalates to a point where he is either fired or he terminates jobs without notice.

In direct contact, he appears immovable and unassailable like a monolith, practically impervious to questions and doubts. Also provocative is an almost generous calmness, which quickly makes one feel powerless and inferior in his presence. In countertransference, one feels the impulse to engage in a struggle for power and control with him but quickly resigns due to his unreachability; ultimately, the dominant feeling as interaction partner is a desire to withdraw from contact.

The selected items for this example are included in the evaluation sheet shown in Figure 7. Based on the illustrated schema, the following relationship dynamic connections can be formulated:

- The patient is convinced that he performs his tasks well and has the right to have his performance respected and acknowledged. However, he experiences that others devalue this (Item 11), dominate him arbitrarily (Item 10), and possibly want to exploit him for their own benefit (Item 14) (P:O). He reacts by stubbornly sticking to his position (Item 18) and eventually just leaves (Item 32).
- Externally, the stubbornness, which the patient portrays as a completely justified response to the impositions from others (Item 17, P: P), appears as an almost non-negotiable claim to dominance (Item 10, O: P); he represents this with superiority (Item 11, O: P) and without any self-doubt.
- This behavior angers others and leads them to respond defiantly (Item 18, O:O), which, however, remains ineffective and deepens their sense of powerlessness (Item 26, O:O). This leads others to break off conversation with him and turn away from him (Item 32,

Perspective A: The patient's experience

Patient experiences themselves (P:P)	Patient experiences others (P:O)
Item no./Text	Item no./Text
17	10
18	11
32	14

Perspective B: The experience of others (including the examiner)

Others experience the patient (O:P)	Others experience themselves (O:O)
Item no./Text	Item no./Text
10	18
11	26
	32

Figure 7. Evaluation sheet case example.

O:O). The examiner/clinician can identify with the patient's superiors, imagining that they, faced with fruitless negotiations, eventually resort to making decisions without consulting him. Similarly, the examiner can envision that his girlfriend chose a moment for the breakup where she could avoid confrontation and fruitless power struggle.
- When others break off contact with the patient (Item 32) and no longer talk with him, it means in his view of the events that he has once again been ignored (Item 11), betrayed (Item 14), and arbitrarily dominated (Item 10).

This final (IV.) connection is consistent, and the dysfunctional relationship pattern describes a vicious cycle that repeatedly occurs in the patient's life.

3.3.3 Clinical Experiences With the OPD-2 Interpersonal Relations Axis (Axis II)

In recent years, the spread of OPD has placed Axis II at the forefront in many ways. Its focus and structure initially allowed for the improvement in capturing and considering interpersonal aspects in clinical situations through continued education and training, helping to develop a corresponding perceptual attitude. Many participants in training sessions found the increased precision in collaboratively working out relationship constellations and interaction patterns beneficial for clinical work. This precision often formed the basis for assessing lifelong conflict themes and structural weaknesses, which could then be addressed in therapy.

In research, experiences with the use of Axis II have been mixed. The large number of items and their lack of gradation and differentiation made reliable assessment significantly difficult. Thus, the initial research results with the Relationship Axis were clinically relevant but lacked reliability. Progress was made with the development of a Q-Sort instrument (Zimmermann et al., 2014) using the items from Axis II, allowing reliable and valid ranking of relationship elements by salience. This approach successfully identified typical patterns in depressed patients. Since such an approach is realistically feasible only in research contexts, the working group began early on to consider how Axis II could be better utilized in research. These considerations have been incorporated into the present revision. Initially, the previous clinical item list was content-reviewed and then it was decided to structure it dimensionally. For each relationship theme or behavior pattern, a "normal" and clinically not relevant variant, an accentuated variant in the said direction, and a dysfunctional variant were formulated. This allows for more precise clinical differentiation and provides a better level of scaling for statistical calculations.

Additionally, the separate research version was created, where the number of choices was halved by combining item pairs at the same circle position. Practically, this means that in the research version, one no longer needs to choose between two adjacent, and thus very similar, items (e.g., 15 "neglecting" and 16 "ignoring") as they are always combined and can only be selected together.

4 Axis III: Conflict

4.1 Summarized Presentation of Axis III

Unconscious conflicts play a central role within psychodynamic understanding. Conflicts involve the clash of opposing positions, the encounter of motives, desires, needs, values, and ideas. Beyond cognitive dissonances the concept of conflicts introduced here addresses unconscious conflicts, which Freud described as the causal factor of neurosis.

What is at the basis of each conception of conflict is the question of psychodynamics ("What moves the soul"). For Freud, this was drive theory.

Advanced conflict psychology is based on psychodynamic motivation and emotion theory: Each conflict starts as an external one (i.e., rooted in an individual's early life history) and becomes internalized over time. It is thus transformed into an intrapsychic conflict theme, which can significantly and persistently influence mental processes. Conflicts represent a cognitive procedural-affective schema of the self and of the relationship with others, activated by external situational factors. The basic human needs (need for attachment, need for safety and control, need for autonomy or individuation, need for self-assertion and exploration, need for sensual pleasure and sexual arousal, need for self-esteem and need for striving, need for identity and meaning in life) all find their way into the description of Conflicts as defined in the OPD:

C1 Dependency vs. Individuation
C2 Submission vs. Control
C3 In Need of Care vs. Self-Sufficiency
C4 Self-Worth Conflict (Self-Worth vs. Object-Worth)
C5 Guilt Conflict (Prosocial Conscience vs. Self-Centered Motives)
C6 Oedipal Conflict
C7 Identity Conflict
C0 Repressed Conflict and Emotion Awareness

Conflicts C1–C7 follow the basic needs, while C0 describes the overarching repression/denial of conflicts and associated affects rather than a motivational system. Conflicts are conceived and structured along the lines of three core elements: the desire (impulse), the associated signal anxiety, and the defense mechanism, which emerges over the course of a person's life in a person's life story as expressed through current problems and transference.

Identifying psychodynamic (unconscious) conflicts requires inductive and deductive approaches. Inductive means using observable phenomena, and recurrent patterns of living and behaving as starting points. Deductive involves the patient's efforts to adaptively/maladaptively resolve conflicts in their life history. Along these lines, four central components for capturing the conflict theme are defined:

1. The repetitive (dys-)functional motivational pattern
2. Core and leading affects (with core affects referring to affective states that are defended against, while leading affects are defined as the typical or frequently occurring, primarily conscious affects, that are present feelings in each conflict mode)

3. Typical triggering situations
4. Typical transference and countertransference dynamics

Each conflict is shaped by the individual's biographically acquired handling in either active (e.g., individuation) or passive mode (e.g., dependency). All conflict themes elaborated here (C1–C7) will be presented as conflict tension, neurotic conflict, and conflict schema. The representation and manifestation of a conflict (phenomenology) are determined by an individual's structural functions (see Axis IV). If, based on a sufficient degree of structural functioning, an adaptive solution is achieved, the conflict theme is accentuated. This conflict tension which arises while psychic flexibility can be maintained, will only cause low degrees of suffering or none. With moderately integrated structural functions, the relevant conflict has a repetitive dysfunctional impact on relationships (neurotic conflict) with rigid/inflexible safeguarding (there is an either-or situation). A low level of structural integration is associated with persistent instability/shifts and extreme manifestations of conflict modes (fear of symbiotic merging and overwhelming fear of separation). The elaboration of the conflict theme at a low level of structural integration, then defined as a conflict schema, represents a significant expansion of OPD-2.

Overall, all operationalized representations are prototypical, highlighting the essential elements. Each conflict operationalization from C1 to C7 and C0 will conclude (close) with a case vignette in the passive mode and active mode, respectively.

4.2 What Are Conflicts?

Unconscious conflicts play a central role within the psychodynamic theory of disorders (alongside self, object, and relationship representations, as well as structural impairments): "Without such a conflict, there is no neurosis" (Freud 1916/1917, p. 293). Every conflict concept must be based on a motivation theory: for Freud, this was drive theory; Freud regarded affects as "drive derivatives." Psychoanalytic motivation theory, as well as emotion theory and thus conflict theory, have made substantial progress. Here, only a basic outline of this development will be presented (for a detailed discussion see Benecke & Brauner, 2017).

Conflict (Latin: collision) involves the encounter of opposing positions, a clash of motives, desires, needs, values, and ideas. Conflicts are universal phenomena, distinguished into external and internal ones.

In general, *external conflicts* are conscious and amenable to being processed and resolved (Schüßler, 2002). The "normal and antinomic conflict" (Dührssen, 1981) refers to the clash of different conscious desires, ideas, and values within a person. What is meant by everyday intra-psychic and/or interpersonal conscious conflicts is, for example, the hedonistic desire to eat well and the simultaneous motivation to remain slim for aesthetic or health reasons. Not all conscious conflicts can be resolved (Dührssen, 1981), because external or internal reasons can remain irreconcilable opposites (such as the desire for a completely unattached, independent life vs. the desire to have a family and children). In such a conflict, resolution can only be achieved through renunciation. Incompatible cognitions (perceptions, thoughts, opinions, attitudes, desires, and intentions) lead to cognitive conflicts (cognitive dissonance). Dissonant states are perceived as unpleasant because of generating internal emotional tensions that lead to stress. The individual tries to resolve these dissonant states of tension through changes in attitude and/or behavior (action) (Festinger, 1957). These essentially conscious cognitive conflicts (dissonances) generate motivation to end this emotional state. In attempting to resolve these dissonances, the individual uses unconscious defense mechanisms (defensive exclusion, denying, devaluing, rationalizing, etc.) to alter the problem so that it will fit cognitive beliefs, or the individual modifies his or her cognitive beliefs so that they fit with behavior. Therefore, cognitive dissonance can essentially be interpreted as a hint at unconscious processing of conflicts and their management.

The concept of *unconscious conflict* is crucial to psychodynamic understanding. Since Freud, unconscious conflicts have been assigned a central role in psychodynamic thinking. When Freud (together with Breuer) described conflicts in "Studies on Hysteria" (Breuer & Freud, 1895/1955), this was the first occasion of defining them as causal factors in the development of neuroses: Neuroses are "to be understood as signs of an interplay of forces in the mind, as a manifestation of purposeful intentions working concurrently or in mutual opposition. We are concerned with a dynamic view of mental phenomena" (Freud 1916/1917, p. 62). Freud's first conflict model assumed that the affect arising in a traumatic situation overwhelms the individual and these distressing thoughts and ideas are repressed (Breuer & Freud, 1895/1955). In his drafts of drive theory, Freud described conflicts between life and death, drives, as well as ego functions. The conflict starts out as an external one (i.e., rooted in an individual's early life history), becomes internalized over time and turns into an internal psychic conflict. The latter often has such a powerful and persistent impact on mental processes that it is easily activated by external situational factors and therefore must be constantly managed and kept at bay. We can assume that if these internal conflicts are activated too strongly (in relation to coping capacity), this often leads to symptoms.

4.2.1 The Unconscious

Freud used the concept of the unconscious in three different interpretations:

1. He described the dynamic unconscious as the repressed unconscious, which includes not only the id but also parts of the ego and superego, encompassing unconscious drive impulses, defensive attitudes, and conflicts.
2. He explained the unconscious as an unconscious part of the ego, elements that are not repressed but have always been unconscious and remain so.
3. The preconscious was the term Freud used to refer to all thoughts and feelings that in principle are accessible to the conscious mind, but which normally remain unconscious (Freud, 1915).

Although this has been hotly disputed over the past 100 years there is now considerable neurobiological and memory-psychological evidence of the unconscious (Schüßler, 2002; Solms, 2015). Most brain activities occur unconsciously, meaning that humans cannot trace how their brain works and how memory or language processes unfold.

The second and most comprehensive part of the unconscious encompasses emotional procedural/implicit processing and associated implicit memory functioning. These processes are predominantly unconscious, partly preconscious, and to a lesser extent, conscious. Therefore, all mental functioning in the brain can be divided into two categories: non-symbolic (implicit-procedural) processes and symbolic-categorical (explicit) pathways. In that, symbolic information processing represents the most complex pathway: symbols are verbal or figurative. Processing is sequential and time-consuming. Sub-symbolic information processing is fast, non-categorical, and occurs simultaneously across multiple information channels. This mode becomes particularly evident in procedural processing (e.g., playing football): a player kicks the ball automatically and cannot (or only after a longer training period) analyze or verbalize the movement. This applies to all such skills (including social and non-verbal processes). Some procedural skills reach a connection to symbolic processing. Substantial parts of social-emotional perception (options for evaluation and action as well as habits) occur in a complex and implicit manner. Fundamental social experiences are acquired implicitly in childhood. Specifically, affective-procedural rules and prototypical experiences are stored implicitly and persist for a lifetime as schemas and internalized self- and object-relationship representations, regardless of the appropriateness of such perception and processing. Procedural-affective self-concepts are cognitively overlaid during development, forming a *cognitive-procedural-affective schema* of the self and relationships with others (Schüßler, 2002; Benecke & Brauner, 2017).

This unconscious system encompasses all abilities and memories, including motor behavior and perceptual properties. Essential social interactions are also stored implicitly. It is important to note that these structures which emerge early in the unconscious do not correspond to the classic unconscious of psychoanalysis but must be seen as non-repressed unconscious. This form of the unconscious is gaining increasing significance in contemporary psychoanalysis, as Bohleber (2013) illustrates when re-assessing the unconscious: "The non-repressed unconscious has been the focus of psychoanalytic interest for some time, primarily due to the discovery of implicit/procedural knowledge. The content of the non-repressed implicit unconscious primarily is formed by early object relationships, reflected as representations or internal objects, as physically anchored (embodied) sensorimotor coordinations, as interaction and action schemas, as fantasies and expectations" (Bohleber, 2013, p. 811).

Explicit (declarative) memory and declarative symbolic processing are predominantly conscious or preconscious, but even here, there are areas that are inaccessible to consciousness, thus unconscious. Our cognitive information processing occurs in symbolic or sub-symbolic processing. However, only symbolic processes are accessible to our consciousness. Consequently, the cognitive sciences also investigate unconscious processes to a considerable extent (Posner & Rothbart, 1989). The "cognitive unconscious" (Kihlstrom, 1999) describes these hidden processes that predominantly occur unconsciously, encompassing: perceptual processes, memories of past events, internal representations, memories of decisions.

The third part of the unconscious is the *psychodynamic unconscious:* Through conscious suppression as well as unconscious defense mechanisms, information may be excluded from consciousness through both conscious suppression and unconscious defense mechanisms, operating throughout the entire processing continuum (from preconscious stages, before awareness arises, to post-conscious phases, wherein the excluded content continues to influence experience and behavior). The dynamic unconscious "contains" impulses, affects, fantasies which are being held unconscious because becoming conscious of them would be or seem unbearable for the individual. For example, because an impulse violates internalized norms, certain affects could overwhelm, or a fantasy contradicts the self-image. However, as these impulses, affects, fantasies are part of the person and linked to the unconscious conflicts that have arisen during the person's life history, they repeatedly force their way into experience and must therefore be "defended" against repeatedly. The psyche must actively work to keep these contents unconscious.

Today, it is no longer necessarily assumed that the unconscious is a place in the psyche categorically separated from the conscious mind. Instead, a continuum between unconscious and conscious cognitive processes is assumed (Vandekerckhove & Panksepp, 2011; Bohleber, 2013; Benecke & Brauner, 2017).

4.2.2 From Drive to Motivation

What is characteristic of the Freudian concept is the duality of opposing, incompatible drives. He introduced the concept of drive in his essays on sexuality (Freud, 1905), initially distinguishing between ego drives (self-preservation) and sexual drives (libido). The biologically derived drive force finds a psychological expression in unconscious "drive representations." Freud called the drive energy itself the libido and its governing principle the pleasure principle. He later added the concept of a death drive (and a life drive). The idea that humans are essentially driven by a few innate drives and basic needs comes mainly from behavioral research (ethology). In this theory, the instinct (natural drive) is the inner basis of the observable behavior of living beings.

The term natural drive (instinct) is now considered outdated and is largely replaced by descriptions such as "innate behavior." The assumption of an "innate behavioral control (drive)" does not do justice to the individually psychosocial and cultural (epigenetic) shaping of human behavior. As the drive concept and the associated "one-person psychology" (everything is rooted in the individual, and the individual is solely oriented toward "pleasure") recede, the intersubjective (apart from the self-related) orientation of motivational systems becomes evident. Conceptually, motivation is more focused on the object than it is on individual drive satisfaction (Fairbairn, 1952). The interpersonal experience of the first relationships creates patterns and prototypes of how one behaves towards close, caring objects and what to expect from them in terms of satisfaction and frustration (Emde, 2005; Stern, 1985). This intersubjective orientation of humans lays the foundation for the internalization of individual experiences; a process that progresses throughout childhood and adolescence. In adulthood, similar relationship experiences activate these prototypes of the "self in relation to others" schemas (Stern, 1985).

Motivation describes the action tendency, which is biologically anchored, yet shaped by the individual's social history. This is what we experience as needs and desires, and largely encompasses experienced and learned patterns. The pursuit of pleasure or avoidance of displeasure (pain vs. cessation of pain) and the anticipation of it drive and motivate humans. Primarily biological motives (hunger, thirst, sexuality) differ from socially oriented motives (attachment or intimacy, power, and achievement). A distinction must be made between usually unconscious motives and conscious drives for action (goals). Based on biological and phylogenetic principles, motives are in their ontogeny socially shaped drives for action, which in part (sometimes altered) go on to merge into conscious goals of adults. Motives and goals can contradict each other (conflict, incongruence, dissonance).

Automated motivational processes are "habits" and inherently contain strong rewards. Holding onto the familiar creates security and reduces the fear of new experiences and failure (repetition compulsion). The anticipation of reward ("I will get something great!") promotes goal-directed behavior. It is pursued according to the expected (hoped-for) reward. Direct reward and the expectation of reward lead to corresponding feelings and behaviors. This is how the mere thought (fantasy) of sexuality can lead to intense activation of the reward-pleasure system.

In general motivational psychology, the model by Maslow (1970) is established, assuming a hierarchy of needs. Its foundation consists of biological needs (food, sexuality), the need for safety, the need for attachment (sense of belonging; living with others and being loved), and the self-worth system (self-esteem and recognition by others). Self-actualization and transcendence are the highest levels of this pyramid. In psychological research, self-efficacy has been empirically confirmed as an important motivational system: the belief of a person that they can successfully handle difficult situations and challenges on their own (Bandura, 1977). Its initially clear closeness to the topic of self-worth (OPD C4) evolved over time into the nowadays central theme of "Self-efficacy: The exercise of control" (Bandura, 1977), which corresponds to OPD C2 *Submission vs. Control.* However, the problem remains that self-efficacy contains many self-worth related beliefs. Bischof (1985, 2009) combines findings from ethology with psychodynamic approaches: attachment desires with striving for security; adventurousness with striving for excitement; need for autonomy (with subsystems: dominance motive, prestige motive, intrinsic worth motive); sexuality; caregiving.

From a neurobiological and "neuropsychoanalytical" perspective, Panksepp (1998; Panksepp and Biven, 2012) distinguishes seven basic motivational systems:

1. SEEKING System
   Function: Exploration, curiosity, motivation, and goal-directed behavior.
   Neurochemistry: Dopamine.
   Associated behaviors: Investigating environment, problem-solving, anticipation of reward.
2. RAGE (Anger) System
   Function: Response to frustration, restraint, or threats.
   Neurochemistry: Substance P, glutamate.
   Associated behaviors: Aggression, defensive behavior, fighting back.
3. FEAR System
   Function: Response to danger, promoting survival via flight or freezing.
   Neurochemistry: Glutamate, CRF (corticotropin-releasing factor).
   Associated behaviors: Avoidance, escape, freezing.
4. LUST System
   Function: Sexual motivation and reproduction.
   Neurochemistry: Estrogen, testosterone, oxytocin.
   Associated behaviors: Mating, sexual attraction, reproduction.
5. CARE System
   Function: Nurturing, maternal behaviors, bonding.
   Neurochemistry: Oxytocin, prolactin.
   Associated behaviors: Parenting, protecting offspring, affection.
6. PANIC/GRIEF System
   Function: Social attachment and distress over separation or loss.
   Neurochemistry: Endogenous opioids, CRF.
   Associated behaviors: Crying, social distress, protest when isolated.
7. PLAY System
   Function: Social joy, rough-and-tumble play, learning social rules.
   Neurochemistry: Possibly opioids, dopamine.
   Associated behaviors: Laughing, play-fighting, social engagement.

These emotions are hardwired and linked to specific brain regions (e.g., amygdala, hypothalamus). The most basic system is SEEKING which can be understood as the most fundamental drive system. Solms (2021) sees strong parallels to Freud's libido. Each system can be modulated by learning and experience but originates from innate circuits.

From very different perspectives (ethology and neurobiology), both Bischof (2009) and Panksepp (1998; Panksepp & Biven, 2012) arrive at very similar basic motivational systems. These also have similarities to motive lists compiled in various clinical-psychotherapeutic theories (e.g., König, 1988; Weinryb & Rössel, 1991; Lichtenberg, 1983; Lichtenberg et al., 2011; Grawe, 2004; Young et al., 2003; overview in Benecke & Brauner, 2017).

Even though no final list exists, the following can likely be counted among these basic motives or needs (see Benecke & Brauner, 2017):

- Need for *attachment*: a primary object-seeking motivation, seeking relatedness, love, and attachment (Fairbairn, 1952; Balint, 1953; Bowlby, 1969; Lichtenberg, 1983).
- Need for *security* (Bischof, 2009): The security principle is considered essential by Sandler (1960), it stands above the pleasure principle and ensures that instinctual impulses perceived as dangerous are brought under control.

- Striving *for autonomy or individuation* is also assumed to be a central motive (Erikson, 1959; Mentzos, 1984).
- Need for *self-assertion and exploration* (Lichtenberg et al., 2011; Bischof, 2009).
- Need for *sensual pleasure* and *sexual arousal* (Bischof, 2009; Lichtenberg et al., 2011).
- Striving for *self-worth enhancement/protection* (Kohut, 1971, 1977; Mentzos, 1984; Grawe, 2004).
- The desire to form an *identity* is attributed a strong motivational component (Erikson, 1959, 1974; Thomä & Kächele, 2006a; Dammann et al., 2011). This component is specifically human.

As mentioned above, the pleasure/unpleasure system is understood as an even more basic system, such that it plays a regulatory role in all these defined motivational systems (Roth, 2001; Panksepp & Biven, 2012; Solms, 2021).

Lichtenberg (1983), like the OPD and many other authors, sees the developmental and motivational goals as a sequence and interaction throughout life. Thus, the overarching goal of intimacy (closeness) can initially be expressed in the need for attachment and later in life be converted into the general need for cooperation and the need for sensual pleasure and sexual arousal. From a developmental perspective, the need for physiological satisfaction, self-preservation, and regulation oriented towards the intersubjective world (curiosity, excitement, security) emerges at the beginning (Stern, 1985). This is followed by attachment needs (Bowlby, 1969; Harlow, 1971) with desires for closeness, security, safety, experience, care, intimacy, and tenderness. Increasingly, these motivational systems clash with endeavors and desires for autonomy, independence, self-assertion, ownership (control, power), and self-efficacy. Building on self-development (Stern, 1985), with the emerging self, the core self, the subjective self, and the verbal self ("I"), the need for self-evaluation together with self-esteem develops in the third and fourth years of life (Schüßler & Bertl-Schüßler, 1992). Self-worth and object-worth are interrelated and arise from successful positive self-object experiences. The sexual motivational system begins with the precursors of physical pleasure and, with the development of gender identity (male/female in relation to parents and social networks) in childhood. Continuing into puberty, it takes the form of sexual activity, seduction, and sexual desire for show and display. In late childhood, adolescence, and young adulthood, self-development with identity formation becomes more pronounced (Seiffge-Krenke, 2012, 2021), a process that ultimately lasts a lifetime: the goal is to achieve a clear, as conflict-free as possible, identity with self-preservation, self-assertion, self-confidence, and social competence. The motivational system of the prosocial conscience unfolds in close interaction with the entire cultural and psychosocial development of the superego.

Using the concept of developmental lines, Anna Freud (1965) was the first to describe how all motivational systems mutually influence each other during development up to the Here and Now. The success of a motivational system depends on the effectiveness of previous systems, and they all intertwine like a woven carpet. One thread (motivational system) begins, intertwines with others, and they ultimately form an individual pattern; the threads are mutually dependent and influence each other.

Even if we can assume that all motivational systems are effective from the beginning to the end of life, they unfold depending on developmental steps (ego function, self-development, symbolization), and certain motivational systems are more significant in specific phases of practice phases than others, e.g., identity formation and related conflicts are more pronounced in adolescence and young adulthood (Mentzos, 1984; Seiffge-Krenke, 2021).

It can be assumed that these systems, as well as the experiences that people have with them in the course of their lives, contribute significantly to the formation of individual personalities and to the development of vulnerabilities and resilience.

4.2.3 Motivation, Emotion, Regulation, and Conflict

The relationship between motivational systems and affects/emotions requires careful consideration. Motives are linked with emotions and are driven by them (Krause, 2012). However, even though they are closely linked, emotions/affects are not the same as motives.

Emotions can be understood as *tools of motives* (Benecke, 2014): they act as indicators and evaluators of various motives. Depending on the activated motivational system, the situation, and the subject's interpretation, emotions are suitable tools in the service of the activated motives. According to Buck (1988), however, emotions serve *no specific function* and do not suggest a specific behavior; rather, they provide "action recommendations" (Frijda, 1996) and form the basis for *the selection of* behavioral alternatives or intrapsychic processes (Bischof, 2009).

Affects/emotions are generally distinguished from feelings (conscious perception). Solms (2021) claims affects are by definition conscious and even the basis of consciousness. Emotions are automatically (sometimes unconsciously?) triggered as internal communication (homeostatic core effects), emotional responses to countless sensory stimuli, and emotional response to and impact of motivation (pleasure/displeasure) (Damasio, 2003). Basic affects include joy, sadness, fear, anger, disgust, and surprise (Ekman, 1992a; 1992b) and sometimes also contempt (Krause, 2012). These are defined from an evolutionary psychological perspective, often searching for the universality of emotional behavior, e.g., for corresponding precursors across all mammals. In evolutionary psychology, emotions are conceptualized as meta-programs that provide a structure and that contribute to adaptive generation of behavior (Cosmides & Tooby, 2000).

Emotions are comprehensive, evolutionary and biologically anchored, physical-mental moods of varying duration, intensity, and closeness to consciousness, coupled with a fundamental impulse to either "move away from" (up to flight) or "move toward" (seeking proximity).

Fear urges avoidance, anger prepares for attack and defense, joy signals motive fulfillment, disgust leads to total rejection and avoidance, interest motivates exploration and curiosity, (erotic) desire motivates seduction and sexuality, and sadness motivates seeking help or withdrawal. These basic emotional patterns are culturally overlaid in their design, form, value, and presentation (emotional display). As a result, both emotions and motivations are socially and culturally influenced, e.g., by being suppressed or repressed and/or by mutually influencing each other.

Emotions integrate and coordinate physiological, cognitive, motivational, behavioral, and subjective responses into patterns that enhance the ability to meet the adaptive demands of internal and external environmental situations. The fundamental value of all emotions is oriented toward pleasure/displeasure and accordingly toward avoidance and approach (Ekman, 1992b). The described emotional responses cause a multitude of further emotions that not only originate from current perception but are retrieved from memory (representations). The recalled representations (memory contents) set programs in motion that, in turn, generate corresponding feelings.

Building on the basic emotions (Ekman, 1992a), far more complex social emotions (shaped by the context of social interaction) emerge such as sympathy, pride, jealousy, envy, love, guilt, and shame. Social, conflict-related emotions are also shaped by cultural and individual influences (e.g., shame- or guilt-oriented cultures). In addition, Lisa Feldman Barrett (Barrett, 2017) has emphasized, in contrast to

Panksepp (1998), the social construction aspect of all emotions.

This evolutionary biological research direction, in which emotion is primarily seen in terms of functional utility, has been criticized from various angles (e.g., Ulich & Mayring, 2003): "We should be careful not to view affects and feelings only in relation to their functional dimension, ... because a highly differentiated and ever-growing inner world has developed, which actually constitutes the essence of our lives" (Mentzos, 2011, p. 26).

The described emotional responses cause a multitude of further emotions that not only originate from current perception but are retrieved from the affective memory. These consciously or unconsciously retrieved representations (memory contents) set programs in motion that generate corresponding feelings. A current interpersonal conflict can be overlaid by the mental affective memory representations of the memory and thus generate an emotional response that does not stem from the here and now but is fed by the past. This development, which has biological and genetic roots, is shaped epigenetically for everyone.

From the sum of all these complex representations and programs, personality groups and culture-specific affective-cognitive individual worlds emerge. In these systems, emotions determine dynamics, while cognitions determine the content and structure of all kinds of psychological and social systems.

Fundamentally, emotion and cognition constantly interact in all psychological and social interactions and processes in a circular manner: cognitions trigger specific emotions, specific emotions influence all cognitions, with emotions having a much stronger influence on cognitions than vice versa (LeDoux 1996, 2002).

Within clinical theories that deal with motivation and emotions, there is a broad consensus that:

- serious violations or prolonged non-fulfillment lead to conflictual "permanent activation" or easy activation of the respective motivational system;
- subsequent activations of these motives are usually associated with the automatic activation of painful emotional states that originate from early experiences and do not function as motive-serving tools;
- the activation of these "old" painful emotions necessitates the use of emotion regulation processes;
- psychopathological experiences and behaviors should be regarded as the end result of these complex processes, and in some cases, emotion- and/or motive-regulating functions are then attributed to the symptomatic experiences and behaviors;
- most of these motivational, emotional, and regulatory processes occur outside of conscious awareness;
- emotion regulation can fail, and
- the competence of emotion regulation is an important aspect of mental health" (Holl et al., 2020, p. 177; cf. Barnow, 2012, 2020; Benecke & Brauner, 2017).

It can be assumed that there is a specific need for regulation when so-called *passive-negative* emotions (panic, fear, sadness, loneliness, shame, guilt, powerlessness, helplessness, despair, etc.) are activated. These emotional states are usually hard to bear, especially over a longer period of time. If the individually dominant motivational systems are linked to such intolerable emotional states due to corresponding negative experiences, the motives themselves become "dangerous," and highly automated regulations usually develop to prevent these motives/desires and the associated emotions from entering subjective experience (cf. Benecke, 2018; Holl et al., 2020). In the process, certain consciously experienced feelings can also be "used" to mask other affects (which unconsciously are experienced as even more painful) (e.g., Wurmser, 1981) – for example, fear can be warded off by anger, as well as anger by fear (e.g., Hoffmann, 2008).

4.2.4 Psychodynamic Conflicts

As mentioned above, the concept of unconscious conflict plays a central role in the psychodynamic approaches to mental illness. Based on clinical material, pioneering work in the systematization of central conflicts was carried out by Malan (1979), Strupp and Binder (1993) in their research on short-term therapies. Both approaches share the assumption that the current problems of the patient are a repetition of the central conflicts between desires and fears. However, the significance of structural factors is overlooked here. In contrast, Perry's (1990) conflict formulation includes not only the conflict with its conscious and unconscious manifestations but also the structural adaptation. In the Psychodynamic Conflict Rating Scales (Perry, 1990), 14 conflicts are defined with the most important wishes and the associated fears. The Karolinska Psychodynamic Profile (KAPP; Weinryb & Rössel, 1991) contains eight motives that can develop into conflicts: intimacy and reciprocity and dependency and separation (essentially corresponds to OPD C1), controlling personality traits (essentially corresponds to OPD C2), alexithymia traits (essentially corresponds to OPD C0), conceptions of bodily appearance and their significance for self-esteem (essentially corresponds to OPD C4), sexual satisfaction (essentially corresponds to OPD C6), sense of belonging (essentially corresponds to OPD C7) and feeling of being needed (essentially corresponds to OPD C3).

The most comprehensive system was developed by Lichtenberg (1989; Lichtenberg et al., 2011). He describes six fundamental, distinct conflicts and motivational systems derived from neurobiology and early childhood research, with the need for physiological satisfaction forming the basis. The conflicts are presented in the following table (Table 25) with their conceptual proximity to OPD conflicts. Like OPD and many other authors, Lichtenberg regards these developmental and motivational goals as a sequence and interaction throughout life. Thus, the overarching goal of intimacy (closeness) can initially be expressed in the need for attachment (OPD C1) and can transition into the general need for cooperation (affiliative needs, OPD C5) and the need for sensory pleasure and sexual arousal (OPD C6) later in life.

Table 25. Conflicts and motivational systems with their conceptual proximity to OPD conflicts

Motivational system/conflict	Conceptual proximity
Need for attachment (attachment, intention of closeness with the caregiver, secure and proximity).	OPD C1
Exploratory/assertive motives correspond essentially to OPD C2. The goals of this motivational system are dominance, power, competition, mastery, exploration, with the main affects being safety and rage (competition, territory).	OPD C2
Caregiving system (care providing/care seeking) as a generalized system derived from maternal care and needs. This system is oriented towards the intentions, needs, and interests of others vs. the suppression of self-interests. It corresponds essentially to OPD C3.	OPD C3
Affiliative motivation system with cooperation vs. competition.	OPD C5
Need for sensory pleasure and sexual arousal.	OPD C6

The systematized psychodynamic conflict concepts are essentially based on three elements, the so-called "conflict triangle," consisting of:

1. The wish (impulse),
2. the corresponding signal anxiety, and
3. the defense (which is reflected in a person's life story, his or her current problems, and in the transference).

An impulse triggers (signal) anxiety, which, in turn, mobilizes the defense (Freud, 1926). With a stable defense, neither the impulse nor the anxiety becomes conscious. The *range of unconscious affect signals triggering defense* has been expanded over time, for example, to include depressive affects (Brenner, 1982), insult (Hoffmann, 1987), or shame (Wurmser, 1981). König (1996) assumes that all affects and moods can trigger defense mechanisms. A given situation (real or imaginary) activates a specific representation and/or an unconsciously conflictual motivational system; the triggered affects (e.g., fear, anger, insult) then mobilize defense processes (intrapsychic and/or behavioral operation). This procedural sequence can, in turn, be related to implicit memory. Unlike other procedural actions, such as driving a car, which are descriptively unconscious and can theoretically become conscious again, *the unconsciousness of what happens in defense processes is precisely the goal of the operation.* The affects involved in triggering defense, or which are themselves warded off are then unconscious, but have not disappeared (they continue to operate in the dynamic unconscious). The conflictual representation, which is being warded off, acts as an input filter, a foil for the unconscious interpretation of a situation, so that the need for defense persists (the unconscious emotions *trigger* the internal defense operations).

These defense operations occur either on an intrapsychic level or are acted out interpersonally, by involving social partners in the defense processes. If the interactional consequences of behavior altered by defense are taken into consideration, it is always both areas that are affected. Therefore, on a fundamental level, we can characterize a *psychological disorder* as an intertwining of intrapsychic and interpersonal processes:

1. Certain motivational systems have individual significance and are easily activated.
2. However, there are only very limited possibilities for interpreting situational circumstances.
3. These are associated with a limited number of (conscious and/or unconscious) emotional states.
4. Only the same processes can be used again and again to regulate them, which leads to the maladaptive behaviors observed in patients, which in turn provoke responses from interaction partners that ...?
5. These responses contribute to the maintenance of the disorder, as they are interpreted by the patients in their "familiar," habitual manner.

The visible manifestations of these processes, which can operate at different structural levels, form the basis for conflict diagnosis.

4.2.5 Conflict and Diagnosis

Unconscious processes or contents cannot be directly measured or captured; they can only be inferred. However, not only the unconscious contents need to be inferred but also conscious ones! Neither do therapists have direct access to the conscious experience of their patients; they have to rely on what their patients report and how they behave. Both the conscious and the unconscious contents must, therefore, be inferred by the observer based on communication and indirect indicators. Assessing these contents is necessary and possible both through intrapsychic experience (what is being reported by the subject, and in which way) and through interpersonal behavior (what is happening and how). Relationship patterns and relationship schemas are represented intrapsychically and manifest themselves in interactions. Conflictual relationship patterns are expressed in relationships and in the transference as manifestations of unconscious and preconscious conditions.

The identification of psychodynamic (unconscious) conflicts requires both an inductive and deductive approach. Based on observable phenomena, *inductive* refers to recurring patterns of experiences and behaviors that can be traced back through the patient's personal history and the course of the illness. *Deductive* describes the patient's efforts to adaptively resolve and understand conflicts (successful life adjustment, work productivity, personal relationships) in their life history. Maladaptive solutions can be recognized by their dysfunctionality in experience and behavior. They lead to social problems (e.g., in couple relationships) that are associated with clinical symptoms and/or personality disorders. Conflicts and associated affects can also be experienced during the assessment process through the analysis of transference and countertransference (Heigl-Evers & Henneberg-Mönch, 1990), e.g., in the patient's narcissistic rage or the therapist's narcissistic injury.

A psychodynamic conflict description must fulfill three basic requirements (Weisman, 1959):

1. The psychodynamic formulation must be based on descriptive-phenomenological observations and psychodynamic conclusions.
2. The description must be precise and allow for general understanding and standardization (operationalization).
3. The psychodynamic conflict formulation must be inferable from a clinical interview (and observation).

4.3 Conflicts in OPD: From Integrated Motivational Systems via Conflict Tensions to Neurotic Conflicts and Conflictual-Motivational Schemas

Based on the theoretical and empirical foundations outlined above, the following biographical repetitive-motivational conflict themes were developed from OPD 1 to OPD 3:

- C1 Dependency vs. Individuation
- C2 Submission vs. Control
- C3 In Need of Care vs. Self-Sufficiency
- C4 Self-Worth Conflict (Self worth vs. Object-worth)
- C5 Guilt Conflict (Prosocial Conscience vs. Self-Oriented Motives)
- C6 Oedipal Conflict
- C7 Identity Conflict
- C0 Warded off Perception of Conflict and Affect

The conflict definitions follow developmental psychological assumptions and are based on the described basic motivational systems, which develop and persist throughout life. Traditional psychoanalytic terminology (e.g., oral or anal conflict) is largely avoided due to detachment from traditional drive theory and due to school-specific ambiguity. The motivational-unconscious conflict model uses the conflictual interaction experience of the individual as its basic unit. This experience is inferred from phenomenology (surface level) and related back to its unconscious meaning through psychodynamics.

4.3.1 Central Characteristics of Conflict Themes

Four central characteristics define each conflict theme:

1. The Repetitive (Dys-)Functional Motivational Pattern: This pattern describes the

specific motivational core of the motivational system ("What is this about?" "What motivates this person?") along with a brief outline of the prototypical (active and passive) modes.
2. Core and Leading Affects: In the Conflict Axis (Axis III) of OPD-2, specific "leading affects" were identified for each conflict and mode. These were not consistently defined: sometimes it was the warded off affect triggering behavior or "solutions," that was listed as the leading affect (e.g., "fear of fusion" in Dependency vs. Individuation in the active mode), whereas in other cases, the consciously experienced feelings, including secondary emotions, which represent the result of defense processes or which themselves serve as a defense against other affects, were listed (e.g., "narcissistic rage" in the Self-Worth Conflict in the active mode). This ambiguous use of terms led to misunderstandings.

In OPD-3, we decided to distinguish between core affects and leading affects and to apply this distinction consistently across all conflicts and modes.

Core affects denote the warded off affective states and are therefore mostly unconscious. Core affects have usually developed early on and are often linked with specific basic motivational systems (Benecke, 2018). The coping modes (with their respective typical self-images, experiences, and behaviors) serve primarily to keep these core affects (often very painful or unbearable) outside of conscious experience.

Leading affects on the other hand, are the consciously experienced feelings typically associated with a particular conflict mode. Leading affects are usually the result of defense processes or serve a defensive function by helping keep the core affects "in check."

Secondary affects arise from interpersonal conflict constellations; for example, if acts of care are not acknowledged (C3), feelings of disappointment and anger may follow.

It is essential to remember that there are no rigid 1-to-1 associations between specific affects and specific conflicts/modes. Only frequently encountered affective ("prototypical") constellations are described. It should also be considered that the same or similar affects may occur in different conflicts/modes, albeit usually with slightly different "colors" (e.g., separation anxiety, fusion anxiety, disappointment rage, narcissistic rage, etc.).

3. Triggering Situations: In a situation of temptation or frustration, the conflict theme is addressed and/or intensified (Dührssen, 1954). Here again, "typical" triggering situations are described without implying a strict 1-to-1 relationship.
4. Transference and Countertransference Dynamics: Conflicts, along with their associated motivational pools/conglomerations and their affects, manifest themselves in the examination situation in transference and countertransference. Here again, only typical transference and countertransference patterns are described. This does not mean, for example, that it is possible to draw conclusions about a specific conflict solely based on a specific countertransference or about the absence of that conflict on the basis of the lack of the described countertransference.

4.3.2 Conflict Dynamics

The respective conflict themes are described in detail regarding their central motivational areas, which persist throughout life and encompass corresponding individual and psychosocial developmental steps. With successful development, a flexible and adaptive approach to the motivational themes is possible, so that no unconscious conflict arises in connection with this motivational system, and the motivational system can be considered psychologically integrated. For example, with C4 (Self-Worth vs. Object-Worth), an individual can ascribe value to both themselves and others, as a matter of course which typically is not given much thought.

If, because of specific life experiences, a motivational theme gains a particular inner-psychic conflictual significance, then this theme is easily activated and mobilizes corresponding coping strategies (defenses). The way in which the conflictual-motivational theme or the conflict dynamics manifests itself in experience and behavior depends, on the one hand, on the (active or passive) coping mode, and on the other hand, on the fundamental level of structural integration of the person.

This conflict dynamic is presented in the field of tension of the respective motivational theme (in the following figure, Self-Worth) and on three levels (Figure 8): conflict tension (upper pole, well-integrated structure), neurotic conflict (moderately integrated structure), and conflict schema (lower structural level).

At a high level of structural integration, the respective theme is present and generates a noticeable conflict tension, in that a somewhat accentuated desire for recognition and appreciation becomes apparent, as well as a tendency toward slight arrogance (active mode) or questioning oneself (passive mode). However, these tendencies can be reflected on and regulated through intrapsychic processes, so they rarely lead to interpersonal problems or critical drops in self-worth. Clinically, this theme may become relevant under significant stress, such as the loss of previous sources of gratification.

In the case of a neurotic conflict (at a moderate level of structural integration), the self-worth theme repeatedly dominates both internal and external experiences: the psyche constantly revolves around the "question of worth," and this question permeates all areas of life and relationships. The modes (passive: self-devaluation and admiration of others; or active: self-aggrandizement and devaluation of others) shape experience and relationships and can be reflected on little or not at all. In a triggering situation, the repetitive-dysfunctional conflict patterns of experience and behavior can

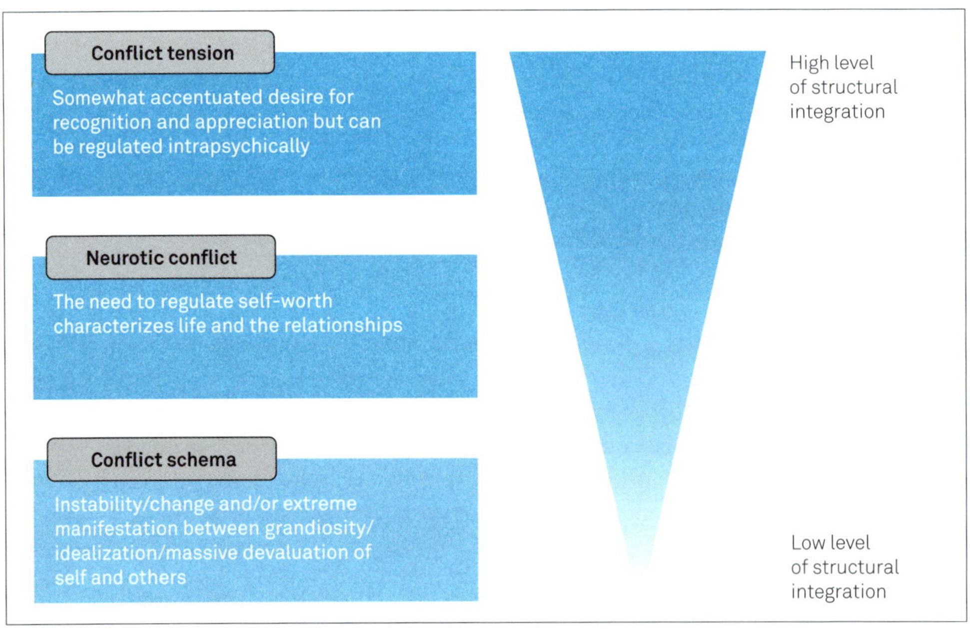

Figure 8. Manifestations of the conflict dynamic "Self-Worth" at varying levels of structural integration.

lead to symptoms. Typically, even minor conflictual stress which, however, has a high individual significance (reactualization), is sufficient to lead to neurotic disorders. On the other hand, neurotic conflicts, if severe, create a conflictual personality (formerly called "character neuroses").

In the case of greater structural impairments, motivational themes manifest themselves as conflict schemas. Motivational conflict themes and structural functions form a complementary series (Mentzos, 1984). Conflict and structure behave like figure and background, or like a stage (structure) on which the play (conflict) is performed: The stage is a prerequisite for the performance of the neurotic conflict. Even people with significant structural impairments in dealing with themselves and others are determined by motivational themes. Activations of the motivational systems contained in the conflict schemas often act as triggers for symptomatic behavior (e.g., self-harm, etc.), which in turn serves the (ultimately dysfunctional) regulation of motives and affect states. At a low level of structural integration, several motivational systems often become dysfunctional and contradictory, however, there is no defined stable neurotic conflict pattern. For instance, in cases of low structural integration, there is no stable self-system, and the Self-Worth vs. Object-Worth Conflict schema alternates, sometimes abruptly, between grandiosity and devaluation or between self-worth and idealization, often even on minimal occasions. Nevertheless, even in such cases, somewhat rigid modes may be found, such as consistently massive self-devaluation or pronounced but "stable" malignant narcissism.

This establishes a dimensional continuum from conflict tension (which typically becomes clinically relevant only under stress) via neurotic conflicts (repetitive-dysfunctional, intrapsychic, and interpersonal patterns) to conflict schemas at a low level of structural integration.

The operationalized descriptions of the individual conflicts allow for the identification of:

- Accentuated motivational themes as Conflict Tension (CT),
- repetitive-motivational neurotic conflicts (NC), and
- conflict-motivational schemas (CMS).

A draft describing the manifestations of conflict-motivational themes with even greater structural impairment (up to disintegration) is available in Section 4.4. We encourage you to look at this draft and provide feedback to the OPD Task Force.

Furthermore, the biographically dominant processing mode and the current processing mode can be determined. As an example, consider an individual whose active self-worth conflict (C4 active, narcissistic) dominated most of his biography, but who, due to a severe current life crisis, switches to a predominantly passive mode in the context of decompensation ("I am useless!"). Thus, the biographically dominant processing mode shifts from active to currently more passive – with the self-worth conflict theme C4 remaining the same.

For each conflict theme, a prototypical description of the manifestation of the neurotic conflict variant in the areas of family of origin, partnership/family, career, social environment, possessions, body/sexuality, and illnesses is also provided. These descriptions can be found in Appendix B.

The operationalization of each conflict concludes with differential diagnosis and distinction/overlap with other conflicts. Finally, prototypical case descriptions are presented for each conflict theme in both active and passive modes.

4.3.3 C1 Dependency vs. Individuation

The *central motives* are the pursuit of affiliation (interpersonal closeness), emotional security, and supportive relationships (attachment) with other people, combined with the desire to experience oneself as an independent and secure individual in the world even without them (individuation and independence). The social-interpersonal orientation (the ability to relate to others) and interpersonal approach (affiliation and attachment) are present from birth (Bowlby, 1969; Stern, 1985; Balint, 1953). Since humans are existentially dependent on relationships (especially infants and young children), this motivation outweighs the desire for individuation in the early years. The interpersonal experiences of the infant and young child with caregivers provide a sense of security and attachment, eventually leading to the development of the specific attachment system (Bowlby, 1951). These experiences with others allow for the development of competences for the regulation of (fear) affects and arousal (Fonagy et al., 2002) and give rise to the ability to be alone. The process of individuation, as part of the journey towards becoming an individual, is the complementary theme (individual socialization). This fundamental motive was described by Margaret Mahler (Mahler et al., 1975) as separation individuation, linked to the development of mental abilities. The individuation process (and motivation) is strongly influenced by cultural factors (depending on culture, there are varying degrees of emphasis on individuality). In childhood, this theme manifests as a closeness-distance conflict (OPD-CA-2 Task Force, 2017).

With *successful development,* a person has a securely anchored trust in their emotional safety in the world (basic trust). One can therefore be emotionally close to and connected with others in an appropriate way without feeling existentially threatened with their own individuality (ability to form attachments). If the other is not present or temporarily away, the stable experience of one's own safety contributes to a sense of security (ability to be alone). The person can form close, emotionally intimate, and deep relationships (dependency) while simultaneously experiencing themselves as separate, autonomous individual (individuation); neither being alone nor being in a relationship triggers (un)conscious fears.

If this *development fails*, there is a pronounced sense of insecurity and existential threat. This is followed by fears of separation or of too much closeness/merging. Life histories are often based on experiences of either overly close or overly distant relationships with significant others.

Consequently, there may be an excessive longing for close relationships (dependence) or fear of them (individuation).

The two coping modes describe typical attempts to manage these issues: Forced emotional distancing in contact with others, in the sense of a counter-phobic emotional pseudo-independence (active mode), is sought as protection against a feared "merging" in the relationship. In the opposite position (passive mode), the individual perceives any distance/separation in the relationship as threatening, so that increasing distance must be avoided at all costs ("I cannot exist without the other").

In relationships with others, the constant question is how close or distant the other can be experienced emotionally without this being perceived as an existential threat.

The relationship with other people is therefore existentially about the question of "having to be alone" or "having to be together," as opposed to the general motivational theme of "being able to be alone" vs. "being able to be together."

In contrast to the following conflict motives, the question of existential dependence or independence from the relationship is described in general, rather than the specifics of individual motivational themes within the relationship. This theme is in line with the known attachment types (disorganized, insecure-avoidant, insecure-ambivalent).

Key Characteristics of the Neurotic Conflict Dependency vs. Individuation

1. Repetitive-Dysfunctional Motivational Pattern: In their self-perception and/or the perception by others, individuals repeatedly

strive to be emotionally highly independent of relationships with others in situations significant to them (active mode) or experience a basic sense of dependence on relationships with others (passive mode). At its core, this is an existential striving for the object that provides support or the denial of such a need (*having to* be alone or *having to* be together).

2. Core and Lead Affects: The core affect is a basic, subjectively unbearable fear of separation or merging. The lead affects, which tend to be more conscious and observable, are a panic in the passive mode, and a strong aversion in the active mode.
3. Trigger Situations: From a biographical perspective, there is a likelihood of recurring experiences of proximity or distance associated with existential fear induced by significant objects in one's life history. The adult individual will seek positions of emotional independence and distance ("active mode") or emotional dependence and closeness ("passive mode") in relationships to compensate for these experiences. In both modes, every effort must be made to prevent the feared closeness (active mode) or the feared separation (passive mode). Situations that hinder these compensatory attempts are typically the ones that are triggering symptoms, albeit through involuntary emotional closeness to someone in the active mode, such as at the birth of a child ("Before the birth, I could have left anytime"), or job loss for an engineer or truck driver who works permanently away from home ("I was able to maintain sufficient distance"). In the passive mode, a typical trigger is the actual or feared loss of a partner in an extremely dependent and close relationship ("I cannot be without a relationship").
4. Transference and Countertransference Dynamics (T-CT): Since closeness or distance in relationships is perceived as dangerous, the affected individual transfers this onto many other object relationships. In treatment, this transference can manifest as a tendency to avoid engaging in treatment, to avoid experiencing emotions, and to be unavailable due to constant scheduling problems (active mode), or through excessive clinging, demanding appointments, and inability to detach (passive mode). In the countertransference feelings of concern and responsibility mix with fears of overwhelming desires for closeness and tendencies of appropriation (passive mode). In the active mode, there is little sense of responsibility, care, or protection. The desire for dependency that the patient is warding off can still be sensed by the examiner.

Active and passive mode and their manifestations: First, a general description of the active and passive modes of Dependency vs. Individuation Conflict is given, followed by descriptions of how the conflict typically manifests itself at different levels of structural integration.

General Description of the Coping Modes of C1

Passive Mode

In the passive mode, the type of forced clinging dominates. Typical is the endeavor to establish very close and secure relationships at (almost) any cost. There is a self-perception of insecurity and threat ("I can't live without you."). The underlying core affect of existential fear (panic) of separation can be compensated for by various behavioral patterns (submission, care, control, clinging) with sometimes aggressive demands ("You mustn't leave me!").

In the countertransference, feelings of concern and responsibility mix with fears of excessive desires for closeness and attempts at appropriation.

Active Mode

In the active mode, there is typically an exaggerated emotional and existential independence from relationships. The areas of life are characterized by the constant struggle for autonomy and independence to ward off the need for attachment, closeness and bonding ("I don't need anyone."). The underlying core effect is the existential fear of closeness and merging. This can be warded off by behavioral patterns of emotional distance (e.g., disinterest in relationships) and also aggressive rejection ("Don't get too close to me").

In the countertransference, there is often a lack of responsibility and a lack of need for care and protection, but a noticeable desire for dependency in the patient.

Manifestations of the Dependency vs. Individuation Conflict (C1) at Different Levels of Structural Integration

The phenomenology of the Dependency vs. Individuation conflict is determined by the level of structural processing. The increase expressed in "conflict tension, neurotic conflict, conflict schema" typically corresponds to decreasing structural integration from "well-integrated, moderate, low" to a level of structural disintegration (Table 26). The upper pole (usually corresponding to a high level of structural integrations) in Figure 9 is characterized by the basic human needs for emotional attachment and independence within relationships that are inherent in all people.

Individuals with conflict tension, for whom the pervasive motivational theme of closeness/distance has been accentuated to some extent, are characterized by a degree of stress in this

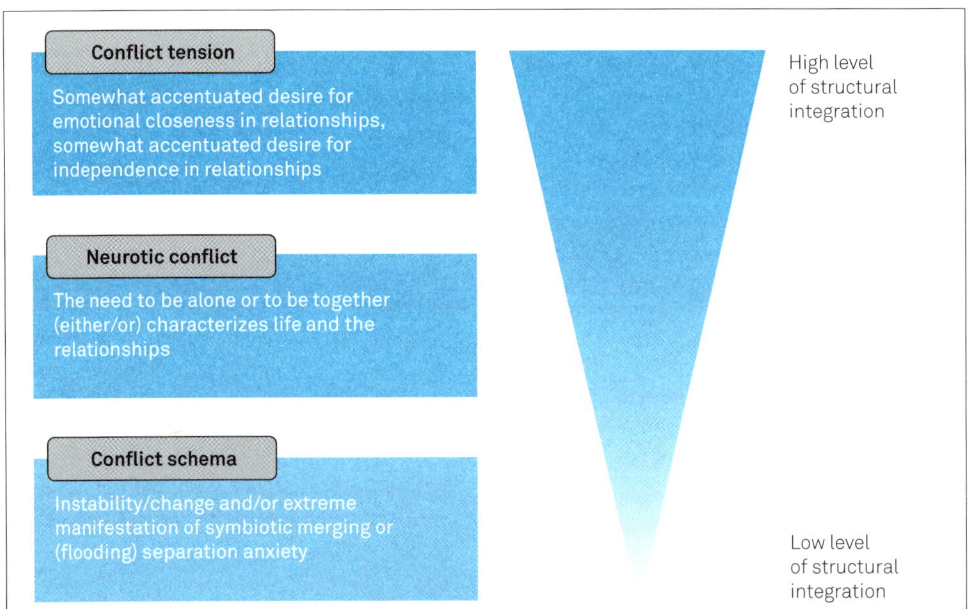

Figure 9. Dependency vs. Individuation and the three levels of structural integration. The three levels of structural integration: Conflict tension (upper pole, high level of structural integration), neurotic conflict (rather moderate level of structural integration) and conflict schema (rather low level of structural integration).

Table 26. Characteristics of C1 on various structural integration levels

Characteristics of C1 at different levels of structural integration	
C1: Characteristics of conflict tension	
(A) Conflict tension in passive mode The individual concerned is more likely to form close relationships. There is a strong emphasis on maintaining attachment and seeking closeness, with a tendency to adapt to the other person or avoid conflict, but not at all costs. The regulation of closeness or distance in relationships is flexible (ambivalent), with an increased desire for closeness in interpersonal relationships. In principle, functional regulation of conflict tension is still possible without clinically significant effects.	**(A) Conflict tension in active mode** The person concerned prefers to adopt a position of independence in relationships. If possible, they prefer activities they can do alone. They tend to remain non-committal and less engaging in relationships with other people. Relationship desires are nevertheless noticeable. If possible, increased emotional closeness is avoided in relationships. In principle, flexible regulation of conflict tension is possible without clinically significant effects.
C1: Characteristics of the neurotic conflict	
(B) Neurotic conflict in passive mode Typically, there is a pronounced striving for dependent positions, although opposing impulses for independence may also be perceived. A sense of dependency or a need to be together dominates ("If I am very close to you, you cannot leave me.") to avoid an (unconsciously) feared separation from the object that provides security. Any separation, real or imagined, triggers existential anxiety and is often met with clinging, accusations or aggressive demands ("You can't leave me."). In crisis situations, the emotional preoccupation can be shifted to other objects.	**(B) Neurotic conflict in active mode** Typically, there is a pronounced striving for emotional independence from relationships; an emotional need to be alone dominates. One's own longing for close relationships and the inherent fear of merging or being abandoned are warded off. In the different areas of life, the individual is mainly looking for independent positions. If emotional distance seems to be threatened, it must be vehemently secured or re-established by means of flight or even aggressively cutting oneself off.
C1: Characteristics of the conflict schema	
Conflict schemas with a low level of structural integration are generally characterized by a pronounced situation/experience dependent instability or even fluctuation. The dysfunctional experience/behavior that is typical of this conflict appears both exaggerated in extreme form and diffuse and alternating between the two modes and is then only vaguely recognizable. For example, the previous tendency towards an intimate relationship can suddenly turn into an aggressive striving for independence – and vice versa. However, you can also find rigid fixations in the passive or active mode	
(C) Conflict schema in passive mode The existential significance of the object is exaggerated to such an extent that existential fears quickly overwhelm the individual in the event of a real or imagined separation. These can often only be handled or prevented by harming oneself and/or others. This can take the form of, for example, enduring violence from the partner or threats of violence towards the partner or oneself ("If you leave me, then ..."). On an interpersonal level, the clinging behavior of the person concerned often triggers strong emotions in the other person.	**(C) Conflict schema in active mode** The existential struggle for emotional independence is so pronounced that emotional relationships are rendered impossible. On an interpersonal level, the person concerned may be experienced as emotionally cold and overly distant. Situations that threaten independence can trigger massive aggression. The other person's response may be mainly to be overly cautious about approaching (and of the threatening aggression) or to make an effort to get close (when experiencing emotional coldness)
For individuals with structural disintegration, even more extreme compensatory mechanisms are possible, sometimes involving a reinterpretation of reality (see Section 4.4).	

area. However, this conflict tension generally causes little to no distress when flexibility is maintained.

With a moderate level of structural integration, relationships become repetitive and dysfunctional in the sense of the neurotic conflict, characterized by the need to inflexibly secure distance or closeness to ward off the resulting basic fear. This is systematically re-iterated below.

With a low level of structural integration and a conflict schema, there may be constant instability or extreme manifestation of the modes, which may be expressed, for example, as a fear of symbiotic merging and an overwhelming fear of separation, and vehement attempts to curb these affects.

In individuals with a disintegrated structural level, even more extreme compensation mechanisms are possible, sometimes involving distortions of reality (see Section 4.4).

Differential Diagnosis of the Dynamics of the Dependency vs. Individuation Conflict

In contrast to the Dependency vs. Individuation Conflict which involves the fundamental question of the patient's ability to relate ("dependency on the relationship"), the other conflicts are about the emotional organization within the relationship (e.g., dependency in the relationship).

Conflict C1 may be confused with the In Need of Care vs. Self-Sufficiency Conflict. However, the latter does not address the question of the fundamental existential significance of a relationship (and therefore leads to the leading affect of fear), but rather that of emotional care and nurturing (or defense against it) with the leading affect of disappointment/grief if this fails to materialize. Even if patients say that they are afraid of separation from their partner, this is about the loss of the emotionally caring object (=disappointment/grief) and not about the loss of the security-providing object (=existential fear). The In Need of Care vs. Self-Sufficiency Conflict is about the thematic organization of the relationship and not about whether a relationship with others can be experienced at all.

Even in cases in which the partner is strongly controlled in a relationship in order to maintain one's own closeness or distance, this should not be mistaken for the underlying theme of striving for dominance in the Submission vs. Control Conflict.

Case Vignettes

Dependency vs. Individuation (Passive Mode)

The Housekeeper: Ms. L. is a 52-year-old, rather unassuming woman who, right at the beginning of the appointment which has been expressly arranged as an initial consultation, asks if there will now be regular weekly sessions with the therapist. She says she came on the advice of her family doctor, who told her in the previous week that she should seek support from a psychotherapist. She had been suffering from depressed feelings, self-esteem doubts, a tendency to cry, feelings of loneliness, fatigue, and exhaustion for a year. She also had trouble sleeping, pain in her joints, and headaches, but her family doctor had not found a cause.

It all started when her 24-year-old daughter moved out and moved in with her boyfriend nearby. Shortly afterwards, her 20-year-old son also moved out because he had started university. Since then, she rarely saw her children, although they previously had a close relationship. She had always been very involved in their lives, supported them, comforting them in times of trouble, and giving lots of advice. She misses both children very much, and the thought of losing them causes her great distress.

Her relationship with her children has always been very important to her, as she has not had an easy marriage for many years. But now they had nearly made it to their silver wedding anniversary. She got married early to get away from home. She would never have managed to move out alone, though her parents wouldn't have objected. In her marriage, everyone has gone their own way for years; there is a lack of warmth, and there is no real cohesion. Her husband had problems with alcohol and repeatedly insulted and sometimes hit her. As a man, he took what he wanted sexually. She had always given in and complied with him even when she didn't want to. Others, including her children, had repeatedly advised her to separate. However, the idea of separation has always been difficult for her, causing anxiety. For her, it was easier to put up with this man than to be alone. Half a year ago, however, he supposedly "got his second wind." He was having an affair again (or at least she believes so) and wanted to move out. The thought of having to be alone terrifies her. She would rather endure his escapades than live alone; she couldn't bear it. In order not to tempt her husband to move out, she herself has moved into the garden house. Her husband now lives in the house, sometimes with his mistress. She cooks, washes for him, and keeps the house clean, if she can stay near him. Sometimes, she is allowed to stay a little longer in the evening and they watch TV together or talk a little. When her husband is away (which he tries to be more and more), she stays in the house, where she feels somewhat comfortable where she can still feel a bit of her husband and children.

Dependency vs. Individuation (Active Mode)

The Salesman: Mr. I., aged 58, comes in for a consultation on the emphatic advice of his family doctor, who has been trying to persuade him to start psychotherapy for a long time. However, he said he could never follow this advice because he works so much and travels frequently, so that he cannot attend regular sessions in person. But his symptoms had worsened recently, forcing him to act. He suffered from periods of depressed feelings, diffuse bad mood, feelings of loneliness, vague fears, and general exhaustion. He has also had tinnitus for several months, especially noticeable in situations involving several people.

In his past, Mr. I. was never able to commit to a stable relationship or job; as a sales representative, he frequently changed employers, residences, and relationships, but he was fully dedicated to his work and very successful. There have certainly been phases in his relationships in which ideas of moving in together or even marriage have arisen. However, this tended to cause him anxiety and things became too close. Once, he even deliberately started an argument to end a relationship.

He said he had maintained a group of friends since school. The others met up more regularly and even went on a skiing vacation together once a year. He had joined them once, but after a few days, he had to go home early because he had felt unwell. Since then, he'd only seen his friends at the regular meetings, which he frequently needed to cancel for work reasons. He did not discuss personal matters with them, and currently, none of them knew how down he was.

The frequent changes have also always been very important to him professionally to move forward. He loves the freedom in his position, where he can decide most things himself if he is successful. Only occasionally does he need to check in with his supervisor, which is always brief meetings. In the past, he was offered promotions, such as team leader positions, but he could never imagine this because they would have involved office work, which he perceived as "imprisoning." Now, however, due to economic reasons, it is planned to reduce the fieldwork, and he is to be transferred to an office role, with a promotion. This is causing him a great deal of stress, and he cannot imagine always being in the same workplace with other people. Due to his age, he cannot find another position, unlike in the past when he always had options.

In the countertransference, there is a feeling of disinterest and an impulse to let the patient go. Yet, there is also a sense of wanting to "take this lonely person under one's wing" and invite him for further conversations.

4.3.4 C2 Submission vs. Control

The *central motivation* is a minimum level of control and security that a person needs over themselves and the key aspects of their environment. "Converging evidence suggests that the need for control is a biological imperative for survival" (Leotti et al., 2010; p. 457). Psychologically, this is referred to as self-efficacy (Bandura, 1977, 1997).

In the context of anal development (Freud) and the "phase of defiance," self-control and external control were referred to as motivations for self-determination (Heimann, 1962) but were not acknowledged as independent motivational systems (rather assigned to the development of libido). Interpersonally, mutual needs clash (self- vs. external control). Historically, the motivation for independence (control) was associated with toilet training ("cleanliness drill"). In today's child-rearing environment, general motor restrictions have largely replaced toilet training. Depending on cultural circumstances and living environment, in developmental extremes, a child's motivation for control is either met with resistance (authoritarian control) or a child is allowed excessive freedom for self-determination (overly laissez-faire approaches). These cultural parenting styles shape successful vs. unsuccessful development. In childhood, this basic conflict often manifests itself as obedience/submission vs. control/rebellion (OPD-CA-2 Task Force, 2017). More generally, it is about the experience of having an impact on the world (vs. being subject to arbitrary action), which is important very early on.

With successful development, a person has a securely anchored sense of self-efficacy. Based on this, the individual can exercise control in a way that is appropriate to the situation and is also able to relinquish control, surrender, and subordinate without experiencing this as submission. This allows for a feeling of satisfaction in realized self-efficacy, which can be situationally replaced by an experience of joy in devotion.

If this development fails, the individual is experiencing a deficit in self-efficacy, which, as they develop, occur in relational contexts and are associated with intense feelings of helplessness. Corresponding biographical experiences make relationships revolve around the dynamic of who is in control or how to avoid the renewed experience of helplessness (core affect). The dominant question is "up or down." The two modes of resolving this question describe typical coping strategies: Aggressive pursuit of dominance (active mode) is an attempt to never relinquish control to eliminate further experiences of helplessness. Conversely, habitual submission (passive mode) achieves defending helplessness by indirectly controlling "the powerful." Submission vs. Control represent the maladaptive poles of "being able to devote oneself" and "being led," on the one hand and "being able to guide others " on the other hand. The potential coexistence of self-efficacy and devotion within the same relationship is hindered by an "either-or" experience of power and powerlessness. An even greater escalation of the conflict involves sheer power (lust for power) vs. the powerless feeling of enslavement up to the lust for submission.

Key Characteristics of the Neurotic Conflict Submission vs. Control

1. Repetitive-Dysfunctional Motivational Pattern: In their self-perception and/or the perception by others, individuals repeatedly strive to exert control over people and situations that are meaningful to them or excessively surrender and submit (either/or). The core motivation is striving for self-efficacy or the defense against helplessness.
2. Core and Leading Affects: The core affect is a subjectively unbearable feeling of helplessness. The observable effects that are accessible to consciousness are anger, defiance, and rage, and the fear of submission or surrender. The striving for dominance and con-

trol in the active mode can develop into a lust for power, while habitual submission in the passive mode can develop into a lust for submission.

3. Trigger Situations: In the person's biography, recurring experiences of helplessness and being at the mercy of others are to be expected, often induced by significant others in his or her life history. Real or imagined experiences in analogous situations in adulthood, with a "powerful other" (partner, superior, sociocultural events), evoke the active impulse to defend one's self-efficacy "by any means (of power) necessary." The fear of losing self-efficacy can escalate into fear of subordination or even enslavement. When feeling hopeless in the face of others' striving for power, submission (passive mode) may serve as a "reasonable compromise," allowing at least indirect influence ("I comply, but ..."). Individuals in passive mode often decompensate (a) when others do not follow the highly regarded supposedly irrevocable rules (e.g., a boss ignores an employee's company anniversary) or (b) when they find themselves in a "powerful" position.
4. Transference and Countertransference Dynamics (T - CT): Because the person's own self-efficacy and security are potentially constantly experienced as being in jeopardy, the person transfers this concern to many other object relationships. During treatment, the therapist may experience in the countertransference the urge to dictate the rules of the therapy setting or to or to be able to introduce affects into therapy only in a very controlled manner. If this underlying transference is not understood, secondary anger and rejection can develop in the countertransference. In the case of a submissive transference offer, the overly compliant behavior does not reflect a genuinely relaxed relationship, as the patient may either be waiting for an opportunity to prove themselves right (indirect control) and/or subconsciously try to reverse roles (possible anger/revenge feelings from the patient, resulting in tension in the countertransference). Furthermore, the patient's passive, overly compliant relationship approach can bring the therapeutic work to a complete standstill (thereby allowing the patient to feel effective again).

General Description of the Coping Modes of C2

Passive Mode

What is typical of the passive mode is passive-aggressive submission. The individual perceives himself or herself as lacking in influence ("The superiors determine everything."), in the sense that you must put up with being "determined'", bow to the "arbitrariness of the powerful" and submit. The associated core affects of helplessness and powerlessness are countered by passive-aggressive behavior (dawdling, delaying, passively undermining requirements) or by "insisting" on irrevocable rules. A considerable degree of control is achieved by only seemingly complying and by precisely registering what makes the determinants tick.

Remaining in the subordinate position is also a protection against the breaking through of lifelong accumulated aggression ("If I ever come to power, then God have mercy on you!") and fantasized desires for revenge.

The submissive and at the same time subliminally aggressive behavior usually quickly provokes anger in the other person. If the passive striving becomes habitual, it can become a secondary motivation in the sense of a "lust for submission."

Active Mode

What is typical of the active mode is an aggressive striving for dominance with the attempt to gain permanent control over others and situations. The striving for power and dominance serves to ward off the fear of being controlled and falling into a state of helplessness. In both professional and private contexts, leadership positions are sought; high motivation ensures control. The easily triggered anger also serves to protect against feelings of powerlessness.

Constructive criticism, dissenting suggestions and the independence of others can also pose a threat and activate the fear of being controlled by others, which quickly leads to interactive "power struggles."

If active striving becomes habitual, it can become a secondary motivation in the sense of "lust for power."

Manifestations of the Submission vs. Control Conflict (C2) at Different Levels of Structural Integration

The phenomenology of the Submission vs. Control Conflict is defined by the relevant level of structural integration. The increase expressed in "conflict tension, neurotic conflict, conflict schema" generally corresponds to a decrease in structural integration, from "good, moderate, low" to a level of structural disintegration (Table 27). The upper pole (typically corresponding to a well-integrated structural level) in Figure 10 is characterized by the basic human need for self-control and control over others, i.e., self-efficacy.

Individuals with conflict tension, in whom the ubiquitous motivational theme of control/self-efficacy is accentuated to some extent, experience some tension in this area. However, this conflict tension usually causes little or no suffering.

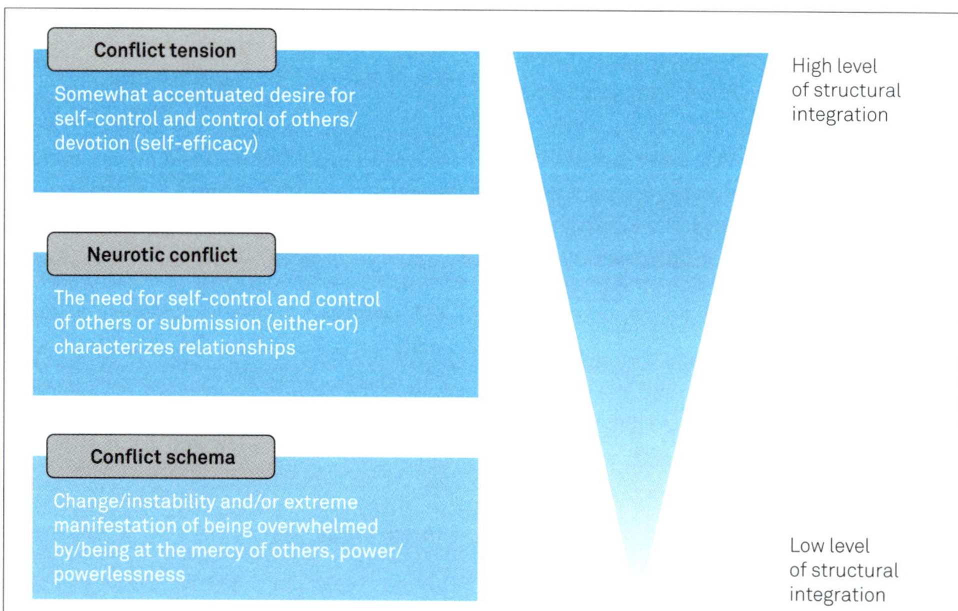

Figure 10. Submission vs. Control and the three levels of structural integration. The three levels: Conflict tension (upper pole, high level of structural integration), neurotic conflict (moderate level of structural integration) and conflict schema (rather low structure level).

In individuals with moderate level of structural integration, who tend to excessively control impulses and affects, relationships are repetitively dysfunctional (neurotic) and shaped by a need for inflexible control (or submission) of self and others to ward off a potential experience of helplessness.

Individuals with a low level of structural integration, have a conflict schema characterized by a lack of impulse and affect control. This can lead to feelings of being overwhelmed, being at the mercy of others, and experiencing powerlessness. There are also rigid fixations in either the passive or active mode, where, for example,

Table 27. Characteristics of C2 on various structural processing levels

Characteristics of C2 at different levels of structural integration	
C2: Characteristics of conflict tension	
(A) Conflict tension in passive mode The person concerned tends to prefer to be "taken along" and led, preferring to take what is suggested and "go with the flow." Leadership roles are avoided. In the case of illness, the feeling of having to endure this fate with patience is prominent. On an interpersonal level, people with this kind of problem tend to be perceived as pleasant, unproblematic and conscientious, perhaps a little lacking in initiative and boring. They can follow and devote themselves to events and people. In principle, flexible regulation of conflict tension is still possible without clinically significant effects.	**(A) Conflict tension in active mode** The person concerned has "always" enjoyed taking on a certain leadership role in important relationships and prefers to be asked. There is a tendency to take things into one's own hands, to control others, and to avoid devotion. As a result, material possessions, for example, can be used to assert their own aspirations, as can the body, which must function. In the event of illness, those affected try to "keep track." In principle, flexibility in regulating conflict tensions is maintained so that there is usually no significant suffering.
C2: Characteristics of the neurotic conflict	
(B) Neurotic conflict in passive mode Although these individuals also perceive opposing impulses, they strive for subordinate positions in order to avoid aggressive tensions which they fear. On an interpersonal level, these individuals will be experienced as yes-men who are not easily trusted and whom other people find difficult to confide in and trust. Rage and anger, which are warded off, can manifest as emphatically slow work, insisting' on irrefutable rules or apparent mistakes that can be understood as "latent opposition." In apparent submission, the "determinant" is accurately controlled. As persistence in the subordinate position also provides protection against aggression breaking through, the subliminally aggressive behavior can make itself felt as anger in the countertransference.	**(B) Neurotic conflict in active mode** Typically, there is an aggressive striving for dominance with the attempt to gain permanent control over others and situations. The striving for power and dominance is a defense against fears of being dominated and falling into a state of helplessness. There are fears of events and people to whom one must submit or surrender. The dominance rage that is easily triggered by permanent tension also protects against feelings of powerlessness. Professionally, they aim for management positions or self-employment. A high willingness to perform ensures control. Interpersonally, constructive criticism, dissenting suggestions and the independence of others can be perceived as a threat, which can quickly lead to "power struggles."

Table 27. Characteristics of C2 on various structural processing levels *(continued)*

Characteristics of C2 at different levels of structural integration	
C2: Characteristics of the conflict schema	
Conflict schemas at a rather low level of structural integration are generally characterized by pronounced instability and even fluctuation depending on the relevant situation and experience, so that the dysfunctional experience/behavior can appear both exaggerated and diffused and is then only passingly recognizable. However, rigid fixations in passive or active mode can also be found.	
(C) Conflict schema in passive mode The attitude of surrendering to others results from the uncertainty of being able to find one's own secure position in relation to oneself and in relationships with others. Surrender allows the maintenance of a bond that reduces anxiety. The experience of being at the mercy of others quickly can have a devastating effect on the person and is sometimes experienced as "enslavement," from which they can only free themselves through massive aggression. Interpersonally, the person concerned can be experienced as a "submissive", annoying trigger, who you may want to push away or who sometimes triggers clear aggressive tendencies in others. Submission/subordination/longing to be dominated can also develop into a feeling of pleasure (secondary motivation) that is repeatedly sought out.	**(C) Conflict schema in active mode** These individuals tend to keep situations and relationship partners "under control" at all costs due to their increased fear of helplessness and feelings of powerlessness. This leads either to chronic feelings of anger or to unexpected outbursts of anger if the person perceives the situation as confusing and uncontrollable. A certain degree of stability can be achieved if a position of power can be attained in which others are at the mercy of this power and arbitrariness. However, this remains a fragile system, so that the position of power must be aggressively "secured" time and again. In the countertransference, a clear sense of threat often manifests itself due to the possibility of sudden dominance or aggression breaking through.
For people with a disintegrated structural level, even more extreme compensatory mechanisms are possible, sometimes involving a reinterpretation of reality (see Section 4.4).	

dominance is exercised aggressively and destructively on a permanent basis or where people remain in a "position of enslavement."

In individuals with a disintegrated structural level, even more extreme compensatory mechanisms are possible, sometimes accompanied by distortions of reality (see Section 4.4).

Differential Diagnosis of Conflict Dynamics Self-Efficacy vs. Self-Worth Experience

Stressful experiences of power and powerlessness (lack of self-efficacy) also influence the experience of self-worth. For this reason, particular attention must be paid to the distinction from self-worth conflicts in the actual sense.

In passive mode, it must be determined whether the shame arises from a feeling of subjugation or if the other person intentionally evoked a sense of devaluation through their interaction.

In active mode, the question is whether the motive of domination and lust for power is in the foreground or rather the need to degrade and devalue the other person (to appear "outstanding" oneself).

It is not uncommon for other conflict dynamics to be warded off with the help of the control/submission theme, e.g., a habitual tendency to control can serve to "keep in check" the fears associated with C1 (of separation, of merging).

Case Vignettes

Submission vs. Control (Passive Mode)

The Administrative Officer: Mr. A., a 45-year-old man, jumps up in the waiting room and greets the examiner with a bow. He begins by talking extensively about his intestinal problems: He cannot get his constipation under control and his bowels force him to spend long periods on the toilet. All the doctors he had consulted so far had been unable to help him, although he had conscientiously taken or followed the prescribed medication and treatments. He had almost resigned himself to the idea that there was no solution and expected nothing from today's consultation. When asked about potential anger, Mr. A. immediately assures, "No, I am not angry, just resigned; I wonder if the doctors are even sufficiently trained or up to date at all?"

He came from a working-class household. His father was very dominant and controlling, and he had been afraid to talk back to him. As the eldest, he was forced by his parents to try to excel in everything he did. Above all, it was important to his parents that he stick to the rules. Statements like "As long as you put your feet under our table, we set the rules!" often formed the basis for such demands. "That's a parenting method I also use with my own children today." During adolescence, he had some arguments with his parents but quickly realized it was important to stick to the rules so that his younger brother wouldn't go astray because of him.

During the conversation, it becomes clear that Mr. A., who works as a civil servant in a surveying department, is threatened with disciplinary proceedings because he has not met work requirements for some time. On the one hand, he must go to the bathroom for long periods at work and on the other hand he tries to do his job, on which legal peace depends, ("avoidance of border disputes") accurately. With a strong voice, Mr. A. emphasizes that he really works himself to the bone, often looking up the relevant regulations, staying at the office longer than necessary, but no one appreciates his commitment! He feels that his new boss, who he has had for two years, is overly controlling his workload. He had already considered submitting a blank sheet of paper instead of the required work reports, to point out that these reports would event take up additional time he urgently needed for his work.

Often, he is exhausted in his free time and is grateful when his family or friends involve him in activities. His wife occasionally reproaches him for not advancing professionally or financially. He has nothing against money himself, but given the choice, conscientious completion of the work takes precedence over career aspirations.

Submission vs. Control (Active Mode)

The Self-Employed Entrepreneur: Mr. B. (56 years old) drops into the chair in the consulting room and immediately spreads out a wealth of documents on the table between himself and the examiner. Amid a flood of symptom complaints, the clinician or interviewer feels overwhelmed by the patient's papers. Attempts to start the usual introductory statement about the course of the session are drowned out by accusations: "I figured right away you wouldn't have enough time to really understand me! It would take you hours ...!"

His internist had advised him to come to the hospital because of his uncontrolled high blood pressure. He had already considered changing doctors, as he found, through internet research, that there were other medicines for high blood pressure.

The immediate reason for the consultation is that his wife has threatened to leave him, saying she feels suffocated by him. Although their children were becoming increasingly independent, he still wasn't allowing her to work, as she was supposed to look after the house perfectly. She has everything she could possibly wish for with him: a beautiful home, a big car, two healthy children. As a self-employed sales representative, he is a successful businessman. After all, he is the one who brings the money home, and therefore he has the right to make the decisions.

Initially, he worked for an insurance company, but the constant "in rank and file" was not for him. He needed freedom and wants to be his own boss. At first, his wife appreciated the money he brought home. Now, however, she apparently wants to "tie him down" and expects him to be more involved with their growing children. He gave the children clear guidelines: every good grade was rewarded with money. "They know that if they don't keep an eye on things, they get nothing! I did the same thing with my parents, when they tried to interfere, I cut off contact." He is furious that his wife has now contacted his parents.

He is involved in numerous clubs and is, therefore, rarely at home. "As a businessman, you must network, you know, and as an entrepreneur, I can award positions, which the others then thank me through business connections ... after all, one hand washes the other! The main thing is that I have the upper hand!" His doctor's advice to "do less" seems unrealistic to him: "I might as well be dead!"

4.3.5 C3 In Need of Care vs. Self-Sufficiency

Numerous neurobiological, psychological, and psychoanalytic motivational theories describe a genuine evolutionary-biologically anchored and socio-culturally malleable object-related need of care (Maslow, 1970; Harlow, 1971; Lichtenberg, 1983; Panksepp, 1998; Emde, 2005; Bischof-Köhler, 2011; Benecke & Brauner, 2017). The basis is the motive and willingness for caregiving and "nurturing" and receiving care (Bischof, 1985, 2009; Bischof-Köhler & Bischof, 2018) as part of the "caregiving system" (Lichtenberg et al., 2011). Initially, psychoanalytic developmental theory described orality as sensory focus on the mouth (oral phase) and subsequently expanded it to include the areas of care and security (Sandler & Dare, 1970). A person's experiences of care and protection, whether positive or negative, shape their need for care and protection, or their capacity (need) for self-care or caring for others. Clinically, care needs can be clearly distinguished from dependency needs, and self-sufficiency needs from individuation needs.

The *central motivation* addresses the basic human need for emotional care and security. This includes material and physical needs. In terms of phenomenology, caring for emotionally close people (e.g., "family-friend group") touches on the psychoanalytic concept of orality but it is not based on its drive theory. Panksepp (1998) reminds us that one may be overly need to care for others to get care for oneself.

With successful development, there is an inner certainty that one has received and will continue to receive adequate care and emotional security. This allows one to care for oneself and seek support without feeling obliged. It also fosters the ability to give affection and emotional security without negative feelings. Giving and receiving come naturally and are balanced, without the constant fear of getting too little, asking for too much, or not giving enough. Flexible oscillation around a middle position between the polar processing modes is possible. These individuals can receive proper care from others just as effectively as they can care for themselves and others.

If this *development fails*, there is a pressing need for emotional security and a sense of deprivation. This may result in either insatiable neediness or excessive giving and self-exploitation, disregarding personal needs. Giving and receiving become imbalanced, driven by fear of inadequacy. Unconscious desires for care can be suppressed by enforced self-sufficiency, often due to fear of unfulfilled needs, dependency, obligation, or being exploited. Forced pseudo-self-sufficiency requires a great deal of effort and carries the risk that, if self-sufficiency fails, the individual might not reliably receive care from others. It is rarely possible to oscillate flexibly between polar processing modes. Instead, idealized, one-sided conflict solutions tend to be favoured as a more bearable option. These individuals struggle to ensure they are well cared for by others and to take care of themselves and others. Desires for care and security, or their defense, shape but do not define relationships. Rather, the structure follows specific desires for emotional care and security, or their defense.

Key Characteristics of the Neurotic Conflict Between In Need of Care vs. Self-Sufficiency

1. Repetitive Dysfunctional Motivational Pattern: Affected individuals often either excessively seek emotional care and security from others or attempt to provide it while avoiding dependence. This pattern is driven by a desire for care and security, or fear of losing it.
2. Core and Leading Affects: The unconscious core affect is a feeling of deprivation, fearing inadequate emotional and material care and security. More conscious leading affects include disappointment, sadness, or depression due to lack or loss of emotional care and security. Resentment can develop over the perceived lack of care, as can envy when others receive better care, or guilt over one's own perceived neediness. Those with a deep-seated sense of inadequacy who reject offers of care often experience loneliness as a result. On one hand, their resilience, self-sacrifice, and independence are impressive. On the other hand, they experience disappointment and envy due to unmet needs for care and attention. They may perceive others as ungrateful, leading to anger and accusations. Defending their own emotional needs can cause self-doubt and feelings of guilt.
3. Trigger Situations: In terms of triggering situations, the issue of emotional deprivation or loss is central. Biographically, problematic object relationships with repeated deprivation (physical, emotional, or material) are to be expected. In adulthood, real or imagined experiences of emotional deprivation (re-)activate neurotic conflict processing. People in passive mode are most likely to decompensate when their strategies for securing care fail and there is no prospect of their excessive neediness being satisfied soon. People in the active mode are most likely to decompensate when their forced pseudo-self-sufficiency strategies collapse, and their previously suppressed desires for emotional care break through. This happens most often in cases of exhaustion or illness. But it can also happen when there are no more objects to care for (altruistic surrender runs into the void, e.g., children moving out, death of previously cared-for relatives).
4. Transference and Countertransference Dynamics (T-CT): The person transfers their own emotional care and security, which they (un)consciously and constantly experience as endangered, or their defense against it, to important object relationships. In therapeutic relationships, which inherently involve care aspects, In Need of Care vs. Self-Sufficiency dynamics is quickly activated in interactions.

In the countertransference, people in the passive processing mode are experienced as excessively needy, as if they could never get enough ("bottomless pit"), up to very demanding, sometimes even "blackmailing" behavior. However, they can also appear constantly disappointed, lamenting, accusatory, with low resilience and in need of rest. In the countertransference, it is therefore difficult to actively make demands on these people. Initial genuine feelings of caring and support increasingly give way to an experience of annoyance and irritation. This often leads to withdrawal tendencies and reinforces the maladaptive interaction cycle.

Individuals in the active processing mode evoke a countertransference of immense strength, self-sacrifice, resilience, and independence, so that little or no inclination to help them arises in the countertransference. At the same time, the underlying longing for care and the disappointment at the lack of emotional support are palpable. Initially, the other person may react with a certain degree of gratitude and even admiration towards these people, but this soon shifts to annoyance and frustration at the over-provision imposed on them. This often leads to withdrawal tendencies, reinforcing the maladaptive interaction cycle.

General Description of the Coping Modes of C3

Passive Mode

The passive mode is characterized by the attempt to compensate for or ward off the inner experience of deprivation through an overly close relationship to an attachment figure that provides care and emotional security. People in this state appear highly dependent, clinging, or demanding.

The "contact hunger" appears as a variant of the passive mode with the attempt to fill the inner experience of lack with as many contacts as possible. In some cases, this can even lead to "parasitic" relationships. Separation is experienced as the loss of an urgently needed care center and of the warmth of a nest.

The leading affects of the subjective experience of deprivation are disappointment, sadness and depression as well as the fear of losing the affection and care of the other person. Envy of others who have not missed out and who are better off is also common. Passive striving can become secondary motivation in the sense of a "desire to complain about having come off badly."

After initial concern, the other person usually reacts to the demanding or even "blackmailing" relationship in an annoyed and defensive manner and may withdraw.

Active Mode

The active mode is characterized by the attempt to compensate for or ward off the inner experience of lack and deprivation through a "pseudo self-sufficiency." When it comes to relationships, this is expressed through excessive modesty, and self-sufficiency in the sense of "I don't need anything for myself!" This self-sufficient care for others allows for "altruistic surrender". There can be a demanding behavior in close relationships, calling for presence and help. Separation is experienced as a threatening loss of the cared-for object, as it deprives the altruistic surrender of its basis.

Concern for others dominates the conscious affective experience of those affected. Behind this, however, their own (un)conscious neediness remains subliminally perceptible as a longing for emotional care and security. This can manifest itself as an experience of ingratitude ("I do so much and get no thanks for it!"), as subliminal envy ("They get everything!") or as an unconscious hope for future compensation ("One day I will be repaid."). However, it is impossible to assert your own needs and the very thought of it usually triggers feelings of guilt.

After initial recognition and gratitude, the other person often reacts to the overprotectiveness with strong tendencies to distance themselves and possibly with withdrawal.

Manifestations of the In Need of Care vs. Self-Sufficiency Conflict at Different Levels of Structural Integration

The phenomenology of the conflict between In Need of Care and Self-Sufficiency is defined by the relevant level of structural integration. The increase expressed in "conflict tension, neurotic conflict, conflict schema" generally corresponds to a decrease in structural integration, from "good, moderate, low" to a level of structural disintegration (Table 28). Figure 11 shows the basic human need for emotional care and security which is manifested differently at different structural levels.

Individuals with a good to moderate level of structural integration, in whom the theme of needing to be taken care of vs. self-sufficiency has only been accentuated to a certain extent, are indeed burdened by conflict and tension due to their unfulfilled desire for care and security. However, this is usually not accompanied by a significant amount of suffering or impairments.

In individuals with a moderate level of structural integration, who tend to overregulate impulses and affects related to the conflict between In need of care and self-sufficiency, the relationship structure is characterized by an either/or (excessive need to be taken care vs. pseudo-self-sufficiency) in the sense of a neurotic conflict. This repetitive-dysfunctional neurotic pattern is usually accompanied by significant distress and symptomatic impairments.

Those with a lower level of structural integration, in whom the In Need of Care vs. Self-Sufficiency issue manifests itself as a conflict schema with a tendency toward under-regulation, are often burdened by abrupt shifts between excessive needs for care and impulses of (pseudo-)self-sufficiency impulses. It can also take the form of fixation in the passive or active modes, such as a chronically parasitic lifestyle (passive mode) or chronic excessive self-exploitation (active mode). This conflict schema can be associated with either significant or entirely absent distress.

In individuals with a disintegrated structural level, even more extreme compensatory mechanisms are possible, sometimes involving distortions of reality (see Section 4.4).

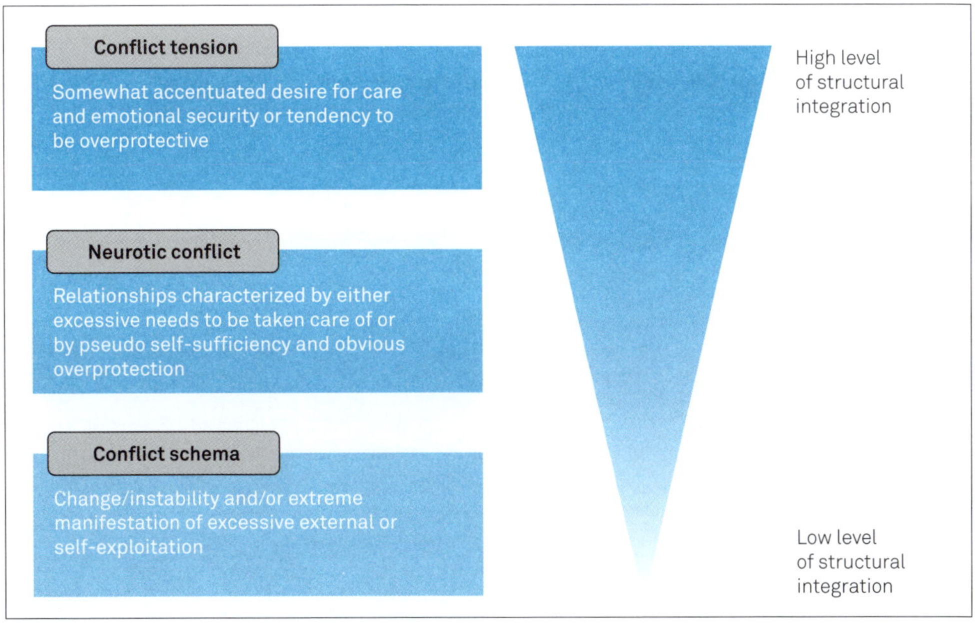

Figure 11. In Need of Care vs. Self-Sufficiency and the three levels of structural integration. The three levels: Conflict tension (upper pole, high level of structural integration), neurotic conflict (moderate level of structural integration) and conflict schema (lower pole, rather low level of structural integration).

Table 28. Characteristics of C3 on various structural processing levels

Characteristics of C3 at different levels of structural integration	
C3: Characteristics of conflict tension	
(A) Conflict tension in passive mode The person concerned tends to attach others more closely to themselves to gain emotional care and security. If the wishes for care are not fulfilled or in case of separation from the care-providing object, this may result in mild disappointment at the loss of affection or even mild annoyance at being "left hanging," which is usually quickly overcome. The person can ensure that his or her social environment provides a sufficient sense of care and security. Interpersonally, the person concerned tends to be perceived as demanding, which can lead to the other person distancing themselves or setting themselves apart ("I am no longer responsible for you"). In principle, flexible regulation of the conflict tension is still possible without clinically significant distress.	**(A) Conflict tension in active mode** The person concerned tends to be particularly caring towards others, putting their own needs aside. If the options for pseudo-self-sufficiency in meeting care needs are limited, slight disappointment and annoyance at the "ingratitude" of others may result, which can usually be quickly overcome. The person succeeds in realizing his or her pseudo-self-sufficient wishes and implementing his or her somewhat overprotective tendencies. In principle, flexible regulation of the conflict tension is still possible without clinically significant distress.
C3: Characteristics of the neurotic conflict	
(B) Neurotic conflict in passive mode The person concerned seeks emotional care and security. They form highly dependent, clinging or demanding relationships. Alternatively, contact appears. This results in temporary and sometimes downright "parasitic" relationships (e.g., "Hotel Mum" in young adults). Rejection of caregiving efforts can result in strong disappointment, sadness and depression as well as fears about the loss of emotional care and affection: all these impress as leading affects. Separation is experienced as a threatening loss of an urgently needed care station and of the warmth of a nest. Secondarily, envy and anger ("But the others get more!") can occur. As a reaction to this behavioral pattern, the examiner initially experiences concern in the countertransference, but this quickly gives way to powerlessness and anger.	**(B) Neurotic conflict in active mode** The person seeks to provide emotional care and security to others, almost to the exclusion of their own care needs. This leads to the formation of relationships in the sense of an "altruistic" basic attitude, i.e., an all-encompassing care for others that may even go as far as sacrifice (e.g., care parentification). At the same time, there is a pronounced modesty and undemanding attitude so as not to "be a burden" to anyone. The conscious experience is dominated by concern for others with a noticeable underlying sadness and longing for care. Secondary anger about the ingratitude of others ("I do so much and get nothing in return!") is also common, often combined with feelings of guilt as soon as one's own neediness becomes apparent. If the possibilities to use pseudo-self-sufficient strategies are restricted, the leading affects can be anger, self-doubt and/or fear of failure and sadness or even depression. In the countertransference, this pattern of behavior ("always doing everything for the other person") evokes an experience of detachment or even being "annoyed," anger, and impulses to withdraw.

Table 28. Characteristics of C3 on various structural processing levels *(continued)*

Characteristics of C3 at different levels of structural integration	
C3: Characteristics of the conflict schema	
Conflict schemas at a rather low level of structural integration are generally characterized by pronounced instability and even fluctuation depending on the relevant situation and experience, so that the dysfunctional experience or behavior can appear both exaggerated and diffuse and then only passingly recognizable. However, rigid fixations in passive or active mode can also be found.	
(C) Conflict schema in passive mode The person concerned is at the mercy of an excessive desire, driven by their own needs, to receive care and emotional security from others. Relationships tend to be impulsively accentuated and are strongly characterized by the manipulative, destructive and exploitative plundering of others. Relationships are characterized by extreme neediness, an almost insatiable "greed" or an almost existential "hunger for contact": "You have to take care of me!" If the desire for care is not fully met or even rejected, the fragile regulatory mechanisms can quickly break down, possibly leading to severe depression or even switching to active mode ("I don't need anything or anyone!"). In the countertransference, feelings of being taken advantage of arise quickly. There is anger and a clear impulse to distance oneself.	**(C) Conflict pattern in active mode** Individuals are at the mercy of the dominant destructive, self-exploitative impulses to be overly caring for others. Relationships are rather impulsively accentuated, and others become obliged to be grateful: "You have to let me take care of you and be grateful!" If the possibilities to manage care needs in a pseudo-autonomous way are limited, the fragile regulatory mechanisms can quickly break down possibly leading to severe depression, a switch to passive mode or even to the termination of the care relationship or even to complete neglect of the other person. The leading affects can be severe disappointment and depression, feelings of meaninglessness and a tendency to withdraw because of the rejected affection. In the countertransference, impulses of dissociation and even massive anger can arise very quickly in response to the imposed overprotectiveness.
For people with a disintegrated structural level, even more extreme compensatory mechanisms are possible, sometimes accompanied by distortions of reality (see Section 4.4).	

Differential Diagnosis of the In Need of Care vs. Self-Sufficiency Conflict Dynamic

The conflict between In need of care and Self-sufficiency must be distinguished from the Dependency vs. Individuation Conflict. Since both motivational systems exist in development from the very beginning and overlap in many ways, it can sometimes be difficult to draw a distinction. While the Dependency vs. Individuation Conflict is about an existential ontological dependence *on* the relationship, the passive mode of the In Need of Care vs. Self-Sufficiency Conflict involves a dependency *in* the relationship, in which the desire for care and security, or the way in which it is processed, is not the basis of the bond and the relationship, but merely a specific feature of it. In one case, it is about the mere availability of an object (C1), while in the other, it is a matter of an object providing care and security (C3).

The In Need of Care vs. Self-Sufficiency topic is related to *self-esteem* issues. Unfulfilled expectations of care or rejected altruistic caregiving efforts can be experienced as insults and be associated with painful disappointments and enduring self-doubt. In the active mode of the In Need of Care vs. Self-Sufficiency Conflict, pseudo-self-sufficient behavior functions as altruistic surrender, serving as a defense against the desire for care and security rather than as a display of one's own significance to stabilize self-esteem, although a certain appreciative recognition is associated with having become indispensable to others. In the passive mode of the In Need of Care vs. Self-Sufficiency Conflict, disappointments, injuries, and self-doubt are linked to experiences of poor care rather than to fundamental appreciation of the individual by others.

Differentiation from the *Guilt Conflict:* Since the altruism-caregiving motivational system (nurturing) unfolds in close interaction with superego development, the In Need of Care vs. Self-Sufficiency Conflict must also be differentiated from guilt-related issues. In the passive mode of the In Need of Care vs. Self-Sufficiency Conflict, secondary guilt feelings may arise when the imbalance and exploitative nature of one's behavior become apparent to the individual. In the active mode, the activation of emotional needs that are fiercely defended against can mobilize intense guilt feelings (as well as self-doubt). These can lead to self-reproach and acts of reparation, sometimes to the point of excessive commitment to others. Atonement for conscious or unconscious guilt and/or self-tormenting, masochistic tendencies must be distinguished.

Case Vignettes

In Need of Care vs. Self-Sufficiency (Passive Mode)

The Judicial Officer: Mr. K. (36 years old) came for treatment due to a year of increasing depression. His depressive feelings of meaninglessness had intensified to the point of suicidal thoughts. Fears (of losing his parents) had existed since childhood. He first experienced clinical symptoms of depression ten years ago when his first wife left him for a new partner. He subsequently underwent three years of psychotherapy. During this time, he remarried, and shortly afterward, their only daughter was born. Since her birth, Mr. K. has had the feeling he is no longer noticed. He attributes his current increase in symptoms to his daughter's growing independence ("She doesn't need me anymore") and to a recent promotion as a judicial officer. With this promotion he has left other colleagues behind and may have to expect a transfer to another place of residence. In interaction, Mr. K. appears dull and unattractive, somewhat unkempt. He quickly clings to the therapist, constantly demanding relief from his "bad" depression: "Why don't you do something for me?!" Affectively, he is dominated by his constant fear that others will leave him, that he may lose others, and that his feelings of depression will increase. He experiences himself dependent on the love and support of others, although he always tries to give something to others. Mr. K. appears very inhibited in expressing his own feelings and needs.

Mr. K. grew up in a small town; his father tried to start his own business and failed. Since then, his mother has had the task of supporting the family of three. Mr. K had a close bond with his mother, idealizing her but seeing her as an unattainable provider. His father was often away as a traveling salesman, strengthening the mother-son relationship. He met his first wife during his apprenticeship. She resembled his mother, and they faced sexual issues in their marriage which led to her having an affair. He later met his second wife, also described as supportive and caring at work. Since their daughter's birth, sexuality has been minimal. Mr. K is professionally steady with good relationships but felt insecure about a recent promotion. Socially, he has few contacts and frequent doctor visits due to his symptoms.

Comment: This is a patient who is fundamentally capable of having a relationship, the experience and organization of which is determined by the in need of care and security issue. Oedipal conflict aspects are also present (C6 passive). Structural functions do not appear significantly impaired.

In Need of Care vs. Self-Sufficiency (Active Mode)

The Father's Hands: Mrs. M. (63 years old) was admitted to inpatient therapy for the second time due to a depressive episode, severe forgetfulness, and multiple joint pains after a legal dispute with her older sister, who had never been in charge of her parents' care, about the parental inheritance. In addition to her obligations as an active, supportive teacher and caring grandmother, as well as her social commitment, she had cared for her physically disabled and demented parents "day and night" at her home for nearly ten years. When a nursing home became unavoidable, she blamed herself for having failed and visited her parents almost daily out of "a sense of duty" and against her impulses. When these parents died in quick succession a few weeks before her admission, she was plagued by severe feelings of guilt because of the relief she felt at the end of the exhausting care she had provided.

She always worked behind the scenes to support her career-oriented husband. She was "always fully there" for her children. For years, she tried to ignore her increasing physical ailments, forcing herself to carry out her daily duties until she could no longer. Even with her leg in a case, she took care of her family. However, she now feels more and more physically and emotionally overwhelmed, when it comes to looking after her two small grandchildren. During her marriage, she felt that she was not "seen" or "valued" enough by her husband who was absorbed in his job. Emotionally and sexually neglected, she entered an affair out of frustration and resentment but returned to her husband after he courted her again.

In conversation, Mrs. M. minimized her sadness, exhaustion, and fear of becoming demented and helpless like her parents. She described herself as reserved, someone who is always there for others and has learned not to need anyone, to handle everything on her own, to fight and endure. Biographically, it emerged that her father was warm-hearted but very strict and achievement oriented. He had lost both hands in the war, a topic never discussed in the family. Instead of spending time with school friends, she did physically demanding work around the house and garden for her multiply disabled father. Proudly, she remarked, "I was my father's hands, his eyes, and his ears." Her idealized father, who never let his physical limitations hold him back, was her great role model. She saw herself as the "caretaker" of the family in partnership with him. She observed her mother's frequent complaints and crying as attempts to seek assistance from others. Her mother's unpredictable and demanding behavior caused her concern. When recounting her longstanding conflicts with her sister, who had always aligned with the mother, she revealed envious and longing desires for security. The patient displayed qualities of self-sacrifice and resilience yet exhibited disappointment due to the lack of acknowledgement for her efforts. During the interview, the examiner did not experience any immediate inclination to help.

Comment: This is a patient who is fundamentally capable of relationships. Behind her pseudo-autonomous facade lies a suppressed, underlying yearning for emotional support and security. There are also indications of self-esteem, guilt, and oedipal conflict components (C4 passive, C5 passive, C6 mixed, primarily passive). Structural functions do not appear significantly impaired.

4.3.6 C4 Self-Worth Conflict (Self-Worth vs. Object-Worth)

The *central motive* is the desire for recognition and appreciation. Everyone aims to develop and maintain self-esteem, which depends on the gap between one's ideal self ("how I want to be") and actual self ("how I am"). A small gap between them is essential for psychological well-being.

Drawing from Greek mythology (Narcissus falls in love with his own image and devalues others), Freud introduced "primary" narcissism into libido theory. Alfred Adler (Adler, 1907/1917) departed from libido theory and saw the experience of inferiority ("organ inferiority") and its physical and psychological processing as essential. Ego and self-psychology subsequently identified the pursuit of self-worth (and avoidance of worthlessness) as the motivation for "a tension-free ego state" associated with well-being (Sandler & Joffe, 1969). Self-psychology (Kohut, 1971) described narcissistic pathology as a motivational neurotic phenomenon, and object psychology (Kernberg, 1975) sees self-object-worth as a structural regulation problem. The pursuit of self-worth enhancement or protection can be found in almost all motivational approaches as a basic human motivational system (for an overview see Benecke & Brauner, 2017).

With successful development, there is an inner certainty about one's own "value" as a person, so the question of "who is worth how much" does not arise, nor is there a need to devalue others. There is an intrinsic balance and naturalness in assigning value to oneself and others, as well as in being able to question oneself and others. The experience of self-worth experiences is dependent on adequate narcissistic supply from significant others. Too much or too little of this supply impairs the internalization of a lasting sense of self-worth that is independent of external validation (see OPD-CA-2 Task Force, 2017).

If this *development fails*, there is an existential insecurity regarding one's worth, up to feelings of inferiority, combined with significant and easily triggered shame and vulnerability. This results in the "value" question or attempts to manage it dominating the psyche in the form of active or passive coping modes. Due to relevant biographical experiences, efforts to secure self-worth in the past or currently have either been excessively intense or insufficient/failed. This manifests in relationships that are dysfunctional in their role of regulating the self-worth issue (active-passive). Conflicts arise between self-value and object-worth, affecting one's ability to question and assign worth. Active coping devalues others while elevating self-worth. Passive coping emphasizes others' worth and highlights personal inferiority.

The motivational system of Self- vs. Object-Worth is influenced by societal trends promoting consistent improvement in all aspects of life, as propagated through media. Repetitive patterns of conflict experiences and behaviors can lead to symptoms in triggering situations and, when significant, may contribute to the development of conflicted personalities, including personality disorders such as narcissistic or avoidant personality disorder, according to DSM-5 criteria.

Key Characteristics of the Neurotic Conflict Self-Worth vs. Object-Worth

1. Repetitive Motivational Pattern: Relationships are used to manage self-worth issues. In active mode, the worth of others is diminished while one's own worth is increased, or people are sought who admire them to stabilize self-worth. In passive mode, the worth of others increases while that of the individual decreases.
2. Core and Leading Affect: The core affect that must be defended against is the intolerable subjective feeling of inferiority, an intense shame/embarrassment. Leading affects include fear of shame, grandiosity, and narcissistic rage if self-worth is questioned/threatened (humiliation) or feelings of inferiority/shame when comparing oneself with others. Narcissistic triumph may be hidden within these feelings ("I'm the biggest loser of all") or avoidance of further shame ("If I make myself small, no one else can"). These leading affects can be conscious, suppressed, or warded off.
3. Trigger Situations: Repeated experiences of either uplifting or devaluing oneself and others are common. Trigger situations that lead to conflict and dysfunctional coping can include imagined or actual experiences of fail-

ure, inadequacy, self-worth humiliation, or temptation where success and failure are closely linked, i.e., success seems possible but is also accompanied by fear of failure.

4. Transference and Countertransference Dynamics: In passive mode, idealizing admiration for others and the therapist can appear in transference, with underlying devaluation sensed, causing countertransference feelings like embarrassment or condescension. In active mode, the therapist's competence may be questioned or devalued, leading to countertransference feelings of humiliation, shame, and defensiveness, possibly followed by anger and the urge to devalue the patient.

General Description of the Coping Modes of C4

Passive Mode

In the passive mode, feelings of inferiority are sometimes outwardly expressed. There is a belief in one's own inability or unattractiveness, which may lead to massive shame. This shame can be managed by abandoning attempts to meet personal ideals and development goals. Individuals may then settle into their existence as a less significant specimen and find some satisfaction in this state. Self-devaluation (e.g., feeling like a perpetual loser) serves as a defense against further shame, failure, and rejection.

In the idealizing admiration of others that is often shown, subtle devaluations are often found (even if this involves showing the other person's susceptibility to the supposed admiration). In narcissistically well-regulated individuals, both self-deprecating and admiring behavior tends to cause embarrassment.

Active Mode

In active mode, the person's forced self-assurance and devaluation of others as an attempt to cope with their own feelings of inferiority and inner shame are impressive. The person may initially seem self-confident, but their insecurity soon shows ("pseudo-self-confidence"). Their fragile self-esteem becomes clear through easily offended behavior, irritability, or 'narcissistic' anger. All actions aim to compensate for this fragility, seeking recognition or admiration. If denied, it triggers anger and devaluation. Others are often devalued to stabilize self-esteem, leading to frequent interpersonal conflicts, mutual offense, and withdrawal behavior.

Manifestations of the Self-Worth vs. Object-Worth Conflict at Different Levels of Structural Integration

The theme of self-worth manifests across different structural levels on a continuum with gradual transitions: from subclinical conflict tension (a high, personality-shaping subjective significance of recognition and appreciation, which is not yet dysfunctional) through neurotic conflicts (repetitive dysfunctional interpersonal and intrapsychic patterns where life and relationships are shaped by the need to manage the self-worth conflict, as described above) to conflict schemas at lower levels of structural integration, where self-worth regulation fluctuates between grandiosity and severe self- and other-devaluation, often oscillating rapidly between these poles.

The desire for recognition and appreciation (as well as the ability to value others) is inherent to every individual. Cultural and individual socialization has led to corresponding personal solutions and internal patterns that recurrently cause conflict tensions (e.g., everyday humiliations affect self-worth), which can largely be handled adaptively.

In the neurotic conflict, biographical experiences have led to unsuitable or one-sided "either-or solutions" (dysfunctional) (e.g., active excessive compensation, active mode of conflict processing). In situations where the self-

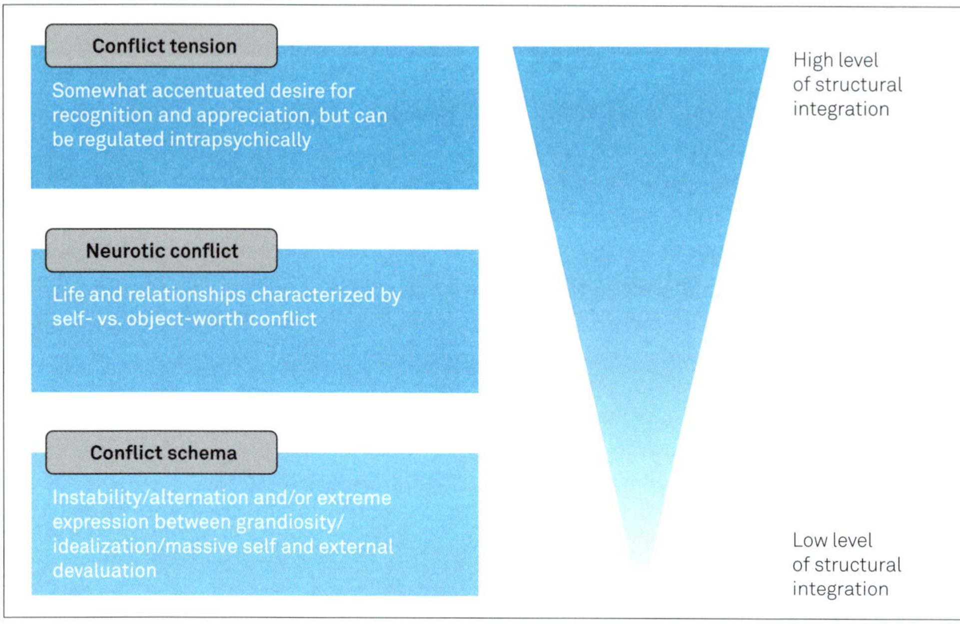

Figure 12. Self-Worth vs. Object-Worth and the three levels of structural integration. The three levels: Conflict tension (upper pole, high level of structural integration), neurotic conflict (moderate level of structural integration) and conflict schema (low level of structural integration).

worth theme is triggered, this leads to repetitive, similar coping patterns with corresponding affects (e.g., narcissistic rage, devaluation of others).

For individuals with lower structural integration, the self-worth system cannot be stably regulated due to issues with self-regulation and realistic self- and object perception. The conflict schema of Self- vs. Object-Worth may abruptly shift between grandiosity and devaluation of others or severe self-devaluation and idealization of others, often in response to minimal triggers or challenges (Figure 12; Table 29). There may also be rigid fixations in either the passive or active mode, such as in severe narcissistic personality disorder (active mode) or chronic severe depressive disorder (passive mode).

For individuals with disintegrated structural levels, even more extreme compensation mechanisms, sometimes involving reality distortion, are possible (see Section 4.4).

Differential Diagnosis of Self-Esteem Conflict Dynamics in Relation to All Other Conflicts

Significant self-esteem conflicts of a person clearly outweigh those narcissistic problems that are contained in other conflict levels. Therefore, what is meant here is not the fundamental grievance or self-esteem stabilization through the involvement of the narcissistic motivation system (narcissistic "tinting") in the occurrence of every other conflict.

Case Vignettes

Neurotic Conflict Self-Worth vs. Object-Worth (Passive Mode)

The Fading One: The 26-year-old patient, who appears pale, shy, and extremely emaciated, speaks in a halting, soft voice and initially avoids eye

Table 29. Characteristics of C4 on various structural integration levels

Characteristics of C4 at different levels of structural integration	
C4: Characteristics of conflict tension	
(A) Conflict tension in passive mode There is an increased need for recognition and appreciation, alongside a tendency to frequently question one's self-worth. Individuals may compare themselves unfavorably with others, experience shame, or admire others. However, these feelings typically do not result in significant or lasting declines in self-esteem that would be considered clinically relevant.	**(A) Conflict tension in active mode** There is a need for recognition and appreciation, often leading to self-exaggeration and slight questioning of others' value or abilities. However, this usually does not result in significant interpersonal problems.
C4: Characteristics of the neurotic conflict	
(B) Neurotic conflict in passive mode When the passive mode predominates, the person experiences a low level of self-esteem or a critical collapse in self-esteem. Narcissistic demands tend to be withdrawn, and the weaknesses and insignificance of one's own person are emphasized. However, accusations are made openly or covertly against others, especially doctors and public institutions. The mode can also be conveyed as a chronic attitude of defense, in which the manifest self-deprecation serves to unconsciously uplift the self. In transference, idealizing admiration for the examiner may cause noticeable embarrassment, sometimes leading to a sense of devaluation. In countertransference, feelings of wanting to support or belittle can emerge.	**(B) Neurotic conflict in active mode** In the predominance of the active mode, a forced self-confidence towards others is impressive as an attempt to overcome a feared or real self-esteem crisis and underlying feelings of inferiority. At first glance, people may appear self-confident, but the underlying insecurity is soon surmised ("pseudo-self-confidence"). Violent affects of irritation and anger ("narcissistic rage") are easily triggered when the positive narcissistic self-image is questioned and the (unconscious) inferiority and shame must be fended off. In the transference or interaction, the analysand is often questioned, even to the point of open devaluation. In the countertransference, feelings of offence and impulses of justification can arise due to the devaluation by the other person, possibly followed by anger and devaluing impulses towards the other person.
C4: Characteristics of the conflict schema	
The design of conflicts at a low structural level is typically marked by instability and fluctuation, depending on the situation and experience. Dysfunctional experiences or behaviors may appear both exaggerated and diffuse and are only passively recognizable, not as a consistently determining and stable theme over time. Different motivational systems can be alternately addressed, causing a conflict theme to fluctuate between active and passive coping attempts. However, there can also be rigid fixations in either passive or active mode behavior.	
(C) Conflict schema in passive mode Massive slumps in self-esteem, inappropriate to the situation/reality, occur even on minor real or imagined occasions and lead to devastating self-criticism and generalized feelings of inferiority. Reactions that seem unduly self-destructive given the context, or in instances where the context is not apparent to others, can lead to feelings of alienation, caution, or devaluation from those impacted.	**(C) Conflict schema in active mode** The person has fantasies of grandeur without sufficient realistic reference. Even small real or fantasized occasions can lead to pronounced narcissistic rage, even to the point of destructiveness, and massive destructive devaluations of the other person, which appear strange, inappropriate to the occasion and incomprehensible to the other person. This can trigger alienation, caution and, if necessary, your own narcissistic anger and devaluation of the other person.
For people with a disintegrated structural level, even more extreme compensation mechanisms are possible, sometimes involving a reinterpretation of reality (see Section 4.4).	

contact with the examiner. She reports that her entire life revolves around food. Due to restrictive eating behaviors, she currently weighs only 39 kg at a height of 1.65 m (BMI of 14.3 kg/m^2). Her lowest weight was 34 kg. However, she still perceives herself as fat and "flabby." She eats very little and avoids high-calorie foods. During the day, she obsessively calculates the calories of any potential food intake, which consumes much of her time and leads to social withdrawal. She denies any compensatory behaviors such as vomiting, laxative use, or excessive exercise.

She has been struggling with an eating disorder for approximately 12 years, though initially she didn't recognize it as an illness. Back then, all the girls in her class started losing weight, and at 58 kg, she felt distinctly overweight. She lost more weight than the others and was admired and envied for it. Eating less became the only thing she could do better than others, and she was proud of her self-control.

She explains that she has felt depressed and unloved since childhood, viewing herself as ugly and stupid. She has an older sister, two years her senior, who is described as very pretty, lively, and successful in school. She was constantly compared to her sister by her grandparents, parents, and teachers. No matter how hard she tried, her sister was always better. Academic performance and the family's public image were very important to her parents. Her mother placed great emphasis on appearance, grooming, and fashionable attire for herself and her daughters. Her weight loss became a major issue for her parents, as they were frequently approached by others about her visible problems, leading to many family conflicts. Her parents took her to a child and adolescent psychiatrist, but she found him uninterested, and nothing changed. Her parents even threatened to have her admitted to a psychiatric hospital, though they never followed through, likely to avoid the embarrassment of having a daughter in a psychiatric institution.

She recalls that she never felt she could meet her parents' expectations, regardless of her efforts. Although her written work in school was good, she always received poor marks for oral participation because she was too afraid to speak up. She had anxiety before tests and was convinced she would fail, though that never happened. She graduated high school with a 3.3 GPA which surprised her.

Despite her teachers' college recommendation, she lacked confidence and chose to apprentice as a bank clerk. She excelled, ranking among the best. Motivated by this, she recently applied for a business administration program and was accepted. This motivated her to recover to increase her chances of succeeding in her studies. However, she already fears failing and worries about making friends at university, feeling uninteresting. She avoids the spotlight and tends to withdraw. She frequently compares herself to others and finds herself inadequate each time.

She has been romantically interested in others multiple times but has never dared to show her interest. Men typically overlook her and choose more attractive and lively women. At 22, she was briefly in her first relationship, which ended after a month when her boyfriend left her for someone else. This outcome didn't surprise her, as she had already questioned what he saw in her.

When the examiner notes that the initial interview is nearing its end after 45 minutes, the patient apologizes for taking up so much time and thanks the examiner, suggesting they probably have better things to do. She accepts the suggestion of inpatient treatment at a specialized eating disorder facility.

Neurotic Conflict Self-Worth vs. Object-Worth (Active Mode)

The Financial Adviser: Mr. D. (52 years old) is referred by his cardiologist, as no organic causes were found for the patient's recurrent heart palpitations, and psychological factors were suspected. When greeted in the waiting room, the patient takes a surprisingly long time to shift his gaze from the magazine he is reading to the examiner, giving the scene an air of an audience. On the way to the examination room, the patient cannot hide his disappointment at the young age of the examiner, stating he had expected to be examined by the chief physician. At the beginning of the conversation, he questions the examiner about the planned procedure and the examiner's qualifications in a critical tone. He goes on to report that he has been feeling down, lacking motivation and energy, and unable to engage in his usual activities. He describes repeated episodes of sudden heart palpitations, sweating, and shortness of breath, coupled with the fear of dying from a heart attack. He doesn't recognize himself this way, having previously always been healthy and taken special care of his fitness.

He explains that he couldn't afford to be ill and had been under significant stress as a self-employed financial advisor. His clients constantly demanded his attention. In this line of work, only those who deliver one hundred percent performance can survive. "When you're juggling other people's millions, you can't afford mistakes." Only upon further questioning about his current professional situation does the patient reveal that he recently experienced bankruptcy shortly before his symptoms began. He lost not only his clients' money but also his private assets in risky financial dealings without safeguards. With difficulty and a sense of shame that appears detached, his dire financial situation with substantial debts and ongoing legal proceedings becomes evident. The patient downplays his problems, claiming he sees no major difficulty in getting out of this "mess:" "After all, Donald Trump managed it too."

Despite his issues, he acknowledges a silver lining: he now realizes what he and his family have gone through because of his work obsession. He neglected them, worked nonstop, and failed to notice how important his family was to him. Without his wife's support, he wouldn't have made it through the past few weeks. He finally recognizes what a wonderful woman she is. She's not only very attractive and the object of every man's desire but also fully supportive of him. She is his "trophy."

Currently, since he is "a bit short on cash," he has realized how little he needs to be happy. He used to value big, flashy cars; now, he drives a used compact car gifted by his brother. It serves its purpose. Luxuries, which used to be essential, are no longer necessary. He finds pleasure in the simple things in life, like flowers along the path.

A detailed biographical history cannot be gathered in the first session, as the patient takes up a lot of time with his narrative. The patient declines a follow-up session to continue diagnostics, stating he can handle his "little problems" himself. With a playful smile, he remarks as he leaves that the examiner has probably learned a lot from his case, but unfortunately, he cannot stay as a practice object. The examiner will have to find another "victim."

4.3.7 C5 Guilt Conflict (Prosocial Conscience vs. Self-Centered Motives)

The *central motivation can be described as follows:* Social cooperation and responsibility (prosocial motivation) are essential behavioral patterns in humans and have a universal foundation. This intrinsic motivation for prosociality (conscience, social norms) supports cooperation and group cohesion: sharing of essential resources, providing instrumental support, emotional assistance, and comfort (Warneken & Tomasello, 2009). The prosocial motivational system leads to shared social well-being and manifests as a positive feeling, even without external rewards. Even more deeply ingrained than prosocial behavior is, across species, self-centered interest, which can reach extreme (greedy) selfishness. Self-centered motives also provide a subjective sense of well-being. Both motivational domains are shaped by human socio-moral development. Cultural and psychosocial frameworks, such as the encouragement of prosocial activities or the condemnation of "selfishness," are an integral part of the internalized conscience (superego, Freud 1940). Social emotions lead to adaptive behavior. Shame and guilt as socio-moral emotions regulate these prosocial motives. Guilt feelings encourage restitution for harm caused (Tangney & Dearing, 2002), and expressions of guilt soothe victims or those harmed.

The feeling of guilt following a harmful action is observable in children as young as two years old (Vaish, 2017). By 30 months, children possess the social-cognitive prerequisites to experience shame and guilt (Barrett, 2005). Initial expressions include fair sharing ("social fairness") and comfort, later evolving in preschool age to flexible prosocial behaviors, such as extended support for others or punishing non-prosocial (even anti-social) intentions (sense of justice). Internalization of (mostly parental and socio-cultural) rules and prohibitions occur with schooling and primarily serves loyalty to parents, to secure this relationship (OPD-CA-2 Task Force, 2017).

When *successfully integrated*, individuals balance prosocial and self-centered motives with internalized values and beliefs (conscience, superego) (Hepach & Warneken, 2018). This balance leads to a fundamental sense of well-being: one can benefit oneself and others (in line with cultural and social norms). The motivational balance shifts based on socio-cultural norms and their internalization. Guilt regulates prosocial conscience; children feel guilty when they cause harm, motivating them to repair the damage and restore damaged relationships (Vaish, 2017). Guilt typically arises when one has truly harmed or compromised another's needs or rights. The degree of internalized norms and resulting guilt is strongly influenced by social and cultural context.

Self-centered actions pursued solely for personal gain ("egoism") are usually accompanied by guilt. Sociocultural conditioning determines whether guilt accompanies selfish actions (e.g., exploiting the environment purely for personal gain).

If this *development fails,* excessive prosocial conscience and tendencies (hypersociality in all aspects of life) with guilt feelings or extreme self-interest and aggressive egoism without guilt feelings may arise. Conflicts stem from the struggle to balance personal interests with prosocial behavior in relationships, as shaped by socio-cultural conscience (socialized guilt). This is not about the biological imperative to care for close ones but about social sharing and conscience. Balancing personal interests with those of the social group is essential. Guilt, when prosocial tendencies are disregarded, may be extreme or repressed and displaced. Guilt is often projected onto others, and the conflict frequently centers on "blaming oneself vs. blaming others." Thus, a fixation can occur, leading to either habitual guilt denial or automatic self-incrimination or guilt acceptance. Excessive prosocial acts can also be a psychodynamic reaction against selfish-aggressive and anti-social tendencies.

Key Characteristics of the Neurotic Conflict Guilt

1. Repetitive Dysfunctional Motivational Pattern: Relationships are dysfunctionally regulated by prosocial vs. egoistic tendencies. In the active mode, individuals appear "coldly" willing to pursue selfish benefits and "without regard for guilt or responsibility" pursue personal gain, even exploiting others and the environment without concern or guilt. Unconscious suppression and denial of guilt are common, and guilt is projected onto others. In the passive mode, individuals display an overly compliant and selfless attitude (hypersociality). These individuals overly accept guilt (penance and atonement), always excuse others, and tend toward self-blame. Self-interest triggers guilt, which is then transformed into hypersociality.
2. Core and Lead Affects: The core affect is subjectively intolerable guilt, which is sup-

pressed in the active mode, or selfish aggression/aggressive (moralistic) self-accusations in the passive mode. In the passive mode, lead affects include (self-)blame, fear of punishment, and sadness. The fear of punishment is unconsciously fueled by forbidden selfish impulses. In the active mode, guilt projection, anger (when blamed), and selfish greed are prominent.

3. Triggering Situations: Biographically, recurring situations of temptation and deprivation related to prosocial and egoistic tendencies are expected, with strong socio-cultural influences (e.g., religious socialization vs. exploitative or "rising star" mentality). Trigger situations for psychological symptoms arise when the suppressed side is activated, and the usual defense fails. In the passive mode, this might also include situations that activate aggressive-egoistic tendencies to the point where they can no longer be suppressed, resulting in heightened feelings of guilt. In active mode, situations in which egoistic tendencies fail can lead to increased exploitative behavior (up to disorder levels), or instances in which repressed guilt "seeps through."
4. Transference and Countertransference Dynamics: In the passive mode, prosocial, self-blaming relationships (including toward the clinician) become evident, although underlying egoistic guilt-avoidant tendencies may be present. In countertransference, compassion, overcautiousness, and efforts to counter the patient's self-blame often emerge, sometimes mixed with aggressive impulses. In the active mode (guilt avoidance), responsibility (guilt) is quickly projected onto others (including the clinician), with predominantly aggressive-cynical defensiveness and justification. Countertransference may include impulses to judge and confront the person quickly or wish them illness (punishment).

General Description of the Coping Modes of C5

Passive Mode

In the passive mode, feelings of guilt are experienced, the guilt is compensated for by self-generated or often only expected punishment and guilt. People tend to reproach themselves because they feel they have done too little or failed in their dealings with their group, institutions or society (church, God, etc.). Subtly perceptible egoistic tendencies are warded off and transformed into hypersociality, e.g., by means of reaction formation. Moralistic aggression is more accessible to experience and is used towards people who do not share the same ideas, laws and rules, but "acting it out" usually also directly triggers feelings of guilt.

Active Mode

In active mode, feelings of guilt are warded off, e.g., denied or projected onto other people. Egoistic tendencies determine behavior. Prosocial tendencies are warded off to be able to pursue one's own benefit and advantage to the point of boundless self-interest "regardless of guilt and responsibility."

The selfish, irresponsible behavior triggers rejection in the other person.

Manifestations of the Conflict Guilt at Different Levels of Structural Integration

The theme of prosocial vs. egoistic tendencies manifests across different structural levels in a continuum with fluid transitions (Figure 13; Table 30).

Conflict tension describes a flexible and adaptive expression of the desire for prosocial vs. egoistic tendencies, with a personal emphasis on one pole but without reaching a dysfunctional extent. Cultural and individual socialization leads to specific personal solutions and internal patterns, which can repeatedly cause conflict tensions (e.g., everyday guilt feelings or temptations toward egoistic tendencies). However, these tensions are largely handled adaptively ("both and" paradigm).

Within neurotic conflicts, repetitive interpersonal/intrapersonal patterns become apparent. Life and relationships are characterized by prosocial or egoistic-aggressive actions with either the acceptance or rejection of guilt (either-or). These patterns are typically quite stable.

With lower-integrated structures or conflict schemas, either overwhelming destructive (self-) blame or an inability to feel guilt (often paired with aggressive egoism) predominates. There is an instability/oscillation and/or extreme expressions of egoistic or prosocial tendencies.

For individuals with a disintegrated structural level, even more extreme compensation mechanisms are possible, sometimes accompanied by distortions of reality (see Section 4.4).

Differential Diagnosis of Conflict Dynamics Between Guilt and Other Conflicts

Self-interest and ego-centeredness must be distinguished from the experience of self-worth, which is involved in all conflicts. In some cultures, in addition to feelings of guilt, prosocial vs. egoistic tendencies are also regulated by feelings of shame to share the common laws and rules or to feel ashamed when this is violated. In our culture, these feelings of shame essentially occur in the "C4 self-esteem experience."

Furthermore, it is important to differentiate between the guilt conflict and "C3 In Need of Care vs. Self-Sufficiency," which is concerned with emotional care and security as a basic theme of human existence, but not with egois-

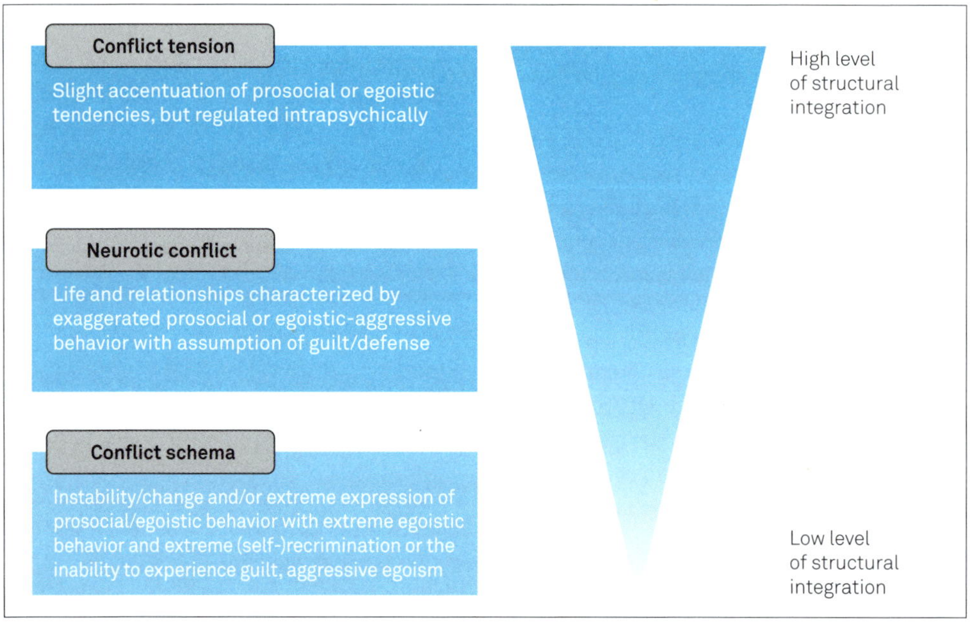

Figure 13. Guilt and the three levels of structural integration. The three levels of structural integration: Conflict tension (upper pole, high level of structural integration), neurotic conflict (rather moderate level of structural integration) and conflict schema (rather low level of structural integration).

Table 30. Characteristics of C5 on various structural integration levels

Characteristics of C5 at different levels of structural integration	
C5: Characteristics of conflict tension	
(A) Conflict tension in passive mode In the balance between prosocial vs. egoistic tendencies, the desire for prosocial behavior predominates. This tendency can lead to a defense against egoistic motives. Feelings of guilt are easily triggered and activate reparation. As a rule, however, there are no critical or persistent and clinically relevant episodes. In critical situations, however, guilt can certainly take on the character of suffering.	**(A) Conflict tension in active mode** There is a predominance of self-centered self-interest with a tendency to blame others for being free from remorse. Egoistic tendencies are easily activated but can also be withdrawn again depending on the situation, so that this does not usually lead to greater restrictions and interpersonal problems.
C5: Characteristics of the neurotic conflict	
(B) Neurotic conflict in passive mode In the neurotic passive mode, the relationship is characterized by strong prosocial behavior with a predominance of assumption of guilt and defense against egoistic motives. Self-interest triggers feelings of guilt or is transformed into reactive prosociality. These people take on guilt in an exaggerated manner. The interactions are characterized by self-blame. In the countertransference, compassion can arise and the desire to work against the patient's self-blame. If this fails, punitive-aggressive impulses can sometimes be felt.	**(B) Neurotic conflict in active mode** When the active mode predominates, the relationship is characterized by egoistic-aggressive behavior, with a defense against prosocial motives and a predominant defense against guilt (either – or). These people pursue their personal advantages selfishly and, if necessary, aggressively ("regardless of guilt and responsibility"). Feelings of guilt are warded off, denied and transferred to others. The behavior and experience serve to avoid fear and (unconscious) feelings of guilt. In the transference or interaction, the other person is very quickly blamed. In the countertransference, impulses of condemnation and confrontation arise in the therapist. Sometimes there is also a tendency to feel guilty by proxy.
C5: Characteristics of the conflict schema	
A pronounced instability/fluctuation depending on the situation and experience applies to the conflicts with a rather low level of structure, so that dysfunctional experience/behavior can appear both exaggerated and diffuse. As the different motivational systems can be addressed alternately and a conflict issue can fluctuate between active and passive attempts to cope, the conflict issues can often only be recognized incidentally. However, there are also rigid fixations of passive or active modes.	
(C) Conflict schema in passive mode The massive feelings of guilt, which are inappropriate to the situation/reality, occur even on insignificant, real or fantasized occasions and lead to destructive self-accusation. The inner value system (conscience, superego) is destructive but fragile and requires external stabilization. Internalized conscience values can replace each other. If this mode is rigid, self-punishing behavior usually manifests itself. The destructive feeling of guilt can be completely hidden and switched off in other situations.	**(C) Conflict pattern in active mode** There are excessively egotistical aspirations up to and including aggressive greed and exploitation ("Only me and everything for me!"). The experience of guilt is often completely suppressed (or not possible), so that behavior patterns that are harmful to others (but also self-harming) are frequent. The subjective values (conscience and superego) only follow the subjective benefit. If this mode is blocked, anti-social behavior usually manifests itself. It can, albeit rarely, lead to the onset of violent or even self-destructive guilt behavior. This, in turn, is usually warded off by destructive behavior.
In people with a disintegrated structural level, even more extreme compensation mechanisms are possible, sometimes involving a reinterpretation of reality (see Section 4.4).	

tic/prosocial motives and feelings of guilt (conscience).

Case Vignettes

Guilt Conflict (Passive Mode)

The Theologian: The patient, a 36-year-old woman, was on sick leave due to severe feelings of sadness, insomnia, rumination, guilt, heart palpitations, and dizziness. She had been treated with antidepressants by an internist, who then referred her for psychotherapy. A year ago, she returned to her hometown after her 90-year-old grandmother had a health crisis. At that time, she withdrew her application and habilitation thesis from a university abroad. Her supervising professor was criticized for allegedly favoring her too much, leading him to distance himself from her. She experienced intense guilt and an urge to escape, ultimately returning home.

Her grandmother was the most important person in her life. Her parents came from a working-class mining family that was both ambitious and resentful of wealth. Since both parents worked, they left her in the care of her grandparents. She never wanted to be with her parents, even when they took her home on weekends, because she saw them as vindictive and "anti-social." She excelled in school and later earned degrees in social sciences and theology. She blamed herself for conflicts with her mother and experienced intense self-reproach over minor disagreements. In her university town, she got a job where she felt increasingly exploited by her supervisor. When she tried to assert herself, she became overwhelmed with guilt. She ended up "draining herself" trying to be unselfish and supporting a colleague she felt was selfish. Eventually, she gave it all up and returned to her grandmother's home to care for her elderly and beloved relative. When her parents also became ill, she took on all the caregiving responsibilities. She was relieved to accept the offer of psychotherapy but simultaneously felt guilty, thinking, "Others are even worse off." In the transference she sought support from the therapist, asking, "Relieve me of my guilt." In the countertransference, she elicited feelings of compassion and respect from the therapist, along with frustration ("Stand up for your abilities and desires!").

Guilt Conflict (Active Mode)

The Wolf of Wall Street: J.B. was born in New York, the son of an accountant, and grew up in modest, middle-class circumstances, under the family motto: "One got to make it and get rich!" He initially studied dentistry but dropped out when he learned that the "golden age" of dentistry was over, and it was no longer a path for those simply wanting to make money. He moved to Wall Street and became a stockbroker, quickly learning that it was not about the client's welfare but about getting rich quickly and claiming the wealth of others and the resources of the world for himself.

He founded his own firm and, in pursuit of greater profits, increasingly operated outside legal boundaries. Employees were trained to follow the "pump-and-dump" scheme (a form of stock fraud), making false claims about stocks to entice investors. Employees were entertained with high bonuses and dehumanizing activities like dwarf-tossing and sexual exploitation.

As his excessive lifestyle drew more attention from the authorities, he was eventually arrested and sentenced to four years in prison. He published his memoirs "without any reflection of guilt." With his two ex-wives, he displayed the same pattern of selfish exploitation. The children were only provided for materially. He repaid only a small fraction of the debts owed to the victims, dismissing the claims of his debts as "lies and accusations."

4.3.8 C6 Oedipal Conflict

The *central motivation* here is the need to gain attention and recognition as a woman or man, along with the experience of physical pleasure and sexual desire, which is seen as fundamental for humans. This includes genital-sexual experiences and the aspiration to be seen as erotically attractive as a woman or man, showing oneself to others, and shaping and enjoying tender erotic interactions. Freud described the development of libido with the "Oedipus complex" as a fundamental aspect of psychoanalysis (Holder, 1982). While Greek mythology (Sophocles – King Oedipus) showed the whole struggle of humanity and (male) rivalry, Freud emphasized erotic-sexual desire. This emphasis on libido-sexuality was rooted in the repression of sexuality in the bourgeois culture of that time.

The basic oedipal basic constellation encompasses the totality of oedipal desires. Freud (1923, 1924) described different oedipal positions for the female child (positive Oedipus: desire for the father, negative Oedipus: desire for the mother) and for the male child (positive Oedipus: desire for the mother, negative Oedipus: desire for the father). The child is faced with the psychological task of transitioning from two-person relationships to those involving three or more people, balancing both positive and negative feelings towards each partner.

The oedipal constellation presupposes the real or imagined presence of three people caught in a field of tension between recognition as woman or man, rivalry, and eroticism/sexuality (triangulation).

The resolution of the Oedipus complex involves relinquishing the desire for parental figures. Consequently, the oedipal constellation incorporates a significant developmental aspect: the redirection of desire towards people outside the family unit.

Successful development includes the ability to triangulate, clarity about generational boundaries, a certainty regarding about being a woman or a man and the associated (sexual) attractiveness, a relaxed and pleasurable approach to eroticism and sexuality (neither forced nor inhibited) balanced attention (neither particularly sought nor avoided), and effortless engagement in rivalry (neither forced nor avoided). *Problematic developments* in this motivational area, classically described as fixations, are now seen as an interactive process involving at least one parent or caregiver with a parental function (e.g., functionalizing the child as a "better partner," etc.).

Such developments lead to fundamental insecurities about one's own attractiveness as a "full" woman or "full" man, as well as about one's own abilities ("I am too small," "I don't belong," "I am too unattractive (sexually)"); triangular relationships are therefore always conflictual: an equal relationship with two or more objects, while simultaneous recognition and acceptance of the relationships between them, is not possible because it reactivates childhood experiences of inadequacy, exclusion, and incompetence for the individual, creating a sense of intense competition.

The two modes illustrate typical solutions: Persistent efforts to gain attention, dramatic-theatrical emotionality, exaggerated eroticism, and rivalry (active mode) serve to are used to counterbalance significant internal uncertainties and affects associated with unresolved Oedipal constellation (exclusion, shame, etc.). The activation of the corresponding affects is prevented by largely or completely warding off this entire motive theme (passive mode).

On the one hand, repetitive conflictual patterns of experience and behavior lead to symptoms in triggering situations, and on the other, they shape a conflictual personality to personality disorder (e.g., histrionic personality disorder).

Key Characteristics of the Neurotic Oedipal Conflict

1. Repetitive-Dysfunctional Motivational Pattern: Self-image and relationship formation involve either consistently seeking attention with heightened emotionality, increased eroticism, and rivalry (active mode), or

avoidance of these behaviors altogether with frequently absent or misguided sexual satisfaction (passive mode).

2. Core and Leading Affects: The core affects that need to be warded off are centered around subjectively unbearable feelings of exclusion and shameful immaturity. Both modes lack a distinct leading affect. In the passive mode, it is rather the lack of appropriate affects in conflict-specific situations that is striking. The only thing the affected individual or the examiner may experience is shyness and a (shameful) fear of living out one's gender-specific abilities. This can go as far as fearing castration and there can be far-reaching desexualization.
3. Triggering Situations: Biographically, it is likely that the individual did not come to terms with the oedipal constellation because, for example, the opposite-sex parent preferred him or her over the other parent, or because the oedipal issue was avoided in the family. Typical triggering situations that can activate the conflict and lead to the appearance of psychological/psychosomatic symptoms as a dysfunctional attempt to find a solution are, for example: situations of perceived or real rejection or exclusion, loss of physical attractiveness (active mode); temptation situations due to sexual interest of potential partners, necessity of rivalry/courtship in case of one's own desire for a relationship and its failure (passive mode).
4. Transference and Countertransference Dynamics (T - CT): In the active mode, affected individuals often display seductive self-staging that creates fascination and (erotic) attraction in the (opposite-sex) counterpart. This can be coupled with irritation or a tendency to not take the affected individual seriously which can turn into annoyance combined with the impulse to send the affected person away. In the passive mode, a lack of awareness regarding sexual topics is usually shown even in the clinical situation, and all forms of eroticized transference are repelled; this may lead to strong boredom and disinterest in the counterpart or may also result in fantasies of "awakening from the Sleeping Beauty sleep" with pronounced sexual passion ("still waters run deep!").

In the active mode we find strongly fluctuating, sometimes dramatically theatrical emotions, eroticization and rivalry to the point of shamelessness as leading affects. These are combined with a tendency to sexualization. In the passive mode, a lack of awareness of sexual topics is usually shown in different situations which includes the clinical one. All forms of eroticized transference are warded off; in the other person, this can lead to extreme boredom and disinterest or also result in fantasies of "liberation from the Sleeping Beauty sleep" with pronounced sexual passion ("Still waters run deep!").

As in other conflicts, feelings of guilt can also arise. However, this involves a conflict-specific tone of guilt, which, for example, in rivalrous aspirations, arises from simultaneous loyalty to both relationship partners and not from guilt in the context of pronounced prosocial or egoistic tendencies.

General Description of the Coping Modes of C6

Passive Mode

The passive mode is dominated by the characteristics of the "gray mouse," harmlessness, childishness, and naivety. The individual experiences themselves as resigned or unaware of the sexual subject, who is at the same time competitive and acknowledging; shyness, fear (of being ashamed), and even "castration anxiety" dominate the individual's emotional experience in relation to the subject. At best, interest in sexuality finds subliminal expression in some coquetry, misbehavior, or is perceivable in the countertransference.

Often, older partners are chosen who are like the preferred primary caregiver, while omitting the sexual aspect in these relationships (in extreme case: a Josephite marriage). Passive avoidance can result in a lack of attraction and an intention towards sexlessness. It is often challenging to fully avoid sexual topics, which can lead to erotically tinged crushes on idols or secret perverse fantasies. In some instances there may also be breakthroughs into behavior.

Active Mode

In active mode, people seek to be the center of attention through their appearance and inappropriately erotic or provocative behavior (especially as a man/woman). These people are driven to put themselves in the spotlight, to be the center of attention, to shine and to seduce (sexually). At the same time, sexual fulfilment and satisfaction may be inhibited.

Relationships are constantly staged to gain attention and approval. The theatrical-emotional, rapidly changing or contradictory sexual behavior (lure and block dynamics, triangular relationships) and strong rivalry cause a great deal of suffering for everyone involved.

Because partner choice is usually based on primary objects, the real partner is often experienced as inadequate and unable to live up to the primary object ("can't hold a candle to Dad"). The active mode is largely consistent with the DSM-5 description of Histrionic Personality Disorder.

Manifestations of the Oedipal Conflict at Different Levels of Structural Integration

The oedipal conflict's phenomenology is determined by the level of structural integration. The progression "conflict tension, neurotic conflict, conflict schema" generally corresponds with decreasing structural integration: "good, moderate, and low" down to the disintegrated structural level (Table 31).

Table 31. Characteristics of C6 on various levels of structural integration

Characteristics of C6 at different levels of structural integration	
C6: Characteristics of conflict tension	
(A) Conflict tension in passive mode There is a tendency toward shyness and avoidance of rivalry. However, the themes of rivalry, recognition, and sexuality are open to conscious experience. There is often a desire for the other person to become active, which is usually met with shy coquetry. Sometimes there is a rapturous infatuation (with "secret" erotic fantasies) in relation to idealized objects. Problems can arise if active rivalry (e.g., in the case of wishes for a relationship, desires, in professional contexts) is required to fulfil desires. This is usually not possible for those affected, so they withdraw in resignation. However, it is usually possible to flexibly regulate the conflict tension without clinically significant consequences. However, conflict tension is typically manageable without clinically significant consequences.	**(A) Conflict tension in active mode** There is a tendency to put oneself in the spotlight as a man/woman and to compete for favor and recognition. Great emphasis is placed on a physically attractive appearance. Relationships often have an underlying sense of rivalry or attraction. Problems arise when existing relationships become "boring" or when those affected do not receive the recognition they desire, leading to disappointment and the search for new "challenges."

Table 31. Characteristics of C6 on various structural processing levels (continued)

Characteristics of C6 at different levels of structural integration	
C6: Characteristics of the neurotic conflict	
(B) Neurotic conflict in passive mode There is a clear desire to hide one's femininity/masculinity and all its implications, from oneself and others. Traits of "gray mouse" and naivety dominate in relation to themes of sexuality, rivalry and recognition-. One's own sexual desires and desires for recognition as a man/woman are usually not allowed to be consciously perceived and are unconsciously tainted with shame and even "castration anxiety". There is a clear desire to hide one's femininity/masculinity and all its implications from oneself and others. Traits of "gray mouse" and naivety dominate in relation to sexual and rivalry recognition issues. One's own sexual desires and desires for recognition as a man/woman are usually not allowed to be consciously perceived and are unconsciously tainted with shame and even castration anxiety. It is not uncommon to find hidden forms of sexuality. Fantasies of intense sexual passion ("Still waters run deep!") can arise in the other person. Sexual interest from others then leads to significant discomfort, often resulting in withdrawal. If withdrawal is not possible or if one's own unconscious desires are activated, it often results in clinically relevant symptoms. Often, older partners are chosen who are similar to the preferred primary caregiver, and the sexual topic is avoided.	**(B) Neurotic conflict in active mode** There is a clear desire to always be the center of attention through physical appearance and overly erotic or provocative behavior and/or exaggerated emotionality. Being ostracized or ignored can be difficult or even impossible to bear, so the staging is intensified to the point of theatrical-dramatic behavior. Not infrequently, those affected try to force themselves into existing relationships ("oedipal explosives"), where the primary goal is usually not sexual fulfillment but "oedipal triumph." Failure to achieve this or loss of physical attractiveness are typical triggers for psychological disorders. Fascination and (erotic) attraction can be created in others, but often also irritation and annoyance due to the contradictory behavior ("lure and block dynamics"), possibly causing withdrawal.
C6: Characteristics of the conflict schema	
Conflict schemas with a low level of structural integration are typically marked by significant situational or experience-dependent instability that can fluctuate. Consequently, dysfunctional experiences or behaviors may appear exaggerated and diffuse or momentarily recognizable. The modes of behavior can change quickly. However, there can also be rigid fixations in either passive or active mode. The traumatic childhood experiences (emotional and/or physical neglect, physical abuse, sexual abuse) that are often present on this level of structural integration frequently affect the entire Oedipal area. They can make sexual desire (one's own and that of others) and self-perception as a man/woman, any desire for tenderness, etc., trigger trauma-related representations and affects.	

Table 31. Characteristics of C6 on various structural processing levels (continued)

Characteristics of C6 at different levels of structural integration	
(C) Conflict schema in passive mode There is a strong tendency towards de-sexualization. Sexual desire is perceived as threatening, as sexuality is associated with complete self-abandonment and a simultaneous longing for but fear of fusion. Rivalry often involves destructive fantasies about the rival, such as fantasies of harming the rival or being harmed by the rival. As a result, this whole set of motives is often completely inhibited, to the point of a self-perception as completely sexless and asexual, with efforts to hide any attractiveness and sexuality. This usually results in a lack of sexual interest from others.	**(C) Conflict schema in active mode** There is a strong tendency to sexualize almost all desires in relationships. Unlike the neurotic mode, sexual fulfillment is often seen as "proof" of one's femininity/masculinity. This can escalate into sex addiction with indiscriminate partners. Triangular constellations are often sought, but frequently ignored, e.g., by massive denial of the existence of rivals. Relationships are often experienced as much more intense than they are. There is a tendency to act out fantasized relationships. Rejections or perceived distancing "afterwards" often result in significant crises, which may involve self-destructive and/or other-destructive behavior.
In people with a disintegrated structural level, even more extreme compensatory mechanisms are possible, in some cases involving distortions of reality (see Section 4.4).	

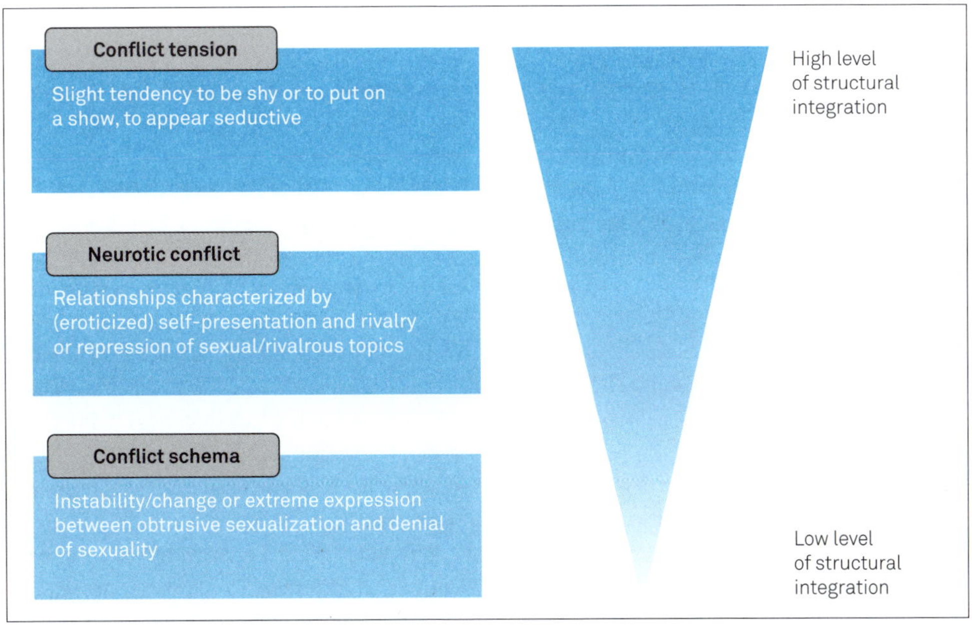

Figure 14. Oedipal Conflict and the three levels of structural integration. The three levels: Conflict tension (upper pole, high level of structural integration), neurotic conflict (moderate level of structural integration) and conflict schema (rather low level of structural integration).

The upper pole in Figure 14 (typically corresponding to a well-integrated structural level) is characterized by the fundamental human need for attention and recognition as a woman or man that is inherent in all people, along with the need for physical and sensual pleasure and sexual desire. Individuals experiencing conflict tension, in whom this ubiquitous motivational theme has been accentuated, often appear stressed in this area and show tendencies like shyness, self-dramatization, or seductive behavior; however, this conflict tension usually does not cause distress and can be managed well by social partners. With a moderate level of structural integration, relationships are characterized by repetitive patterns of, neurotic conflict. These conflicts are driven by a rigid need for self-dramatization or the avoidance thereof in order to ward off a threatening experience of "smallness/immaturity/exclusion" as well as one's own sexual desire. Individuals with a low level of structural integration often experience instability or extreme manifestations of both modes. For these patients, the oedipal theme (the oedipal conflict schema) is often interwoven with other conflictual themes, Dependency vs. Individuation. Triangular relationship constellations can hardly be tolerated and evoke intense emotions. Sexualization can be either invasive (active mode) or completely denied (passive mode). The modes are often unstable and may alternate quickly. In individuals with a disintegrated structural level, even more extreme compensatory mechanisms are possible, sometimes accompanied by distortions of reality (see Section 4.4).

Differential Diagnosis of Oedipal Conflict Dynamics vs. Self-Esteem Experience

The Oedipal (C6) and Self-worth (C4) themes can be hard to separate. Ask if it concerns overall self-worth or recognition as a man/woman. In passive mode, determine if the shame is from general inferiority (self-worth) or specifically about being a man/woman, sexual attractiveness, and avoiding rivalry (Oedipal).

In the passive mode, a distinction must be made as to whether the shame stems from a comprehensive experience of inferiority (self-worth) or relates specifically to the issues of being a man/woman, sexual attractiveness, and avoiding rivalry (oedipal).

In the active mode, the question is whether putting oneself in the spotlight and "wanting to win" serves to create or maintain an experience of grandiosity, usually associated with a clear devaluation of others (self-worth), or to secure attention, especially as a woman/man.

Case Vignettes

Oedipal Conflict (Passive Mode, Moderate Level of Structural Integration)

The Student: Ms. C., a 26-year-old law student came to the interview due to depressive symptoms. She appeared as a rather pale, childlike young woman, dressed mostly in dark tones, speaking softly and generally giving a very lifeless, unappealing impression. The examiner did not sense marked depression; instead, shyness, inhibition, and shame predominated. During the interview, she was extraordinarily passive, only timidly speaking about her concerns, prompting the interviewer to repeatedly ask follow-up questions.

The symptoms began gradually about two years ago. In her studies, she increasingly had to compare herself with other students, but she avoided these comparisons. Moreover, a fellow student in her study group showed interest in her. To avoid this erotic temptation, she attempted to conceal herself more, hide, and present herself as a woman in inconspicuous clothing. Her attempt to maintain "just a good friendship" with him led to him eventually choosing another classmate.

This confirmed her feelings of inferiority and unattractiveness. At that time, the depressive withdrawal intensified, although the patient cannot see any direct connection. Since then, she has intensified her already strong familial relationships, calling her parents daily and spending every weekend with them. She described both her father and mother lovingly but as somewhat colorless and bland. Her relationship with her father is described as "affectionate and friendly," more like a lifelong best friend than a father. The mother appears to play a rather subordinate role in the family balance. No conflicts seem to exist. The entire family atmosphere is described as conservatively protective. Since childhood and adolescence, the patient has enjoyed being with friends, but in social relationships, she preferred to remain "inconspicuous." Since puberty, she has predominantly chosen female friendships, though she remains more on the sidelines. Gender-specific developmental steps like dance classes were taken because "that's what you do," but she mostly felt that it was "far too early" and not fitting for her. In subsequent years, no man showed erotic interest in her until the triggering situation. This did not consciously bother her, yet she also wished for protection and security (less sexual desire) from a partner.

Oedipal Conflict (Active Mode, Level of Structural Integration Between Moderate and Low)

The Emergency Patient: Ms. A., aged 30, was admitted via the emergency department due to hyperventilation tetany. Over the past two years, she had experienced these attacks with increasing frequency, sometimes occurring almost daily. The first attack occurred when she heard from a friend on the phone that the friend had given birth to a son.

Ms. B. bubbled over in conversation. She was attractive and began to act out with the male doctor, sometimes laughing completely inappropriately or suddenly becoming depressed and crying. She had been reported as an emergency, causing considerable concern in the outpatient clinic and necessitating the urgent involvement of a specialist. The medical staff felt both attracted to her and irritated by her (inappropriate) dramatic behavior.

Her life story was a series of "wild" experiences and "crazy" plans. Coming from a simple family, she was the only girl among six siblings and her father's favorite. However, he was marginalized in the family, chronically ill since her birth, and retired, while her mother was an ailing housewife. Despite strong family bonds, there was constant competition for attention and care. At the age of 19, she moved in with her first boyfriend 9: pregnancy, miscarriage, and a "wild party life" followed, which led her to drink more and more alcohol.

After meeting her future second husband, she broke up with her boyfriend and stopped drinking. In between this, she was once married because of a crazy plan (first marriage), she married this man to "free" him from prison. Today, she does not understand why she married him; she divorced him soon after without ever being intimate with him. She met her current husband on her own initiative, and they slept next to each other for a long time without any intimacy; he is very nice, reserved, and shy.

Since marrying, she has longed for children but hasn't conceived. Professionally, her jobs have often been below her capabilities. She has many friends, but no one (except for her husband) with whom she can share her worries. Although she considers herself physically attractive, she sometimes feels overwhelmed by men's attention.

Oedipal Conflict (Active Mode, Moderate Structural Level)

The Artist: 55-year-old Mr. B. comes on the advice of his family doctor, whom he consulted due to insomnia and "restlessness" he had been experiencing since his significantly younger partner left him about six months ago.

The tall patient, dressed in a light-colored linen suit and hat, greets the much younger interviewer "gallantly," with a firm but slightly too long handshake and look. The word "stately comes to the interviewer's mind."

The patient begins to talk about the relationship and its separation, which "traumatized" him, without beating around the bush and with many gestures. As a concert pianist, he had traveled a lot, his partner had known this, and now she wanted him to have a child and become more "domestic." They had discussed this repeatedly, but he could not warm up to the idea.

Since she had brought up the topic, he had often been "weak in bed." During his last concert tour, she had simply moved out. Since then, he had been "constantly thinking about her, her beauty, her charm, her grace." However, he also often thinks of other women and has met with young female colleagues several times. With a penetrating look, he says, "There are a lot of very beautiful women in my profession," and with a smile, "Someone like you!" He often fantasizes about this and that, which helps him with his "infinite sadness and disappointment." When asked if he has gone beyond mere imagination with any of these women, Mr. B. replies, "Once, yes, but it didn't really do anything for me," as he "wasn't fully engaged."

Mr. B. is the only child of a "very musically gifted and refined" mother and a "rather simple" father. His father, a self-employed businessman, was frequently away; he passed away about a year ago. Mr. B. remarks that he did not feel much as he hardly knew him. His mother, on the other hand, had devoted herself entirely to him, and they had a very close relationship; he still visits her regularly as much as possible, and they play music together as they always have. He admires her "grace" and her "fine intellect," qualities he has yet to find in any other woman.

During his youth, alongside school and piano training, he also dedicated himself intensively to sports. He did not want to be just the "pretty boy," so he developed a considerable ambition in sports as well. He greatly enjoyed outdoing other "boys" in several areas and being assured of the "admiration of the ladies." This continued throughout his life. He has had "an incredibly exciting and fulfilling life," enjoyed "fascinating engagements," and "conquered incredibly amazing women." However, the relationships usually did not last long; he is unsure why, perhaps because he "never really committed" and quickly found daily life in a relationship too dull.

4.3.9 C7 Identity Conflict

We understand the "self" as the complete inner image a person has of itself (Jung, 1921/1971). This self-identity system is associated with states of tension-free existence, well-being, and a sense of security (Sandler & Joffe, 1970). Identity is formed through experiences and developmental processes. Identity is created by the internalization of experiences/interactions into self-representations. Social identity is shaped by social roles (role identities) and is constructed in interactional processes, expressed in the expectations others have of me and fears about how others see me (Mead, 1934). Social identity also refers to the values of an (ethnic) group and culture, as well as all their interactions. This creates a sense of belonging to a community, a nation with a shared history. This social-ethnic identity can be replaced or modified by other group identities. The primary task of the motivational system of identity is to maintain a coherent and continuous self-image while seeking meaningfulness (Frankl, 1955, 1998). For Erikson (1959, 1968), the search for identity (meaning) with preservation of continuity and coherence was the primary motivational task of the ego. Grawe (2004) also describes the overarching goal of striving for identity consistency. Thomä & Kächele (1989) refer to resistance against identity change (following the need for security) as identity resistance. Overall, the pursuit of temporally continuous and coherent identity can be attributed great motivational significance (see Dammann et al., 2011; Benecke & Brauner, 2017).

Identity is not a static construct; it is constantly reshaped (Köber et al., 2015). Adaptation to familial-social living conditions, acquisition of gender identity, confrontation with aging and death, all of which lead to lifelong identity work that unfolds in the tension between culturally and socially developed patterns.

The theme of identity is closely linked to the availability of structural capacities (e.g., Kernberg, 1975). Dammann et al. (2011) describe a continuum along structural integration: mature identity, identity tension, identity crisis, identity conflict, identity diffusion, and eventually identity fragmentation. For Kernberg (1975) and in the Alternative Model of Personality Disorders of DSM-5, such manifestations of identity or its disturbances are central indicators of an individual's personality organization or level of functioning. On the OPD-3 Structure Axis (Axis IV), the "identity" facet is found under the "self-perception" dimension (see Section 5.5.6).

In contrast to maturity-oriented "structural" conceptions of identity issues, which fundamentally focus on the capacity for differentiation and integration in relation to self-image, the Conflict Axis (Axis III) here, pertains to the basic human need/motivation for a reasonably consistent self-image and sense of meaning, the affects that arise when this consistent self-image and sense of meaning could not develop or had been conflictually shaped, as well as the typical "solutions" in such cases. The individual's coping options strongly depend on their level of structural integration.

The central motivation is as follows. Lifelong, individuals strive to build an identity system characterized by continuity, coherence, and meaningfulness. Coherence is the strongest motivational drive in the realm of identity; our identity must be cohesively constructed, newly each day. Following this is the drive for continuity, where the individual experiences themselves as stable across different situations over time. All of this enables meaningfulness in one's worldview. Building coherence, continuity, and meaningfulness is achieved through recurring narrative constructions. Inadequate consistency is met with identity resistance, particularly rationalization, repression, denial, etc. (Belke & Landoll, 2000), which strongly depends on the availability of structural functions.

When development is successful, it leads to a "feeling of ego identity ... the accumulated trust ... of uniformity, the continuity one holds in the eyes of others, an ability ... to maintain an inner unity and continuity" (Erikson, 1959, p. 107). A person's overall identity is divided into various parts, often significantly contradictory sub-identities, frequently tied to specific situations (being a father/mother/professional identity/erotic identity, etc.). The human body is an important component in identity work. Successful identity leads to a sense of uniqueness, affirmation, and meaningfulness in one's life (Keupp, 1999). Successful identity work enables, as Erikson described a sense of belonging to a group alongside personal individuality. It allows one to realistically adapt to the current situation while maintaining one's identity. In successful development, alignment with reality is achieved. A coherent and stable sense of identity provides the motivational-emotional foundation: "Why I have become who I am and why I feel and act as I do." Today, this identity development extends into the 18–30 age range, meaning it has shifted into young adulthood (Seiffge-Krenke, 2012, 2021).

Life phase transitions (e.g., entering a career, parenthood, aging) can be associated with significant identity upheavals, necessitating corresponding identity work for the individual. Today, the digital world offers significantly expanded possibilities for shaping outward images: the so-called "digital identity," which also affects psychological identity and can be used for regulating identity issues.

If this development fails, resulting in a lack of a coherent, stable, and multifaceted self-image, this leads to feelings of insecurity, alienation, and/or meaninglessness, which are difficult to bear. Those affected typically respond either by avoiding a well-defined identity (passive mode) or by forcibly creating a rather constructed sense of identity (active mode).

As people often acquire different (sub-)identities over the course of their development, both conscious and (often even more pronounced) unconscious contradictory self-representations come into play. Disturbances can occur among all (sub-)identities: body, gender, family, ethnic, religious, social, political, emotional, and professional identities. Conflicts arise not only among these sub-identities but also within them, such as among different professional identities. Identity conflicts are often prevalent in the realm of body image identities: athlete vs. feminine body, disabled body vs. bodily integrity, young vs. old, but also postoperative states, e.g., after mastectomy. Traditional societies rely on stable, predetermined social structures such as family, gender, kinship systems, and the like. In modern societies, individuals have increasingly fewer predefined (sub-)roles and (sub-)identities and building and harmonizing contradictions among these requires considerable effort and is prone to disruption. Failure in identity work is associated with anxiety, insecurity, alienation, and/or feelings of meaninglessness.

Key Characteristics of the Neurotic Identity Conflict

1. Repetitive-Dysfunctional Motivational Pattern: Life and relationship structuring are marked by attempts to manage uncertainties regarding one's identity and sense of meaning (Who am I, really? What is my purpose? Where do I belong?"). In the active mode, these individuals have a general tendency to actively cover up their identity uncertainty or to actively deny and repress a sub-identity. The hallmark of this coping attempt is a compensatory approach (over-identification) across various identities, avoiding identity dissonance. In the passive mode, it's about avoiding commitment to any sub-identity. Coping strategies include minimizing, rationalizing, and even denial, which can appear as a complete lack of identity or over-adaptation to identities (chameleon effect).
2. Core and Lead Affects: Core affects are the subjectively unbearable feelings of insecurity, alienation, and/or meaninglessness ("I don't know who I am, and my life is meaningless"), which must be defended against. Clinically, lead affects include anxiety, self-devaluation, depressive affects in the passive mode, but also anger and aggression toward excluded identities ("They aren't human beings!") in the active mode.
3. Trigger Situations: Biographically, one expects persistent and conflict-laden identity formations within a life story, with sociocultural influences, e.g., forced identification with the loss of an original identity. Trigger situations that activate the latent conflict often involve comparison between parts of the identity system on the one hand and on the other the alignment of (sub-)identities with social and sociocultural demands.
4. Transference and Countertransference Dynamics (T-CT dynamics): In the active, compensated mode, these individuals appear self-assured, content, and identified with themselves and their reference group. Underneath, insecurity and doubt ("this can't be quite right") become noticeable to both the affected person and the counterpart. In the decompensated state, this strong insecurity and internal conflict become apparent to the counterpart. In the passive mode, rationalization to the point of denial, identity uncertainty, and dissonance appear. The counterpart perceives a sense of arbitrariness, blandness, and lack of identity contours, even to the point where it feels like "there are no interests or (sub-)identities." In countertransference, feelings of pity and support arise. With perceived arbitrariness (chameleon effect), one senses irritation, as well as feelings of devaluation ("He doesn't know what he wants and only wants to please me."). Here, over-adaptability becomes apparent ("How should I be for you?").

General Description of the Coping Modes of C7

Passive Mode

In passive mode, an attempt is made to overcome the unclear or recurring, chronic feeling of identity uncertainty or contradiction ("Who am I, I can't decide, what is my purpose?") by avoiding the whole question of identity. Any form of definition ("This is who I am!") is avoided, everything is kept vague.

The other person can sense feelings of (self-) insecurity, fear and even a sense of meaninglessness.

Active Mode

In active mode, there is a tendency to compensate for uncertainty regarding one's identity. Some aspects of conflicting identities may be minimized or ignored, while other aspects are highlighted or expanded. This leads to an approach that overcompensates in terms of role identities. Conversely, the other person may feel uncertain and conflicted in a decompensated state.

Manifestations of the Identity Conflict (and Identity Dissonance) at Different Levels of Structural Integration

The theme of identity formation and its contradictions manifests on different structural levels within a continuum of fluid transitions (Figure 15; Table 32).

The term conflict tension refers to the flexible and adaptive management of both conscious and unconscious tensions experienced by individuals, often emphasizing one aspect (active or passive) or one identity vs. another,

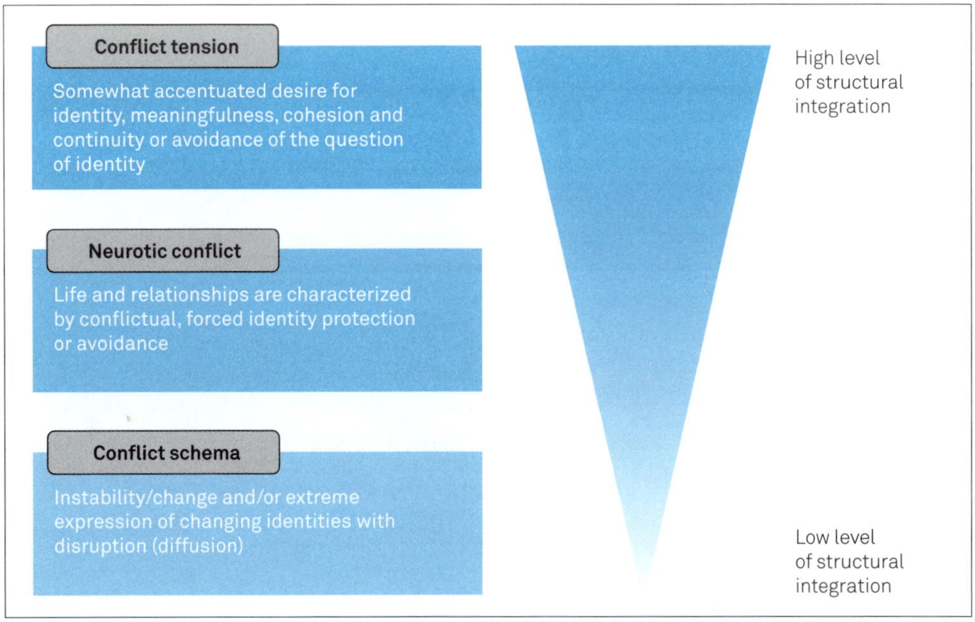

Figure 15. Conflict dynamics of the Identity Conflict and the three levels of structural integration. The three levels of structural integration: Conflict tension (upper pole, high level of structural integration), neurotic conflict (rather moderate level of structural integration) and conflict schema (rather low level of structural integration).

without reaching a dysfunctional level. Cultural and individual socialization contribute to personal solutions and internal patterns. Life events and disruptions can lead to conflict tensions, such as balancing the identity of a working woman with that of a mother. These tensions are generally managed adaptively. The pursuit of self-identity and meaningfulness, while maintaining self-cohesion and continuity, is achieved even when one aspect is emphasized.

In neurotic-dysfunctional conflicts, repetitive patterns show a struggle with forced identity or avoiding identity commitment. In low-structure patterns, identity diffusion leads to severe self-image distortions, instability, and fluctuating or extreme sub-identities that are poorly perceived and regulated. At the disintegrated structural level, identity fragmentation and extreme reality reinterpretations may occur (see Section 4.4 for further research on dilemmas and conflicts).

Table 32. Characteristics of C7 on various structural integration levels

Characteristics of C7 at different levels of structural integration	
C7: Characteristics of conflict tension	
(A) Conflict tension in passive mode A sense of identity with personal goals, plans, values, hopes and feelings ("This is my meaning") is basically successful in important areas. Time and again, however, there is an increased experience of identity doubts about (parts of) identity and crises of meaning. There is a tendency to avoid the question of identity, but without this reaching clinical proportions. Tendencies to (over)adapt are also noticeable and identifiable, but it is always possible to maintain one's own core identity.	**(A) Conflict tension in active mode** With a fundamentally coherent and continuous identity in the essential areas, there is a noticeable tendency towards uncertainty or inconsistency in sub-areas: e.g., contradictions in the (sub-) identity area of the body or between (sub-) identity areas such as career and parental role. There is a tendency to emphasize a partial identity. However, it is always possible to actively process the existing contradictions.
C7: Characteristics of the neurotic conflict	
(B) Neurotic conflict in passive mode When passive mode predominates, there is an unclear or recurring chronic feeling of a lack of identity with a lack of contours and disorientation with the attempt to compensate for this by adapting. The existing (partial) identities are contradictory. Any form of definition ("This is who I am!") is avoided, everything is kept vague. Fear, self-deprecation and even depressive moods appear as leading affects. In the countertransference, interest ("There must be something to find") and pity, but also feelings of boredom and anger are possible.	**(B) Neurotic conflict in active mode** In the active mode, there is generally a tendency to actively cover up the insecurity of the (partial) identities or to actively deny or suppress contradictions in the (partial) identities. The overcompensatory (over-)identification is groundbreaking ("as-if"). The leading affect is often anger or even aggression towards others who do not correspond to this identity. These people appear overly sure of themselves, their goals and their purpose. In a decompensated state, anxiety and inner turmoil are evident. In the countertransference, the examiner has feelings of "He knows where his life is going!" with a simultaneous tendency to question the other person, to doubt everything and to (aggressively) confront the other person.

Table 32. Characteristics of C7 on various structural integration levels (continued)

Characteristics of C7 at different levels of structural integration	
C7: Characteristics of the conflict schema	
A pronounced instability/fluctuation depending on the situation and experience applies to the form of the conflicts at a rather low structural level, so that dysfunctional experience/behavior can appear both exaggerated and diffused. Since (partial) identity systems and changes can be addressed and the confrontation can fluctuate between active and passive attempts at coping, the conflictual areas of identity can often only be recognizable passively (as a theme that is not constant and stable over time). However, there are also rigid fixations in the passive or active mode, e.g., chronic identity diffusion in the passive mode or rigid one-sided as-if identity in the active mode.	
(C) Conflict schema in passive mode Due to the poorly integrated self and object representations, there is no coherent and stable self-image. This lack of identity (identity diffusion) results in a lack of identification and adoption of (partial) identities in the external world that are appropriate to the situation and reality. The resignative-passive failure in the endeavor to build an identity system with partial meaningfulness is noticeable. With external support, the identity can at least be partially "held stable" over a longer period.	**(C) Conflict schema in active mode** Due to the poorly integrated self and object representations, it is not possible to create a coherent and continuous image of oneself. Identity diffusion leads to severe distortions in the image of oneself in comparison to the image that others have of one, whereby the contradictions and ambivalences can only be partially experienced. Overcompensatory, changing (partial) identities are constructed based on external identity provisions (e.g., exclusive role identity) or inner, unstructured desires. The endeavor and struggle for a self-image and meaning in the CTis palpable. When failure is experienced, depressive feelings alternate with violent aggression.
At the disintegrated structural level, there is often a fragmentation of identity, but also extreme manifestations, sometimes with a reinterpretation of reality (see Section 4.4).	

Axis III

Differential Diagnosis of Conflict Dynamics Identity to Other Conflicts

The passive mode C7 has certain similarities with the passive mode C1: In both cases, patients tend to adapt strongly to others/partners. However, while this happens in C1 to tame existential separation anxiety, a dominant C7 adapts to avoid having to feel their missing or contradictory identity and the associated insecurities and feelings of alienation.

The active mode C7 can have similarities to the active mode C4: in both cases, those affected can appear "overconfident." However, while this happens in C4 to ward off inner inferiority, a dominant C7 attempts to dispel their own doubts about their created "as-if" identity through a forced self-confident demeanor, both towards others and towards themselves.

Invented or heavily manipulated identities are sometimes also found in a dominant C5 in active mode. However, these are used to take advantage of others, which is not the focus of a dominant C7.

The distinction from the "identity" structural facet has already been described above.

Case Vignettes

Identity Conflict (Mixed, Predominantly Active Mode)

The Swiss Abroad: The 36-year-old patient came to the initial consultation independently and reported difficulties in her relationship: her husband told her that she did not know what she wanted. She had studied and been in a successful position for years but now wanted to study psychology and start over again. This pattern, he said, was evident in many areas. He said she was searching for something, didn't know what, and was never satisfied with what she had. These accusations led to conflicts in the relationship.

The patient appeared dressed in a style typical of boardrooms, feminine and tasteful. Outside of work, she said, she dressed almost like a man ("They have it easier").

The patient was born in Switzerland and grew up in Zurich. However, she speaks flawless standard German. As the daughter of a traditional Swiss family, she has lived in Germany with her German husband for six years since their marriage. When asked about this, she smiled and said that this was her way of over-adapting, something she does in all areas of her life. Many admired this ability in her, though she viewed it more skeptically. She provided many examples. At work, everyone assumed she was a lawyer, although she had studied economics. Her father was a lawyer, but she had tried to distance herself from his wish that she followed his profession ("It seems I wasn't entirely successful at that").

Her boss asked her to evaluate the statements of legal experts. The in-house legal counsel probably hated her for that. It was almost given that her husband was also a lawyer. Her desire to study psychology was another attempt to differentiate herself and not be mistaken for others and to better understand herself ("With the way I've handled things so far, I should make a great psychologist").

She was the youngest after three older brothers ("You had to adapt to survive"). Her father was a successful corporate lawyer, and her mother was a housewife. Her childhood memories seemed oddly colorless. All three brothers studied law, though they worked in different professions. She claimed to be unable to tolerate the sight of blood, which ruled out the medical profession, a field her father would have still tolerated. Economics, which she thought little of, became the compromise. The father and his language were apparently the identity markers within the family. He was a Swiss nationalist and supported a xenophobic party.

The patient oscillated between adaptation (+) and resistance (-). Her husband is German (-) and a lawyer (+). Economics is insignificant (-) but carries no signs of rebellion (+). People assume she is a lawyer (+), but she cannot claim that title (-). She is Swiss by birth (+) but adapts to foreigners so thoroughly that she is no longer recognizable as Swiss (-). She has the "wrong" gender (-) but does not want children, which somewhat mitigates the damage (+).

At 36, the patient stands on the threshold of a new attempt at finding her identity, and this time her concept is somewhat revolutionary (-). She is also considering studying law after all, which she believes would not be difficult for her (++), saying, "Then I'd just have to learn proper Swiss German again!"

In countertransference, feelings of confusion and fuzziness dominated. The described dynamics only gradually emerged over several diagnostic sessions and were presented in a bland manner. Alongside signs of an Oedipal-sexual conflict, the identity conflict is prominent. The primary domain is her career and (to a lesser extent) her nationality. Underlying, and more inferred than confirmed, is a conflict of gender identity, she feels she is in the wrong skin no matter which profession she chooses.

Comment: Besides Oedipal aspects (C6), there is a predominantly active struggle for identity.

Zelig

In his film "Zelig," Woody Allen refers to the writings of F. Scott Fitzgerald, who describes encountering a charming individual at a garden party in New York, someone with refined language and exquisite attire. This person adapted their identity to the gestures of high society and spoke with a Boston accent, sharing their views, only to then switch in the kitchen to a different tone with the service staff and adopt their views. Later, Fitzgerald encounters him as a baseball player who calls himself Zelig, and still later as a member of Al Capone's gang, and finally as a jazz musician in a black band. Woody Allen's film (1983) adapts this story, portraying Zelig as an inconspicuous, identity-less man with the ability to adjust his appearance to fit those around him, influenced by them ("as-if" chameleon). The psychiatrist at the clinic where he is treated discovers that the root of his complete identity adaptation is his overwhelming desire to be accepted and approved. She improves his self-esteem, at which point he turns into an intolerant person, only to revert to his former identity-overadapting self after the therapy fails. Zelig possesses the remarkable ability, driven by insecurity around others, to mentally and physically adjust to each environment. As he becomes more famous, he flees to Germany, where the circumstances turn him into a Nazi.

Zelig appears as a person whose emotions do not differ from others', overly adapted, a person who takes adaptation to an extreme degree. Zelig's fundamental problem is that he cannot claim any identity as his own. Due to this complete lack of identity, he has (unconsciously) developed the ability to adopt other identities when faced with a strong personality. When in the company of a Native American, he becomes a Native American. In therapy with his psychiatrist, he turns into an outstanding psychiatrist.

Comment: Self-esteem aspects are also present (C4 active), with an overriding active search for identity and meaning, but with a complete lack of continuity. Structural functions appear limited but not severely integrated.

Identity Conflict (Active Mode)

The Musician: The 45-year-old Spanish violinist, Mr. S., presents himself after being unable to sccure a permanent position with the regional orchestra despite several temporary contracts, resulting in pronounced depressive moods. In the first interview, he seemed upbeat, seeking emotional, intense contact with his counterpart and discussing his struggle with his career in music.

He followed his older brother to Germany at 18 and began studying violin and cello at the Mozarteum. His brother transitioned to a salsa band and enjoyed significant financial success there for many years. After completing the Mozarteum, Mr. S. played in classical orchestras for an extended period, aiming to secure a permanent position with the regional orchestra. This led to two temporary positions, each lasting five years, but ultimately no permanent role was available. In response to his unemployment, he began a music education program at the college, stating, "I can only make and live for music." Forced into a deep existential crisis by unemployment, he developed depressive symptoms, and as his unemployment benefits were about to expire, he found himself living at the social minimum.

Mr. S. comes from a family where music is everything. His father was a conductor and concertmaster, his mother a singer, and even his aunts and uncles were involved in music, often professionally. He has eight siblings, all of whom are musicians, fully devoted to music. After several interested questions about other interests or potential career paths, Mr. S. revealed that he had enjoyed playing soccer immensely in his youth and had even considered a career in soccer. However, this was never taken seriously in his family, and it was effectively impossible, to the point that he no longer even engages in any sports or soccer as a hobby.

Comment: Self-worth aspects are also present (C4 active, now decompensated into passive). The life history is overwhelmingly dominated by an identity centered around MUSIC within the entire family.

4.3.10 C0 Repressed Conflict and Emotion Awareness

The *central motivation* is to prevent intrapsychic and interpersonal conflicting tensions from reaching consciousness, to ward off the associated anxiety or other unpleasant (anhedonic) feelings. Therefore, excessive defense functions as a protective mechanism, rather than an unconscious conflicting motivational system. It theme. Behind this defense, the entire spectrum of conflicts (C1 – C7) may be hidden.

With *successful development*, a person can also perceive, tolerate, and use conflicting, contradictory drives, unpleasant feelings, and interpersonal tensions to some extent. However, the flexible and adequate defensive handling (coping) of tensions is a necessary and important element of human experience and behavior.

When this *development fails,* there is a heightened defense against intrapsychic and interpersonal tensions. This prevents the conflicting motivational systems and associated interpersonal tensions or conflicts, as well as unpleasant affects, from reaching conscious awareness. As a result, individuals may overlook internal and relational conflicts and have difficulty perceiving feelings and needs in themselves and others.

Normative sociocultural aspects, such as the stigma of mental illnesses, the necessity of "functioning" in work and private life, and gender roles, have a significant influence. This category is related to the concept of alexithymia, which may also have neurobiological foundations.

Typically, one or more neurotic conflicts (C1–C7) are hidden behind this defense. They only emerge when the person is able, possibly with therapeutic help, to gradually loosen their defenses.

Key Characteristics of the Repressed Conflict and Emotion Awareness

1. Repetitive-Dysfunctional Pattern: In these individuals' accounts, their life and relationships with others appear free of tension and strongly governed by conventions, even though the observer may sense underlying tensions and conflicts. They describe their life as if there have never been any problems up to the present. Their own experiences and external circumstances are often dismissed with "everything is normal." They either mention very few feelings and conflicts in relation to others ("Everything is fine, I'm doing well," "We get along, there are no problems") or handle conflicts technically ("I can manage it all," "We settle it sensibly"). Intense feelings, whether their own or others', are perceived as disruptive and insignificant. Stressful life circumstances or events are mostly managed through denial strategies with rational action. Occasionally, the patient also expresses satisfaction with being a "steadfast person" who is not easily shaken. When their individual defense mechanisms fail, they primarily experience and present somatic symptoms. Psychological symptoms may be noted by the observer, because the patient tends to hide them.
2. Core and Leading Affects: The core affect corresponds to the underlying conflict (C1 to C7, see above), but it is usually not immediately recognizable due to strong defense. Due to the absence and suppression of affects and conflict-specific coping modes, there are usually only a few recognizable leading affects, most commonly hints of anxiety or diffuse tension states. Defense mechanisms (typically repression and denial; rationalization and affect isolation) are mainly aimed at avoiding unpleasant affects, which may be noticeable to others. Pleasant affects are less involved in the defense mechanisms.
3. Triggering Situations: These situations correspond to neurotic conflicts, but strong defenses often make them hard to identify directly. They usually become clear through external history-taking or prolonged observation, making them understandable psychodynamically.
4. Transference and Countertransference Dynamics (T–CT): In transference, the patient often expects the examiner to provide a technical solution to their (psycho-)somatic issues. The affectively monotonous description or rationalized account makes it difficult for the examiner to gain a nuanced picture of the individual and their inner life. In countertransference, feelings of disinterest and boredom can easily arise, or the examiner might experience the feelings that the patient omits or covers with rationality. The pa-

tient's defensive presentation may also evoke irritation in the examiner. As defense is dynamic, intense questioning or prolonged observation can trigger conflictual elements that are quickly re-defended. This may initially interest the examiner but can lead to frustration. In psychotherapy, patients may be seen as "unmotivated" and "difficult."

Since the defense against underlying conflicts and emotions is paramount, there is no active and passive mode. Therefore, the following Section only describes how the defended conflict and emotion awareness typically manifests.

Manifestations of the Repressed Conflict and Emotion Awareness at Different Levels of Structural Integration

Individuals with a high structural level exhibit flexible and functional defense. They may tend to present as "too rational," for example, by quickly proposing a "technical" solution to emotional matters or emphasizing the need for a "reasonable solution" (Figure 16; Table 33).

"Repressed Concflict and Emotion Awareness" in terms of exaggerated (but stable) neurotic defense can, by definition, only manifest at least in the moderately integrated structural level, or at most in the transitional range to neighboring structural integration levels.

For individuals with a low structural level, defense is generally not sufficiently stable to protect them from awareness and flooding by often undifferentiated and intense affects. They have reality-distorting defense mechanisms (projection, splitting, dissociation). Consequently, their affect and impulse tolerance is low, which results in interpersonal conflicts that the individual often perceives as problematic and describes as such. A defended conflict and emotion awareness can be diagnosed in individuals with a poorly integrated structure if there is a chronic or prolonged "shutdown" of affects ("chronic emptiness").

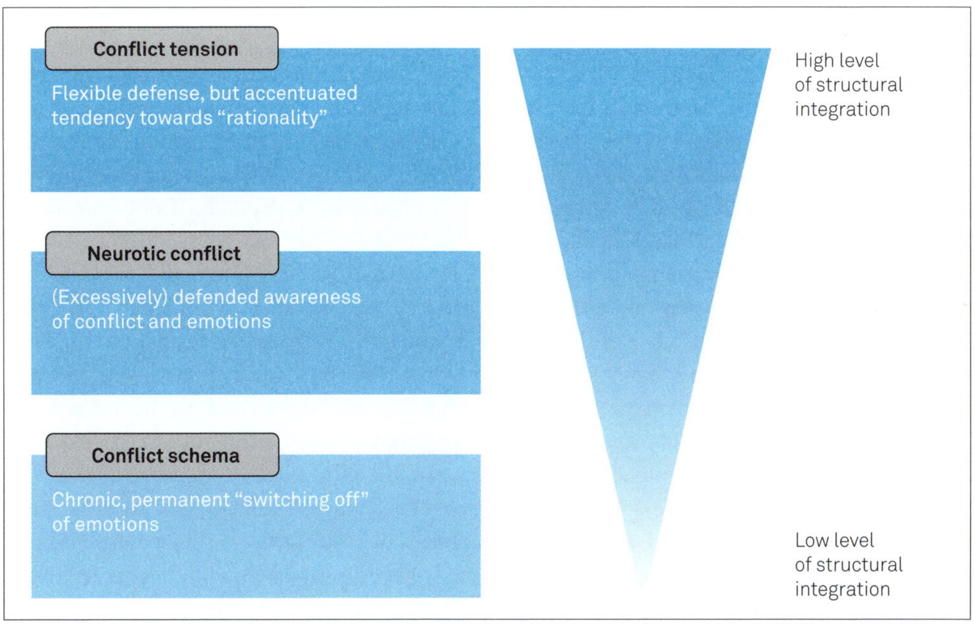

Figure 16. The manifestations of defense on different structural levels. The different structural levels and manifestation: Flexible defense (well-integrated structure), defended awareness of conflict and emotions (rather moderately integrated structure), and failure of defense (rather low structural level).

Table 33. Characteristics of CO on various structural integration levels

Characteristics of the awareness of conflict and emotions at different levels of structural integration
Characteristics of the awareness of conflict and emotions at a good structural level
Flexible and functional defense
Characteristics of the defensed awareness of conflict and emotions
Due to the exaggerated, rigid defense with a predominance of repression and denial; rationalization and isolation of affect, anhedonic affects and the description of interpersonal problems are absent.
Characteristics of conflict and emotion awareness at low integrated structural levels
Conflict schemas with a rather low level of structure are generally characterized by a pronounced situation/experience-dependent instability or even fluctuation. A defenseless awareness of conflict emotions with a low level of integrated structure can manifest itself in a chronic or long-lasting, arrested "switching off" of affects ("chronic emptiness").
In people with a disintegrated structural level, even more extreme compensation mechanisms are possible, sometimes involving a reinterpretation of reality (see Axis IV).

At a disintegrated structural level, even more extreme compensation mechanisms may be present, sometimes with reinterpretations of reality (see Axis IV, Chapter 5).

Case Vignette

Repressed Conflict and Emotion Awareness

The Normal One: Ms. A., aged 50, was referred for consultation from the gastroenterology department of the university hospital. She reported abdominal complaints for approximately one year, characterized by cramping pain, alternating episodes of diarrhea and constipation, frequent bowel movements, and mucus discharge. Extensive gastroenterological examinations did not identify an organic cause for her symptoms, leading to a diagnosis of "irritable bowel syndrome." Ms. A. expressed confidence in her physicians' ability to eventually diagnose and treat the underlying cause of her symptoms, indicating she was not particularly concerned about the abdominal issues.

When queried about the reason for her consultation, Ms. A. expressed confusion, stating that her problem was gastrointestinal rather than psychological. She emphasized that she felt well otherwise. Ms. A., a housewife, has two children; her younger child moved out approximately one year ago. When asked about her feelings regarding this change, she responded pragmatically, noting it as a natural part of life. Her husband, employed as an electrical installer, is frequently away on assignments, which she accepted as part of his job. Ms. A. stated that they have a positive relationship and experience no significant issues.

She keeps her household neat and values good relationships with neighbors, as her parents taught her. She trained as a sales assistant successfully in her youth. After her son moved out, she worked in a bakery but was recently dismissed due to complaints from coworkers, though she doesn't understand their reasons. She avoided gossip and focused on doing her job well. The investigator felt bored during the examination, suppressing yawns.

In a follow-up session, the investigator learned from the patient's husband that he had recently confessed to an affair and was considering separation. His wife refused to discuss it. She had always been functional in essential areas but emotionally distant. She focused more on household and garden tasks than spending time with him. Despite 30 years of marriage, he knew little about her background. Her sister revealed they were superficially cared for, received little emotional support, and were often beaten as children.

4.3.11 The OPD Conflict Rating Sheet

Figure 17 shows the OPD conflict rating sheet. The significance assessment reflects the extent to which the respective conflict topic influences a person's life. Looking at the manifestations of conflict in various areas of life (see Appendix B) can help with this assessment.

Very significant would be given if a conflict appears in three or more of the seven areas of life, *significant* in two areas, and *not very significant* in one area. However, this classification should not be applied too rigidly. The decisive factor is the clinical assessment of how strongly the person is dominated by the respective conflict topic.

4.4 Proposed for Further Research: Dilemma and Conflict

In OPD-1 and OPD-2, the definition of conflicts primarily focused on neurotic conflicts, with the conflict rating centered on the moderately integrated structural level. It was assumed that in cases of severely impaired structure, specific conflicts would be scarcely discernible (affecting nearly all topics), and that these conflict-related topics would hold little therapeutic significance for such patients; thus, the emphasis should be on structural impairments. However, OPD-3 proposes an expansion wherein conflicts should be considered diagnostically across all structural levels, although identifying specific conflict-related motivational themes in patients with very severe structural impairments can be challenging or, in some instances, impossible. Nonetheless, we believe that identifying conflict-related motivational themes in these patients is valuable. Additionally, psychodynamic literature has long provided a conflict concept for patients with severe mental disorders, such as Mentzos' (2002) concept of dilemmas and dilemmatic dispositions.

Since not all members of the OPD working group have yet come to accept this concept's integration into Axis III (Conflict axis), this integration attempt is presented in the corresponding chapter.

Mentzos (2002, 2015) described dilemmas as a concept for capturing the psychodynamics of psychotic disorders. The difference between a dilemma and a neurotic conflict is not in the content-related motivational themes and tendencies but in the level of threat involved, which in a dilemma concerns psychic survival and very restricted solutions available due to the lack of psychological representability of the dilemma. A dilemma is essentially a type of conflict involving an existential threat from an unresolved antagonism and specific defense mechanisms.

The dilemmatic disposition is an inherent potential of this conflict-related motivational theme that may remain latent under favorable conditions. However, if it is activated/triggered/intensified in specific activating situations, leading the disposition to become a concrete, life-threatening dilemma in the here and now ("collapse"), those affected may often only "free" themselves from the dilemma through extreme compensations, often involving reality distortions (e.g., "delusional reconstruction" with psychotic symptoms).

The motivational theme of a dilemmatic disposition or a dilemma is the same as with conflict tension, neurotic conflict, or conflict schema; the oppositional and incompatible nature is also the same, as is the character of vulnerability. The level of threat and coping abilities determine the differences in manifestations across structural levels (well-integrated, moderately integrated, and low-integrated). As the threat intensifies, capacities for representation, integration, and regulation decrease or become more specific. In psychosis, the psychic space and latitude almost vanish, allowing "problem processing" only under reality loss conditions.

If the dilemmatic disposition is not excessively activated, the person may not necessarily be classified at the disintegrated structural level. However, in phases when this disposition is activated, such as when the "psychotic dilemma" manifests in a "collapse," posing a con-

OPD-3 Rating Sheet Axis III: Conflict.											
	Biographical-repetitive-motivational conflict issues						Biographically dominant processing mode				
	• Conflict tensions (CT) • Neurotic conflicts (NC) • Conflictual-motivational schemata (CMS)	Non-existent	Little significant	Significant	Very significant	Not applicable	Mainly passive	Mixed, rather passive	Mixed, ambivalent	Mixed, rather active	Mainly active
C1	Dependence vs. Individuation	⓪	①	②	③	⑨	p+	p	p/a	a	a+
C2	Submission vs. Control	⓪	①	②	③	⑨	p+	p	p/a	a	a+
C3	In Need of Care vs. Self-Sufficiency	⓪	①	②	③	⑨	p+	p	p/a	a	a+
C4	Self-Worth Conflict	⓪	①	②	③	⑨	p+	p	p/a	a	a+
C5	Guilt Conflict	⓪	①	②	③	⑨	p+	p	p/a	a	a+
C6	Oedipal Conflict	⓪	①	②	③	⑨	p+	p	p/a	a	a+
C7	Conflict of Identity	⓪	①	②	③	⑨	p+	p	p/a	a	a+
C0	Repressed conflict and emotion awareness	⓪	①	②	③	⑨	p+	p	p/a	a	a+

	Current main conflict	Structure				Current processing mode				
						Mainly passive	Mixed, rather passive	Mixed, ambivalent	Mixed, rather active	Mainly active
1	.... /	CT	NC	CMS		p+	p	p/a	a	a+
2	.... /					p+	p	p/a	a	a+

Certainty of the conflict assessment	Not sure				Very sure
	①	②	③	④	⑤

Figure 17. OPD-3 rating sheet Axis III: Conflict (also available in the online material).

crete, deadly, and unavoidable threat to identity, with the ensuing "psychotic solutions," this generally corresponds to a structural level between low-disintegrated or disintegrated. Because of the variability in the availability of structural functions for these (and other) patient groups, the Structure Axis (Axis IV) has been diversified (see Axis IV).

A dimensional line can thus be drawn, from conflict tension (typically clinically relevant only under stress) through neurotic conflicts (repetitive-dysfunctional intrapsychic and interpersonal patterns) and conflict schemas (in patients with lower-integrated structures) to dilemmas (in patients with more disintegrated structures).

Mentzos (2002, 2015) described and associated dilemmas with certain disorder groups, particularly with CC1 (schizophrenic psychoses) and C4 (affective psychoses). However, manifestations of other conflicts as dilemmatic dispositions are equally plausible. The OPD fundamentally does not assign specific conflict-related motivational themes to particular disorders. Instead, we assume that manifestations of conflict-related motivational themes at very low integration levels may accompany a variety of severe mental disorders, and conversely, that patients with the same nosological diagnosis can substantially differ in their dominant conflict themes and structural impairments (cf. Henkel et al., 2018).

The following descriptions of manifestations of conflict-related motivational themes in cases of severe structural impairment as dilemmas are proposed as suggested supplements or expansions to the respective conflict descriptions in this chapter.

4.4.1 C1 Dependency vs. Individuation as a Dilemma

With a more disintegrated structure, there can be an extreme antagonism between the self-pole and object-pole, making any compromise between individuation and dependence (Table 34) impossible (dilemmatic disposition). Due to the fragile self-object differentiation, there is a threat of existential loss through symbiotic merging or an "autistic" withdrawal. When the dilemma is activated, it leads to a further breakdown of structural abilities, for example, a breakdown of reality orientation. In a sub-

Table 34. C1 Dependency vs. Individuation as a dilemma

Dependency vs. Individuation as a dilemma	
In people with a rather disintegrated structural level, the conflictual-motivational issue manifests itself as an existential and extremely threatening dilemma: extremely threatening antagonism between dependency and individuation/autonomy, psychologically unrepresentable, therefore under stress there is a threat of a further collapse of the structure with consecutive reconstruction, ignoring the reality check.	
Dilemma in passive mode The behavior can be clinging and dependent, any decision of one's own can be impossible, or others are made to take responsibility. Behind this superficial behavior of being controlled by others lies an inability to argue and compromise. There is a lack/deep weakness of one's own intentionality; the experience of action and authorship is reduced. There are emotions without mental (metacognitive) distance. A leading affect may be missing, identity and emotional world may appear borrowed or "borrowed." These people usually trigger intense feelings in the other person (aversion or infantilizing appropriation).	**Dilemma in active mode** The behavior can appear cold, unassailable and extremely autonomous. There may be strong intellectualization and an inability to get in touch with one's own feelings. Dependencies (e.g., to the parental home) are not recognized and are treated as if they do not exist. It is also possible to withdraw extensively into esotericism/philosophy and reduce the interpersonal sphere. The leading affect can appear to be "deleted." In the countertransference, feelings of fear of overstepping one's own boundaries, injury and loss (due to the withdrawal of the affected person) but also fusional fears and longing can arise.

sequent phase, a psychotic reconstruction of reality occurs, meaning an ego, an object, and a relationship between ego and object are re-established, for example, within the framework of delusional experiences. This reconstruction can be understood as a compromise attempt to re-establish experiential coordinates after the "end of the world." Here, reality testing is subordinated to the re-creation of a connection to reality and self, however tenuous. The unreconciled aspects of reality (the "inner rejected," Freud, 1911, p. 308) reappear, albeit usually veiled, within the psychotic symptom.

4.4.2 C2 Submission vs. Control as a Dilemma

In people with a rather disintegrated structural level, the conflictual-motivational issue appears as a dilemma (Table 35): extremely threatening antagonism between extreme submission and "total" control, psychologically unrepresentable, therefore manifestation in the form of interpersonal patterns, changing or arrested, e.g., persistence in bizarre/dangerous action dialogues.

4.4.3 C3 In Need of Care vs. Self-Sufficiency

In people with a rather disintegrated structural level, chronic parasitic lifestyles or chronic excessive self-exploitation/asceticism are frozen in an unrepresentable concretization (Table 36). Occasionally overvalued or unrealistic ideas are found (examples: impoverishment delusion; patient who wants to survive with "light fasting").

Table 35. C2 Submission vs. Control as a dilemma

Submission vs. Control as a dilemma	
In people with a more disintegrated structural level, the conflictual-motivational issue manifests itself as an existential and extremely threatening dilemma, sometimes with more extreme compensation mechanisms, sometimes with reinterpretations of reality: Extremely threatening antagonism between extreme subjugation and "total" control, psychologically unrepresentable, therefore manifestation in the form of interpersonal patterns, changing or arrested, e.g., persistence in bizarre/dangerous action dialogues.	
Dilemma in passive mode The experience of one's own wishes is practically erased, the focus is on the other person (partner) and their wishes are the only orientation. This avoids difference and therefore separation. One's own desires can then only appear delusional or hallucinatory, as coming from outside. Arrested submission and "enslavement" without a sense of suffering and basic self-protection. Finalized, sometimes highly expressive suicidality as a source of power and control. In the countertransference, powerlessness or admiration for the extreme self-abandonment to the point of questioning one's own person, but also pronounced aggression, a tendency also to torment or a desire to destroy this lie.	**Dilemma in active mode** The experience of the other's wishes is practically erased. Difference and separation are avoided through extreme control. Feeling that one's own point of view is absolute law, another point of view is betrayal. Maintaining power and control while abandoning basal self-protection and empathy. If the wishes of the other arise, the reaction is withdrawal, defense or delusional resistance: bizarre forms of dominating and torturing other living beings as a source of power and "total" control. Subjective "entitlement" to exercise violence. Countertransference: Experience of threat, fear of the uncanny, bewilderment, powerlessness or even tendencies to revolt against this coercive system. Alternatively, submission and fear of others controlling oneself.

4.4.4 C4 Self-Worth Conflict as a Dilemma

People with a rather disintegrated structural level face an unrepresentable dilemma between the value they attribute to themselves and the value that others possess or attribute to them; Self-Worth vs. Object-Worth (Table 37). If you follow what is existential for your own self-worth ("your star"), you completely lo contact with the esteem of others (and your superego). If you follow the values of others, you lose your self-worth and experience the destruction of your narcissism. The dilemma allows only two extremes: to become completely independent of the superego and the value that others give you, or to give yourself up and completely sacrifice your self-worth.

4.4.5 C5 Guilt Conflict as a Dilemma

Unrealistic feelings of guilt may either become deeply entrenched, potentially leading to delusions of guilt or sin, or egotistical tendencies may deepen (Table 38), possibly resulting in delusional transgression.

4.4.6 C6 Oedipal Conflict as a Dilemma

At a more disintegrated structural level, a dilemma manifests itself between an urge for completely obtrusive sexualization and the complete denial/destruction of sexuality (Table 39). This can manifest itself, for example, as a sexualized "relationship mania" or a completely uninhibited display of sexuality, or, on the other hand, can involve a complete negation of one's own sexuality, even to the point of destroying one's own genitals.

Table 36. C3 In Need of Care vs. Self-Sufficiency as a dilemma

In Need of Care vs. Self-Sufficiency as a dilemma	
In people with a more disintegrated structural level, the conflictual-motivational issue manifests itself as an existential and extremely threatening dilemma with sometimes extreme compensation mechanisms, sometimes with reinterpretations of reality:	
Extremely threatening antagonism between parasitism and self-exploitation/asceticism, psychologically unrepresentable, therefore manifestation in the form of interpersonal patterns, alternating or arrested, e.g., greedy exploitation, life-threatening asceticism, etc.	
Dilemma in passive mode The individual is viewed as a provider of psychological and material support, who is expected to be available without question. Frustrations are often met with aggressive responses, and the individual's contribution to care may be seen as an undue expectation. There may be behavior that disregards the circumstances of other people, treating them as extensions of oneself. In the countertransference there are feelings of guilt for not meeting expectations, aggressive feelings towards a demanding person, and tendencies to fail to meet the other person's needs.	**Dilemma in active mode** The psychological and material goods of others are seen as inappropriate or dangerous and not appropriate to what is needed. This applies, for example, to food, which has to be very special, to the point where there is a risk of malnutrition and undernourishment. Psychological "food" is also considered unnecessary. There is a threat of withdrawal, unreflected asceticism and loss of social connection. In the countertransference one experiences helplessness because you must watch someone "starve" for lack of connection to others, alternatively a tendency to "feed" them by force or even violently.

Axis III

Table 37. C4 Self-Worth conflict as a dilemma

Self-Worth conflict as a dilemma	
In people with a more disintegrated structural level, the conflictual-motivational issue manifests itself as an existential and extremely threatening dilemma, sometimes with more extreme compensation mechanisms, sometimes with reinterpretations of reality: Extremely threatening antagonism between Self vs. Object-Worth, psychologically unrepresentable, therefore only either destructive self-devaluation or absolute grandiosity (e.g., "manic revolt").	
Dilemma in passive mode Often complete renunciation of experiencing their own wishes, let alone asserting them. Own pain, suffering or excessive demands are often practically not recognized for a long time. Offences go unnoticed and lead to depressive states that often cannot be attributed to the situation. Unrepresentable, sometimes unrealistic self-devaluation leads to psychotic-depressive states and even negativistic delusions. The subjective psychological strain can even decrease (anosognosia) or be arrested in a solidified, unconscious. narcissistic triumph ("queen of suffering", "luminary killer"). In the countertransference, the dominant tendencies are either to be infected by despair and hopelessness and to feel like a harmful and incompetent therapist, or to deny the affect or to devalue the affected person themselves.	**Dilemma in active mode** Insults are not recognized and lead to hyperactivity or the start of unrealistic projects. Busyness, restlessness, and permanent preoccupation with new things must not be interrupted, as this triggers anxiety. An unrepresentable urge to overcompensate for the fragile experience of self-worth can lead to the apparent inflation of self-worth through manic defense, even to symptomatic mania with possible delusions of grandeur. Maintaining self-esteem is sometimes only possible by breaking out into mania. In the countertransference, envy, anger or boredom can appear, or admiration and allowing oneself the denial of one's own feelings of inferiority.

Table 38. C5 Guilt conflict as a dilemma

Guilt conflict as a dilemma	
In people with disintegrated structural level, the conflictual-motivational issue manifests itself as an existential and extremely threatening dilemma with sometimes extreme compensation mechanisms, sometimes with reinterpretations of reality: Extremely threatening antagonism between prosociality vs. egoism, psychologically unrepresentable, therefore only destructive and possibly delusional developments possible, e.g., delusion of guilt, querulous paranoia.	
Dilemma in passive mode Feelings of guilt can also occur on trivial occasions in an arrested and excessive form and become entrenched to the point of delusions of guilt or sin. It is not possible to differentiate between what one is responsible for and what one is not. Atonement or self-punishing actions can be demanded by means of psychotic symptoms. In the countertransference there is usually compassion and a tendency to appease and exonerate, or alternatively to lose patience, accuse or punish.	**Dilemma in active mode** The experience of guilt can be completely cancelled out, complete impossibility of acknowledging one's own guilt. Experiences that suggest guilt are completely ignored, or there may be persistent attempts to externalize one's own guilt, such as querulous paranoia. Aggression in the countertransference, tendency to confront or even punish, alternatively own sense of guilt.

Table 39. C6 Oedipal conflict as a dilemma

Oedipal conflict as a dilemma	
In people with a more disintegrated structural level, the conflictual-motivational issue manifests itself as an existential and extremely threatening dilemma with sometimes extreme compensation mechanisms, sometimes with reinterpretations of reality: Extremely threatening antagonism between an urge for completely obtrusive sexualization and complete denial/destruction of sexuality, psychologically unrepresentable, therefore only realizable through concrete action.	
Dilemma in passive mode The dyad in the primary relationship is defended against the threat posed by the "third party," the father, who is perceived as a threat to their existence. He is devalued or even declared irrelevant to the parentage. Rejection of the father, the "thirdness." A delusional reaction to the intruder is also possible. One's own sexuality can be sacrificed to an asexual dyad – regarded as the highest – through the complete negation of sexuality, in extreme cases the destruction of one's own genitals. In the countertransference, there may be despair, a feeling of being completely excluded, helplessness, pity, and tendencies towards an aggressive separation of the dyad.	**Dilemma in active mode** The position of the one who stands above all laws ("father of the primordial horde") and to whom all women/men should be loyal is taken – sometimes delusionally. This can be associated with the urge for completely obtrusive sexualization, uninhibited display of sexuality, or sexualized "relationship mania." In the countertransference, there may be despair, pity, and disgust, an urge to restore "order" and limit omnipotence. Alternatively, envy of those who can enjoy being above the law.

4.4.7 C7 Identity Conflict as a Dilemma

Individuals with fragmented self-structure often face a conflict between wanting to have an identity and a tendency to negate their own existence (Table 40). As this dilemma cannot be represented psychologically, what remains is either a devastating self-annihilation or an unrepresentable tendency to take on roles and clichéd "identities" without any real connection to the self.

This proposal suggests integrating conflict-motivational issues in cases of severe structural impairment into OPD as dilemmas. We hope this approach will be widely tested for its meaningfulness and usefulness. Early applications indicate it could be beneficial in clinical practice (Sell et al., 2021).

Table 40. C7 Identity conflict as a dilemma

Identity conflict as a dilemma	
In people with a more disintegrated structural level, the conflictual-motivational issue manifests itself as an existential and extremely threatening dilemma with sometimes extreme compensation mechanisms, sometimes with reinterpretations of reality: Extremely threatening antagonism between the "need to be someone" and the tendency to negate one's own existence, dilemma cannot be represented psychologically, therefore only either destructive self-annihilation or the assumption of roles and clichéd "identities" without a real connection to the self.	
Dilemma in passive mode Complete lack of identity, of meaning, up to the complete negation of one's own existence. Attempt to be completely incomprehensible can also include inaudible or incomprehensible speech. Countertransference: Confusion, emptiness, boredom, feeling of not being able to get in touch, patient does not remain "perceptible" or intangible, is forgotten and overlooked, alternatively fear, insecurity regarding one's own identity.	**Dilemma in active mode** Unrepresentable tendency to assume (better: concretize) roles and clichéd "identities" without any real reference to self and own values. Attempt to compensate for the lack of reference to one's own feeling, the feeling of being real and alive, by "borrowing identity," adopting details (e.g., clothing, voice, posture) of another person. Often clichéd language and separation of affect and intellect. CT: Agonizing feeling of not being able to make contact, anger, not being able to see behind the "shimmering wall," helplessness, alternatively insecurity of one's own identity, resignation or dropping the other person.

5 Axis IV: Structure

5.1 Summarized Presentation of Axis IV

Structure represents the basic framework of personality – the more constant traits and responses, the intrapsychic and interpersonal competencies. It is less about individual coloring and more about the basic abilities and dispositions that usually provide regulatory functions. Structure becomes visible in the way one deals with oneself, with relationships, and with the world, so that diagnostically relevant information is found mostly in challenging situations (under stress) and mostly in the interpersonal realm (including the clinical examination itself). Axis IV comprises five dimensions, four of which are divided into sub-dimensions related to the self and objects/relationships, respectively. Only the third dimension, "Defense," spans both areas as it (almost) always combines intrapsychic and interpersonal aspects.

The five dimensions are:

1. Perception
2. Regulation
3. Defense
4. Communication
5. Attachment

Each of the dimensions, except for defense, contains 2 × 3 facets, with defense having 1 × 3, which are rated on a seven-point scale and represent the smallest units of the rating (a total of 27 facets in 9 domains). The maturity or integration of the structure ranges from "good" (1) through "moderate" (2) to "low" (3) and "disintegrated" (4). The OPD-3 structure rating allows for the capture of clinically relevant temporal variability (e.g., due to episodes of illness) as well as divergent structural levels in different areas of life (e.g., in psychosis or trauma-related disorders).

Axis IV is closely related to the new conceptions of personality function in DSM-5 (American Psychiatric Association, 2013) as well as the severity determination in personality disorders of ICD-11 (Blüml & Doering, 2021; Hörz-Sagstetter et al., 2021). This is not surprising, as the as the new alternative model for personality disorders draw on psychoanalytic models of structure or personality organization. Thus, Axis IV can easily be used for personality diagnostics from a descriptive-phenomenological perspective, even though it conceptually and in terms of its content breadth goes far beyond that.

5.2 What Is Structure?

5.2.1 Definition

Structure encompasses the fundamental abilities of personality to deal with oneself, relationships, and others in a complex and appropriate manner. It does not capture the contents of experiences, thoughts, and actions but their prerequisites. Structure can be developmentally impaired, which forms the basis for a variety of mental disorders, known as structural disorders, and is of utmost importance for personality disorders. Structural disorders can occur in a variety of mental disorders; conversely, a well-integrated structure is a protective factor for mental health.

Synonyms include personality functioning or organization. Structure is operationalized along a continuum of integration levels of various personality aspects; in other words, the adaptivity of personality functions. Strictly speaking, the terms structure and organization refer to an invisible intrapsychic form of organization, while functions represent the observable manifestations of the underlying structure. However, the terms are usually used synonymously.

5.2.2 Structure and Current Trends in Classification and Research

Since the publication of OPD-1 in 1996 (English: OPD Task Force, 2001) with the initial conceptualization of the Structure Axis (Axis IV), the topic has received unexpected international attention and dissemination. What was originally understood as a psychoanalytic idiosyncrasy has since made its way into mainstream psychiatric diagnostics. The DSM-5 of the American Psychiatric Association (2013) included in its "Section III" a diagnosis of personality function that largely corresponds to the OPD Axis IV – the Scale of Personality Functioning (SEFP; American Psychiatric Association, 2013, pp. 775–778) appears like an adoption of the OPD structure checklist (OPD Task Force, 2008, p. 360–367). Last but not least, the SEFP of DSM-5 has further accelerated the boom of the structure topic: diagnostic instruments are springing up like mushrooms, and a large number of clinical studies are now focusing on "personality function." Axis IV can rightly be seen as a pioneer of structural diagnostics that significantly influenced and participated in the development of various concepts and instruments.

Of course, Axis IV was also overtaken by the zeitgeist – since the early 1990s and the publication of ICD-10 and DSM-IV with their phenomenological-descriptive diagnostics and symptom focus, the realization has gained ground in international psychiatry that there are relevant categories of mental health and illness beyond symptoms. It has become clear, for example, that merely reducing depressive symptoms does not necessarily mean that patients are satisfied with themselves, their relationships, their work, and their life. This development has likely been contributed to by the relative decline in the importance of psychopharmacology and the significant strengthening of psychotherapy: Almost all current guidelines for various mental and psychosomatic disorders consider psychotherapy essential, if not the first choice of treatment. The psychotherapeutic engagement with the patient quickly makes it clear that what Freud (1904) formulated as the goal of psychoanalysis, namely the restoration of "capacity for work and enjoyment" (Freud, 1904, p. 8; often cited slightly differently as the ability to love and work), is a treatment goal across all schools of thought for every patient (and therapist). While structural diagnostics in DSM-5 and also in ICD-11 (World Health Organization, 2018, 2024; Oltmanns & Widiger, 2019; Bach & Simonsen, 2021) are still limited to the diagnosis of personality disorders, the endeavor to also consider personality and functional aspects in other disorders has long since begun (see e.g., Doering et al., 2018).

Another interesting parallel can be found between structural diagnostics, such as in OPD, and the so-called P-factor by Caspi et al. (2014) and Fonagy et al. (2017a; Fonagy et al., 2017b) or the G-factor by Carla Sharp (Sharp et al., 2015), which both stand for a "general personality pathology" and provide an empirically generated underpinning of the concept of personality functions. Although this has not yet been empirically tested, it is assumed that there are extensive overlapping areas with the structure concept.

In OPD-3, Axis IV largely follows the structure and content of the previous OPD-2. Some facets have been renamed and described in more detail; all texts of the Axis IV checklist have been supplemented or reworded. The most significant change is the manualization of all seven levels of structure – previously only the four "main levels" were presented and the three "intermediate levels" were not specifically formulated. In addition, more space has been given to defense, as a separate dimension on Axis IV. Furthermore, the Axis IV checklist was supplemented with so-called "core sentences." These are intended to clarify which central aspects are contained in each (sub-) dimension and how these change on a continuum from good integration to disintegration.

Even more attention was paid to the formulation of the facets to ensure that the disintegrated level does not simply depict the psychopathology, e.g., symptomatology of psychotic or dissocial disorders. Rather, the underlying structure should be captured independently of the diagnosis. Lastly, a variability rating of the structure was introduced, which can be used optionally, for example, with psychotic patients. This accounts for the fact that the structure does not always remain completely stable but can be impaired depending on stressful influences such as trauma or episodes of illness.

The following Section will first generally define the concept of structure as well as its psychological and psychoanalytic definitions and developmental lines before describing the operationalization of OPD.

5.2.3 The Concept of Structure in General

In general, structure is understood as the ordered arrangement of parts within a whole; structures can be described and defined using the rules of their functioning and their developmental history. In this sense, the concept of structure is used in many different disciplines, for example, in terms such as the "geological structure of the Rhine rift valley," the "molecular structure of a crystal," the "age structure of the population," the "power structure of a society," the "structure of texts, sign systems, languages, communication," and others (Küchenhoff, 2002; Küchenhoff, 2012).

To understand structures as meaningful and functional, a reference to their developmental history is usually made, i.e., to the origin of their construction and functioning during childhood. Since only hypotheses can be formed about the function, construction, and history of structures, and the structures are not accessible to direct observation or investigation, the structural dimensions should be regarded as models and explanatory constructs. These can only be formulated within the framework of theoretical assumptions. Therefore, such structural models are always related to specific theories and formulated in their terminology. Dealing with structural concepts, thus, requires constant critical examination of the underlying theoretical assumptions.

Structures can usually be understood as compositions of substructures, and these, in turn, as parts of overarching frameworks in a network of influencing factors. They represent an ensemble of information that organizes experiences and their processing. Here lies the proximity to the concept of a system, which emphasizes the dynamic processes of homeostatic balance in the sense of feedback loops and the effectiveness of nonlinear processes.

5.2.4 The Psychological Concept of Structure

Structure in the psychological sense refers to the holistic configuration of psychological dispositions. They encompass everything that runs regularly and repetitively in an individual's experience and behavior (conscious or unconscious). Structure establishes the enduring personal style (Shapiro, 1965) in which the individual repeatedly restores their intrapsychic and interpersonal balances. An unimpaired structure flexibly and creatively disposes of functions that regulate or adapt intrapsychically and interpersonally.

Structure is not rigid and unchangeable but develops over the lifespan. However, the speed of change in these processes is so slow that the impression of constancy prevails, similar to concepts such as identity, character, or personality. To counteract a too static conception of structure, reference should be made to the arguments that suggest viewing structure from dynamic perspectives: Psychological structures are dynamic when viewed from a developmental perspective because they are formed over the course of life. Although they are based on genetically anchored personality dispositions, they are only shaped during childhood and are subject to significant changes during the course of life development.

Psychological structures are dispositions and, as such, are not directly observable; they only manifest in concrete, current situations as functions from which enduring structural characteristics are inferred. Such inferences are never exhaustive; the description of personality structures is always provisional and unfinished. Furthermore, the concept of structure implies a temporal stability, which may be limited at the psychological level: Based on the assumption of potentially lifelong possible growth of personality, the concept of structure also includes aspects of developmental dynamics with temporal, albeit slow, potential for change. Structures change through the integration of new experiences, thereby establishing regularity until they change again through the integration of different experiences.

5.2.5 The Psychoanalytic Concept of Structure

As in other sciences, a unified concept of structure cannot be found in psychoanalytic literature. However, several focal points can be distinguished in the historically evolved discussion (see also Rudolf, 2020):

The *topographical structural model:* Freud, for example, in *The Ego and the Id* (1923) or in the *New Introductory Lectures* (1933), speaks of the "structural relationships of the mental personality" when describing the interplay of the Id, Ego, and Superego. The aim of this structural model is not to describe individual contents but the interplay of different contents, the rule system of psychic functioning in the topography of the "psychic apparatus," for example, to distinguish between conscious/unconscious systems.

Character structure: These are terms that, in a reduced form, describe typologies of character attitudes. The typologies are theoretically based, derived from metapsychology and developmental psychology (oral personality, anal character, etc., see Abraham, 1925/1927). As a diagnostic category, the concept of character neurosis forms a counterpart to that of conflict neurosis. There are transitions to what is described in contemporary diagnostic systems as personality disorder.

Neurosis structure: In his neurosis-psychological concept Schultz-Hencke (1951) describes hysterical, obsessive, depressive, and schizoid structures of neurosis. It is a drive-theoretical concept that describes the characteristic consequences of certain drive repressions. Clinically, a coexistence of several structural components (e.g., depressive-hysterical neurosis structure) is usually diagnosed (see also Schwidder, 1972a, 1972b).

Ego structure: After the formulations of psychoanalytic ego psychology (Hartmann, 1958), it became possible to systematize ego functions (Bellak & Hurvich, 1969) and later operationalize them, thus deriving an assessment of ego-structural functioning ("ego strength, ego weakness").

Structure and object relations: The psychoanalytic theory of internalization processes with its developmental stages of establishing self and object representations was, based on the work of authors like Melanie Klein, Donald Winnicott and Wilfred Bion, systematically laid out by Kernberg within his object relations theory and made clinically and therapeutically useful concerning personality disorders (Kernberg,

1970, 1976, 1980, 1984). Since Kernberg's conception is strongly based on developmental psychological models, the developmental psychology of structure is presented in the following chapter.

In Rudolf's conceptualization of structure, alongside object relations theory and ego psychology, developmental psychology and attachment theory play a significant role (Rudolf et al., 2002; Rudolf, 2020). His model has been central to the conceptualization of Axis IV from the beginning and is therefore essentially represented in Section 5.4

5.2.6 The Developmental Psychology of Structure

The study of infants and young children, in the light of developmental psychology and attachment research, has been of particular importance for understanding the concept of structure. Towards the end of the 20th century, psychoanalysts increasingly adopted this research (Dornes, 1997; Emde 1981; Fonagy et al., 1998; Fonagy et al., 2002; Grossmann et al., 1989; Lichtenberg, 1983; Stern, 1977, 1985). Findings emphasize the infant's innate object-seeking activity and their early-developed competence to involve the caregiving adult in social interactions. These(mostly) pleasurable interactions include bodily care, nutrition, and emotional security processes, which the classic Freudian theory (in terms of oral and early libidinal relationships) emphasized. In these early developmental stages, the ego begins to organize itself by being interested, ready to act, and emotionally oriented towards the non-self, i.e., the world of objects (intentional-communicative function of the ego, see Rudolf, 1977). The repetitive interactions between the infant and their available, emotionally supportive objects involve practicing structural functions, particularly through the experience of empathetic understanding and appropriate treatment. The development of the self's structure is then provisionally completed when the ego can look at itself as an object and thus refer reflexively to itself (Stern, 1985). The associated establishment of a demarcated inner psychic space and the beginning of conceptual-symbolic representation of the experiential world can be observed around the 18th month of age. Fonagy's group emphasizes the aspects of increasing psychological integration and mentalization, which ultimately express themselves in the availability of the self-reflective functioning (Fonagy et al., 2002).

In the constant relationship with the object world, the controlling, organizing function of the ego is differentiated furthermore, and images of the self and important objects (self-representations and object representations) are created. Objects are experienced as separate from the self, recognized, affectively charged, and internalized. The emotional attitudes experienced from significant objects and, particularly, the affectively charged interactions between the child and the caregiver color not only their image and attitudes toward them but also the self-image as well as self-esteem. The structure of the self and the structure of object relations mature in intense reciprocity. The self gains increasing coherence, demarcation, and the ability of self-organization. Simultaneously, the ability to bond with others that provide security is strengthened. The security of object attachment, in turn, favors the development of self-autonomy, which in further steps leads to the strengthened self beginning to detach from and confront the objects. At the end of the development there is an autonomous self which has developed a sense of identity and which is able to regulate its self-image, self-esteem, and ability to control and act.

Kernberg's object relations theory model also focuses on the development of what he calls "personality organization" (see, e.g., Kernberg, 1984). He assumes that early relationship experiences are internalized, with initially only partial aspects of the self and the object being experienced and stored in memory (partial self, partial object). These are either only good or only bad and are associated with a corresponding positive or negative affect. These partial object relationship dyads are the building blocks of personality. By the end of the third year of life, the internalized partial aspects of the self and the objects are integrated, and the defense mechanism of splitting between positive and negative parts is lifted. This identity integration leads to complete, gestalt-like internal images of the self and objects, characterized by shades of gray (as opposed to black-and-white views) and the emergence of ambivalent affects. In Kernberg's model, people with a structural disorder ("borderline organization level") have not undergone this integration, resulting in identity diffusion, wherein adults still represent idealized and devalued self and object parts unconnected. This is the case, for example, in patients with borderline personality disorder. Empirical evidence has shown (Doering et al., 2013) that Kernberg's neurotic organization level corresponds to the moderately integrated structural level of OPD, while the borderline organization level corresponds to the poorly integrated structural level.

Developmental psychological and psychoanalytic structural models are also available for diagnosing and treating psychotic disorders (Dümpelmann, 2018; Küchenhoff, 2012, 2012/2018; Lempa et al., 2017). The OPD-3 Structure Axis (Axis IV) contains descriptions that attempt to account more precisely for psychotic illnesses than in earlier versions. This primarily relates to the disturbed or unstable ability for self-constitution and authorship, the symbolic communication of psychic experiences, and the resulting peculiarity of reacting to conflicts, which in psychoses take on a dilemmatic form (Mentzos, 2015), with sometimes radical denial of reality and externalizations, and dissolution of ego boundaries and fusion, or with withdrawal of investment and isolation (Dümpelmann, 2018; Lempa et al., 2017). Further developments in this area are to be expected and are necessary due to the clinical significance of psychotic disorders.

5.3 Empirical Approaches to Measuring Structure

To operationalize personality structure, a variety of theoretical approaches were available as precursors to the standardization of psychodynamic structural diagnostics, which the authors of the first OPD Manual could rely on. Clarkin (2004) lists among them Sullivan's conceptualization of the Psychiatric Interview in 1954. This was followed by "The initial interview in psychiatric practice" by Gill et al. (1954) and the "Tavistock Interview" by Balint & Balint (1961). The "Metapsychological Developmental Profiles for Children and Adults" published by Anna Freud from 1963 represents early approaches to operationalizing personality structure, as did the classification system of the "Hampstead Index for Children" by Sandler (1962). In the German-speaking area, the "Psychoanalytic Initial Interview" by Argelander (1970/1976) was widespread, as well as the "Biographical Anamnesis" by Dührssen (1981) and the "Guidelines for Psychiatric Examination" by Kind (1973).

The actual operationalization of components of structure, such as defense mechanisms (Vaillant, 1971), ego strength in the Menninger project (Kernberg et al., 1972), and ego functions (Bellak et al., 1973) further paved the way for the Axis IV. However, the concepts of character and structure remained vague for a long time. It was argued that psychological structure should always be related to a character diagnosis. Hoffmann combined structural and characterological features in a two-dimensional operationalization design to describe the extent and nature of pathology (Hoffmann, 1984).

A significant starting point for modern psychodynamic thinking is Kernberg's innovative concept of psychic structure. Here, the term structure captures basic regulation types or the entire organization of psychological functioning along a developmental and maturity gradient, oriented by dimensional characteristics regarding resilience under stress or pathological processes. Described are global levels or layers of functioning that correspond to a specific organization. His dimensionally oriented classification of personality structure was groundbreaking, encompassing dimensions for mature and pathological developments of ego and superego structures, internalized object relations, development of libidinal and aggressive drive derivatives, and defense mechanisms, including the nature of pathological character traits. In an early, less known version, three structural levels of character pathology were already distinguished (Kernberg, 1970).

This classification inspired other groups: In Sweden, a standardization of Kernberg's previously unstructured clinical "Structural Interview," resulted in the "Karolinska Psychodynamic Profile (KAPP)" (Weinryb & Rössel, 1991). In Germany, a group developed the "Heidelberg Rating" based on constructs such as psychosexual development level, aspects of ego functions and superego structure, development of narcissism, and emotional expressiveness (Engel et al., 1979). An understanding of psychovegetative disorders as an ego-structural problem emerged with the "Structural Developmental Level" (Ermann, 1982). This was followed by the "Multiaxial Diagnostics in Psychosomatics" (Schüßler et al., 1990), also referencing Kernberg's work (for the theory development of personality structure, see Pouget-Schors, 2014).

Two operationalized models can be seen as direct precursors of Axis IV: The "Munich Structural Level of Personality Organization" developed a systematic approach to Kernberg's early 1970 model (Lohmer et al., 1992). This distinguished on the construct level a three-tier structural level of personality organization to differentiate early disorders as an intermediate structural level from more mature neuroses or borderline personality disorders. Evaluated were the following: nature and pathology of object relationships, ego structure and defense mechanisms, superego development, handling of libidinal and aggressive drive impulses, quality of anxiety, and the patient-therapist relationship. The operationalization of the structural dimensions based on this was first presented in Heidelberg in 1993, in the Structure Axis working group of the OPD (Pouget, 1993).

Gerd Rudolf's Heidelberg group developed the 17-Item ISO scales ("Ich-Selbst-Objekt-Beziehungs-Items"), a solution approach on the item-cluster level with scaled gradations (Rudolf, 1995). Congruences of both models formed the basis of the OPD-1 Structure Axis, after modifications by the authors of the OPD working group who also considered other preliminary work and new developments, especially the Swedish "Karolinska Psychodynamic Profile KAPP" (Weinryb & Rössel, 1991), until the publication of the OPD-1 manual (OPD Task Force, 1996).

As described, Kernberg's "Structural Interview" was one of the first systematized approaches to clinical structural diagnosis. His later conceptualization oriented itself to the triad of identity diffusion, primitive defense, and reality testing as the parameters enabling the distinction between neurotic, borderline, and psychotic structural levels (Kernberg, 1981; Buchheim et al., 1987). Later, this unstructured clinical interview was primarily developed for research purposes into the "Structured Interview for Personality Organization" (STIPO; Clarkin et al., 2004), which in its revised form (STIPO-R, Clarkin et al., 2016) comprises six dimensions (identity, object relations, primitive defense mechanisms, higher-level defense mechanisms, aggression, moral values). Wallerstein created the "Scales of Psychological Capacities" (SPC; Wallerstein, 1996) to capture structural changes in psychotherapy research, translated and validated in German by Huber et al. (2006) as "Scales of Psychological Competencies" (SPK).

Important sub-aspects of structure related to attachment and derived mentalizing ability are captured by the "Adult Attachment Interview" (AAI; George et al., 1985), allowing the determination of adult attachment style. Based on the AAI, the "Reflective Functioning Scale"

(RF-Scale; Fonagy et al., 1998) can be used to assess mentalizing ability.

Two interviews were recently developed to capture personality function according to DSM-5: the "Structured Clinical Interview for the DSM-5 Alternative Model for Personality Disorders" (SCID-5-AMPD; First et al., 2018) and the "Semi-Structured Interview for the Assessment of DSM-5 Personality Functions" (Zettl et al., 2019). Although the DSM-5 does not explicitly refer to psychoanalytic models, it is evident that almost all of its content has its antecedents in psychoanalytic/psychodynamic theory building. There are also several questionnaires to capture the structural level. The three validated and established questionnaires in German are the "OPD Structure Questionnaire" (OPD-SF; Ehrenthal et al., 2012; Schauenburg et al., 2012), the "Borderline Personality Inventory" (BPI, Leichsenring, 1997; Salzer & Leichsenring, 2012), and the "Inventory of Personality Organization" (IPO; Clarkin et al., 2000) constructed by the Kernberg group and conceptually corresponding to the Structural Interview and STIPO. All three instruments capture closely related constructs and show high intercorrelations (König et al., 2016).

Recently, three questionnaires have also been presented directly targeting the assessment of personality function according to DSM-5: the "Level of Personality Functioning Scale - Self-Report" (LPFS-SR; Morey, 2017), the "General Assessment of Personality Disorder" (GAPD; Livesley, 2009; Zimmermann et al., 2015), and the "Standardized Assessment of Severity of Personality Disorder" (SASPD; Olajide et al., 2018).

The structure construct is extremely robust (Hörz-Sagstetter et al., 2021). The various short questionnaires for measuring structure or personality function can be interchanged (Zimmermann et al., 2020). The interviews correlate relatively well with each other (Doering et al., 2013; Doering et al., 2014), and the questionnaires also show high agreement with the interviews, justifying their use for screening. So, although questionnaires on structure aspects are relatively reliable, they have the disadvantage that they provide only general clinical information. For this reason, they can never replace clinical diagnosis, and a positive screening e.g., should be followed by clinical evaluation for indication and therapy planning.

5.4 Operationalization of Structure in the OPD

The OPD strives to integrate the above-mentioned psychodynamic structure concepts while largely avoiding the use of traditional psychoanalytic terms, instead aiming to capture the behavior and experience of patients as observationally close as possible. This leads to a functional description of the structure as the self in its relationship to the objects (Rudolf, 1995; Rudolf et al., 2002), which can be found in large areas in the much younger "Scale for Assessing the Level of Personality Functioning of the DSM-5" (American Psychiatric Association, 2013). Similarly, all structural functions can be related both to the inner psychological world and to the outer social reality, i.e., to the self and to objects.

The Structure of the Self: According to Stern (1985), the self develops from a core self through a subjective self to a verbal self. This mature self is characterized by its reflective function (self-reflection): The ego takes itself as the object of inner perception. This results in a self-image and, in its constancy and coherence, an experience of identity. The self integrates all psychological functions and dispositions into a whole and regulates internal processes (affect regulation, impulse control). The availability of flexible defenses with reference to an internalized value system is part of the regulatory process. As a result of significant relationship experiences, internalization processes occur from an early age, which not only establish an inner image of important objects (object representations) but also shape the self-image (self-representations).

The reference to internalized, sufficiently good objects is crucial for the function of self-regulation and affect regulation, especially self-soothing and self-comforting. The self-reflective reference to one's inner world structurally means the ability for inner communication, an inner dialogue, where one's emotionality, needs, fantasy world, and experiences of physical sensations (Küchenhoff, 2012; Küchenhoff & Argawalla, 2013) are of particular importance.

The Relation to Objects: All mentioned aspects of the self find their counterpart in the relationship to external objects. Developmentally, relationship experiences form the basis for the development and regulation of the self. Parallel to the reflective perception of the self, the realistic perception of objects can be described. Realistically, in an adult sense, it becomes so through the secure differentiation of self and object, through the demarcation of both and the acceptance that the object possesses its own reality independent of the self. Here, there are parallels to the concept of mentalization, where several structural dimensions converge.

The processes of self-regulation correspond to the structural ability to shape relationships in such a way that one's own and others' interests are appropriately considered, while simultaneously protecting an emotionally significant relationship from one's own disturbing impulses and affects. As the name suggests, the two regulation dimensions correspond to the concept of emotion dysregulation, which is often thought of less in terms of relational dynamics (see, e.g., Linehan, 1993).

The fact that others can be experienced as distinct objects requires (since they are not one and know everything about each other) making oneself communicatively understandable. This happens through emotional expression that must reach the other or being emotionally touched by the other; here, the ability to temporarily empathize with the inner world of the other plays a crucial role.

Structure can thus be described according to OPD in five dimensions, each distinguishing between the relation to the self and the relation to the objects. Each dimension has two sub-dimensions (self- and object-directed), each described by three facets (see Table 41), except for defense, which spans the boundaries between self and object (see the next section).

The structural dimensions are not independent of each other. They reflect structural aspects from different perspectives and capture complex functional patterns in various contexts. One has to take into account, however, that these dimensions have been shown to statistically correlate moderately to highly with each other (see, e.g., Benecke et al., 2009; Doering et al., 2013).

Most of the operationalizations from OPD-2 have been retained and slightly expanded in OPD-3. Special emphasis was placed on formulating the operationalization of the structural dimensions independently of aspects of mental disorders or psychopathological symptoms. This proved particularly relevant for the disintegrated structural level. With the new formulation, it should be possible to capture both, patients with rather psychotic disintegration and those with rather psychopathic disintegration.

For each of the 27 facets, two or more so-called "core sentences" were formulated. These summarize the central themes of the facet in one sentence each, from good to increasingly lower integration. The core sentences are aids for understanding or rating but are not rated themselves.

Defense occupies a special position because it regulates both the self and relationships, involves both emotional and cognitive aspects, and has both functional and substantive characteristics. In contrast to general regulatory abilities, defense always involves an effort to keep distressing affective content temporarily or permanently out of consciousness. Defense pervades all structural dimensions and thus represents a central element of neurotic conflicts – more precisely, of conflict resolution, for which it provides the tools to transform affective conflict tension into neurotic conflict by shifting

Table 41. Overview of the dimensions and facets of structure

Self		Object/relationships	
Self-perception		**Object perception**	
ST1.1	Self-reflection	ST1.4	Self-object differentiation
ST1.2	Affect differentiation	ST1.5	Object related affect differentiation
ST1.3	Identity	ST1.6	Integrated object perception
Self-regulation		**Relationship regulation**	
ST2.1	Impulse control	ST2.4	Protecting relationships
ST2.2	Affect tolerance	ST2.5	Anticipation
ST2.3	Self-esteem regulation	ST2.6	Balancing of interests
Defense			
ST3.1 Living and experiencing possibilities			
ST3.2 Interpersonal impact			
ST3.3 Mechanisms			
Internal communication		**Communication with the external world**	
ST4.1	Experience of affects and fantasies	ST4.4	Making emotional contact
ST4.2	Experience of joy	ST4.5	Intimacy
ST4.3	Bodily self	ST4.6	Empathy
Attachment to internal objects		**Attachment to external objects**	
ST5.1	Internalization	ST5.4	Ability to form attachments
ST5.2	Use of introjects	ST5.5	Trust
ST5.3	Variability	ST5.6	Ability to separate

Note. ST = structure.

one pole into the unconscious and thus withdrawing it from life and ongoing consciousness. Relationship behavior is usually characterized by defense mechanisms (moderately integrated level) or is a direct expression of defense (low/disintegrated level). Of course, the experience of illness and expectations of treatment are also shaped by defense mechanisms. Thus, defense essentially influences and shapes all axes of the OPD-3. This omnipresence of defense and the fact that it is so difficult to objectify because it is never seen directly, but only its results, can be seen as the reason for the traditionally volatile fate of the operationalization of defense. In OPD itself, it was a distinct structural dimension in OPD-1, then seemingly disappeared from OPD-2, only to reappear implicitly in individual structural facets – most prominently in the "Protecting relationships" facet, where it at least appeared in parentheses. It has now returned to OPD-3 as its own dimension and, as in OPD-1, is ranked third among the dimensions. Defense mechanisms have had a similar fate in the DSM: they were included in DSM-IV as the "Defense Mechanisms and Coping Styles Scale" in the Appendix for further research but are absent in DSM-5 because this scale was barely researched and did not make it into the "Personality Functioning Scale." OPD-3 now gives defense as a central ego function a place as its own dimension on Axis IV, recognizing that defense is more than just a structural feature. It has deliberately not been assigned to another structural dimension as a separate facet, as it permeates all structural dimensions. It is strategically located in the middle of Axis IV, spanning self and relationship domains between perception and regulation on the one hand, and communication and attachment on the other. In terms of content, the operationalization focuses on functional rather than content aspects, in line with the general OPD definition of structure. Three facets are defined, each focusing on different aspects of defense: maintaining or giving up the ability to experience different aspects of life and experience possibilities, intrapsychic vs. interpersonal defense, and the specific defense mechanisms used for defense. Defense reveals the variability of structure in two ways: first, it undergoes micro-fluctuations dependent on everyday states of mind. For example, in relationship conflicts, most people reach a point where they use projective identifications and other mechanisms of the low integrated structural level. However, they can return to a better functioning level after a manageable time and reflect on what happened, provided their overall structure level is moderate or good. We also observe interpersonal regulatory mechanisms at a good structural level that are not considered dysfunctional but contribute to a mature stabilization of, for instance a couple, while material can be shifted into the unconscious (collusively), it is debatable whether the term "defense" is suitable for these processes.

Second, defense is subjected to variability due to episodes of illness, as captured in the structure variability rating. In a psychotic episode, a patient may employ low or disintegrated defense in some or all life areas, while functioning moderately in the interval. The operationalization of defense requires rating the prevailing level under usual everyday conditions.

The three facets of defense focus primarily on the functionality of defense: how high is the price for achieving (relative) stability. In other words, how many life and experience possibilities must the individual sacrifice to stabilize? For mature personalities, these losses are minimal; as the structural level decreases, they grow larger, up to giving up fulfilling relationships or professional performance. There are artists who, despite their psychosis, can create great art (e.g., art brut), but only as long as they live in a sheltered institution and avoid emotionally disturbing relationship experiences. They have retreated to a "small island in the big ocean," living and experiencing very limitedly but functioning artistically and in everyday life.

Another functional aspect of defense is how much others must be involved in the individual's defense efforts to achieve (relative) stability. The central mechanisms of interpersonal defense (splitting and projective identification) typically appear from the low integrated structural level onwards (apart from the micro-regressions of more mature personalities). The lower the structural level, the stronger the defense-induced distortions of social reality perception, up to an exclusively constructed social reality.

5.5 Diagnostic Procedure

5.5.1 The Diagnostic Material

The structural patterns inherent in the patient manifest themselves in interactive actions. This means that the diagnostician experiences something of the patient's structure in the immediate situation of the encounter and that they get an image of the patient's structure from the patient's descriptions of their everyday life and life history. Structural diagnostics are facilitated by the possibility of letting the patient speak spontaneously or upon request about introspectively obtained assessments of their own person and behavior.

The recognition of psychological structure is necessarily linked to verbal and non-verbal communication. The prerequisite for assessing structural aspects is a diagnostic interview that enables the development of a relationship between patient and diagnostician. To reflect and interpret the phenomena, the diagnostician needs basic knowledge about personality theory and development as well as diagnostic experience. They should ideally have self-experience to switch between observation and introspection in experiencing and evaluating their own countertransference.

Structure constitutes itself from the self and its relationships to objects, specifically from the availability of psychic functions in regulating the self and its relationship to internal and external objects. The degree of availability or restriction of the respective functions determines the structural integration level.

The constructs of structure and conflict describe different psychological aspects. Conflict, as a repetitive pattern, describes content-related, motivational system-related psychodynamic aspects of events, and thus also conditions for triggering symptoms. Structure refers to the vulnerability of personality due to impaired availability of basic psychic abilities, to the disposition to illness due to the varying or limited capacity to process internal conflicts and external stress experiences.

The same conflict themes appear differently at different structural levels (e.g., different quality of affects, different images of self and objects, different quality and intensity of needs, different mature defenses, etc.). Empirical evidence found an association of individual conflicts with specific structural levels: individuation-dependence conflict and self-worth conflict at reduced structural levels, oedipal-sexual conflicts at better-integrated structural levels (Grande et al., 1998). This should not be misunderstood as implying that the respective conflict themes cannot also be found at other structural levels. The lower the structural level, the more difficult it becomes to identify stable conflict patterns. At low to disintegrated structural levels, the same motivationally conflicting patterns are present, but they are not neurotically organized in the sense that one pole can be stably and permanently defended; instead, both poles are alternately activated, and there can be arrested extremes here as well. In previous OPD versions, conflict rating was sometimes omitted. OPD-3 now provides for rating conflict themes at every structural level. Although these are not neurotically configured conflicts at low or disintegrated levels, the same motivational themes are active and influence the psychological events and symptoms, so their significance (and coping attempts) should also be marked on the Conflict Axis (Axis III) at low or disintegrated levels if possible.

The clinical material to be examined from a structural perspective includes:

- The interactions and experiences reported by the patient from their life.
- The structural abilities displayed in the diagnostic relationship.
- The countertransference experienced by the therapist and the experience of the "here and now."
- The patient's introspective assessments of their own person and behavior, either spontaneously or upon request.

For structure assessment, the OPD interview obligatorily includes generating a self-description and an object description from the patient. This technique, already included in Kernberg's Structured Interview (Kernberg, 1981; Buchheim et al., 1987), is discussed in more detail in Chapter 7 on conducting the OPD interview.

5.5.2 The Time Window

The time window for assessing structure is generally 5 years. Processes before this period should not be included in the rating. For adolescents, the time window should be shortened, for example, a time window of one or two years for a 19-year-old patient would be reasonable, as this prevents puberty-related changes in structural abilities from distorting or complicating the rating too much. Similarly, for certain scientific questions, the time window can be shortened. This applies, for example, to follow-up studies where treatment effects are to be captured over a shorter period. If the treatment period is one year, the time window for OPD interviews can be shortened to 6 months.

In order to reflect on and interpret the phenomena, the diagnostician needs basic knowledge of personality theory and development as well as diagnostic experience. Ideally, the diagnostician should have the self-experience to alternate between observation and introspection in experiencing and evaluating his or her own countertransference. When temporal variability in structure occurs, it may be within the 5-year window or extend over a longer period. In such cases it may be useful to extend the time window. This is true, for example, of patients with addictive disorders in whom deterioration of the structural level has occurred over many years as a result of substance use. Here, the time window may be extended to 6, 7, or even 10 years. More detailed explanations of the temporal dynamics of structural changes can be found in the OPD-2 module on addictive disorders (Arbeitskreis OPD – Abhängigkeitserkrankungen, 2013) and as explained by Jakobsen (2014).

5.5.3 Assessing the Variability of Structure

The structural level of personality is still considered relatively stable over time, and many conceptualizations of structure assume that the various structural dimensions are highly correlated with each other and that structural deficits typically manifest across all life areas. There is ample empirical evidence supporting the first assumption (see validation studies of Axis IV, e.g., Benecke et al., 2009; Doering et al., 2014), and the second is reflected in criterion B of the general diagnostic criteria for personality disorders in DSM-5, which considers "impairments in social, occupational, and other important areas of functioning" (American Psychiatric Association, 2013, p. 885).

Recently, however, there has been growing recognition that structure may be less stable than previously assumed. Long-term studies of patients with personality disorders, such as the Collaborative Longitudinal Personality Disorders Study (CLPS; Skodol et al., 2005), support this view. Hopwood et al. (2009) found that the diagnostic criteria for borderline personality disorder were far from stable over time. Clinical reality also shows that many patients experience temporary or permanent changes in their structural level over the course or following episodes of illness or chronic mental disorders, thanks to the more precise structural diagnostic perspective provided by OPD. For instance, patients with psychoses, trauma-related disorders, addictions, or brain-organic disorders may experience these "fluctuations" in structure. To capture these fluctuations, a variability rating was developed for patients who cannot be adequately described by a single structural level within the usual five-year window.

Different patterns of progression are possible:

1. A patient may enter the five-year window at a relatively low structural level due to a long-term, possibly chronic illness (e.g., schizophrenic psychosis) and then experience a temporary or permanent remission that improves their structural level. Similarly, a patient with substance addiction may achieve abstinence and subsequently regain their structural functions.
2. The second course pattern involves a temporary deterioration: a patient with an affective psychosis may experience a severe depressive episode within the five-year window, significantly worsening their structural level for a few months, but then returning to their baseline level after the depressive episode subsides.
3. The third course pattern is a change in structural level occurring within the five-year window and still present at the time of OPD diagnosis, meaning the patient has not returned to the baseline level (although this does not imply a prognosis, as remission in the future can never be ruled out).

This conceptualization of the structural level's time-axis fluctuation assumes a uniform change across all dimensions of the overall structural level, thus only the overall structural level is considered in the rating.

Clinical reality also shows differential changes in structure, where specific life areas are affected differently, remaining largely unaffected in other areas. This is seen, for example, in patients with psychoses who function at a high level professionally but decompensate dramatically in personal relationships either temporarily or permanently. Similar situations occur in trauma-related disorders, where trauma-relevant areas (e.g., traffic or sexuality) are massively impaired in terms of structural functionality, while other life areas remain largely intact.

This variability or divergence of structure is organized orthogonally to the initially mentioned forms of fluctuation, resulting in different structural levels in different life areas. Therefore, no predominant level can be determined under usual everyday conditions, rather, there is a "side-by-side" of different structural levels, a kind of "double bookkeeping." The corresponding variability rating is conducted for the individual life areas defined on OPD's Conflict Axis (Axis III). It is important to note that temporal progression plays no role in this rating. Chronically stable conditions should also be described, even if they have not changed over the five-year window. This can apply, for instance, to patients with schizophrenia exhibiting "double bookkeeping," characterized by permanent or long-lasting divergent structural levels in different areas of life (e.g., professional life vs. partnership).

Rating 1, Temporal Variability Rating: The temporal fluctuation results from a mental illness (e.g., psychosis, brain-organic disorder, addiction) and/or trauma. Remission of fluctuation can occur spontaneously or be attributed to treatment or other influencing factors.

The temporal variability rating assumes a change in integration level from a baseline level. The baseline level refers to functioning under usual everyday conditions and outside of illness episodes impacting the structural level (see rating sheet in Section 5.6). The fluctuations in structural level must (a) occur within the defined time window of Axis IV (usually the past five years), (b) have significant impacts on everyday life (affecting relationships or work ability), and (c) last at least 4 weeks. If "no" is checked for Criterion A (variability of structural level), the remaining temporal variability rating is omitted.

Criterion B indicates the current structural level. Is it changed compared to the baseline level and if so, in which direction?

Example 1: A patient with bipolar disorder had a depressive episode three years ago, worsening her structural level from moderate (2.0) to low to disintegrated (3.5). They have been functioning at her baseline level of 2.0 for the past two years. In this case, "baseline level" is checked for criterion B.

Example 2: A patient was kidnapped and repeatedly raped two years ago. Since then, her originally good to moderate structural level (1.5) has dropped to a low structural level (3.0), and she suffers from severe PTSD that remains unchanged at the time of assessment. Here, "worse" is checked.

Example 3: A patient with heroin addiction has been abstinent for 1.5 years, no longer using any drugs. He has taken a job as a warehouse worker, performs diligently, and moved in with his new partner. The partnership is described as a bit complicated but stable. During active drug use, his structural level was low (3.0) with some short-term breaks. Now, his overall structural level is stable at moderate to low (2.5). Here, "better" is checked. If the illness began at an early age and lasted more than five years, the structural level that existed five years ago (start of the time window) is considered the baseline level. In such cases, no fluctuations within the time window are rated.

Criterion C, assesses the extent of the fluctuation, rated in 1-point steps (as in the ratings for the structural dimensions of Axis IV) rounding up to the next whole step if necessary. A finer granularity is not practical given the need to retrospectively estimate the baseline level. The direction of fluctuation is derived from criterion B. The rating in example 1 would thus be "±2," in example 2 it would also be "±2," and in example 3 it would be "±1."

Criterion D, describes the duration of the fluctuation, referring to the current or last structural change, thus "6–12 months" in example 1, "1–2 years" in examples 2 and 3.

Criterion E, documents the cause of this fluctuation in the form of diagnosis and/or trauma, "depressive episode, bipolar disorder," "PTSD after severe trauma for 1.5 years," or "abstinence for 1.5 years, opioid addiction, " for the examples.

Rating 2, Variability Rating by Life Areas: The variability rating by life areas can be conducted with or without the preceding temporal variability rating. If the variability lasts longer than the five-year window, the temporal variability rating is omitted. If it begins within the window, both variability ratings are conducted.

Starting from the overall structural level, which with different structural levels in life areas can only be an average value, the variability rating notes which life areas the patient is rated worse or better than the overall structural level. The overall structural level may correspond to most life areas, so only one or two divergent life areas are marked, or it may lie between 3–4 better and 3–4 worse life areas, so all life areas are rated either worse or better compared to the overall structural level.

Finally, the cause of the fluctuation is also recorded.

Example 1: A 45-year-old patient has suffered from paranoid psychosis since age 18. After an initially dramatic course, he has been relatively stabilized for about 12 years (under antipsychotic medication). He resumed his acting career and is successful in leading roles at a reputable state theater. The patient lives alone, takes care of himself, and has a large circle of friends where he is well integrated. However, he still tends to react paranoically when he falls in love or gets physically close to a woman, affecting him not so much that he has to call in sick at the theater. His structural level in "partnerships and family" and "body and sexuality" is low to disintegrated (3.5), while in all other life areas he is moderate. His overall structural level is assessed as moderate to low (2.5), with the variability rating marking five life areas as "better" and the two mentioned as "worse." The cause of variability is "paranoid psychosis."

Example 2: A 34-year-old bus driver experienced an accident three years ago, hitting an older man who later died from the injuries. Since then, she has suffered from PTSD and cannot work, taking early retirement. In all other areas of life, she functions well, caring devotedly for her husband and two children. She no longer drives, which she doesn't mind as her husband drives her or she uses public transport. She is well integrated socially within her circle of friends and extended family. The structural level in the "work" life area is low (3.0), but it remains good (2.0) in all other life areas. The variability rating marks only the "work" life area as "worse." The temporal variability rating does not apply as her overall structural level (2.0) has not changed due to PTSD. The cause of variability is PTSD.

Example 3: A 73-year-old patient has suffered from hypochondriacal delusion for 4 years after being previously healthy and well-structured (2.0). The delusion severely impacts her in the "body/sexuality" and "illnesses" life areas as she frequently visits doctors, obsessively concerned about her "innards," fearing irreversible damage from accidentally drinking a sip of dish soap; her structural level is disintegrated (4.0). Despite spending a lot of time alone at home preparing "healing elixirs," she is socially unremarkable, interacting normally with her children and grandchildren. Her overall structural level has been moderately to low integrated (2.5) since the onset of delusional disorder. Thus, both variability ratings are completed. The cause of variability is "hypochondriacal delusion."

5.5.4 Levels of Integration of Structure

As already in OPD-2, the OPD-3 Structure Axis (Axis IV) distinguishes seven levels of structure: four "main levels" and three "intermediate stages." Unlike OPD-2, OPD-3 operationalizes all seven stages in detail. The general characteristics of the seven levels are presented below (see Table 42).

Level: Good integration. The well-integrated psychic structure provides a psychic inner space where psychic experiences (cognitions, affects, fantasies, memories, decisions, etc.) can be perceived in a differentiated manner. Conflicts can also be managed intrapsychically; these occur between different needs and between need impulses on the one hand and internalized norms (in the form of a mature superego) and ideals on the other. The well-integrated structural level is characterized by the fact that the regulating functions are generally available to the patient and can be maintained or regained over longer periods, even in situations of internal and external stress. Thus, the well-integrated structural level represents a central psychological resilience factor. The central fear concerns the loss of the love of the object. The countertransference to such patients is characterized by the awareness of emotional responses that relate to the revival of biographically relevant experiences with previously experienced persons.

Level: Good to moderate integration. At this intermediate level, the functions of good integration are essentially present, but they are temporarily lost in situations and phases of significant stress (here meaning life events rather than illness episodes). During these times, the functioning of the individuals approaches that of the moderate structural level but returns to good functioning once the stressful situation ends.

Level: Moderate integration. The moderately integrated level is characterized by the availability of the described abilities and functions in principle, but they are reduced. Here, too, intrapsychic conflicts prevail, but they have a different configuration and management compared to the well-integrated level: on the wish side, there are unconscious impulses of greedy neediness, domination, and submission; on the opposing side, there are rigid and punitive norms ("immature superego") and exaggerated ideals. This "overregulation" of impulses, wish-

Table 42. General description of the levels

Levels	Description
1 Good	Stable presence of structural capabilities that are readily available even under stress.
1.5 Good to moderate	Good availability of structural abilities, although these may occasionally be interrupted in individual areas. Under stress, the full flexibility of the capabilities may be lost.
2 Moderate	There is a lack of flexibility and constrictions; there is a permanent overregulation. Rarely, outbreaks with intensive counter-regulation can occur.
2.5 Moderate to low	Clear limitations in structural abilities are recognizable. However, the abilities are maintained under favorable conditions or with the help of others.
3 Low	Severe limitations in structural capabilities. Typically characterized by under-regulation.
3.5 Low to disintegrated	Structural skills are barely available. A certain amount of compensation is possible without denying reality.
4 Disintegrated	Structural skills are no longer available, compensation is only possible by denying reality.

es, affects, and fantasies is usually quite stable, with occasional breakthroughs that are immediately over-regulated again. The central fear concerns the loss of the object or separation from the important object and the fear of one's own intense impulses. The corresponding countertransference is characterized by intermittently hard-to-endure experiences that, with consistent therapeutic self-reflection, can be traced back to the relevant relationship experiences for the patient.

Level: Moderate to low integration. This level is characterized by impaired functioning, restricted regulatory capacity, and interpersonal defense. Under stabilizing conditions, better functioning can be possible for certain periods (e.g., at a well-structured workplace or in a supportive living environment). The affected individuals can then utilize the abilities of the moderate level, but when stabilizing conditions are removed, their functioning level decreases again even under everyday stresses. In psychotic disorders, there can already be limited denials of reality at this level.

Level: Low integration. Unlike the previously described structural levels, the availability of regulating functions here is significantly reduced, either permanently (in the sense of a developmental deficit) or repeatedly in connection with stress situations (structural vulnerability). Unlike the previously mentioned structural levels, the psychic inner space is underdeveloped. The self is very needy, very vulnerable, very impulsive, and the images of objects are threatening, persecutory, or longingly idealized. The normative structure (in the sense of superego) is dissociated. Unconscious wish impulses are not bound intrapsychically but are directed outward. The hallmark is "underregulation." Thus, intrapsychic conflicts occur less frequently, with interpersonal conflicts prevailing instead (in partnership, work, and social environment). Reality denials can occur. Alternatively, there can be a withdrawal into the inner world, with the self, appearing need-free, untouchable, empty, unenergetic, and thereby extremely over-regulated, all at the cost of giving up further life and experience areas. The central fear concerns the destruction of the self by the bad object or the loss of the good object. The countertransference is characterized by intensity, abruptness of experience, and feelings that linger beyond the real presence of the patient. These patients also repeat biographically relevant conflicts with their counterpart, but mainly through projective identifications that mobilize psychic experiences in the other, which are unconscious and unbearable for them.

Level: Low to disintegrated. At this level, there is essentially disintegration. However, the affected individuals can at least stabilize on a nearly low-integrated level for certain phases, and sometimes even over longer periods, with limited distortions of reality.

Level: Disintegration. Disintegration does not mean disorganization. The permanent lack of coherence of the self and the overwhelming emotionality can be covered in the sense of restitution through post-psychotic, post-traumatic, psychopathic, etc., organizational forms. Self and object images appear confused, empathic object perceptions are almost impossible, and responsibility for one's impulsive actions is often not experienced (things just happen). Disintegration can occur both in the context of psychotic disorders and states, as well as in antisocial or psychopathic personalities. It is particularly important to note here that the structural level is independent of the presence of individual symptoms or syndromes. Defense is generally interpersonal and characterized by pronounced introjective and projective mechanisms. Reality denials are common and can be both promising and threatening. Interpersonal relationships can be experienced and structured symbiotically or completely avoided. The central fear concerns uncanny objects, which appear more medial than objectual, as well as the fear of ego loss and self-dissolution. The countertransference can be characterized by the experience of the incomprehensible, strange, and threateningly uncanny.

5.5.5 The Rating

For the rating, there are both a clinical and a research version. The clinical rating is done along the nine sub-dimensions, with the evaluation of a sub-dimension being formed by the assessment of the three associated facets, which are individually operationalized. The clinical rating sheet can be found in Section 5.6. For specific scientific questions, it may be important to also rate all facets individually; this purpose is served by the research version of the rating sheet. In both cases, an overall structural level rating is performed at the end. The overall level will generally correspond to the arithmetic mean of the ratings of the nine sub-dimensions. However, it is also possible to weight the assessments of the sub-dimensions so that the overall structural level deviates by a 0.5 level up or down from the arithmetic mean. This must be well justified if needed.

5.5.6 Operationalization of the Structure Facets

The following are the operationalizations of the individual structure facets, where three facets are assigned to each of the nine sub-dimensions that are to be assessed on the rating sheet. The dimension "Defense" is the only one that lifts the polarization into self vs. object/relationship focus of the Structure Axis (Axis IV), including both areas. So-called "core sentences" were formulated for each sub-dimension. They define the respective themes and summarize the range of associated facets from healthy functioning to significant impairment in the corresponding area in the form of a polarity. The themes described in the core statements are understood dimensionally, with the operationalizations offering seven manifestations on this continuum. The following list will describe the sub-dimensions and associated facets and highlight their corresponding tables within the book.

1. The sub-dimension of self-perception includes the facets self-reflection (Table 43), affect differentiation (Table 44), and identity (Table 45).
2. The sub-dimension of object-perception includes the facets self-object differentiation (Table 46), object-related affect differentiation (Table 47), and integrated object perception (Table 48).
3. The sub-dimension of self-regulation includes the facets impulse control (Table 49), affect tolerance (Table 50), and self-esteem regulation (Table 51).
4. The sub-dimension of relationship regulation includes the facets protecting relationships (Table 52), anticipation (Table 53), and balancing of interests (Table 54).
5. The sub-dimension of defense includes the facets of living and experiencing possibilities (Table 55), interpersonal impact (Table 56), and mechanisms (Table 57).
6. The sub-dimension of internal communication includes the facets of experience of affects and fantasies (Table 58), experience of joy (Table 59), and bodily self (Table 60).
7. The sub-dimension of communication with the external world includes the facets making emotional contact (Table 61), intimacy (Table 62), and empathy (Table 63).
8. The sub-dimension of attachment to internal objects includes the facets internalizations (Table 64), use of introjects (Table 65), and variability (Table 66).
9. The sub-dimension of attachment to external objects includes the facets ability to form attachments (Table 67), trust (Table 68), and ability to separate (Table 69).

The tables on the following pages can be understood as the full text of the operationalization of the structure facets. A condensed short checklist of Axis IV can be found in Appendix C.

Table 43. Operationalization of self-reflection (ST1.1 in Table 41)

1 Good	1.5	2 Moderate	2.5	3 Low	3.5	4 Disintegrated
The ability to focus on oneself is available. It is possible to realistically recognize what kind of person one is and what is going on inside oneself. This can be conceptualized. Feedback from others is included, relativized or rejected in an appropriate manner. This often leads to new insights.	The ability to focus on oneself and to perceive oneself authentically is generally present, but at times (under pressure) impaired. Terms are only available to a limited extent at times. Abstract attributions rather than vivid situations are described. If something is questioned by another person, irritation arises, but this can usually be resolved.	The ability to self-reflect is limited and inflexibly follows the same paths. It is primarily focused on the acting self (what the person has said and done). The self-image appears less differentiated, but coherent. It is difficult to find appropriate linguistic terms. The person reacts to the other person's relativizing remarks with offence, incomprehension or withdrawal.	Self-reflection is often not possible under stress (emotional situations, criticism). Only under favorable conditions or with support the acting self can be reflected upon and a coherent, albeit less differentiated self-image can be created. With empathic support and suggestions from the other person, the self-image can become clearer and more comprehensible, while critical feedback can significantly increase instability.	Self-reflective perception is hardly possible; even with support, the person cannot create a coherent picture of themselves and their inner situation; contradictory aspects of the self are juxtaposed. No terms for inner processes or drastic and incomprehensible descriptions of affective states and situations. Interest can be interpreted as an attack. Critical feedback leads to massive self-deprecation, uncritical acceptance or is completely rejected.	Self-reflective perception is severely impaired and threatens the coherence of the self. Affective flooding or levelling can occur. Rudimentary aspects of the self exist, but cannot be connected with each other. Reflection of the acting self is only possible under supportive conditions. Feedback remains inconsequential or provokes violent defense reactions. Alternatively, they lead to fundamental questioning or loss of integration of the self.	Attempts at self-reflection are avoided or can lead to affective overload. There is no coherence of the self. The inner and outer world cannot be distinguished, the self can no longer be recognized as distinct. In extreme cases, it is no longer possible to reflect on the authorship of the self. Feedback comes to nothing or reinforces the fragmentation of the self.

		Good integration	With increasing impairment …
Core sentences	**Self-reflection**	Good self-reflection (mental and physical aspects).	less differentiated self-image and body image, contradictory self-aspects unconnected, some self-aspects alienatingly in the foreground, up to a complete lack of reflection on the self as author.
	Feedback	Feedback is used appropriately.	defense against feedback, increasing collapse in self-image up to complete ignoring/blanking out.

Table 44. Operationalization of affect differentiation (ST1.2 in Table 41)

1 Good	1.5	2 Moderate	2.5	3 Low	3.5	4 Disintegrated
Affects can be perceived in a differentiated way and have great variability. Contradictory affects can be integrated, i.e., they can be perceived in their ambivalence. Affects can be understood within the context and situational aspects, i.e., one can react emotionally adequately and flexibly in contact.	In moments of stress and great emotional pressure, emotions are occasionally avoided and their variability is temporarily restricted. The ability to perceive and integrate contradictory affects can be limited under emotional pressure. An affective context of understanding cannot always be established in stressful situations.	Affects are only perceived to a limited extent and are also avoided in difficult situations in order to maintain stability. The variability of affects and the experience of ambivalent affects are limited; being torn between different affects. The affective experience characterizes the inner life in a mostly negative way. Contexts of experience are difficult to understand; the control of behavior through affects is limited.	Affects can often not be perceived in a differentiated way and show hardly any variability. An integrating perception of ambivalent affects is only possible to some extent, but this can be lost even under low levels of stress. This leads to irritability and affective flooding, and it is then no longer possible to understand contextual relationships. The proximity of an object can be supportive, but also stressful.	Affects cannot be perceived in a differentiated way or named in a comprehensible way. Affects are experienced as undifferentiated states that can be of great intensity and duration or change rapidly. Alternatively, there is a stereotypical expression of affect that pushes itself to the fore. Mixed affects rarely occur. Affects express themselves either in excitement, alienation or lack of affect. Affects can hardly be understood situationally and used for targeted behavior control.	No inner distance to one's own feelings and no reflexive perception of affects and affect correlates. Being at the mercy of intense, undeveloped and often agonizing emotional states that cannot be expressed in words; or a void of affect. Contradictory affects exist simultaneously and side by side without being perceived as such. Situationally appropriate emotional reactions are only possible to some extent with support.	No inner distance to one's own feelings and no reflexive perception of affects and affect correlates. Affects express themselves as somatic arousal or unnamable agony. Alternatively, affects and affectively significant events are completely erased, not experienced at all or experienced completely inadequately and/or only appear externalized in the outside world. No situationally appropriate emotional response is possible.

		Good integration	With increasing impairment …
Core sentences	**Affect variability**	Affects can be perceived and named in a differentiated way and with great variability.	less to no differentiated and variable perception of affect, instead undifferentiated affect states predominate.
	Affect integration	Ambivalent affects can be tolerated and integrated.	reduced ability or even inability to integrate and tolerate ambivalent affects.
	Contextuality	Affects can be placed in a contextual context of understanding and are action-guiding.	detachment of affects from situation and context, action control by affects no longer possible.

Table 45. Operationalization of identity (ST1.3 in Table 41)

1 Good	1.5	2 Moderate	2.5	3 Low	3.5	4 Disintegrated
The self-image is multi-faceted and comprehensive, so that a coherent picture of oneself can be created. Contradictory aspects of the self can be experienced cognitively and affectively and can be endured well. The self-image is stable, i.e., it is related to one's biographical origins and is orientated towards the future.	The self-image is differentiated and comprehensive; limitations in coherence and diversity can occur under pressure. Occasional difficulty in continuously maintaining the self-image. Occasional struggles with oneself. Biographical references can be plausibly established and point to the future.	Although the self-image is coherent, it appears constricted and rigid. "Shades of grey" of the self can only be perceived, represented and endured to a limited extent. Certain conflictual aspects can be hidden in a stable manner. The self-image is fundamentally stable but can be called into question due to conflict. A connection between the past and the future can be established.	Under favorable conditions, the self-image is coherent and comprehensible. However, even slight frustration, for example, has a clear and lasting effect on this image. Various aspects of the self can be incorporated into the self-image with support. In difficult situations, the self-image becomes unstable or distorted. This is accompanied by an impaired relationship to the past and future.	No coherent image of oneself. Different aspects of the self are unconnected to one another and are significantly reduced in their complexity. The person has "different faces." Different aspects of the self come to the fore at different times. It remains unclear what behavior and experiences have arisen from and how they will develop in the future.	The self-image is not coherent and not very complex; however, distortions and fragmentations can be partially corrected with support and stabilized in phases. Aspects of identity are deposited in unconnected ideas. Biographical references made by others can be traced. Continuity from the past into the future cannot be established.	Lack of a coherent self-image. Instead, fragmentation, distorted or clichéd attributions of characteristics. Identity can be accommodated in substitute formations. Biographical descriptions appear fantasy-led. Future plans are non-existent or seem absurd.

		Good integration	With increasing impairment …
Core sentences	**Coherence**	A creative and integrated self-image can be developed.	appearance of unconnected and fantasized aspects of the self that cannot be integrated.
	Complexity	Diverse parts of the self can be experienced cognitively and affectively at the same time. Shades of grey can emerge.	reduced complexity of the self-image. The cognitive-emotional experience of the self is increasingly black and white or diffuse.
	Stability	There is a clear continuity of self-image over time.	occurrence of changes in the self-image. The person has different faces and changes abruptly or appears fixed in fantasized substitute images.

Table 46. Operationalization of self-object differentiation (ST1.4 in Table 41)

1 Good	1.5	2 Moderate	2.5	3 Low	3.5	4 Disintegrated
Affects, impulses, and thoughts can be reliably differentiated in terms of their assignment to the self or to objects; the person can reliably differentiate themselves and perceive the other from the outside. Others are experienced as people with their own wishes and goals, which may differ from their own.	Affects, impulses and thoughts can in principle be assigned to themselves or to objects. There is occasional confusion in the area of neurotic conflict as to which impulse came from whom. Others can usually be experienced as independent individuals.	In the area of conflict, the allocation of affects, impulses and thoughts in relation to the self and objects is impaired. The distanced perception of others is permanently impaired. Sometimes it is no longer clear who is being spoken about.	Self and object are partially confounded or confounded in certain areas. Under stable conditions, self and object can be perceived in a differentiated way. Under stress, this ability is lost. Others are then no longer experienced as distinct persons.	Self and object are often confounded and are frequently confused with each other; those affects that are unbearable for the self are attributed to the object. Unrealistic attributions (projective identifications) can often be observed. Blurring of ego boundaries in close relationships	Threatening fusion of self and object aspects; there is a lack of certain awareness that the other is separate from the self and has its own desires, impulses, and needs. Others are perceived as extensions of the self or seem non-existent. Under certain circumstances, an attempt at demarcation by means of a radical withdrawal into inner worlds.	Due to persistent fusion and consolidation of self and object aspects, the object is not perceived as separate from the self; dissolution of ego boundaries. Loss of a sense of selfhood and authorship. Alternatively, experience of omnipotence and/or complete abandonment of object occupation. Inner and outer world(s) cannot be distinguished.

		Good integration	With increasing impairment …
Core sentences	**Differentiation**	Secure differentiation between self and object through secure allocation of affects, impulses and thoughts to the self or to the objects.	uncertain allocation of affects, impulses and thoughts, confounding and even confusion or fusion.
	Boundary	Safe demarcation and ability to perceive the other person as an independent person from the outside.	insecure to lacking demarcation and ability to distinguish the other from the self.

Table 47. Operationalization of object-related affect differentiation (ST1.5 in Table 41)

1 Good	1.5	2 Moderate	2.5	3 Low	3.5	4 Disintegrated
The affective inner world of others can be perceived accurately and described in a differentiated and lively way. Affects of objects can be brought into a context of understanding with situational aspects and their behavior.	Under pressure, it is sometimes the case that the emotions of others can only be perceived to a limited extent. The connection between the situational context and the perceived emotions of others is then partially lost. Understanding the behavior of others is then temporarily more difficult.	Conflict-related affects of others are only perceived to a limited extent and in difficult situations are also suppressed in order to maintain stability. Context-related understanding of the experience and behavior of others is thus restricted, but can be loosened with the help of others.	At times, the emotions of others cannot be perceived in a differentiated way. The understanding of the affective inner world of others is quickly lost. This often leads to misinterpretation of the experience and the behavior of others, but this can be approximately corrected under stabilizing conditions or with the help of the interviewer.	The affects of others cannot be perceived in a differentiated way and can only be described in broad categories. Accordingly, the affective inner world of others is predominantly incomprehensible or is "made comprehensible" projectively. Contradictions between attributed affects and behavior cannot be integrated and resolved.	The affective inner world of others can only be perceived with considerable distortions. The situational context and the affective experience of others are interpreted against the background of one's own wishes and fears. This often leads to massive misinterpretations of the behavior of others.	The emotions of others can usually not be perceived at all, let alone understood. Instead, threatening or promising affects are attributed to others in a distorted way. The behavior of others can usually only be attributed meaning by denying reality.

		Good integration	With increasing impairment ...
Core sentences	**Affect perception**	The emotions of others can be perceived in a differentiated way and with great variability.	less or no differentiated and variable perception of affect possible; distortion in the direction of negative or inadequate affects.
	Contextuality	The affects of others can be placed in a contextual context of understanding.	detachment of the attributed affects from situation and context.
	Explanation of behavior	Affects of others can be associated with their behavior.	failure to understand the behavior of others; inadequate explanation of the behavior of others.

Table 48. Operationalization of integrated object perception (ST1.6 in Table 41)

1 Good	1.5	2 Moderate	2.5	3 Low	3.5	4 Disintegrated
Object perception is coherent. Different sides of other people can be integrated into a vivid and realistic picture. You can imagine the people described, understand their motives and behavior, which makes the descriptions lively and interesting. The perception of the other person is not affected by conflicts, it remains stable.	Object perception is coherent. Others are always experienced and portrayed as people with their own goals, wishes and demands. Under pressure, this ability is temporarily limited and different sides cannot always be integrated into a vivid picture. The portrayal of others is then emotionally colored by one's own conflicts and temporarily unstable.	Object perception is coherent, but can be impaired by conflict. Others are then not perceived in their complexity and inconsistency, but are experienced according to their own wishes. As a result, the descriptions appear one-sided and incomplete. The perception of others is impaired by the conflict and becomes temporarily unstable.	Coherent object perception is often not possible. In difficult situations, the coherence of perception is lost and a splitting tendency with a black and white view prevails. Other people are then portrayed in a clichéd or flat but still partially comprehensible way. A change from coherence to incoherence is typical.	A coherent perception of objects is not possible. Others are experienced in extremes, particularly good or bad. Contradictions cannot be integrated. The description of others is often no longer comprehensible and appears empty or alienating. The behavior of others can hardly be understood in a situational context, a distance to the objects is still possible. It is typical for idealization to turn into devaluation.	No coherent object perception. Extremes predominate. Others are experienced in phases as predominantly aggressive, unjust and threatening. Alternatively, the object is symbiotically appropriated and can only be experienced as good. The descriptions are unrealistic. Under stabilizing conditions, a distance to the objects can still be maintained.	The perception of objects is not coherent. Others are quickly experienced as aggressively persecutory and threatening or idealized. Individual characteristics stand for the whole object. Own fears, anxieties and desires determine perception and interpretation; the other person is no longer experienced as a securely demarcated counterpart.

		Good integration	With increasing impairment ...
Core sentences	**Holistic approach**	Others are experienced coherently with positive and negative components, shades of grey appear, a gestalt-like image emerges.	loss of coherence with black and white vision and fragmentation.
	Comprehensibility	The image of the other is comprehensible and is in line with the reality of the person concerned and their biographical development.	distortion of the image of the other to the point of arbitrariness or lack of perception of the other.
	Stability	The other is perceived stably over time in the same or a similar way.	occurrence of frequent or abrupt changes in the perception of others.

Table 49. Operationalization of impulse control (ST2.1 in Table 41)

1 Good	1.5	2 Moderate	2.5	3 Low	3.5	4 Disintegrated
Aggressive, sexual, and oral impulses and desires can be experienced and controlled in a differentiated and graduated way. Needs can be postponed but also satisfied. Loss of control can occur to a small extent and can be tolerated.	Aggressive, sexual, and oral impulses and desires can be experienced, postponed and satisfied in a differentiated and graduated manner. Overcontrol can occur under pressure. Limited loss of control occurs and tends to be poorly tolerated.	Impulses and desires are experienced and sometimes perceived as agonizing. They are predominantly inhibited by overcontrol. Needs are chronically postponed or suppressed. Rarely can impulses break through, which is reacted to with overcontrol.	Impulses and desires are experienced as urgent or suppressed. Under stabilizing circumstances there is an overcontrol, in difficult situations an undercontrol. Needs cannot be postponed well. Loss of control occurs in tense situations, which is experienced as failure.	Urging impulses and desires cannot be regulated (chronic undercontrol). It is not possible to postpone the fulfilment of needs, at best they are denied. Massive loss of control often leads to actions that endanger oneself or others, which is usually experienced as failure. Unrealistic beliefs can at times serve as a means of control.	Impulses are immediate and massively urgent or cancelled or negated. Massive loss of control can lead to serious self-destructive and other-destructive behavior. Alternatively, one's own intentionality is reduced. Excessive doubt and empty reflection can paralyze action.	The ability to control and regulate impulses is cancelled or may be linked to unrealistic and/or bizarre beliefs. Needs can be directly translated into action without taking the context into account, possibly abandoning reality. Dramatic loss of control can occur, possibly resulting in serious harm to self and others. Alternatively, impulses and desires may be completely absent.

		Good integration	With increasing impairment ...
Core sentences	**Control of impulses and wishes**	Impulses and wishes can be experienced and taken into account as appropriate to the situation, but can also be postponed or abandoned.	inappropriate consideration of impulses and wishes, either in the form of over- or under-control.
	Postponing gratification	Needs can be experienced, satisfied but also postponed.	rigidity or failure of postponing.
	Loss of control	Loss of control only occurs to a small extent and can be tolerated.	fear of loss of control and/or actual occurrence of loss of control.

Axis IV

Table 50. Operationalization of affect tolerance (ST2.2 in Table 41)

1 Good	1.5	2 Moderate	2.5	3 Low	3.5	4 Disintegrated
Affects, even if they are intense, can be experienced as appropriate to the situation. Spontaneous, appropriate strategies for counteracting and balancing are available. Ambivalent emotions can be experienced and tolerated.	Strong affects can usually be maintained, but over-regulated under pressure. Compensatory strategies occasionally in the form of overcontrol. Ambivalent affects can be experienced and endured, avoidance only in rare cases.	Affects are experienced in a restricted way. Strong and especially negative affects are difficult to bear and are usually over-regulated. The experience of ambivalent affects is often suppressed in stressful situations.	Affects can flood and trigger impulsive behavior. Under stabilizing conditions, overcontrol with suppression of ambivalent affects is successful, which can also happen with the help of unrealistic beliefs.	Affects often flood and are experienced as so unbearable that they trigger impulsive behavior or withdrawal; alternatively, they are ignored. Counter-regulation is usually dysfunctional. Ambivalent affects cannot be experienced.	Even less intense emotions cannot be tolerated and trigger diffuse, highly agitated feelings and pressure to act. Counter-regulation occurs through the most violent internal and external reactions. Alternatively, states of emptiness and affective disengagement can occur, in which case affects are barely experienced.	Violent reflexive counteractions even with minimal intensity of affect. Ambivalence does not occur, only ambivalent tendencies. Frequently flooded by undifferentiated affects. Alternatively, affects can be completely switched off.

		Good integration	With increasing impairment ...
Core sentences	**Experience and endure emotions**	Affects can be experienced, endured and regulated.	acting out or fading out intense emotions.
	Experience ambivalent affects	Ambivalent emotions can be experienced and endured.	loss of the ability to tolerate ambivalent affects and the occurrence of undifferentiated affects.
	Counter-regulation	Adequate spontaneous strategies of inner balance to ensure well-being.	fewer counter-regulatory strategies and flooding by affects, possibly lack of affect experience or externalization.

Table 51. Operationalization of self-esteem regulation (ST2.3 in Table 41)

1 Good	1.5	2 Moderate	2.5	3 Low	3.5	4 Disintegrated
Self-esteem can be maintained with realistic limitations and fluctuations and can be regained appropriately quickly after being challenged.	Self-esteem can usually be maintained. Noticeable fluctuations in the event of conflictual questioning, in which case restoration is possible with effort.	Self-esteem is disruptible, which manifests in sensitivity, self-exaggeration, -devaluation, or -punishment, withdrawal. Realistic assessment is difficult; confirmation from others is required.	Self-esteem is very fragile even in the case of minor injuries. Offendedness, shame, disgust and devaluation are common, habitual self-judgement. In favorable situations or with support, however, self-esteem can be stabilized with difficulty.	Self-esteem is very fragile, which manifests in great vulnerability, unrealistic ideas of greatness, shame, disgust with oneself, devaluation of others, relationship breakdowns, and an inability to accept one's own limits. Severe fluctuations in self-esteem or an inflexible fixation of self-perception. Attempts to stabilize self-esteem are increasingly dysfunctional.	Self-esteem can hardly be regulated or restored even after minor challenges. This is reflected in considerable and persistent distortions of one's own self-esteem (grandiosity or chronically low self-esteem), as well as in markedly dysfunctional, even interpersonal attempts to compensate.	Self-esteem seems to be replaced by an inner unrealistic system of self-esteem control. Rigid, distorted self-attributions of grandiosity or a general lack of self-esteem are frequent or alternate. A stable, balanced self-esteem experience is not available, attempts to stabilize self-esteem are dysfunctional or seem alienating.

		Good integration	With increasing impairment …
Core sentences	**Stability of self-esteem**	Self-esteem is flexible, generally positively colored and stable across situations.	impairment of the stability of self-esteem with excessive offending behavior and even threats to the self.
	Adaptivity of the self-esteem experience	Self-esteem is variable and deflectable according to the occasion.	very strong alternation of idealization and devaluation or rigidity with extreme fixations of self-experience.
	Regaining self-esteem	Self-esteem can be appropriately restored after everyday offenses as well as major challenges to it.	dysfunctional attempts to restore self-esteem with strong distortions in relation to the self and objects.

Table 52. Operationalization of protecting relationships (ST2.4 in Table 41)

1 Good	1.5	2 Moderate	2.5	3 Low	3.5	4 Disintegrated
The others are taken into account regardless of their own current needs. Maintaining identification with the relationship and constructive efforts to make amends, even in the event of conflicts of interest.	Under pressure, the other person is temporarily lost from view. Ruptures in the relationship can be repaired after crises with certain difficulties, and identification with the relationship can be restored.	In conflictual areas, others cannot be recognized as separate persons independent of the self. They fulfill a function for the regulation of one's own inner conflicts. Instead of active endeavor, there is an acceptance of a lack of closeness and relatedness in circumscribed areas.	The ability to consider others as independent persons is increasingly lost and is usually only possible under stabilizing conditions. Significant areas of the relationship remain excluded from identification and reparative reapproach and cannot be lived together.	The other person can only be experienced in relation to oneself and one's own needs. Relationships can sometimes be maintained in the long term; this happens either by largely excluding shared experiences or by merging closeness after stormy crises (on-off relationship).	The other is predominantly a self-object, alternating between threat and idealization. They do not appear as an independent person. Commitment to the relationship occurs in a dysfunctional way, occasionally through self-destructive or other-destructive actions, e.g., dominating control in order to maintain the relationship.	Others are either an extension of the self or non-existent. The ability to protect relationships is largely lost. The protection of or from relationships only takes place in self-worldliness and fantasy. The experience of the relationship is strongly determined by one's own ideas, which are overvalued. Under certain circumstances, drastic, highly destructive actions to "protect" relationships.

		Good integration	With increasing impairment ...
Core sentences	**Keep the relationship in mind**	The other person is recognized and respected as an independent person.	losing sight of the other.
	To actively engage	Actively and constructively endeavoring to maintain the relationship. Successful reparation after crises.	inability to protect the relationship by constructive means.

Table 53. Operationalization of anticipation (ST2.5 in Table 41)

1 Good	1.5	2 Moderate	2.5	3 Low	3.5	4 Disintegrated
The ability to anticipate the consequences of one's own actions. This influences their own actions in a constructive way. One's own position can be seen from different perspectives; empathizing with the perspective of others on a trial basis makes the relationship more flexible.	The ability to anticipate the consequences of one's own actions may be temporarily restricted in stressful situations. Perspective-taking and empathy with the experience of others can be more difficult when central inner conflicts are activated and temporarily impair relationship behavior.	The anticipation of the consequences of one's own actions is limited or distorted by unresolved inner conflicts; this influences behavior. In the area of neurotic conflicts, the capacity of adopting a perspective is limited; this restricts the ability to relate one's own actions to others.	Anticipating the consequences of one's own actions is clearly limited and usually only possible temporarily under stabilizing conditions. Only then and to a limited extent can anticipation be used to control behavior. Perspective-taking is severely restricted without help, which often results in rigidity in relationship behavior.	It is almost impossible to anticipate the consequences of one's own actions. The reactions of others to one's own actions are often experienced as surprising. Perspective-taking hardly ever takes place, and if it does, it leads to distortions and misinterpretations. Behavior in relationships is often dysfunctional.	There is no anticipation of the consequences of one's own actions. There is no genuine adoption of the perspective of others, the relationship is rigid and/or manipulative and purposeful or disorganized.	The anticipation of the consequences of one's own actions is controlled by inner convictions, which can be bizarre. These replace an assumption of perspective and determine the relationship behavior. Alternatively, disorganized or autistic relationship behavior.

		Good integration	With increasing impairment ...
Core sentences	**Anticipate**	Anticipation is possible.	the inability to anticipate and the distortion caused by unrealistic inner conviction systems and disorganization.
	Use anticipation	Anticipation makes a constructive contribution to managing relationship behavior.	inability to anticipate the consequences of one's own behavior on others.
	Perspective taking	Perspective-taking enables empathy with others and thus flexibility in behavior and experience in relationships.	loss of the ability to empathize with others and development of dysfunctional and unrealistic or autistic relationship behavior.

Table 54. Operationalization of balancing of interests (ST2.6 in Table 41)

1 Good	1.5	2 Moderate	2.5	3 Low	3.5	4 Disintegrated
In relationships, one's own interests can be upheld and those of others taken into account appropriately. Actions are determined by stable internalized values. Respect for the needs and the mental and physical integrity of others is central. The value system can be followed flexibly and appropriately to the situation. Actions that run counter to the value system are experienced as culpable.	In relationships, it is usually possible to maintain one's own interests and take appropriate account of the interests of others. Due to conflict, a more altruistic or a more selfish attitude can occur in some cases. Balancing interests can then be significantly more difficult. Internalized values determine actions. Depending on the situation and the conflict, however, there may be restrictions on the flexibility of action, whereby more rigid standards are applied and "misdemeanors" can lead to increased, sometimes inappropriate feelings of guilt.	One's own interests or those of others are permanently in the foreground, so that difficulties arise in balancing interests or a strongly one-sided tendency prevails. The internalized values are rigid. Especially in conflicts, a flexible, situation-appropriate approach to values is no longer possible. "Misbehavior," but also desires and ideas that contradict the values, trigger intense, excessive feelings of guilt.	The relationship is fundamentally characterized by the feeling that one's own interests are threatened and a lack of understanding of the other person's interests. However, with a careful and considerate counterpart, it is partially possible to reconcile interests. Inner values become fragile and this can lead to circumscribed actions that contradict one's own value system. These can either be responded to with strong feelings of guilt or be ignored while avoiding the experience of guilt. Under stabilizing conditions, the inner values can be maintained.	The relationship is characterized by the feeling that one's own interests are under threat and a lack of understanding of the other person's interests. It is not always possible to fall back on internalized values. Although these exist, they are not securely and stably anchored. Actions repeatedly contradict one's own value system. Desires, impulses, and behavior are not consistently and adequately linked to the experience of guilt; this can be both, extensively destructive and largely eliminated. There may also be highly idealized and inflexible values that are not suitable for everyday life.	Overvalued and existential experience of one's own interests, which are often difficult to understand. Fanatical pursuit of overriding interests. Stable internalized values hardly exist and if they do, then in an overvalued, difficult to understand form. The unrealistic value system is rigid and inappropriate to the situation, but can also be temporarily suspended in response to personal desires and impulses. The experience of guilt can be tied to one's own "code of honor." The experience of guilt can be completely suppressed or lead to severe self-destruction.	Own or other interests are pursued or denied following an inner system regardless of the interpersonal reality. An exchange does not take place. The inner system is often bizarre and difficult to understand. A stable inner value system does not exist or is bizarrely organized. If desires, impulses and behavior violate the rudimentary/bizarre value system, this leads to strong feelings of shame and guilt, which can trigger self-destruction or the destruction of others. Alternatively, feelings of shame, guilt, and remorse may be completely absent.

Table 54. Operationalization of balancing of interests (ST2.6 in Table 41) *(continued)*

1 Good	1.5 / 2 Moderate	2.5 / 3 Low	3.5 / 4 Disintegrated
		Good integration	**With increasing impairment ...**
Core Sentences	**Consideration of own interests**	Own interests can be maintained and expressed flexibly in contact with others, and other people's interests can be taken into account.	distortion of one's own interests and, in extreme cases, complete overlooking or exaggeration of the interests of others.
	Consideration of values	There is a secure, internalized value system that guides their actions.	the fragility of the value system through to unrealistic ideas that guide behavior.
	Flexibility/rigidity	Flexibility allows us to adapt our actions to the situation without compromising our commitment to our own value system.	narrowing the scope for action by rigidly binding values that do not take the situation into account or abolishing value-led action by making the value system extremely flexible.
	Experience of guilt	Guilt and remorse are adequately experienced in the event of misbehavior.	inappropriately strong feelings of guilt or loss of feelings of guilt and remorse.

Table 55. Operationalization of living and experiencing possibilities (ST3.1 in Table 41)

1 Good	1.5	2 Moderate	2.5	3 Low	3.5	4 Disintegrated
Stressful internal and external processes can be recognized and overcome. Experience of various aspects of life remain fully intact.	Over-regulation during stressful internal and external processes with the abandonment of some experiential aspects of experience of life.	Certain areas of life and experience are given up in order to maintain inner stability. Stressful processes are then no longer consciously perceived and cannot be dealt with adaptively.	Considerable opportunities to live and experience life are lost. Under supportive conditions, splitting processes can be reversed and a distance to the content can be created.	Stabilization is only possible by excluding large areas of experi-ence and usually only for a short time. Internal and external processes can take on a threatening, persecutory or merging character.	Stressful internal and external processes can only be coped with under considerable distortion of reality; stabilization is only possible by giving up other areas of experience.	Stabilization is only possible in very limited "islands of experience" and/or with a distortion or reinterpretation of reality. There are breakdowns of defense with flooding by stressful experiences and impulsive reactions.
			Good integration		**With increasing impairment ...**	
Core sentences	**Preserving experience of various aspects of life**		Full spectrum of experiencing various aspects of life.		loss of capacity to experience various aspects of life; impulses, affects, fantasies must be kept away from experience, polarize, flood, or fragment it.	

Table 56. Operationalization of interpersonal impact (ST3.2 in Table 41)

1 Good	1.5	2 Moderate	2.5	3 Low	3.5	4 Disintegrated
Intrapsychic flexible defense is basically available and can be used flexibly. (Social) reality can be adequately perceived. Interpersonal mechanisms are adaptive at best, whereby they can expand the possibilities of experience.	Intrapsychic defenses are predominantly available, but are sometimes somewhat inflexible. Under stress, interpersonal mechanisms with a less adaptive function can come into play, but important relationships are hardly affected.	The defense is usually intrapsychic, but rigid. (Social) reality can be perceived in a distorted way under stress. Stress can lead to the temporary emergence of interpersonal mechanisms that can put a strain on relationships in the short or long term.	Interpersonal but also intrapsychic defense. Depending on the extent of the stress, there is a shift from intrapsychic to interpersonal defense, which then leads to a distorted perception of social reality in certain phases.	Stress can hardly be dealt with intrapsychically. Interpersonal defenses dominate, the effects of which place a heavy burden on relationships. The overall picture of the defenses is unstable and changeable (dysfunctional flexibility) or even locked in place. The (social) reality is predominantly perceived in a distorted way and also reconstructed.	Relationships are characterized by distinctly dysfunctional interpersonal defense processes. The environment is experienced as threatening or promising.	Mature intrapsychic defense processes are lost, and interpersonal defenses hardly lead to stabilization. Interpersonal reality is usually no longer accessible. Drastic protection from or escape into unrealistic relationship constructs.

		Good integration	With increasing impairment ...
Core sentences	**Intrapsychic vs. interpersonal**	Defense is usually intrapsychical.	interpersonal defense and loss of the ability for intrapsychic defense.
	Rigidity	Defense is flexible.	inflexible defense.
	Distortion of reality	Social reality can be adequately perceived.	distortion of the perception of reality through to an exclusively constructed social reality.

Table 57. Operationalization of mechanisms (ST3.3 in Table 41)

1 Good	1.5	2 Moderate	2.5	3 Low	3.5	4 Disintegrated
Prevalence of mature defense mechanisms with good adaptivity, such as sublimation or humor; good adaptivity.	Predominantly mature defenses with some limitations of adaptivity, e.g., repression, rationalization, intellectualization.	Relatively mature defenses whose adaptivity is permanently restricted, e.g., chronic repression, reaction formation, turning against the self, intellectualization, affect isolation.	Under stress, immature mechanisms emerge which can, however, be abandoned again under stable conditions, e.g., splitting tendencies and projective identification, but also forms of repression.	Predominantly dysfunctional and immature mechanisms occur, typically splitting, idealization, devaluation and projective identification, sometimes in rapid alternation.	Altered constructions of reality and/or persistent splits, massive projections and interpersonal acting out are common.	The imaginary world is threatened by fragmentation, de-symbolization, concretism, autistic withdrawal and/or bizarre interpersonal defenses.

		Good integration	With increasing impairment ...
Core sentences	**Dominant mechanisms**	Sublimation, humor; predominance of mature mechanisms that are used flexibly.	use of immature mechanisms such as splitting, idealization, devaluation, projective identification, autistic withdrawal, and even abandonment of reference to reality.
	Adaptivity	Good adaptivity.	loss of adaptivity and increase in dysfunctionality.

Table 58. Operationalization of experience of affects and fantasies (ST4.1 in Table 41)

1 Good	1.5	2 Moderate	2.5	3 Low	3.5	4 Disintegrated
Affects can be allowed and experienced in their diversity. This makes a lively experience possible. There is a feeling of liveliness and a playful, curious contact with one's own inner world. The inner spaces of experience can be expanded through fantasies. This allows for creative solutions to be developed.	Affects can be allowed and experienced in their diversity. They are only experienced to a limited extent under particular pressure. Under pressure, vitality and contact with the inner world can be temporarily restricted. Fantasies are temporarily suspended in stressful situations. It is then difficult to develop creative solutions.	Affects are experienced in a limited way and presented in a normative way. Access to inner processes, curiosity and vitality are limited. Fear of losing control inhibits vitality. Fantasies are only rarely able to expand inner spaces of experience. They are often avoided and warded off in order to maintain stability. Creative solutions are put aside in favor of "safe" alternatives.	One-sided affects usually predominate and it is difficult to distance oneself from them. Under favorable circumstances, they can decrease without this leading to general relief. They oscillate between a colorless, inanimate, threateningly overflowing or curiously impulsive approach to their own inner world. Fantasies are almost absent or are dramatically creative. Stabilization sometimes results in creative, but also dysfunctional solutions.	One-sided, negative or positive affects (panic, anger, disgust, contempt or ecstasy etc.) impose themselves and persistently occupy the inner experience and the construction of psychological reality. Inner worlds are increasingly colored in a threatening way. Contact with the inner experience is intense and can be very invigorating. It quickly leads to flooding, anxiety and discomfort. Fantasies range from threatening to enraptured to agonizing inner emptiness. The solutions are rarely creative, mostly avoidant or destructive.	Individual affects can come to the fore in an alienating way; alternatively, persistent affective uninvolvement. No contact with inner emotional processes, or these are experienced as massively threatening or promising. Experiencing reality and fantasies cannot be reliably separated. Fantasies can become unsettling certainties. Under stabilizing conditions, a selective reference to reality can be made possible. Creative solutions do not emerge; tense inner emptiness or massive impulsiveness.	Individual emotions dominate or alternate with other individual emotions. A persistent lack of emotion can also occur. Contact with inner emotional processes is either blocked or overflowing; massively threatening or tempting. Reality and fantasies cannot be distinguished. Fantasies become unsettling certainties and can mobilize massive fears and the experience of boundaries being broken; bizarre form. Creative solutions are only possible by giving up reality.

Table 58. Operationalization of experience of affects and fantasies (ST4.1 in Table 41) *(continued)*

1 Good	1.5	2 Moderate	2.5	3 Low	3.5	4 Disintegrated
			Good integration		**With increasing impairment ...**	
Core sentences	**Liveliness**		A variety of lively emotions enrich our existence. Negative affects can also be valued.		rigidity of affects up to flooding or complete fading out.	
	Affect quality		Positive emotions prevail and support the person even in difficult moments.		prevalence of one-sided affects up to massive and permanent impairment of the experience of affect.	
	Curiosity about emotional inner processes		Liveliness and a playfully curious approach to one's own inner world.		loss of vitality and curiosity, instead increasing experience of threat or unrealistic promise, in extreme cases loss of perception of the mental.	
	Fantasy		Inner spaces of experience can be expanded through fantasies.		blurring of fantasy and reality, threatening and fearful or promising experience of fantasies decoupled from reality.	
	Creativity		Creative solutions can be developed.		inability to develop creative solutions without giving up reality.	

Table 59. Operationalization of experience of joy (ST4.2 in Table 41)

1 Good	1.5	2 Moderate	2.5	3 Low	3.5	4 Disintegrated
One's own body can be experienced with pleasure. Eroticism and sexual arousal can be experienced (alone or with a partner) in a satisfying way. Sensual, spiritual, cultural, culinary or natural experiences can be experienced as pleasurable and enriching.	In stressful situations, the possibilities for experiencing one's own body, eroticism and sexuality as well as non-sexual pleasures are temporarily restricted.	The pleasurable experience of one's own body, of eroticism and sexuality is rigidly and normatively limited. Non-sexual pleasure is also limited in its intensity, spontaneity and expansiveness, but can take place in a thoroughly satisfying way within predetermined structures with sublimatory connotations.	Pleasurable interaction with one's own body, eroticism and sexuality is either avoided or occurs impulsively and can be overwhelming and occasionally trigger anxiety. Non-sexual pleasure can be experienced, possibly very intense and intoxicating, but can also remain inaccessible or mobilize discomfort and anxiety. Under favourable conditions, joyful experiences can succeed in phases.	One's own body, eroticism and sexuality can either not be experienced in a pleasurable way and remain lifeless or the experience is very intense and overflowing. Violent feelings of disgust, disappointment, anger or fear of merging can occur. Non-sexual pleasures are either experienced as intoxicating, sometimes threatening or remain inaccessible.	Their own body and sexuality are either inaccessible to a pleasurable experience or there is a massive diffuse arousal with dissolution of boundaries and possibly fear of self-loss. The latter can be experienced as very threatening. The arousal may be tied to partial objects. Pronounced sexual inhibitions are possible. Non-sexual pleasures can be experienced intensely, but can also quickly tip over into excess or boredom and inner emptiness.	Physical experience and sexuality are characterized by intensely pressing ideas that can quickly take on a threatening character. The intensity of the experience can cause fears of self-loss and/or destructive fantasies and impulses. Alternatively, interpersonal pleasure is avoided due to massive fears of closeness and intimacy, up to and including general anhedonia. The non-sexual capacity for pleasure is also extremely excessive or depleted.

		Good integration	With increasing impairment ...
Core sentences	**Joyful experience of body and sexuality**	The body, eroticism, and sexuality can be experienced in a pleasurable and satisfying way.	inability to experience the body and sexuality as pleasurable, instead avoidance or threat and flooding by the inner experience.
	Non-sexual pleasure	Sensual, spiritual, cultural, culinary, or natural experiences are pleasurable and enriching.	loss of the ability to experience non-sexual pleasures as joyful.

Table 60. Operationalization of bodily self (ST4.3 in Table 41)

1 Good	1.5	2 Moderate	2.5	3 Low	3.5	4 Disintegrated
One's own body is experienced as vital, positive and whole, and as belonging to oneself. Attention to the body changes according to the situation and there is an appropriately self-caring approach to one's own body.	Under pressure, the body is sometimes experienced as inanimate; the feeling of wholeness and connection with the body remains. Situationally, attention can become fixated on the body; in most cases, dealing with one's own body is characterized by appropriate self-care.	The body can sometimes be perceived as lacking vitality and as a burden. It is experienced as a whole, but an experience of strangeness can occur in the short term. Focusing attention on physical processes can last for a long time. Occasionally, the body is neglected.	Outside of stabilizing conditions, the experience of the body is always less vivid or alien and can become stressful or threatening. The experience of the body as a whole is lost at times. Attention may be focused on physical (dys-)functions over a longer period of time. The body is occasionally neglected or damaged.	The body is repeatedly experienced as frozen, burdensome, fragmented, or alien; however, the experience of the body can also be excessively vivid. It is easy to become fixated on physical dysfunctions and even to objectify an alienated body. The body is neglected or – often damagingly – made the object of various manipulations.	The body is repeatedly experienced as dead, fragmented or separated from the mind. Sensitive perception of the body can be temporarily altered. Attention is focused on physical dysfunctions and is accompanied by panic and despair. The body is massively neglected or permanently damaged by exaggerated and disfiguring measures.	The body is predominantly perceived as dead, fragmented or influenced by others. There is often a rigid focus of attention on altered, often negative aspects of the body. The connection between psyche and soma seems to be largely lost. The body can be massively damaged or neglected directly, for which there is often a lack of awareness.

		Good integration	With increasing impairment …
Core sentences	**Vitality**	A lively and affirming body feeling.	feeling of rigidity and burden.
	Integrity	Integrated (coherent) body image.	fragmentation of the body image.
	Sense of self	Integration of the body into the self-image.	alienation of the bodily experience.
	Attention focusing	Flexibility in the way you treat your own body.	fixation in the observation of one's own body.
	Self-care	Ability to care for, nourish, and exercise physically.	neglect and damage to the body.

Table 61. Operationalization of making emotional contact (ST4.4 in Table 41)

1 Good	1.5	2 Moderate	2.5	3 Low	3.5	4 Disintegrated
The person can make lively contact. Through affective participation, communication is lively, interesting, and fruitful. Conflicts are moderated and dealt with authentically; they do not have a lasting negative impact on communication.	There is the ability to make lively contact. Through affective involvement, communication can be fruitful when there is agreement; when negative emotions are involved, communication becomes difficult at times. In conflicts, withdrawal and fear of confrontation are noticeable.	The search for contact is noticeable, but making contact is nevertheless inhibited. A reduced expression of affect makes it difficult to communicate vividly. Communication is difficult due to increased sensitivity (e.g., defensive, retentive, demanding, reproachful behavior).	Interest in contact and establishing a relationship fluctuates greatly but can succeed under stabilizing conditions. Reduced affect expression or the prevalence of negative affect can make it difficult for the person to communicate. Communication is then difficult due to considerable vulnerability.	Avoidance of contact or urgent, distanced contact behavior. As the mood changes quickly or is inappropriately arrested, the other person receives contradictory or incomprehensible affective messages. The other person may experience confusion, emptiness, distance, a feeling of as-if, lack of relatedness and alternating between over-commitment and resignation.	When establishing contact, massive changes in affectivity and relatedness or inappropriate arresting behavior can make communication unpredictable or irritating. Reduced expression of affect, lack of involvement, lack of warm affect or excessive affect make communication very difficult. The other person regularly experiences confusion, emptiness, distance, a feeling of as-if, lack of relatedness and alternating between over-involvement and powerlessness.	Contact is not possible or follows stereotypical patterns. Communication is often refused or avoided. Under certain circumstances, emotional contact can be parathymic or completely absent. Affects are easily mobilized, but cannot be controlled and symbolized, so that diffuse excitement can easily occur and the frame may be violated; alternatively, contact may seem lifeless and walled in. The other person experiences intense feelings of being completely isolated or highly involved.

		Good integration	With increasing impairment …
Core sentences	**Making contact**	Interest in and desire for contact.	avoidance or failure of emotional contact.
	Affectivity	Liveliness of communication.	reduction of the affective modulation of communication.
	Conflict ability	Ability to deal with conflict when dealing with others.	vulnerability and communicative ambiguities.

Table 62. Operationalization of intimacy (ST4.5 in Table 41)

1 Good	1.5	2 Moderate	2.5	3 Low	3.5	4 Disintegrated
There is the ability to create and tolerate tender feelings and sexual closeness at the same time. Dependence can be endured well and also experienced in a satisfying way. The ability to establish and maintain an intimate emotional bond with other people is linked to the ability to harmonize giving and receiving. There is a lively and flexible openness and trust in one another.	The ability to build up intimacy and maintain it both emotionally and sexually is impaired in stressful situations. Dependence tolerance may be limited at times. In certain situations, the ability to continue verbal and non-verbal dialogue and to balance interests is temporarily lost. Reciprocal trust may be limited in stressful situations.	Tender feelings and sexuality can be combined, but one or the other is restricted. There is a fear of being hurt in intimate relationships. Dependence is avoided or clinging takes place. However, flexible giving and taking is only possible to a limited extent; one or the other takes center stage. There is a tendency to inflexibly define ways and boundaries of intimacy.	It is very difficult to combine tender feelings and sexuality. Limited emotional flooding can easily occur. Relationship experience and behavior tilt into splits between sexuality and emotional closeness with avoidance of sexuality in the partnership and/or living out sexual relationships without emotional closeness. There is pronounced dependency avoidance or clinging. Reciprocal give and take is hardly possible. Intimate issues are sometimes anxiously withheld or shared uncontrollably.	Division into desexualized love relationships and sexual activity without emotional commitment. The coincidence of intimacy and emotional closeness leads to flooding, a feeling of self-loss, and often to impulsive behavior. Dependence cannot be tolerated in the long term. In intimate situations, only one's own experience is perceived; alternatively, intense submission and self-abandonment. Intimate details are mistrustfully concealed or revealed unthinkingly, one-sidedly and impulsively.	Neither sexual nor emotional intimacy is tolerated. Both lead to emotional flooding and the threat of self-loss. Alternatively, radical avoidance of closeness or massive manipulation of the object. Dependency avoidance or highly dysfunctional dependency relationships. Sexuality predominantly in dependent or perverse arrangements. Divergent experiences lead to a high degree of confusion, emotional flooding and experiences of threat, possibly with loss of self. It is not possible to open up to each other.	Intimacy cannot be lived. Closeness leads to fusion and loss of self; or the other is used as a thing, possessed and controlled. Alternatively, closeness is completely avoided. Dependency is radically avoided or symbiotic arrangements are used. The perception of a separate counterpart is impossible. The experience of the object is ignored or subject and object are fused. It is not possible to open up to one another.

		Good integration	With increasing impairment ...
Core sentences	**Integration of sexuality and love**	Sexual desire and love can be combined.	problems combining sexuality and loving feelings.
	Dependence tolerance	Dependence can be endured and experienced as enriching.	difficulty experiencing dependency positively or tolerating it at all.
	Mutual give and take	A flexible alternation of give and take is possible.	one-sidedness, economization and rigidity in giving and receiving.
	Being able to open up to each other	Mutual confiding, opening up and sharing is possible.	difficulty opening up without fear and experiencing the other person.

Table 63. Operationalization of empathy (ST4.6 in Table 41)

1 Good	1.5	2 Moderate	2.5	3 Low	3.5	4 Disintegrated
Communication is characterized by the desire and ability to empathize with others. Empathy and identification with the other person's inner world are easily possible. Emotional understanding can be communicated to the other person in a sympathetic way.	The desire and ability to empathize with others characterizes communication but is limited in stressful situations. In principle, the ability to temporarily identify with the inner world of the other person exists. In general, understanding can be communicated to the other person.	Empathizing with others is more difficult due to conflict. Sympathy and identification with the other person are limited under the pressure of one's own wishes and fears. It is always difficult to communicate understanding to the other person.	Empathy with others is noticeably limited and usually only possible under stabilizing conditions. Identifying with the inner experience of others is often difficult. Sympathy and understanding are difficult to communicate adequately.	It is difficult to empathize with the experiences of others. It is almost impossible to sympathize and identify with others. Excessively sensitive understanding can be possible but always remains linked to one's own wishes and fears. In most cases, this is not a truly sympathetic understanding.	Empathizing with and identifying with the inner world of others is generally not possible. Instead, unquestioned, erroneous, or oversensitive attributions dominate, which are characterized by their own fears or desires. Attributions are communicated that trigger irritation and/or a feeling of intrusion in the other person. Alternatively, communication is avoided.	Empathizing with others is not possible or leads to symbiotic states. The inner world of the other person is not accessible. The experience of the other is determined by massive attributions. Instead of identification, there is often a fusion with the projectively charged object. Alternatively, there is no conception of psychological inner worlds, communication is de-emotionalized, functionalized, or remains in the concrete.

		Good integration	With increasing impairment …
Core sentences	**Empathize with the emotional world of others**	Ability to empathize with communication partners.	inability to empathize with the other person.
	Identifying with the inner world of others	Ability to sympathize.	problems making the other person's world their own.
	Being able to communicate understanding to the other person	It is possible to communicate emotional understanding and empathy to the other person.	inability to communicate understanding and empathy.

Table 64. Operationalization of internalization (ST5.1 in Table 41)

1 Good	1.5	2 Moderate	2.5	3 Low	3.5	4 Disintegrated
The ability to create and maintain emotionally stable internal images of important people is consistently present. The central fear is to lose the love of the object.	The ability to create and maintain emotionally stable internal images of important people is usually present. It can be temporarily restricted under pressure or in conflict situations. The central fear is to lose the love of the object.	The ability to create stable internal images of important people and thus be more independent of their external presence is more difficult: internal images can fade or be limited in their differentiation after a short time or in conflictual situations. The central fear is losing the important, supporting, controlling object.	Relationships with other people rarely leave consistent positive internal images. Insecure object images predominate. The central fear of damage, emptiness and being lost can be temporarily overcome with the help of a counterpart through special effort and adaptation.	Relationships with other people leave hardly any positive internal images. If they do exist, they are idealized in a one-sided way or aversive object images predominate. The central fear is of being damaged by the objects.	Stable internal images of others do not exist. Idealized or threatening partial aspects of others are internalized. These are sparse and arbitrary. The internal (partial) objects often display aggressive or sadistic qualities. The central fear is of fusion and/or annihilation by the object.	The lack of constant images of others can lead to inner emptiness or be replaced by inner, sometimes magical worlds. The internal (partial) objects can be bizarre, uncanny, seductive, or even lifeless. Partial aspects can stand for the whole person. The central fear concerns the destruction of self and identity.

		Good integration	With increasing impairment …
Core sentences	**Stability and quality of internal images**	Internal images of important others are stable, coherent, differentiated, and generally rather positive.	instability and disintegration of these images due to strong fears of loss through to massively threatening ideas of objects.
	Internal working model of relationships	Images of the self and important others in relationships are stable, coherent, differentiated and generally positive. There is a fundamental certainty that others can be there for you.	uncertainty as to whether others can be there for one. Increasing difficulties in attributing an emotional meaning to the object without its real presence, fear of annihilation and/or fusion.

Table 65. Operationalization of use of introjects (ST5.2 in Table 41)

1 Good	1.5	2 Moderate	2.5	3 Low	3.5	4 Disintegrated
As a consequence of internalized good experiences in relationships, it is possible to refer to the internalized objects in difficult situations (to enter into an "inner dialogue"), to take care of oneself, to calm oneself down and to stand up for oneself. Being alone with oneself can be well tolerated and, if self-chosen, also enjoyed over a longer period of time.	Under pressure, it is sometimes less possible to use the internalized good objects to stand up for oneself and calm oneself down; the objects then become more demanding and critical at times. Being alone with oneself can be tolerated in stressful phases but often cannot be experienced positively.	The inner objects tend to be driving, criticizing, demanding or neglectful. This makes it difficult to stand up for oneself and calm down. A relieving "inner dialogue" with objects is usually not possible. Being alone with oneself can be tolerated but is experienced as a burden or a relief depending on the conflict.	It is only rarely possible to relate to positive inner objects. As these are experienced as very critical, demanding, sometimes devaluing and neglectful, it is not possible to calm down in crises. Under stabilizing conditions, being alone with oneself can be tolerated at times. However, this can be lost, resulting in inner emptiness, anxiety, and restlessness.	The inner objects tend to be aversive or over-exciting, so they cannot be used to calm down. An "inner dialogue" creates either unrealistic ideal or torturous images. Being alone with oneself has the character of a form of survival in a certain isolation or quickly takes on a threatening quality, which can lead to impulsive action in the sense of self-harm or sexualization of a lack of relationship.	The internalized sub-objects have a distinctly threatening or over-exciting quality or are not experienced. They lead to violent, sometimes abrupt states of agitation, feelings of powerlessness and confusion. Being alone can cause severe crises, which are coped with dysfunctionally, e.g., by not recognizing the isolation at all or by creating fantasized substitute relationships.	Being at the mercy of inner part-objects that have acquired a predominantly autonomous form. This can lead to intense agitation and typically to inner certainties that are completely removed from reality. Being alone with oneself is either not tolerated or it takes on a fantastic quality through the denial of reality.

		Good integration	With increasing impairment …
Core sentences	**Self-calming through positive inner objects**	Internalized good relationship experiences facilitate self-calming.	inability to calm down because the inner images of others are driving, criticizing, and neglectful, or very threatening.
	Encourage oneself to take care of oneself	Internalized good relationship experiences facilitate and enable one to develop inner strength for decisions and actions and/or to treat oneself kindly.	inability to encourage or care for oneself because helpful internal images are either not used or not available.
	Being alone with oneself	Internalized good relationship experiences make it possible to cope well with oneself, to be at peace with oneself, to like oneself, even in situations of loneliness.	inability to cope well with oneself, to be at peace with oneself, to like oneself. This often becomes clear when a person is thrown back on themselves, especially in situations of loneliness.

Table 66. Operationalization of variability (ST5.3 in Table 41)

1 Good	1.5	2 Moderate	2.5	3 Low	3.5	4 Disintegrated
Internal images of important others are different and diverse. Depending on the other person and the situation, the relationships vary in terms of intensity, quality, closeness, and content that is shared. It is quite possible to represent different relationships with different people at the same time, i.e., to have emotional access to them: Triadic relationships can be maintained.	The internal images of important others are different and diverse. In stressful situations, the ability to perceive others in their diversity and variety and to represent them in a differentiated way can be limited. If the ability for triadic relationships is otherwise good, dyadic constellations are then increasingly sought.	Important others are represented in a less differentiated way, the internal images are more similar. The quality and intensity of relationships are also less diverse and more dyadic. Rivalry is avoided in relationships where possible or is the focus of attention due to conflict. Existing triadic relationships are easily disrupted.	There is little variability about the internal images of important others, and these are predominantly negative in tone. Triadic relationships can only be represented under stabilizing conditions, otherwise only one person at a time is inwardly accessible and can also be experienced emotionally.	Relationships appear functionalized – very often only that which is significant in relation to the self is perceived by the other. As a result, the inner images of others are often barely distinguishable and hardly recognizable in their individuality. They are also characterized by splits or fragmentation. Triadic relationships cannot be represented.	Inner images of others are clichéd and highly functionalized; the representations do not reveal individual differences. Relationships are experienced and represented on a level characterized by regressive impulses. Triadic relationships cannot be represented and are experienced as threatening.	The inner images of others are largely based on their own fantasies, are threatening or promising and have little or no connection to reality. Attachments exist predominantly to the fantasized others, real relationships are irritating and threatening, are purely functional or are avoided. Triadic relationships do not seem to exist.

		Good integration	With increasing impairment ...
Core sentences	**Differentiation**	Different degrees of closeness, distance, and relationship quality can be experienced with different objects.	tendency not to recognize existing differences, so that the other person becomes increasingly interchangeable, even to the point of creating unrealistic fantasized internal images.
	Diversity	In relationships, the diversity and change of objects can be perceived and represented internally	functionalization of relationships and self-centred internal images that are not variable and are characterized by splitting or fragmentation.
	Triadic relationships	Different relationships to different objects can be tolerated and represented at the same time.	preference for dyadic relationships to prevalence of interchangeable, seemingly clichéd internal images and and a lack of triangulation ability.

Table 67. Operationalization of ability to form attachments (ST5.4 in Table 41)

1 Good	1.5	2 Moderate	2.5	3 Low	3.5	4 Disintegrated
Others have emotional significance; there is the ability and desire to attach to them. Relationships are actively protected, and closeness is flexibly organized according to the situation. The feelings of dependency resulting from emotional significance can be tolerated and enjoyed well.	Others have emotional significance; there is the ability and desire to attach to them. Under pressure, the ability to organize closeness is limited. Conflict can lead to distancing or temporary excessive dependence, which can no longer be flexibly organized and experienced positively.	Attachment and lasting relationships are usually possible, but dependency and closeness can often not be enjoyed and flexibly organized. Instead, the emotional significance of the significant other is either exaggerated or avoided. Relationships are characterized by conflict or are partially emotionally drained.	Relationships are either characterized by dramatic collapses and violent conflicts or there is a lack of emotional distance. Alternatively, attachments are often avoided or replaced by frequently changing short-term relationships. Dependence can be tolerated temporarily under stabilizing conditions and the other person can be granted emotional significance.	It is not possible to maintain a permanent object-centeredness. Dependence is either avoided completely or experienced very intensely, which ultimately becomes threatening and can lead to forced distancing (on-off relationship). Nevertheless, unstable and dramatic relationships can exist over a long period of time. Alternatively, frequently changing intensive but unsustainable relationships or chronic isolation.	Symbiotic relationships or rigid and anxious preservation of autonomy and pronounced avoidance of object attachments. Highly dysfunctional relationships that often do not last. The experience of dependency is met with dysfunctional (often aggressive or destructive) attempts to control the object, alternatively extensive, sometimes masochistic self-sacrifice.	Dependence cannot be tolerated. When relationships exist for a short time, they are either functionalized, without the other being given emotional significance, or symbiosis-like, whereby the other is possessed like a thing and controlled dysfunctionally, sometimes aggressively. Alternatively, there is complete subjugation. The other is less a real person than a powerful fantasized internal object.

		Good integration	With increasing impairment ...
Core sentences	**Object-relatedness**	Close relationships can be established, the desire to commit exists, the other person can be experienced and respected as an independent person.	exaggeration of the emotional significance of the objects up to symbiosis-like relationships, or pronounced avoidance of contact.
	Giving objects an emotional meaning	Important others become emotionally significant.	threats from others that take on emotional significance.
	Dependence tolerance	Feelings of dependency in important relationships are tolerated and can be enjoyed.	avoidance of dependency, dysfunctional control of the object, or complete relinquishment of independence.

Table 68. Operationalization of trust (ST5.5 in Table 41)

1 Good	1.5	2 Moderate	2.5	3 Low	3.5	4 Disintegrated
There is a secure basic trust in other people. Others are believed in an appropriate manner; other people can be utilized as good objects.	Given a basic level of trust, other people can usually be used as good objects in difficult life situations. Under great pressure or in conflict-relevant situations, there is a tendency to primarily want to help oneself.	Trust in others is limited; alternatively, there may be uncritical trust in others. Determined by inner conflict issues, it may be difficult to find and accept support even when there is inner need.	There is no secure basic trust in others. This can be compensated for by exaggerated trust. Due to strong mistrust, help from others can be re-jected suspiciously and aggressively. Help may be cautiously accepted for a short time with special effort on the part of the other person.	Due to strong mistrust, supportive help from others is rejected reflexively, fearfully, suspiciously, or aggressively. No secure trust in others and no idea that others could be helpful without ulterior motives. Alternatively, dysfunctional trust and surrendering to others.	Help is difficult to differentiate from an attack on the core of the personality. No idea of helpful others. Offers of help are fiercely rejected or ignored as potential manipulations or attacks. In other cases, there is a submissive surrender to others.	Help is equated with destruction and/or empowerment. Help can only be expected from fantasized omnipotent figures or is unimaginable. It is also possible to identify with an all-powerful savior to whom one can surrender oneself unconditionally.
			Good integration		**With increasing impairment …**	
Core sentences	**Object quality**		Basic trust and realistic confidence in the goodwill of others.		coloring of expectations of the objects through own wishes up to pronounced, habitual mistrust. Alternatively, dysfunctional surrender	
	Give credence		Offers of support from others are believed in a realistic manner; commitment, reliability, and reciprocity are internalized values of experi-ence.		difficulties in realistically assessing others as credible and reliable, to the point of being unable to even imagine that others mean what they say.	
	Accept help		Others can be regarded as good and support-ive objects.		fearful, mistrustful, or aggressive rejection of offers of support from others despite being in need.	

Table 69. Operationalization of ability to separate (ST5.6 in Table 41)

1 Good	1.5	2 Moderate	2.5	3 Low	3.5	4 Disintegrated
Separations can be tolerated, brought about and overcome with an appropriate feeling of sadness. The affective cathexis of the lost object can be withdrawn, whereby an appropriately positive inner image can be retained. This creates an inner freedom for new relationships.	In principle, separations can be endured, brought about and overcome with an appropriate feeling of sadness. Affective cathexis can be withdrawn from lost objects while maintaining an appropriately positive inner image. Occasionally, feared or real conflictual losses can lead to increased clinging or denial of the separation.	Farewells are ignored or people cling to objects to avoid feared losses. This can lead to persistence in conflictual relationships. After separations, the affective preoccupation cannot be removed for a long time; positive inner images are warded off after a separation. This can put a strain on new relationships.	The inner experience of separation and saying goodbye while grieving only exists to a very limited extent. With the active support of others, grief can be partially endured; however, real separations often harbor an increased risk of symptom formation or compensatory impulsive actions. Persistence in dysfunctional relationships or separation with destruction of inner objects.	The inner experiences of separation and parting under grief are not possible; nevertheless, real separations often trigger symptom formation or compensatory impulsive actions. The affective cathexis cannot be withdrawn from the lost object; internal objects are destroyed or maintained in an idealized form.	Separations are seemingly accepted without emotion or denied by turning to pure objectivity. Separations can trigger massive and sometimes disturbing reactions such as sudden suicidal behavior or aggression towards others. Symbiotic relationships are dissolved by destroying the internal objects; alternatively, an idealized inner image remains.	In the case of separation, there is no reaction to the loss, but rather an increased focus on inner, fantasized worlds. Visible emotional reactions are usually absent; however, the turning away from reality is often massively intensified. Alternatively, the inner object is destroyed, possibly leading to the destruction of the real object and/or suicidal behavior.

		Good integration	With increasing impairment ...
Core sentences	**Initiating separations and farewells**	Affective cathexis of objects can be withdrawn.	clinging to the object and/or denial of real losses, through to sudden, difficult to understand acts of separation.
	Dealing with separations and farewells	Separations and farewells can be tolerated, endured and appropriately mourned.	massive internal and external reactions, or avoidance, or denial of affective reactions to separation and loss.

5.6 Rating Sheet Structure Axis (Axis IV)

The rating sheets of Axis IV are given in Figure 18 (clinical version) and Figure 19 (research version) (both figures are available in the online material).

OPD-3 Rating Sheet Axis IV: Structure (Clinical Version).

Time window: ☐ 5 years ☐ shortened/extended to: ____________ n/a = not applicable

	Good ①	Good to moderate 1.5	Moderate ②	Moderate to low 2.5	Low ③	Low to disinte-grated 3.5	Disinte-grated ④	Not applicable ⑨
1a Self-perception	①	○	②	○	③	○	④	⑨
1b Object perception	①	○	②	○	③	○	④	⑨
2a Self-regulation	①	○	②	○	③	○	④	⑨
2b Relationship regulation	①	○	②	○	③	○	④	⑨
3 Defense	①	○	②	○	③	○	④	⑨
4a Internal communication	①	○	②	○	③	○	④	⑨
4b Communication with the external world	①	○	②	○	③	○	④	⑨
5a Attachment to internal objects	①	○	②	○	③	○	④	⑨
5b Attachment to external objects	①	○	②	○	③	○	④	⑨
Structure total	①	○	②	○	③	○	④	⑨

Temporal variability rating

Variability of structure	no ⓪			yes ①			n/a ⑨

Continue, if yes ①:

Current structural level	Baseline level ⓪		worse ①		better ②		n/a ⑨
Extent of the fluctuation	±1 ○		±2 ○		±3 ○		n/a ⑨
Duration of the fluctuation	<3 ○ months	3–6 ○ months	6–12 ○ months	1–2 ○ years	>2–3 ○ years	>3 ○ years	n/a ⑨
Cause of the fluctuation (disorder/trauma)							n/a ⑨

Variability rating by life areas

Divergence of structure	no ⓪	yes ①	n/a ⑨

Better functioning	Life areas	Worse functioning
○	Family of origin	○
○	Partnership/family	○
○	Profession	○
○	Social environment	○
○	Possessions	○
○	Body/sexuality	○
○	Illnesses	○
Cause of the fluctuation (disorder/trauma)		

Figure 18. OPD-3 rating sheet Axis IV: Structure (clinical version).

OPD-3 Rating Sheet Axis IV: Structure (Research Version).								
Time window: ☐ 5 years ☐ shortened/extended to: ____________ n/a = not applicable								
	Good ①	Good to moderate 1.5	Moderate ②	Moderate to low 2.5	Low ③	Low to disintegrated 3.5	Disintegrated ④	Not applicable ⑨
Self-perception	①	◯	②	◯	③	◯	④	⑨
ST1.1 Self-reflection	①	◯	②	◯	③	◯	④	⑨
ST1.2 Affect differentiation	①	◯	②	◯	③	◯	④	⑨
ST1.3 Identity	①	◯	②	◯	③	◯	④	⑨
Object perception	①	◯	②	◯	③	◯	④	⑨
ST1.4 Self-object differentiation	①	◯	②	◯	③	◯	④	⑨
ST1.5 Object-related affect differentiation	①	◯	②	◯	③	◯	④	⑨
ST1.6 Integrated object perception	①	◯	②	◯	③	◯	④	⑨
Self-regulation	①	◯	②	◯	③	◯	④	⑨
ST2.1 Impulse control	①	◯	②	◯	③	◯	④	⑨
ST2.2 Affect tolerance	①	◯	②	◯	③	◯	④	⑨
ST2.3 Self-esteem regulation	①	◯	②	◯	③	◯	④	⑨
Relationship regulation	①	◯	②	◯	③	◯	④	⑨
ST2.4 Protecting relationships	①	◯	②	◯	③	◯	④	⑨
ST2.5 Anticipation	①	◯	②	◯	③	◯	④	⑨
ST2.6 Balancing of interests	①	◯	②	◯	③	◯	④	⑨
Defense	①	◯	②	◯	③	◯	④	⑨
ST3.1 Living and experiencing possibilities	①	◯	②	◯	③	◯	④	⑨
ST3.2 Interpersonal impact	①	◯	②	◯	③	◯	④	⑨
ST3.3 Mechanisms	①	◯	②	◯	③	◯	④	⑨
Internal communication	①	◯	②	◯	③	◯	④	⑨
ST4.1 Experience of affects and fantasies	①	◯	②	◯	③	◯	④	⑨
ST4.2 Experience of joy	①	◯	②	◯	③	◯	④	⑨
ST4.3 Bodily self	①	◯	②	◯	③	◯	④	⑨
Communication with the external world	①	◯	②	◯	③	◯	④	⑨
ST4.4 Making emotional contact	①	◯	②	◯	③	◯	④	⑨
ST4.5 Intimacy	①	◯	②	◯	③	◯	④	⑨
ST4.6 Empathy	①	◯	②	◯	③	◯	④	⑨
Attachment to internal objects	①	◯	②	◯	③	◯	④	⑨
ST5.1 Internalization	①	◯	②	◯	③	◯	④	⑨
ST5.2 Use of introjects	①	◯	②	◯	③	◯	④	⑨
ST5.3 Variability	①	◯	②	◯	③	◯	④	⑨
Attachment to external objects	①	◯	②	◯	③	◯	④	⑨
ST5.4 Ability to form attachments	①	◯	②	◯	③	◯	④	⑨
ST5.5 Trust	①	◯	②	◯	③	◯	④	⑨
ST5.6 Ability to separate	①	◯	②	◯	③	◯	④	⑨
Structure total	①	◯	②	◯	③	◯	④	⑨

Figure 19. OPD-3 rating sheet Axis IV: Structure (research version).

6 Interplay of Axes and Individual Psychodynamics

6.1 Basic Considerations

With its four Axes Operationalized Psychodynamic Diagnosis (OPD) is a multiaxial approach. A multiaxial approach offers the possibility of better depicting the complex constellation of conditions that we find in most mental phenomena and mental disorders.

In mathematical-theoretical concepts, descriptive axes are fundamentally independent of each other and thus stand perpendicular to each other in a mathematical space (e.g., X- and Y-axes). This does not apply to different clinical axes, in which mental phenomena of varying depths (conscious/unconscious experiences and behaviors) are recorded. Rather, the multiaxial approach of the OPD resembles the famous Indian parable of several blind men feeling an elephant: All parts belong to the elephant, all parts interact, and each person perceives a different part correctly, but not the whole. The Axes I to IV of the OPD are therefore not independent of each other in what and how they capture phenomena; rather, they capture different parts of the person or deeper phenomena (the unconscious) from different perspectives, which naturally interact with each other.

The following is an attempt to explain the interaction of the axes with each other in the most important elements.

6.2 Process of Gathering and Integrating Diagnostic Material

Two opposing movements can be traced for the diagnostic process based on the OPD. The path to acquiring and recording diagnostic material begins with aspects that concern the basic accessibility of the patient for diagnostic exploration and are part of what is described in Axis I "Mental Disorders, Experience of Illness, and Prerequisites for Treatment." Important here are, for example, their complaints/symptoms, the patient's illness model, and their (lack of) openness to a psychological approach to their complaints. The examination subsequently focuses on the patient's relational experiences, which serve as a key diagnostic pathway to psychodynamic understanding and are systematically explored in the OPD interview.

Both from the relationship descriptions and the immediately perceptible relationship design of the patient, their typical interpersonal scenarios or arrangements can be deduced, which are depicted in Axis II. These relationship patterns represent a surface in which conflict predispositions are reflected, which are compromise-managed in the encounter with others. The form and quality of this management finally directs attention to the functional equipment of the patient, i.e., their structural possibilities and limitations, which provide a stable framework for the dynamic play of mental forces.

The path to integrating diagnostic material leads in the opposite direction (Figure 20). It begins with the structural prerequisites. These

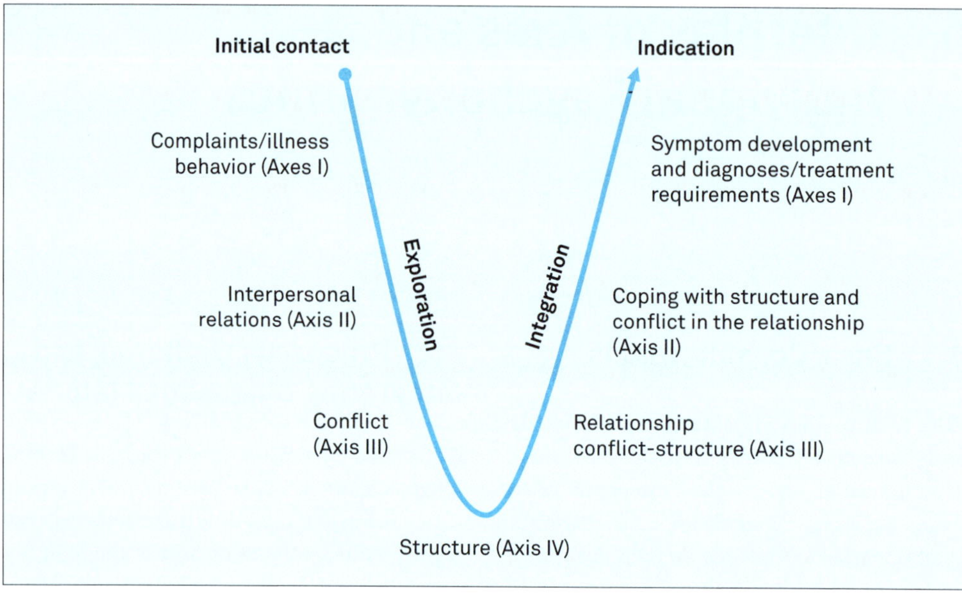

Figure 20. Obtaining and integrating the diagnostic materials. Illustration of the diagnostic process starting on the top left with the collection and recording of diagnostic material and towards the investigation of structural requirements, followed by the integration of the axis-related findings into a coherent overall picture as the basis for the indication (axis-related results).

represent a fundamental diagnostic dimension according to the understanding of the OPD, which significantly (co-)determines the quality and character of the other features described by the OPD. The extent of structural impairment influences and limits the weight that lifelong acquired conflict dispositions have in the development and maintenance of complaints. It influences the quality of affects, which become increasingly "archaic" and more difficult to regulate with greater structural impairment. It shapes habitual relationship patterns, which become increasingly inefficient and fragile with greater structural limitation, making it increasingly difficult or impossible to establish lasting relationships. The structural condition of an individual further determines whether the "illness" is significant in the sense of neurotic symptom formation or whether the nature, variety, intensity, and variability of the complaints indicate that basic mental functions are impaired, and the individual's regulatory possibilities are constantly overwhelmed. All these points ultimately touch on the prerequisites and possibilities of a potential psychotherapeutic treatment, which must be consistently adapted to the type and weight of the structural difficulties.

6.3 The Relationship Between the Axes

6.3.1 Conflict and Structure (Relationship of Axes III and IV)

The conflict diagnostics in OPD-3 is closely intertwined with structural diagnostics. For each conflictual-motivational theme, the manifestations at different structural levels are described, from conflict tension through neurotic conflicts to conflict schemas (and dilemmas; see Chapter 4). Conflict and structure represent poles of a clinical complementary series (Mentzos, 1984).

Structural diagnostics describe a continuum of structural integration with the poles of secure availability of structural (i.e., personality) functions and abilities on one side and severe functional limitations on the other. If a patient can easily access these functions, they usually do not become the focus of diagnostic interest and instead form the background for the conflict dynamics that capture most of the attention. On the other hand, if the functions are limited or fail, the diagnostic focus shifts from the contents of the conflict dynamics (the unconscious motives, fears, and defenses) to the structural equipment of the patient. Conflict and structure relate to the "why" and the "how" of a disorder. If the structure holds, content and meanings dominate; if it is fragile, the disturbed functional processes come to the fore. However, mental events are also determined by the "why," the content, even when structural impairment is significant, though it may be difficult or impossible to recognize this.

A stage metaphor (see Rudolf and Grande, 2002) illustrates this: Imagine going to the theater without any prior knowledge of the play. In this case, you would involuntarily search for dramatic content that explains the actions of the characters on stage, i.e., the conflicting motives and action strategies of the protagonists. This corresponds to conflict orientation. It is assumed that the performance is not disturbed or even determined by influences unrelated to the play's content: e.g., loose stage sets or props that need to be avoided, misaligned or broken furniture, unprepared or unsuitable players, etc. In the case of structurally induced problems, the search for a dramatic event that makes the stage action understandable would be difficult, as one would be constantly irritated by inappropriate occurrences and would eventually realize that an attempt of a play is being made, but it is so disturbed by functional impairments of the stage setup or the protagonists that coherent content is hardly recognizable. This would be the moment when those frame elements come to the fore, which otherwise form the natural background of the action and should serve it effortlessly. This corresponds to a structure orientation.

When a mental disorder is present, dysfunctional conflicts and structural impairments can be responsible to varying degrees. If a low or disintegrated structural level predominates, conflict signs are more often assigned to the so-called conflict themes (or dilemmas), which (in the metaphor) merely represent the "attempt of a performance" but are repeatedly severely disturbed by the unsuitable and damaged stage. Conflictual stressors can often play a role in revealing a structural anomaly, as they address and overwhelm individual structural functions: The motivational themes then somewhat trigger the structural dysfunction, which can cause the motivational themes to become almost unrecognizable or manifest in extreme forms (e.g., closeness becomes fusion, control becomes enslavement, self-worth becomes grandiosity). Even if a patient's structural vulnerability is the primary problem, it is worth simultaneously looking at the associated motivational-conflict dynamics, if only to work with the patient to better understand the occasions and internal triggers of their structural overload. To stay with the metaphor: it is the affects linked to the motivational dynamics that, for example, cause the chair on stage to collapse (the chair not just collapsing on its own), and at the same time, the collapsing chair can have a regulating function, for example, by braking an even stronger flood of affect, or preventing other dangerous actions. The functional interactions between conflict and structure vary at all structural levels.

With better structural equipment, conflicts come more to the fore, increasingly determining the stage action as a latent script and making it understandable. But also, the configuration and management of neurotic conflicts, typically with moderately integrated structure, are determined by this moderate integration: the rigidity of defense, the oversteering of affects and desires, the functionalization of significant others for one's conflict management are the hallmarks of the structural level. This means that working on conflicts is also working on the structure (e.g., in terms of defense making defense more flexible, improving the ability to perceive self and others, deepening emotional communication, changing relationship representations, etc.).

In this respect, these are always mixed forms, some of which place high demands on the diagnostician/psychotherapist. While some conflictual-motivational issues can be easily identified at all structural levels defined in the OPD (e.g., Dependency vs. Individuation; Self-Worth), other issues are found less frequently in cases of severe structural impairment (Grande et al., 1998) or in a very distorted form. Nevertheless, current empirical results suggest that individual conflictual-motivational profiles can be determined even in cases of severe structural impairment (Henkel et al., 2022). And even in very severely structurally impaired patients with psychotic disorders, individually significant conflictual motivational themes can be identified and integrated into an overall psychodynamic understanding (see Sell et al., 2021).

6.3.2 On Coping With Conflict and Structure in Relationship Patterns (Connections to Axis II)

According to our understanding, habitual relationship patterns that appear dysfunctional from an external perspective are primarily adaptive regulatory efforts in the interpersonal realm through which patients attempt to cope with both their conflict inclinations and structural vulnerabilities. The (unconscious) "goal" is to steer interpersonal situations in such a way that the maximum satisfaction of interpersonal needs and interests is achieved while providing sufficient protection for the self. The resulting habitual relational behavior is often conceptualized as a compromise formation between desires and fears (e.g., Luborsky, 1984). From the perspective of Operationalized Psychodynamic Diagnosis, however, it should be noted that protective measures relate not only to fears arising from conflictual desires but also to structurally experienced anxieties and threats (Rudolf, 2000). Moreover, it must be considered that different conflict dispositions and/or structural sensitivities may be managed simultaneously in relational behavior. Considering these possibilities, several principles emerge that affect the formation of relationship patterns:

- *Simple compromise formations:* In primarily conflict-related disorders, relationship patterns can be understood as compromise formations between desire and fear. Example: A patient unconsciously experiences his need for care as unbearable for others, fears rejection, and therefore presents himself as particularly unneedy and caring for others. His compromise formation consists in intensively trying to be helpful for others, with the unconscious claim of receiving care in return.
- *Conflict intersections:* In the example just described an additional conflict issue around control or submission can lead to the altruistic attitude on the one hand impressing as servile and duty-bound, but at the same time helping others satisfies unconscious needs for control.
- *Protection of structural vulnerabilities*: In more structurally based disorders, relationship patterns may serve to protect particularly vulnerable aspects of a patient that are touched upon in interactions with others. These patterns can also be described as compromise formations, where, however, several needs often come into unspecified tension with anxieties and threats that arise due to the overstrain of structural functions in contact with other people. Such anxieties arise, for example, in situations of impending closeness, dependency, intimacy or, conversely, in the event of the unavailability of important objects. In these situations, specific relationship patterns may provide protection. Additionally, performance demands in

general represent a stress test for structural functions.

- *Conflict-structure intersections:* Another clinically significant constellation arises when structural weaknesses are compensated for with the help of relationship figures that seem primarily conflict-motivated on the surface. For example, in a relationship pattern characterized by a control theme, it may be overlooked that constant power struggles effectively manage structurally based fear of closeness (e.g., with insecure self-object differentiation). Structural limitations are also often associated with massive self-worth problems, so that associated motives (envy, resentments, rivalry) can give relationships a conflictual character that manifests in relational behavior.

When analyzing dysfunctional relationship patterns, it is also important to consider that patients can only use the abilities they structurally possess in their coping efforts. For example, a relationship pattern characterized by a pronounced conflict around submission/control may differ significantly in its manifestation, depending on how well-developed the abilities for empathy or impulse control are. Therefore, the structural state or level of personality functioning of a patient determines their relationships in two ways: first, through the vulnerabilities that must be protected in interactions with others, and second, through the functional equipment used to manage both conflict dispositions and structural vulnerabilities.

As various authors have shown, relationship patterns function like maladaptive, self-reinforcing cycles (Strupp & Binder, 1984; Schacht & Henry, 1994). These cycles account for their stability, intrusiveness, and resistance to change. At the core of these cycles are partially unconscious, dysfunctional beliefs about oneself and others, shaped by personal relationship history. These beliefs act as unconscious guiding principles, leading individuals to arrange relationships in ways that elicit confirmation of the unconscious belief from others (Strupp & Binder, 1984). This view complements the principles explained above, as it explains the formation and maintenance of dysfunctional relationship patterns in situ. In the case of severe structural impairments, it can be expected that maladaptive cycles appear more disorganized (e.g., sporadic and variable), as emotional self-regulation fails faster, and abrupt defensive reactions become necessary. In cases of pronounced structural disorder, it may then seem that a contoured, repetitively occurring relationship pattern hardly exists and instead a pattern of abrupt relationship terminations can be diagnosed, which constantly repeats itself. Nevertheless, even here the working hypothesis is useful that such abrupt and/or intense relationship behaviors also conceal "patterns," for example, in that recurrent inner processes that lead to the abrupt terminations or similar behaviors, and even chaotic relationship behavior that follows an inner dynamic and "logic."

6.3.3 Pathways of Symptom Formation (Connections to ICD and DSM)

Based on the previous explanations, the following pathways of symptom formation can be described (see also Rudolf, 2000, p. 137). In specific cases, it is assumed that several of these principles interact and symptoms are thus determined in multiple ways:

Regarding disorders with a conflict-dynamic background, a distinction must be made between a neurotic, conflictual personality disorder and people with repetitive and dysfunctional neurotic conflicts. In the case of a conflictual personality, the pronounced motivational tension leads to a clinically relevant impairment of experience and behavior, for example due to pronounced avoidance attitudes, rigidity or anxiety.

The associated constrictions of experience, interpersonal relationships, and scope of action can be so significant that they become symptomatic. An example would be Obsessive-Compulsive Personality Disorder with no symptoms but relevant disturbances in experience and behavior. An important aspect of the neurotic conflictual personality is the characteristic habitual dysfunctional relationship pattern in which conflict-related desires and fears are managed through compromise, and the manner of this management becomes symptomatic. In Kernberg's model, these would be personality disorders at a neurotic level (for example see Caligor et al., 2009).

The traditional neurotic conflict is accompanied by clinical symptoms that have an intrapsychic and/or interpersonal effect. In situations of temptation and deprivation, threshold situations and situations with internal and external triggers (trigger situations), motivational ambivalences are intensified, resulting in the destabilization and collapse of a previously successful balance. Symptoms develop that can be understood as compromises between the conflicting forces (desires, fears and defenses) and therefore have the positive aspect of an adaptive achievement from a psychodynamic point of view. The characteristics in the context of a structural disorder, which are not "masked" by coping, can themselves become symptomatic. These include, for example, impulse breakthroughs, affect flooding, distortions in object perceptions, or pronounced susceptibility to injury. Symptoms of this type are particularly common in the so-called "dramatic" personality disorders (DSM-IV/-5, Cluster B), e.g., borderline personality disorder.

Structural vulnerabilities are rarely overt, as they are reshaped through processing and thus made bearable. As described in the last section, an important aim of such processing is to regulate relationships with other people in such a way that sufficient protection for the self and its vulnerabilities is guaranteed. However, the processing patterns developed in this way can shape behavior and experience in a way that is symptomatic. This is the case, for example, in severely schizoid or narcissistic relationships. In contrast to the concept of the "conflictual personality disorder" mentioned above, this involves defensive forms of coping that are designed to protect structural vulnerabilities, while the conflictual personality presents itself as a complex, characteristically solidified form of compromise formation, in which active, drive- or desire-driven strivings and their defense are incorporated. The possible interconnections between structural sensitivities and conflict readiness in habitual relationship patterns were described in the previous section. As Rudolf (2000) emphasizes, symptoms often arise due to the failure of coping. Compensatory coping efforts are exhausting, leading to fatigue over time and often do not withstand the inevitable changes and stressors in life or to offer "appropriate" coping mechanisms for new life situations. The collapse of coping leads to various symptom formations: for example, to acute and dramatic symptoms as in the case of suicidal crises in narcissistic personalities or to chronic symptom formations, e.g., in patients with a somatization disorder.

When the acute stressors that cause the collapse of coping are significant or extreme, the assessment may be justified that a clinically noticeable disorder would not have arisen without the external event. In this case, an adjustment disorder in the sense of conflict-related stress occurs, meaning the stress conveys a conflictual motivational contradiction that leads to illness. In this case, the disorder may not be the result of a long-standing repetitive pattern with both life-defining and dysfunctional character. Nevertheless, conflictual motivational themes can now be of current significance and determine psychological events, including symptom formation.

6.3.4 Mental Disorders, Experience of Illness, and Prerequisites for Treatment (Connections to Axis I)

The experience of illness and the expectation of change are often determined and derived not only from the mental characteristics listed in the OPD (structure, conflict, and relationship). Besides the personal variables, of which the OPD characteristics represent a selection, the experience of illness and the motivation for change are influenced by psychosocial context factors interacting with personal characteristics. These include societal norms and values related to illness and treatment, conveyed through the personal social network of the patient, the media, or the healthcare provider.

When assessing the experience of illness and the preconditions for treatment, numerous characteristics are captured that reflect how a patient positions themselves in relation to the clinician, i.e., what expectations they have of them and what tasks they assign to them. Indirectly, this addresses their habitual relationship inclinations, thereby establishing a fundamental connection to the OPD relationship diagnosis. However, this connection cannot be specified in detail, as the diagnosis of habitual dysfunctional relationship patterns is individualized. Connections to Axis I must therefore be examined on a case-by-case basis; they cannot be discussed in general terms without further ado. However, it is to be expected, for example, that patients with a dominant relationship behavior of "submitting/bow to" also have corresponding expectations of the clinician, from whom they passively expect a therapeutic "application," or that patients with withdrawal tendencies have more difficulties in establishing a committed working relationship and are therefore less compliant. Regarding the Conflict Axis (Axis III), connections can indeed be described. In this axis, dealing with illness is one of those areas for which the OPD Manual explicitly formulates criteria. Thus, a direct interface is immediately given. For each conflict, specific complications typically occurring in the encounter with illness and healthcare providers are presented. A distinction is made between a passive and active mode of processing:

In the passive mode, regressive forms of conflict processing predominate, while in the active mode, more reaction-formation, counterphobic, or compensatory forms prevail. Comparing these criteria for the different conflicts shows that the prevailing mode of *conflict processing* plays a significant role in the experience of illness and as a prerequisite for treatment:

- Generally, patients with a predominantly *passive conflict mode* (regardless of the type of conflict) highlight their suffering and complaints more clearly and place the clinician, as mentioned, in an active, responsible role. This suggests that they are more likely to report complaints whose causes lie outside their responsibility and influence. Consequently, their concept of illness should more often include somatic or social (external) stress factors, with corresponding expectations of somatic treatment or changes in external circumstances. If psychotherapy is desired, it is more likely to be associated with the expectation of active support or receiving advice. Due to the passive stance, there is a fundamental risk that elements of secondary gain from illness significantly contribute to maintaining the disorder.
- In cases of a predominantly *active mode* across various conflicts, different risks arise. These patients perceive their illness more as a threat to their autonomy, self-determination, and control. They tend to balance this threat by trivializing their difficulties, rejecting help, or controlling the clinician. If they prefer a somatic model of illness, it may serve to fend off the anticipated questioning and uncertainty associated with a psychological approach. If they endorse psychotherapy, they may prefer a form of treatment they perceive as controllable or one that promises to impart the skills to regain a sense of self-determination. Suitable for this are ap-

proaches promising skill acquisition or insight-oriented treatments, which in the patients' view enable cognitive control or self-optimization.

Axis I "Mental Disorders, Experience of Illness, and Prerequisites for Treatment " certainly has many connections to the Structure Axis (Axis IV). It can be generally expected that all dimensions included in the Structure Axis will impact the experience of illness to varying extents. Central to the treatment preconditions in the context of mental or psychosomatic disorders is the question of whether the patient perceives their problems more on the mental and/or somatic level. This, alongside the nature of the complaints and problems, crucially depends on the ability for self-reflection. The extent to which an individual has developed or can develop access to their "inner world" is partly determined by how and to what extent affects are mentally organized. In our view, a "vivid inner world," where affects and mental themes/conflicts/motives or ambivalences can be experienced and accepted, is primarily an expression of a relatively "good" structure, i.e., a high level of personality functioning. The ability for self-reflection significantly influences what conceptions patients form about their difficulties and what models of illness and change they develop. Willingness to engage in cognitive or affective dissonances also plays a considerable role. Another important structural dimension thus addressed is the ability for self-regulation, which encompasses functions of affect tolerance, self-esteem regulation, and impulse control. The patient's ability for self-regulation forms a foundation for treatment-promoting traits such as perseverance and endurance.

The experience of illness and preconditions for treatment are also influenced by the type of symptomatology. Somatic complaints initially suggest a somatic concept of illness. If this attribution to the somatic is further reinforced by doctors and somatic diagnostic and therapeutic measures, it can lead to a corresponding consolidation of this concept and the associated somatic treatment expectations. In this case, "the body" and "the treatment" may become fields of action where individual conflicts, relationship patterns, and structural difficulties manifest.

Overall, it becomes clear that the OPD axes should not be considered in isolation (with exception of research, for example structural diagnostics) if a psychodynamic understanding of a mental problem is sought. Therefore, an OPD diagnosis will always encompass all axes.

7 The OPD Interview

After presenting the axes of OPD in the previous chapters, this chapter focuses on how to obtain the required information to assess the specific areas of each axis. During the development of OPD-1, it had become clear that it was rarely possible to obtain a comprehensive rating of all OPD axes based on a typical clinical psychodynamic initial interview (Freyberger et al., 1996). Therefore, we conceptualized an OPD interview and provided corresponding interview guidelines. In short, the OPD interview is a synthesis of a psychodynamic interview with a series of more structured interview strategies borrowed and adapted from existing diagnostic systems. In the following, we will first describe the psychodynamic interview with its specific characteristics and its development history. Then, we will discuss other interview systems relevant to the OPD interview. Thereafter, we will present its implementation based on general interview strategies and in the form of specific interview guidelines.

7.1 Theory of the Psychodynamic Interview

There are two fundamentally different approaches available for conducting a diagnostic interview:

1. An *exploratory* approach that aims to collect facts by asking specific questions, which has its roots in biologically oriented psychiatry;
2. A *relational-dynamic* approach that gains relevant information based on a genuinely psychoanalytic attitude from the "reconstruction of infantile object relationships in the transference-countertransference between psychotherapist and patient" (Janssen et al., 1996).

The development of the diagnostic interview in psychiatry and psychotherapy over the past 100 years has taken place between these two poles.

At the beginning of the 20th century, scientific psychiatry regarded patients as "objects of observation" and aimed to "identify and describe signs of illness with the greatest possible exactitude" (Kind, 1973, p. 2, translated by E.R.). Kraepelin (2005, p. 356) already regretted that "investigation of psychopathic symptoms appeared up to now to be so unpromising and unsatisfactory." Sigmund Freud also showed a noticeable diagnostic restraint (Freud, 1913). On the one hand, he wanted to prevent the formation of an overly intense transference in the patient even before therapy began. On the other hand, he did not believe that diagnostic exploration could be helpful for the indication for psychoanalysis and recommended an analysis on trial lasting one to two weeks (Freud, 1913). At that time, Freud could afford such "diagnostic freedom" because no psychotherapeutic alternatives to psychoanalysis existed. He only had to make sure that the indication was appropriate: Is the patient suitable for psychoanalysis or not? To answer this question, a trial analysis was a suitable means. Given the multitude of different forms of psychotherapy available today, we must however make a differential indication, which means we must ask ourselves which form of psychotherapy may be suitable for the patient. From this modern plurality of psychotherapeutic treatment alternatives, it follows that neither pure symptom exploration nor merely determining the "analyzability" of a patient can be sufficient for the diagnostic interview. The development towards modern, multimodal, and multiaxial interview forms took place in several steps, briefly outlined here (see also Janssen, 1994).

The first to develop was F. Deutsch's (Deutsch, 1939; Deutsch & Murphy, 1955) so-called Associative Anamnesis, in which the interviewer should adopt a restrained, listening attitude to enable the patient to unfold their inner conflict world. He applied his method particularly to psychosomatic patients.

Shortly afterward, the models of Sullivan (1954) and Gill et al. (1954) followed. Sullivan emphasized the interpersonal process nature of the conversation and the interviewer's role as a "participant observer" in his predominantly structured technique of the Psychiatric Interview. Collecting information about the patient's biography and living conditions plays a much stronger role in Sullivan's interview than in the approach of Gill et al. (1954). These authors conceptualized their Initial Interview in Psychiatric Practice as a social-psychological situation separate from treatment, where the relationship between interviewer and patient should become a central theme; an important goal was to explore the patient's motivation for treatment. Here, for the first time, this highlights not only the diagnostic but also the therapeutic function of the initial interview. It was the psychiatrist Hans Kind (Kind, 1973, 1978), who reimported psychodynamic interview approaches into European psychiatry. Under the title "Guideline for Psychiatric Examination," he first published a monograph in 1973, mainly based on Sullivan's work, which remains popular in constantly revised form until today (Haug & Kind, 2008).

Parallel to this American development, mainly in psychiatry, a similar process occurred within psychoanalysis in Europe. In her groundbreaking article from 1950, Paula Heimann first explicitly pointed out the enormous significance of countertransference as a psychoanalytic diagnostic tool (Heimann, 1950): "My thesis is that the analyst's emotional response to his patient within the analytic situation represents one of the most important tools for his work. The analyst's countertransference is an instrument of research into the patient's unconscious. [...] the analyst's unconscious understands that of his patient. This rapport on the deep level comes to the surface in the form of feelings which the analyst notices in response to his patient, in his 'counter-transference'" (pp. 81–82).

Although Paula Heimann did not make these remarks regarding a diagnostic interview, they significantly shaped the further development of psychoanalytic diagnostics. M Balint and E. Balint emphasized in their Diagnostic Interview, developed at the London Tavistock Clinic (Balint & Balint, 1961), that it is an examination of interpersonal relationships and explicitly highlighted the significance of countertransference for the diagnostic process. H. Argelander (Argelander, 1970/1976) further developed this approach in his monograph "The Initial Interview in Psychotherapy." He differentiated three levels of gathering information: *objective, subjective,* and *scenic*. While the first two levels have verbal content, verifiable facts on an objective level and verbal communications about the patient's inner experience on a subjective level, the scenic information level refers to non-verbal messages in the form of "scenes" (what does the patient do, how do they say what they say). The experience of the familiar other glides along the track of colloquial communications, while that of the foreign other is only revealed through a hermeneutic work process sui generis, which does not take the communicative material at face value. Argelander saw this third level as the most important for the diagnostic initial interview: "The basic framework of the initial interview, the creatively formulated scene, is the basic information for the understanding of an alien happening. According to its nature, it has a dynamic or a drama of its own, which it feeds from unconscious sources." (Argelander, 1970/1976, p. 85/96).

The concept of countertransference has evolved into a comprehensive model since its introduction (Gabbard, 1995). While Freud only addressed the therapist's countertransference in terms of the therapist's unconscious conflicts, and Heimann primarily saw it as "general" diagnostic tool for understanding the patient's unconscious processes, countertransference today, together with transference, is understood as a mutual, interactive process between patient and therapist. It is a complex interaction of real, actual experiences and "neurotic transferences" from both patient and therapist.

To enable the relevant intrapsychic processes of the patient to be enacted on the stage of the initial interview, the therapist must be available as a co-actor, becoming a "two-person play." Since the therapist does not initially know the "play", they must develop a floating readiness to take on roles (Sandler, 1976), enabling them to recognize and accept the role assigned to them, based on their current countertransference.

Today, a widespread position in psychoanalysis places scenic understanding entirely and exclusively at the center of the psychoanalytic interview (see, for example, Mertens, 1992). Laimböck (2000) argues that biographical data should merely "support further relationship diagnosis without being its basis" (p. 11). She warns against mixing "psychoanalytic conducting of an initial interview" with "diagnosing" and recommends a clearly recognizable separation between scenic and question-asking procedures (p. 17).

Especially in Germany, due to the application procedures specified in rules and regulations governing psychotherapy, the "depth-psychological-biographical anamnesis" forms another essential building block of psychodynamic diagnostics. This anamnesis scheme was designed in the 1940s by Schultz-Hencke (1951) in Berlin and further developed by various authors (Dührssen, 1981; Rudolf, 1981). This diagnostic approach is based on the classic model of neurosis, understanding a mental disorder as a consequence of the re-actualization of a defended-against conflict in the life history of the patient. Both a neurotic disposition acquired early in life and a triggering situation matching the key-lock principle play a role (see, for example, Doering, 2003). Understanding these associations requires information about the patient's social situation and their developmental history. These are collected in the depth-psychological-biographical anamnesis in the areas of personal relationships, romantic relationships, family life, family of origin, occupational problems, learning difficulties, experiences with and behavior towards material possessions, and the surrounding socio-cultural environment. Finally, a hypothesis about the interaction of early experiences and the current triggering situation is formulated from the gathered data in the form of a "psychodynamic picture" (Dührssen, 1981).

Recently, integrative interview models have been presented, especially intended for use in clinical settings, where differential therapy indication and referral are central, unlike in private practice. Janssen (1994) introduced a psychoanalytic initial examination technique combining psychoanalytic initial interview, biographical anamnesis, and psychoanalytic developmental diagnosis. This approach allows for the formulation of both a psychodynamic and a descriptive ICD diagnosis. Similarly eclectic, Doering & Schüßler (2004) described the psychodynamic initial examination as a sequence of a psychoanalytic initial interview, an exploratory psychopathological examination, and a biographical anamnesis.

Otto F. Kernberg, during his tenure at the Menninger Clinic in Topeka in the 1960s and 1970s, found that neither the classic psychoanalytic treatment technique nor the usual psychoanalytic initial interview suited his patient clientele. In his work with structurally severely disturbed borderline patients, it was hardly possible for him to remain in a state of free-floating attention for an hour, and it was equally difficult to obtain a complete biographical overview in a reasonable time. Specifically for the diagnostics of structurally disturbed patients, Kernberg developed his Structural Interview (Kernberg, 1981, 1984). The adjective "structural" indicates that this interview primarily aims to assess a patient's structural level. Kernberg distinguishes a neurotic, a borderline, and a psychotic level of personality organization (= structural level). Typical for a borderline level of integration are the presence of a non-integrated identity (= identity diffusion) and primitive defense mechanisms, however, with intact reality testing. A special feature of the structural interview technique is the cyclical alternation of more unstructured parts with a highly exploratory interview style. The focus is on the patient's interpersonal relationships, particularly the transference relationship. Through the alternation of analytical and structured interview styles, both the enactment of internalized relationship experiences in the transference relationship as well as information about how the patient perceives themself, others, and their relationships, whether these perceptions are realistic, how they handle professional demands, and how they deal with sexuality and moral values, are obtained. Buchheim et al. (1987) rightly referred to how the second generation of diagnostic interviews, as exploratory and relational-dynamic interview styles were not merely juxtaposed, but received a new integrated form based on a new cyclical interview concept.

Under the pressure of evidence-based science, which forces psychotherapy (almost worldwide) to provide quantifiable proof of effectiveness, a series of research-oriented structured diagnostic interviews have been developed, referred to by Buchheim and colleagues as the third generation of interview methods (Buchheim et al., 1987). Examples of these instruments include the *Structured Clinical Interview for DSM-IV* (SCID-I and -II; First et al., 1997; First et al., 1996), designed to capture phenomenological DSM-IV diagnoses by sequentially querying the individual DSM-IV operationalization items. The *Adult Attachment Interview* (AAI; George et al., 1985) is a semi-structured interview used for attachment diagnostics in adults, aiming to capture current representations of early attachment experiences. It poses 18 questions about relationships with parents or early attachment figures and one's own children. The interview is evaluated based on transcripts, with the main criterion being the coherence of the discourse. The *Core Conflictual Relationship Theme* Method (CCRT; Luborsky & Crits-Christoph, 1998; Luborsky et al., 1991) inquires according to clearly defined criteria for relationship episodes, narrative material that is then processed to measure the internalized relationship structures shaping interpersonal behavior. The Structured Interview for Personality Organization (STIPO; Clarkin et al., 2004; Doering, 2004; Doering et al., 2013) attempts to operationalize Kernberg's structural interview. In a structured form, 100 items on seven dimensions of personality structure are assessed, rated on a six-point scale of personality organization. The revised version (STIPO-R; Clarkin et al., 2016) includes only 55 items on five dimensions and an additional narcissism score.

These formalized interview approaches represent the opposite end of the spectrum from the psychoanalytic initial interview, emphasizing the collection of relationship-dynamic material in the here-and-now. The latter provides a stage for the unfolding of a scene in the transference relationship, while the operationalized interview forms forego this relationship-dynamic material in favor of reliably assessing small and smallest measurable psychopathological units. Continuing the Buchheim et al. (1994) typology, the OPD interview can thus be described as the fourth generation of psychodynamic interviews (Dahlbender, Grande et al., 2004). It attempts to synthesize the previous generations of interviews. Initially, it requires a psychoanalytic stance as a basis that allows for the "recreation of infantile object relationships in the transference-countertransference between psychotherapist and patient" (Janssen et al., 1996, p. 298, translated by the authors). However, similar to Kernberg's structural interview, the unstructured approach is cyclically interrupted by more exploratory interview phases. These are partially borrowed from existing instruments, such as the identification of relationship episodes according to the CCRT method. Additionally, the OPD interview includes structured passages of biographical anamnesis and possibly captures psychopathological symptoms. The OPD interview is *multiaxial* and *multimodal*, collecting material for assessing the axes by applying different modes of interview methods (Dahlbender, Grande et al., 2004). From a psychoanalytic perspective, the OPD interview has been criticized for sacrificing too much scenic material through its multimodal interview approach, as structured interview portions may not allow a transference-countertransference relationship to fully develop (Mertens, 2004b). While this argument is not entirely unfounded, we believe that a sufficiently sensitive psychodynamic stance in the OPD interview still leaves enough room for the development of a diagnostically valuable transference activation. Targeted interventions, as Kernberg uses in his structural interview, may even promote this (Dahlbender, Grande et al., 2004).

7.2 Conducting the OPD Interview

7.2.1 Preconditions

The aim of the OPD interview is to generate material to reliably assess all items and dimensions of the four axes. To facilitate this, the interviewer can use specific interview strategies, which require the following preconditions:

1. The interviewer must have a basic psychodynamic understanding. This does not necessarily require advanced training in psychodynamic psychotherapy, although it is certainly advantageous. Rather, a *capacity to empathize* is needed, allowing the interviewer to recognize and understand relational aspects in the here-and-now of the interview situation and to connect symptom formation with relevant experiences from the past (the there-and-then). This demands the interviewer to open up to his or her own experiences in the interview relationship in the sense of Sandler's (1976) "free-floating role responsiveness."
2. The interviewer must have a good knowledge of the contents of Axes I to IV to know during the interview which areas have already been adequately covered and where more material is needed. This competence can usually be sufficiently acquired in the context of three, 20 hour OPD training courses (for a total of 60 hours), provided that the learned material is practiced and applied between the courses.
3. If the assessment of symptomatic diagnoses is planned within the framework of the OPD interview, the interviewer must be familiar with the diagnostic criteria of ICD-10/-11 or DSM-IV/-5 and either have sufficient clinical experience or have attended training courses on the application of the classification schemes. However, it is advisable to separate classificatory disorder diagnosis from the actual OPD interview.

7.2.2 Principles

As mentioned earlier, the OPD interview involves a multimodal and multiaxial approach with phases of structured passages. The primary stance of the interviewer is that of a psychodynamic initial interview, providing a stage for a scenic development in the interview relationship, proceeding unstructured and non-exploratory. Although this attitude is temporarily abandoned in the more structured interview passages, it is a fundamental principle of the OPD interview to return to it continually. This approach can be best described as oscillating between a relational-dynamic and an exploratory interview stance, employing varying degrees of structure:

- An open, unstructured conversational style that serves the spontaneous unfolding of the inner experience and the relational offers of the patient.
- A moderately structured approach that focuses on specific topics in the interview and gives the patient gentle nudges in certain directions, such as when taking a biographical history or examining relationship episodes, self-perception, and perception of others.
- A structured approach that queries specific details, such as exploring psychopathological signs and symptoms to determine the syndromal ICD-10/-11 diagnosis.

The individual interview phases, into which the OPD interview is divided, should be initiated with an open conversational stance as much as possible. The patient should decide which content to prioritize, what to elaborate on in detail, and what to mention. Additionally, the unstructured interview phases allow for the development of an "enactment" of the transference and countertransference. In these phases, the interviewer should pay attention not only to the manifest content of what is said but also to scenic material, such as the patient's facial expressions and gestures, subjective judgments, emphases, and omissions. Contradictions often arise at psychodynamically relevant places between the content of what is said and the affective tone. Special attention of course should be given to the patient's relational offers to the therapist and the therapist's emotional reaction to them. From this relational dynamic, hypotheses about the patient's neurotic conflicts and dysfunctional relational patterns can be derived, which can then be further explored in more structured interview sections.

In terms of structural diagnostics, less emphasis is placed on the overt or covert *meanings* of statements and enactments but rather on the structural *abilities or limitations* implicitly described in the patient's report or directly demonstrated in the interview situation. The way the patient handles stress and conflicts shows the extent to which they can accurately perceive themselves and others, their regulatory capabilities, and how well they connect with themselves and others. Therefore, the diagnostician focuses less on unconscious *content* and more on the *form* in which the patient manages the demands posed by the interview.

In the unstructured-open parts of the interview, familiar psychodynamic intervention strategies can be applied: clarification, confrontation, and interpretation.

Clarification involves exploring aspects of the patient's presentation that remain diffuse, unclear, or contradictory. These contents are discussed but not yet questioned, representing the closest and most "factual" level of interaction.

Example: "You told me that you like to go out with other women occasionally. Last week you had a terrible fight with your partner over this topic. Is your girlfriend extremely jealous, or was there more reason for her anger?"

Confrontation goes a step further by pointing out unconscious or preconscious content to the patient that is contradictory but considered unproblematic by them. This often involves defense mechanisms, contradictory representations of self and object, or structural incapacity. Confrontation can provoke the patient since it implies a clear questioning of their perception and behavior, creating a situation where the patient's structural capabilities (e.g., affect and self-worth regulation, perception) can be directly examined.

Example: "You say you definitely don't want to lose your partner, yet you keep having intimate contacts with other women and tell your partner about them. How does that fit together?"

Interpretation is the intervention aiming most at the unconscious level. Here, not only conflicting aspects are highlighted, but also hypotheses are offered about the motives and psychodynamic backgrounds involved in the problem's development. In an OPD interview, interpretations must be cautiously given as diagnostic preliminary interpretations to avoid destabilizing the patient.

Example: "We've seen that you start 'side relationships' whenever you feel particularly close to your partner. You also emphasized to me during an especially intense moment of our conversation that you want to schedule at least two more initial meetings with other therapists. Could it be that you open a 'side relationship' whenever the closeness in an important relationship becomes too great and thus too threatening?"

In the moderately structured conversation sections, the interviewer presents or focuses on specific topics. It is essential not to abruptly switch to closed questions but initially address the respective area as openly as possible. In the context of a biographical anamnesis, this might sound like: "Can you please describe how you grew up, how your childhood was."

Subsequently, it may be necessary to focus more precisely: "Please explain with an example how the relationship with your father was when you were a child."

And possibly even more specifically to clarify the child's real situation: "Did your father ever hit you with objects, a belt, stick, or similar?"

Such structuring and focusing is also applied in interview sections to capture relationship patterns, self- and object-perception.

A particularly structured approach is needed in the interview for exploring psychopathological signs and symptoms for syndromal ICD-10 diagnosis. Here, it may even be necessary to ask closed or selection questions to clarify matters unequivocally.

In addition to these general interview strategies, the OPD interview requires specific diagnostic procedures. These include stimulating relationship episodes for assessing Axis II and self- and other-description for evaluating perception of self and others on Axis IV. These techniques are explained in the following Section.

7.2.3 Interview Process

The interview is divided into different phases, with each phase being introduced by a question or intervention as described. The structure is minimal at the beginning and may increase as the interview progresses. Within each phase, structuring questions may be used if necessary. It has been found that a complete OPD interview can hardly be conducted in less than 90 minutes; sometimes, two to three hours may be required. For the first conversation, the therapist should plan for at least one hour. If sufficient information for clinical diagnosis, and to address the criteria of the four axes cannot be obtained in this time, one or two more sessions with the patient should be arranged. Between the sessions, the therapist can reflect on which areas of the OPD diagnosis still lack information.

The Opening Phase

In the opening phase, the patient should be informed about the aim of the conversation and the time frame, for example, with the following wording:
"We have one hour for this conversation. The aim is to understand your illness/problem. We will look at different areas of life, what is happening now, how you grew up, and so on. Let's start with you telling me what is currently bothering you the most."

The patient will typically begin with descriptions of their complaints since they come up with specific mental or somatic problems to discuss with the therapist. The patient should have the opportunity to speak freely and openly about their symptoms. (If the nosological diagnosis is planned in the same interview session, the therapist should be able to identify the core symptoms according to ICD-10/-11. If he/she is not sure, cautious questions are possible here without going into a pure exploration.) In this phase, the therapist will be able to make an initial assessment of the severity of the mental and/or somatic illness and the patient's level of distress. The therapist will gain first impressions regarding the impairment of the patient's current life situation and self-experience. Not too early but still in temporal association with the complaint/illness descriptions, an important aspect of Axis I can be asked, for example:

- "What do you think: Where does this come from?"
- "How do you explain these changes to yourself?"

The assessment of the complaints and the current life situation is not only about the patient's experience but also about the facts of their current psychosocial situation, such as their relationship with their partner or capacity to work. It may also be possible to identify life-determining conflicts in several areas, which can then be explored in more depth later in the interview. The therapist should also note whether the onset of the symptoms is related to specific triggering situations, such as threshold events like leaving the parental home, starting vocational training, moving into a leadership position, starting a family, or retirement.

- Patient A. says after the initial phase: "Now I'm sitting here ..." She describes her fears, depressive mood, and helplessness in detail, as well as her efforts to take initiative, especially her inner tensions after returning from inpatient psychosomatic treatment when encountering her husband. This phase ends with her tearful statement: "I can't take it anymore."
- Patient B. accurately and unemotionally describes the previous examinations and somatic treatments for ulcerative colitis. She shows the X-rays given to her by the referring doctor. She emphasizes her expectation of healing by turning to a new form of treatment, psychotherapy, even though the previously treating internist advised against it.
- Patient C. comes due to a crisis during a vocational retraining activity. He is suicidal and depressed; during the conversation about the current professional failure, his great sensitivity to being hurt becomes apparent. He expresses disappointment and anger about the conditions of his retraining. His description of external circumstances is confusing, and his illness experience is marked by helplessness and despair.

Even in the initial encounter between patient and therapist, the "initial scene" (Wegener, 1992), and in the following opening phase, the interviewer must pay close attention to the patient's scenic presentations, as they are already expressed during the contact, the description of complaints, the illness experience, and how the patient deals with the illness. The therapist can orient themselves to these scenic representations for the further course of the interview.

- For example, Patient A. opens the interview by presenting a referral form with a diagnosis she cannot read. She asks the examiner to decipher and explain the illegible writing. She thus establishes a relationship with the examiner by presenting herself as uninformed and seeking enlightenment from the examiner. The modality of this relational structure is determined by her wishes for dependency, which also manifest in her relationship with her husband and father.

Patient B.'s descriptions are oriented towards a role-based normative adaptation to the medical examination situation. Hardly any relational figures can be discovered in her presentation.

Patient C. immediately emphasizes his great sensitivity to and connects it with a psychosocial situation (retraining).

Once the patient has finished their initial description of complaints (whether solely symptoms or otherwise), it is advisable to broaden the perspective:
"Are there any other areas, apart from what you have mentioned, where things are not going well, where you are dissatisfied, or where problems exist?"

Often, descriptions that more strongly concern relational aspects (e.g., within partnerships or at work) will emerge at this point. This often provides a smooth transition to capturing relationship episodes and the experience of objects.

Relationship Episodes and Object Experience

When working out relationship experiences and episodes, the therapist must consider two perspectives. On the one hand, they must be able to use the analysis of the current transference-countertransference, and on the other hand, they must draw on the analysis of current or biographical relationship experiences. The latter essentially involves the narration of episodes in relationships with significant others. The therapist is particularly interested in dysfunctional, ongoing, or repetitive (habitual) relationship patterns. They will primarily focus on neurotic repetitions, overgeneralizations, discontinuities, and contradictions in relationships, as well as the differentiation of objects in the patient's experience. To do this, they can refer to specific experienced interactions and cumulative interaction experiences in a typifying overview of repetitive patterns.

To gather this material, it is mandatory to collect relationship episodes as part of the OPD interview. This is done following the CCRT method (Luborsky & Crits-Christoph, 1998; Luborsky et al., 1991), where narratives of specific relationship interactions that were difficult, conflictual, or stressful for the patient are requested. For the OPD interview, at least two to three relationship episodes should be obtained.

Collecting relationship episodes can be well combined with capturing the relational object's experience, e.g.,
"You mentioned XY earlier, can you describe your relationship with them in more detail?"

Then, specific singular interactions should be described in detail. *Actively* ask about *wishes, expectations, fears, thoughts, and feelings* (also those of others). Examples:

- "How do you interact with each other? Are there ever any arguments or conflicts?"
- "I can't quite imagine the relationship with X yet. Can you describe a specific example? What was the situation, who said or did what? What were you thinking and feeling?"

The therapist should always be interested in singular interactions, that means examples of relationship experiences, especially with patients who, for defensive reasons, only provide overviews or abstract statements.

To work out the motivating relationship dynamics more precisely, it can be important to specifically ask about expectations, wishes, fears (possibly concerning themselves and others), as well as externally visible behavioral reactions and internal experiences, emotional or cognitive reactions to the relationship event. Suitable questions include:

- "Can you tell me what you and/or your counterpart did or said at that moment?"
- "When XY said that to you, what were you thinking and feeling?"
- "How do you think XY felt at that moment?"
- "Can you say what you feared from X at that moment?"
- "What did you actually wish for in that situation?"
- "Why is that so important to you?"

When asking about relationship episodes, the therapist can pick up on first hints about relational objects from the preceding interview sections and ask about the specific relationship situation, or they can transition from the description of complaints to the description of relationship experiences by asking about the reactions of others to their illness if the patient does not mention the relationship persons themselves.

- For patient A., the relationship with her husband reveals an ambivalence conflict regarding dependency desires and tendencies for independence.
- For patient B., it is the relationship with her daughter. She was born out of wedlock. The patient made great efforts to be a good mother with significant concern. The daughter has so far "prevented" the patient from realizing a partner relationship.
- Patient C. describes how he repeatedly seeks relationships with idealized women and subsequently experiences severe disappointments. This pattern is not limited to partners but extends to all objects, for instance, also to training institutions. It is therefore of great importance for possible therapy.

The therapist can also delve into more detail or be more interested in the typical or the temporal development and accordingly ask questions about the development of relationships then or now. They can form a picture of whether the described relationship has a unique character or whether it is comparable to other relationships.

Although the focus on relationship episodes comes to the fore, starting from current relationship situations, and the therapist can initially roughly estimate the patient's position towards relational objects, what they expect and fear, and how others behave towards them, further opportunities to ascertain relationship experiences will also arise in later phases, especially in the third and fourth phases. The therapist should also pay attention to specific examples, for instance, relationship episodes, in later phases of the conversation.

In the relationship episodes, much of the necessary information about the existence of repetitive conflict patterns will already become apparent. Overall, conflicts are not to be explored in the narrow sense. Their trace runs through the entire interview, content-wise and scenically. Clarifying (i.e., hypothesis/testing) questions help to verify the assumed conflict in other areas of life ("Does this also show up at work/with other people? Do you take after your father or your mother in this regard? Am I right in thinking that the illness brings you back to a similar situation?").

It is likely that relationship experiences will always be described in relation to the objects. Nevertheless, the therapist should always focus again on the perception and experience of the objects. They should work out how the patient sees the others in the "here and now." A specific object description can be initiated with the question:

"You've already told me a lot about your relationship with XY. Describe them to me: What kind of person are they? What qualities do they have? What makes them special?"

The therapist should build on the previous descriptions of the objects. But if the patient has not yet provided detailed accounts of life areas, clarifying and guiding questions will need to be asked to encourage the patient to talk about relationships and life themes of the present and the past.

Some patients may omit life areas when speaking freely and non-reflectively. To identify life-determining conflicts, it is necessary to cover multiple life areas. For example, the following question may be necessary:

"You've given me a good impression of your family life. But I can't quite imagine how you're doing at work. Can you give me an idea of that?"

The therapist must always bear in mind that it is less about obtaining "historical truth" and more about capturing the patient's subjective experience and memories, especially the experience of relational objects. In some cases, it is likely that the patient will only give hints about important situations. The therapist should remember these but not necessarily push the patient to share very uncomfortable information that they might only be able to share later. Likewise, significant situations and relationships with important objects will likely remain unmentioned or possibly repressed. The therapist can address this, but they must recognize that sometimes they will only get hints or encounter resistance to describing the "real" relationships.

For patient A., the significant important object is the husband; for patient B., it is the daughter. From these objects, the interview for patient A. leads to the father, who is very idealized and who died shortly before the patient got married. For patient B., the path leads from the daughter to the mother, who is also very idealized and who died shortly before the onset of the illness. Patient A. describes her father as an ideal object; she could always turn to him, and he had understanding for everything. She had not yet processed his death.

For patient B., it is the mother who did everything for the family, sacrificed herself, and was always there for the children, from whom the patient could hardly separate. The patient expresses intense guilt, as the mother died when she could not visit the family.

For patient C., a realistic perception of other people is very difficult. He oscillates between the extreme poles of great idealizing hope and bitter disappointment. An inner emotional bond to individual important persons is hardly recognizable. This also applies, for example, to the two teenage children from a failed marriage.

When exploring the structural dimensions, which essentially include self and object perception, it is necessary for poorly structured patients to leave the initially open and unstructured conversation stance to offer the patient an active approach to what might be going on inside them, as these patients are often not able to perceive and name their internal processes and deficits. It can be helpful to use metaphors, stories, or even film scenes for illustration.

Experience of Sexuality and the Body

Since the previous Section (Relationship Episodes and Object Experience) usually already conveys some information about partnerships (whether present or not) and potentially their quality, a transition to the topic of sexuality and body experience often arises naturally. For example:

- "For many people, sexuality is an important and sometimes not entirely unproblematic area. How is it for you? How do you experience sexuality?"
- "Is sexuality an important area in your life personally?"
- "Can you describe what you find particularly enjoyable and what you find particularly difficult in the area of sexuality?"
- "How do you think your partner experiences it?"
- "Do difficult feelings arise for you in the area of sexuality?"
- "Was it the same in previous relationships? How was it before?"

If the patient is not currently sexually active: "Has it always been like this?", "No interest?", "Masturbation?", "Any fantasies?"

If the patient does not want to talk about it: "What makes it difficult to talk about?"

From the experience of sexuality, a transition to other forms of possible pleasurable experiences is sensible. Questions here might be (depending on how sexuality was experienced):

- "Are there other areas where you can experience something like enjoyment or pleasure?"
- "What do you particularly like, what do you like less?"

Subsequently, the transition to the general experience of one's own body is usually easy. Questions here might be:

- "How would you describe your overall relationship with your body?"
- "What do you like about your body? What do you not like at all?"
- "What feelings arise when you, for example, look at yourself in the mirror?"

A Typical Dream

It is often informative to have a dream described. Ideally, the dream that comes to the patient's mind spontaneously. If no spontaneous idea comes up, you can ask about a subjectively significant dream from any time, one "that you might have had more often in a similar way or one that has remained in your memory."

Here too, like capturing relationship episodes, you can ask further questions: "What was the emotion in the dream? How did it end? What do you think about it?"

Childhood and Primary Family

Here, the exploration of the individual's developmental history can then be connected. Some information about the experienced and factual life areas (family of origin, own family, work and professional world, if not already spontaneously told before) should be obtained as part of the biographical anamnesis.

Note that the questions about childhood, mother, father, and so forth, are important on the one hand, but on the other hand they quickly take up a lot of space and the interview gets out of hand. Therefore, it is about the subjective experience and the processing of these experiences, and not all questions have to be asked in the following way.

Possible questions might be:

- "We have mostly talked about your current life situation so far. The next questions will be about your childhood."
- "How did you grow up? Can you give a rough description: What was the family situation like? Were there siblings? Etc."
- "Who was the most important person in your childhood?"

The relationship with the *mother* or, if the mother was not present, the person who most took on the mother role should be discussed. It is also about the object description of the mother and then about the description of the relationship:

- "How would you describe your mother/XX?"
- "Can you describe your relationship with her a bit more closely? How was she towards you?"
- "Can you describe a typical event that perhaps best illustrates your relationship (this aspect)?"

Then the same for *father*/YY: describe the object, relationship experience, typical events.

The relationship between the parents (or primary caregivers) with each other should also be inquired about unless it becomes spontaneously clear.

If time allows, questions from the Adult Attachment Interview (George et al., 1985) could be included here, for instance:

- "What do you think: Why did your parents behave that way?"
- "Has the relationship with your parents changed since your childhood?"
- "Do you believe that the experiences from your childhood influence how you are today? How?"

Questions about early separation experiences, deaths, or traumatic experiences can also be well integrated here.

Worst Experience

If patients make corresponding hints, we should offer them to talk about it.
"You mentioned earlier that there was something very stressful. Would you like to say what that was?"

If there have been no indications of traumatic experiences up to this point, the simple question is often effective:
"What was the worst thing you have experienced so far?"

This event can then be freely explored.

Self-Perception, Self-Experience, and Emotions

At the latest now, the focus should be on the patient's experience of themselves, essentially assessing structural features (Axis IV). Explicitly asking for a self-description of the patient is (together with capturing relationship episodes and object descriptions) another mandatory interview strategy that must be included in every OPD interview. This technique was also used by Otto F. Kernberg in his structural interview (Kernberg, 1981, 1988). The self-description can be initiated with the following questions:

- "We have already discussed a lot about how you are doing today, how you grew up, etc. Now, if you look at yourself again: What kind of person are you? How would you describe yourself?"
- "How do you see yourself, what is typical for you, what distinguishes you from others?"
- "How do you see yourself now and how did you see yourself before?"

If contradictions appear (also compared to statements from previous sections), they should be addressed (see above: *confrontation*), for example by asking: *"How does that fit together?"*

From the descriptions, the therapist will not only see whether the patients can describe themselves in a differentiated manner but also whether they can distinguish themselves from the objects, and whether they have a clear self-concept. As patients usually describe themselves in certain situations, the therapist will often also learn more about family or professional life areas. Here, through in-depth questions, it is possible to gather more precise biographical situations, for instance the relationship with parents, siblings, partner, superiors, and colleagues, as well as the patient's self-experience in these social and biographically defined situations. This part of the interview can be very extensive, and further clarifications may be necessary in subsequent interview sessions.

For instance, more detailed questions about the patient's satisfaction in the family, at work in their past and current activities, about burdens, remuneration, relationships with superiors, and relationships with colleagues are possible. The therapist should address several life areas in a way that life-determining conflicts may broadly present themselves.

For patient A., the current self-experience is determined by the perceived inability to plan and carry out independent undertakings and by being bound in marriage. From the previous marriage, which she entered after her father's death, she describes that the husband locked her up until he returned from work. He justified this by saying that she did not need to do anything, and he could do everything for her. The patient found this "amusing" at the time. She felt like a "precious jewel." Subsequently, there are various attempts to separate and distance herself after an agoraphobic symptomatology, but they fail. The marital relationship is particularly strained by the husband's illness.

For patient B., the self-experience is shaped by adaptation at work, concern for her daughter, and guilt feelings that she is not a good mother, but also by her willingness to be available for the primary family. She sacrifices herself for others.

Patient C. sees himself as a victim who is repeatedly "tricked"; his great efforts are not recognized. Although he learned a craft despite his physical disability, he lost the job to his own surprise. His current career goal is to pursue a social worker profession, "because there are so many difficulties in the world." The patient cannot convey a current picture of himself and his real situation.

The examples clearly show that this phase of the interview reveals essential aspects for assessing conflicts (Axis III) and structural elements (Axis IV).

Following the self-description, it is advisable to explore more closely the experience of emotions and dealing with difficult emotions. For example:

- "You have now described a picture of yourself. I would now like to focus more on your feelings. You have (often) mentioned experiencing feelings of ... Is this a frequent/difficult feeling for you?"
- "What is the most difficult feeling you often experience?"
- "How would you describe it yourself?"
- "In what situation does this feeling arise? What precedes it?"
- "What do you do then? How do you get out of it?"

If not mentioned spontaneously, anger/rage should be asked about. Does it exist? How is it experienced? What thoughts/fantasies arise? How is it dealt with?

Also often informative is the following question:
"What is the most beautiful feeling you know?"
"Can you describe it? In what situations do you experience it?"

Motivation for Psychotherapy and Preconditions

Towards the end of the interview, the therapist should once again go through the scenes and stories of the patient. The therapist should determine how they have experienced the patient so far and identify the main problems. Based on the collected material, the therapist should formulate an intervention. Depending on the structural level of the patient being examined, this can also be an interpretation that refers to transference aspects using countertransference.

This intervention could be for patient A.:
"You want to be able to live independently, but you feel tied and dependent on your husband, and as our conversation shows, on me as well. You expect me to help you out of this difficult situation."

The intervention for patient B. might be formulated as:
"You have hidden your grief and guilt after the loss of your mother for years, and now in the conversation with me, they have resurfaced. This seems to upset you because you think you do not have enough control over yourself."

For patient C., the response might be:
"You have had a very tough life. Despite your efforts, you have often ended up empty-handed and have fallen on your face many times. I think it might be important to find out what this is all about. Maybe you have missed something here and there, perhaps you have not quite perceived certain sides of others."

Such summarizing interventions aim to "tentatively" introduce the patient to their problem and examine their reactions to such interventions. This is essential for capturing internal conflicts or the structure, as well as for assessing their willingness to engage in a clarifying treatment process. The therapist must therefore investigate whether the patient can work with such interventions and to what extent it is possible to recognize and work on the reactivation of conventional experiences in the current relationship based on a common understanding. On the other hand, these interventions should also give something back to the patient. Michael Balint is attributed to the saying: "The patient should also gain something from the diagnostics." Ideally, the patient should leave an OPD interview enriched, stimulated, and motivated.

In this phase of the interview, besides the conflicts and structural level, aspects of Axis I that have not yet been clarified are also addressed. Above all, the patients' ideas about change should also be discussed, e.g.,
"What do you expect from therapy? What do you want to achieve/change? What do you think could particularly help you?"

If the therapist feels able to assess the *structure, conflicts, relationships*, as well as the *experience of illness* and *treatment conditions* at the end of this phase, they can conclude the examination. Otherwise, further interview sessions should be arranged.

If this examination is conducted as the initial interview, it should not end without giving the patient an indication of the further course of action. It should be briefly discussed with the patient what has been clarified so far and what still needs to be clarified. Furthermore, if possible after completing the previous phases, the therapist should provide an indication for a psychotherapeutic procedure and communicate this to the patient.

7.3 Excursus: Diagnostic Assessment of Mental and Psychosomatic Disorders

A descriptive clinical diagnosis of mental disorders according to ICD-10/-11 or DSM-IV/-5 requires a complete diagnostic assessment or verification of the core symptoms of each ICD-10/-11 section, including the collection of their course and stability over time. In principle, the core symptoms can be examined for each patient and diagnostically mapped to the relevant Section if corresponding symptoms are present. However, this should be followed by complete symptom exploration. This complete symptom exploration cannot be carried out without abandoning the previously described approach for the OPD interview in favor of a structured procedure.

The therapist must be familiar with the diagnostic guidelines or research criteria of ICD-10/-11. Appropriate diagnostic training is recommended, as shown by various application and reliability studies on ICD-10 (Dittmann, Dilling, et al., 1992; Dittmann, Freyberger, et al., 1996; Freyberger et al., 1990; Schneider et al., 1993). It is obvious that in many clinical situations, for instance in private practice, these separate diagnostic processes may develop along an initial therapeutic context and may take much longer time.

In the context of clinical research questions, symptom checklists can also be used as a supplement (e.g., Dittmann et al., 1996). These are external assessment procedures that should be supplemented with other information sources, such as information from third-party interviews, behavioral observations, etc. The relevant individual symptoms or symptom clusters are usually assessed in these symptom checklists in a diagnosis-related manner, so that post hoc collection of information with supplementary interviews are possible with detailed knowledge of the patients.

If research questions suggest conducting structured or standardized diagnostic interviews in addition to the OPD interview (e.g., homogeneous sample, comorbidity), they should be conducted separately from the OPD interview and preferably by another interviewer to impair the relationship with the OPD interviewer as little as possible during the exploration.

8 Focus Formulation and Therapy Planning

Since the publication of the first manual in 1996, the OPD has evolved from a diagnostic system into a tool that can structure and plan practical therapeutic work. An important step in this direction was two therapy studies (Grande et al., 2001; Grande et al., 2003), in which the OPD was used to measure change beyond the level of symptoms. For this purpose, specific foci are defined for each patient based on OPD ratings, which guide the observation of the treatment course and the monitoring of therapeutic progress. The details of this procedure for assessing change are described in Section 9.1 ("Heidelberg Structural Change Scale").

This procedure can be easily applied to practical therapeutic work. OPD findings are used to identify particularly problematic aspects that cause or maintain the disorder, and these aspects become the focus of therapeutic work. The selection of such foci also affects the therapeutic approach, including the choice of appropriate settings, therapeutic stance, and suitable interventions. The differentiation between the conflictual and structural components of the disorder, their interplay, and the resulting treatment implications play a crucial role (see Rudolf, 2004; Rudolf, 2020; Benecke, 2014, 2018; Doering, 2016; Henkel et al., 2018; Sell et al., 2021). It should be possible to formulate specific guidelines for each focus constellation that can guide treatment. This is a very extensive and complex program. The basic decision steps for focus formulation will be introduced for each axis. First, the conceptualization of the treatment indication based on Axis I will be presented.

8.1 Treatment Indication Based on OPD Axis I

Axis I aims to provide treatment indication for a patient based on the nature and severity of their mental disorder or problem, the way they experience their disorder, subjective illness concepts, and treatment expectations. In this phase of the indication process, the primary goal is to determine whether psychotherapy is appropriate, if further psychosomatic diagnostics or guidance is needed, if a somatically oriented therapy is indicated (potentially supported by motivating measures), or whether no further treatment is required at all. The question of differential indication for psychotherapy (which kind of psychotherapy) cannot be answered solely based on Axis I but must consider the results of the whole OPD diagnostic process.

If psychotherapy is indicated, the next step involves treatment planning, which includes formulating therapeutic goals (foci) and selecting suitable psychotherapeutic approaches to achieve them. The process of formulating therapy goals is iterative, meaning that at different phases of the therapeutic process, sequential therapeutic goals or foci are typically developed. This chapter outlines the selection and decision-making processes for formulating foci for the Axes of Relationship, Conflict, and Structure after presenting the assessment rules for indicating psychotherapy based on Axis I.

The following decision steps are necessary when clarifying the differential indication based on Axis I.

1. Determine whether there is a significant mental disorder or problem that requires psychosomatic treatment or psychotherapy. If the patient has a mental disorder or problem that requires treatment, the following aspects must be examined.

- Assess whether the subjective suffering of the patient constitutes a sufficient motivational basis (suffering pressure: "I need to change!") to seek treatment.
- Examine whether the patient's problem representation includes psychosocial aspects.
- Ensure that the patient considers psychosocial factors in their subjective illness concept.
- Evaluate the patient's motivation for psychotherapy.
- Determine if the patient has sufficient personal resources to participate constructively in psychotherapy.
- Identify any substantial internal or external barriers to starting or consistently participating in psychotherapy, including secondary gain from the illness.

The items of Axis I have a different relevance for differential indication: Diagnosing mental disorders according to ICD/DSM and ratings of current severity and duration of the mental disorder/problem primarily indicate whether there is a treatable condition, with relevant physical functional impairments and (psychosocial) adaptation issues (GAF). Generally, a higher severity level and more functional impairments and adjustment issues suggest a more-in-depth psychosomatic diagnosis/guidance or psychotherapy.

The degree of suffering item is indirectly related to the indication question. A patient with a high degree of suffering shows probably a higher motivation for change; their change goals and therapy expectations need to be assessed through other Axis I items. A minimum degree of suffering is necessary for any treatment (psychotherapy or organ-centered) to be indicated.

Two ideal-typical item configurations illustrate the significance of items from Sections 4 (Illness Concepts) to 7 (Psychotherapy - Change Strategies and Goals) of Axis I for the indication question. One configuration characterizes a patient who is well-prepared (Table 70) for psychotherapy (psychotherapy-oriented patient), and the other depicts a patient more oriented towards somatic illness concepts (Table 71) and treatment expectations.

Table 70. Example for psychotherapy-oriented patient

Items with medium to high scores (2–4)
External-social illness concept
Intrapsychic illness concept
Psychotherapeutic treatment concept
Burden of suffering
Symptom reduction
Reflection and clarification
Emotional support
Active guidance
Items with Low Scores (0–1)
External impediments for change
Internal impediments for change
Secondary gain

Note. For detailed descriptions/comparison see Chapter 2.

Table 71. Example for somatically oriented patient

Items with medium to high scores (2–4)
Somatic illness concept
Somatic treatment concept
External impediments for change
Internal impediments for change
Secondary gain
Items with low scores (0–1)
Coping resources
Openness

Note. For detailed descriptions/comparison see Chapter 2.

In general, patients will exhibit "mixed" feature distributions/ratings. That means some of the item characteristics of a specific patient indicate a more somatic orientation, while other item characteristics signal a stronger orientation towards psychotherapy. In such cases, it is possible to compare the number of items with different focuses (somatic orientation vs. psychotherapeutic orientation). If the patient shows a clear tendency towards a somatic orientation across all items, the question of psychotherapy indication should be treated cautiously. In such a case, it may be necessary to first implement a measure to enhance psychotherapy motivation for patients whose condition or problem essentially indicates a need for psychotherapy.

The "key items" for the indication of psychotherapy are the items related to *change and treatment concepts* (Psychotherapy Concept, see Chapter 2) and *change resources* (Burden of Suffering, Openness, see Chapter 2). If the patient shows a psychotherapeutic orientation in these areas from the examiner's perspective, psychotherapy or, depending on the issue, psychosomatic treatment should be indicated.

Positive statements regarding psychotherapy indication can, however, be relativized by the Items "External Impediments for Change," "Internal Impediments for Change," and "Secondary Gain." For instance, pronounced external impediments for change (e.g., lack of therapy or cost coverage) can lead to a well-motivated patient not receiving appropriate treatment. A high degree of secondary gain will also lead to a low motivation and willingness for change in a patient with a "psychosocial illness concept"; this applies to both psychotherapeutic and somatic measures.

8.2 Focus Formulation Based on OPD Axes II–IV

Therapeutic foci are selected based on the diagnostic findings from the three psychodynamic OPD axes: Relationship, Conflict, and Structure. The logic of formulating a focus is briefly summarized here:

Psychotherapy planning with the determination of therapeutic foci and strategies can take place once the treatment prerequisites are clarified, an indication for psychotherapy is given, and the treatment can be agreed upon with the patient. The characteristics recorded in Axis I (including the degree of suffering, the subjective illness concept, the patient's ideas for change, the desired form of treatment, barriers to change, and secondary gain from illness) have been important or even decisive factors for the examiner's decisions and negotiations with the patient up to this point. They now stand back to considerations concerning the content and objectives of the planned therapy. At this point, the more strictly psychodynamic OPD Axes Relationship, Conflict, and Structure come into focus. Together, they represent psychodynamic findings and thus form the basis for selecting the foci that will guide the therapeutic work. The procedure for choosing the foci and the subsequent therapeutic strategy considerations are explained below. First, however, the connection to the results of the diagnostic process is made by briefly summarizing the central components of the psychodynamic findings according to OPD.

8.2.1 Relationship

Figure 6 (see Dysfunctional Relationship Pattern, Section 3.2.1) shows the schema for the diagnostic assessment of dysfunctional relationship patterns. The upper right field (in "Dysfunctional Relationship Pattern" in Section 3.2.1) is the entry point into the pattern: The patient usually perceives the behavior of others as a bother or disappointment to which they must react. They typically see themselves as passive or responsive, meaning not as proactive and therefore not responsible (Connection I). In contrast, others perceive that the patient is by no means merely reactive but rather makes a challenging relational offer (II). This offer suggests certain responses that become noticeable as impulses in the countertransference (III). When others give in to these impulses and respond accordingly, the patient is likely to experience this as a repetition of the disappointment they have always expected or feared from others (IV). This creates a self-reinforcing maladaptive cycle.

An example of a relational dynamic formulation developed using this schema might read: “The patient perceives others as demanding and fears failing to meet these demands and being shamed. She tries to avoid this by adapting and making great efforts to please others. In contrast to this self-view, she appears demanding, critical, and exacting to the outside world. This prompts others to either to be careful with her and self-protective around her or to correct her in an offensive manner. There is a risk that the patient will perceive either of these responses as a sign that she has not met expectations and has failed.”

8.2.2 Conflict

On the one hand, deriving potential conflict foci from the OPD findings is straightforward: Foci can fundamentally include the two conflicts rated as the main and second most important one (see Section 4.2).

- C1. Dependency vs. Individuation
- C2. Submission vs. Control
- C3. In Need of Care vs. Self-Sufficiency
- C4. Self-Worth Conflict
- C5. Guilt Conflict
- C6. Oedipal Conflict
- C7. Identity Conflict
- C0. Repressed Conflict and Emotion Awareness

However, the therapist should not stop simply naming one or more conflicts. The respective modes of processing should also be considered, as well as possible differences between the biographically dominant processing mode and the currently prevailing mode. It should always be kept in mind that the modes of defense/coping constellations serve a functional role within mental organization. Thus, the focus should not be limited to the defense/coping constellations but also include the possible repressed motives and core affects. Additionally, the functional interplay of various conflicts should be considered (e.g., C2 to cope with C1, an example of which can be found in Section 8.3).

8.2.3 Structure

When selecting structural foci, the first step is to assess the extent to which structural limitations contribute to the patient's current disorder and accordingly, how motivational conflict themes and maladaptive relationship patterns manifest. The weight of structural limitations can be judged when the diagnostic evaluation of the nine structural dimensions, including the overall level of structural integration and the intensity of conflicts, are available (see Rating Sheet Structure, Section 5.6, and Rating Sheet Conflict, Section 4.3.11). The captured interaction between structural and conflictual diagnoses reveals the significance of structural features for diagnostic understanding and therapeutic goal setting. If structural aspects are to be therapeutically focused on, they can be specified based on the list of structural abilities (Section 5.3). Items believed to significantly contribute to or sustain the patient's limitations are marked. These also describe the problem areas to be addressed in psychotherapeutic work and whose modification constitutes an important therapeutic goal.

8.3 Principles of Focus Selection and Composition

Selecting a focus for psychotherapeutic work involves many aspects that are not solely related to the nature of the mental disorder but also to the framework conditions of psychotherapy. For example, psychotherapy may be time-limited, requiring the therapeutic task to be formulated so it can be resolved within the given time. Certain aspects of a mental disorder may also become particularly prominent in therapy if they are triggered by specific life circumstances and events. Additionally, it may be beneficial to start working on problems where the patient already has some insight and can easily form a therapeutic alliance where, for instance, their free associations begin. In these and similar cases, one would choose from a range of possible foci those that are most pertinent due to the special circumstances and then later address other, potentially more fundamental aspects of the disorder.

On the other hand, it is crucial to initially examine a disorder without restrictive considerations and identify the fundamental difficulties a patient has in their relationships, conflicts, and structural characteristics, what they should change about them, and consequently, what psychotherapeutic work is necessary. The OPD findings provide significant support for this analysis. The foci can be those features of the OPD findings that cause and maintain the disorder and thus play a determining role in the psychodynamics of the clinical picture. This implies that something must change concerning these foci to achieve substantial and sustainable therapeutic progress. Under this premise, one or more foci can be selected from the OPD findings. As experiences in the studies mentioned above have shown, several foci are usually needed to fully depict a disorder in its various aspects (e.g., Grande et al., 2001).

To select therapeutically relevant foci, the therapist must form a picture of the *dynamic interrelationships and dependencies between the various aspects of the disorder* captured in the OPD findings. These aspects may be interconnected and interact with each other. For example, a problematic conflict theme may initially seem prominent to the psychotherapist, which, upon closer examination, mainly serves to manage another underlying conflict or a structural vulnerability, representing the actual or deeper issue.

Example: A 40-year-old patient behaves in a domineering and controlling manner in relationships, leading to frustrating power struggles and eventual breakups in past partnerships (Conflict: Submission vs. Control). A more profound analysis reveals that the patient uses this behavior to manage closeness and distance in relationships, thus coping with the fear of losing their boundaries and being overwhelmed by intimate closeness with another person (Dependency vs. Individuation as a deeper conflict and therefore the primary focus).

Selecting structural foci can sometimes be challenging when several or many of a patient's structural abilities are similarly limited, raising the question of which focus to prioritize. This difficulty arises because different structural features are often closely linked and interdependent, meaning that the limitation of one function leads to deficits in other functions. Thus, focus selection must determine which specific functional limitations *primarily* cause overall structural impairment. Other structural difficulties usually derive from these primary limitations and are therefore secondary, making them less suitable as therapeutic foci.

Example: A patient's deficient object perception might be due to a fragile identity, making them feel "lost" in interactions with others. Developing and differentiating their "own" self would be a prerequisite for gaining stability in relation to the object world and navigating it more securely. This would imply that limitations in self-perception (identity) should be the primary focus compared to deficits in object perception. These deficits can be expected to change "on their own" once the primary focus is addressed.

According to the OPD-3 concept, even in cases of severe structural impairment, motivational conflict themes should be considered. Including a conflict theme in the focus should be considered for all patients. This often deepens the understanding of which motivational (relational) themes and potentially in which life areas the structural impairments manifest.

Example: A 29-year-old patient manages well as long as she does not enter an intimate relationship: she works regularly, exercises, and has a few friends she meets with but does not let anyone get too close (C1 active). Once she enters an intimate relationship, she becomes highly emotionally dependent (C1 passive), causing various structural functions to deteriorate: she loses self-object differentiation, does not know who she is, has difficulty regulating impulses and affects, and is overwhelmed by fear of loss, among other things.

In such cases, the (dys-)functional interplay between conflict and structure should be included in the focus.

As described in Section 6.3.2, On Coping with Conflict and Structure in Relationship Patterns, all conflict dispositions and structural difficulties of a patient are condensed into a complex form in the dysfunctional relationship pattern. Therefore, the relationship pattern is fundamentally always in focus for therapeutic work. However, the type of therapeutic work on the relationship will significantly differ depending on whether it is more determined by structural features or conflicts.

When determining the foci from the other two psychodynamic Axes III and IV, it should be noted that depending on the type of disorder, the weight of structural or conflict components will vary and that this ratio should be reflected in the focus selection. In clear cases, only conflict or only structural foci may be chosen. However, both aspects are usually significant, so mixed foci are the standard. Studies have also shown that at an overall low level of structural integration, certain conflicts (Dependency vs. Individuation, Self-Worth Conflict) are particularly common. Conversely, at a high level of integration, oedipal-sexual conflicts are relatively more frequent (Grande et al., 1998; Rudolf, Grande et al., 2004). However, it is essential to emphasize that no automatism (e.g., "always C1/C4 for structural disorders" or "C6 only for better structure") can be derived from these results: As extensively described in Chapter 4, all conflict themes can, in principle, occur on all structural levels.

Based on previous experience, we suggest selecting a total of 5 foci with the following distribution:

- The dysfunctional relationship pattern summarized in the relational dynamic formulation is mandatory and always forms one of the foci.
- Up to 4 additional foci can be taken from the Axes "Conflict" and "Structure," with the respective number varying depending on the extent of structural or conflict-related limitations. This means that in extreme cases, all 4 foci can be taken from Axis IV, but all other combinations are also possible. In cases clearly determined by conflicts, it may be sufficient to describe the disorder with 2 or 3 conflicts, and structural foci may be omitted entirely. This is possible and may result in selecting only 3 or 4 foci instead of 5.
- The dynamic interplay between conflict and structure should, if possible, also be included in the focus formulation.

8.4 Therapy Planning and Therapeutic Goal Setting

Using Axis I, it is diagnostically clarified whether, given the type and intensity of the patient's mental disorder, psychotherapy is fundamentally indicated and what attitudes and expectations the patient has towards it. If psychotherapy is generally appropriate, the next step is to choose the appropriate form of treatment based on the diagnostic findings and formulate therapeutic goals for it.

Therapeutic difficulties often arise from the fact that structural limitations are significant in a patient and make it difficult to address the conflict dynamics. This aspect is particularly clearly articulated in OPD through elaborate conflict and structural diagnostics. This makes it possible to assess the relative weights of conflict-related and structural components of the disorder and their dynamic interplay. We recommend, in planning therapy based on this assessment, initially making a strategic decision on whether the principal therapeutic orientation should be more conflict- or structure-focused. Additionally, in structurally impaired patients, it is essential to assess the extent to which conflict-motivational themes play a role in psychodynamics.

The answer to this question can then inform therapeutic strategies that may be more structuring or more conflict-mobilizing/processing, or a combination of both. These strategies concern:

- the therapeutic setting
- the therapeutic stance
- the prioritization of selected foci
- dealing with dysfunctional relationship patterns
- psychodynamic and other psychotherapeutic techniques (interventions)

Depending on the importance of conflict-related or structural limitations, one can typify (1) predominantly conflict-processing strategies, (2) predominantly structure-supporting strategies, and finally (3) predominantly structural-dynamic strategies (addressing conflict-motivational components in structural disorders).

In all cases, the (dys-)functional interplay between conflict and structure, as well as their manifestations at the level of relationship patterns, should be considered.

8.4.1 Predominantly Conflict-Related Disorder

In this type, psychological processes occur at a well or moderately integrated structural level; the disorder is considered primarily conflict related. In this case, psychodynamics is primarily understood as expressions of unconscious motives, affects, fantasies, and their defenses.

Setting: Given the extensive availability of an inner mental space and structural functions, therapeutic work can be carried out in individual or group psychotherapy settings. Depending on the indication, treatment can occur in the regression-promoting, transference-focused setting of psychoanalysis/psychodynamic psychotherapy or the focal conflict-revealing, regression-limiting setting of psychodynamic psychotherapy or (analytical) short-term therapy. Due to the extensive availability of structural functions, the therapeutic framework does not have primarily structuring, limiting, or supporting tasks, meaning that missing or underdeveloped structural functions do not need to be provided from outside. Since conflict-oriented work should foster the patient's latent capabilities, such support would not challenge the patient to a sufficient degree. Instead, the setting defines the conditions under which therapy takes place by agreement and maintains these conditions even when tensions arise. Boundary violations can be therapeutically addressed and interpreted as transference or resistance phenomena based on the current unconscious conflict dynamics.

Therapeutic stance: The therapist can assume that the patient transfers their unconscious conflictual experiences onto them. Therefore, the therapist focuses on their own countertransference and examines what unconscious wishes the patient is directing at them. A key therapeutic option is to address these wishes or the associated fears and bring them to the patient's awareness. The assumption is that the patient can fundamentally take responsibility for their actions and gain greater freedom in thinking, feeling, and acting if they understand their unconscious motives and bring the associated affects (including previously repressed core affects) into conscious experience. Therapeutic work should promote this ability of patients and actively challenge it. It is therefore conducted in an attitude of benevolent abstinence, which does not protect the patient through primarily supportive and holding therapeutic offers, potentially not challenging them enough.

Focus prioritization: A hypothesis must be formed about which conflict constitutes the core of the disorder and which other conflicts are related to or derived from the core conflict. Such conflict overlaps are common and can be more easily analyzed with OPD because it helps to make complex clinical pictures transparent as layers of distinguishable simple conflicts. Uncovering conflict processing can begin with the secondary or derivative conflict, whose manifestation often has coping character concerning the core conflict. The coping effort involved can be validated in a first step. By balancing the costs of coping efforts, the approach to the core conflict becomes possible in the second step. Initially, this core conflict is interpreted in its defensive aspects before interventions approach the defended against unconscious wishes and core affects.

Example: A depressive patient mainly exhibits a In Need of Care vs. Self-Sufficiency Conflict derived from biographical relationships with parents and shapes all current relationships with spouse, children, and friends. Also noticeable, although less significant and derived from the need for care, are a self-worth and a guilt conflict. Relative to the core conflict of need for care and self-sufficiency, these have a more reparative character. The uncovering work (relief of guilt feelings, stabilization of self-worth) begins with the derived conflicts because this approach does not touch and unsettle the patient's central self-concept, as direct addressing of the need for care and self-sufficiency conflict would, but rather initially provides relief and stabilization. Addressing the central conflict with the repressed core affects often becomes possible "as if by itself:" the deep feeling of lack, of always falling short, and the attempts to "make these nagging affects go away" can then usually be well processed.

Working on dysfunctional relationships: The therapist examines which relationship wishes and fears the patient directs at them and others. They form a hypothesis about how the relationship offers can be understood as a compromise formation. In their countertransference, the therapist discovers the feelings and impulses triggered by the patient; they can then imagine the entanglements that would arise if they gave in to these feelings and impulses. Together with the patient, the therapist examines their fears regarding others and the therapist differentiates the associated affects. In a further step, the focus is on the patient's efforts to protect themselves in relationships based on their fears (in the therapeutic relationship and other relationships). The therapist accepts and validates these efforts. They then also show the patient the dysfunctional side of their efforts, particularly the likelihood that their defensive behavior leads to others reacting disappointingly, fulfilling the feared outcome, leaving their real relationship wishes unmet, and establishing a stable, self-perpetuating vicious cycle. It may be important to show the patient which feelings and impulses they trigger in others and the therapist and what consequences this has or might have if others react accordingly.

The central hypothesis is that dominant conflicts are processed as compromises in relationship patterns, with the relationship patterns being the manifestation field of unconscious conflicts and their coping attempts. Therefore, addressing relationship patterns is a good starting point for working on unconscious conflicts, the associated (often painful) core affects, and their defenses.

Interventions: Therapeutic interventions can be used to promote and challenge the patient's fundamentally existing but disguised and limited possibilities by defense and compromise formations. All interventions that animate and actualize the unconscious conflict process are suitable for this. These include techniques of affect mobilization. In long-term psychodynamic therapies, interventions and therapeutic strategies can be used to promote regression and intensify the transference process. Since symptoms and difficulties, which have the quality of a symptom of the patient are triggered by situational features that have a subjectively specific meaning developed historically and determined by unconscious conflicts, interpretations or understandings that bring out such meanings and activate affects ("emotional insight") are essential. The conflict-oriented intervention techniques have been extensively elaborated in psychoanalytic literature (e.g., Mertens, 2000, 2004a; Thomä & Kächele, 2006a, 2006b; Benecke & Staats, 2016; Körner, 2015); practical compilations for psychodynamic psychotherapy can be found, for example, in Wöller & Kruse (2018) and Gumz & Hörz-Sagstetter (2018).

8.4.2 Predominantly Structure-Related Disorder

Various treatment strategies have been developed for the psychodynamic treatment of patients with structural disorders. An overview can be found in Benecke (2014), who fundamentally distinguishes between structure-stabilizing and structure-dynamic approaches.

Structure-Stabilizing Therapy Strategies

The disorder is primarily determined by the limited availability of structural functions (e.g., the ability for self-reflection and affect differentiation, realistic object perception and empathy, self-regulation and mature defense function, emotional communication, and internalization of relationships). The overall structural level is low (moderately to poorly integrated, poorly integrated, poorly to disintegrated, and disintegrated). Conflict themes may be recognizable, but they are diverse and not always clearly contoured and initially do not constitute a therapeutic focus. For understanding the psychodynamics, it is crucial to comprehend the patient's difficulties primarily because of a developmental restriction and disruption in self-regulation and relationship formation.

Setting: The more severe the structural disorder, the more likely it is necessary to provide external structures (possibly an indication for inpatient treatment, partial hospitalization, rehabilitation measures, fostered living in the community) and to promote competence-enhancing measures and opportunities for social learning (e.g., educational and recreational activities). In outpatient psychotherapies, a stable structure (reliable and long term availability) must be offered, while being relatively flexible in responding to the patient's fears, need for reassurance and crisis-like mood swings. The external form of treatment and the substantive approach of the therapy must be carefully discussed and well agreed upon; specific essential points can be regulated in "contracts" (e.g., regarding suicidal behavior, eating behavior, substance abuse, and other forms of self-harm). All these structure-providing external conditions must be embedded in a (therapeutic) relationship and represented by the therapist (or a therapeutic team) as (a) person(s), so that the provided (auxiliary ego) functions (e.g., control in the service of care, setting of limits, tolerating difficult affects) can be adopted by the patient as structural abilities (e.g., as the ability of regulation in the service of self-care, settings limits, affect tolerance). Rule violations are not examined for hidden intentions of the patient but are addressed with boundary setting and firmness. It must always be checked whether the patient is possibly overburdened and cannot adhere to the rules because they are assigned self-responsibility that exceeds their structural possibilities; this would require the next level of stronger structuring.

Therapeutic stance: Given the patient's tendencies to withdraw or their often devaluing and destructive relationship behavior, the primary goal is to develop a therapeutic stance that helps ensure that the therapeutic relationship and collaboration are not made impossible or destroyed. This includes "parenting" attitudes, particularly at the start of therapy, suggesting the therapist should contain, take on auxiliary ego functions, take care, mirror and respond to their perceptions and emotions, or firmly set boundaries. It is also important to address the patient's active possibilities to constructively or destructively cope with their structural difficulties. This requires the therapist to learn to see the patient's behavior as a problematic pattern of experience and behavior that the patient needs to learn to cope with better. The "parenting" attitude also involves responding to the patient's expressions in a "child-appropriate" manner through a more active therapeutic attitude. Therapeutic abstinence is still maintained by responding not only as a personal counterpart but also from a supportive parental function.

Focus prioritization: Initially, it is necessary to determine which structural functions the patient primarily needs therapeutic support in to regulate themselves and their relationships. The more severe the structural disorder, the more the focus is on the aspects of the self, described in the OPD (self-perception, self-regulation); the therapist's task here is to promote the patient's self-relation and autonomy. Often, it becomes evident that relationships with objects improve without additional assistance when patients gain more orientation and stability within themselves. With less severe structural disorders, the focus shifts to the relationship with objects (object perception, communication) and can be therapeutically addressed directly in interpersonal interactions. The therapist can promote the therapeutic process by more clearly positioning themselves as a counterpart or "other." The more severe the disorder, the more central the characteristics described in the OPD structural dimension of attachment become; this level of experience is often only imperfectly reached by verbal content, so in such cases, the therapist's attitude and behavior (e.g., reliability, firmness, benevolence) are more important for therapeutic effectiveness than the (conceptual) content of the conversation.

Working on dysfunctional relationship patterns: The therapist works with the patient to identify the structural difficulties, limitations, and vulnerabilities reflected in their relationship behavior. The therapist does not take problematic relationship offers personally but strives for a relational stance where the problem arising in the therapeutic contact is objectified and examined as something third, side by side with the patient. The therapist supports the patient in taking responsibility for and managing their relationship behavior with the knowledge gained. Especially in cases of aggressive and destructive behaviors, it can be helpful to consider these as expressions of an "id," that means parts or forces within the patient that are not yet integrated and controllable (Benjamin, 1996). This view facilitates the triangulation mentioned and helps the patient distinguish themselves from their behavior. If the patient cannot yet make this distinction (i.e., seems identical with their behavior), the therapist must still internally develop a model that maintains this difference.

If patients with structural limitations develop secondary coping forms that are aggressive, devaluing, or destructive due to an experience of insufficiency, this causality should be acknowledged: Not the "id" acts, but the patient, along with the validating acknowledgment of the regulatory function of this behavior. Relationship patterns based on structural limitations are not always aggressive but are often defensive or avoidant. Withdrawal and rigid control of relationships can serve to protect structural sensitivities (e.g., a fragile identity, low self-esteem). The therapist works with the patient to articulate vulnerability and finds words for it. Specifically, the therapist identifies which situational circumstances and relationship situations touch these vulnerabilities. The therapist accepts and validates the patient's way of protecting their vulnerability in relationships, thus highlighting their coping competence. In a further step, it can become clear that this self-protection also has "costs," such as unfulfilled relationship wishes.

Interventions: The more severe the structural disorder, the more care and reservation are required regarding affect-mobilizing techniques, and the less regression- and dependency-promoting therapy offers are made (e.g., couch setting, higher session frequency). Instead, techniques are used that convey basic stabilization of the self, while object-directed interactional aspects are intensified in a later therapy phase. Nonverbal procedures are often better suited than verbal interventions to give the patient an authentic sense of their own person. Since structural limitations often manifest through nonspecific stressors, i.e., not primarily conflict-neurotic through triggering situations with a life-historically developed individual meaning, interpretations of something "underlying" (unconscious motives, unconscious affects, biography) play a lesser role in the outlined structure-stabilizing treatment strategy. The focus is on the "how" (i.e., on the objectification and differentiation of the limitation) and not on the "why" (Grande, 2002). The patient should not be "questioned" but learn to distance themselves from their difficulty and manage it. The specific sequences of therapeutic action, largely determined by the therapeutic attitude described above, are detailed in Rudolf (2020).

Structure-Dynamic Therapy Strategies

Conflict-motivational themes often play a significant role even in patients with clear or severe structural impairments (see Axis III; also, Section 6.3.1), for example, in a way that the individually dominant motivational themes frequently trigger structural dysfunctions. The activation of unconscious aspects (such as wishes, affects, etc.) often forms the inner contexts of structural dysfunctions. Conversely, structural impairments and the resulting actions and experiences of the patient are attributed an inner-psychic regulatory function, for example, in that limited self-perception "protects" from perceiving certain aspects of oneself that would be perceived as unbearable, or in that the predominance of splitting protects against the feared "annihilation" of the good, by destructive parts of the self or the object. Similarly, activating a "purely bad" object image protects against a feared and simultaneously desired fusion, which would again be experienced as complete self-abandonment, etc.

Such complex motive-affect-structure intertwining must also be recognized and understood in the transference and worked out together with the patient.

Setting: The setting corresponds in essential points to the structure-stabilizing strategy described above: Here, too, regression-promoting aspects are avoided, the therapist is more active, "contracts" are concluded, etc. A difference lies in handling setting rule violations (in structure-dynamic approaches), these are indeed interpreted concerning transference meanings, often in the sense that patients want to protect themselves or "test" the therapist through these rule violations (e.g., repeated lateness) (cf. the concept of testing the limits by Weiss & Sampson, 1986). Given the structural impairments, the possible overburdening of the patient must always be kept in mind. A preliminary or intermediate inpatient treatment may be indicated.

Therapeutic stance: The therapist makes themselves available as a counterpart with whom such patterns are enacted while striving together with the patient to understand these patterns. The fundamental attitude is one of technical neutrality (e.g., Doering, 2016). This can and must be deviated from when serious threats (e.g., to health or life, or to the therapy) are feared. However, even then, these deviations should subsequently be understood interpretatively, for instance: What dynamic function did it serve for the therapist to intervene massively with boundary setting? What transference constellation was established by this? Etc.

Focus prioritization: The focus here is not on one axis or the other but on the individual interplay between relationship, conflict, and structure. Which motivational theme is functionally linked with which structural facet, and how does this manifest (potentially as a coping attempt) in relationship behavior and experience? The investigation of currently self-, other-, or therapy-damaging tendencies and their psychodynamic background in the here and now has priority. Special attention should be paid to affect-related structural aspects. Affects often form the core of current structure-dynamic processes, and a primary goal is to bring affects (even painful ones, etc.) into mental experience without having to "get rid" of them immediately (cf. also the concept of mentalized affectivity by Fonagy et al., 2002).

Handling dysfunctional relationships: Focus on manifestations of structurally and affectively based dynamics within the therapeutic relationship or external relationships. The transference relationship is seen as the field where structural impairments, underlying conflict themes, affects, and their defenses manifest and are accordingly addressable. The often very problematic relationship patterns are viewed as dysfunctional functionalities: They are functional because they help the patient manage structural impairments or conflict-motivational themes, but they are also dysfunctional because they have high mental (and sometimes material) "costs" and tend to maintain the disturbance constellation.

Interventions: Interpretations of the here-and-now dynamics aim to promote the integration of self- and object-representations and enhance mentalization and mental control over often intense affective dynamics. The current affects and acting out are understood as results of defense processes or self-protection, and interpretive work seeks to identify the currently defended "part-object relationship dyad" along with the associated affects (Yeomans et al., 2015) or "the emotional precursors" (Bateman & Fonagy, 2008, p. 314) that triggered the current reaction. Given that such interventions are often affect-activating, great caution is required, and potentially related structural impairments should be addressed directly. The specific therapeutic procedures are also extensively described (e.g., Yeomans et al., 2015; Doering, 2016; Bateman & Fonagy, 2004; Benecke, 2018).

Structure-stabilizing and structure-dynamic interventions can be combined. It is important that the therapist is always clear about why they are doing what they are doing and that they remain vigilant about how the patient responds to each intervention.

9 Measuring Change With OPD

In line with its psychodynamic orientation, the OPD captures those aspects of a disorder that belong to the personality of the affected individual and are relatively stable (Grande et al., 2000). This is reflected in the manual, among other things, by specifying a relatively large time window of 5 years for structural diagnosis; in connection with conflict diagnosis, there is explicit mention of "temporally enduring conflicts." This stability over time of OPD findings appears appropriate in view of the underlying psychoanalytic model of illness. However, this characteristic poses a difficulty for measuring change because therapeutic effects can only be mapped if they are reflected in a change in the relationship, conflict, or structural diagnosis. Smaller therapeutic steps cannot be captured, at least not based on the OPD alone.

A more fundamental problem arises from the fact that the personality traits captured by the OPD often do not change in terms of "reduction of a trait," even if the treatment was successful. Axis III diagnoses life-determining and dysfunctional conflicts. Successful psychotherapy may result in a conflict theme remaining life-determining but being so successfully processed that it can be constructively shaped and productively used by the patient in life. The change would, in this case, not be measured by the degree of reduction or elimination of the pathogenic conflict but by the degree of its successful integration (i.e., change in salience or change in structural level of the conflict theme). Similarly, for structural limitations (or vulnerabilities) and dysfunctional relationship patterns, the sign of positive therapeutic change is not their elimination or reduction but the improved ability to manage and constructively handle them.

Overall, it can be assumed that sustainably successful psychodynamic therapies lead to better availability of structural functions, reduced significance of individual conflict themes, and less dysfunctional relationship behavior. This has already been demonstrated for structural functions (Cropp et al., 2016; Lübke et al., 2021).

9.1 The Heidelberg Structural Change Scale (HSCS)

The aforementioned peculiarities of the relationship between psychodynamic constructs and symptomatology lead to the consideration of detecting progress in the psychotherapy process as changes in a patient's handling of their central problem areas. This approach implies two methodological steps. In the first step, the characteristics from the OPD findings spectrum of a patient that are significant for their disorder are selected. In the second step, how the patient deals with them and how their handling changes over time is recorded.

1. Focus Selection: The central problem areas are referred to as foci because they serve as reference points for measuring change. (They can be identical to the therapeutic foci, but they do not have to!) Those problem areas considered central are those that cause and maintain a patient's disorder, so something must change about them to achieve lasting success. In principle, the

number of foci to be selected can be determined as needed. However, our studies suggest that selecting a maximum of 5 features from the findings spectrum of the Axes II, III, and IV is sufficient to fully capture a patient's problem. It is recommended that the habitual dysfunctional relationship pattern always forms one focus, while the remaining foci are chosen from the areas of conflict and structure (see Chapter 8). As stated in Section 8.3, in some cases, fewer than 5 foci may suffice to describe the relevant aspects of the disorder. This can be the case, for example, when a disorder is clearly conflict-based, and only 2 (or 3) significant conflicts can be identified in addition to the relationship focus.

2. Heidelberg Structural Change Scale (Rudolf et al., 2000): The scale shown in Figure 21 is used to capture how a patient deals with the foci. It is a revised form of the "Assimilation of Problematic Experiences Scale (APES)" by Stiles and colleagues (Stiles et al., 1990), modified towards a closer alignment with a psychoanalytic process and change model (Rudolf et al., 2000). The scale describes, in 7 (main) stages, different modalities of a patient's handling of a focus problem, starting with cutting it off from perception, through its gradual perception and interested exploration, to efforts at its active management. The upper stages describe the process of therapeutic destabilization of habitual defense attitudes and the

1. Not recognizing the focus problem	1 1+	Complete defense or avoidance of the focus area, there is "no problem"	
2. Involuntary preoccupation with the focus	2– 2 2+	Symptom pressure, interpersonal difficulties: Impositions, experienced from external sources	
3. Vague focus perception	3– 3 3+	Passive engagement with the focus, rudimentary recognition, sense of personal responsibility	Mastering
4. Recognizing the focus	4– 4 4+	Interested understanding of the problem, working relationship, active "mastering," action	Mastering
5. Dissolution of old structures in the focus area	5– 5 5+	Defense becomes fragile, process becomes a "passion:" grief, being at the mercy of others, confusion	Structural change
6. Restructuring in the focus area	6– 6 6+	Reconciliatory experience, new experiences/behavioral possibilities arise spontaneously	Structural change
7. Resolving the focus	7– 7	Integration, self-congruence, realistic experience, reorganization	Structural change

Figure 21. Heidelberg structural change scale (HSCS). Translated with permission from "Die Heidelberger Umstrukturierungsskala: Ein Modell der Veränderung in psychoanalytischen Therapien und seine Operationalisierung in einer Schätzskala [The Heidelberg restructuring scale. A model of changes in psychoanalytic therapies and its operationalization in an estimating scale]" by G. Rudolf, T. Grande, & C. Oberbracht, *Psychotherapeut, 45*, 237–246. © 2000 Springer Nature.

resulting reorganization of the personality. They capture changes addressed in the psychoanalytic concept of "restructuring" or "structural change."

The foci selected for a patient are evaluated independently at each measurement point using this scale, where the intermediate stages shown in Figure 21 can also be chosen. A particular feature of the HSCS is that positive therapeutic changes in the sense of "coping" are conceptually possible as early as stages 3 and 4, provided that a patient, based on the insight gained at this level, makes active efforts to manage the problem. In contrast, the changes described at the stages 5 to 7 refer to more fundamental transformations of the personality structure, which typically occur spontaneously, without effort, and often surprisingly for the individuals themselves (see Rudolf et al., 2000). Due to this construction principle, treatment outcomes can be categorically assigned to the "coping" mode of change at stage 4 and the "restructuring" mode at stages 5 and 6.

Various studies have found good to very good interrater reliabilities of r=.77 to r=.88 (Rudolf et al., 2000; Rudolf et al., 2012; Leuzinger-Bohleber et al., 2019) by trained raters (partly students) and clinicians. In a study of inpatients, the global success assessments of the therapeutic team highly correlated with the mean scale value of the foci at the end of treatment and with the pre-post difference, higher than with all other success measures (Grande et al., 2001). In the same study, high positive correlations were found between the mean scale values of the foci at the beginning of therapy and prognostically favorable characteristics such as "therapy motivation," "emotional responsiveness," and others. In a follow-up study, it was shown that the mean absolute restructuring value of the foci at the end of treatment significantly correlated with progressive steps in the patients' external lives after discharge from the clinic and was the only outcome measure that could predict such steps (Grande et al., 2003). Schneider et al. (2015) also found that stronger restructuring after inpatient psychotherapy was associated with better outcomes in the follow-up. A study by Rudolf et al. (2012) shows that patients in high-frequency long-term analytical therapy significantly more often achieve restructuring in the sense of the scale (i.e., reaching stage 5 or higher) than patients in only one-hour psychodynamic therapy. The LAC study also showed that analytical long-term therapy leads to stronger restructuring than cognitive-behavioral therapies (Leuzinger-Bohleber et al., 2019).

The Heidelberg Structural Change Scale can also be applied in clinical practice once one or more problem areas have been selected from the OPD findings that cause or maintain the disturbance and therefore need to be therapeutically altered. Under this condition, the scale is also easily applicable for practitioners. At the beginning of therapy, it can be used to check how far a patient has come in dealing with their central problem areas and where the therapeutic work can begin. At stage 2, "Unwanted Engagement with the Focus," there is already distress, but the difficulty is experienced as something imposed from the outside, so the patient is more passive and primarily expects the treatment to remove this imposition. A genuine psychotherapeutic collaboration is therefore only possible when the patient at least has a vague focus awareness (stage 3) in the sense that they sense and partly acknowledge their own involvement and responsibility for the difficulty. The trial sessions or preliminary talks for therapy serve, among other things, to establish a vague focus awareness for at least one of the various focus areas.

During the treatment, the therapist can use the scale to see how far they have progressed with a patient concerning the various problem areas. As mentioned above, reaching both stage 4 ("Acknowledgment and Exploration of the Focus") and stage 6 ("Restructuring in the Focus Area") can be considered valid therapy goals. At stage 4, the patient gains insight into their difficulties and acquires the ability to manage them; this mode of change is referred to as coping in Figure 21.

Stage 5 describes a process of therapeutic destabilization that leads to habitual forms of coping and defense no longer working. This creates a situation where the patient no longer "does" therapy but "suffers" it. Their condition is accordingly characterized by confusion, doubt, sadness, or even hopelessness connected to several of the foci. At the same time, however, they may already be perceived as positively changed by others (including the therapist), for instance as softer, more transparent, and more authentic. For the patient themselves, this positive turn becomes noticeable only later, at the end of stage 5 or the beginning of stage 6. They typically experience the changes occurring at that time as something that happens spontaneously and without their will. They find that they can suddenly do and feel things that were previously inaccessible or entirely unknown to them. These are indicators that a fundamental change and reorganization of the personality has occurred, which is sought in intensive psychoanalytic long-term treatments and referred to as "restructuring" or "structural change." Often a new set of foci such as a higher-level conflict, relating and structuring may emerge for a new phase of the treatment.

Just as in research applications, focus-related changes can also be captured in *therapeutic practice* by assessing the restructuring status at the beginning of therapy and repeating this assessment during and at the end of treatment. This makes the therapeutic effect visible as the progression of the foci on the scale.

A detailed description of the HSCS with illustrative case examples can be found in Stasch et al. (2026).

9.2 OPD Questionnaires for Measuring Change

In recent years, self-assessment instruments have been developed for Axis III (OPD Conflict Questionnaire, OPD-KF; Benecke et al., 2018) and Axis IV (OPD Structure Questionnaire, OPD-SF; Ehrenthal et al., 2012). The OPD Structure Questionnaire is also available in a short form (OPD-SFK, Ehrenthal et al., 2015).

Change sensitivity could be demonstrated for the OPD-SFK, especially for patients with more severe structural impairments (Lübke et al., 2021).

A first publication with pre-post data (mostly from time-limited in-patient stings) from the OPD Conflict Questionnaire is in preparation (Henkel et al., 2024).

10 Further Fields of Application of OPD

10.1 OPD in Different Clinical Settings

The main application of OPD is in the clinical field. OPD findings are obtained in various clinical settings to gain a structured and clinically action-guiding picture of the psychodynamics of patients with mental and psychosomatic disorders. Here, the specifics and experiences of applying OPD in different clinical settings, especially in German speaking countries, are briefly outlined.

10.1.1 OPD in Inpatient Psychosomatics

Most of the psychodynamically oriented hospital departments for Psychosomatic Medicine and Psychotherapy in Germany systematically work with the OPD-3 and use its potential, e.g. through pre-post rating of therapy foci based on the Heidelberg Structural Change Scale (HSCS, see Section 9.1) for critical quality management of the outcome quality of inpatient courses. In addition to the socio-demographic data collection based on a German documentation system (Psy-BaDo; Heuft & Senf, 1998; Heymann & Tritt, 2018), the indication for inpatient treatment is based on syndromal diagnostics (ICD-10, ICD-11), supplemented by a severity assessment (BSS; GAF; Lange & Heuft, 2002) and OPD diagnostics. OPD diagnostics is mandatory for coding (and billing) a psychodynamic psychosomatic-psychotherapeutic complex treatment according to the German OPS catalog of procedures (Code 9–63) (BfArM, 2022). The Structure (Axis IV) diagnosis plays a guiding role in terms of differential therapy indication (Rudolf, 2020; Rudolf, Jakobs et al., 2004). Dysfunctional repetitive relationship and conflict patterns recognized already during the outpatient pre-diagnosis can be communicated clearly to the patient in the medical letter and with the inpatient treatment team for treatment planning: "Mr. A. suffers from a self-esteem conflict in the active mode with a well to moderately integrated structural level. He will probably easily become actively involved in offensive dynamics on the ward, but is very likely to be able to make good use of the cognitive agreement reached with him before admission to hospital to consistently point out his own part in such conflicts, which he is still largely unaware of (HUS: stage 2), if it is communicated to him with empathy." Alternatively, the treatment team could prepare for a patient with a poorly integrated structure at the beginning of therapy as follows: "The patient will probably feel high pressure even with minor conflict tensions and react with repeated binge-purge episodes, developing dangerous hypokalemia." This example demonstrates the role of OPD in planning inpatient treatments, which always have the character of focal therapy within the framework of an outpatient-inpatient-outpatient overall treatment plan. The treatment foci of the inpatient treatment phase can refer to problem areas of Axes II, III, and IV. In the mentioned example, the progress in achieving therapy goals would be described as: "Recognizing own part in developing offending dynamics" (HSCS: Stage 3), and: "Successfully anticipating alternatives to such escalations" (HSCS: Stage 4). The necessity of inpatient therapy duration and the treatment success can thus be represented via the HSCS.

The reassessment of the severity of the diagnoses in the light of the treatment completed and the individual therapy goals (ITZ, German abbreviation for "Individuelle Therapieziele"; Heuft & Senf, 1998) formulated in terms of experience and behavior (possibly together with the patient) complete the final documentation, which also provides external audits, with meaningful insights into the curative course of treatment. The next steps planned are institutional comparative studies with the aim of clarifying how much time a defined patient group needs on average and at which therapy dose to reach which levels on the HSCS? And: Which treatment successes prove to be stable?

Other possible areas of application are the consultation and liaison service for patients in other (somatic) hospital departments: What influence does the psychological comorbidity and the psychological structure (Axis IV) of a hospital patient have on length of stay, compliance and the course of treatment and rehabilitation (Burgmer et al., 2004)? For example, it is advisable to advise a patient on dialysis who has considerable difficulty in self-control (dimension of Axis IV) to undergo structural psychotherapy before his wife accepts a living kidney donation, so that the kidney transplant can serve him for longer with his increased ability to adhere to therapy because of the treatment.

10.1.2 OPD in Psychosomatic Rehabilitation Treatment

Medical rehabilitation has the German social law mandate to support people with chronic illnesses in coping with illness-related limitations and to be able to perform their professional functions and roles in family and society again as best as possible. This general objective is based on the experience that in the case of chronic illnesses and their consequences, it is often no longer possible to achieve full recovery. In contrast to the primarily curative mission of hospital treatment, medical rehabilitation therefore focuses primarily on improving the limited state of health as far as possible or at least halting the progression of the disease process, reducing functional and activity disorders that have already occurred and effectively preventing impairment of participation or the occurrence of permanent disadvantages (Gerdes & Weis, 2000).

This view of the tasks and objectives of rehabilitation is essentially based on the disease impact model of the "International Classification of Injuries, Disabilities and (Social) Impairments" (ICIDH) of the World Health Organization from 1980 (WHO, 1980), which was conceptually expanded considerably in 2001 (WHO, 2001, 2018) with the "International Classification of Functioning, Disability and Health" (ICF) and is closely oriented towards the biopsychosocial disease and health concept of psychosomatic medicine. The basic concept of the ICF is functional health, which, in addition to the bio-medical aspects (bodily functions and structures) relating to the biological level of the organism, also includes the psychosocial aspects of the person as an active subject (activities) and as a self-determined and equal individual in society and the environment (participation). Furthermore, the contextual factors of the person concerned, i.e. all external circumstances of the world in which they live, as well as all their personal characteristics and attributes (e.g., age, gender, education, motivation, and willingness to perform) are taken into account. The ICF has is of significant importance for medical (and particularly psychosomatic) rehabilitation (Bassler et al., 2016). It is a crucial instrument in determining individual rehab needs, functional diagnostics, rehab management, intervention planning, and evaluating rehabilitative measures. Due to the specific structural and organizational framework conditions, rehabilitation treatment planning must closely align with the goal of setting as concrete and quality-assured verifiable therapy goals as possible. Since in the German Mental Health System only an average treatment duration of 5 weeks is available, the therapy goals primarily focus on specific occupational conflicts and overload situations, as well as specific work and performance disorders. More comprehensive psychotherapy goals, such as "improvement of conflict management" or "improvement of ego-structural deficits," are, from the perspective of pension insurance, not within the scope of psychosomatic rehabilitation but are primarily the responsibility of the curative care sector. In clinical practice, however, specific and general therapy goals often cannot be as sharply distinguished from each other as quality assurance programs of pension insurance require.

Given limited personnel resources, most psychosomatic rehabilitation clinics have adopted multimodal treatment concepts with a group therapy focus (Schauenburg & Hildenbrand, 2017; Köllner & Bassler, 2021). The traditional distinction between psychodynamic and cognitive-behavioral therapy orientation has lost importance as more and more rehabilitation clinics combine elements from both therapy methods. The psychodynamically influenced treatment programs are primarily based on the principles of focal short-term psychotherapy (Tschuschke & Mattke, 1997). Specifically, the group therapeutic work aims to make habitual dysfunctional relationship patterns, as they particularly manifest in the occupational but also other social relationships of the patient, directly experienceable for them (Strauß & Mattke, 2017). Through this approach, social integration disorders are favorably influenced, and a self-esteem stabilizing development of occupational performance skills is enabled.

The OPD has not been implemented in the existing quality assurance program of the German Pension Insurance, as this is primarily based on the ICF (Deutsche Rentenversicherung, 2018). However, as part of a clinic's own internal quality management system, OPD can make a valuable contribution to improving process and outcome quality, even if it requires additional time on the part of the therapist:

1. OPD diagnostics to work out the psychodynamics, in developing an understanding of "difficult" treatment courses and for focus development in the rehab team (process quality).
2. OPD diagnostics for assigning patients with different structural levels (Axis IV) to a differentiated treatment program: (1.) for patients with a good – moderately integrated structural level: groups for working on conflict pathology; (2.) for patients with a low integrated structural level: groups for working on specific ego-structural deficits (subsequent development of impaired ego functions, enabling corrective emotional experience (Strauß & Mattke, 2017).
3. OPD diagnostics in the socio-medical assessment to estimate the potential for change depending on the structural level and the degree of chronicity of the conflict dynamics (Bückers et al., 2001).
4. OPD diagnosis in the basic documentation (in addition to ICD-10 in the initial and final diagnosis), to be able to take relevant change processes into account in the final socio-medical assessment.

10.1.3 OPD in Assessment in Psychosomatic Medicine and Psychotherapy and in Legal Contexts

In the German field of Psychosomatic Medicine and Psychotherapy, the importance of assessment tasks in various legal contexts (e.g., criminal law, civil law, or social law) is growing. For all these legal areas, OPD, alongside descriptive psychiatric diagnostics, can provide a better understanding of the mental development of the individuals being assessed. A forensic assessment that lacks access to the relevant individual mental development lines from a psychodynamic and/or behavioral therapeutic perspective will be limited in its ability to make statements about the motives or causes underlying a "critical behavior" (e.g., a criminal act) or make prognoses.

Social law issues include, for example, the question of the need for treatment or rehabilitation for health limitations and their possible consequences, such as disability or inability to work (see e.g., International Classification of Functioning; WHO, 2001). When it comes to assessing the performance and operational capacity of an individual in the context of pension insurance or health insurance, it becomes the task in social compensation law or statutory and private accident insurance to assess the causality of damaging events.

Currently, there are no uniform standards for assessment in the various legal fields regarding the psychosocial dimensions and methods to be regularly considered. However, representatives of different assessment focuses have each strictly and stringently formulated their procedures. There are several publications for assessment in criminal law and forensic sexual medicine topics (see e.g., Kröber & Steller, 2005; Venzlaff et al., 2020).

We have primarily focused on assessment in the fields of social and civil law and have also been scientifically engaged with these topics. In 2019, the revised version of the Taskforce of the Scientific Medical Professional Societies (AWMF, German abbreviation for "Arbeitsgemeinschaft wissenschaftlicher medzinischer Fachgesellschaften") guidelines for the medical expert opinion of mental and psychosomatic disorders were published (AWMF, 2019), led by the German Society for Psychosomatic Medicine and Psychotherapy and the German Society for Neuroscientific Assessment, in cooperation with seven other medical and mental health professional societies. These guidelines include fundamental aspects and methods in various legal areas in its general part, explicate the principles of assessing occupational capacity in the second part, and standards for assessing causality questions in trauma-related disorders in the third Section (AWMF registry number 051-029; Schneider et al., 2015).

The assessment in Psychosomatic Medicine and Psychotherapy encompasses descriptive disorder-related diagnostics, which serve to map psychiatric and psychosomatic symptoms or syndromes. Currently, we work with ICD-10, but in the future, ICD-11 will be used, which will be tested in a transition phase from January 1, 2022. In certain cases, such as questionable trauma-related disorders, DSM-5 will also be used beyond ICD.

In addition, appropriate and comprehensive medical diagnostics, including physical, laboratory, and instrumental examinations, are naturally applied. Regarding mental problems, test-psychological procedures are often indicated.

The Operationalized Psychodynamic Diagnosis (OPD) allows for more differentiated access to psychosocial and particularly psychodynamically relevant features, enabling a deeper understanding of potentially significant mental or psychosocial factors for the respective issues. Maladaptive relationship patterns, conflict patterns, or structural features, as well as behavioral dimensions, open access to the important developmental conditions or contexts of the specific issue of the individual being assessed. They allow the significant factors for decision-making to be worked out and transparently communicated to the client or court. These approaches are required in almost all psychosomatic, psychotherapeutic, or psychiatric assessment issues across various legal fields. Additionally, in some cases, the question of assessing contextual conditions also arises.

Psychodynamic backgrounds (e.g., conflicts or structural features) can be crucial in assessing somatoform (pain) disorders. These diagnostic concepts can further provide insights into current experience, relationship, and behavior patterns, allowing statements about resources or obstacles that offer explanatory value for the relevant questions. For example, the increased vulnerability (i.e., "structure" or personality functioning) of an employee on long-term sick leave who subjectively feels bullied can have prognostic significance for assessing the likelihood of returning to work.

Axis I of the OPD examines the experience of illness (psychological distress, secondary illness gain) and focuses on aspects relevant to change, such as the respondent's access to intrapsychic and interpersonal factors in the illness process and their consequences for performance assessment. Against this background, both the prognosis of the illness and future performance can be worked out. Aspects of coping with illness are important for many issues. For example, in the assessment of chronic mental or psychosomatic illnesses in the context of social law assessments or in private occupational disability insurance, as chronic disorders or problems are usually present in an assessment for reduced earning capacity under social law.

The question of causality assessment requires an analysis of any trauma. It must be checked whether the event fulfills the criteria that are applied to trauma in the relevant psychiatric diagnosis systems (DSM-5 and ICD-10/ICD-11).

Furthermore, an in-depth insight into the psychological development of the person being assessed is always indicated. It is usually not enough to check whether mental or psychosomatic conditions that are worthy of illness were diagnosed or treated before the confrontation with the event. The OPD diagnosis is well suited to determining the extent to which the person being assessed has an increased vulnerability to developing a mental health problem after confrontation with the specific event due to certain developmental obstacles. For this question, all axes of the OPD represent important diagnostic approaches with different focal points. The Structure Axis (Axis IV), which provides information on the resources or obstacles to coping with stress at the level of affective, cognitive and motivational processing, is of particular importance.

Particularly about the topic of traumatization, while of great importance in current psychoanalytic thinking, it must be taken into account that this problem is currently very popular, as traumatization is repeatedly widely reported in the media and, if compensation is granted, this can be of a financial nature or include other forms of relief such as retirement. It is certainly often necessary to clarify whether a trauma sequelae disorder can be justifiably assumed or whether it is pretended to be a secondary illness gain. The aspect of whether traumatization is present is particularly explosive, as it is often linked to ethical and political-ideological aspects in particular contexts. For example, the issue of sexual abuse or violence against children and women, the issue of granting asylum and more. This tends to put pressure on the experts to proceed in a "politically correct" manner. This requires a methodologically sound and comprehensive assessment, for which the OPD diagnostic tool is a suitable additional module. In addition, the OPD is also well suited to making the expert's reasoning and decision-making process transparent.

10.1.4 OPD in Group Therapy

Clinical group psychotherapy research provides convincing evidence of its effectiveness in many studies across different mental disorders (Burlingame et al., 2016; Strauß et al., 2016). Psychodynamic group therapists emphasize inherent group-specific effectiveness factors (Yalom, 1970; Bion, 1959). Not least due to a high level of acceptance among the population (Burlingame et al., 2016) and an assumed high level of health economic cost efficiency (Strauß et al., 2016), outpatient group psychotherapy has been upgraded in the new German Psychotherapists Act (translated from German term Gemeinsamer Bundesausschuss; Gemeinsamer Bundesausschuss, 2020). The specialist training regulations for the P-subjects now also include an independent group qualification (Janssen & Kruse, 2019) and group psychotherapy is a central component of the integrative model of psychodynamically oriented psychotherapy in inpatient and day-care settings – alongside the concept of the "therapeutic community" (Main, 1946; Janssen, 2016).

The vision of the "OPD and Group" task force group is to conceptualize the Operationalized Psychodynamic Diagnostic (OPD) for a diagnostic assessment of therapeutic (small) groups (OPD-G). The primary goal is to provide psychodynamic group therapists and researchers with a diagnostic system based on the OPD that operationalizes the three primary aspects of group dynamics of therapeutic groups – the individual dynamics, the interpersonal dynamics and the dynamics of the group. This should help to make it easier to grasp these three perspectives in therapeutic group processes in the here-and-now of the group situation by reducing complexity. The aim is to anchor existing psychodynamic concepts of groups within the OPD. The aim is to find a common language for psychodynamically oriented group therapists, supervisors and researchers across different traditions. By providing an instrument for the assessment of groups, a binding reference framework for diagnostics and documentation is to be provided to record therapeutic processes and developments of and in groups and to promote research activity in this area. At the same time, the operationalization should help to perceive group processes more clearly and ultimately influence them constructively.

By applying it to psychodynamic group psychotherapy, the OPD not only expands its traditional clinical field, but also its theoretical premises. Historically, it thus ties in with the construct of a "multi-person psychology" (Bion, 1959) and is based on the original contributions of Bion and Foulkes and their successors (Bion, 1959; Foulkes, 1957; Heigl-Evers & Heigl, 1994; Hopper, 2009; Schlapobersky, 2016). In addition to dyadic relationships, polyadic relationships are becoming increasingly important, with the horizontal "sibling" axis coming to the fore alongside the vertical "parent-child" axis (Kaës, 2017). The step "from the couch to the circle of chairs" (Schlapobersky, 2016) is associated with a conceptual challenge that has new and specific characteristics in the group situation that are not present in the individual situation and must therefore be formulated as "group-analytical equivalents" (Foulkes, 1964). The main challenge for the task force group is to find group-related equivalents for concepts that have been formulated in the individual sphere, in terms of relationships, conflict and structure. For the observation period in the sense of a diagnostic assessment, OPD-G is meant to provide for one group session at a time.

Axis-III-G: Conflictual Group Theme

The OPD describes psychodynamic conflicts of the individual on Axis III. These life-determining, unconscious intrapsychic conflicts are defined as a collision or better, lack of integration of opposing motivational systems (e.g., basic need for Dependency vs. Individuation), with each Conflict characterized by a typical main motive, a core affect, and an active or passive coping mode. These individual intrapsychic conflicts are also recognizable in the group situation.

As a manifestation of intrapsychic conflicts, "the neurotic conflict of the individual in the group situation appears in a dynamic, and even dramatized form" (Foulkes, 1964). Freud suggested that the group is more governed by the unconscious than the individual (Freud, 1921). The individual conflicts of the group members are continuously externalized, dramatized, personified, and staged in and through the group process. In this way each group member reenacts their typical conflict situations by using other group members, including the leader, and endowing them with characteristics of people from their lives, from the past and present, thereby bringing intrapsychic conflicts to the stage of the group. In the group situation, something beyond-individual and new emerges, described in psychoanalytic family therapy as the "dominant theme" (Cierpka & Windaus, 2007) or as the "common group theme" (Foulkes & Anthony, 1957). Thus, intrapsychic conflicts find expression that confluence in the social field of a multilateral transference disposition into a common, dominant group theme, which can be observed in scenes – the conflictual group theme. The scenic relationship design in the here and now always contains effective elements of the past. Identifying malignant affective exchange patterns and symptomatic interaction sequences in the current group process and linking them with individual biographical experiences and focusing on the group's conflictual theme helps to elaborate and make the underlying group conflict and structural dynamics accessible to the group members.

Conflictual group themes are conscious and unconscious group-determining themes – not "life-determining," as in the individual. Conflictual group themes are thus collective scenes, narratives, or discourses that revolve around a thematic conflict core corresponding to OPD conflicts and can be described under different aspects: the theme, the basic question, the core and/or leading affect, the basic and pathological polarity, associated roles, the group's task, and the interaction. For example, the conflict of Submission vs. Control appears in the conflictual group theme as a "one up-one down dynamic." The basic question is who controls or steers the group. The core affect is a (to be avoided) helplessness, which manifests as helpless anger or fear of being controlled. An active or passive processing mode may prevail. In the active mode, there is a striving for dominance, especially to control the topics of conversation, group rules, as well as the framework and boundaries, experiencing power over others or fearing being controlled by others. In the countertransference, the group leader feels annoyed, dominated, or exposed by open aggression and dominance. In the passive mode, passive-aggressive submission predominates. Here, other group members or the leader or the group's rules are seemingly followed without asking critical questions or revealing their own views and desires; instead, they are subordinated or remain hidden. Aggressive contact is feared, expressed in refusal to speak, withdrawal, or lateness. The apparent friendliness and lack of aggression, combined with the underlying often strong aggression, generate restrained resentment in the leader as countertransference, and given the hidden aggression, guilt feelings arise. The localization of conflictual group themes can occur both within and outside the group. Within the group, the conflictual theme can be located between group members, between the leader and one or more members, between the group as a whole and individual members, and between subgroups.

Axis-IV-G: Structure of the Group as a Whole

In the OPD, Axis IV describes the individual's personality structure differentiated in five dimensions: perception, control, defense, communication, and attachment at different integration levels, which are regarded as more or less stable states in individuals. The group equivalent for the respective individual mental structure/level of functioning can be seen in the model of the working group function (Bion, 1959). The object of the investigation is the group, i.e., the group as a social system. The phenomenon of the group-as-a-whole has been described by various authors. All authors share the view that groups are seen as organizations characterized by common experience and behavior (e.g., Bion, 1959; Foulkes, 1957; Hopper, 2009).

All approaches distinguish between highly structured and task-oriented behavior on the one hand and irrational, primitive, and non-task-oriented behavior on the other. Dimensionally, two opposing modes of group functioning can be distinguished. One pole represents the working group, primarily characterized by a stable conscious focus on reality, its task, and its fulfillment using highly differentiated means ("sophisticated means"). The other pole is defined as several "Basic Assumption Groups," which revolve around its most elementary, unconscious drive experience at the cost of losing task fulfillment, role assumption, and reality recognition, characterized by irrational collective experience and behavior (Dependency G., Fight-Flight G., Pairing G.). Bion proposes that the concept of the working group should be understood as the group equivalent of the psychoanalytic concept of ego function (Bion, 1959). Thus, the group can be seen as a complex system between the poles of differentiation and dedifferentiation. The group's functionality is reflected in maintaining the group's specific task, relevant roles, upholding a culture of joint exploration and investigation of unconscious mental and social processes, and the group's willingness to interact appropriately with its environment. This perspective is particularly suitable for operationalizing the group structure – its degree of integration is crucial for how the group can handle its conflictual group themes. The following are brief descriptions of individual overall structure assessments.

1. Well-integrated group structure:
   A well-integrated group ("work group") has the unconscious ideal of wanting to overcome challenges together (motto: "We think, feel, and reflect together, therefore we are"). The group is constantly focused on its task and uses methods such as reflection in the group mirror, interpersonal conflict processing, giving and receiving feedback, and is aware that interpersonal events need to be clarified. Reflection and self-reflection are highly valued in the group and are desired or required by members among themselves. Monologue flexibly transitions to dialogue and finally to group discourse, which is characterized by the externalization of the various internal objects of an individual encountered in the group (Schlapobersky, 2016). Communication is characterized by free-flowing discussion. Differences in values and norms and between group members can be negotiated, coexist, and enrich the group. If the group process is hindered by internal conflicts or external obstacles, these events can be creatively integrated for the benefit of all, or the path to task completion can be realistically adjusted within the same session. In this way, the group grows out of its temporary "dysfunctional states." Roles are assumed according to the group situation and adjusted as needed. The group is trusted so that fantasies, dreams, and ventures can be shared and realized together. There is a sense of belonging (cohesion), emotional warmth (group climate), and realistic hope. The leader receives positive attributions, but can also be critically questioned by the group, of which he is still largely unaware (HUS: Stage 2), if this is communicated to him with empathy.
2. Moderately integrated group structure:
   A moderately integrated group ("grumbling group") has the unconscious guiding principle that it is all about task fulfillment, but the group behaves ambivalently because it is not sure of itself (motto: "We think, but struggle with our feelings, so we doubt and come together insecurely"). In principle, the group feels committed to its task and has it in mind for long stretches. However, it can happen that fantasies, emotional states or arguments interfere with the fulfillment of tasks. The group members are less able to reflect on themselves in the mirror of the group, as the flexibility to switch between the role of participant and observer of the group is limited. Free-floating discussion in the group is also restricted. The role of the person who speaks, listens and asks questions is distributed among different group members, which limits the possibility of spontaneously responding to the conflicts of others. Dialogue is the predominant language pattern (Schlapobersky, 2016). Various phenomena can occur: The group is stuck in an argument that seems unsolvable, the group does not stick to the

primary task but gets lost in secondary tasks or becomes entrenched in passivity or a grumpy attitude of entitlement. The task is questioned, people rationalize why something cannot be done and conditions are placed on the work that cannot be achieved. Sometimes it seems as if the group is actively avoiding something which can be expressed by individuals working on behalf of others. New requirements that reality demands are overlooked, misinterpreted or put off for far too long. The path to the common goal is arduous, often at the expense of joy. Role behavior is not consistently placed in the "service of the group," but alternates with individualized behavior. The group is not really trusted, so that many things are kept secret, fantasies and important things are kept inside the individual. Self-criticism and fear of the disapproval and rejection of others prevail when aggression is shared, and one exposes oneself in the group. The leader is followed and/or condemned for failure.

3. Poorly integrated group structure:
   A poorly integrated group ("tumult group") has the unconscious guiding principle that the group is more of a tense ordeal than an accomplishment (motto: "We are taken in by our feelings or don't realize them, thinking is difficult, so we often deceive ourselves and lose our bearings"). The group is hardly task-oriented and cannot organize itself without leadership. It is almost the rule that fantasies, emotional states or emotional arguments make it impossible to complete tasks over several sessions. Members are unable to switch between their roles as participants and observers. The group members can hardly reflect themselves in the mirror of the group, or there is a fear of a malicious reflection in the group, which acts as a destructive force (Zinkin, 1983). Various phenomena can occur that are often associated with splitting processes: The group is stuck in a dispute that seems unsolvable, the group looks for a task that is far removed from reality, roles are no longer taken in the interests of the group, the group becomes entrenched in passivity or begins to fight against each other (scapegoat phenomenon). The group and other group members can be perceived as a threat to one's own self. Supposed opponents and enemies from outside are also identified and attacked verbally and in the imagination. New demands that challenge reality are no longer perceived and are interpreted irrationally and unrealistically. The tension is high but can hardly be verbalized. The mood is characterized by high dissatisfaction, resignation or mutual accusation and conflict. This leads to the formation of subgroups that fight each other or are internally withdrawn or dissociated and blocked. The group is either mistrusted to such an extent that people no longer want to reveal anything about themselves or there is a damaging lack of shame - cohesion does not develop. The group's containing and supportive function cannot be maintained. There are regular violations of the setting, participants leave the group or turn up late or irregularly. The framework is fragile and difficult to maintain. The leader can be perceived as exaggerated due to messianic attributions or be persistently devalued, attacked or disempowered.
4. Disintegrated group structure:
   A disintegrated group ("confusion group") has the unconscious model of an apocalypse, the group thinks irrationally and acts instinctively and haphazardly (motto: "I am being persecuted and threatened with extinction, and everyone here is fighting for their existence"). The group can only experience itself as a rudimentary group and is primarily concerned with differentiating between self and non-self. The group only suspects that there is a task but has no concept that a group could be there to fulfill a task. There is a dilemma between loss of self through object dependence or loss of self through fusion with the group (Mentzos, 2011; Hopper,

2009). In mirroring, the differentiation between group members has collapsed and there is a fear of persecution or extinction; the mirror function reflects highly distorted images. The speech pattern is monolithic, and leaves others confused, empty or frightened. The ability to take on roles is concretistically limited. The group's containing and supporting function exists only in a rudimentary form and has been suspended. The group is fragmented, there is no longer any balance or other recognizable patterns, a chaotic coexistence is typical. Speechlessness, untargeted aggression and panicked fears are observed. The often idiosyncratic and private communication must be actively supported and related to the group to counteract the paranoia that would otherwise arise. There is no trust, but it must be built up again and again in a non-confrontational and protective way. The leader is no longer perceived as such or glorified; there may also be great fear of him. The group finds it difficult to keep to the framework and may have to be reminded to participate. The leader must actively intervene to provide structure and create an adjustment to reality; the maintenance of group life and the principle of hope are of central importance for the mental survival of the group.

Case Vignette

A group with nine members has been meeting for almost two years. Shortly after the session begins, a member playfully shares the fantasy of taking the leader's seat by sitting in the spot habitually occupied by the leader. The individual group members respond to the conflictual staging of the Submission vs. Control theme according to their inner conflicts and structural possibilities. Some members cheerfully anticipate a reaction from the leader and consider doing the same. Other members describe feelings of fear and the impulse to withdraw. The protagonist then talks about his authority conflicts outside the group and engages with feedback from the more passive, submissive members, who in turn find inspiration in the courage to rebel against the authorities. The group talks about the leader's chair, which symbolizes the desire to be in a powerful position and the fear of being punished for this desire, especially if it is put into practice. The group then talks about testing boundaries, experiencing powerlessness at work and the desire to question the power and decisions of leaders and the fantasy of being protected from one's own experience of powerlessness/helplessness as long as one "has the power." The group appears to be well integrated in this discussion and works on its task, examining the interactions and their resonance with the common group theme. The free-floating communication follows a discursive pattern in which members spontaneously associate with each other. Although emotions such as anger and powerlessness are addressed and there is a certain "tension" in the air, the atmosphere is essentially playful and creative.

10.1.5 OPD in Couple and Family Therapy

Building on the established OPD instruments for adults and for children and adolescents (OPD Task Force, 2008; OPD-KJ 2, 2017), concepts have been developed in recent years to extend the multiaxial diagnostic system to relationship systems (Stasch et al., 2012). The diagnostics of conflict and structure in couples and families will be outlined here.

Conflict Diagnostics

In psychoanalytic terms, "conflict" refers to the unsuccessful integration of conflicting intrapsychic or interpersonal motivational systems (desires, interests, demands, and their realization). Conflict, as an unconscious event, is to be distinguished from predominantly consciously experienced tensions. Unconscious conflicts that persist over time are derived from the clinical description of observable behaviors and experiences. They manifest at both the subject and object levels (intrapsychically as well as in relationship formation) and are associated with conflict-typical leading affects). The scenic representation of relationship formation and biographical data provide the diagnostician with important diagnostic information in the clinical situation.

Special attention is given to the analysis of the family's transference readiness and the therapist's countertransference experience (according to OPD):

- Dependency vs. Individuation
- Submission vs. Control
- In Need of Care vs. Self-Sufficiency
- Self-Worth
- Oedipal Conflict
- Identity

An example from the Manual for Psychoanalytic Infant-Parent Psychotherapy (Cierpka, Hirschmüller et al., 2007) illustrates the *In Need of Care vs. Self-Sufficiency Conflict:* The handling of the need for care shapes object relationships in such a way that the experience and formation of relationships follow the need for care and security or their defense in a conflictual manner. The associated leading affect is (prolonged) sadness and depression because the significance of the failing object (fear) is constantly perceived. Clinically significant is the theme of loss, denial, or envy. The caregiving theme may, for example, take the form of altruistic renunciation (defense) in the early time with the baby; or the partner may be coerced in a demanding, blackmailing way to provide security and care. The infant may also be used to satisfy "contact hunger." In the countertransference, feelings of anxiety and helplessness become apparent, along with feelings of sadness or longing for care in identification with a part of the parent's self. Often, there is a collusive conflict staging in couple relationships when both partners manifest the same conflict (usually complementarily, such as closeness/distancing) or when the same central relationship theme is unconsciously passed down through generations in families. However, various conflict mixes can also be observed in relationship systems. For example, a man with a basic desire for merging (regressive coping with a conflict of Dependency vs. Individuation, according to OPD) may sacrifice himself very altruistically for the children, thereby relieving his very performance-oriented and autonomy-focused wife (active coping with a care-self-sufficiency conflict according to OPD) of her own repressed care desires.

In couple and family systems, all individuals are assessed individually in their predominant conflict situation after understanding the observable interactional coping of the relationship system, which usually manifests a common dominant theme. The so-called "dominant theme" (Stern, 1998) is characterized by occupying a lot of space and time in the representational world of the participants and being highly relevant to behavior and experience. This theme can be related to unconscious intrapsychic conflicts or express the coping with severe familial crises or traumas (Fraiberg et al., 2003). The dominant theme influences both perception and interaction and is thus identified in relationship formation. The heuristic of the dominant theme provides a very helpful entry into the more differentiated psychodynamic diagnostics of central conflict dynamics. These must be distinguished from current stressors that can influence the relationship system in various ways:

- Presence of ubiquitous developmental challenges (e.g., school enrollment, partner loss)
- Currently effective stressors of potentially traumatic proportions (migration, death, war experiences)
- Past stressors of extraordinary traumatic magnitude that are transgenerationally active
- Ongoing conflicts regarding cultural-religious identity

- Subclinical conflict manifestations as a developmental risk (e.g., the child's school enrollment triggers object loss fears in the parents but can still be adequately managed)

Structural Diagnostics

Structure in the OPD sense describes the availability of regulatory functions of the psyche and distinguishes four functional levels: well-integrated, moderately integrated, poorly integrated, and disintegrated. The structural assessment was previously carried out in the OPD-2 version (OPD Task Force, 2008) for

- the ability of the patient for self- and object-perception,
- the ability for affective self-regulation and relationship regulation,
- the ability of intrapsychic and interpersonal communication,
- the ability for internal object attachment and external relationships.

In these eight structural dimensions (four each relating to the self and the objects), 24 structural items are described, comprehensively operationalized to depict the structural capabilities of an individual. Structural diagnostics with the OPD always also understand itself as relationship diagnostics, as the possibilities of the self unfold in its relationship to the objects (and thus also in the relationship to the diagnostician).

For the diagnostic view of relationship systems, this perspective, which is very oriented towards the individual's internalization achievements, is no longer sufficient. The functionality of the psyche must be understood as the functionality of the system, which also has further facets. Additionally, group dynamic processes must be considered. A group or relationship system can only function sustainably if the individual members settle at the functional level of the structurally weakest member. Family research has developed some models relevant for developing the Structure Axis (Axis IV) of the "Family OPD" (e.g., Steinhauer et al., 1984; Stasch & Cierpka, 2006).

Just as in individual-centered OPD, the structural functional levels of relationship systems are described as ranging from "well-integrated" (healthy), "moderately integrated" (neurotic-conflictual), "poorly integrated" (clear structural deficits) to "disintegrated" (significant structural deficits), depicted in Table 72.

These different functional levels are defined for each of the six structural dimensions:

- Control and responsibility function
- Task fulfillment
- Role behavior
- Communication
- Emotional relationship formation
- Values and norms

An exemplary illustration of the structural dimension of the *control and responsibility function (CAR*, translated from German "Kontrolle und Verantwortung") is provided:

Definition CAR: refers to a family system's ability to organize various tasks necessary for the functioning of cohabitation, thus maintaining the individual members' sense of security. This includes everyday activities like children's school attendance, keeping appointments, and ensuring physical care (nutrition, health care, housing). Additionally, control also refers to adaptive abilities to face new life challenges and adapt to changes in family life cycles.

The quality of CAR derives from the fit between mental, sociocultural, and material resources and societal conditions. In the interaction of family members, it is considered whether the behavior of individual family members is predictable or reliable even under stress. CAR assesses whether the control ability is consistent and constructive, whether there is a capacity for taking responsibility for family members, and how it is implemented.

CAR can be situated at different functional levels:

1. Well-integrated: The family system has a good control and responsibility function

Table 72 Structural functional levels of relationship-systems

Functional level	Description
Well-integrated	The relationship system is characterized by warmth, respect, positive relatedness, and the ability to resolve conflicts constructively. Communication and interpersonal boundaries are clear. Conflictual limitations may occur but are not persistent.
Moderately integrated	Communication is relatively clear but shaped by conflict-related desires and fears. Interpersonal control to ensure a "good" atmosphere is excessive and dysfunctional. Affects such as anger, fear, and depression are predominant. Ambivalence is responded to with repression.
Poorly integrated	Alternating between chaotic and rigid-tyrannical control efforts. Interpersonal boundaries fluctuate between permeable and rigid. Predominance of distant unrelatedness or boundary violations. Under-regulation in the sense of affective outbursts predominates.
Disintegrated	Permeable boundaries, contradictory-confusing communication, no common attentional focus, stereotypical "mechanistic" handling of family "rules." Denial of ambivalence, feelings of hopelessness and cynicism. Possibly psychotic constructions of perception and experience.

even under emotional stress and unplanned changes in everyday life. There is room for self-regulation among family members, and the family system can adapt flexibly to internal and external changes. Responsibility-taking is reliable and possible in alternative constellations, appropriate to family members' abilities, age-appropriate, and developmental-promoting. Tasks can be flexibly assumed, and there is considerable room for self-regulation in the family system – various societal resources and systems can be used flexibly to meet existential basic needs.

2. Moderately integrated: The family system's CAR is limited under emotional stress and especially during sudden changes, tending towards rigid over-regulation or laissez-faire as regressive conflict avoidance. There is little room or encouragement for self-regulation; family members often must conform to a "family creed." Responsibility-taking/task fulfillment happens schematically, limitedly authentically, and inflexibly; for example, adaptability in threshold situations of the life cycle is impaired. CAR limits development opportunities but does not make them impossible.
3. Poorly integrated: The control and responsibility function (CAR) of the family system is predominantly dysfunctional, and daily tasks cannot be reliably managed. There may be risks to child welfare. The family's CAR may be impaired to the extent that external assistance is necessary. Interpersonal reactions during conflicts are emotionally charged, unpredictable, or predictably destructive. Self-regulation of family members and the family system is limited, with no reliable patterns for conflict resolution. Maintaining the image of a family unit is predominantly achieved through projective-facade mechanisms. Internally, the family breaks down into dyads and highly conflictual coalitions. Emerging needs are urgent and cannot be postponed due to limited control abilities. Individual family members may try to ensure a minimum level of CAR (e.g., through parentification). Overall, there is a tendency towards potentially destructive under- and/or over-control.
4. Disintegrated: The control and responsibility function (CAR) of the family system is highly dysfunctional. For the examiner, the needs of the family appear very urgent, while responsibility-taking is not evident. Task fulfillment no longer succeeds, so that, in contrast to the poorly integrated level, such fam-

ily systems regularly require external help. Interpersonal reactions in conflicts appear bizarre, unpredictable, and barely comprehensible. Self-regulation of family members and the family system is either non-existent or severely impaired. Maintaining the image of a family unit is often only possible within a segregated construction of reality for the outside world, while the internal space appears fragmented.

On the evaluation sheet, in addition to the four main levels, the three unspecified intermediate levels (1.5, 2.5, and 3.5) can also be assessed.

10.1.6 The Addiction Module

The Addiction Module (Arbeitskreis OPD – Abhängigkeitserkrankungen, 2013; Jakobsen, 2014) is an addition to the OPD for substance abuse or dependence. It is intended for all diagnosticians and is particularly helpful when substances play a role, even if one does not work in a specialized addiction clinic.

It allows for a differentiated diagnostic assessment for patients with substance abuse and dependence. With the modern, empirically oriented system, relevant psychodynamic considerations in addiction disorders can be easily recorded, communicated, and utilized for therapy. The standardization of terminology optimizes information transfer, and the adoption allows for a more transparent understanding of the therapy process. It is fully manualized and can be trained in an OPD training course. It is based on OPD-2 and can also be easily used with OPD-3 (only the numbering of Axis I varies slightly). Previous experiences suggest easy applicability both in a specialized clinic and in a psychotherapeutic practice.

The following tools are included:

- The Addiction Spiral (as a concept of addiction dynamics and a clinically useful rating instrument)
- Focus Selection (as a link between personality and addiction dynamics)
- Acquisition (as an assessment of the starting point of therapy and its progress)
- Illness Experience and Treatment Prerequisites: Addiction-specific supplements to Axis I (as a checklist for severity, duration, and possibilities of change)

The concept of the "Addiction Spiral" (Figure 22) allows for a psychodynamically based assessment of the development, maintenance, and autonomy of addiction, capturing it in text and rating form. The central assumption is that consumption behavior initially fulfills specific mental functions, which over time can develop into their own dynamics. This process is described as "autonomization" and is assessed in its extent.

With the inclusion of the "focus selection" (OPD), it is also possible to link personality and addiction dynamics. This requires knowledge of the OPD diagnostics of relationships, conflicts, and structure. This enables the linkage of personality with disorder-specific symptoms and dynamics (see Jakobsen, 2014, 2017).

With the "acquisition" according to Sporn (2005), it is possible to make assessments of the degree of recognition of the addictive disorder by the patient at the beginning of therapy and the progress of therapy. This is particu-

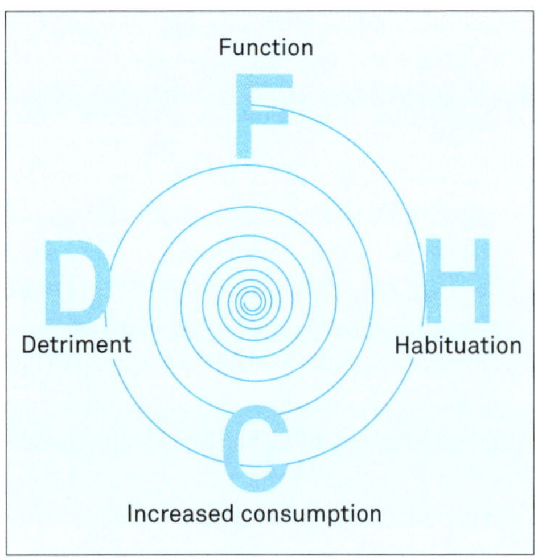

Figure 22. Addiction spiral (Arbeitskreis OPD – Abhängigkeitserkrankungen, 2013).

larly helpful for mapping the therapeutic process.

Axis I, with the addition for addiction disorders provides an important checklist. For specialized, experienced colleagues who routinely check the "pitfalls," it can facilitate daily work. For all colleagues who are not specialized in addiction disorders, it proves very useful in treatment planning and indication setting.

It records:

- whether there is an addiction and its severity;
- which phases of e.g. alcoholism may be present;
- which change concepts need to be considered;
- which special obstacles may exist;
- which treatment goals are pursued;
- which external demands exist;
- the family situation.

It is therefore useful in counseling and therapy in outpatient and (partially) inpatient settings. It helps to decide between outpatient and inpatient treatment. It tries to better take into account the patient's attitude towards the disease and to assess the influence of personality and addiction dynamics on the chances of substance abstinence. In an outpatient setting, it makes it possible to classify the extent of the addiction and to outline the sequence of steps. In an inpatient setting, realistic goals can be set that take into account the patient's personality. Treatment tasks and their progress can be easily mapped, which is useful during treatment and helpful in reports and legal psychotherapy applications.

10.1.7 OPD in Forensic Psychiatry

Rehabilitation Model

Since the 1990s, diagnostics and interventions in the forensic context have been influenced mainly by a rehabilitation model – the Risk, Need, Responsivity (RNR) Model by Bonta & Andrews (2007). The basic idea of this model is that interventions – such as psychotherapy – for people at risk of committing (or recommitting) crimes should align with these three principles to be as effective as possible (e.g., Hilton & Radatz, 2021; Olver et al., 2020; Mikolajewski et al., 2021).

The *risk principle* means that the extent of therapeutic interventions should be higher the greater the person's risk of recidivism. This can manifest, for example, in the number of hours and duration dedicated to therapy to manage the risk adequately. The range spans from no therapy offer for low-risk individuals to multi-year therapies with over 350 hours. The *need principle* refers to identifying the criminogenic needs that are significantly important for the risk (and were significant) and directing the treatment towards influencing these needs. Many of these factors are so-called stable dynamic risk factors, meaning that while they are fundamentally changeable, they generally do not change without interventions and remain stable. Examples could be a sexually sadistic symptomatology or antisocial attitudes. These factors should be identified, prioritized, and focused on in therapy. The *responsivity principle* means that the intervention is tailored to the individual's abilities with treatment needs so that they can benefit from the intervention. Factors such as language barriers, motivation, abilities, and strengths of the person play a role here.

The advantage of this theory-led approach is that various therapy forms and therapy schools can be associated with it. The prognosis assessment in the criminal justice context is now mainly based on this approach.

Approaches for the OPD Forensic Module

The basic idea of the planned OPD Forensic Module is to relate the various axes of the OPD to the RNR model, thereby making psychodynamic theory, diagnostics, and practice useful for prognosis assessment, therapy planning, and the implementation of psychodynamically informed or based therapies.

On Axis I, it will focus on the particularly *significant forensic diagnoses* – especially those that significantly increase the risk of recidivism: antisocial personality disorder, substance-related disorders, and paraphilic disorders. As an objective measure of severity, the static risk, as measured by actuarial static risk assessment instruments (e.g., VRAG, static-99; overview, e.g., by Rettenberger et al., 2013), will be used.

Axis II will assess relational capacity as both a static factor (always able to form long-term relationships) and a dynamic risk factor (building relationships, social network), as well as a factor of responsiveness. The central issue here is which transference and countertransference constellations can endanger or even harm therapy, as the context of mostly involuntary treatment paired with typical primitive defense mechanisms presents a series of challenges for forensic psychotherapies. These are particularly better understood with a psychodynamic understanding, as is the clarification of the reenactment of risk-relevant constellations inside and outside therapy.

In working with Axis III, the focus is on translating central conflicts into criminogenic needs, i.e., the question of how each conflict might be related to dynamic risk factors. For example, experiencing guilt in antisocial personality traits can be denied in an active mode. A person with pedophilic sexual interests may experience inferiority in the passive mode of the self-worth conflict. Sadomasochistic interests can be associated with Submission vs. Control conflicts and can also manifest massively and variably on the level of the therapeutic relationship.

Finally, Axis IV, the Structure Axis, or its various facets, forms the core of the translation work into the RNR model, because, of course, self and object perception, but especially self-regulation and relationship regulation, are often severely impaired in people with forensic-relevant disorders and thus pose a major challenge for any therapy.

The integration of OPD-3 with the RNR model in the forensic module is expected to provide practical benefits in three ways:

1. With this combination, diagnosis, case conceptualization, and treatment planning can be done according to the forensic state of the art (RNR), taking into account unconscious processes. The therapy could be a psychodynamically oriented forensic psychotherapy (MBT for ASP or TFP for borderline disorder). The findings from the case conceptualization can also be used for team intervision or supervision.
2. In particular, Axis IV could also be useful in assessing criminal responsibility, especially in assessing the severity of impairment (see Dobbrunz et al., 2020). Unconscious processes could be used transparently in the translator's work with the court.
3. Whether the OPD – especially with regard to structural impairments – can also make prognostically significant statements and, in particular, take more account of unconscious aspects (Briken, 2019) will be an empirically testable hypothesis.

Overall, the forensic module will mean a manageable translation of psychodynamic into forensic knowledge and vice versa regarding the additional effort, which will be of great practical benefit, especially for psychodynamically working practitioners.

10.1.8 OPD and Trauma-Related Disorders

Over the years, the application of OPD has proven particularly effective in the diagnosis and treatment planning for "neurotic" and/or "structural" patients, helping therapists and patients develop an understanding of the causal and symptom-maintaining factors. Ideally, this leads to a shared understanding of which life-history risk factors have developed and why a mental disorder has occurred at a certain point, influenced by further biological and social factors. This individualized case conceptualization is essential for any psychotherapeutic treatment, as mere psychiatric symptom classification according to ICD and DSM does not provide sufficient information for actual psychotherapeutic treatment planning. The goal of OPD is to understand the patient's individual psychodynamics, which can form a risk constellation leading to various psychopathological syndromes.

But what about disorders where bio-social factors seem obvious and psychodynamic factors are much harder to discern? Can OPD also be a useful tool for diagnosis and treatment planning here? This tension seems particularly relevant for the group of so-called trauma-related disorders, as one or more external life events, initially independent of the patient, are known to directly and causally lead to the development of the mental disorder. Can a psychodynamically informed approach, which examines neuroses or "structural disorders," contribute anything meaningful for a previously mentally healthy person who develops Post-Traumatic Stress Disorder (PTSD) after a severe and nearly fatal robbery? Especially since there are very successful treatment methods like EMDR or trauma-focused cognitive behavioral therapy, which completely forgo a psychodynamic understanding?

At its core, distressing life experiences represent potential threat situations that can endanger the individual's pre-existing physical, social, or mental integrity. The goal of intrapsychic engagement with external stressors is thus to secure or restore the previously existing physical, social, and mental balance. Fundamentally, people are equipped with biological, social, and mental mechanisms that help the affected individual counteract the threat and manage it without resulting in long-term consequences. Comparable to a homeostatic regulatory system, if there is a "balance" between the extent of life stress and the available resources, one would expect no or comparatively few long-term negative consequences for the individual. Thus, it is also understandable from a psychodynamic perspective that even with stressors that meet the criteria of a traumatic event, the majority of those affected do not suffer lasting negative bio-psycho-social consequences if they have sufficient internal and external resources to cope with them. At the same time, it also makes clear that what we define as a traumatic event is always something that exceeds coping possibilities, at least temporarily. For these reasons, it seems relevant for the psychodynamic assessment of trauma and its consequences to clearly distinguish between the traumatic event itself and any resulting traumatization, as not every event leads to the individual's traumatization. Unfortunately, this distinction is often not sufficiently made in practical psychotherapeutic work. Besides blurring category boundaries, especially affecting indication and treatment planning, prematurely categorizing a person with life stressors as "traumatized" also overlooks potential strengths and coping strategies and also "earlier" and important traumatization.

The OPD extension on trauma aims to sketch an explicitly psychodynamic perspective on trauma-related disorders, adopting a clear both-and stance: Instead of delineating psychodynamics and psychotraumatology, it examines how both traditions and concepts can be integrated in clinical practice. The focus is on describing psychodynamic vulnerabilities and resources in terms of OPD that an individual carries at the time of a traumatic event and their impact on disorder development and disease progression, as well as aspects of treatment planning.

According to the OPD systematics, an Operationalized Psychodynamic Diagnosis should address the psychodynamically significant factors for the development and maintenance of a trauma-related disorder. Therefore, it is initially important to strive for a clear definition (operationalization) of what is understood as trauma and how it differs from other psychosocial stressors. It is further necessary to define, given the heterogeneity of traumatic events, how they can be operationalized, differentiated, and quantified. Additionally, it is essential to characterize the psychodynamic resources needed for "processing" trauma, as well as the hindering vulnerabilities, and to identify potential consequences of trauma for the psychodynamics of the affected individuals. Thus, three psychodynamic dimensions of trauma and traumatization considerations can be presented, which the book will address:

1. How can trauma be defined from a psychopathological and psychodynamic perspective (trauma vs. life event)?
2. What are the central intrapsychic mechanisms of trauma processing?
3. What are the psychodynamic consequences of trauma?

The OPD trauma processing module has been elaborated in detail and with illustrative case examples by Burgmer et al. (2023).

10.2 OPD in Quality Assurance

10.2.1 OPD in the Expert Review Procedure of Guideline-Based Psychotherapy

The expert review procedure for guideline-based psychotherapy makes an important contribution to quality assurance in psychotherapeutic care by having an expert review the therapist's expertise on the illness and the psychotherapeutic treatability of the patient considering the psychotherapy guidelines (Rudolf & Schmutterer, 2003). Therapists formulate their clinical judgment, their psychodynamic hypotheses about the disorder, their therapeutic goals, and treatment planning, as well as their prognostic assessment, for a planned therapy for their patient. The expert reviews this text against the backdrop of the psychotherapy guidelines, i.e., the agreements on the necessity, appropriateness, and cost-effectiveness of defined psychotherapy procedures for a specified catalog of disorders. The expert examines the insurance company's obligation to provide benefits in the specific case and may recommend covering the costs for a certain number of hours.

Questions regarding diagnostic procedures and classification are not undisputed in the field of psychodynamic and analytic psychotherapy (Rudolf, 2001). Is the use of the OPD system suitable for improving the quality of diagnostics, therapy planning, and indication decisions? It also needs to be clarified how experts react to the use of OPD formulations in reports. An overview of initial applications for therapy reveals that 30–40 % of initial applications use OPD formulations with varying emphasis:

Patient characterizations on the Interpersonal Relations Axis (Axis II) of the OPD, are comparatively rare. When they are present, they indicate that therapists are interested and capable of providing a very detailed depiction of interpersonal dynamics, especially the therapeutic relationship.

OPD Conflicts (Axis III) are mentioned more frequently, with the Autonomy vs. Dependency Conflict (OPD-2: Dependency vs. Individuation) being cited in most cases. The terms autonomy and dependency seem to tempt many to diagnostically label various life problems related to attachment needs and efforts towards independence with this term, regardless of OPD's operational definitions for this conflict. (Examples from therapy applications: "The close, denied dependency on the mother with an almost absent, anxiety-inducing father prevented the resolution of the early autonomy-dependency conflict;" "The patient has a strong autonomy-dependency conflict in terms of partnership. He wants to pursue his need for autonomy and distance himself from his partner's overwhelming demands, but fears losing his wife.")

Therefore, it is not surprising that experts sometimes critically comment on the use of the term "autonomy-dependency," especially where it is used descriptively and associatively without a plausible psychodynamic explanation. This difficulty is observed more often in applications for psychodynamic therapy than for psychoanalytical therapy. In contrast, other, less commonly used OPD conflicts (e.g., In Need for Care vs. Self-Sufficiency, Guilt, Oedipal Conflict) are often very precisely presented in psychodynamic contexts, often with detailed therapeutic goals. Similarly frequent as the OPD conflict theme is the mention of structural level in terms of the Axis IV. This term is usually used in connection with assessing the severity of the disorder and the therapeutic goals. The discussion of structural features, their diagnostic and prognostic significance, and their impact on treatment techniques can be found equally in applications for psychodynamic and analytic therapies. Usually, structural diagnostics are also mentioned in follow-up reports: whether and how structural stabilization has been therapeutically achieved. Some therapists refer to structure-related modifications of psychodynamic and psychoanalytic therapy (Rudolf, 2004).

When OPD formulations are used as psychodynamic codes without the corresponding psychodynamics in the OPD sense, the same problem arises as with the occasional use of diagnostic terms such as borderline personality disorder, somatoform disorder, or posttraumatic stress disorder, etc.: they are not used in their operational definition, but in their private contextual meanings. It is up to the professionals to insist on the precise use of diagnostic terms that justify treatment planning for the benefit of the patient. Where specific OPD experience is available, these categories are used to set diagnostically sound psychodynamic accents in the areas of relationship design, conflict experience, and structural level, and to precisely tailor the treatment plan and therapeutic approach. With the book "OPD-3 in Psychotherapy Application," Stasch et al. (2026) provided a guide, including informative case examples, for using OPD in case formulation in the "report to the expert."

10.2.2 The Quality Assurance Project QPP

The Quality Assurance Project QPP is based on OPD and is developed for outpatient psychoanalytic and psychodynamic psychotherapy. It includes a questionnaire-based evaluation of therapy outcomes from the perspective of patients and therapists. This represents an additional effort towards quality assurance/management and aims to enable a procedure-specific form of quality assurance under practical conditions.

The goal of the project is to provide therapists with systematic individual case feedback, which, combined with their detailed knowledge from treatment, enables them to assess progress, identify long-term "good" and "problematic" outcomes. The underlying idea is that appropriate quality assurance is only meaningfully possible with the therapist's knowledge of the individual process.

Procedure: QPP builds on the experiences and materials of the Berlin Psychotherapy Study (Practice Study Analytic Long-term Therapy, PAL Study) and experiences with individual case feedback on a ward of the Psychosomatic Clinic at the University of Heidelberg including OPD.

Several surveys are conducted, at least at the beginning and end of therapy. A follow-up survey on the patient side is also recommended.

The therapist receives initial written feedback after the first survey, supplemented by further individual case feedback after each subsequent survey. This feedback helps assess the therapy against the therapist's individual experience with the patient. Modifications are possible.

Goals:

- Practice-oriented evaluation and critical accompaniment of outpatient psychotherapies

- Validation of outcome assessment by linking patient and therapist perspectives
- Evaluation of the feasibility and usefulness of the approach (survey of participating therapists)
- Certification of practices participating in quality assurance

There is no direct influence on the therapeutic process and no undifferentiated comparison of procedures. *Note:* This procedure is not intended to accompany the therapeutic process with the aim of indicating acute crisis developments.

Recording psychodynamic aspects: Patient self-assessments have a symptom-focused accent. Here, subjective suffering, interpersonal impairments, and (dis)satisfaction with quality of life are described. The final questions to the patient allow them to evaluate the therapy and changes from their perspective, express their satisfaction with the changes achieved, or complain about what was not achieved.

The therapist also describes the type and extent of the patient's symptoms. However, a significant addition is that at the beginning of treatment, the therapist can select from the spectrum of conflicts and structural limitations those issues whose change they consider particularly important for improving the patient's situation. They thus formulate individualized observation focuses on a psychodynamic basis (OPD focus selection). The therapeutic approach is determined by the therapist.

Using the Heidelberg Structural Change Scale (HSCS), they can then depict the therapeutic restructuring process during and at the end of therapy. Thus, they have an assessment possibility of therapeutic change on a psychodynamic basis beyond symptom reduction. Differences in change between short-term and long-term therapy as well as between psychodynamic and psychoanalytic therapy can be well depicted. The treatment outcomes achieved from the perspectives of therapists and patients are systematically related to each other, providing interesting starting points for further understanding.

Advantages of the proposed approach:

- Qualified assessment of therapy progress is the responsibility of the therapist.
- The instruments used are appropriate to the subject.
- The collected patient data "belong" to the practice, and the patient's anonymity is protected from third parties.
- Comparisons of patient and clinician ratings at the beginning and end of therapy (outcome) are possible.
- Follow-up surveys of patient ratings are easy to implement and complement the evaluation.
- Provides an overall view of practice quality over time
- Minimal impact on ongoing therapy and minimization of effort through a centralized evaluation center
- Clear, timely feedback on individual treatments for therapists
- Practical and feasible in an outpatient setting

Critical points:

- QPP is a lot of work. Each patient and each measurement require about 30 minutes of the therapist's time.
- Implementation is costly (license fees, postage, evaluation, etc.).
- Legislation requires quality assurance.
- Third parties have no access to the data (no external comparisons).
- Patients who only attend trial sessions do not participate.
- It is important to record dropouts and their reasons, but this is not done here.
- Interim surveys are useful for long-term therapy.

The procedure, based on OPD and the PAL study, was used voluntarily in 71 psychodynamic practices in Germany and Switzerland from 2001 to around 2010. It proved feasible and content appropriate. The practices covered the minor costs themselves. About 340 patients were evaluated with this system, and the data was processed and fed back to the therapists. Although designed for OPD-2, it can also be fundamentally combined with OPD-3, although this increases the time required.

Contact: Dipl. Psych. Thorsten Jakobsen, Rebgasse 28, CH 4058 Basel, jakobsen@gmx.de

10.3 OPD in Human Resources

The OPD was developed for use in clinical-psychotherapeutic contexts. However, the OPD is now also used in non-clinical areas. Particularly in the fields of personnel selection and personnel development/coaching, extensive experience has been gained, and the OPD has been successfully adapted (see Kotte et al., 2019; Gisch et al., 2020; Benecke & Möller, 2019). For the application of OPD in work psychology contexts, the central psychodynamic axes of Relationship, Conflict, and Structure were maintained but terminologically adapted for the respective application area.

Thus, on Axis III, the fundamental motivational themes are emphasized (which can develop into conflicts under unfavorable conditions). These fundamental motivational themes are:

- Attachment/autonomy
- Self-efficacy
- Care
- Self-worth
- Responsibility
- Competition
- Identity

These motivational themes are considered regarding their influence on professional life and tasks (e.g., leadership tasks and problems), and alongside the active and passive modes, the balanced ("integrated") mode is also always described.

The structural functions on Axis IV have also been reformulated and simplified in the context of assessing leadership qualities as "basic mental abilities," depicted in Table 73.

With the help of OPD-based personnel selection, evaluation, and development diagnostics, it is possible to derive a *person-job fit*, predict potential complications, and address them in a timely manner, formulate focuses for job-related coaching, and identify personalized

Table 73. Short description of the basal psychological skills (modified from Benecke & Möller, 2019)

Basic ability	Short description
Self-perception	Ability for self-reflection; ability to differentiate one's own affects; ability to become clear about the mental backgrounds of one's own behavior.
Perception of others	Ability to develop a coherent image of others; ability to connect others' behavior with mental processes (their wishes and feelings).
Self-experience	Ability to engage in emotionally lively contact with oneself; thereby feeling alive.
Affect regulation	Ability to experience, "hold," and regulate affects (even very negative ones) mentally without having to "recruit" the outside world/relationships for the regulation of one's own affects.
Empathy	Ability to empathize with the affective inner world of others and to share in their emotions; ability to communicate this emotional understanding and empathy sensitively to the other person.
Reciprocity ("we-feeling")	Ability to establish emotional contact with others, which is sustained by a mutual "we-feeling."

Note. Modified with permission from "OPD-basierte Diagnostik im Coaching [OPD-based diagnostics in coaching]" by C. Benecke, & H. Möller, in A. Ryba & G. Roth (Eds.), *Coaching und Beratung in der Praxis: Ein neurowissenschaftlich fundiertes Integrationsmodell* (pp. 127–147). © 2019 Klett-Cotta.

development topics or tasks. The OPD Task Force is currently developing a new assessment instrument for groups (see above), which will also be applicable in the human resources field for evaluating and coaching teams and team processes.

11 Training in OPD

The complexity of the OPD requires that it be taught in special training seminars, even if some of the categories are already known. Experience has shown that such training and continuous application within the framework of supervised diagnostics leads to a continuous improvement in diagnostic quality. This learning process also allows for feedback on criticism, objections, and suggestions for change. From the outset, the OPD Task Force has placed great emphasis on the continuous provision of training seminars and other educational activities, like the successful introduction of ICD-10 and other psychiatric diagnostic instruments.

After the publication of the OPD-1 manual in 1996, interest in OPD, first in the German speaking countries then internationally, grew in the following years, as reflected in the demand for training opportunities. Initially, the most interested groups included younger colleagues in psychiatric and psychosomatic-psychotherapeutic training, as well as established colleagues with long clinical experience. It was often stimulating that colleagues with no background in psychodynamic diagnostics could learn psychodynamic thinking through engagement with OPD. This experience contrasted with the original conception that the system was primarily for psychotherapists with extensive experience in the field. Over the years, psychotherapeutic training institutes (initially for depth psychology-based therapy, later increasingly for psychoanalysis) also joined, often conducting training with the multipliers, i.e., the teaching staff of the respective institutes.

Another group consisted of younger scientists who learned the method for application in research projects. Following the publication of translations into various languages, interest in seminars also developed abroad (e.g., Italy, UK, Denmark, Sweden, Hungary, Chile, China).

11.1 OPD Training Seminars

11.1.1 Structure of OPD Training

There is a traditional difficulty in developing uniform diagnostic habits in psychodynamic methods. This is partly because psychodynamic diagnostics have particularly evolved concerning the therapeutic process, rather than descriptive and symptom-oriented aspects. The diagnostic process was seen as an opportunity to initiate and test a relationship with the patient and also served to motivate the patient for psychotherapy. Only in this context was the elaboration of relevant psychodynamic constructs intended. Training within the framework of OPD must try to integrate these two central aspects of diagnostics, namely categorical and interactional components.

Training and further education seminars should have the following tasks: Conveying the content of the OPD axes; highlighting and discussing previous diagnostic habits of the participants; immediate practical testing of the new system.

The training is divided into a basic course and two advanced courses, each comprising

20 hours. These time specifications have proven effective but can also be adjusted to local specifics in various ways. Overall, this is the same amount of time as is required for most psychiatric diagnostic systems.

Structure of an OPD Basic Course:
1. Introduction to the features and history of psychodynamic diagnostics and OPD
2. Presentation of the axes, including their tradition of origin and categories using video material
3. Rating and discussion of one to two complete interviews (video or live)
4. Final discussion
5. Optional: special section on interview techniques

Structure of an OPD Advanced Course:
1. Deepening knowledge of the individual axes through selected case material and video clips
2. Evaluation and discussion of complete exemplary video films or live interviews
3. Final discussion
4. Depending on the need, discussion of special clinical questions and research topics, e.g., change measurements with the Heidelberg Structural Change Scale, focus finding using the Interpersonal Relations Axis (Axis II), and application in a scientific project

Other forms of instruction include:
- Simple information events, which can be conducted as short lectures or "taster afternoons" by authorized trainers, for example, for clinics or institutes
- Training seminars for entire clinic teams, often conducted over longer periods as regular OPD-oriented supervision offers, usually over whole or half days
- Targeted seminars for training institutes or lecturers (as multipliers)
- Research-oriented supervision in projects that apply OPD as a method, etc.

Content Focuses of Training

It is important to note that the OPD maps relevant aspects of personality from different theoretical and clinical traditions. Its historical origins lie in general health psychology and illness experience (Axis I), research on interpersonal patterns (Axis II), traditional psychoanalytic drive and object relationship theory (Axis III), and ego and object relationship theory (Axis IV). It forms the basis of the overall understanding of the system and is presented in the introductions to the seminars.

This is followed by a discussion of the information needed to answer the OPD Rating or the data sources used. On the one hand, "objective" information from clinical examination results and medical findings as well as "hard" biographical data are taken into account. On the other hand, information resulting from the interview, its content, verbal and non-verbal elements, and the resulting "scenic" information is considered. In many seminars, the OPD interview (see Chapter 7) is taught and discussed in a separate block.

The purpose of the OPD is to help capture and categorize characteristics using descriptive and illustrative categories. To do this, it must consciously and intentionally reduce the complexity of the original theory to make it testable and communicable. Therefore, OPD users are required to critically accept this reduction in complexity from the outset. Only then is it possible to adhere closely to the given definitions and operationalizations and thus approach the criteria of reliability and validity required by test theory. The discussion of this topic is initially carried out in the context of teaching the individual axes. Extensive material on edited videos, supporting scripts (e.g., checklists, slides, etc.) is now available for teaching in this area, which should facilitate application in clinical practice. Overall, case work has proven to be the best basis for discussion and assessment. Over the years, the OPD group has documented and evaluated "standardized" cases on video, allowing seminar participants to relate their assessments to the "expert group." Furthermore, often, for example in clinics and other institutions, the possibility is utilized to conduct live interviews with clinic patients. This allows a good introduction to interview technique problems and quasi case-related supervision for the involved therapists. In this context, work on focus formation and change assessment (Heidelberg Structural Change Scale; Rudolf et al., 2000) has also been established.

11.1.2 Certification

The standardized cases are also used to certify individual participants for use in scientific studies upon completion of the three courses. This certification requires a sufficiently reliable evaluation of a previously evaluated case by the working group. The criteria for "passing" the reliability test have been continuously adapted and developed based on the experience of past years.

Of course, participants who do not work in scientific projects can also undergo such certification or test their familiarity with the OPD system. For example, court-appointed experts can refer to the certificate as legitimation for using the OPD criteria in court. Certificates are issued by the OPD Training Coordinator upon receipt of the appropriate participation or reliability certificates.

11.1.3 Previous Experience With OPD Training

The groups interested in the seminars have been described above. In recent years, several thousand psychotherapeutic colleagues have been trained in open training seminars, seminars within psychotherapeutic training weeks, and in clinics and in institutes. In many clinics, OPD has established itself as a permanent, supervised component in the promotion of the "diagnostic culture" and in specialist training and psychological education. The growing interest in OPD in forensic psychiatry and among reviewers in the context of psychotherapy guidelines has also opened new fields.

Our experience over the years has shown that OPD and case-oriented training seminars are helpful for many colleagues. The use of OPD allows the classification of highly complex characteristics into an appropriately reducing category system. Discussion of specific cases allows reflection on one's own diagnostic habits and discussion of controversial issues with colleagues at the same level rather than at a hierarchical level. Many objections to individual categories raised in the training seminars were taken up by the trainers and the working group and considered in the development of OPD-2.

A frequently expressed wish was for the diagnostic classification to be more directly related to clinical-therapeutic practice. At the same time, the development of the Heidelberg Structural Change Scale made it possible to incorporate the focus work with OPD into OPD-2. Our initial concern that the OPD would lead to "under-complex" diagnoses has not, in our opinion, been confirmed. The discussion in the training seminars showed that the orientation to the "OPD framework" leaves enough room for individual constellations to be considered and even encourages and facilitates them. The present OPD-3, with its even stronger integration of the different axes, especially Conflict and Structure, will help even more to represent the complexity of psychological processes.

Training Centers

The OPD task force has designated regional training centers that regularly offer OPD courses. Requests, for example, for in-house courses, can also be directed to the training centers or their leaders. Naturally, the certified trainers can also be contacted directly (see: https://www.opd-online.net/opd-seminare/coordinators_international).

The OPD task force has designated regional training centers in Germany and some other countries that regularly offer OPD courses. Requests, for example, for in-house courses, can also be directed to the training centers or their leaders. Naturally, the certified trainers can also be contacted directly on the homepage: https://www.opd-online.net/opd-seminare/coordinators_international

Appendix A

Relationship Item Checklist: Description of All Items on the Interpersonal Relations Axis (Axis II) Across All Levels of Expression

The Relationship Item Checklist (Table A1) explains and thus improves understanding, what is meant by the individual items of Axis II and their gradations. It is to a certain extent a reference work that is intended to help resolve uncertainties.

Note: The column "OPD relationship theme" contains a general description of what is meant by the theme. "Unremarkable =0" shows what the OPD considers to be "normal" or "healthy" about the topic. Columns [=1] and [=2] contain examples of accentuated and then dysfunctional behaviors. For reasons of readability, only the masculine form is used.

In the left-hand column, the general topic is put in front. This is intended to facilitate DD: e.g., dysfunctional behavior is about too much care (7) or too close contact (8).

Table A1. Relationship item checklist

OPD relationship theme	Unremarkable/clinically not relevant (=0)	Accentuated (= 1)	Dysfunctional (= 2)
1 Give freedom (+)	**Give others freedom**	**Give a lot of freedom**	**Just let do**
The axis of interdependence is about the amount of freedom granted to the other person. DD: In contrast to (2–10 below), this is about allowing or not allowing the active behavior of the other person.	Others are allowed to develop according to their wishes and needs within healthy boundaries.	Others tend to be given too much freedom, healthy boundaries for development are too loose.	The other person can develop excessively but is also without a guiding framework due to the lack of healthy boundaries.
2 Guide others (–)	**Guide little**	**Guide very little**	**Not guide at all, avoid influencing**
The axis of interdependence is about the degree of interactional control exerted on others. DD: In contrast to (1/9), this is about actively "ordering" the other person to do something or not.	This shows a basic attitude that the other person is coping well and needs little control or guidance.	Although the other person actually needs more rules, control and guidance, they tend to be given too little.	Although the other person clearly needs clear rules, control and guidance, they are not given these at all.
3 Acknowledge others (+)	**Acknowledge friendly**	**Idealize**	**Completely overestimate**
This is about the fundamental value that is conceded to the other.	The fundamental value of the other is adequately recognized, with a tendency to praise.	The value of the other tends to be overestimated and thus idealized.	The value of the other is completely overestimated, seen in a highly distorted way as an ideal object.
4 Hold responsible (–)	**Hold responsible**	**Hold little accountable**	**Completely excuse inappropriately**
This is about the concrete guilt and responsibility that is given to another.	The other person is given an appropriate degree of responsibility for their behavior, so they may be more or less to blame in specific situations.	The other person tends to be excused, even though he or she is responsible for problematic behavior.	The other person is always excused, even if they have clearly behaved culpably on their own responsibility.
5 Show affection (+)	**Show affection**	**Overwhelm with affection**	**Stalk with love**
The axis of affiliation is about the amount of affection/love you have for the other person.	An adequate amount of affection/love is shown to the other person, a tendency towards affection.	Too much affection/love tends to be shown to the other person, which puts pressure on them.	A completely inadequate amount of affection/love is shown to the other person. This can lead to blind love or "stalking."

Table A1. Relationship item checklist *(continued)*

OPD relationship theme	Unremarkable/clinically not relevant (= 0)	Accentuated (= 1)	Dysfunctional (= 2)
6 Show aggression (–)	**Show little aggression**	**Avoid conflicts, downplay**	**Over-harmonize, ignore conflicts**
The axis of affiliation is about the extent to which appropriate aggressive behavior is shown towards others.	On the whole, a healthy level of aggressive behavior towards others is rather low.	There is inadequate aggressive behavior towards others, conflict-averse, too concerned with harmony.	Adequate aggression is not shown at all, completely exaggerated harmonization and denial of conflicts.
7 Care (+)	**Care**	**Care a lot**	**Care excessively**
It is about the extent of (im)material care that is given to the other person.	The other person receives an adequate level of care, is neither undersupplied nor oversupplied and gets what they need.	The other tends to be oversupplied.	The other is completely inadequately oversupplied, spoilt far too much.
8 Make contact (+)	**Make contact**	**Be tactless, push**	**Violate boundaries, be intrusive**
It's about the appropriate contact that is made with the other person, the right amount of distance or closeness.	Contact is made with the other person at an appropriate proximity or distance, with a tendency towards closeness.	The tendency is to get too close to the other.	Boundaries are completely ignored, there is a lack of distance and assault.
9 Give freedom (–)	**Get involved**	**Interfere**	**Constantly patronize**
The axis of interdependence is about the degree of freedom granted to the other person. DD: In contrast to (2/10), this is about allowing or not allowing the active behavior of the other person.	Others are allowed to develop according to their wishes and needs within the framework of healthy boundaries, but the boundaries are constantly being introduced.	Others tend to be given too little freedom, the boundaries for development are too tight.	The other cannot develop at all, is completely restricted in their free space.
10 Guide others (+)	**Guide appropriately**	**Guide or control a lot**	**Constantly guide or control**
The axis of interdependence is about the degree of interactional control exerted on others. DD: In contrast to (1/9), this is about actively "ordering" the other person to do something or not.	This shows a basic attitude that the other person always needs (gentle) controlling impulses or guidance in order to cope.	The other tends to receive too many rules, control and guidance, even though they doesn't actually need them (to that extent).	The other is constantly controlled, determined, receives inadequate permanent guidance ("orders").

Table A1. Relationship item checklist *(continued)*

OPD relationship theme	Unremarkable/clinically not relevant (= 0)	Accentuated (= 1)	Dysfunctional (= 2)
11 Acknowledge others (–)	**Critically acknowledge**	**Criticize a lot, question**	**Devalue, humiliate**
This is about the fundamental value that is conceded to the other.	The fundamental value of the other is adequately recognized, tendency to criticise.	The value of the other tends to be underestimated and overly criticised.	The other person's value is greatly diminished. This can take the form of direct devaluation or humiliation or the constant lack of recognition of value (e.g., when achievements are "never" seen).
12 Hold responsible (+)	**Hold responsible**	**Blame, reproach**	**Persecute with guilt accusations**
This is about the concrete guilt and responsibility that is given to another.	The other person is given an appropriate degree of responsibility for their behavior, so they may be more or less to blame in specific situations.	The other person tends to be blamed even though they have no (or little) responsibility for problematic behavior.	The other person is always blamed, even if they are clearly not at fault or responsible.
13 Show affection (–)	**Keep distance**	**Show little affection**	**Show no affection at all**
The axis of affiliation is about the amount of affection/love you have for the other person.	The other person is shown an appropriate amount of affection/love, but affection can also be shown with restraint.	The other person tends to receive less affection/love than would actually be appropriate.	The other person is treated completely unlovingly, receives no love/affection whatsoever.
14 Show aggression (+)	**Show anger**	**Meet angrily**	**Threaten, attack, harm**
The axis of affiliation here is about the extent to which inappropriate aggressive behavior is shown towards others.	Appropriate aggressive behavior/anger towards others is also shown to a healthy degree.	There is a tendency to show too much aggressive behavior towards others, expressing anger too quickly.	The other person is constantly met with manifest aggression, they are (psychologically/physically) attacked.
15 Care (–)	**Limit help**	**Deny help, abandon**	**Completely neglect**
It is about the extent of (im)material care that is given to the other person.	The other person receives an adequate level of care and is neither undersupplied, nor oversupplied. However, not every care request is catered for in the same way.	The other person tends to receive too little care and does not get (enough) of the help they need.	The other receives no care at all, their neediness is not considered at all.

Table A1. Relationship item checklist *(continued)*

OPD relationship theme	Unremarkable/clinically not relevant (= 0)	Accentuated (= 1)	Dysfunctional (= 2)
16 Make contact (–)	**Limit contact**	**Make little contact**	**Ignore others, completely overlook**
It's about the appropriate contact that is made with the other person, the right amount of distance or closeness.	It is about the extent of (im)material care that is given to the other person.	Contact with the other person tends to be too loose, inadequate and relatively distant.	There is no contact with the other person, although this would actually be appropriate.
17 Develop freely (+)	**Develop independently**	**Claim a lot of freedom or independence**	**Insist too much on independence**
The axis of interdependence is about the extent of freedom that the person claims for themselves. DD: In contrast to (18/26), this is about actively developing.	The person develops according to their wishes and needs within healthy boundaries.	The person tends to claim too much freedom and questions healthy boundaries excessively.	The person completely inadequately takes any freedom, rigidly insists on independence and disregards any healthy boundaries.
18 Submit (–)	**Assert oneself, resist**	**Often resist**	**Defy, constantly resist**
The axis of interdependence is about the extent of resistance/subordination in relation to interactional control by others. DD: In contrast to (17/25), this is about how someone reacts to control by others.	The person reacts adequately to interactional control by others, tendency to healthy resistance (resisting).	The person has a clear tendency to resist interactional control by others. Rules and guidance are questioned too much.	The person permanently and inadequately resists interactional control by others and is always defiant. Rules and guidance are not accepted at all.
19 Assert oneself (+)	**Assert oneself**	**Assert a lot**	**Constantly make oneself important, put in the center**
This is about the fundamental value that a person ascribes to themselves.	The person can adequately recognize their own value, tendency to healthy self-esteem enhancement.	The person tends to exaggerate their self-worth. In interactions, they tend to come across as arrogant.	The person exaggerates their self-worth completely inadequately and is very arrogant in interactions.
20 Acknowledge guilt (–)	**Examine own responsibility**	**Rather reject guilt**	**Not acknowledge your own guilt at all**
This is about the specific guilt and responsibility that a person ascribes to themselves.	The person attributes an adequate degree of responsibility for their behavior to themselves, so they can attribute guilt to themselves in specific situations. Tendency towards a healthy defense against guilt.	The person tends to reject their own guilt, even though they are responsible for problematic behavior.	The person always rejects guilt, even if they have clearly behaved culpably on their own responsibility.

Table A1. Relationship item checklist *(continued)*

OPD relationship theme	Unremarkable/clinically not relevant (= 0)	Accentuated (= 1)	Dysfunctional (= 2)
21 Accept affection (+)	**Accept affection**	**Accept too much affection**	**Lose oneself in others' affection**
The axis of affiliation here is about the extent to which the person engages with affection/love from others.	The person can allow adequate affection/love from others.	The person tends to rely too much on affection/love from others.	The person blindly and completely uncritically accepts the affection/love of others.
22 Protect oneself (–)	**Open up**	**Protect little**	**Put oneself in danger, not protect from aggression**
The axis of affiliation here is about how the person protects themselves from inappropriate aggression from others.	The person opens up to others if they are not aggressive.	The person tends to protect themselves too little from inappropriate aggression by others.	The person does not protect themselves from inappropriate, possibly dangerous aggression from others. The boxer has no cover, even though a punch is being thrown.
23 Lean on (+)	**Show own needs**	**Lean a lot, show neediness**	**Cling, show helplessness**
It is about the extent of (im)material care that the person claims for themselves.	The person demands adequate care for themselves. They do not want to be under- or overprovided for and demand what they are "entitled to.	The person tends to demand too much care for themselves, wants too much and is quickly disappointed if they don't get "enough".	The person claims far too much care for themselves, always appears over-needy and under-supplied.
24 Allow contact (+)	**Allow contact**	**Set few boundaries**	**Not set boundaries, allow too much**
It's about the appropriate contact that the person allows from the other person, the right amount of distance or closeness.	The person allows contact from the other person at an appropriate proximity or distance, tendency towards close-ness.	The person tends to let others get too close.	The person does not draw boundaries with others who are/can be assaultive without distance.
25 Develop freely (–)	**Develop independently**	**Avoid independence**	**Be completely dependent**
The axis of interdependence is about the extent of freedom that the person claims for themselves. DD: In contrast to (18/26), this is about actively developing.	The person develops according to their wishes and needs within healthy boundaries.	The person tends to claim too little freedom and questions problematic boundaries too little.	The person takes no freedom at all, behaves completely independently and blindly accepts problematic boundaries.

Table A1. Relationship item checklist *(continued)*

OPD relationship theme	Unremarkable/clinically not relevant (= 0)	Accentuated (= 1)	Dysfunctional (= 2)
26 Submit (+)	**Submit somewhat**	**Adapt a lot**	**Completely give up, subordinate**
The axis of interdependence is about the extent of resistance/ subordination in relation to interactional control by others. DD: In contrast to (17/25), this is about how someone reacts to control by others.	The person reacts adequately to interactional control by others, tendency to subordinate within a healthy frame-work.	The person has a clear tendency to subordinate themselves to interactional control by others. Rules and guidance are not scrutinised enough.	The person permanently and inadequately submits to interactional control by others. They follow rules and instructions without question.
27 Assert oneself (–)	**Question oneself**	**Belittle oneself**	**Devalue/hate oneself**
This is about the fundamental value that a person ascribes to them-selves.	The person can adequately recognize their own value, tendency to healthy self-criticism.	The person tends to self-deprecation. In interactions, they tend to hide their light under a bushel.	The person permanently and inadequately devalues themselves. In interactions, they always consider them-selves to be worth less than others.
28 Acknowledge guilt (+)	**Acknowledge own responsibility**	**Often blame oneself**	**Mostly take sole blame**
This is about the specific guilt and responsibility that a person ascribes to themselves.	The person attributes an adequate degree of responsibility for their behavior to themselves, so they can attribute guilt to themselves in specific situations. Tendency to recognize guilt in a healthy way.	The person tends to blame themselves, even though they have no (or little) re-sponsibility for problematic behavior.	The person constantly and inadequately blames themselves, even if they have clearly not behaved culpably and are not responsible.
29 Accept affection (–)	**Examine affection**	**Accept little affection**	**Close oneself off from affection**
The axis of affiliation is about the extent to which the person engages with affection/love from others.	The person can allow adequate affection/love from others but tests it within healthy limits.	The person tends not to accept adequate affection/love from others and tends to close themselves off from it.	The person completely shuts them-selves off from any affection/love, even if it is adequate and good.
30 Protect oneself (+)	**Protect oneself**	**Be very cautious**	**Distrust excessively, always be on guard**
The axis of affiliation is about how the person "protects" themselves from others, even though they are not aggressive in themselves.	The person can protect themselves from others if they are aggressive.	The person tends to "protect" themselves too much from others, even if they are not aggressive.	The person constantly and excessively "protects" themselves from others, even if they are not aggressive. The boxer takes cover even though no punch is expected.

Table A1. Relationship item checklist *(continued)*

OPD relationship theme	Unremarkable/clinically not relevant (= 0)	Accentuated (= 1)	Dysfunctional (= 2)
31 Lean on (–)	**Show own needs**	**Show little own needs**	**Seem completely unneedy, claim no help**
It is about the extent of (im)material care that the person claims for themselves.	The person demands adequate care for themselves. They do not want to be under- or overprovided for and can demand what they are "entitled" to.	The person tends to claim too little care for themselves and does not demand what they are "entitled" to. They are too self-sufficient.	The person claims no care for themselves at all, always showing themselves to be unneeded. They are completely overly self-sufficient.
32 Allow contact (–)	**Limit contact**	**Allow little contact**	**Completely reject contact, withdraw**
It's about the appropriate contact that the person allows from the other person, the right amount of distance or closeness.	The person allows contact from the other person at an appropriate proximity or distance, tending towards distance.	The person tends to withdraw from contact with others.	The person withdraws completely from contact with others and does not allow any closeness.

Appendix B

Manifestations of Neurotic Conflicts in Different Areas of Life

In parallel to the detailed descriptions of all items on Axis II, this Section provides a prototypical description for each conflict theme on Axis III, illustrating the manifestation of the neurotic conflict variant across the life areas of:

- family of origin;
- partnership/family;
- profession;
- social environment;
- possessions;
- body/sexuality;
- illnesses.

A prototype is the ideal, representative description of a concept. Prototypical means a description of the fundamental elements that should be significantly (though not completely) fulfilled in individual cases.

The selection of life areas presented here is primarily based on A. Dührssen's concept (Dührssen, 2010) but has been further expanded. Following the recommendations for psychodynamic/psychodynamic anamnesis, the functionality or conflict-laden nature of relationship formation in these life areas (including how one deals with their own body as an object relationship) should be actively explored.

C1: Dependency vs. Individuation in the Areas of Life

The following description (Table A2) of the "Dependency vs. Individuation" Conflict is provided for the neurotic conflict across the seven described life areas.

Table A2. Neurotic conflict Dependency vs. Individuation areas of life

Passive mode	Active mode
Family of origin	
In the early family of origin, the child's experience of not being able to detach predominates. Close and intensive relationships with the family are sought and functional developmental steps that would mean independence and detachment are avoided ("nestling").	There is a sometimes forced detachment from the family of origin from a very early age, even if this means accepting losses and disadvantages ("fleeing the nest"). The emotional significance of the primary caregivers tends to be denied and played down.
Partnership/family	
Existing partnerships must be secured and maintained at all costs. Even massive problems in the relationship are easier for patients to tolerate than the existential threat of a separation. As a result, problems may be denied, rationalized or harmonized. Even temporary distancing of the partner, e.g., when travelling on business, can hardly be endured alone or must be cushioned by other caregivers, e.g., children.	Due to their own striving for independence, relationships can only be tolerated if they guarantee sufficient emotional or temporal independence. If both partners have similar desires for independence, relationships can appear very stable for years. However, these are jeopardized if divergent aspirations are present and lead to conflicts. Conflicts may have to be "consciously" provoked again and again to keep an emotional distance.
Profession	
At work, patients seek positions that ensure proximity to colleagues. Conflicts, competition or even opportunities for advancement are avoided in order not to jeopardize this closeness. Under the possible guise of team spirit and cohesion, their own fears are concealed so that they may stay in the same job for a long time, even in times of crisis.	At work, independence must be secured at all costs. Under certain circumstances, opportunities for advancement are also avoided if they would require greater proximity to colleagues. People tend to look for jobs that favor "lone riders." Even in teams, independent and self-determined positions are sought, which can lead to conflicts.
Social environment	
In the social environment, groups that traditionally emphasize their own cohesion and/or a strong ideological background are preferred. The feeling of belonging, of being part of the community and an overly strong identification with the group are at the center of the experience. A great deal is invested in preserving these basic principles to prevent the group from breaking apart.	Group membership or close social contacts are avoided; non-binding contacts are favored. As a rule, social obligations or norms tend to be avoided. In situations with a predetermined distance, e.g., via the anonymity of the internet, some of the averted longings for closeness can be actively acted out, but only in these safe, because distanced, conditions.
Possessions	
Money and possessions are used to maintain emotional closeness. This can either be dispensed with or deliberately used to prevent distancing.	A sufficient economic basis ensures independence from other people. Financial obligations are avoided as they can create dependencies. In extreme cases, a lack of possessions can also be strived for as an ideal of complete independence.

Table A2. Neurotic conflict Dependency vs. Individuation areas of life *(continued)*

Passive mode	Active mode
Body/sexuality	
The needs of one's own body are often neglected to maintain closeness in relationships. Physical restrictions can also be used to ensure closeness ("I am dependent on you"). Sexuality may be functionalized to ensure closeness.	Physical needs are generally ignored, and physical performance is cultivated as the ideal image of independence. The physical limitations that occur with age must be negated or can be concealed in an "exaggerated" youthfulness and fitness but can also be the basis for the development of symptoms if this is no longer possible. Sexuality tends to be lived in an attachment-free manner or avoided.
Illnesses	
Illnesses offer a good opportunity to live out dependency to a greater extent. If this is not sufficiently successful in the primary circle of relationships, close and "loyal" relationships with the medical support system can be sought. To avoid a feared detachment from the doctor who provides security, treatment attempts may also be boycotted to remain in the stable sick role.	Illness represents a strong threat to one's own independence and is therefore ignored/denied and or fought at all costs. Medical treatments and the obligations and closeness they entail are avoided or undermined. This can lead to poor compliance. The doctor-patient relationship tends to remain distant and factual. It is not uncommon for patients to be overlooked in their neediness.

C2: Submission vs. Control in the Areas of Life

The following description (Table A3) of the "Submission vs. Control" Conflict is given for the neurotic conflict across the seven areas of life described.

Table A3. Neurotic conflict Submission vs. Control areas of life

Passive mode	Active mode
Family of origin	
The predominant basic attitude is to allow oneself to be taken along and led in decisions and, despite discomfort, to be satisfied overall with a lower experience of one's own self-efficacy. Hierarchically structured relationships within the family are also accepted into adulthood. This also applies to any family relationships that continue over generations, which are defined by obligations and tasks that people do not dare to question. A tense subordination to any older siblings, primary objects experienced as dominant or other important reference persons in the primary family can be observed. Reactive, possibly dawdling or occasionally refusing behavior, e.g., also in school/professional contexts. Relationship episodes in which rebellious behavior would be understandable are considerably less detectable or absent altogether. The less integrated the structure is, the more likely it is that constant chasing or asking, e.g., from parents, appears superficially as fear, but is motivated by excessive conformity to actual or perceived demands. Submission can then be perceived as "essential for survival."	The person concerned usually takes the initiative (e.g., in everyday decisions: "This is how it's done;" "Dinner is at ...," but also in games: "I only play when ..."). This leads to frequent conflicts that cannot always be reconciled. In adulthood, the person concerned may not be too happy to be involved in planning, as they are perceived as being relatively dominant throughout. There is a tendency to assert oneself over the people in the family of origin at all costs and to determine interactional events as far as possible. Rigid rules that prevail across generations are enforced. Under certain circumstances, the exercise of power is rationalized through arguments of care. In the event of (cross-generational) tensions, relationships can also break down radically with violent expressions of anger ("I won't be told what to do!"). Balancing interests appears to be much more difficult, as it is difficult for those affected to categorize them appropriately. To ward off feelings of powerlessness, attempts are made to gain and maintain control over the family members almost "at any cost." This can sometimes lead to abrupt movements of liberation by such "controlled" objects, which in turn can be met with massive outbursts of anger and even violence.
Partnership/family	
On the surface, the people concerned appear modest in their partnership and seem content with their subordinate position. Resistance is expressed indirectly through hesitation, dawdling, stubbornness, etc. and is often largely unconscious. This behavior is perceived as resistance by social partners, which can result in anger.	Complementary partners are sought. Derived from the family of origin, a "dictatorial power" is assumed and re-enacted, for example, through rigid rules. The partnership is used to express power (authoritarian control). This can go as far as the violent enforcement of claims to power, to which the relationship partner must submit.
Profession	
Despite possible opportunities for advancement, subordinate positions are maintained; independence and decisions are avoided in order not to have to determine/control. Requirements can also be passively undermined by carrying out work too precisely and very slowly. In the mixed, predominantly passive mode, the position of the "typical successful second" is also conceivable. Subordination can go as far as complete exploitation of the person concerned.	In the hierarchy, people strive for leading positions (to be able to control; "power") or positions with a high degree of independence (in order not to have to categorize/subordinate themselves). This can also be found in freelance work or in "niches" of self-determination. The management style is often experienced by others as "overbearing." Even constructive criticism or suggestions from others (in the sense of professional authority) are misinterpreted as a threat to one's own self-efficacy. The desire to dominate can escalate into an extreme desire for power that does not tolerate any contradiction.

Table A3. Neurotic conflict Submission vs. Control areas of life *(continued)*

Passive mode	Active mode
Social environment	
A subordinate position is assumed in the neighborhood, community, clubs and friendship groups. This can go as far as complete submission to group norms. Via these "diversions," the person concerned can then "reconnect to power" via the group and its leaders.	Social groups, clubs and friends are assessed in terms of whether they serve to increase or exercise power and influence. A loss of control is experienced as very unpleasant. Claims to power and dominance by others in the group can be experienced as a threatening risk of losing one's own power.
Possessions	
Although possessions and money play a central role in life, there is a seemingly docile willingness to give them away. Sometimes this relates to a defined part of the possessions, while a "core area" is extremely guarded to reduce anxiety and maintain self-efficacy.	Property and money are seen as important means of power to realize one's own ideas: "Money is power; Others will do anything for me for money!" The less well-off can be ruthlessly pushed to the side as "have-nots."
Body/sexuality	
The person concerned has the feeling that they are at the mercy of their body. The body does what it wants with them. Medical instructions must be followed exactly. A possible critical distance to this is at best possible through passive refusal ("forgetting the medication"). Submission ("drooping shoulders") can also be communicated non-verbally via body language. There is a tendency to submit to the sexual demands of others or to unconsciously refuse them, for example through "dysfunction" or "discomfort/ displeasure."	One's own body and sexuality must "function" according to one's own ideas (control). The body is therefore an object on which power is exercised to the point of self-exploitation. The body can also be used to exercise power over others. Physical training is primarily aimed at mastering one's own body and overcoming the "inner bastard."
Illnesses	
Illness is seen as a fate to which one must submit and surrender. In the doctor-patient relationship, docility predominates, but orders and agreed co-operation in treatment can also be passively undermined. In the case of severe illnesses, these patients can suffer considerable side effects during treatment without consulting a doctor. As the patient did not have the courage to contact the doctor earlier ("I thought everything was so right!"), secondary accusations are then levelled at the doctor who prescribed this medication and thus "caused" the side effect. This can escalate to the feeling that they are just a "guinea pig" for the medicine.	The "fight against the illness" is fought with all means at their disposal according to the motto: "I won't let it get me down" and "I mustn't be weak." Beyond a fundamentally positive, active approach to coping with the disease, the patient's doggedness leads to inflexibility. Relapses and setbacks can be difficult or even impossible to bear. The doctor-patient relationship can be colored by disputes over the right to "self-determination". The power struggle can also be directed against the hospital or the institution. In the case of serious illnesses, defiant reactions ("Now more than ever!") can develop against the threat of loss of control.

C3: In Need of Care vs. Self-Sufficiency in the Areas of Life

The following description (Table A4) of the conflict "In Need of Care vs. Self-Sufficiency" is given for the neurotic conflict across the seven areas of life described.

Table A4. Neurotic conflict In Need of Care vs. Self-Sufficiency areas of life

Passive mode	Active mode
Family of origin	
The pronounced striving for care can lead to young adults remaining in the close family circle for too long and too loyal, e.g., also in their free time, to maintain the previously secure care and security of the family. The delayed separation from the family is justified by a variety of necessities. The problem is largely not recognized. Remaining in the family can sometimes even occur across generational boundaries.	The pronounced striving for self-sufficiency can lead on the one hand to an early separation from the family of origin ("fleeing the nest") or on the other hand to selfless care and concern for parents or relatives, possibly even to the point of self-sacrificing care, to experience further care and security within the family as part of an altruistic cession. Possible relief is excluded or warded off by rationalization.
Partnership/family	
The pronounced desire to provide can lead to their own needs for care and security dominating the partnership, resulting in considerable closeness in the relationship, which is usually rationalized. Since "you" are dependent on each other, separation from your partner seems impossible. Even the partner's own separation fantasies or efforts to distance themselves can lead to violent accusations and even outbursts of anger towards the partner but can also trigger depressive episodes. This can reactively intensify the need to cling. The partners react to this overprotective, demanding relationship, which is often experienced as "blackmailing", either over-protectively or latently defensively and aggressively. If the partner also has a strong desire for care and security, symptoms can develop on both sides that mutually justify the right or obligation to care for the other.	The pronounced striving for self-sufficiency can lead to a strong denial of one's own desire for care and security in the partnership, possibly even completely. In the partnership, the person concerned is particularly self-sufficient and self-sacrificing for the other person, whereby the unconscious desire for future retribution for the other person always remains noticeable. In order to always "be there" for the other person, a particularly close relationship can be constellated, whereby the partner must allow themselves to be cared for. If the partner also has a strong desire for self-sufficiency, symptoms can develop on both sides.
Profession	
The pronounced desire to provide can lead to those affected seeking work situations that provide support and a sense of security. Those affected always look for allies and helpers, avoid independent decisions and often even endeavor to climb the social ladder so as not to jeopardize their social security. They therefore often fall well short of their potential. Demands on them can be experienced as a loss of support and responded to with dejection and/or refusal.	The pronounced striving for self-sufficiency can lead to the person appearing at work as an irreplaceable, self-sacrificing and hard-working employee who does not spare themselves. However, they also expect constant goodwill in return. If this reward is not forthcoming, there is a risk of considerable dejection and even deep self-doubt. In an increasingly unbounded world of work, the people concerned are at considerable risk to their health and especially their mental health (e.g., burn-out) due to their constant professional self-exploitation.

Table A4. Neurotic conflict In Need for Care vs. Self-Sufficiency areas of life *(continued)*

Passive mode	Active mode
Social environment	
The pronounced striving to provide can lead to the person concerned becoming socially withdrawn and focusing on a few close, caring and emotionally secure relationships. They are often perceived by others as demanding and exhausting because they often only express their care needs indirectly in the social sphere and their resulting noticeable disappointment is experienced by others as a reproach.	The pronounced striving for self-sufficiency can lead to the person concerned being more socially orientated towards relationships that care for others. Social commitment is often done in the service of altruistic fulfilment. This is often accompanied by envy of those being cared for. Those affected often do not receive the attention and appreciation they deserve for their commitment but are instead exploited. A loss of control is experienced as very unpleasant. Claims to power and dominance by others in the group can be experienced as a threatening risk of losing one's own power.
Possessions	
The pronounced desire to provide can lead to the person concerned also experiencing their possessions as being cared for and secure. They must therefore be protected and defended and any "giving away" must be avoided with fear. Both things and people are "owned" or taken possession of. However, just like all allowances, all possessions are never enough to provide a lasting feeling of being cared for and protected, resulting in a hunger for more possessions.	The pronounced striving for self-sufficiency can lead to those affected also dealing selflessly with their possessions, although self-sacrifice often contains a component of unconscious calculation. Despite sometimes considerable material disadvantages, the anger over the loss is usually rationalized to maintain the caring-altruistic pattern.
Body/sexuality	
The pronounced striving for care can lead to the person concerned communicating their emotional care and attention needs to others via the special needs of their own body: "My body needs ..." Their own body is thus a constant source of caring attention, primarily from others, while the person concerned often does not give it much real self-care. The body is primarily cared for with food, addictive substances, etc. Sexuality can be lived as a way of being cared for, which can be functionalized to the point of "sex hunger."	On the one hand, the pronounced striving for self-sufficiency can lead to the person concerned taking excessive care of their body, insofar as they make it an object, just like everything else, but not necessarily giving it adequate care. On the other hand, it can lead to them not perceiving their body with its needs, signals and limits appropriately, but as something that merely has to "function". Constantly overstepping physical boundaries can be dangerous to health. Sexuality can also be lived in the sense of caring primarily for others, while putting one's own needs aside.
Illnesses	
The pronounced striving for care can lead to a tendency for those affected to regress in the event of illness to demand even more care and attention. In their passive, clinging expectations of doctors, therapists and carers, those affected by their excessive needs are often experienced as "exhausting" and "troublesome" and sometimes trigger intense anger. It is usually difficult to promote an active-rehabilitative approach to the illness. A secondary gain from the illness is often sought directly (e.g., pension), whereby the claim is subjectively experienced as completely justified due to the illness.	On the one hand, the pronounced striving for self-sufficiency can lead to the person concerned acting inadequately independently and being insufficiently able to accept help and support in their role as a patient. At the same time, however, the unconscious need for care often manifests itself in dissatisfaction with the actual care or in that other patients in the clinic are often given demonstrative and altruistic assistance, as a kind of unconscious criticism of the care provided by the clinic or its staff. As a result, they sometimes cause severe anger among doctors, therapists and caregivers.

C4: Self-Worth Conflict in the Areas of Life

The following description (Table A5) of the conflict "Self-Worth" is given for the neurotic conflict across the seven areas of life described.

Table A5. Neurotic conflict Self-Worth areas of life

Passive mode	Active mode
Family of origin	
In the family tradition, the negative self-image is often passed down through the generations. People are often the bearers of compensatory expectations, whereby despite their own efforts and endeavors, the myth of being set back and their own inferiority persists. Alternatively, the person may tend to constantly devalue themselves against the background of overvalued achievements of their family of origin that they could never achieve.	The narrative about the family of origin is used to boost self-esteem. Either the family of origin and one's own biography are highly idealized, the person feels like a worthy offspring of the family, experiences the family's mission to be something special and is proud of it. Alternatively, humble origins may be barely mentioned, trivialized or denied to the point of oblivion.
Partnership/family	
In relationships and partnerships, it is not uncommon for such people to form strong bonds with partners in which a history of slights, humiliations and other burdens that are problematic for self-esteem, particularly in the field of social prestige, are dealt with together. The partnership is stabilized through the shared feeling of "always being disadvantaged" and the demarcation from others who seem to have it better. Alternatively, people can look for an idealized partner in whose "sun" they can stabilize themselves.	Relationships and the choice of partner serve to stabilize self-esteem and are designed in such a way that one is admired ("we are something special") or the partner is so admirable (in the hope of being enhanced by them). Constantly devaluing your partner can also serve to enhance your own self-esteem ("I don't know why I put up with someone like that").
Profession	
Some people show a pronounced willingness to work and perform at work to receive recognition as compensation for offences. Due to the increased vulnerability that lies behind this when the commitment is not honored, the onset of symptoms is often directly linked to professional setbacks or insults. Some people are more likely to show a refusal to work and perform, which coincides with their self-image ("I can't do it anyway!").	At work, there is a tendency to overestimate one's own position and performance and therefore strive for ever higher positions, which can lead to failure. Alternatively, problems in the workplace and deficits in one's own performance can be denied or blamed on others. The real professional positions are sometimes not good because people can be prone to relationship breakdowns and loss of performance or symptom formation due to their vulnerability.
Social environment	
They tend to seek subordinate positions in social groups, either with real or perceived disadvantaged people. However, people often withdraw in resignation at an early stage and only rely on themselves or a few trusted people. New social experiences tend to be avoided.	Social groupings or contacts with celebrities or well-known personalities are particularly sought after ("I belong to the elite"). People also often must actively distance themselves from supposed "failures" for fear of the "rubbing off" of others' shortcomings.

Table A5. Neurotic conflict Self-Worth areas of life *(continued)*

Passive mode	Active mode
Possessions	
The lack or possible presence of possessions, a home and the like can be experienced as inferior to that of others or unconsciously compensate for the feeling of inferiority. They do not provide a basis for narcissistic satisfaction but often confirm the subjective feeling of being worthless.	Possessions and money serve as representative attributes for self-affirmation ("I've made it") or external image ("wealth fetishes"). However, these attributes may be more present in the person's desires and fantasies than available.
Body/sexuality	
People experience their own body as inferior, which often leads to it being neglected ("The body gets what it deserves"). Alternatively, frustrating, sometimes repeated attempts to correct different parts of the body with the help of surgical procedures can serve to enhance their own self-image ("If only my nose was straight, then ..."). These people are predominantly convinced of their own (also sexual) unattractiveness.	When dealing with the body, there is a strong tendency to make it appear young, beautiful and attractive to compensate for supposed or possibly real weaknesses. In connection with sport, body worship and other phenomena, there are indications of a fantasized physical invulnerability and a pronounced libidinous preoccupation with the body. Ageing regularly leads to problems and attempts to compensate. One's own sexual potency/attractiveness is overemphasized as a tonic for self-esteem.
Illnesses	
Illnesses or the relationship with doctors often confirm the deficient self-perception ("No wonder this is happening to me!"; "I'm not worthy of your treatment"). The symptom can be ascribed a self-esteem-threatening effect (I am no longer worth anything) that goes far beyond the clinically comprehensible extent. Consequently, life can be "organized" around the illness and the inferiority experienced as a result.	Illnesses, even trivial ones, threaten self-esteem and can lead to a breakdown. In any case, they require strong defense and compensation efforts, far beyond the actual cause. The symptom can be ascribed to a self-esteem stabilizing effect that goes far beyond the clinically comprehensible extent and this can serve as an explanation for the real or imagined failure in other areas of life ("Without the pain I would be the boss today"; "What could I have achieved if I hadn't become ill ...") (so-called narcissistic seal). Dealing with the symptom/illness can also have a stabilizing effect on self-esteem (the "admirable" way of coping with the illness, the "very special" illness).

C5: Guilt Conflict in the Areas of Life

The following description (Table A6) of the conflict "Guilt" is given for the neurotic conflict across the seven areas of life described.

Table A6. Neurotic conflict Guilt areas of life

Passive mode	Active mode
Family of origin	
In the family, the blame for internal and external problems and difficulties is quickly assumed or assigned within the family (black sheep). There is a fundamental family attitude of selflessness with underlying feelings of envy and strongly moralizing aggression. Guilt is often compensated for by self-generated or assumed punishment. The severity of this (self-)punishment often bears witness to suppressed anger and resentment.	There is an attitude in the family– which also affects relatives – that "personal benefit is the most important thing!" Feelings of guilt are suppressed and shifted onto others (usually outsiders). Family of origin and generational conflicts are usually judged and portrayed from the point of view of self-righteousness.
Partnership/family	
There is a tendency to take the blame and excuse the partner and the children, to accuse oneself or even to create situations in which one continues to appear the guilty party. At the same time, there is often a moralizing, aggressive attitude towards selfish tendencies in the family and partnership, or selfish tendencies are delegated "you are allowed to do what I am not allowed to do."	Selfish and possessive behavior towards the partner and children is justified and guilt is hardly ever acknowledged; if it is, then there is usually an immediate qualification (yes, but ...). The blame is sought from partners and children and is literally collected in the context of "bookkeeping."
Profession	
Social advancement and career success often lead to "feelings of guilt" (taking something away from the other person) and result in symptoms or a return to the old position. There is a tendency to seek and accept blame for the mistakes of others. Adequate financial compensation is often not demanded, and work is done "below value."	Overbearing egotistical behavior is associated with a defense against feelings of guilt. In extreme cases, it can lead to inconsiderate, boundary-crossing, exploitative behavior towards others. Own misbehavior and performance problems are attributed to the guilt of others. Accounts of guilt are collected and held against colleagues. Envy is a common feeling. Material favors are aggressively demanded.
Social environment	
Social commitment is pronounced, and groups are favored in which guilt can be "worked off". However, people who do not belong to their own social groups are left out. Due to their prosocial commitment, there is a risk of being abused by others for their own benefit, and often even despised.	While avoiding feelings of guilt, there is a tendency to take social advantage and even to exploit other people – often on the borderline of legality ("It's not my fault!"). The blame for one's own selfish tendencies is attributed to the social environment.
Possessions	
Giving and taking as well as possession are conflictual ("Am I even entitled to this in comparison to others?"). A guilty conscience leads to the obligation to repay immediately and to keep one's own debt account "low."	The accumulation of possessions and selfish behavior is perceived as justified and necessary. However, possessions are always too few. People try to own more than others and trick others, constantly looking for bargains ("Stinginess is cool!"). Nevertheless, there is a tendency to often feel taken advantage of, disadvantaged or cheated ("It's their fault!").

Table A6. Neurotic conflict Guilt areas of life *(continued)*

Passive mode	Active mode
Body/sexuality	
Dealing with the body and its needs – including sexuality – is problematic in a guilt-ridden or normative community ideology. Depending on the cultural background, physical needs – especially sexual ones – can trigger feelings of guilt and even efforts to atone. Basic physical needs are often disregarded ("My body and I do not deserve this"). Bad health behavior is often the result.	One's own body is often exploited, as one's own responsibility is denied and projected ("The tobacco industry is to blame for my nicotine addiction!"). The body can also be greedily lavished with material things (e.g., food). Sexuality is usually something that one is entitled to guilt-free; for transgressive sexual behavior and exploitation, others are blamed.
Illnesses	
Illnesses are often seen because of one's own misbehavior, as guilt or even as punishment. Medical interventions are endured and rarely complained about, dissatisfaction is rarely expressed. Inadequacies in treatment are trivialized. In the doctor-patient relationship, orders are complied with docilely so as not to provoke criticism or reprimands. In hospitals, these people tend to be "easy to care for" and apologize for the work they cause the staff.	Illnesses are usually the responsibility of others, and too little is often done for the person affected ("Others get much more!"). Doctors are often blamed, while their own misconduct or health-damaging behavior is trivialized and denied. It goes without saying that rights are also claimed to the detriment of other patients.

C6: Oedipal Conflict in the Areas of Life

The following description (Table A7) of the "Oedipal" conflict is given for the neurotic conflict across the seven areas of life described.

Table A7. Neurotic Oedipal conflict areas of life

Passive mode	Active mode
Family of origin	
The relationship with a primary caregiver is often idealized in a "childlike" way and eroticized, while at the same time the other real or imagined caregiver is marginalized. The family history seems grey and not very lively, family conflicts and (sibling) rivalries are suppressed, sexuality is taboo.	There are often highly emotionalized relationships in the family, usually with special attention and recognition of the opposite-sex parent. The patient usually carries the role of one parent's "favorite" into adulthood or constantly fights for it. There is fierce rivalry in sibling relationships.
Partnership/family	
In the most stable partner relationships, the appreciative, rivalrous and erotic area is often left out (extreme: so-called Mary/Joseph marriage), instead it is mostly about protection and security. As a result, older partners are often chosen. These often resemble the preferred primary caregiver. Crises can arise in old age with the feeling of "not having lived"; on the other hand, old age can serve as protection (I do not need that anymore.	In relationships, too, there is constant staging to gain attention and recognition. The theatrical-emotional or contradictory sexual behavior (lure-block, triangular relationships) causes a lot of suffering for everyone involved. As the choice of partner is usually orientated towards the primary objects, the partner is often experienced as inadequate ("doesn't come close to mother"). Crisis-like developments occur because of the adjustments required by advancing age, which are hardly compatible with the active mode (e.g., "Lolita" or "the party girl" becomes a mother, "Don Juan" becomes a father).
Profession	
Rivalry is also avoided in working life. As a result, relationships are usually inconspicuous and often good, but in which personal, especially interpersonal skills are not practiced. As a result, they tend to occupy subordinate positions.	Professional recognition and attention are sought through staging, sometimes eroticizing behavior rather than through consistent performance. Excessive seductive competition puts a strain on the professional situation. This leads to frequently changing professional constellations and positions.
Social environment	
In social groups, stable, inconspicuous relationships are favored that put aside or avoid the rivalry-sexual moment (harmonious, sibling-like relationship; "tuck tail"). This can mean that these people are sometimes not unpopular, but do not make an impression.	Social groups, clubs and friends are used in the service of their own seductive staging and may be changed quickly. Relationships are often judged to be more personal than they are. There are also triangular destructive constellations in which the desire to destroy other people's relationships is the predominant motive.
Possessions	
On the surface, people avoid using possessions in the service of their own attractiveness and rivalry. Nevertheless, it can serve as a silent and unconscious substitute.	Possessions and money are used to seduce and be the center of attention, to rival and gain recognition. Accordingly, it must be a particularly conspicuous house, car, clothes, fashion, etc., whereby the things are interchangeable depending on the situation and often no inner attachment to them can be felt ("props" for the seductive staging).

Table A7. Neurotic Oedipal conflict areas of life *(continued)*

Passive mode	Active mode
Body/sexuality	
Little attention is paid to physicality and physical appearance without neglecting its care. Attempts are even made to disguise, hide or conceal possible attractiveness, sexuality and rivalry in order to omit recognizably rivalrous and erotic areas. This problem can persist into old age, whereby the renunciation of physicality is then justified by "age" ("At my age, you don't need that anymore!"). In extreme cases, there is sexual disinterest.	The body or parts of it are used to gain recognition and compete seductively. As a result, it is given an enormous amount of attention, it is lustfully and sometimes provocatively "dressed up" and "put on show." The limits or loss of physical attractiveness (e.g., in old age) therefore represent a major threat and may be overplayed to the point of caricature ("young at any price"). There is a pronounced interest in sexuality but often limited sexual satisfaction.
Illnesses	
Complaints and suffering offer an unconscious opportunity to gain the Oedipal attention and recognition that has been warded off. In the illness, people appear weak and pseudo-regressive, sometimes seeking therapeutic procedures that serve as a silent substitute for recognition or sexual satisfaction.	Illnesses can be used with a dramatic effect that captivates everyone to receive oedipal attention and care. At the same time, however, no healthcare provider is really in a position to fulfil these needs, so that new experts must always be sought. The doctor-patient relationship is also often erotically charged or sexualized ("in love with the doctor").

C7: Identity Conflict in the Areas of Life

The following description (Table A8) of the conflict "Identity" is given for the neurotic conflict across the seven areas of life described.

Table A8. Neurotic conflict Identity areas of life

Passive mode	Active mode
Family of origin	
The family identity appears colorless, dull or visibly broken. There were few attractive and supporting roles for which identification would have been possible. The entire family is told of unclear or contradictory identities, for example the father may have been a successful businessman, a broke bankrupt and a humiliated welfare recipient all at the same time ("Everything without meaning"). In their social environment, these people often appear to be chameleons because of their search for meaning and avoidance of identity, but at the same time appear rather colorless. This is presumably why they are not respected very much. They also make great efforts to adapt culturally in order to "fit in." This can involve adopting a wide variety of identities, including negative ones. First and second-generation migrants often find themselves in (unconscious) conflict between their family culture and their social and cultural identifications. There is often a dissonance (conflict) between a traditional, patriarchal, sometimes religiously interpreted, family-centered sense and style of life on the one hand and a Western, individualistic sense and style of life on the other. ("I don't know whether I'm Turkish or German, I'm something in between. I don't feel comfortable in Turkey, I don't feel comfortable here. I need a Turkish-Germany or something like that," Habermas & Reese, 2015, p. 50).	Identity contradictions in the family sphere are glossed over and denied. The history of the family is often idealized. With a family of origin that is often experienced as meaningless, the unconscious desire to set oneself apart, to rise, to start anew dominates. Group affiliations are sought and cultivated for their meaning and identity-creating function ("We punks!"). These compensatory endeavors usually lead to exaggeration. First and second-generation migrants often find themselves in (unconscious) conflict between their family culture and the social and cultural identifications of meaning. There is often a dissonance (conflict) between a traditional, patriarchal, sometimes religiously interpreted, family-centered sense and style of life on the one hand and a Western, individualistic sense and style of life on the other. There is either a forced adoption of the traditional lifestyle ("I only follow the rules of my religion and the commandments of my family, that's me and that's my purpose, I don't want anything else") or, on the other hand, the forced adoption of a group (gang) identity ("We, the motorbike gang").
Partnership/family	
On the one hand, partners are sought who can be identity-forming; in this case, the person often subordinates his or her identity to that of the partner in complete alignment. On the other hand, precisely such partners can be avoided as people in order not to feel the discrepancy between their own identity insecurity and the security of their partner. With partners who also have identity insecurity, there are constant "as-if constructions" in which the meaning of life and identities alternate and thus become conflictual.	As a rule, partners, relationships and families are sought who can support the patient in the area of their dissonant identity and, in favorable cases, lead to long-term stable solutions. However, this forced acceptance of a new sense of life and identity can also lead to maladjustments and further intense conflicts.

Table A8. Neurotic conflict Identity areas of life *(continued)*

Passive mode	Active mode
Profession	
They often appear unreal and/or unstable in their professional roles and functions. Sometimes they try out many roles and positions without inner satisfaction and a lack of purpose. To be successful, they lack inner consistency and role security.	The world of work takes on a role that creates meaning and identity ("My job is me"). Other interests and areas are faded out and suppressed. This leads to the impression of an overvalued idea. The necessary factual reference and task-orientation take a back seat to the relationship with one's own person and identity.
Possessions	
Possessions can serve to replace the sense of security that is lacking in identity ("having instead of being"). Nevertheless, these people often know little about what to do with the money they earn ("No interests, what should I do?").	Ownership serves to stabilize one's own identity ("My alternative energy house ...", "My car ...," "My red wine collection ..."). Ownership is sought because of the identity-forming function. This must be distinguished from (narcissistic) self-esteem.
Body/sexuality	
Colorlessness and helplessness in relation to their own identity lead to an indifferent approach to body and clothing. Biographical and cultural coincidences shape the external image ("Everyone wears jeans, but I don't care what I wear"). There are often changing orientations, also about outward appearance ("You have to go with every fashion."). This indicates a rather passive identity. Sexual body identity (man vs. woman) is often uncertain or avoided. This also applies to sexual orientation. People generally adapt to partners with a strong sexual identity and orientation.	Dealing with one's own body/clothing can have an identity-forming function. Clothing has always established identity and camouflaged the insecure ("Clothes make the man!"). Uniforms, traditional costumes and branded products ("We ...") stabilize identity just as much as appropriate grooming (complete shave) or physical signs such as tattoos. The active mode is characterized by fixed emphasis, which leads to limited choice and (over)adaptation. Insecurities in a gender role are overcompensated for ("My body has to be that of a superwoman.") and sexual identities are expanded and defended to the point of aggression ("I'm straight and I hate homos!"). Body and sexuality are overly meaningful ("Sex is my goal in life").
Illnesses	
Due to role insecurity and passivity, it is difficult for patients to find and accept a new, adequate patient role on their own when they become ill. They avoid confrontation and are usually passively adapted, but helpless.	Patients tend to actively shape their sick role; if they were nothing before, they are now – sick! On the other hand, there is the enforced refusal of the sick role because it cannot harmonize with the patient's ideas of their own identity ("They can't put me in bed!").

C0: Repressed Conflict and Emotion Awareness

The following is a description (Table A9) of "Repressed Conflict and Emotion Awareness" at a neurotic level across the seven life domains.

Table A9. Repressed Conflict and Emotion Awareness areas of life

Family of origin
The relationships are portrayed in a uniform, unemotional, matter of fact and "unproblematic" manner, even when difficult circumstances prevail in reality. Dealing with each other is characterized by objectivity and conventions. Conspicuous intergenerational conflicts are either negated or people try to resolve them on a rational level. Separation from or remaining in the family of origin appears to be a matter of course and without friction.
Partnership/family
Normality and functionality of family life take center stage. Changes in relationships and, above all, separations are reported as facts. Obvious problems and conflicts are negated or rationalized.
Profession
In working life, these people often look for professions with a pronounced functional orientation. They can achieve above-average success if their relationships with other people are functionally organized. They are valued by colleagues and superiors for their competence and factual orientation. However, as they do not adequately recognize emotions in relationships, they occasionally get into conflicts that are incomprehensible to them.
Social environment
These people also organize their social life in a purely factual way, avoiding emotional and conflictual areas.
Possessions
Dealing with possessions seems rational and factual. There is often a noticeably more emotional relationship with material things than with living objects.
Body/sexuality
People deal with their own bodies in a matter of fact, rational way. The body should function like a machine. Emotional, pleasurable physicality is often made difficult, but sexuality is important as an expression of normality. The emotional significance of change and ageing processes is denied.
Illnesses
Illnesses are experienced as a fateful event without much emotional involvement or as a problem to be solved technically. Although the patients support the doctors' "repair efforts" in their experience, the emotional denial can lead to insufficient compliance. These people are rather difficult to motivate to undergo psychosocial-psychotherapeutic treatment measures.

Appendix C

Short Checklist for Axis IV Structure

The following is a condensed description of the operationalizations of the individual structural facets, omitting the description of the intermediate stages:

- *Self-perception* (Table A10): The subdimension self-perception contains the facets self-reflection, affect differentiation, and identity.
- *Object perception* (Table A11): The subdimension object perception contains the facets self-object differentiation, object-related affect differentiation, and integrated object perception.
- *Self-regulation* (Table A12): The subdimension impulse control contains the facets impulse control, affect tolerance, and self-esteem regulation.
- *Relationship regulation* (Table A13): The subdimension relationship regulation contains the facets protecting relationships, anticipation, and balancing of interests.
- *Defense* (Table A14): The subdimension defense contains the facets possibilities of experience, interpersonality, and mechanisms.
- *Internal communication* (Table A15): The subdimension internal communication contains the facets experience of affects and fantasies, pleasure experience, and bodily self.
- *Communication with the external world* (Table A16): The subdimension communication with the external world contains the facets making emotional contact, intimacy, and empathy.
- *Attachment to internal objects* (Table A17): The subdimension attachment to internal objects contains the facets internalization, use of introjects, and variability.
- *Attachment to external objects* (Table A18): The subdimension attachment to external objects contains the facets ability to form attachments, trust, and ability to separate.

Table A10. Self-perception

	1 Good	2 Moderate	3 Low	4 Disintegrated
1.1 Self-reflection	It is possible to realistically recognize what kind of person one is and what is going on inside one-self. This can be conceptualized. Feedback from others is considered in an appropriate manner.	The ability to self-reflect is limited. It is primarily focused on the acting self. It is difficult to find appropriate linguistic terms. Feedback causes offence, lack of understanding, or withdrawal.	Self-reflective perception is hardly possible; even with support, the person cannot create a coherent picture of themselves and their inner situation; contradictory aspects of the self are juxtaposed. No terms for inner processes. Critical feedback leads to self-deprecation, uncritical acceptance, or is rejected.	Attempts at self-reflection are avoided or can lead to affective overload. There is no coherence of the self. The inner and outer world cannot be distinguished, the self can no longer be recognized as distinct. Feedback comes to nothing or reinforces the fragmentation of the self.
1.2 Affect differenti-ation	Affects can be perceived in a differentiated way and have great variability. Contradictory affects can be integrated, i.e., they can be perceived in their ambivalence. Affects can be understood within the context and situational aspects.	Affects are only perceived to a limited extent and are also avoided in difficult situations to maintain stability. The variability of affects and the experience of ambivalent affects are limited. Contexts of experience are difficult to understand.	Affects cannot be perceived in a differentiated way or named in a comprehensible way. Affects are experienced as undifferentiated states. Mixed affects rarely occur; excitement, alienation, or affectlessness. Affects can hardly be understood situationally and used for targeted behavior control.	No inner distance to one's own feelings and no reflexive perception of affects and affect correlates. Affects express themselves as somatic arousal, unnamable agony or can be completely erased, not experienced at all, or experienced completely inadequately and/or only appear externalized in the outside world. No situationally appropriate emotional response is possible.
1.3 Identity	The self-image is multi-faceted and a coherent picture of oneself can be created. Contradictory aspects of the self can be experienced cognitively and affectively and can be endured well. The self-image is stable, i.e., it combines biographical origins and the future.	The self-image is coherent, but narrowed and rigid, with only limited "shades of grey". Conflicting aspects can be faded out. The self-image is stable, but can be called into question due to conflict. There is a connection between the past and the future.	No coherent image of oneself. Different aspects of the self stand side by side, unconnected and reduced in their complexity. Different aspects of the self come to the fore at different times. It remains unclear what behavior and experiences have arisen from and how they will develop in the future.	Lack of a coherent self-image. Instead, fragmentation, distorted or clichéd attributions of characteris-tics. Identity can be accommodated in substitute formations. Biographical descriptions appear fantasy-led. Future plans are non-existent or seem absurd.

Table A11. Object perception

	1 Good	2 Moderate	3 Low	4 Disintegrated
1.4 Self-object differentiation	Affects, impulses and thoughts can be reliably differentiated regarding their assignment to the self or to objects; the person can reliably differentiate themselves and perceive the other from the outside. Others are experienced as people with their own wishes and goals.	In the area of conflict, the allocation of affects, impulses and thoughts in relation to the self and objects is impaired. The distanced perception of others is permanently impaired. Sometimes it is no longer clear who is being spoken about.	Self and object are often confounded and confused with each other; the affects that are unbearable for the self are attributed to the object. Unrealistic attributions (projective identifications) can often be observed. Blurring of ego boundaries in close relationships.	Due to persistent fusion and consolidation of self and object aspects, the object is not perceived as separate from the self; dissolution of ego boundaries. Alternatively, experience of omnipotence and/or complete abandonment of object occupation. Inner and outer world cannot be distinguished.
1.5 Object-related affect differentiation	The affective inner world of others can be perceived accurately and described in a differentiated and lively way. Affects of objects can be brought into a context of understanding with situational aspects and their behavior.	Conflict-related affects of others are only perceived to a limited extent and, in difficult situations, are also suppressed in order to maintain stability. Context-related understanding of the experience and behavior of others is restricted but can be loosened with the help of others.	The affects of others cannot be perceived in a differentiated way and can only be described in broad categories. The inner world of others is largely incomprehensible. Contradictions between attributed affects and behavior cannot be integrated and resolved.	The affects of others can usually not be perceived and understood. Instead, threatening or promising affects are attributed to others in a distorted way. The behavior of others is interpreted unrealistically.
1.6 Integrated object perception	Object perception is coherent. Different sides of other people can be integrated into a vivid and realistic picture. You can visualize the people described in a lively and interesting way. The perception of the other person is not affected by conflicts, it remains stable.	Object perception is coherent but can be impaired by conflict. Others are then not perceived in their complexity and contradictions but are experienced according to their own wishes. Descriptions then appear one-sided and incomplete; the perception of others is impaired and becomes temporarily unstable.	A coherent perception of objects is not possible. Others are experienced in extremes, particularly good or bad. Contradictions cannot be integrated. The description of others is often no longer comprehensible. The behavior of others can hardly be understood situationally. It is typical for idealization to turn into devaluation.	The perception of objects is not coherent. Others are quickly experienced as aggressively persecutory and threatening or idealized. Individual characteristics stand for the whole object. Own fears, anxieties and desires determine perception and interpretation; the other person is no longer experienced as a securely demarcated counterpart.

Table A12. Self-regulation

	1 Good	2 Moderate	3 Low	4 Disintegrated
2.1 Impulse control	Aggressive, sexual, and oral impulses and desires can be experienced and controlled in a differentiated and graduated way. Needs can be postponed but also satisfied. Loss of control can occur to a small extent and can be tolerated.	Impulses and desires are experienced and sometimes perceived as agonizing. They are predominantly inhibited by over-control. Needs are chronically postponed or suppressed. Rarely can impulses break through, which is reacted to with overcontrol.	Urging impulses and desires cannot be regulated (under-control). It is not possible to postpone the fulfilment of needs, at best they are denied. Actions that jeopardize self and others and are experienced as failure. Unrealistic beliefs can at times serve as a means of control.	The ability to regulate impulses is cancelled or may be linked to unrealistic and/or bizarre beliefs. Needs can be directly translated into action by abandoning reality. Loss of control with severe damage to self and others. Alternatively, complete absence of impulses and desires.
2.2 Affect tolerance	Affects can be experienced as appropriate to the situation. Spontaneous, appropriate strategies for counteracting and balancing are available. Ambivalent affects can be experienced and tolerated.	Affects are experienced in a restricted way. Strong and especially negative affects are difficult to bear and are over-regulated. The experience of ambivalent affects is often suppressed in stressful situations.	Affects often flood and trigger impulsive behavior or withdrawal; alternatively, they are ignored. Counter-regulation is usually dysfunctional. Ambivalent affects cannot be experienced.	Violent reflexive counteractions even with minimal intensity of affect. Ambivalence does not occur, only ambivalent tendencies. Frequently flooded by undifferentiated affects. Alternatively, affects can be completely switched off.
2.3 Self-esteem regulation	Self-esteem can be maintained or quickly regained with realistic restrictions.	Self-esteem is disruptible, which manifests in sensitivity, self-exaggeration, devaluation, or self-punishment, withdrawal. Confirmation from others is required.	Self-esteem is very fragile, which manifests in great vulnerability, unrealistic ideas of greatness, shame, disgust with oneself, devaluation of others, relationship breakdowns and an inability to accept one's own limits.	Self-esteem seems to be replaced by an inner unrealistic system of self-esteem control. Grandiosity or a general lack of self-esteem are frequent or alternate.

Table A13. Relationship regulation

	1 Good	2 Moderate	3 Low	4 Disintegrated
2.4 Protecting relationships	The others are considered regardless of their own current needs. Maintaining identification with the relationship and constructive efforts to make amends, even in the event of conflicts of interest.	In conflictual areas, others cannot be recognized as separate people independent of the self. They fulfil a function for the regulation of one's own inner conflicts. Instead of active endeavor, there is an acceptance of a lack of closeness and relatedness in circumscribed areas.	The other person can only be experienced in relation to oneself and one's own needs. Relationships can sometimes be maintained in the long term; this happens either by largely excluding shared experiences or by merging closeness after stormy crises (on-off relationship).	Others are either an extension of the self or non-existent. The ability to protect relationships is largely lost or only possible in fantasies of the self. The experience of the relationship is strongly determined by overvalued and existential ideas. Drastic, highly destructive actions to "protect" relationships.
2.5 Anticipation	The consequences of one's own actions can be anticipated. This influences their own actions in a constructive way. One's own position can be seen from different perspectives; empathizing with the perspective of others makes relationships more flexible.	The anticipation of the consequences of one's own actions is limited or distorted by inner conflicts. In the area of neurotic conflicts, the capacity of adopting a perspective is limited; this restricts the ability to relate one's own actions to others.	It is almost impossible to anticipate the consequences of one's own actions. The reactions of others to one's own actions are often experienced as surprising. Perspective-taking hardly takes place, at best with distortions and misinterpretations. Behavior in relationships is often dysfunctional.	The anticipation of the consequences of one's own actions is controlled by inner convictions, which can be bizarre. These replace perspective-taking and determine the relationship behavior. Alternatively, disorganized or autistic relationship behavior.
2.6 Balancing of interests	Interests can be maintained in relationships and others can be considered appropriately. Stable internalized values. Respect for the needs and mental and physical integrity of others. The value system can be followed flexibly and appropriately to the situation. Actions that run counter to the value system are experienced as culpable.	One's own interests or those of others are permanently in the foreground, difficulties in balancing interests. Internalized values are rigid. Particularly in conflicts, a flexible, situation-appropriate approach to values is no longer possible. "Misbehavior" but also wishes and ideas that contradict the values trigger intense, excessive feelings of guilt.	The relationship is characterized by the feeling that one's own interests are under threat and a lack of understanding of the other person's interests. Internalized, highly idealized and inflexible values exist, but are not securely and stably anchored; actions repeatedly contradict one's own value system. The experience of guilt can be both extensively destructive and largely eliminated.	Own or other interests are pursued or denied following an inner system regardless of interpersonal reality. A stable inner value system does not exist or is bizarrely organized. If desires, impulses and behavior violate the value system, this leads to strong feelings of shame and guilt, which can trigger self-destruction or the destruction of others. Alternatively, feelings of shame, guilt and remorse may be completely absent.

Table A14. Defense

	1 Good	2 Moderate	3 Low	4 Disintegrated
3.1 Living and experiencing possibilities	Stressful internal and external processes can be recognized and overcome. Experience of various aspects of life remain fully intact.	Certain areas of life and experience are given up maintaining inner stability. Stressful processes are then no longer consciously perceived and cannot be dealt with adaptively.	Stabilization is only possible by excluding large areas of experience and usually only for a short time. Internal and external processes can take on a threatening, persecutory or merging character.	Stabilization is only possible in very limited "islands of experience" and/or with a distortion or reinterpretation of reality. There are breakdowns of defense with flooding by stressful experiences and impulsive reactions.
3.2 Interpersonal impact	Intrapsychic flexible defenses are basically available. (Social) reality can be adequately perceived. Interpersonal mechanisms are adaptive at best, whereby they can expand the possibilities of experience.	The defense is usually intrapsychic but rigid. Stress can lead to the temporary use of interpersonal mechanisms and distorted (social) perceptions of reality, which can put significant strain on relationships.	Stress can hardly be dealt with intrapsychically. Interpersonal defenses dominate, which places a heavy burden on relationships. Defenses are unstable and changeable (dysfunctional flexibility) or locked in place. The (social) reality is predominantly perceived in a distorted way and reconstructed.	Mature intrapsychic defense processes are lost, and interpersonal defenses hardly lead to stabilization. Interpersonal reality is usually no longer accessible. Drastic protection from or escape into unrealistic relationship constructs.
3.3 Mechanisms	Predominance of mature defense mechanisms with good adaptivity, such as sublimation or humor, good adaptivity.	Relatively mature defenses whose adaptivity is permanently restricted, e.g., chronic repression, reaction formation, turning against the self, intellectualization, affect isolation.	Predominantly dysfunctional and immature mechanisms occur. Typically splitting, idealization, devaluation and projective identification.	The imaginary world is threatened by fragmentation, desymbolization, concretism, autistic withdrawal and/or bizarre interpersonal defenses.

Table A15. Internal communication

	1 Good	2 Moderate	3 Low	4 Disintegrated
4.1 Experienc of affects and fantasies	Affects can be allowed and experienced in their diversity; a lively experience is possible. There is a feeling of liveliness and a playful, curious contact with one's own inner world. The inner spaces of experience can be expanded through fantasies. This allows for creative solutions to be developed.	Affects are experienced in a limited way and presented in a normative way. Limited access to inner processes, curiosity and vitality; fear of losing control; restricted imaginative activity. Fantasies are often avoided and defended against in order to maintain stability. Creative solutions are postponed in favor of "safe" alternatives.	One-sided, negative or positive affects (panic, anger, disgust, contempt, ecstasy) impose themselves and persistently occupy the inner experience. The inner worlds are increasingly colored in a threatening way. There is flooding, fear and discomfort. Fantasies range from threatening to enraptured to agonizing inner emptiness. The solutions tend to be avoidant or destructive.	Individual affects dominate, which can change, or persistent numbness. Contact with inner emotional processes is blocked or experienced as massively threatening or tempting. Reality and fantasies cannot be distinguished. Fantasies can mobilize massive fears and the experience of boundaries being broken, or they can take on bizarre forms. Creative solutions can only be found by giving up reality.
4.2 Experience of joy	One´s own body can be experienced with pleasure. Eroticism and sexual arousal can be experienced (alone or with a partner) in a satisfying way. Sensual, spiritual, cultural, culinary or natural experiences can be experienced as pleasurable and enriching.	The pleasurable experience of one's own body, of eroticism and sexuality is rigidly and normatively limited. Non-sexual pleasure is also limited in its intensity, spontaneity and expansiveness, but can take place in a thoroughly satisfying way within predetermined structures with sublimatory connotations.	The body, eroticism and sexuality cannot be experienced in a pleasurable way and remain lifeless, or the experience is very intense and overwhelming. Violent feelings of disgust, disappointment, anger or fear of merging can occur. Non-sexual pleasures are either experienced as intoxicating, sometimes threatening or remain inaccessible.	Physical experience and sexuality intensely pressing and quickly threatening; fears of self-loss and/or destructive fantasies and impulses. Alternatively, interpersonal pleasure is avoided due to massive fears of closeness and intimacy, up to and including general anhedonia. The non-sexual capacity for pleasure is also extremely excessive or depleted.
4.3 Bodily self	One's own body is experienced as vital, positive and whole and as belonging to oneself. Attention to the body changes according to the situation and there is an appropriately self-caring approach to one's own body.	The body can sometimes be perceived as lacking vitality and as a burden. It is experienced as a whole, but an experience of strangeness can occur in the short term. Focusing attention on physical processes can last for a long time. Occasionally, the body is neglected.	The body is repeatedly experienced as frozen, burdensome, fragmented or alien; however, the experience of the body can also be excessively vivid. It is easy to become fixated on physical dysfunctions. The body is neglected or – often damagingly – made the object of various manipulations.	The body is perceived as dead, fragmented or influenced by others. Rigid focus of attention on altered, often negative aspects of the body. The connection between psyche and soma seems to be largely lost. The body can be massively damaged or neglected, for which there is often a lack of awareness.

Table A16. Communication with the external world

	1 Good	2 Moderate	3 Low	4 Disintegrated
4.4 Making emotional contact	The person has the ability to make lively contact. Through affective participation, communication is lively, interesting, and fruitful. Conflicts are moderated and dealt with authentically; they do not have a lasting negative impact on communication.	The search for contact is noticeable, but making contact is nevertheless inhibited. A reduced expression of affect makes it difficult to communicate vividly. Communication is difficult due to increased sensitivity (e.g., defensive, retentive, demanding, reproachful behavior).	Avoidance of contact or urgent, distanced contact behavior. The rapidly changing or arrested mood can create confusion, emptiness, distance, a feeling of "as-if," lack of relatedness and alternation between over-commitment and resignation in the other person.	Making contact is not possible or follows stereotypical patterns or can be parathymic. Affects are easily mobilized, but cannot be controlled and symbolized; diffuse excitement and violation of the frame; alternatively lifeless and walled in. Feelings of being isolated or highly involved arise in the other person.
4.5 Intimacy	Tender feelings and sexual closeness can be established and tolerated at the same time. Dependence can be experienced in a satisfying way. An intimate emotional connection to others can be maintained. Giving and receiving can be harmonized; lively and flexible openness and trust in one another.	Tender feelings and sexuality can be combined, but some are restricted. Fear of being hurt in intimate relationships. Dependence is avoided or clinging takes place. However, flexible giving and taking is only possible to a limited extent; one or the other takes center stage. There is a tendency to inflexibly define ways and boundaries of intimacy.	Division into desexualized love relationships and sexual activity without emotional commitment. The coincidence of intimacy and emotional closeness leads to flooding, feelings of self-loss and impulsive behavior. Dependence cannot be tolerated in the long term. One's own experience of intimacy dominates; alternatively, submission and self-abandonment. Intimate details are mistrustfully concealed or revealed unilaterally and impulsively.	Intimacy cannot be lived. Closeness leads to fusion and loss of self, or the other is used as a thing and controlled. Dependency is radically avoided, or symbiotic arrangements are used. The perception of a separate counterpart is impossible. The experience of the object is ignored, or subject and object are fused. It is not possible to open to one another.
4.6 Empathy	Communication is characterized by the desire and ability to empathize with others. Empathy and identification with the other person's inner world are easily possible. Emotional understanding can be communicated to the other person in a sympathetic way.	Empathizing with others is more difficult due to the conflict. Sympathy and identification with the other person are limited under the pressure of one's own wishes and fears. It is always difficult to communicate understanding to the other person.	It is difficult to empathize with the experiences of others. Identification with others is hardly possible. Excessively sensitive understanding can be possible but always remains linked to one's own wishes and fears. In most cases, this is not a truly sympathetic understanding.	Empathizing with others is not possible or leads to symbiotic states. The experience of the other is determined by massive attributions. Often fusion instead of identification. Alternatively, no idea of the psychological inner worlds of others; communication is de-emotionalized, functionalized or concretistic.

Table A17. Attachment to internal objects

	1 Good	2 Moderate	3 Low	4 Disintegrated
5.1 Internalization	The ability to create and maintain emotionally stable internal images of important people is consistently present. The central fear is to lose the love of the object.	The ability to create stable internal images of important people and thus be more independent of their external presence is more difficult: internal images can fade or be limited in their differentiation after a short time or in conflictual situations. The central fear is of losing the important, supporting, controlling object.	Relationships with other people hardly leave any positive internal images. If they do exist, they are one-sidedly idealized. Aversive object images predominate. The central fear is of being damaged by the objects.	The lack of constant images of others can lead to inner emptiness or be replaced by inner, magical worlds. The internalized (partial) objects can be bizarre, uncanny, seductive, or even lifeless. Partial aspects can stand for the whole person. The central fear concerns the destruction of self and identity.
5.2 Use of introjects	As a consequence of internalized good experiences in relationships, it is possible to refer to the internalized objects in difficult situations, to take care of oneself, to calm oneself down and to stand up for oneself. Being alone with oneself can be well tolerated and enjoyed over a longer period.	The internal objects tend to be driving, criticizing, demanding or neglectful. It is difficult to stand up for yourself, to calm down. A relieving "inner dialogue" with the objects is usually not possible. Being alone can be tolerated, but is experienced as a burden or a relief, depending on the conflict.	The internal objects tend to be aversive or over-exciting and cannot be utilized. An "inner dialogue" creates either unrealistic ideal or torturous images. Being alone is a form of survival or takes on a threatening quality; impulsive action in the sense of self-harm or sexualization of lack of relationship.	Being at the mercy of internal sub-objects that have acquired a predominantly autonomous form. This can lead to intense agitation and typically to inner certainties that are completely removed from reality. Being alone with oneself is either not tolerated or it takes on a fantastic quality through the denial of reality.
5.3 Variability	Internal images of important others are different and diverse. Depending on the other person and the situation, the relationships vary in terms of intensity, quality, closeness and content that is shared. It is quite possible to represent different relationships with different people at the same time; triadic relationships can be maintained.	Important others are represented in a less differentiated way, the internal images are more similar. The quality and intensity of relationships are also less diverse and more dyadic. Rivalry is avoided in relationships where possible or is the focus of attention due to conflict. Existing triadic relationships are easily disrupted.	Relationships appear functionalized – very often only that which is significant in relation to the self is perceived by the other. The internal images of others are often barely distinguishable and are characterized by splits or fragmentation. Triadic relationships cannot be represented.	The internal images of others are orientated towards their own fantasies, are threatening or promising, with little reference to reality. Attachments exist predominantly to fantasize others, real relationships are irritating and threatening, purely functional or avoided. Triadic relationships do not seem to exist.

Table A18. Attachment to external objects

	1 Good	2 Moderate	3 Low	4 Disintegrated
5.4 Ability to form attachments	Others have emotional significance; there is the ability and desire to attach to them. Relationships are actively protected, and closeness is flexibly organized according to the situation. The feelings of dependency resulting from emotional significance can be tolerated and enjoyed.	Attachment and lasting relationships are usually possible, but dependency and closeness can often not be enjoyed and flexibly organized. Instead, the emotional significance of the significant other is either exaggerated or avoided. Relationships are characterized by conflict or are partially emotionally drained.	Permanent object-centeredness cannot be maintained. Dependence is either avoided completely or experienced very intensely, which becomes threatening and can lead to forced distancing (on-off relationship). Unstable, dramatic relationships can last a long time; alternatively, frequently changing relationships or chronic isolation.	Dependence cannot be tolerated. When relationships exist for a short time, they are either functionalized or symbiotic, with the other person being possessed like a thing and controlled dysfunctionally, sometimes aggressively. Alternatively, there is complete subjugation. The other person is less a real person than a powerful fantasized internal object.
5.5 Trust	There is a secure basic trust in other people. Others are believed in an appropriate manner; other people can be utilized as good objects.	Trust in others is limited; alternatively, there may be uncritical trust in others. Determined by inner conflict issues, it may be difficult to find and accept support even when there is inner need.	Help from others is rejected reflexively, suspiciously or aggressively. No secure trust in others and no idea that others could be helpful without ulterior motives. Alternatively, dysfunctional trust and surrendering to others.	Help is equated with destruction and/or empowerment. Help can only be expected from fantasized omnipotent figures or is unimaginable. It is also possible to identify with an all-powerful savior to whom one can surrender oneself unconditionally.
5.6 Ability to separate	Separations can be tolerated, brought about and overcome with an appropriate feeling of sadness. The affective cathexis of the lost object can be withdrawn, whereby an appropriately positive internal image can be retained. This creates an inner freedom for new relationships.	Farewells are ignored or clinging takes place to avoid feared losses. This sometimes leads to persistence in conflictual relationships. After separations, the affective cathexis cannot be removed for a long time; positive inner images are warded off after a separation. This can put a strain on new relationships.	The inner experiences of separation and parting under grief are not possible; nevertheless, real separations often trigger symptom formation or compensatory-impulsive actions. The affective cathexis cannot be withdrawn from the lost object; internal objects are destroyed or maintained in an idealized form.	In the case of separation, there is no reaction to the loss, but rather an increased focus on inner, fantasized worlds. Visible emotional reactions are usually absent; however, the turning away from reality is often massively intensified. Alternatively, the inner object is destroyed, possibly leading to the destruction of the real object and/or suicidal behavior.

References

Abraham, K. (1927). Psycho-analytical studies on character-formation. In *Selected papers of Karl Abraham* (D. Bryan & A. Strachey, Trans., pp. 370–417). Hogarth Press. (Original work published 1925).

Adler, A. (1917). *Study of organ inferiority and its psychical compensation. A contribution to clinical medicine* (S. E. Jelliffe, Trans.). The Nervous and Mental Disease Publishing Company. (Original work published 1907). https://doi.org/10.1037/10734-000

Ainsworth, M., Blehar, E., Waters, E., & Wall, S. (1978). *Patterns of attachment: A psychological study of the strange situation.* Erlbaum.

Albani, C., Blaser, G., Körner, A., König, S., Marschke, F., Geissler, I., Geyer, M., Pokorny, D., Staats, H., Benninghofen, D., Dahlbender, R., Cierpka, M., & Kächele, H. (2002). Zum Zusammenhang zwischen der Valenz von Beziehungserfahrungen und der Schwere der psychischen Beeinträchtigung [The connection between affective evaluation of recollected relationship experiences and the severity of psychic impairment]. *PPmP – Psychotherapie, Psychosomatik, Medizinische Psychologie, 52*(6), 282–285. https://doi.org/10.1055/s-2002-32248

Albrecht, R., Löwe, B., Brünahl, C.A., & Riegel, B. (2015). Chronische Unterbauchschmerzen und Persönlichkeit – Zusammenhänge zwischen körperlichen Beschwerden und psychischer Struktur [Chronic pelvic pain syndrome and personality – Association of somatic symptoms and psychic structure]. *PPmP – Psychotherapie, Psychosomatik, Medizinische Psychologie, 65*(11), 418–425. https://doi.org/10.1055/s-0035-1554692

American Psychiatric Association. (2000). *Diagnostic and statistical manual of mental disorders DSM-IV-TR.* American Psychiatric Publishing.

American Psychiatric Association. (2013). *Diagnostic and statistical manual of mental disorders: DSM-5.* American Psychiatric Publishing. https://doi.org/10.1176/appi.books.9780890425596

Arbeitsgemeinschaft medizinischer wissenschaftlicher Fachgesellschaften (AWMF). (2019). *S2k-Leitlinie Begutachtung bei psychischen und psychosomatischen Störungen* [S2k guideline: Assessment in cases of mental and psychosomatic disorders]. https://register.awmf.org/de/leitlinien/detail/051-029

Arbeitskreis OPD. (1996). *Operationalisierte Psychodynamische Diagnostik. Grundlagen und Manual* [Operationalized Psychodynamic Diagnosis. Foundations and manual]. Huber.

Arbeitskreis OPD – Abhängigkeitserkrankungen. (2013). *OPD-2 Modul Abhängigkeitserkrankungen: Das Diagnostik-Manual* [OPD-2 module dependency disorders: The diagnostic manual]. Huber.

Argelander, H. (1976). *The initial interview in psychotherapy* (H. F. Bernays, Trans.). Human Sciences Press. (Original work published 1970).

Bach, B., & Simonsen, S. (2021). How does level of personality functioning inform clinical management and treatment? Implications for ICD-11 classification of personality disorder severity. *Current Opinion in Psychiatry, 34*(1), 54–63. https://doi.org/10.1097/YCO.0000000000000658

Baie, L., Hucklenbroich, K., Hampel, N., Ehrenthal, J.C., Heuft, G., & Burgmer, M. (2020). Steht das strukturelle Integrationsniveau nach OPD-2 in Zusammenhang mit der Symptomschwere einer Posttraumatischen Belastungsstörung (PTBS)? Eine Kohortenstudie bei Patienten einer Trauma-Ambulanz [Level of personality functioning (OPD-2) and the symptom severity of posttraumatic stress disorder: A cohort study]. *Zeitschrift für Psychosomatische Medizin und Psychotherapie, 66*(1), 5–19. https://doi.org/10.13109/zptm.2020.66.1.5

Bales, R.F., & Cohen, S.P. (1979). *SYMLOG – A system for multiple level observation of group.* The Free Press.

Balint, M. (1953). *Primary love and psycho-analytic technique.* Liveright Publishing Corporation.

Balint, M., & Balint, E. (1961). *Psychotherapeutic techniques in medicine.* Travistock.

Bandura, A. (1977). Self-efficacy: Toward a unifying theory of behavioral change. *Psychological Review, 84*(2), 191–215. https://doi.org/10.1037/0033-295X.84.2.191

Bandura, A. (1997). *Self-efficacy: The exercise of control.* Freeman.

Barnow, S. (2012). Emotionsregulation und Psychopathologie: Ein Überblick [Emotion regulation and psychopathology. An overview]. *Psychologische Rundschau, 63*(2), 111–124. https://doi.org/10.1026/0033-3042/a000119

Barnow, S. (Ed.) (2020). *Handbuch Emotionsregulation – Zwischen psychischer Gesundheit und Psychopathologie* [Handbook of emotion regulation – Between mental health and psychopathology]. Springer.

Barrett, K.C. (2005). The origins of social emotions and self-regulation in toddlerhood: New evidence. *Cognition & Emotion, 19*(7), 953–979. https://doi.org/10.1080/02699930500172515

Barrett, L.F. (2017). *How emotions are made: The secret life of the brain.* Houghton Mifflin Harcourt.

Bassler, M., Köllner, V., Paar, G., Grohmann, S., & Rüddel, H. (2016). Psychosomatische Rehabilitation [Psychosomatic rehabilitation]. In K. Köhle, W. Herzog, P. Joraschky, J. Kruse, W. Langewitz, & W. Söllner (Eds.), *Uexküll, Psychosomatische Medizin* (8th ed., pp. 561–568). Elsevier.

Bateman, A., & Fonagy, P. (2004). *Psychotherapy for borderline personality disorder: Mentalization-based treatment.* Oxford University Press. https://doi.org/10.1093/med:psych/9780198527664.001.0001

Belke, D.R., & Landoll, S.L. (2000). Striving for a consistent life story: Cognitive reactions to autobiographical memories. *Social Cognition, 18*(3), 292–318. https://doi.org/10.1521/soco.2000.18.3.292

Bellak, L., & Goldsmith, L.A. (1984). The broad scope of ego function assessment. In L. Bellak & L.A. Goldsmith (Eds.), *The broad scope of ego function assessment* (pp. 268–290). Wiley.

Bellak, L., & Hurvich, M. (1969). A systematic study of ego functions. *The Journal of Nervous and Mental Disease, 148*(6), 569–585. https://doi.org/10.1097/00005053-196906000-00001

Bellak, L., Hurvich, M., & Gediman, H.K. (1973). *Ego functions in schizophrenics, neurotics, and normals.* Wiley.

Benecke, C. (2014). *Klinische Psychologie und Psychotherapie: Ein integratives Lehrbuch* [Clinical psychology and psychotherapy: An integrative textbook]. Kohlhammer.

Benecke, C. (2018). *Negative Affekte in der Psychotherapie* [Negative affects in psychotherapy]. Kohlhammer.

Benecke, C., Bock, A., Wieser, E., Tschiesner, R., Lochmann, M., Küspert, F., Schorn, R., Viertler, B., & Steinmayr-Gensluckner, M. (2011). Reliabilität und Validität der OPD-KJ-Achsen Struktur und Konflikt [Inter-rater reliability and validity of the OPD-CA axes structure and conflict]. *Praxis der Kinderpsychologie und Kinderpsychiatrie, 60*(1), 60–73. https://doi.org/10.13109/prkk.2011.60.1.60

Benecke, C., & Brauner, F. (2017). *Motivation und Emotion: Psychologische und psychoanalytische Perspektiven* [Motivation and emotion: Psychological and psychoanalytic perspectives]. Kohlhammer.

Benecke, C., Henkel, M., Doering, S., Jakobsen, T., Stasch, M., Dahlbender, R., Alhabbo, S., & Zimmermann, J. (2018). Der OPD-Konfliktfragebogen [The OPD conflict questionnaire]. *Zeitschrift für Psychosomatische Medizin und Psychotherapie, 64*(4), 380–393. https://doi.org/10.13109/zptm.2018.64.4.380

Benecke, C., Koschier, A., Peham, D., Bock, A., Dahlbender, R., Biebl, W., & Doering, S. (2009). Erste Ergebnisse zu Reliabilität und Validität der OPD-2 Strukturachse [First results on the reliability and validity of the OPD-2 axis structure]. *Zeitschrift für Psychosomatische Medizin und Psychotherapie, 55*(1), 84–96. https://doi.org/10.13109/zptm.2009.55.1.84

Benecke, C., & Möller, H. (2019). OPD-basierte Diagnostik im Coaching [OPD-based diagnostics in coaching]. In A. Ryba & G. Roth (Eds.), *Coaching und Beratung in der Praxis: Ein neurowissenschaftlich fundiertes Integrationsmodell* (pp. 127–147). Klett-Cotta.

Benecke, C., & Schauenburg, H. (2020). Psychodynamik und Operationalisierung [Psychodynamics and operationalization]. *PDP – Psychodynamische Psychotherapie, 19*(1), 36–48. https://doi.org/10.21706/pdp-19-1-36

Benecke, C., & Staats, H. (2016). *Psychoanalyse der Angststörungen: Modelle und Therapien* [Psychoanalysis of anxiety disorders: Models and therapies]. Kohlhammer.

Benjamin, L.S. (1974). Structural analysis of social behavior. *Psychological Review, 81*(5), 392–425. https://doi.org/10.1037/h0037024

Benjamin, L.S. (1993). *Interpersonal diagnosis and treatment of personality disorders.* Guilford.

Benjamin, L.S. (1996). Introduction to the special section on structural analysis of social behavior.

Journal of Consulting and Clinical Psychology, 64(6), 1203–1212. https://doi.org/10.1037/0022-006X.64.6.1203

Benjamin, L.S., Rothweiler, J.C., & Critchfield, K.L. (2006). The use of structural analysis of social behavior (SASB) as an assessment tool. *Annual Review of Clinical Psychology, 2,* 83–109. https://doi.org/10.1146/annurev.clinpsy.2.022305.095337

Berens, S., Schaefert, R., Ehrenthal, J.C., Baumeister, D., Eich, W., & Tesarz, J. (2021). Different dimensions of affective processing in patients with irritable bowel syndrome: A multi-center cross-sectional study. *Frontiers in Psychology, 12,* Article 625381. https://doi.org/10.3389/fpsyg.2021.625381

Bettighofer, S. (1998). *Übertragung und Gegenübertragung im therapeutischen Prozeß* [Transference and countertransference in the therapeutic process]. Kohlhammer.

Bion, W. (1959). *Experiences in groups and other papers.* Tavistock.

Bischof, N. (1985). *Das Rätsel Ödipus: Die biologischen Wurzeln des Urkonfliktes von Intimität und Autonomie* [The oedipus riddle: The biological roots of the fundamental conflict between intimacy and autonomy]. Piper.

Bischof, N. (2009). *Psychologie: Ein Grundkurs für Anspruchsvolle* (2nd ed.) [Psychology: A fundamental course for the ambitious]. Kohlhammer.

Bischof-Köhler, D. (2011). *Soziale Entwicklung in Kindheit und Jugend: Bindung, Empathie, Theorie of Mind* [Social development in childhood and adolescence: Attachment, empathy, and theory of mind]. Kohlhammer.

Bischof-Köhler, D., & Bischof, N. (2018). Self-recognition, empathy and concern for others in toddlers. In N. Roughley & T. Schramme (Eds.), *Forms of fellow feelings* (pp. 78–105). Cambridge University Press. https://doi.org/10.1017/9781316271698.003

Blanck, G., & Blanck, R. (1974). *Ego psychology I: Theory and practice.* Columbia University Press.

Blanck, G., & Blanck, R. (1979). *Ego psychology II: Theory and practice.* Columbia University Press.

Blaser, A. (1977). *Der Urteilsprozeß bei der Indikationsstellung zur Psychotherapie* [The decision-making process in determining the need for psychotherapy]. Huber.

Blüml, V., & Doering, S. (2021). ICD-11 personality disorders: A psychodynamic perspective on personality functioning. *Frontiers in Psychiatry, 12,* Article 654026. https://doi.org/10.3389/fpsyt.2021.654026

Bock, A., Huber, E., & Benecke, C. (2016). Levels of structural integration and facial expressions of negative emotions. *Zeitschrift für Psychosomatische Medizin und Psychotherapie, 62*(3), 224–238. https://doi.org/10.13109/zptm.2016.62.3.224

Bock, A., Huber, E., Peham, D., & Benecke, C. (2015). Negative mimische Affekte im Kontext klinischer Interviews: Entwicklung, Reliabilität und Validität einer Methode zur Funktionsbestimmung negativer Affektmimik [Facial expressions of negative emotions in clinical interviews: The development, reliability and validity of a categorical system for the attribution of functions to facial expressions of negative emotions]. *Zeitschrift für Psychosomatische Medizin und Psychotherapie, 61*(3), 247–261. https://doi.org/10.13109/zptm.2015.61.3.247

Boeker, H., Himmighoffen, H., Straub, M., Schopper, C., Endrass, J., Kuechenhoff, B., Weber, S., & Hell, D. (2008). Deliberate self-harm in female patients with affective disorders: Investigation of personality structure and affect regulation by means of operationalized psychodynamic diagnostics. *The Journal of Nervous and Mental Disease, 196*(10), 743–751. https://doi.org/10.1097/NMD.0b013e3181879daf

Bohart, A.C., & Wade, A.G. (2013). The client in psychotherapy. In M.J. Lambert (Ed.), *Bergin and Garfield's handbook of psychotherapy and behavior change* (6th ed., pp. 219–257). John Wiley & Sons.

Bohleber, W. (2013). Der psychoanalytische Begriff des Unbewussten und seine Entwicklung [The psychoanalytic concept of the unconscious and its development]. *Psyche – Zeitschrift für Psychoanalyse, 67*(9–10), 807–816. https://doi.org/10.21706/ps-67-9-807

Böker, H., Schopper, C., Straub, M., Himmighoffen, H., Endrass, J., Küchenhoff, B., Weber, S., & Hell, D. (2007). Automutilistisches Verhalten bei Patientinnen mit affektiven Störungen: Untersuchung der Persönlichkeitsstruktur und Affektregulation mittels Operationalisierter Psychodynamischer Diagnostik (OPD) [Automutilistic behaviour in female patients with affective disorders: Investigation of personality structure and affect regulation by means of Operationalized Psychodynamic Diagnostics (OPD)]. *PPmP – Psychotherapie, Psychosomatik, Medizinische Psychologie, 57*(8), 319–327. https://doi.org/10.1055/s-2006-952033

Bonta, J., & Andrews, D.A. (2007). *Risk-need-responsivity model for offender assessment and treatment* (User Report No. 2007-06). Public Safety Canada.

Both, L.M., Favaretto, T.C., Freitas, L.H.M., & Crempien, C. (2019). Cross-cultural adaptation of the module for assessment of domestic violence, adapted from Axis I of the operationalized psychodynamic diagnosis (OPD-2), with a sample of Bra-

zilian women, victims of domestic violence. *Trends in Psychiatry and Psychotherapy, 41*(3), 283–291. https://doi.org/10.1590/2237-6089-2018-0075
Bowlby, J. (1951). *Maternal care and mental health.* World Health Organization.
Bowlby, J. (1969). *Attachment and loss. Vol. I: Attachment.* Basic Books.
Bowlby, J. (1988). *A secure base: Clinical applications of attachment theory.* Routledge.
Brenner, C. (1982). *The mind in conflict.* International University Press.
Breuer, J., & Freud, S. (1955). Studies on Hysteria. In J. Strachey (Ed. & Trans.), *The standard edition of the complete psychological works of Sigmund Freud* (Vol. 2, pp. 1–312). Hogarth Press. (Original work published 1895).
Briken, P. (2019). Wiederholungszwang, Selbstvertauschungsagieren und Pädophilie [Compulsion to repeat, self-exchange and paedophilia]. *Psyche, 73*(5), 363–390. https://doi.org/10.21706/ps-73-5-363
Buchheim, P., Cierpka, M., Kächele, H., & Jimenez, J. P. (1987). Das "Strukturelle Interview" – ein Beitrag zur Integration von Psychopathologie und Psychodynamik im psychiatrischen Erstgespräch [The "structural interview" – A contribution to the integration of psychopathology and psychodynamics in the psychiatric initial interview]. *Fundamenta Psychiatrica, 1*, 154–161.
Buchheim, P., Dahlbender, R.W., & Kächele, H. (1994). Biographie und Beziehung in der psychotherapeutischen Diagnostik [Biography and relationship in psychotherapeutic diagnosis]. In P.L. Janssen & W. Schneider (Eds.), *Diagnostik in Psychotherapie und Psychosomatik* (pp. 105–134). Fischer.
Buck, R. (1988). *Human motivation and emotion.* Wiley.
Bückers, R., Kriebel, R., & Paar, G. (2001). Der „geschickte" Patient in der psychosomatischen Rehabilitation – Leitlinien für die sozialmedizinische Beurteilung und Behandlung von fremdmotivierten Patienten [Patients "sent" for psychosomatic rehabilitation – Guidelines for sociomedical assessment and management of extrinsically motivated patients]. *Rehabilitation, 40*(2), 65–71. https://doi.org/10.1055/s-2001-12483
Bundesinstitut für Arzneimittel und Medizinprodukte (BfArM). (2022). *Federal board for pharmaceuticals and medical products. Coding systems.* https://www.bfarm.de/DE/Kodiersysteme/_node.html
Burgmer, M., Ehrenthal, J.C., Heyng, M., Klauck, G., & Wrenger, M. (2023). *OPD-3 Manual zur Ereignis- und Traumaverarbeitung* [OPD-3 module life-event and trauma processing]. Hogrefe.
Burgmer, M., Fiori, W., Bunzemeier, H., Roeder, R., & Heuft, G. (2004). Komorbidität psychischer Störungen im G-DRG-System – Einfluss auf die Verweildauer und Erlössituation an einem deutschen Universitätsklinikum [Comorbidity of mental disorders in the German G-DRG System – Effect on length of stay and revenue situation at a university hospital]. *Zeitschrift für Psychosomatische Medizin und Psychotherapie, 50*(3), 306–316. https://doi.org/10.13109/zptm.2004.50.3.306
Burlingame, G.M., Seebeck, J.D., Janis, R.A., Whitcomb, K.E., Barkowski, S., Rosendahl, J., & Strauss, B. (2016). Outcome differences between individual and group formats when identical and nonidentical treatments, patients, and doses are compared: A 25-year meta-analytic perspective. *Psychotherapy, 53*(4), 446–461. https://doi.org/10.1037/pst0000090
Caligor, E., Kernberg, O.F., & Clarkin, J. (2009). *Handbook of dynamic psychotherapy for higher level personality pathology.* American Psychiatric Publishing.
Caspar, F. (2007). *Beziehungen und Probleme verstehen: Eine Einführung in die psychotherapeutische Plananalyse* (3rd rev. ed.) [Understanding relationships and problems: An introduction to psychotherapeutic plan analysis]. Huber.
Caspi, A., Houts, R.M., Belsky, D.W., Goldman-Mellor, S.J., Harrington, H., Israel, S., Meier, M., Ramrakha, S., Shalev, I., Poulton, R., & Moffitt, T.E. (2014). The p factor: one general psychopathology factor in the structure of psychiatric disorders? *Clinical Psychological Science, 2*(2), 119–137. https://doi.org/10.1177/2167702613497473
Castonguay, L.G. (2011). Psychotherapy, psychopathology, research and practice: Pathways of connections and integration. *Psychotherapy Research, 21*(2), 125–140. https://doi.org/10.1080/10503307.2011.563250
Cierpka, M. (1992). Die Entwicklung des Familiengefühls [The development of the family bond]. *Forum der Psychoanalyse, 8*, 32–46.
Cierpka, M. (2003). *Handbuch der Familiendiagnostik* (3rd ed.) [Handbook of family diagnostics]. Springer.
Cierpka, M., Grande, T., Rudolf, G., Tann, M. von der, & Stasch, M. (2007). The operationalized psychodynamic diagnostics system: Clinical relevance, reliability and validity. *Psychopathology, 40*(4), 209–220. https://doi.org/10.1159/000101363

Cierpka, M., Grande, T., Stasch, M., Oberbracht, C., Schneider, W., Schüßler, G., Heuft, G., Dahlbender, R., Schauenburg, H., & Schneider, G. (2001). Zur Validität der Operationalisierten Psychodynamischen Diagnostik (OPD) [About the validity of the Operationalized Psychodynamic Diagnosis (OPD)]. *Psychotherapeut, 46,* 122–133. https://doi.org/10.1007/s002780100145

Cierpka, M., Hirschmüller, B., Israel, A., Jahn-Jokschies, G., Kalckreuth, B. von, Knott, M., Stasch, M., Wiesler, C., & Windaus, E. (2007). Manual zur psychoanalytischen Behandlung von Regulationsstörungen, psychischen und psychosomatischen Störungen bei Säuglingen und Kleinkindern unter Verwendung des Fokuskonzeptes [Manual for psychoanalytic treatment of regulatory disorders, mental and psychosomatic disorders in infants and young children using the focus concept]. In M. Cierpka & E. Windaus (Eds.), *Psychoanalytische Säuglings-Kleinkind-Eltern-Psychotherapie: Konzepte-Leitlinien-Manual* (pp. 87–214). Brandes & Apsel.

Cierpka, M., Strack, M., Benninghoven, D., Staats, H., Dahlbender, R., Pokorny, D., Frevert, G., Blaser, G., Kächele, H., Geyer, M., Körner, A., & Albani, C. (1998). Stereotypical relationship patterns and psychopathology. *Psychotherapy and Psychosomatics, 67*(4–5), 241–248. https://doi.org/10.1159/000012286

Cierpka, M., & Windaus, E. (Eds.). (2007). *Psychoanalytische Säuglings-Kleinkind-Eltern-Psychotherapie: Konzepte-Leitlinien-Manual* [Psychoanalytic infant-child-parent psychotherapy: Concepts-guidelines-manual]. Brandes & Apsel.

Clarkin, J.F. (2004). Assessment of the psychiatric patient with a semi-structured interview. In R. Dahlbender, P. Buchheim, & G. Schüßler (Eds.), *Lernen an der Praxis: OPD und die Qualitätssicherung in der psychodynamischen Psychotherapie* (pp. 30–40). Huber.

Clarkin, J.F., Caligor, E., Stern, B., & Kernberg, O.F. (2004). *Structured Interview of Personality Organization (STIPO).* Weill Medical College of Cornell University.

Clarkin, J.F., Caligor, E., Stern, B.L., & Kernberg, O.F. (2016). *Structured Interview of Personality Organization-Revised (STIPO-R).* Weill Medical College of Cornell University.

Clarkin, J.F., Foelsch, P.A., & Kernberg, O.F. (2000). *Inventory of Personality Organization.* Weill College of Medicine of Cornell University.

Cosmides, L., & Tooby, J. (2000). Evolutionary psychology and the emotions. In M. Lewis, & J.M. Haviland-Jones (Eds.), *Handbook of emotions* (2nd ed., pp. 91–115). Guilford.

Cramer, P. (2006). *Protecting the self: Defense mechanisms in action.* Guilford Press.

Crempien, C., Grez, M., Valdés, C., López, M.J., La Parra, G. de, & Krause, M. (2017). Role of personality functioning in the quality of life of patients with depression. *The Journal of Nervous and Mental Disease, 205*(9), 705–713. https://doi.org/10.1097/NMD.0000000000000676

Cropp, C., Salzer, S., & Streeck-Fischer, A. (2016). Veränderungen der psychischen Struktur im Verlauf der stationären psychodynamischen Behandlung von jugendlichen Patienten mit einer kombinierten Störung des Sozialverhaltens und der Emotionen [Changes in OPD-CA axis structure during inpatient psychodynamic treatment of adolescents suffering from comorbid disorders of conduct and emotions]. *Praxis der Kinderpsychologie und Kinderpsychiatrie, 65*(5), 328–339. https://doi.org/10.13109/prkk.2016.65.5.328

Dagnino, P., Ugarte, M.J., Morales, F., González, S., Saralegui, D., & Ehrenthal, J.C. (2020). Risk factors for adult depression: Adverse childhood experiences and personality functioning. *Frontiers in Psychology, 11,* Article 594698. https://doi.org/10.3389/fpsyg.2020.594698

Dahlbender, R., Buchheim, P., & Schüßler, G. (Eds.). (2004). *Lernen an der Praxis: OPD und die Qualitätssicherung in der psychodynamischen Psychotherapie* [Learning from practice: OPD and quality assurance in psychodynamic psychotherapy]. Huber.

Dahlbender, R.W. (2002). *Schwere psychischer Erkrankungen und Meisterung internalisierter Beziehungskonflikte* [Severe mental illness and mastering internalized relationship conflicts]. Profund.

Dahlbender, R.W., Grande, T., Buchheim, P., Schneider, W., Perry, J.C., Oberbracht, C., Freyberger, H.J., Janssen, P.L., Schauenburg, H., & Doering, S. (2004). Qualitätssicherung im OPD-Interview: Entwicklung eines Interviewleitfadens [Quality assurance in OPD interview: Development of an interview guide]. In R. Dahlbender, P. Buchheim, & G. Schüßler (Eds.), *Lernen an der Praxis* (pp. 41–66). Huber.

Damasio, A. (2003). *Looking for Spinoza: Joy, sorrow, and the feeling brain.* William Heinemann.

Dammann, G., Walter, M., & Benecke, C. (2011). Identität und Identitätsstörungen bei Borderline-Persönlichkeitsstörungen [Identity and identity disorders in borderline personality disorders]. In B. Dulz, S.C. Herpertz, O.F. Kernberg, & U. Sachsse (Eds.), *Handbuch der Borderline-Störungen* (2nd ed., pp. 275–285). Schattauer.

Deutsch, F. (1939). The associative anamnesis. *The Psychoanalytic Quarterly, 8,* 354–381. https://doi.org/10.1080/21674086.1939.11925396

Deutsch, F., & Murphy, W. F. (1955). *The clinical interview. Volume one: Diagnosis.* International Universities Press.

Deutsche Rentenversicherung. (2018). *Sozialmedizinische Beurteilung bei psychischen und Verhaltensstörungen.* [Social medical assessment of mental and behavioral disorders; Update 2018]. Retrieved January 27, 2026, from https://www.deutsche-rentenversicherung.de/DRV/DE/Experten/Infos-fuer-Aerzte/Begutachtung/begutachtung.html

Dinger, U., Fuchs, M., Köhling, J., Schauenburg, H., & Ehrenthal, J. C. (2021). Change of emotional experience in major depression and borderline personality disorder during psychotherapy: Associations with depression severity and personality functioning. *Journal of Personality Disorders, 35*, 1–20. https://doi.org/10.1521/pedi_2019_33_420

Dinger, U., Löw, C. A., & Ehrenthal, J. C. (2021). The functional domain of self-criticism. In G. de la Parra, P. Dagnino, & A. Behn (Eds.), *Depression and personality dysfunction: An integrative functional domains perspective* (pp. 171–192). Springer Nature Switzerland AG. https://doi.org/10.1007/978-3-030-70699-9_7

Dinger, U., Schauenburg, H., Hörz, S., Rentrop, M., Komo-Lang, M., Klinkerfuß, M., Köhling, J., Grande, T., & Ehrenthal, J. C. (2014). Self-report and observer ratings of personality functioning: A study of the OPD system. *Journal of Personality Assessment, 96*(2), 220–225. https://doi.org/10.1080/00223891.2013.828065

Dittmann, V., Dilling, H., & Freyberger, H. J. (Eds.). (1992). *Psychiatrische Diagnostik nach ICD-10: Klinische Erfahrungen bei der Anwendung. Ergebnisse der ICD-10 Merkmallistenstudie* [Psychiatric diagnostics according to ICD-10: Clinical experiences in application. Results of the ICD-10 feature list study]. Huber.

Dittmann, V., Freyberger, H. J., Mombour, W., & Dilling, H. (1996). *Die ICD-10 Merkmalliste: Instrument und Manual* [The ICD-10 feature list: Instrument and manual]. Huber.

Dobbrunz, S., Daubmann, A., Müller, J. L., & Briken, P. (2020). Predictive validity of operationalized criteria for the assessment of criminal responsibility of sexual offenders with paraphilic disorders – A randomized control trial with mental health and legal professionals. *Frontiers in Psychology, 11,* Article 613081. https://doi.org/10.3389/fpsyg.2020.613081

Doering, S. (2003). Wo steht der Neurosenbegriff heute? [The concept of neurosis today?]. *Persönlichkeitsstörungen: Theorie und Therapie, 7,* 176–187.

Doering, S. (2004). *Strukturiertes Interview zur Persönlichkeitsorganisation* [Structured Interview for Personality Organization; German version: STIPO-D]. University of Münster.

Doering, S. (2016). *Übertragungsfokussierte Psychotherapie (TFP)* [Transference-focused psychotherapy (TFP)]. Vandenhoeck & Ruprecht.

Doering, S., Blüml, V., Parth, K., Feichtinger, K., Gruber, M., Aigner, M., Rössler-Schülein, H., Freidl, M., & Wininger, A. (2018). Personality functioning in anxiety disorders. *BMC Psychiatry, 18*(1), Article 294. https://doi.org/10.1186/s12888-018-1870-0

Doering, S., Burgmer, M., Heuft, G., Menke, D., Bäumer, B., Lübking, M., Feldmann, M., & Schneider, G. (2014). Assessment of personality functioning: Validity of the Operationalized Psychodynamic Diagnosis axis IV (structure). *Psychopathology, 47*(3), 185–193. https://doi.org/10.1159/000355062

Doering, S., Burgmer, M., Heuft, G., Menke, D., Bäumer, B., Lübking, M., Feldmann, M., Hörz, S., & Schneider, G. (2013). Reliability and validity of the German version of the Structured Interview of Personality Organization (STIPO). *BMC Psychiatry, 13*, Article 210. https://doi.org/10.1186/1471-244X-13-210

Doering, S., Hoerz, S. (Eds.). (2012). *Handbuch der Strukturdiagnostik: Konzepte, Instrumente, Praxis* [Handbook of structural diagnostics: Concepts, instruments, practice]. Schattauer.

Doering, S., & Schüßler, G. (2004). Theorie und Praxis der psychodynamischen Diagnostik, Indikationsstellung und Therapieplanung [Theory and practice of psychodynamic diagnosis, indication and therapy planning]. In W. Hiller, S. K. D. Sulz, & F. Leichsenring (Eds.), *Lehrbuch der Psychotherapie – Ausbildungsinhalte nach dem Psychotherapeutengesetz (PsychThG)* (pp. 3–31). CIP-Medien.

Döll-Hentschker, S., Reerink, G., Schlierf, C., & Wildberger, H. (2006). Zur Einleitung einer Behandlung: Die Frequenzwahl [Commencing treatment: The choice of frequency]. *Psyche: Zeitschrift für Psychoanalyse und ihre Anwendungen, 60*(11), 1126–1144. https://doi.org/10.21706/ps-60-11-1126

Dornes, M. (1997). *Die frühe Kindheit: Entwicklungspsychologie der ersten Lebensjahre* [Early childhood:

Developmental psychology of the first years of life]. Fischer.

Dührssen, A. (1954). Das Problem der auslösenden Konfliktsituation in der Diagnostik psychogener Erkrankungen [The problem of the triggering conflict situation in the diagnosis of psychogenic disorders]. *Zeitschrift für Psychosomatische Medizin und Psychoanalyse, 1,* 45–51.

Dührssen, A. (1981). *Die biographische Anamnese unter tiefenpsychologischen Aspekten* [The biographical anamnesis from a depth psychological perspective]. Vandenhoeck & Ruprecht.

Dührssen, A. (2010). *Die biografische Anamnese unter tiefenpsychologischem Aspekt: Mit einer Einführung von Gerd Rudolf und Ulrich Rüger* [The biographical anamnesis from a depth psychological perspective: With an introduction by Gerd Rudolf and Ulrich Rüger]. Schattauer.

Dümpelmann, M. (2018). *Psychodynamische Behandlung psychotischer Störungen: Wenn die Grenze der Fall ist* [Psychodynamic treatment of psychotic disorders: When the border is the case]. Kohlhammer.

Dunlop, W. L., Lind, M., Harake, N., Lee, D., Sedano, A., Ring, C., & Davis, J. P. (2022). Motivational and affective themes in the life stories of underserved emerging adults: A pilot study. *The International Journal of Reminiscence and Life Review, 9*(1), 1–8.

Eagle, M. N. (1991). Kritische Rezension: A. Grünbaums "The foundation of psychoanalysis: A philosophical critique" (1984) [Critical review: A. Grünbaum's "The foundation of psychoanalysis: A philosophical critique" (1984)]. In A. Grünbaum (Ed.), *Kritische Betrachtungen zur Psychoanalyse* (pp. 217–241). Springer.

Ehlers, W., Hettinger, R., & Paar, G. (1995). Operational diagnostic approaches in the assessment of defense mechanisms. *Psychotherapy and Psychosomatics, 63*(2), 124–135. https://doi.org/10.1159/000288948

Ehlers, W., & Peter, R. (1990). Entwicklung eines psychometrischen Verfahrens zur Selbstbeurteilung von Abwehrkonzepten (SBAK) [Development of a psychometric instrument for self-assessment of defense concepts (SBAK)]. *PPmP – Psychotherapie Psychosomatik, Medizinische Psychologie, 1,* 1–19.

Ehrenthal, J. C. (2014). Strukturdiagnostik – neue Ergebnisse aus der Forschung für die Praxis [Measuring structural integration – New results from research for practical settings]. *Psychodynamische Psychotherapie, 13,* 103–114.

Ehrenthal, J. C., & Benecke, C. (2019). Tailored treatment planning for individuals with personality disorders: The operationalized psychodynamic diagnosis (OPD) approach. In U. Kramer (Ed.), *Case formulation for personality disorders: Tailoring psychotherapy to the individual client* (pp. 291–314). Elsevier Academic Press. https://doi.org/10.1016/B978-0-12-813521-1.00015-1

Ehrenthal, J. C., & Dinger, U. (2019). Strukturdiagnostik in der Praxis – von der Indikation zur Therapieplanung [Assessing levels of personality functioning – From indication to treatment-planning]. *Ärztliche Psychotherapie, 14,* 32–40.

Ehrenthal, J. C., Dinger, U., Horsch, L., Komo-Lang, M., Klinkerfuß, M., Grande, T., & Schauenburg, H. (2012). Der OPD-Strukturfragebogen (OPD-SF): Erste Ergebnisse zu Reliabilität und Validität [The OPD structure questionnaire (OPD-SQ): First results on reliability and validity]. *PPmP: Psychotherapie Psychosomatik Medizinische Psychologie, 62*(1), 25–32. https://doi.org/10.1055/s-0031-1295481

Ehrenthal, J. C., Dinger, U., Schauenburg, H., Horsch, L., Dahlbender, R. W., & Gierk, B. (2015). Entwicklung einer Zwölf-Item-Version des OPD-Strukturfragebogens (OPD-SFK) [Development of a 12-item version of the OPD-structure questionnaire (OPD-SQS)]. *Zeitschrift für Psychosomatische Medizin und Psychotherapie, 61*(3), 262–274. https://doi.org/10.13109/zptm.2015.61.3.262

Ehrenthal, J. C., Düx, A., Baie, L., & Burgmer, M. (2019). Levels of personality functioning and not depression predict decline of plasma glucose concentration in patients with type 2 diabetes mellitus. *Diabetes Research and Clinical Practice, 151,* 106–113. https://doi.org/10.1016/j.diabres.2019.04.011

Ehrenthal, J., & Grande, T. (2014). Fokusorientierte Beziehungsgestaltung in der Psychotherapie von Persönlichkeitsstörungen [Focus-oriented relationship building in the psychotherapy of personality disorders – An integrative model]. *PiD – Psychotherapie Im Dialog, 15*(03), 80–85. https://doi.org/10.1055/s-0034-1388644

Ekman, P. (1992a). An argument for basic emotions. *Cognition and Emotion, 6*(3–4), 169–200. https://doi.org/10.1080/02699939208411068

Ekman, P. (1992b). Are there basic emotions? *Psychological Review, 99*(3), 550–553. https://doi.org/10.1037/0033-295X.99.3.550

Emde, R. (1988). Development terminable and interminable. I. Innate and motivational factors from infancy. *The International Journal of Psychoanalysis, 69,* 23–42.

Emde, R. (2005). A developmental orientation for contemporary psychoanalysis. In E. Person, A. Cooper, & G. Gabbard (Eds.), *Textbook of psycho-*

analysis (pp. 117–130). American Psychological Association.

Emde, R.N. (1981). Changing models of infancy and the nature of early development: Remodelling the foundations. *Journal of the American Psychoanalytic Association, 29*, 179–219. https://doi.org/10.1177/000306518102900110

Engel, K., Haas, E., Rad, M. von, Senf, W., & Becker, H. (1979). Zur Einschätzung von Behandlungen mit Hilfe psychoanalytischer Konzepte (Heidelberger Rating) [Assessing treatments using psychoanalytic concepts (Heidelberg rating)]. *Medizinische Psychologie, 5*, 253–268.

Erikson, E.H. (1959). *Identity and the life cycle.* International Universities Press.

Erikson, E.H. (1968). *Identity: Youth and crisis.* Norton.

Erikson, E.H. (1974). *Dimensions of a new identity.* Norton.

Ermann, M. (1982). Die psychovegetativen Störungen als ich-strukturelles Problem [Psycho-vegetative disorders as an ego-structural problem]. *Zeitschrift für Psychosomatische Medizin und Psychoanalyse, 28*(3), 255–265.

Ermann, M. (1992). Die sogenannte Realbeziehung [The so-called real relationship]. *Forum der Psychoanalyse, 8*, 281–294.

Etkin, A., Büchel, C., & Gross, J.J. (2015). The neural bases of emotion regulation. *Nature Reviews Neuroscience, 16*(11), 693–700. https://doi.org/10.1038/nrn4044

Fairbairn, W.R. (1952). *Psychoanalytic studies of the personality.* Tavistock/Routledge.

Ferber, J., Schneider, G., Havlik, L., Heuft, G., Friederichs, H., Schrewe, F., Schulz-Steinel, A., & Burgmer, M. (2014). Blended-Learning in der Psychosomatik und Psychotherapie – Erhöhung der Zufriedenheit und Fachkompetenz Studierender durch Einsatz eines web-basierten E-Learning-Tools [Blended learning in psychosomatics and psychotherapy – increasing the satisfaction and knowledge of students with a web-based e-learning tool]. *Zeitschrift für Psychosomatische Medizin und Psychotherapie, 60*(4), 310–323. https://doi.org/10.13109/zptm.2014.60.4.310

Ferro, A., & Civitarese, G. (2018). *A short introduction to psychoanalysis.* Routledge.

Festinger, L. (1957). *A theory of cognitive dissonance.* Standford University Press. https://doi.org/10.1515/9781503620766

First, M.B., Gibbon, M., Spitzer, R.L., Williams, J.B.W., Smith Benjamin, L. (1997). *Structured clinical interview for DSM-IV axis II personality disorders (SCID-II).* American Psychiatric Association.

First, M.B., Skodol, A.E., Bender, D.S., & Oldham, J.M. (2018). *Structured clinical interview for the DSM-5 alternative model for personality disorders (SCID-5-AMPD).* American Psychiatric Association.

First, M.B., Spitzer, R.L., Gibbon, M. & Williams, J.B. (1996). *Structured clinical interview for DSM-IV Axis I disorders (SCID-I).* American Psychiatric Association Publishing.

Flenreiss-Frankl, K., Unterrainer, H.-F., & Fuchshuber, J. (2021). Die Beziehung zwischen Trauma, Traumafolgen und Persönlichkeitsstruktur: Eine Mediationsanalyse [The relationship between trauma, consequences of trauma and personality structure: A mediation analysis]. *Zeitschrift für Psychosomatische Medizin und Psychotherapie, 67*(2), 114–131. https://doi.org/10.13109/zptm.2021.67.oa3

Fonagy, P., Gergely, G., Jurist, E.L., & Target, M. (2002). *Affect regulation, mentalization, and the development of the self.* Other Press.

Fonagy, P., Luyten, P., Allison, E., & Campbell, C. (2017a). What we have changed our minds about: Part 1. Borderline personality disorder as a limitation of resilience. *Borderline Personality Disorder and Emotion Dysregulation, 4*(1), Article 11. https://doi.org/10.1186/s40479-017-0061-9

Fonagy, P., Luyten, P., Allison, E., & Campbell, C. (2017b). What we have changed our minds about: Part 2. Borderline personality disorder, epistemic trust and the developmental significance of social communication. *Borderline Personality Disorder and Emotion Dysregulation, 4*(1), Article 9. https://doi.org/10.1186/s40479-017-0062-8

Fonagy, P., Target, M., Steele, H., & Steele, M. (1998). *Reflective-functioning manual, version 5.0 for application to adult attachment interviews.* University College London.

Foulkes, S.H. (1957). *Introduction to group-analytic psychotherapy. Studies in the social integration of individuals and groups.* Heinemann.

Foulkes, S.H. (1964). *Therapeutic group analysis.* George Allen & Unwin.

Foulkes, S.H., & Anthony, E.J. (1957). *Group psychotherapy: The psychoanalytic approach* (2nd ed.). Penguin.

Fraiberg, S., Adelson, E., & Shapiro, V. (2003). Gespenster im Kinderzimmer: Probleme gestörter Mutter-Säugling-Beziehungen aus psychoanalytischer Sicht [Ghosts in the nursery: Problems of disturbed mother-infant relationships in a psychoanalytic perspective]. *Analytische Kinder- und Jugendlichen-Psychotherapie, 34,* 465–504.

Frankl, V.E. (1955). *The doctor and the soul – From psychotherapy to logotherapy.* Alfred A. Knopf. (Original work published 1946).

Frankl, V.E. (1998). *Logotherapie und Existenzanalyse: Texte aus sechs Jahrzehnten* [Logotherapy and existential analysis: Texts from six decades]. Psychologie Verlags Union.

Freier, A., Kruse, J., Schmalbach, B., Zara, S., Werner, S., Brähler, E., Fegert, J.M., & Kampling, H. (2022). The mediation effect of personality functioning between different types of child maltreatment and the development of depression/anxiety symptoms – A German representative study. *Journal of Affective Disorders, 299*, 408–415. https://doi.org/10.1016/j.jad.2021.12.020

Freud, A. (1965). Normality and pathology in childhood: Assessments of development. In A. Freud (Ed.), *The writings of Anna Freud.* International Universities Press.

Freud, S. (1904). The Freudian psychoanalytic method. In J. Strachey (Ed. & Trans.), *The standard edition of the complete psychological works of Sigmund Freud* (Vol. 7, pp. 249–254). Hogarth Press.

Freud, S. (1905). Three essays on the theory of sexuality. In J. Strachey (Ed. & Trans.), *The standard edition of the complete psychological works of Sigmund Freud* (Vol. 7, pp. 125–245). Hogarth Press.

Freud, S. (1910). The future prospects of psycho-analytic therapy. In J. Strachey (Ed. & Trans.), *The standard edition of the complete psychological works of Sigmund Freud* (Vol. 11, pp. 139–151). Hogarth Press.

Freud, S. (1911). Psychoanalytic notes on an autobiographically described case of paranoia (dementia paranoides). In J. Strachey (Ed. & Trans.), *The standard edition of the complete psychological works of Sigmund Freud* (Vol. 12, pp. 3–82). Hogarth Press.

Freud, S. (1912). The dynamics of transference. In J. Strachey (Ed. & Trans.), *The standard edition of the complete psychological works of Sigmund Freud* (Vol. 12, pp. 97–108). Hogarth Press.

Freud, S. (1913). On beginning the treatment (Further recommendations on the technique of psychoanalysis I). In J. Strachey (Ed. & Trans.), *The standard edition of the complete psychological works of Sigmund Freud* (Vol. 12, pp. 121–144). Hogarth Press.

Freud, S. (1915). The unconscious. In J. Strachey (Ed. & Trans.), *The standard edition of the complete psychological works of Sigmund Freud* (Vol. 14, pp. 159–215). Hogarth Press.

Freud, S. (1916–1917). Introductory lectures on psycho-analysis. In J. Strachey (Ed. & Trans.), *The standard edition of the complete psychological works of Sigmund Freud* (Vols. 15–16). Hogarth Press.

Freud, S. (1921). Group psychology and the analysis of the ego. In J. Strachey (Ed. & Trans.), *The standard edition of the complete psychological works of Sigmund Freud* (Vol. 18, pp. 65–143). Hogarth Press.

Freud, S. (1923). The ego and the id. In J. Strachey (Ed. & Trans.), *The standard edition of the complete psychological works of Sigmund Freud* (Vol. 19, pp. 1–66). Hogarth Press.

Freud, S. (1924). The dissolution of the Oedipus complex. In J. Strachey (Ed. & Trans.), *The standard edition of the complete psychological works of Sigmund Freud* (Vol. 19, pp. 171–179). Hogarth Press.

Freud, S. (1925). An autobiographical study. In J. Strachey (Ed. & Trans.), *The standard edition of the complete psychological works of Sigmund Freud* (Vol. 20, pp. 1–74). Hogarth Press.

Freud, S. (1926). Inhibitions, symptoms and anxiety. In J. Strachey (Ed. & Trans.), *The standard edition of the complete psychological works of Sigmund Freud* (Vol. 20, pp. 75–175). Hogarth Press.

Freud, S. (1933). New introductory lectures on psycho-analysis. In J. Strachey (Ed. & Trans.), *The standard edition of the complete psychological works of Sigmund Freud* (Vol. 22, pp. 1–182). Hogarth Press.

Freud, S. (1940). An outline of psycho-analysis. In J. Strachey (Ed. & Trans.), *The standard edition of the complete psychological works of Sigmund Freud* (Vol. 23, pp. 139–207). Hogarth Press.

Freyberger, H., Dierse, B., Schneider, W., Strauß, B., Heuft, G., Schauenburg, H., Pouget-Schors, D., Seidler, G.H., Küchenhoff, J., & Hoffmann, S.O. (1996). Operationalisierte Psychodynamische Diagnostik (OPD) in der Erprobung: Ergebnisse einer multizentrischen Anwendungs- und Praktikabilitätsstudie [Testing Operationalized Psychodynamic Diagnosis (OPD): Results of a multicentric acceptability and practicability study]. *PPmP – Psychotherapie, Psychosomatik, Medizinische Psychologie, 46,* 356–365.

Freyberger, H.J., Dittmann, V., Stieglitz, R.D., & Dilling, H. (1990). ICD-10 in der Erprobung: Ergebnisse einer multizentrischen Feldstudie in den deutschsprachigen Ländern [Trials with ICD-10: Results of a multicenter field study in German speaking countries]. *Der Nervenarzt, 61*(5), 109–127.

Frijda, N.H. (1996). Die Gesetze der Emotionen [The laws of emotion]. *Zeitschrift für Psychosomatische Medizin und Psychotherapie, 42,* 205–221.

Gabbard, G.O. (1995). Countertransference: The emerging common ground. *International Journal of Law and Psychiatry, 76,* 475–485.

Gebhardt, C., Zimmermann, J., Peham, D., Bock, A., Mitte, K., & Benecke, C. (2016). Written on the face: Self- and expert-rated impairments in personality functioning are differently related to the expression of disgust toward an interviewer. *Journal of Personality Disorders, 30*(3), 408–418. https://doi.org/10.1521/pedi_2015_29_199

Gee, D.G., DeYoung, K.A., McLaughlin, K.A., Tillman, R.M., Barch, D.M., Forbes, E.E., Krueger, R.F., Strauman, T.J., Weierich, M.R., & Shackman, A.J. (2022). Training the next generation of clinical psychological scientists: A data-driven call to action. *Annual Review of Clinical Psychology, 18,* 43–70. https://doi.org/10.1146/annurev-clinpsy-081219-092500

Gemeinsamer Bundesausschuss. (2020). *Neue Regelungen zur Förderung der Gruppentherapie* [New rules for the advancement in group therapy]. https://www.g-ba.de/presse/pressemitteilungen-meldungen/913/

George, C., Kaplan, N., & Main, M. (1985). *Adult attachment interview* [Unpublished manuscript]. University of California.

Gerdes, N., & Weis, J. (2000). *Zur Theorie der Rehabilitation: Themen, Strategien und Methoden der Rehabilitationsforschung* [On the theory of rehabilitation: Topics, strategies, and methods of rehabilitation research]. Springer.

Gill, M.M. (1982). *Analysis of the transference, volume I: Theory and technique.* International Universities Press.

Gill, M.M. (1979). The analysis of the transference. *Journal of the American Psychoanalytic Association, 27*(Suppl), 263–288.

Gill, M.M., & Hoffman, I.Z. (1982). A method for studying the analysis of aspects of the patient's experience of the relationship in psychoanalysis and psychotherapy. *Journal of the American Psychoanalytic Association, 30*(1), 137–167. https://doi.org/10.1177/000306518203000106

Gill, M., Newman, R., Redlich, F.C., & Sommers, M. (Collaborator). (1954). *The initial interview in psychiatric practice, with phonograph records available to professional persons and institutions.* International Universities Press, Inc. https://doi.org/10.1037/11130-000

Gisch, H., Perlinger, J., Zimmermann, J., & Kretschmar, T. (2021). Die latente Struktur von psychodynamischen und psychologischen Persönlichkeitsmodellen: Eine gemeinsame Untersuchung von OPD-KF, OPD-SFK und BFI-2 [The latent structure of psychodynamic and psychological personality models: A joint analysis of the OPD-KF, OPD-SFK, and BFI-2]. *Zeitschrift für Psychosomatische Medizin und Psychotherapie, 67*(3), 241–255. https://doi.org/10.13109/zptm.2021.67.oa5

Gisch, H., Zimmermann, J., & Kretschmar, T. (2020). Ödipus vs. Big-Five: Kann eine psychoanalytisch fundierte Persönlichkeitsdiagnostik einen inkrementellen Beitrag über die Big-Five-Persönlichkeitsfacetten hinaus zur Vorhersage von psychischer Gesundheit und Zufriedenheit am Arbeitsplatz liefern? [Oedipus versus the big five: Do psychoanalytically based assessments of internal conflicts provide incremental validity over the big five personality facets for the prediction of employees' mental health and job satisfaction?]. *Zeitschrift für Arbeits- und Organisationspsychologie, 64*(4), 263–277. https://doi.org/10.1026/0932-4089/a000319

Grande, G., Rudolf, G., & Oberbracht, C. (2000). Veränderungsmessung auf OPD-Basis: Schwierigkeiten und ein neues Konzept [Measurement of change based on OPD: Challenges and a new concept]. In W. Schneider & H.J. Freyberger (Eds.), *Was leistet die OPD? Empirische Befunde und klinische Erfahrungen mit der Operationalisierten Psychodynamischen Diagnostik* (pp. 121–138). Huber.

Grande, T. (2002). Therapeutische Haltung im Umgang mit „Struktur" und „Konflikt" [A therapeutic approach to dealing with "structure" and "conflict"]. In G. Rudolf, T. Grande & P. Henningsen (Eds.), *Die Struktur der Persönlichkeit* (S. 236–248). Schattauer.

Grande, T. (2007). Wie inszenieren sich dysfunktionale Beziehungsmuster in der Therapeut-Patient-Interaktion? [How are dysfunctional relationship patterns re-enacted in the therapist-patient interaction?]. *PPmP – Psychotherapie, Psychosomatik, Medizinische Psychologie, 57*(2), 61–69. https://doi.org/10.1055/s-2006-951921

Grande, T., Oberbracht, C., & Rudolf, G. (1998). Einige empirische Zusammenhänge zwischen den Achsen „Beziehung", „Konflikt" und „Struktur" [Some empirical correlations between the axes "relationship", "conflict", and "structure"]. In H. Schauenburg, H.J. Freyberger, M. Cierpka, & P. Buchheim (Eds.), *OPD in der Praxis: Konzepte, Anwendungen, Ergebnisse der Operationalisierten Psychodynamischen Diagnostik* (pp. 121–138). Huber.

Grande, T., Rudolf, G., Oberbracht, C., & Jakobsen, T. (2001). Therapeutische Veränderungen jenseits der Symptomatik: Wirkungen stationärer Psychotherapie im Lichte der Heidelberger Umstrukturierungsskala [Therapeutic changes beyond symptoms: Effects of inpatient treatment in the view of the Heidelberg Structural Change Scale]. *Zeitschrift für Psychosomatische Medizin und Psychotherapie, 47*, 213–233. https://doi.org/10.13109/zptm.2001.47.3.213

Grande, T., Rudolf, G., Oberbracht, C., & Pauli-Magnus, C. (2003). Progressive changes in patients' lives after psychotherapy: Which treatment effects support them? *Psychotherapy Research, 13*(1), 43–58. https://doi.org/10.1093/ptr/kpg006

Grawe, K. (2004). *Neuropsychotherapie* [Neuropsychotherapy]. Hogrefe.

Grenyer, B.F.S., & Marceau, E.M. (2022). Helping patients master core conflictual relationship themes in psychotherapy. *Journal of Clinical Psychology, 78*(3), 386–395. https://doi.org/10.1002/jclp.23314

Grossmann, K.E., August, P., Fremmer-Bombik, E., Friedl, A., Grossmann, K., Scheuerer-Englisch, H., Spangler, G., Stephan, C., & Suess, G. (1989). Die Bindungstheorie [Attachment theory]. In W. Keller (Ed.), *Handbuch der Kleinkindforschung* (pp. 101–122). Springer.

Gumz, A., & Hörz-Sagstetter, S. (Eds.). (2018). *Psychodynamische Therapie in der Praxis* [Psychodynamic therapy in practice]. Beltz.

Habermas, T., & Reese, E. (2015). Getting a life takes time: The development of the life story in adolescence, its precursors and consequences. *Human Development, 58*(3), 172–201. https://doi.org/10.1159/000437245

Hans, G., Krause, R., & Steimer, E. (1986). Interaktionsprozesse bei Schizophrenen [Interaction processes in schizophrenics]. In E. Nordmann & M. Cierpka (Eds.), *Familienforschung in Psychiatrie und Psychotherapie*. Springer.

Harlow, H.F. (1971). *Learning to love.* Albion.

Hartmann, H. (1958). *Ego psychology and the problem of adaptation* (D. Rapaport, Trans.). International Universities Press. (Original work published 1939). https://doi.org/10.1037/13180-000

Haug, H.-J., & Kind, H. (2008). *Psychiatrische Untersuchung: Ein Leitfaden für Studierende, Ärzte und Psychologen in Praxis und Klinik* [Psychiatric examination: A guide for students, doctors, and psychologists in practice and clinic] (Version 7). Springer Medizin Verlag Heidelberg.

Heigl-Evers, A., & Heigl, F. (1994). Das Göttinger Modell der Anwendung der Psychoanalyse in Gruppen unter besonderer Berücksichtigung der psychoanalytischen-interaktionellen Methode [The Göttingen model for the application of psychoanalysis in groups with special consideration of the Psychoanalytic-interactional Method]. *Gruppenpsychotherapie und Gruppendynamik, 30*, 1–29.

Heigl-Evers, A., & Henneberg-Mönch, U. (1990). Die Bedeutung der Affekte für Diagnose, Prognose und Therapie [The importance of affects for diagnosis, prognosis, and therapy]. *PPmP - Psychotherapie, Psychosomatik, Medizinische Psychologie, 40*, 39–47.

Heimann, P. (1950). On countertransference. *International Journal of Psychoanalysis, 31*, 81–84.

Heimann, P. (1962). Notes on the anal stage. *International Journal of Psychoanalysis, 43*, 406–414.

Henkel, M., Benecke, C., Masuhr, O., Jaeger, U., & Spitzer, C. (2022). Reliabilität und Validität des OPD-Konfliktfragebogens bei stationären Psychotherapiepatient*innen [Reliability and validity of the OPD conflict questionnaire in an inpatient treament sample]. *Zeitschrift für Psychosomatische Medizin und Psychotherapie, 68*(1), 39–53. https://doi.org/10.13109/zptm.2022.68.1.39

Henkel, M., Zimmermann, J., Huber, D., Staats, H., Wiegand-Grefe, S., Taubner, S., Frommer, J., & Benecke, C. (2019). Patient characteristics in psychodynamic psychotherapies. *Psychoanalytic Psychology, 36*(1), 1–8. https://doi.org/10.1037/pap0000165

Henkel, M., Zimmermann, J., Künecke, J., Remmers, C., & Benecke, C. (2018). Same same but different: Das Potential der Operationalisierten Psychodynamischen Diagnostik für ein differenziertes Verständnis von Persönlichkeitsstörungen [Same same but different: The potential of the Operationalized Psychodynamic Diagnosis for a differentiated understanding of personality disorders]. *Zeitschrift für Psychiatrie, Psychologie und Psychotherapie, 66*(2), 107–117. https://doi.org/10.1024/1661-4747/a000346

Henkel, M., Benecke, C., Volz, M., Cropp, C., & Spitzer, C. (2024). Veränderungen in der Konfliktpathologie während stationärer Psychotherapie und ihr Zusammenhang mit Symptomreduktion [Changes in conflict pathology during inpatient psychotherapy and their relationship to symptom reduction]. *Zeitschrift für Psychosomatische Medizin und Psychotherapie, 70*(3), 266–282. https://doi.org/10.13109/zptm.2024.70.3.266

Hentschel, U., Smith, G.J., Draguns, J., & Ehlers, W. (Eds.). (2004). *Defense mechanisms: Theoretical, research and clinical perspectives.* Elsevier.

Hepach, R., & Warneken, F. (2018). Early development of prosocial behavior: Revealing the foundation of human prosociality. *Current Opinion in Psychology, 20*, iv–viii. https://doi.org/10.1016/j.copsyc.2018.02.001

Hettich, N., Beutel, M.E., Ernst, M., Schliessler, C., Kampling, H., Kruse, J., & Braehler, E. (2022). Conspiracy endorsement and its associations with personality functioning, anxiety, loneliness, and sociodemographic characteristics during the COVID-19 pandemic in a representative sample of the German population. *PLoS ONE, 17*(1), Article e0263301. https://doi.org/10.1371/journal.pone.0263301

Heuft, G., & Senf, W. (1998). *Paxis der Qualitätssicherung in der Psychotherapie: Das Manual zur Psy-BaDo* [Practice of quality assurance in psychotherapy: The manual for Psy-BaDo]. Thieme.

Heymann, F. von, & Tritt, K. (2018). *Psy-BaDo-PTM.* (Version 4.13). [System for quality management]. IQP.

Hiebler-Ragger, M., Perchtold-Stefan, C.M., Unterrainer, H.F., Fuchshuber, J., Koschutnig, K., Nausner, L., Kapfhammer, H.P., Papousek, I., Weiss, E.M., & Fink, A. (2021). Lower cognitive reappraisal capacity is related to impairments in attachment and personality structure in poly-drug use: An fMRI study. *Brain Imaging and Behavior, 15*(4), 2187–2198. https://doi.org/10.1007/s11682-020-00414-3

Hilton, N.Z., & Radatz, D.L. (2021). Criminogenic needs and intimate partner violence: Association with recidivism and implications for treatment. *Psychological Services, 18*(4), 566–573. https://doi.org/10.1037/ser0000450

Hörz-Sagstetter, S. & Doering, S. (2021). *Strukturiertes Interview zur Persönlichkeitsorganisation* (Revision STIPO-R, deutsche Version). [Structured interview on personality organization, revision STIPO-R, German version] [Unpublished manuscript].

Hoffmann, I.Z., & Gill, M.M. (1988). A scheme for coding the patient experience of the therapist (PERT): Some applications, extensions, and comparisons. In H. Dahl, H. Kächele, & H. Thomä (Eds.), *Psychoanalytic process research strategies* (pp. 67–108). Springer. https://doi.org/10.1007/978-3-642-74265-1_5

Hoffmann, S.O. (1984). *Charakter und Neurose: Ansätze zu einer psychoanalytischen Charakterologie* [Character and neurosis: Approaches to a psychoanalytic characterology]. Suhrkamp.

Hoffmann, S.O. (1987). Forschungstendenzen im Bereich von Psychotherapie und Neurosenlehre in den letzten fünfzehn Jahren [Research trends in the field of psychotherapy and neurosis theory in the last fifteen years]. *PPmP – Psychotherapie, Psychosomatik, Medizinische Psychologie, 37*, 10–14.

Hoffmann, S.O. (2008). *Psychodynamische Therapie von Angststörungen: Einführung und Manual für die kurz- und mittelfristige Therapie* [Psychodynamic therapy for anxiety disorders: Introduction and manual for short- and medium-term therapy]. Schattauer.

Holder, A. (1982). Der Ödipuskomplex [The oedipus complex]. In D. Eicke (Ed.), *Tiefenpsychologie (Bd. 1): Sigmund Freud – Leben und Werk* (pp. 602–609). Beltz.

Holl, J., Oeten, R. von, & Benecke, C. (2020). Emotionsregulation bei psychischen Störungen und in der Psychotherapie [Emotion regulation in mental disorders and psychotherapy]. In S. Barnow (Ed.), *Handbuch Emotionsregulation – Zwischen psychischer Gesundheit und Psychopathologie* (pp. 175–206). Springer. https://doi.org/10.1007/978-3-662-60280-5_12

Hopper, E. (2009). The theory of basic assumption of incohesion: Aggregation/massification or (BA) I:A/M. *British Journal of Psychotherapy, 25*, 214–229. https://doi.org/10.1111/j.1752-0118.2009.01116.x

Hopwood, C.J., Newman, D.A., Donnellan, M.B., Markowitz, J.C., Grilo, C.M., Sanislow, C.A., Ansell, E.B., McGlashan, T.H., Skodol, A.E., Shea, M.T., Gunderson, J.G., Zanarini, M.C., & Morey, L.C. (2009). The stability of personality traits in individuals with borderline personality disorder. *Journal of Abnormal Psychology, 118*(4), 806–815. https://doi.org/10.1037/a0016954

Horowitz, L.M., Strauß, B., & Kordy, H. (2000). *IIP-D: Inventar zur Erfassung interpersoneller Probleme – Deutsche Version* (2nd ed.) [IIP-D: Inventory for the assessment of interpersonal problems – German version]. Beltz Test.

Horowitz, M.J. (Ed.). (1991). *Person schemas and maladaptive interpersonal patterns.* The University of Chicago Press.

Hörz-Sagstetter, S., Ohse, L., & Kampe, L. (2021). Three dimensional approaches to personality disorders: A review on personality functioning, personality structure, and personality organization. *Current Psychiatry Reports, 23*(7), Article 45. https://doi.org/10.1007/s11920-021-01250-y

Huber, D., Klug, G., & Wallerstein, R.S. (2006). *Skalen Psychischer Kompetenzen (SPK): Ein Messinstrument für die therapeutische Veränderung in der psychischen Struktur* [Scales of psychological competence (SPK): A measuring instrument for therapeutic change in psychological structure]. Kohlhammer.

Immel, N., Dagnino, P., & Hunger-Schoppe, C. (2021). Associations between patient personality, symptomatic change and therapy dropout. *Clinical Psychology & Psychotherapy, 29*(3), 922–932. https://doi.org/10.1002/cpp.2670

Jacobs, T.J. (1986). On countertransference enactments. *Journal of the American Psychoanalytic Association, 34*(2), 289–307. https://doi.org/10.1177/000306518603400203

Jacobsen, E. (1964). *The self and the world of objects*. International Universities Press.

Jakobsen, T. (2014). Abhängigkeitsdynamik, Konflikt und Struktur in der Operationalisierten Psychodynamischen Diagnostik (OPD-2) [Addiction dynamics, conflict, and structure within the Operationalized Psychodynamic Diagnosis (OPD-2)]. *Persönlichkeitsstörungen: Theorie und Therapie, 18*(2), 75–87.

Jakobsen, T. (2017). Psychodynamische Überlegungen zur Abhängigkeit [Psychodynamic considerations on dependency]. *PiD – Psychotherapie im Dialog, 18*(1), 28–33. https://doi.org/10.1055/s-0042-121752

Janssen, P.L. (1994). Zur psychoanalytischen Diagnostik [On psychoanalytic diagnostics]. In P.L. Janssen & W. Schneider (Eds.), *Diagnostik in Psychotherapie und Psychosomatik* (pp. 77–103). Fischer.

Janssen, P.L. (2016). Psychoanalytisch und gruppenanalytisch begründete stationäre Psychotherapie in der Psychosomatischen Medizin [Psychoanalytical and group-analytical founded inpatient psychotherapy in psychosomatic medicine]. *Gruppenpsychotherapie und Gruppendynamik, 52*(1), 24–35. https://doi.org/10.13109/grup.2016.52.1.24

Janssen, P.L., Dahlbender, R.W., Freyberger, H.J., Heuft, G., Mans, E.J., Rudolf, G., Schneider, W., & Seidler, G.H. (1996). Leitfaden zur psychodynamisch-diagnostischen Untersuchung [Guideline for psychodynamic-diagnostic examination]. *Psychotherapeut, 41*(4), 297–304. https://doi.org/10.1007/s002780050038

Janssen, P.L., & Kruse, J. (2019). Was bringt die Musterweiterbildungsordnung 2018? [What are the implications of the 2018 model continuing education regulation?]. *Ärztliche Psychotherapie, 14*(2), 127–142.

Jauk, E., & Ehrenthal, J.C. (2020). Self-reported levels of personality functioning from the Operationalized Psychodynamic Diagnosis (OPD) system and emotional intelligence likely assess the same latent construct. *Journal of Personality Assessment, 103*(3), 365–379. https://doi.org/10.1080/00223891.2020.1775089

Jung, C.G. (1971). Psychological types. In H. Read, M. Fordham, G. Adler, W. McGuire (Eds.), *The collected works of C.G. Jung* (Vol. 6). Princeton University Press. (Original work published 1921).

Kaës, R. (2017). Der Geschwisterkomplex [The sibling complex]. *Psyche, 71*(9/10), 780–811. https://doi.org/10.21706/ps-71-9-780

Kaplan, A.H. (1981). From discovery to validation: A basic challenge to psychoanalysis. *Journal of the American Psychoanalytic Association, 29*(1), 3–26. https://doi.org/10.1177/000306518102900101

Kati, A., Stumpf, A., Heuft, G., Burgmer, M., & Schneider, G. (2015). Personale Ressourcen in stationärer Fachpsychotherapie–Zusammenhänge und Entwicklung [Personal resources in inpatient psychotherapy–relationships and development]. *Zeitschrift für Psychosomatische Medizin und Psychotherapie, 61*(2), 139–155. https://doi.org/10.13109/zptm.2015.61.2.139

Kaufhold, J., Negele, A., Leuzinger-Bohleber, M., Kallenbach, L., & Bahrke, U. (2017). Zur Konfliktdynamik bei chronischer Depression – Ergebnisse zur Konflikt- und Strukturachse der OPD in der LAC-Studie [Conflict dynamics in chronic depression – Results of the conflict and structure axis using the OPD in the LAC study]. *Zeitschrift für Psychosomatische Medizin und Psychotherapie, 62*(2), 151–162. https://doi.org/10.13109/zptm.2017.63.2.151

Kehyayan, A., Best, K., Schmeing, J., Axmacher, N., & Kessler, H. (2013). Neural activity during free association to conflict-related sentences. *Frontiers in Human Neuroscience, 7,* Article 705. https://doi.org/10.3389/fnhum.2013.00705

Kernberg, O.F. (1970). A psychoanalytical classification of character pathology. *Journal of the American Psychoanalytic Association, 18*(4), 800–822. https://doi.org/10.1177/000306517001800403

Kernberg, O.F. (1975). *Borderline conditions and pathological narcissism*. Jason Aronson.

Kernberg, O.F. (1976). *Object relations and clinical psychoanalysis*. Jason Aronson.

Kernberg, O.F. (1980). *Internal world and external reality: Object relations theory applied*. Jason Aronson.

Kernberg, O.F. (1981). Structural interviewing. *The Psychiatric Clinics of North America, 4*(1), 169–195. https://doi.org/10.1016/S0193-953X(18)30944-4

Kernberg, O.F. (1984). *Severe personality disorders: Psychotherapeutic strategies*. Yale University Press.

Kernberg, O.F. (1988). *Schwere Persönlichkeitsstörung. Theorie, Diagnose, Behandlungsstrategien* [Severe personality disorder: Theory, diagnosis, and treatment strategies]. Klett-Cotta.

Kernberg, O.F., Burstein, E.D., Coyne, L., Appelbaum, A., Horowitz, L.M., & Voth, Z. (1972). Psychotherapy and psychoanalysis: Final report of the Menninger foundation's psychotherapy research project. *Bulletin of the Menninger Clinic, 36*(1), 3–275.

Kessler, H., Stasch, M., & Cierpka, M. (2013). Operationalized psychodynamic diagnosis as an instrument to transfer psychodynamic constructs into neuroscience. *Frontiers in Human Neuroscience, 7*, Article 718. https://doi.org/10.3389/fnhum.2013.00718

Kessler, H., Taubner, S., Buchheim, A., Münte, T.F., Stasch, M., Kächele, H., Roth, G., Heinecke, A., Erhard, P., Cierpka, M., & Wiswede, D. (2011). Individualized and clinically derived stimuli activate limbic structures in depression: An fMRI study. *PLoS ONE, 6*(1), Article e15712. https://doi.org/10.1371/journal.pone.0015712

Keupp, H. (1999). *Identitätskonstruktionen. Das Patchwork der Identitäten in der Spätmoderne* [Identity constructions. The patchwork of identities in late modernity]. Rohwolt.

Kihlstrom, J. (1999). The psychological unconscious. In L.A. Pervin & O.P. John (Eds.), *Handbook of personality: Theory and research* (2nd ed., pp. 424–442). Guilford.

Kind, H. (1973). *Leitfaden für die psychiatrische Untersuchung* [Guide to psychiatric examination]. Springer.

Kind, H. (1978). Das psychiatrische Erstinterview [The psychiatric initial interview]. *Der Nervenarzt, 49*, 255–260.

Köber, C., Schmiedek, F., & Habermas, T. (2015). Characterizing lifespan development of three aspects of coherence in life narratives: A cohort-sequential study. *Developmental Psychology, 51*(2), 260–275. https://doi.org/10.1037/a0038668

Köhling, J., Moessner, M., Ehrenthal, J.C., Bauer, S., Cierpka, M., Kämmerer, A., Schauenburg, H., & Dinger, U. (2016). Affective instability and reactivity in depressed patients with and without borderline pathology. *Journal of Personality Disorders, 30*(6), 776–795. https://doi.org/10.1521/pedi_2015_29_230

Kohut, H. (1971). *The analysis of the self: A systematic approach to the psychoanalytic treatment of narcissistic personality disorders*. International Universities Press.

Kohut, H. (1977). *The restoration of the self*. International Universities Press.

Köllner, V., & Bassler, M. (Eds.). (2021). *Praxishandbuch psychosomatische Medizin in der Rehabilitation* [Practical handbook of psychosomatic medicine in rehabilitation]. Elsevier.

König, K. (1982). Interaktioneller Anteil der Übertragung und phobische Persönlichkeitsstruktur [Interactive aspects of transference and phobic personality structure]. *Praxis der Psychotherapie und Psychosomatik, 27*, 25–32.

König, K. (1988). Basale und zentrale Beziehungswünsche [Basic and central relationship desires]. *Forum Psychoanalyse, 4*, 177–185.

König, K. (1996). *Abwehrmechanismen* [Defense mechanisms]. Vandenhoeck & Ruprecht.

König, K., Dahlbender, R.W., Holzinger, A., Topitz, A., & Doering, S. (2016). Kreuzvalidierung von drei Fragebögen zur Strukturdiagnostik: BPI, IPO und OPD-SF [Cross-validation of three questionnaires for structural diagnosis: BPI, IPO, and OPD-SQ]. *Zeitschrift für Psychosomatische Medizin und Psychotherapie, 62*(2), 177–189. https://doi.org/10.13109/zptm.2016.62.2.177

Koops, T.U., Wiessner, C., Ehrenthal, J.C., & Briken, P. (2021). Assessing psychodynamic conflicts and level of personality functioning in women diagnosed with vaginismus and dyspareunia. *Frontiers in Psychology, 12*, Article 687369. https://doi.org/10.3389/fpsyg.2021.687369

Körner, J. (2015). *Die Deutung in der Psychoanalyse* [Interpretation in psychoanalysis]. Kohlhammer.

Kotte, S., Bick, E., Benecke, C., & Möller, H. (2019). Operationalisierte Psychodynamische Diagnostik im Arbeitskontext: Entwicklung eines berufsbezogenen OPD-Konflikt-Fragebogens [Operationalized psychodynamic diagnostics at the workplace: Development of a work-related OPD-conflict-questionnaire]. *Organisationsberatung Supervision Coaching, 26*(1), 67–83. https://doi.org/10.1007/s11613-019-00587-x

Krakau, L., Tibubos, A.N., Beutel, M.E., Ehrenthal, J.C., Gieler, U., & Brähler, E. (2021). Personality functioning as a mediator of adult mental health following child maltreatment. *Journal of Affective Disorders, 291*, 126–134. https://doi.org/10.1016/j.jad.2021.05.006

Kraus, B., Dammann, G., Rudaz, M., Sammet, I., Jeggle, D., & Grimmer, B. (2021). Changes in the level of personality functioning in inpatient psychotherapy. *Psychotherapy Research, 31*(1), 117–131. https://doi.org/10.1080/10503307.2020.1763493

Krause, R. (2012). *Allgemeine psychodynamische Behandlungs- und Krankheitslehre: Grundlagen und Modelle* [General psychodynamic treatment and disease theory: Fundamentals and models]. Kohlhammer.

Kraepelin, E. (2005). The directions of psychiatric research. *History of Psychiatry*, *16*(3), 350–364. https://doi.org/10.1177/0957154X0501600306

Kröber, H.-L., & Steller, M. (2005). *Psychologische Begutachtung im Strafverfahren: Indikationen, Methoden, Qualitätsstandards* [Psychological assessment in criminal proceedings: Indications, methods, quality standards]. Steinkopff.

Küchenhoff, J. (2002). In Strukturen denken: Strukturkonzepte in Philosophie, Psychiatrie und Psychoanalyse und ihre praktischen Auswirkungen [Thinking in structures: Structural concepts in philosophy, psychiatry, and psychoanalysis and their practical implications]. In G. Rudolf, T. Grande, & P. Henningsen (Eds.), *Die Struktur der Persönlichkeit* (pp. 68–80). Schattauer.

Küchenhoff, J. (2012). *Körper und Sprache: Theoretische und klinische Beiträge zu einem intersubjektiven Verständnis des Körpererlebens* [Body and language: Theoretical and clinical contributions to an intersubjective understanding of body experience]. Psychosozial-Verlag.

Küchenhoff, J. (2018). *Understanding psychosis*. Routledge. (Original work published 2012). https://doi.org/10.4324/9781351025942

Küchenhoff, J., & Argawalla, P. (2013). *Körperbild und Persönlichkeitsstörung: Die klinische Evaluation des Körpererlebens mit der Körperbildliste* [Body image and personality disorder: The clinical evaluation of body experience with the body image list]. Springer. https://doi.org/10.1007/978-3-642-32577-9

La Parra, G. de, Dagnino, P., Valdés, C., & Krause, M. (2017). Beyond self-criticism and dependency: Structural functioning of depressive patients and its treatment. *Research in Psychotherapy (Milano)*, *20*(1), Article 236. https://doi.org/10.4081/ripppo.2017.236

Laimböck, A. (2000). *Das psychoanalytische Erstgespräch* [The psychoanalytic initial interview]. Brandes & Apsel.

Lambert, M. J. (2013). *Bergin and Garfield's handbook of psychotherapy and behavior change*. John Wiley & Sons.

Lange, C. & Heuft, G. (2002). Die Beeinträchtigungsschwere in der psychosomatischen und psychiatrischen Qualitätssicherung: Global Assessment of Functioning Scale (GAF) vs. Beeinträchtigungs-Schwere-Score (BSS) [Psychic impairment in psychosomatic and psychiatric quality assessment: Global assessment of functioning scale (GAF) vs. impairment score (IS)]. *Zeitschrift für Psychosomatische Medizin und Psychotherapie, 48*, 256–269. https://doi.org/10.13109/zptm.2002.48.3.256

Langer, E. J. & Abelson, R. P. (1974). A patient by any other name ...: Clinician group difference in labeling bias. *Journal of Consulting and Clinical Psychology, 42*(1), 4–9. https://doi.org/10.1037/h0036054

Leary, T. (1957). *Interpersonal diagnosis of personality*. Ronald Press.

LeDoux, J. (1996). *The emotional brain: The mysterious underpinnings of emotional life*. Simon & Schuster.

LeDoux, J. (2002). *Synaptic self - How our brains become who we are*. Penguin.

Leichsenring, F. (1997). *Borderline-Persönlichkeits-Inventar (BPI): Manual* [Borderline Personality Inventory (BPI): Manual]. Hogrefe.

Leichsenring, F., Beutel, M. E., & Leibing, E. (2008). Psychoanalytisch-orientierte Fokaltherapie der sozialen Phobie: Ein Behandlungsmanual auf der Grundlage der supportiv-expressiven Therapie Luborskys [Psychodynamic short-term therapy of social phobia: A treatment manual on the basis of Luborsky's supportive-expressive therapy]. *Psychotherapeut, 53*(3), 185–197. https://doi.org/10.1007/s00278-007-0573-7

Leichsenring, F., & Salzer, S. (2014). *Generalisierte Angststörung: Psychodynamische Therapie* [Generalized anxiety disorder: Psychodynamic therapy]. Hogrefe.

Lempa, G., Haebler, D. von, & Montag, C. (2017). *Psychodynamische Psychotherapie der Schizophrenien* [Psychodynamic psychotherapy of schizophrenia]. Psychosozial-Verlag.

Leotti, L. A., Iyengar, S. S., & Ochsner, K. N. (2010). Born to choose: The origins and value of the need for control. *Trends in Cognitive Sciences, 14*(10), 457–463. https://doi.org/10.1016/j.tics.2010.08.001

Leuzinger-Bohleber, M., Kaufhold, J., Kallenbach, L., Negele, A., Ernst, M., Keller, W., Fiedler, G., Hautzinger, M., Bahrke, U., & Beutel, M. (2019). How to measure sustained psychic transformations in long-term treatments of chronically depressed patients: Symptomatic and structural changes in the LAC Depression Study of the outcome of cognitive-behavioural and psychoanalytic long-term treatments. *The International Journal of Psychoanalysis, 100*(1), 99–127. https://doi.org/10.1080/00207578.2018.1533377

Lichtenberg, J. D. (1983). *Psychoanalysis and infant research*. Analytic Press.

Lichtenberg, J. D. (1989). *Psychoanalysis and motivation*. Analytic Press.
Lichtenberg, J. D., Lachmann, F. M., & Fosshage, J. L. (2011). *Psychoanalysis and motivational systems: A new look*. Routledge/Taylor & Francis Group. https://doi.org/10.4324/9780203844748
Linehan, M. M. (1993). *Cognitive-behavioral treatment of borderline personality disorder*. Guilford.
Lingiardi, V., Lonati, C., Delucchi, F., Fossati, A., Vanzulli, L., & Maffei, C. (1999). Defense mechanisms and personality disorders. *The Journal of Nervous and Mental Disease, 187*(4), 224–228. https://doi.org/10.1097/00005053-199904000-00005
Lingiardi, V., & MacWilliams, N. (Eds.). (2017). *Psychodynamic diagnostic manual (PDM-2)* (2nd ed.). Guilford Press.
Livesley, W. J. (2009). *General assessment of personality disorder (GAPD)*. Sigma Assessment Systems.
Lohmer, M., Klug, G., Herrmann, B., Pouget, D., & Rauch, M. (1992). Zur Diagnostik der Frühstörung: Versuch einer Standortbestimmung zwischen neurotischem Niveau und Borderline-Störung [On the diagnosis of early disorder: An attempt to locate between neurotic level and borderline disorder]. *Praxis Psychotherapie Psychosomatik, 37*, 243–255.
Lorenzini, N., de la Parra, G., Dagnino, P., Gomez-Barris, E., Crempien, C., & Ehrenthal, J. C. (2021). Chilean validation of the operationalized psychodynamic diagnosis-structure questionnaire (OPDSQ) for personality structure. *BMC Psychology, 9*, Article 139. https://doi.org/10.1186/s40359-021-00640-4
Lübke, L., Flemming, E., Mestel, R., Masuhr, O., Jaeger, U., & Spitzer, C. (2021). Veränderungsmessung mit der Kurzform des OPD-Strukturfragebogens (OPD-SFK) [Measurement of change with the short version of the OPD Structure Questionnaire (OPD-SQS)]. *PPmP – Psychotherapie, Psychosomatik, Medizinische Psychologie, 71*(11), 456–463. https://doi.org/10.1055/a-1425-7618
Luborsky, L. (1984). *Principles of psychoanalytic psychotherapy: A manual for supportive-expressive treatment*. Basic Books.
Luborsky, L., Albani, C., & Eckert, R. (1991). *Manual zur ZBKT-Methode (deutsche Übersetzung mit Ergänzung der Ulmer ZBKT-Arbeitsgruppe)* [Manual for the CCRT method (German translation with additions from the Ulm CCRT working group)]. University of Ulm.
Luborsky, L., & Crits-Christoph, P. (1998). *Understanding transference: The core conflictual relationship theme method* (2nd ed.). Basic Books. https://doi.org/10.1037/10250-000
Mahler, M., Pine, F., & Bergmann, A. (1975). *The psychological birth of the human infant*. Basic Books.
Main, T. F. (1946). The hospital as a therapeutic institution. *Bulletin of the Menninger Clinic, 10*, 66–95.
Malan, D. H. (1979). *Individual psychotherapy and the science of psychodynamics*. Butterworths.
Maslow, A. H. (1970). *Motivation and personality*. Harper & Row.
McCallum, M., & Piper, W. E. (Eds.). (1997). *Psychological mindedness: A contemporary understanding*. Lawrence Erlbaum Associates Publishers.
McCullough, J. P. (2000). *Treatment for chronic depression: Cognitive Behavioral Analysis System of Psychotherapy (CBASP)*. Guilford.
Mead, G. H. (1934). *Mind, self & society*. University of Chicago Press.
Mentzos, S. (1984). *Neurotische Konfliktverarbeitung* [Neurotic conflict processing]. Fischer.
Mentzos, S. (2002). *Psychodynamische Modelle in der Psychiatrie* (5th ed.) [Psychodynamic models in psychiatry]. Vandenhoeck & Ruprecht.
Mentzos, S. (2011). *Lehrbuch der Psychodynamik: Die Funktion der Dysfunktionalität psychischer Störungen* (5th ed.) [Textbook of psychodynamics: The function of dysfunctionality in mental disorders]. Vandenhoeck & Ruprecht.
Mentzos, S. (2015). Dilemmatische Gegensätze im Zentrum der Psychodynamik der Psychosen [Dilemmatic conflicts at the center of the psychodynamics of psychoses]. *Forum Der Psychoanalyse, 31*(4), 341–352. https://doi.org/10.1007/s00451-015-0216-5
Mertens, W. (1992). *Kompendium psychoanalytischer Grundbegriffe* [Compendium of psychoanalytic basic terms]. Quintessenz.
Mertens, W. (2000). *Einführung in die psychoanalytische Therapie* [Introduction to psychoanalytic therapy] (3rd ed., Vol. 1). Kohlhammer.
Mertens, W. (2004a). *Einführung in die psychoanalytische Therapie* [Introduction to psychoanalytic therapy] (3rd ed., Vol. 2). Kohlhammer.
Mertens, W. (2004b). Von der Theorie zur Praxis: Operationalisierung und die Tiefe von Bedeutung am Beispiel der OPD-Konfliktachse [From theory to practice: Operationalization and the depth of meaning using the example of the OPD conflict axis]. In R. Dahlbender, P. Buchheim, & G. Schüßler (Eds.), *Lernen an der Praxis: OPD und die Qualitätssicherung in der psychodynamischen Psychotherapie* (pp. 229–237). Huber.

Mikolajewski, A.J., Allan, N.P., Merrill, L., Carter, M.C., & Manguno-Mire, G. (2021). Employing the risk-need-responsivity (RNR) model and predicting successful completion in an alternative drug court program: Preliminary findings from the Orleans Parish Drug Court. *Journal of Substance Abuse Treatment, 131*, Article 108453. https://doi.org/10.1016/j.jsat.2021.108453

Morey, L.C. (2017). Development and initial evaluation of a self-report form of the DSM-5 Level of Personality Functioning Scale. *Psychological Assessment, 29*(10), 1302–1308. https://doi.org/10.1037/pas0000450

Nikendei, C., Mölle, C., Fischer, K., Granov, M., Huber, J., Dinger, U., Herzog, W., Schauenburg, H., & Ehrenthal, J.C. (2020). Persönlichkeitsstruktur und Bindungsstil als Prädiktoren für die erfolgreiche Aufnahme einer ambulanten psychotherapeutischen Behandlung [Level of personality functioning and attachment style as predictors for the successful referral to outpatient psychotherapy]. *Zeitschrift für Psychosomatische Medizin und Psychotherapie, 66*, 178–192. https://doi.org/10.13109/zptm.2020.66.2.178

Nitzgen, D., & Brünger, M. (2000). Operationalisierte Psychodynamische Diagnostik in der Rehabilitationsklinik Birkenbuck: Einsatz und Befunde [Operationalized Psychodynamic Diagnosis in the rehabilitation clinic Birkenbuck: Application and findings]. In W. Schneider & H.J. Freyberger (Eds.), *Was leistet die OPD? Empirische Befunde und klinische Erfahrungen mit der Operationalisierten Psychodynamischen Diagnostik* (pp. 229–237). Huber.

Niv, N., Cohen, A.N., Sullivan, G., & Young, A.S. (2007). The MIRECC version of the global assessment of functioning scale: Reliability and validity. *Psychiatric Services, 58*(4), 529–535. https://doi.org/10.1176/ps.2007.58.4.529

Obbarius, A., Ehrenthal, J.C., Fischer, F., Liegl, G., Obbarius, N., Sarrar, L., & Rose, M. (2021). Applying item response theory to the OPD structure questionnaire: Identification of a unidimensional core construct and feasibility of computer adaptive testing. *Journal of Personality Assessment, 103*(5), 645–658. https://doi.org/10.1080/00223891.2020.1828435

Olajide, K., Munjiza, J., Moran, P., O'Connell, L., Newton-Howes, G., Bassett, P., Akintomide, G., Ng, N., Tyrer, P., Mulder, R., & Crawford, M.J. (2018). Development and psychometric properties of the Standardized Assessment of Severity of Personality Disorder (SASPD). *Journal of Personality Disorders, 32*(1), 44–56. https://doi.org/10.1521/pedi_2017_31_285

Oltmanns, J.R., & Widiger, T.A. (2019). Evaluating the assessment of the ICD-11 personality disorder diagnostic system. *Psychological Assessment, 31*(5), 674–684. https://doi.org/10.1037/pas0000693

Olver, M.E., Marshall, L.E., Marshall, W.L., & Nicholaichuk, T.P. (2020). A long-term outcome assessment of the effects on subsequent reoffense rates of a prison-based CBT/RNR sex offender treatment program with strength-based elements. *Sexual Abuse: A Journal of Research and Treatment, 32*, 127–153. https://doi.org/10.1177/1079063218807486

Østergård, O.K., Fenger, M., & Hougaard, E. (2019). Symptomatic distress and effectiveness of psychological treatments delivered at a nationwide student counseling service. *Counselling Psychology Quarterly, 32*(2), 150–168. https://doi.org/10.1080/09515070.2017.1410696

OPD Task Force. (1996). *Operationalisierte Psychodynamische Diagnostik. Grundlagen und Manual* [Operationalized psychodynamic diagnosis: Basics and manual]. Huber.

OPD Task Force. (2001). *Operationalized psychodynamic diagnostics (OPD): Foundation and manual.* Hogrefe & Huber.

OPD Task Force. (2008). *Operationalized Psychodynamic Diagnosis, OPD-2: Manual of diagnosis and treatment planning.* Hogrefe.

OPD-CA-2 Task Force. (2017). *Operationalized Psychodynamic Diagnosis in childhood and adolescence.* Hogrefe.

Panksepp, J. (1998). *Affective neuroscience: The foundations of human and animal emotions.* Oxford University Press. https://doi.org/10.1093/oso/9780195096736.001.0001

Panksepp, J., & Biven, L. (2012). *The archaeology of mind: Neuroevolutionary origins of human emotion.* W.W. Norton & Company.

PDM Task Force. (2006). *Psychodynamic diagnostic manual (PDM).* Alliance of Psychoanalytic Organizations.

Perry, J.C. (1990). *The psychodynamic conflict rating scales.* Cambridge Hospital.

Perry, J.C., Augusto, F., & Cooper, S.H. (1989). Assessing psychodynamic conflicts: I. Reliability of the idiographic conflict formulation method. *Psychiatry: Interpersonal and Biological Processes, 52*(3), 289–301.

Perry, J.C., & Cooper, S.H. (1989). An empirical study of defense mechanisms: I. Clinical interview and life vignette ratings. *Archives of General Psychiatry,*

46(5), 444–452. https://doi.org/10.1001/archpsyc.1989.01810050058010

Pieh, C., Frisch, M., Meyer, N., Loew, T., & Lahmann, C. (2009). Validierung der Achse III (Konflikt) der Operationalisierten Psychodynamischen Diagnostik (OPD) [Validation of axis „conflicts" of the Operationalized Psychodynamic Diagnosis (OPD)]. *Zeitschrift Für Psychosomatische Medizin und Psychotherapie, 55*(3), 263–281. https://doi.org/10.13109/zptm.2009.55.3.263

Pincus, A. L., & Wright, A. G. C. (2010). Interpersonal diagnosis of psychopathology. In L. M. Horowitz & S. Strack (Eds.), *Handbook of interpersonal psychology: Theory, research, assessment, and therapeutic interventions* (pp. 359–381). John Wiley & Sons, Inc. https://doi.org/10.1002/9781118001868.ch22

Posner, M. I., & Rothbart, M. K. (1989). Intentional chapters on unintended thoughts. In J. S. Uleman & J. A. Bargh (Eds.), *Unintended thought: Limits of awareness, intention, and control* (pp. 450–469). Guilford.

Pouget, D. (1993). *Schematische Übersicht zum "Münchner Strukturniveau der Persönlichkeitsorganisation"* [Schematic overview of the "Munich structural level of personality organization"] [Unpublished manuscript].

Pouget-Schors, D. (2014). Persönlichkeit, Persönlichkeitsstruktur [Personality, personality structure]. In W. Mertens & B. Waldvogel (Eds.), *Handbuch psychoanalytischer Grundbegriffe* (4th ed., pp. 714–724). Kohlhammer.

Rabin, R., & De Charro, F. (2001). EQ-SD: A measure of health status from the EuroQol group. *Annals of Medicine, 33*(5), 337–343. https://doi.org/10.3109/07853890109002087

Rathgeber, M., Sommer, T., & Seiffge-Krenke, I. (2014). Die Achse Konflikt der Operationalisierten Psychodynamischen Diagnostik im Kindes- und Jugendalter: Reliabilität und klinische Validität [The conflict axis of Operationalized Psychodynamic Diagnosis in childhood and adolescence OPD-CA) – Reliability and clinical validity]. *Kinderanalyse, 22*, 26–47. https://doi.org/10.1007/s00278-012-0956-2

Rettenberger, M., & von Franqué, F. (Eds.). (2013). *Handbuch kriminalprognostischer Verfahren* [Handbook of criminal prognostic procedures]. Hogrefe.

Reymann, G., Zbikowski, A., Martin, K., Tetzlaff, M., & Janssen, P. L. (2000). Erfahrung mit der Anwendung von Operationalisierter Psychodynamischer Diagnostik bei Alkoholkranken [Experience with the application of operationalized psychodynamic diagnosis in alcoholics]. In W. Schneider & H. J. Freyberger (Eds.), *Was leistet die OPD? Empirische Befunde und klinische Erfahrungen mit der Operationalisierten Psychodynamischen Diagnostik* (pp. 229–237). Huber.

Rohde, J., Hofmann, T., Voigt, B., Rose, M., & Obbarius, A. (2019). Measurement of personality structure by the OPD structure questionnaire can help to discriminate between subtypes of eating-disorders. *Frontiers in Psychology, 10*, Article 2326. https://doi.org/10.3389/fpsyg.2019.02326

Rost, R. (2011). *Subtypen depressiver Persönlichkeitsdiagnostik zur Validierung der Konfliktachse der OPD-2* [Subtypes of depressive personality diagnosis for validation of the conflict axis of OPD-2] (Doctoral dissertation, Universität Heidelberg). https://doi.org/10.11588/heidok.00013061

Roth, G. (2001). *Fühlen, Denken, Handeln: Wie das Gehirn Verhalten steuert* [Feeling, thinking, acting: How the brain controls behavior]. Suhrkamp.

Rudolf, G. (1977). *Krankheiten im Grenzbereich von Neurose und Psychose: Ein Beitrag zur Psychopathologie des Ich-Erlebens und der zwischenmenschlichen Beziehungen* [Diseases on the borderline between neurosis and psychosis: A contribution to the psychopathology of ego experience and interpersonal relationships]. Vandenhoek & Ruprecht.

Rudolf, G. (1981). *Untersuchungen und Befund bei Neurosen und psychosomatischen Erkrankungen* [Investigations and findings in neuroses and psychosomatic disorders]. Beltz.

Rudolf, G. (1995). Diagnostik struktureller Störungen [Diagnosis of structural disorders]. In G. Schneider & G. H. Seidler (Eds.), *Internalisierung und Strukturbildung in Psychoanalyse und Psychotherapie* (pp. 313–328). Westdeutscher Verlag.

Rudolf, G. (Ed.). (2000). *Psychotherapeutische Medizin und Psychosomatik* [Psychotherapeutic medicine and psychosomatics]. Thieme.

Rudolf, G. (2001). Wie analytische Psychotherapeuten Diagnosen handhaben: Eine Bestandsaufnahme und ein Plädoyer [How analytical psychotherapists work with diagnoses. A summing-up and pleading]. *Psychotherapeut, 46*, 102–109. https://doi.org/10.1007/s002780100142

Rudolf, G. (2004). *Strukturbezogene Psychotherapie: Leitfaden zur psychodynamischen Therapie struktureller Störungen* [Structural psychotherapy: Guide to psychodynamic therapy of structural disorders]. Schattauer.

Rudolf, G. (2020). *Strukturbezogene Psychotherapie (SP): Leitfaden zur psychodynamischen Therapie struktureller Störungen* (4th ed.) [Structural psychotherapy (SP): Guide to psychodynamic therapy of structural disorders]. Schattauer.

Rudolf, G., & Grande, T. (2002). Struktur der gesunden Persönlichkeit [Structure of the healthy personality]. *Persönlichkeitsstörungen: Theorie und Therapie, 6*, 174–185.

Rudolf, G., Grande, T., & Henningsen, P. (Eds.). (2002). *Die Struktur der Persönlichkeit* [The structure of personality]. Schattauer.

Rudolf, G., Grande, T., & Jakobsen, T. (2004). Struktur und Konflikt: Gibt es strukturspezifische Konflikte? [Structure and conflict: Are there structure-specific conflicts?]. In R. Dahlbender, P. Buchheim, & G. Schüßler (Eds.), *Lernen an der Praxis: OPD und die Qualitätssicherung in der psychodynamischen Psychotherapie*. Huber.

Rudolf, G., Grande, T., & Oberbracht, C. (2000). Die Heidelberger Umstrukturierungsskala: Ein Modell der Veränderung in psychoanalytischen Therapien und seine Operationalisierung in einer Schätzskala [The Heidelberg restructuring scale. A model of changes in psychoanalytic therapies and its operationalization in an estimating scale]. *Psychotherapeut, 45*, 237–246. https://doi.org/10.1007/PL00006720

Rudolf, G., Grande, T., Oberbracht, C., & Jakobsen, T. (1996). Erste empirische Untersuchungen zu einem neuen diagnostischen System: Die Operationalisierte Psychodynamische Diagnostik (OPD) [A preliminary study on a new diagnostic system: The Operationalized Psychodynamic Diagnosis (OPD)]. *Zeitschrift für Psychosomatische Medizin und Psychotherapie, 42*, 343–357. https://doi.org/10.1007/978-3-642-51501-9_22

Rudolf, G., Jakobs, E., Micka, R., & Schumann, E. (2004). Störungsbezogene Ergebnisse psychodynamisch-stationärer Psychotherapie [Results of psychodynamic inpatient psychotherapy in relation to diagnosis]. *Zeitschrift für Psychosomatische Medizin und Psychotherapie, 50*, 37–52. https://doi.org/10.13109/zptm.2004.50.1.37

Rudolf, G., Jakobsen, T., Keller, W., Krawietz, B., Langer, M., Oberbracht, C., Stehle, S., Stennes, M., & Grande, T. (2012). Umstrukturierung als Ergebnisparadigma der psychodynamischen Psychotherapie – Ergebnisse aus der Praxisstudie Analytische Langzeittherapie [Structural change as an outcome paradigm in psychodynamic psychotherapy – Results of the PAL-Study (long-term psychoanalytic psychotherapy study)]. *Zeitschrift für Psychosomatische Medizin und Psychotherapie, 58*(1), 55–66. https://doi.org/10.13109/zptm.2012.58.1.55

Rudolf, G., & Schmutterer, J. (2003). Gutachterverfahren vor Psychotherapien: Qualitätssichernde Therapiebegleitung [Expert opinion procedures before psychotherapies: Quality-assuring therapy support]. *Deutsches Ärzteblatt, 2*, 13–15.

Rudolf, G., & Stille, D. (1984). Der Einfluss von Krankheitsbild und Krankheitsverhalten auf die Indikationsentscheidung in der Psychotherapie [The influence of disease pattern and disease behavior on the indication decision in psychotherapy]. *Praxis Psychotherapie Psychosomatik, 29*, 115–128.

Salzer, S., & Leichsenring, F. (2012). Das Borderline-Persönlichkeits-Inventar (BPI) [The borderline personality inventory]. In S. Doering & S. Hoerz (Eds.), *Handbuch der Strukturdiagnostik: Konzepte, Instrumente, Praxis* (pp. 256–268). Schattauer.

Sandler, J. (1960). The background of safety. *International Review of Psychoanalysis, 41*, 352–356.

Sandler, J. (1962). Research in psycho-analysis: The Hampstead Index as an instrument of psychoanalytic research. *The International Journal of Psychoanalysis, 43*(4–5), 287–291.

Sandler, J. (1976). Countertransference and role-responsiveness. *The International Review of Psycho-Analysis, 3*, 43–47.

Sandler, J. (1983). Reflections on some relations between psychoanalytic concepts and psychoanalytic practice. *International Journal of Psychoanalysis, 64*, 35–45.

Sandler, J., & Dare, C. (1970). The psychoanalytic concept of orality. *Journal of Psychosomatic Research, 14*(3), 211–222. https://doi.org/10.1016/0022-3999(70)90046-2

Sandler, J., & Joffe, W. G. (1969). Toward a basic psychoanalytic model. *International Journal of Psychoanalysis, 50*(1), 79–90.

Sandler, J., & Joffe, W. G. (1970). Discussion towards a basic psychoanalytical model. *International Journal of Psychoanalysis, 51*, 183–193.

Schacht, T., & Henry, W. (1994). Modeling recurrent patterns of interpersonal relationship with structural analysis of social behavior: The SASB-CMP. *Psychotherapy Research, 4*(3–4), 208–221. https://doi.org/10.1080/10503309412331334042

Schauenburg, H. (2000). Zum Verhältnis zwischen Bindungsdiagnostik und psychodynamischer Diagnostik [On the relationship between attachment diagnosis and psychodynamic diagnosis]. In W. Schneider & H. J. Freyberger (Eds.), *Was leistet die OPD? Empirische Befunde und klinische Erfahrungen mit der Operationalisierten Psychodynamischen Diagnostik*. Huber.

Schauenburg, H., & Cierpka, M. (1994). Methoden zur Fremdbeurteilung interpersoneller Beziehungsmuster [Methods for external assessment of interpersonal relationship patterns]. *Psychotherapeut, 39*, 135–145.

Schauenburg, H., Dinger, U., Komo-Lang, M., Klinkerfuß, M., Horsch, L., Grande, G., & Ehrenthal, J. C. (2012). Der OPD-Strukturfragebogen (OPD-SF) [The OPD structure questionnaire (OPD-SF)]. In S. Doering & S. Hoerz (Eds.), *Handbuch der Strukturdiagnostik: Konzepte, Instrumente, Praxis* (pp. 284–307). Schattauer.

Schauenburg, H., & Grande, T. (2010). Interview measures of interpersonal functioning and quality of object relations. In L. M. Horowitz & S. Strack (Eds.), *Handbook of Interpersonal Psychology* (pp. 343–356). Wiley. https://doi.org/10.1002/9781118001868.ch21

Schauenburg, H., & Hildenbrand, G. (2017). Stationäre Psychotherapie und Psychosomatik [Inpatient psychotherapy and psychosomatics]. In K. Köhle, W. Herzog, P. Joraschky, J. Kruse, W. Langewitz, & W. Söllner (Eds.), *Uexküll Psychosomatische Medizin: Theoretische Modelle und klinische Praxis* (pp. 545–554). https://doi.org/10.1016/b978-3-437-21833-0.00050-4

Schlapobersky, J. R. (2016). *From the couch to the circle: Group-analytic psychotherapy in practice.* Routledge/Taylor & Francis Group. https://doi.org/10.4324/9781315670096

Schmeing, J., Kehyayan, A., Kessler, H., Lam, A. T. a. D., Fell, J., Schmidt, A., & Axmacher, N. (2013). Can the neural basis of repression be studied in the MRI scanner? New insights from two free association paradigms. *PLoS ONE, 8*(4), Article e62358. https://doi.org/10.1371/journal.pone.0062358

Schneider, W., Freyberger, H. J., Muhs, A. & Schüssler, G. (Eds.). (1993). *Diagnostik und Klassifikation nach ICD-10 Kapitel V (F). Eine kritische Auseinandersetzung. Ergebnisse der ICD-10-Forschungskriterienstudie aus dem Bereich Psychosomatik/Psychotherapie* [Diagnostics and classification according to ICD-10 Chapter V (F). A critical analysis. Results of the ICD-10 research criteria study in the field of psychosomatic medicine/psychotherapy]. Vandenhoek & Ruprecht.

Schneider, W., & Hoffmann, S. O. (1992). Diagnostik und Klassifikation neurotischer und psychosomatischer Störungen [Diagnosis and classification of neurotic and psychosomatic disorders]. *Fundamenta Psychiatrica, 6*, 137–142.

Schneider, W., Klauer, T., & Freyberger, H. J. (2008). Operationalized psychodynamic diagnosis in planning and evaluating the psychotherapeutic process. *European Archives of Psychiatry and Clinical Neuroscience, 258*(S5), 86–91. https://doi.org/10.1007/s00406-008-5014-2

Schneider, G., Mendler, T., Heuft, G., & Burgmer, M. (2008a). Der Körper in der Konflikt- und Strukturdiagnostik der Operationalisierten Psychodynamischen Diagnostik – Bezug zu Körperkonzepten in der Selbstauskunft [The body in Operationalized Psychodynamic Diagnosis (OPD) – its representation on the axes "conflict" and "structure" and the correlation to self-assessment]. *Zeitschrift für Psychosomatische Medizin und Psychotherapie, 54*(2), 132–149. https://doi.org/10.13109/zptm.2008.54.2.132

Schneider, G., Mendler, T., Heuft, G., & Burgmer, M. (2008b). Validität der Konfliktachse der Operationalisierten Psychodynamischen Diagnostik (OPD-1) – empirische Ergebnisse und Folgerungen für die OPD-2 [Validity of axis III "conflict" of Operationalized Psychodynamic Diagnostics (OPD-1) – Empirical results and conclusions for OPD-2]. *Zeitschrift für Psychosomatische Medizin und Psychotherapie, 54*(1), 46–62. https://doi.org/10.13109/zptm.2008.54.1.46

Schneider, G., Tiemann, M., Stumpf, A., & Heuft, G. (2015). Dimensions of the operationalized psychodynamic diagnosis system that predict long-term outcome after inpatient psychotherapy. *Psychopathology, 48*(2), 101–113. https://doi.org/10.1159/000368311

Schneider, G., & Heuft, G. (2018). Operationalized psychodynamic diagnosis system and outcome of psychodynamic inpatient psychotherapy in male and female patients. *Zeitschrift für Psychosomatische Medizin und Psychotherapie, 64*(3), 281–297. https://doi.org/10.13109/zptm.2018.64.3.281

Schultz-Hencke, H. (1951). *Lehrbuch der analytischen Psychotherapie* [Textbook of analytical psychotherapy]. Thieme.

Schüßler, G. (2002). Aktuelle Konzeption des Unbewussten – Empirische Ergebnisse der Neurobiologie, Kognitionswissenschaften, Sozialpsychologie und Emotionsforschung [The current conception of the unconscious – Empirical resultsof neurobiology, cognitive sciences, social psychology and emotion research]. *Zeitschrift für Psychosomatische Medizin und Psychotherapie, 48*, 192–214. https://doi.org/10.13109/zptm.2002.48.2.192

Schüßler, G., & Bertl-Schüßler, A. (1992). Neue Ansätze zur Revision der psychoanalytischen Entwicklungstheorie [New approaches to revising psychoanalytic development theory]. *Zeitschrift für Psychosomatische Medizin und Psychotherapie, 38*(2), 101–114.

Schüßler, G., & Bertl-Schüßler, A. (Eds.). (2011). *Medizinische Psychologie, Psychosomatik und Psychotherapie systematisch* (4th rev. ed.) [Medical psychology, psychosomatics, and psychotherapy systematically]. UNI-MED Verlag.

Schüßler, G., Leibing, E., & Rüger, U. (1990). Multiaxiale Diagnostik in der Psychosomatik [Multiaxial diagnosis in psychosomatics]. *Zeitschrift für Psychosomatische Medizin und Psychotherapie, 36*, 343–354.

Schwidder, W. (1972a). Klinik der Neurosen [Clinic of neuroses]. In K. P. Kisker, J. E. Meyer, M. Müller, & E. Strömgren (Eds.), *Psychiatrie der Gegenwart II/1* (pp. 351–477). Springer. https://doi.org/10.1007/978-3-642-65278-3_11

Schwidder, W. (1972b). Neopsychoanalyse [Neo-psychoanalysis]. In G. Bally (Ed.), *Grundzüge der Neurosenlehre* (pp. 563–612). Urban & Schwarzenberg.

Seiffge-Krenke, I. (2012). *Therapieziel Identität* [Therapy goal identity]. Klett-Cotta.

Seiffge-Krenke, I. (2021). Identität und Beziehungen: Auswirkungen der veränderten Identitätsentwicklung auf Partnerschaften [Identity and relationships: Effects of changing identity development on partnerships]. *Psychodynamische Psychotherapie, 20*(1), 17–27. https://doi.org/10.21706/pdp-20-1-17

Sell, C., Gröning, F., & Benecke, C. (2021). "Zur weiteren Forschung vorgesehen:" Verstehen psychotischer Patient*innen mittels der Operationalisierten Psychodynamischen Diagnostik ["Intended for further research:" Using Operationalized Psychodynamic Diagnosis for a psychodynamic understanding of patients with psychosis]. *Persönlichkeitsstörungen: Theorie und Therapie, 25*(2), 139–152. https://doi.org/10.21706/ptt-25-2-141

Shapiro, D. (1965). *Neurotic styles*. Basic Books.

Shapiro, T. (Ed.). (1991). *The concept of structure in psychoanalysis*. International Universities Press.

Sharp, C., Wright, A. G. C., Fowler, J. C., Frueh, B. C., Allen, J. G., Oldham, J., & Clark, L. A. (2015). The structure of personality pathology: Both general ('g') and specific ('s') factors? *Journal of Abnormal Psychology, 124*(2), 387–398. https://doi.org/10.1037/abn0000033

Simmonds, J., Constantinides, P., Perry, J. C., Drapeau, M., & Sheptycki, A. R. (2015). Assessing psychodynamic conflict. *Psychodynamic Psychiatry, 43*(3), 349–377. https://doi.org/10.1521/pdps.2015.43.3.349

Skodol, A. E., Gunderson, J. G., Shea, M. T., McGlashan, T. H., Morey, L. C., Sanislow, C. A., Bender, D. S., Grilo, C. M., Zanarini, M. C., Yen, S., Pagano, M. E., & Stout, R. L. (2005). The collaborative longitudinal personality disorders study (CLPS): Overview and implications. *Journal of Personality Disorders, 19*(5), 487–504. https://doi.org/10.1521/pedi.2005.19.5.487

Solms, M. (2015). Sigmund Freud heute – eine neurowissenschaftliche Perspektive auf die Psychoanalyse [Sigmund Freud today – a neuroscientific perspective on psychoanalysis]. In M. Leuzinger-Bohleber, H. Böker, T. Fischman, G. Nordhoff & M. Solms (Hrsg.), *Psychoanalyse und Neurowissenschaften: Chancen-Grenzen-Kontroversen* (S. 56–88). Kohlhammer.

Solms, M. (2021). *The hidden spring. A journey to the source of consciousness*. Profile Books.

Spitzer, C. (2004). Zum Zusammenhang zwischen OPD-Merkmalen der Persönlichkeitsstruktur und symptombezogenen sowie interpersonalen Behandlungsergebnissen stationärer Psychotherapie [On the relationship between OPD features of personality structure and symptom-related and interpersonal outcome of inpatient psychotherapy]. *Zeitschrift für Psychosomatische Medizin und Psychotherapie, 50*(1), 70–85. https://doi.org/10.13109/zptm.2004.50.1.70

Sporn, H. (2005). Aneignung der Suchterkrankung [Appropriation of addiction]. *Psychotherapeut, 50*(5), 347–353. https://doi.org/10.1007/s00278-005-0437-y

Stasch, M. (2002). Assessing reenactment in inpatient psychodynamic therapy. *Psychotherapy Research, 12*(3), 355–368. https://doi.org/10.1093/ptr/12.3.355

Stasch, M., & Cierpka, M. (2006). Beziehungsdiagnostik mit der GARF-Skala: Ein Plädoyer für die interpersonelle Perspektive nicht nur in der Mehr-Personen-Psychotherapie [Rational diagnostics by the GARF-scale. Pleading for the interpersonal perspective not only in multiperson-psychotherapy]. *Psychotherapie in Psychiatrie, Psychotherapeutischer Medizin und Klinischer Psychologie, 11*, 56–63.

Stasch, M., Cierpka, M., Dahlbender, R. W., Grande, G., Hillenbrand, E., Kraul, A., & Schauenburg, H. (2004). OPD und Repräsentation interpersonellen Beziehungsverhaltens: Ein Ansatz zur Konstruktvalidierung [OPD and representation of interpersonal relationship behavior: An approach to construct validation]. In R. Dahlbender, P. Buchheim, & G. Schüßler (Eds.), *Lernen an der Praxis: OPD und die Qualitätssicherung in der psychodynamischen Psychotherapie* (pp. 85–94). Huber.

Stasch, M., Cierpka, M., & Windaus, E. (2012). Fokusorientierte Psychotherapie von Familien mit Säuglingen und Kleinkindern [Focus-oriented psychotherapy for families with infants and toddlers]. In M. Cierpka (Ed.), *Frühe Kindheit 0–3 Jahre: Beratung und Psychotherapie für Eltern mit Säuglingen und Kleinkindern* (pp. 441–454). Springer.

Stasch, M., Grande, T., Janssen, P.L., Oberbracht, C., & Rudolf, G. (2026). *OPD-3 im Psychotherapie-Antrag* [OPD-3 in psychotherapy application]. Hogrefe.

Steinhauer, P.D., Santa-Barbara, J., & Skinner, H. (1984). The process model of family functioning. *The Canadian Journal of Psychiatry, 29*(2), 77–88. https://doi.org/10.1177/070674378402900202

Stern, D.N. (1977). *The first relationship: Infant and mother.* Harvard University Press.

Stern, D.N. (1985). *The interpersonal world of the infant.* Basic Books.

Stern, D.N. (1998). *The motherhood constellation: A unified view of parent-infant psychotherapy.* Basic Books.

Stiles, W.B., Elliott, R., Llewelyn, S.P., Firth-Cozens, J.A., Margison, F.R., Shapiro, D.A. & Hardy, G. (1990). Assimilation of problematic experiences by clients in psychotherapy. *Psychotherapy: Theory, Research, Practice, Training, 27*(3), 411–420. https://doi.org/10.1037/0033-3204.27.3.411

Stolorow, R., Brandchaft, B., & Atwood, G. (1987). *Psychoanalytic treatment: An intersubjective approach.* The Analytic Press.

Strauß, B., Barkowski, S., Schwartze, D., & Rosendahl, J. (2016). Aktueller Stand der Gruppenpsychotherapieforschung [Current state of group psychotherapy research]. *Psychotherapeut, 61*, 364–375. https://doi.org/10.1007/s00278-016-0120-5

Strauß, B., & Mattke, D. (Eds.). (2017). *Gruppenpsychotherapie: Lehrbuch für die Praxis* (2nd ed.) [Group psychotherapy: Textbook for practice]. Springer.

Strupp, H.H., & Binder, J.L. (1984). *Psychotherapy in a new key: A guide to time-limited dynamic psychotherapy.* Basic Books.

Strupp, H.H., & Binder, J.L. (1993). *Kurzpsychotherapie* [Brief psychotherapy]. Klett-Cotta.

Sullivan, H.S. (1954). *The psychiatric interview.* W.W. Norton & Co.

Szende, A., Janssen, B., & Cabases, J. (Eds.) (2014). *Self-reported population health: An international perspective based on EQ-5D.* Springer. https://doi.org/10.1016/j.jval.2013.08.812

Tangney, J.P., & Dearing, R.L. (2002). *Shame and guilt.* Guilford Press.

Taubner, S., Hörz, S., Fischer-Kern, M., Doering, S., Buchheim, A., & Zimmermann, J. (2013). Internal structure of the Reflective Functioning Scale. *Psychological Assessment, 25*(1), 127–135. https://doi.org/10.1037/a0029138

Thomä, H. (1981). *Vom spiegelnden zum aktiven Analytiker* [From the mirroring to the active analyst]. Suhrkamp.

Thomä, H., & Kächele, H. (1989). *Lehrbuch der psychoanalytischen Therapie. Band 1: Grundlagen* [Textbook of psychoanalytic therapy. Vol. 1: Fundamentals]. Springer-Verlag.

Thomä, H., & Kächele, H. (2006a). *Lehrbuch der psychoanalytischen Therapie. Band 1* [Textbook of psychoanalytic therapy. Vol. 1]. Springer-Verlag.

Thomä, H., & Kächele, H. (2006b). *Lehrbuch der psychoanalytischen Therapie. Band 2: Praxis* [Textbook of psychoanalytic therapy. Vol. 2: Practice]. Springer-Verlag.

Tress, W. (Ed.). (1993). *SABS – Die strukturale Analyse sozialen Verhaltens: Ein Arbeitsbuch für Forschung, Praxis und Weiterbildung in der Psychotherapie* [SABS – The structural analysis of social behavior: A workbook for research, practice, and further training in psychotherapy]. Asanger.

Tschuschke, V., & Mattke, D. (1997). Kurzgruppenpsychotherapie: Entwicklung, Konzept, und aktueller Forschungsstand [Short-term group psychotherapy: Development, concept, and current research status]. *Gruppenpsychotherapie und Gruppendynamik, 33*, 36–54.

Tyrer, P., Mulder, R., Kim, Y.R., & Crawford, M.J. (2019). The development of the ICD-11 classification of personality disorders: An amalgam of science, pragmatism, and politics. *Annual Review of Clinical Psychology, 15*(1), 481–502. https://doi.org/10.1146/annurev-clinpsy-050718-095736

Ulich, D. & Mayring, P. (2003). *Psychologie der Emotionen* [Psychology of emotions] (2., rev. & ext. ed.). Kohlhammer.

Uzdawinis, D., Edel, M., Özgürdal, S., Von Haebler, D., Marta, H., Witthaus, H., Gudlowski, Y., Heinz, A., & Juckel, G. (2010). Operationalisierte Psychodynamische Diagnostik (OPD) bei Patienten im schizophrenen Prodromalstadium – Eine explorative Studie [Operationalized Psychodynamic Diagnostics (OPD) in patients in a prodromal state of schizophrenia – An explorative study]. *Zeitschrift für Psychosomatische Medizin und Psychotherapie, 56*(2), 150–162. https://doi.org/10.13109/zptm.2010.56.2.150

Vaillant, G.E. (1971). Theoretical hierarchy of adaptive ego mechanisms. *Archives of General Psychiatry, 24,* 107–118. https://doi.org/10.1001/archpsyc.1971.01750080011003

Vaillant, G.E., Bond, M., & Vaillant, C.O. (1986). An empirically validated hierarchy of defense mechanisms. *Archives of General Psychiatry, 43,* 786–794. https://doi.org/10.1001/archpsyc.1986.01800080072010

Vaish, A. (2017). The prosocial functions of early social emotions: the case of guilt. *Current Opinion in Psychology, 20,* 25–29. https://doi.org/10.1016/j.copsyc.2017.08.008

Vandekerckhove, M., & Panksepp, J. (2011). A neurocognitive theory of higher mental emergence: From anoetic affective experiences to noetic knowledge and autonoetic awareness. *Neuroscience & Biobehavioral Reviews, 35*(9), 2017–2025. https://doi.org/10.1016/j.neubiorev.2011.04.001

Vanegas-Osorio, J.H., Chindoy-Luna, E.H., Patiño-González, J.E., Pérez-Atehortúa, C.A., Rincón-Ospina, F.H., & Jiménez-Hernández, J.A. (2020). Contributions of OPD-2 in Colombia: Training and practice. *Revista Brasileira de Psicoterapia, 22,* 45–53. https://doi.org/10.5935/2318-0404.20200022

Venzlaff, P., Foerster, K., Dreßing, H., & Habermeyer, E. (2020). *Psychiatrische Begutachtung* (7th ed.) [Psychiatric assessment]. Elsevier.

Vicente, C.S., Oliveira, R.A., Silva, F., Ferrajão, P., Augusto, S., Oliveira, S., Senra, H., Oliveira, R., & Krieger, D. (2012). Cross-cultural adaptation of the Operationalized Psychodynamic Diagnosis (OPD-2) in Portugal. *Trends in Psychiatry and Psychotherapy, 34*(3), 129–138. https://doi.org/10.1590/s2237-60892012000300004

Waage, M., Vogel, M., Hake, K., & Schneider, W. (2011). Die Operationalisierte Psychodynamische Diagnostik (OPD-2): Validität der Achse I „Krankheitserleben und Behandlungsvoraussetzungen" [Operationalized Psychodynamic Diagnostics system (OPD-2): Validity of Axis I "experience of illness and prerequisites for treatment"]. *PPmP – Psychotherapie, Psychosomatik, Medizinische Psychologie, 61*(03/04), 154–161. https://doi.org/10.1055/s-0030-1261874

Wagner-Skacel, J., Bengesser, S., Dalkner, N., Mörkl, S., Painold, A., Hamm, C., Pilz, R., Rieger, A., Kapfhammer, H., Hiebler-Ragger, M., Jauk, E., Butler, M.I., & Reininghaus, E.Z. (2020). Personality structure and attachment in bipolar disorder. *Frontiers in Psychiatry, 11,* Article 410. https://doi.org/10.3389/fpsyt.2020.00410

Wallerstein, R.S. (1996). *The scales of psychological capacities.* (Version 1) [Unpublished manual].

Warneken, F., & Tomasello, M. (2009). The roots of human altruism. *British Journal of Psychology, 100,* 455–471. https://doi.org/10.1348/000712608X379061

Wegener, P. (1992). Zur Bedeutung der Gegenübertragung im psychoanalytischen Erstinterview [On the significance of the countertransference in the psychoanalytic initial interview]. *Psyche, 46*(3), 286–307.

Weinryb, R., Rössel, R.J., & Schauenburg, H. (1999). Eine deutsche Version des "Karolinska Psychodynamic Profile – KAPP" [A German Version of the "Karolinska Psychodynamic Profile – KAPP"]. *Psychotherapeut, 44,* 227–233. https://doi.org/10.1007/s002780050170

Weinryb, R.M., & Rössel, R.J. (1991). Karolinska Psychodynamic Profile KAPP. *Acta Psychiatrica Scandinavica, 83,* 1–23. https://doi.org/10.1111/j.1600-0447.1991.tb10573.x

Weisman, A. (1959). The psychodynamic formulation of conflict. *Archives of General Psychiatry, 1,* 288–309. https://doi.org/10.1001/archpsyc.1959.03590030072010

Weiss, J., Sampson, H., & Mt Zion Psychotherapy Research Group. (1986). *The psychoanalytic process: Theory, clinical observations, and empirical research.* Guilford Press.

Wendt, L.P., Wright, A.G.C., Pilkonis, P.A., Nolte, T., Fonagy, P., Montague, P.R., Benecke, C., Krieger, T., & Zimmermann, J. (2019). The latent structure of interpersonal problems: Validity of dimensional, categorical, and hybrid models. *Journal of Abnormal Psychology, 128*(8), 823–839. https://doi.org/10.1037/abn0000460

Werner, C., & Langenmayr, A. (2005). *Das Unbewusste und die Abwehrmechanismen* [The unconscious and defense mechanisms]. Vandenhoeck & Ruprecht.

World Health Organization. (1980). *International classification of impairments, disabilities, and Handicaps: A manual of classification relating to the consequences of disease.*

World Health Organization. (2001). *International classification of functioning, disability and health.* https://icd.who.int/dev11/l-icf/en

World Health Organization. (2018). *International classification of functioning, disability and health.* https://icd.who.int/dev11/l-icf/en

World Health Organization. (2024). *Clinical descriptions and diagnostic requirements for ICD-11 mental, behavioral and neurodevelopmental disorders.* https://www.who.int/publications/i/item/9789240077263

Widiger, T.A., & Simonsen, E. (2005). Alternative dimensional models of personality disorder: Finding a common ground. *Journal of Personality Disorders, 19*(2), 110–130. https://doi.org/10.1521/pedi.19.2.110.62628

Wiggins, J.S. (1982). Circumplex models of interpersonal behavior in clinical psychology. In J.C. Kendall & J.N. Butcher (Eds.), *Handbook of research methods in clinical psychology* (pp. 183–221). Wiley.

Wiswede, D., Taubner, S., Buchheim, A., Münte, T.F., Stasch, M., Cierpka, M., Kächele, H., Roth, G., Erhard, P., & Kessler, H. (2014). Tracking functional brain changes in patients with depression under psychodynamic psychotherapy using individualized stimuli. *PLoS ONE, 9*(10), Article e109037. https://doi.org/10.1371/journal.pone.0109037

Wöller, W., & Kruse, J. (2018). *Tiefenpsychologisch fundierte Psychotherapie: Basisbuch und Praxisleitfaden* [Depth-psychologically oriented psychotherapy: Basic book and guide]. Klett-Cotta.

Wurmser, L. (1981). *The mask of shame.* The Johns Hopkins University Press.

Yalom, I.D. (1970). *The theory and practice of group psychotherapy.* Basic Books.

Yeomans, F.E., Clarkin, J.F., Kernberg, O.F. (2015). *Transference-focused psychotherapy for Borderline personality disorder. A clinical guide.* American Psychiatric Publishing.

Young, J.E., Klosko, J.S., & Weishaar, M.E. (2003). *Schema therapy. A practitioner's guide.* The Guilford Press.

Zeeck, A., von Wietersheim, J., Weiss, H., Hermann, S., Endorf, K., Lau, I., & Hartmann, A. (2020). Self-criticism and personality functioning predict patterns of symptom change in major depressive disorder. *Frontiers in Psychiatry, 11*, Article 225. https://doi.org/10.3389/fpsyt.2020.00147

Zettl, M., Taubner, S., Hutsebaut, J., & Volkert, J. (2019). Psychometrische Evaluation der deutschen Version des Semistrukturierten Interviews zur Erfassung der DSM-5 Persönlichkeitsfunktionen (STiP-5.1) [Psychometric evaluation of the German version of the Semi-Structured Interview for Personality Functioning DSM-5 (STiP-5.1)]. *PPmP – Psychotherapie, Psychosomatik, Medizinische Psychologie, 69*(12), 499–504. https://doi.org/10.1055/a-1010-6887

Zettl, M., Volkert, J., Vögele, C., Herpertz, S.C., Kubera, K.M., & Taubner, S. (2020). Mentalization and criterion a of the alternative model for personality disorders: Results from a clinical and nonclinical sample. *Personality Disorders: Theory, Research, and Treatment, 11*(3), 191–201. https://doi.org/10.1037/per0000356

Zimmermann, J., Benecke, C., Bender, D.S., Skodol, A.E., Krueger, R.F., & Leising, D. (2013). Persönlichkeitsdiagnostik im DSM-5 [Personality assessment in DSM-5]. *Psychotherapeut, 58*(5), 455–465. https://doi.org/10.1007/s00278-013-1009-1

Zimmermann, J., Dahlbender, R.W., Herbold, W., Krasnow, K., Turrión, C.M., Zika, M., & Spitzer, C. (2015). Der OPD-Strukturfragebogen erfasst die allgemeinen Merkmale einer Persönlichkeitsstörung [The OPD structure questionnaire captures the general features of personality disorder]. *PPmP – Psychotherapie, Psychosomatik, Medizinische Psychologie, 65*(2), 81–83. https://doi.org/10.1055/s-0034-1395626

Zimmermann, J., Ehrenthal, J.C., Cierpka, M., Schauenburg, H., Doering, S., & Benecke, C. (2012). Assessing the level of structural integration using Operationalized Psychodynamic Diagnosis (OPD): Implications for DSM-5. *Journal of Personality Assessment, 94*(5), 522–532. https://doi.org/10.1080/00223891.2012.700664

Zimmermann, J., Ehrenthal, J.C., Hörz, S., Rentrop, M., Rost, R., Schauenburg, H., Schneider, W., Waage, M., & Cierpka, M. (2010). Neue Validierungsstudien zur Operationalisierten Psychodynamischen Diagnostik (OPD-2) [New validation studies on Operationalized Psychodynamic Diagnosis (OPD-2)]. *Psychotherapeut, 55*(1), 69–73. https://doi.org/10.1007/s00278-009-0717-z

Zimmermann, J., Müller, S., Bach, B., Hutsebaut, J., Hummelen, B., & Fischer, F. (2020). A common metric for self-reported severity of personality disorder. *Psychopathology, 53*(3–4), 168–178. https://doi.org/10.1159/000507377

Zimmermann, J., Stasch, M., Grande, T., Schauenburg, H., & Cierpka, M. (2014). Der Beziehungsmuster-Q-Sort (OPD-BQS): Ein Selbsteinschätzungsinstrument zur Erfassung von dysfunktionalen Beziehungsmustern auf Grundlage der Operationalisierten Psychodynamischen Diagnostik [Maladaptive interpersonal patterns Q-sort (MIPQS): A self-report method for assessing maladaptive interpersonal patterns based on Operationalized Psychodynamic Diagnosis]. *Zeitschrift für Psychiatrie Psychologie und Psychotherapie,*

62(1), 43–53. https://doi.org/10.1024/1661-4747/a000177

Zinkin, L. (1983). Malignant mirroring. *Group Analysis, 16*(2), 113–126. https://doi.org/10.1177/053331648301600204

Zuccarino, M. L., Zuglian, P., Magni, M., Rossetti, A., Manna, G., Gentile, M. G., Nichelatti, M., Fava, E. D., Bondi, O. E. D. M. G., Ferrario, D., Greco, M., Mentasti, G., Monea, T., Testa, A., Cadeo, F., Cafagna, P., Piemontese, V., & Marco. (2012). Eating disorder subtypes in a young female sample using the Operationalized Psychodynamic Diagnosis System: Preliminary results. *Adolescent Psychiatry, 2*(4), 333–344. https://doi.org/10.2174/2210676611202040333

Online Material

DOWNLOAD

The following materials for your book can be downloaded free of charge once you register on the Hogrefe website.

OPD-3 Rating Sheet Axis I
OPD-3 Item List Rating Sheet Axis II (Clinical Version): Relationship Topics
OPD-3 Item List Rating Sheet Axis II (Research Version): Relationship Topics
OPD-3 Evaluation Sheet Axis II: Dysfunctional Relationship Patterns; with the four interpersonal perspectives, the relation between perspectives (curved arrows), and empty fields for relationship dynamic formulation.
OPD-3 Rating Sheet Axis III: Conflict
OPD-3 Rating Sheet Axis IV: Structure (Clinical Version)
OPD-3 Rating Sheet Axis IV: Structure (Research Version)

How to proceed:
1. Go to www.hgf.io/media and create a user account. If you already have one, please log in.
2. Go to My supplementary materials in your account dashboard and enter the code below. You will automatically be redirected to the download area, where you can access and download the supplementary materials.

Code: **B-1SJU8K**

To make sure you have permanent direct access to all the materials, we recommend that you download them and save them on your computer.

OPD-3 Rating Sheet Axis I: Axis I: Mental and psychosomatic disorders		
Mental disorders/behavioral disorders	ICD or DSM	
Main diagnosis		
Additional diagnosis 1		
Additional diagnosis 2		
Additional diagnosis 3		
Additional diagnosis 4		
Additional diagnosis 5		
Physical illnesses	ICD	
Main diagnosis		
Additional diagnosis 2		
Additional diagnosis 3		
Additional diagnosis 4		
Additional diagnosis 5		
Age: ___ years	Gender: m/f/___	Assessment date ___/___

Axis I: Experience of illness & treatment requirements						
2.4 Current severity of symptomatology/disorder						
Global severity of the disorder	⓪	①	②	③	④	⑨
GAF: Highest value of the last 7 days Psychological symptoms Occupational functions Social functions	 ___ ___ ___					⑨
EQ-5D-modified Sum: _______ item scores →	1.___	2.___	3.___	4.___		⑨
2.5 Duration and course of the illness/problem						
Duration of the current mental disorder	◯ <6 months	◯ 6–24 months	◯ 2–10 years	◯ >10 years		⑨
Other pre-existing conditions	Were there any prior mental conditions? Which? ___________					⑨
Chronic course of the current mental symptomatology	Course of symptom severity (trend) • stable • decreasing • progressive Additional course information: • without fluctuations • fluctuating • episodic-remitting • relapsing progressive					⑨

This is a **preview** of the content that is available in the downloadable material of this book.
Please see p. 319 for instructions on how to obtain the full-sized, printable PDF.

Illness and change concepts						
2.6 Illness concepts						
Somatic illness concept	⓪	①	②	③	④	⑨
External-social illness concept	⓪	①	②	③	④	⑨
External-alternative illness concept	⓪	①	②	③	④	⑨
Intrapsychic illness concept	⓪	①	②	③	④	⑨
2.7 Change and treatment concepts						
Somatic treatment concept	⓪	①	②	③	④	⑨
External-social treatment concept	⓪	①	②	③	④	⑨
External-alternative treatment concept	⓪	①	②	③	④	⑨
Psychotherapeutic treatment concept	⓪	①	②	③	④	⑨

Change resources/impediments for change/psychotherapy goals						
2.8.1 Change resources						
Burden of Suffering	⓪	①	②	③	④	⑨
Coping resources	⓪	①	②	③	④	⑨
Psychosocial support	⓪	①	②	③	④	⑨
Openness	⓪	①	②	③	④	⑨
2.8.2 Impediments for change						
External impediments for change	⓪	①	②	③	④	⑨
Internal impediments for change	⓪	①	②	③	④	⑨
Secondary gain	⓪	①	②	③	④	⑨
2.9 Psychotherapy: Change strategies and goals						
Symptom reduction	⓪	①	②	③	④	⑨
Reflection and clarification	⓪	①	②	③	④	⑨
Emotional support	⓪	①	②	③	④	⑨
Active guidance	⓪	①	②	③	④	⑨

Note. I.0 = not present, 2 = moderately present, 4 = very highly present, 9 = not applicable.

OPD-3 Item List Rating Sheet Axis II (Clinical Version): Relationship Topics

	OPD relationship theme	P:O	P:P	O:P	O:O	Res	Unremarkable/clinically not relevant (= 0)	Accentuated (= 1)	Dysfunctional (= 2)	
1	*Give freedom (+)*					1	Give others freedom	Give a lot of freedom	Just allow it to happen/ignore	1
2	*Guide others (–)*					2	Guide little	Guide very little	Not guide at all, avoid influencing	2
3	*Acknowledge others (+)*					3	Acknowledge friendly	Idealize	Completely overestimate	3
4	*Hold responsible (–)*					4	Hold responsible	Hold little accountable	Completely excuse inappropriately	4
5	*Show affection (+)*					5	Show affection	Overwhelm with affection	Stalk with love	5
6	*Show aggression (–)*					6	Show little aggression	Avoid conflicts, downplay	Over-harmonize, ignore conflicts	6
7	*Care (+)*					7	Care	Care a lot	Care excessively	7
8	*Make contact (+)*					8	Make contact	Be tactless, push	Violate boundaries, be intrusive	8
9	*Give freedom (–)*					9	Get involved	Interfere	Constantly patronize	9
10	*Guide others (+)*					10	Guide appropriately	Guide or control a lot	Constantly guide or control	10
11	*Acknowledge others (–)*					11	Critically acknowledge	Criticize a lot, question	Devalue, humiliate	11
12	*Hold responsible (+)*					12	Hold responsible	Blame, reproach	Persecute with guilt accusations	12
13	*Show affection (–)*					13	Keep distance	Show little affection	Show no affection at all	13
14	*Show aggression (+)*					14	Show anger	Meet angrily	Threaten, attack, harm	14
15	*Care (–)*					15	Limit help	Deny help, abandon	Completely neglect	15
16	*Make contact (–)*					16	Limit contact	Make little contact	Ignore others, completely overlook	16
17	*Unfold (+)*					17	Unfold independently	Claim a lot of freedom or independence	Insist too much on independence	17
18	*Submit (–)*					18	Assert oneself, resist	Often resist	Defy, constantly resist	18
19	*Assert oneself (+)*					19	Assert oneself	Assert a lot	Constantly make oneself important, putting oneself in the center	19
20	*Acknowledge guilt (–)*					20	Examine own responsibility	Rather reject guilt	Not acknowledge own guilt at all	20
21	*Accept affection (+)*					21	Accept affection	Accept too much affection	Lose oneself in others' affection	21
22	*Protect oneself (–)*					22	Open up	Protect little	Put oneself in danger, not protect from aggression	22
23	*Lean on (+)*					23	Show own needs	Lean a lot, show neediness	Cling, show helplessness	23
24	*Allow contact (+)*					24	Allow contact	Set few boundaries	Not set boundaries, allow too much	24
25	*Unfold (–)*					25	Unfold independently	Avoid independence	Be completely dependent	25
26	*Submit (+)*					26	Submit somewhat	Adapt a lot	Completely give up, subordinate	26
27	*Assert oneself (–)*					27	Question oneself	Belittle oneself	Devalue/hate oneself	27
28	*Acknowledge guilt (+)*					28	Acknowledge own responsibility	Often blame oneself	Mostly take sole blame	28
29	*Accept affection (–)*					29	Examine affection	Accept little affection	Close oneself off from affection	29
30	*Protect oneself (+)*					30	Protect oneself	Be very cautious	Distrust excessively, always be on guard	30
31	*Lean on (–)*					31	Show one's own needs	Show little of one's own needs	Seem completely unneedy, claim no help	31
32	*Allow contact (–)*					32	Limit contact	Allow little contact	Completely reject contact, withdraw	32

Patient ID:

Date:

Therapist:

Narrative:

Note. P:O = patients' experience others, P:P = patients' experience themselves, O:P = others' experience patients, O:O = others experience themselves.

This is a **preview** of the content that is available in the downloadable material of this book.
Please see p. 319 for instructions on how to obtain the full-sized, printable PDF.

OPD-3 Item List Rating Sheet Axis II (Research Version): Relationship Topics.

OPD relationship theme		P:O	P:P	O:P	O:O	Res	Unremarkable/clinically not relevant (= 0)	Accentuated (= 1)	Dysfunctional (= 2)	
Give freedom (+)	1					1	Give others freedom	Give a lot of freedom	Just allow it to happen/ignore	1
Guide others (–)	2					2	Guide little	Guide very little	Not guide at all, avoid influencing	2
Acknowledge others (+)	3					3	Acknowledge friendly	Idealize	Completely overestimate	3
Hold responsible (–)	4					4	Hold responsible	Hold little accountable	Completely excuse inappropriately	4
Show affection (+)	5					5	Show affection	Overwhelm with affection	Stalk with love	5
Show aggression (–)	6					6	Show little aggression	Avoid conflicts, downplay	Over-harmonize, ignore conflicts	6
Care (+)	7					7	Care	Care a lot	Care excessively	7
Make contact (+)	8					8	Make contact	Be tactless, push	Violate boundaries, be intrusive	8
Give freedom (–)	9					9	Get involved	Interfere	Constantly patronize	9
Guide others (+)	10					10	Guide appropriately	Guide or control a lot	Constantly guide or control	10
Acknowledge others (–)	11					11	Critically acknowledge	Criticize a lot, question	Devalue, humiliate	11
Hold responsible (+)	12					12	Hold responsible	Blame, reproach	Persecute with guilt accusations	12
Show affection (–)	13					13	Keep distance	Show little affection	Show no affection at all	13
Show aggression (+)	14					14	Show anger	Meet angrily	Threaten, attack, harm	14
Care (–)	15					15	Limit help	Deny help, abandon	Completely neglect	15
Make contact (–)	16					16	Limit contact	Make little contact	Ignore others, completely overlook	16
Unfold (+)	17					17	Unfold independently	Claim a lot of freedom or independence	Insist too much on independence	17
Submit (–)	18					18	Assert oneself, resist	Often resist	Defy, constantly resist	18
Assert oneself (+)	19					19	Assert oneself	Assert a lot	Constantly make oneself important, putting oneself in the center	19
Acknowledge guilt (–)	20					20	Examine own responsibility	Rather reject guilt	Not acknowledge own guilt at all	20
Accept affection (+)	21					21	Accept affection	Accept too much affection	Lose oneself in others' affection	21
Protect oneself (–)	22					22	Open up	Protect little	Put oneself in danger, not protect from aggression	22
Lean on (+)	23					23	Show own needs	Lean a lot, show neediness	Cling, show helplessness	23
Allow contact (+)	24					24	Allow contact	Set few boundaries	Not set boundaries, allow too much	24
Unfold (–)	25					25	Unfold independently	Avoid independence	Be completely dependent	25
Submit (+)	26					26	Submit somewhat	Adapt a lot	Completely give up, subordinate	26
Assert oneself (–)	27					27	Question oneself	Belittle oneself	Devalue/hate oneself	27
Acknowledge guilt (+)	28					28	Acknowledge own responsibility	Often blame oneself	Mostly take sole blame	28
Accept affection (–)	29					29	Examine affection	Accept little affection	Close oneself off from affection	29
Protect oneself (+)	30					30	Protect oneself	Be very cautious	Distrust excessively, always be on guard	30
Lean on (–)	31					31	Show one's own needs	Show little of one's own needs	Seem completely unneedy, claim no help	31
Allow contact (–)	32					32	Limit contact	Allow little contact	Completely reject contact, withdraw	32

Patient ID:

Date:

Therapist:

Narrative:

Note. P:O = patients' experience others, P:P = patients' experience themselves, O:P = others' experience patients, O:O = others experience themselves.

This is a **preview** of the content that is available in the downloadable material of this book.
Please see p. 319 for instructions on how to obtain the full-sized, printable PDF.

Dysfunctional Relationship Pattern

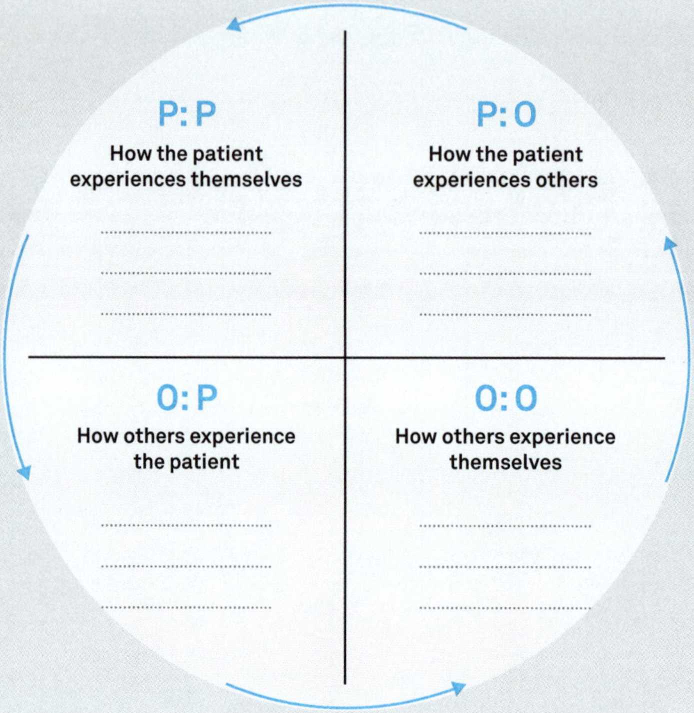

How the patient experiences others time and again:	
How the patient reacts to this typically:	
Which is the (unconscious) relational offer:	
Which are typical answers elicited through the offer:	
How is the patient experiencing the situation, if others answer as elicted:	

This is a **preview** of the content that is available in the downloadable material of this book. Please see p. 319 for instructions on how to obtain the full-sized, printable PDF.

OPD-3 Rating Sheet Axis III: Conflict.

	Biographical-repetitive-motivational conflict issues						Biographically dominant processing mode				
	• Conflict tensions (CT) • Neurotic conflicts (NC) • Conflictual-motivational schemata (CMS)	Non-existent	Little significant	Significant	Very significant	Not applicable	Mainly passive	Mixed, rather passive	Mixed, ambivalent	Mixed, rather active	Mainly active
C1	Dependence vs. Individuation	0	1	2	3	9	p+	p	p/a	a	a+
C2	Submission vs. Control	0	1	2	3	9	p+	p	p/a	a	a+
C3	In Need of Care vs. Self-Sufficiency	0	1	2	3	9	p+	p	p/a	a	a+
C4	Self-Worth Conflict	0	1	2	3	9	p+	p	p/a	a	a+
C5	Guilt Conflict	0	1	2	3	9	p+	p	p/a	a	a+
C6	Oedipal Conflict	0	1	2	3	9	p+	p	p/a	a	a+
C7	Conflict of Identity	0	1	2	3	9	p+	p	p/a	a	a+
C0	Repressed conflict and emotion awareness	0	1	2	3	9	p+	p	p/a	a	a+

Current main conflict		Structure				Current processing mode				
						Mainly passive	Mixed, rather passive	Mixed, ambivalent	Mixed, rather active	Mainly active
1	.... /	CT	NC	CMS		p+	p	p/a	a	a+
2	.... /					p+	p	p/a	a	a+

Certainty of the conflict assessment	Not sure				Very sure
	1	2	3	4	5

This is a **preview** of the content that is available in the downloadable material of this book. Please see p.319 for instructions on how to obtain the full-sized, printable PDF.

OPD-3 Rating Sheet Axis IV: Structure (Clinical Version).

Time window: ☐ 5 years ☐ shortened/extended to: ______________ n/a = not applicable

	Good ①	Good to moderate 1.5	Moderate ②	Moderate to low 2.5	Low ③	Low to disinte-grated 3.5	Disinte-grated ④	Not applicable ⑨
1a Self-perception	①	◯	②	◯	③	◯	④	⑨
1b Object perception	①	◯	②	◯	③	◯	④	⑨
2a Self-regulation	①	◯	②	◯	③	◯	④	⑨
2b Relationship regulation	①	◯	②	◯	③	◯	④	⑨
3 Defense	①	◯	②	◯	③	◯	④	⑨
4a Internal communication	①	◯	②	◯	③	◯	④	⑨
4b Communication with the external world	①	◯	②	◯	③	◯	④	⑨
5a Attachment to internal objects	①	◯	②	◯	③	◯	④	⑨
5b Attachment to external objects	①	◯	②	◯	③	◯	④	⑨
Structure total	①	◯	②	◯	③	◯	④	⑨

Temporal variability rating							
Variability of structure	no ⓪			yes ①			n/a ⑨
Continue, if yes ①:							
Current structural level	Baseline level ⓪		worse ①		better ②		n/a ⑨
Extent of the fluctuation	±1 ◯		±2 ◯		±3 ◯		n/a ⑨
Duration of the fluctuation	< 3 ◯ months	3–6 ◯ months	6–12 ◯ months	1–2 ◯ years	>2–3 ◯ years	>3 ◯ years	n/a ⑨
Cause of the fluctuation (disorder/trauma)							n/a ⑨
Variability rating by life areas							
Divergence of structure	no ⓪			yes ①			n/a ⑨

Better functioning	Life areas	Worse functioning
◯	Family of origin	◯
◯	Partnership/family	◯
◯	Profession	◯
◯	Social environment	◯
◯	Possessions	◯
◯	Body/sexuality	◯
◯	Illnesses	◯
Cause of the fluctuation (disorder/trauma)		

This is a **preview** of the content that is available in the downloadable material of this book.
Please see p.319 for instructions on how to obtain the full-sized, printable PDF.

OPD-3 Rating Sheet Axis IV: Structure (Research Version).								
Time window: ☐ 5 years ☐ shortened/extended to: ______________ n/a = not applicable								
	Good ①	Good to moderate 1.5	Moderate ②	Moderate to low 2.5	Low ③	Low to disinte-grated 3.5	Disinte-grated ④	Not applicable ⑨
Self-perception	①	○	②	○	③	○	④	⑨
ST1.1 Self-reflection	①	○	②	○	③	○	④	⑨
ST1.2 Affect differentiation	①	○	②	○	③	○	④	⑨
ST1.3 Identity	①	○	②	○	③	○	④	⑨
Object perception	①	○	②	○	③	○	④	⑨
ST1.4 Self-object differentiation	①	○	②	○	③	○	④	⑨
ST1.5 Object-related affect differentiation	①	○	②	○	③	○	④	⑨
ST1.6 Integrated object perception	①	○	②	○	③	○	④	⑨
Self-regulation	①	○	②	○	③	○	④	⑨
ST2.1 Impulse control	①	○	②	○	③	○	④	⑨
ST2.2 Affect tolerance	①	○	②	○	③	○	④	⑨
ST2.3 Self-esteem regulation	①	○	②	○	③	○	④	⑨
Relationship regulation	①	○	②	○	③	○	④	⑨
ST2.4 Protecting relationships	①	○	②	○	③	○	④	⑨
ST2.5 Anticipation	①	○	②	○	③	○	④	⑨
ST2.6 Balancing of interests	①	○	②	○	③	○	④	⑨
Defense	①	○	②	○	③	○	④	⑨
ST3.1 Living and experiencing possibilities	①	○	②	○	③	○	④	⑨
ST3.2 Interpersonal impact	①	○	②	○	③	○	④	⑨
ST3.3 Mechanisms	①	○	②	○	③	○	④	⑨
Internal communication	①	○	②	○	③	○	④	⑨
ST4.1 Experience of affects and fantasies	①	○	②	○	③	○	④	⑨
ST4.2 Experience of joy	①	○	②	○	③	○	④	⑨
ST4.3 Bodily self	①	○	②	○	③	○	④	⑨
Communication with the external world	①	○	②	○	③	○	④	⑨
ST4.4 Making emotional contact	①	○	②	○	③	○	④	⑨
ST4.5 Intimacy	①	○	②	○	③	○	④	⑨
ST4.6 Empathy	①	○	②	○	③	○	④	⑨
Attachment to internal objects	①	○	②	○	③	○	④	⑨
ST5.1 Internalization	①	○	②	○	③	○	④	⑨
ST5.2 Use of introjects	①	○	②	○	③	○	④	⑨
ST5.3 Variability	①	○	②	○	③	○	④	⑨
Attachment to external objects	①	○	②	○	③	○	④	⑨
ST5.4 Ability to form attachments	①	○	②	○	③	○	④	⑨
ST5.5 Trust	①	○	②	○	③	○	④	⑨
ST5.6 Ability to separate	①	○	②	○	③	○	④	⑨
Structure total	①	○	②	○	③	○	④	⑨

This is a **preview** of the content that is available in the downloadable material of this book.
Please see p.319 for instructions on how to obtain the full-sized, printable PDF.

Peer Commentaries

Lucid, structured, and clinically resonant, OPD-3 bridges the gap between descriptive diagnosis and psychodynamic understanding. It delivers depth without unwieldiness and clarity without reductionism, supported by an expanding evidence base. A major contribution to contemporary diagnostic practice.

Christopher J. Hopwood, PhD, Professor of Psychology, University of Zurich, Switzerland

Based upon the clinical experience of a community of mental health experts, the OPD-3 is a unique and exemplary assessment guide. Its definitional clarity of psychoanalytic concepts enhances both research efforts and clarity of communication among clinicians. The instrument provides practitioners with an empirically tested structure for assessment, and it presents patients with an opportunity to begin reflection on their patterns of self-destructive functioning that can be the forerunner of therapeutic change.

John F. Clarkin, PhD, Emeritus Professor, Weill Cornell Medical College, New York, NY, USA

This volume is a landmark achievement. It is simply the best and most comprehensive account of psychodynamic diagnosis and treatment planning currently available. Rigorous, clinically insightful, and remarkably current, it comes at a pivotal time when psychodynamic approaches are experiencing renewed influence. OPD-3 is therefore destined to become the standard reference in the field and an indispensable guide for clinical practice.

Patrick Luyten, PhD, Professor of Clinical Psychology, University of Leuven, Belgium and University College London, UK

A comprehensive guide to modern psychodynamic thinking that distills abstract concepts into jargon-free operational definitions and rating scales that can be very helpful in diagnostic assessment and treatment. OPD-3 significantly contributes to the goal of making high quality psychodynamic psychotherapy practice more generalizable.

Richard D. Lane, MD, PhD, Professor of Psychiatry, Psychology and Neuroscience, University of Arizona, Tucson, AZ, USA